Presented to ....

....

From..

Date ....

Other Goodword Books on
Islamic Spain

Spanish Islam:
A History of the Muslims in Spain

The Travels of Ibn Jubayr

The Muslims in Spain

The Moriscos of Spain

THE STORY OF
ISLAMIC SPAIN

Syed Azizur Rahman

Goodword
B·O·O·K·S

First published in 2001
Reprinted 2002
© Goodword Books 2002

Goodword Books
1, Nizamuddin West Market,
New Delhi 110 013
Tel. 435 5454, 435 1128, 435 6666
Fax 435 7333, 435 7980
e-mail: info@goodwordbooks.com
http://www.goodwordbooks.com

In Loving Memory of
My Father, Syed Amin ur Rahman
and
My Mother, Amna Begum

Not to know what happened before we were born is
to remain perpetually a child.

(Cicero)

The weather vane on the palace of Badis son Habbus was
in the shape of a warrior mounted on a horse
with a lance in one hand. The meaningful
couplet in Arabic inscribed on it may be
translated as follows :

Said al-Badis, son of Habus —
"Thus shall vanish al-Andalus"

(Al-Maqqari/Gayangas, Vol. 2, p. 548)

Contents

Part I

Rise and Fall of Islamic Spain

Part II
Hispano-Muslim Culture

Appendix

Preface

I have been interested in the history of Al-Andalus or Muslim Spain for a long time. During the course of my study, I came across only a few books covering the entire period of eight centuries of Muslims' presence in Iberian peninsula. In 1820-21 Dr. Condé, Spain's first Arabist wrote a history of the period using Arabic sources, but his book (whatever its shortcomings) stopped at the fall of the kingdom of Granada in the 15th century. Lane-Poole's brief history appeared in 1886, and went through a dozen editions. S.P. Scott's History of the Moorish Empire in Europe was published in Philadelphia in 1904. These books are now out of print. The scientific study of Muslim Spain was undertaken by the Dutch orientalist R. Dozy. His books are, still relevant. In more recent time, the French orientalist, Lévi Provençal planned to write a complete history in six volumes. On my enquiry in 1953 he replied, in an affectionate letter, that the third volume of his book was in the press. After a few years he died. Both Dozy and Provençal did not go beyond the fall of the Umayyad kingdom. The book before the reader covers the entire period from Tariq's landing in Spain to the expulsion of the Muslims in the first decade of the 17th century. Part II of the book deals with Hispano-Muslim culture. The subject is, no doubt, fascinating. It was a pleasure to write the book, and I would deem it a privilege if I can share some of my joy with the readers.

I should like to thank Khwaja Munir Ahmad, Librarian of the Indian Council for Cultural Relations, for his generous cooperation. My thanks are also due to the Makkah-educated Maulana Muhammad Iftikhar Hussain of the Madrassa Rahmia of Delhi.

Last of all, I must express my deep gratitude to my parents. My father (junior Architect in the C.P.W.D. during the time when Lutyens and Baker were building the magnificent Secretariat in New Delhi) introduced me to the aesthetics of Muslim architecture. My mother, introduced me to the history of Muslim Spain. I was barely 15 years of age, when she presented me an Urdu translation of Al-Maqqari's Nafh at-tib. In reading this book, I felt the same joy and excitement which Keats experienced on his first looking into Chapman's Homer. I have, therefore, dedicated this book to them. It is a small recompense for the abundant love they gave to their only son.

One final word. I am grateful to Iqbal Jahan Begum, my wife, who looked after me with devotion and gentleness, when I was busy with this work. I am sorry she did not live to see the book in its present format.

Syed Azizur Rahman

Ghaziabad, India
17 March 2001

Chapter 1

A Brief Introduction

The Iberian peninsula now divided into two sovereign states of Spain and Portugal is in fact a single geographical entity. This mass of land, pentagonal in shape, was given different names in the past. The Greeks called it Iberia, the Romans named it Hispania, while to the Muslims it was known as Al-Andalus[1]. The Pre-historic age of Spain is rather dim, but it is about the eleventh century B.C. that we see her within a clear historical perspective. Since then she received wave after wave of invaders, colonisers and conquerors. Her fertile valleys and mineral wealth attracted the Greeks, the Celts, the Carthaginians, the Romans, the Vandals, the Goths and last of all the Muslims.

After the second Punic war (201 B.C.) Carthage lost Spain to Rome, and the whole peninsula became a part of the Roman empire. The coming of the Romans in Spain was a great civilizing influence. Here, as elsewhere, they set up a strong government. They constructed walled towns, elegant villas, theatres and baths. They exploited the mines, and built imposing acquaducts for irrigation. They connected the country by a network of roads. They introduced Latin out of which grew up Spanish of today. Some of the greatest names in Roman history — Seneca the lawyer, Martial the poet, Quintilian the orator, hailed from Spain. However, under the later Caesers, Spain presented a sorry spectacle of decay. The Romans lost their warlike spirit and tenacity. The Roman aristocracy sank into luxury, while the subjects (mostly slaves and serfs), groaned under heavy taxation. A government of corrupt and pleasure loving ruling class, and impoverished people, could not endure very long. Roman Spain fell a prey to the Gothic hordes, like a house built on sand, in the fifth century B.C.

The social and economic ills of the Roman days aggravated with the coming of the Goths. Like the Romans, the Goths too abandoned themselves to luxury and vice once power rested securely into their hands. The Gothic nobility thrived on the labour of the middle class. The big landlords (called *Latifundia*) who owned vast estates were exempted from taxation. The tax paying middle class created money which the privileged tax-free nobles squandered on luxurious living. At the bottom of the society was the vast multitude of serfs and slaves. Since the days of the Romans large number of people, driven under economic distress, were giving themselves up voluntarily as slaves to the big landlords. Under the Goths, slavery became more rampant than it was under the Romans. There was hardly a Gothic nobleman who did not own an army of slaves. Apart from the slaves there were the serfs in large numbers who constituted the agricultural labour of the state. They were permanently attached to the soil by hereditary rights. They had no other occupation open to them. A serf was no better than the ordinary slave. Neither the serf nor the slave could marry without the consent of his master. When a serf married a woman belonging to another nobleman, the offsprings were shared by the two masters. The advent of Christianity in Gothic Spain did not improve the prevailing social and economic conditions, as the high officials of the church were themselves partners in the

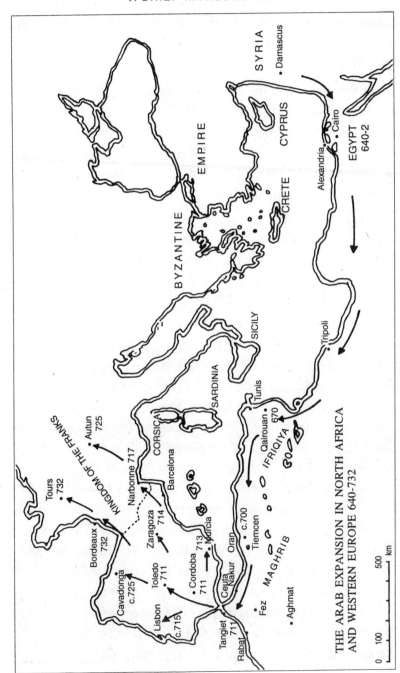

THE ARAB EXPANSION IN NORTH AFRICA
AND WESTERN EUROPE 640-732

exploitation of the masses. The priests were princes of the church. They lived a life of ease and luxury, caring little for their flock.

At the time when the Muslims appeared on the Spanish soil the Goths had been in occupation of the country for some centuries. The last Gothic monarch to rule Spain was Roderick. He was, probably the governor of Baetica i.e., south Spain, but in 710 A.D., he usurped the throne after the death of king Witiza of the legitimate dynasty.

Long before Roderick seized the Spanish throne, the Muslims were firmly established in north Africa. A history of the world — shaking conquests of the Muslims in the middle of the 7th century would be a long story to narrate. Their sudden eruption from the *Arabia Deserta*, which gave them undisputed sway over three continents from walls of China and the Indus in India to the Pyrenees, is one of the miracles of history. Long before anybody could dream of aeroplanes, speeding cars and electronic media, the pagan Arabs converted to Islam built the world's greatest empire in history. The Arab empire comprised dozens of nationalities, diverse climates, cultures and faiths. The historians have debated the causes of this cataclysmic event. A discussion on the subject is beyond the scope of this book. We are concerned here with their conquests beyond the Red Sea which brought them to the farthest corner of north Africa, and ultimately to Spain, with spectacular rapidity. The conquest of Egypt was effected by Amar ibn al-'As. Taking his route through the Sinai peninsula along the coast trodden by the patriarch Abraham, he set his foot on the Nile land in July 639 A.D. City after city succumbed in quick succession — Babylonia in July 640, Nikio in May 641, and finally the fabulous Alexandria about the middle of November 641. The fall of

Egypt left the Byzantine provinces of north Africa almost vulnerable. The Muslim armies pushed on to Barca and reached Tripoli.

The land beyond Tripoli was inhabitated by the Berbers, a Hamitic branch of the Caucasian race. The whole region was a part of the Byzantine empire. For some thousands of years the Berbers had lived in this region, but their condition had remained unchanged from the time they emerged from the neolithic age. The Pheonician, the Greek and the Roman colonists concentrated mainly on the coast. They assimilated the Berbers, but in the interior they lived in a state of savage independence. Although ethnically different, the Berbers resembled the Muslim Arabs in their tribal organisation, their extreme individualism, their race — consciousness and inflammable temper. They offered stubborn resistance to the Arabs. Only after years of warfare they laid their arms and recognised Arab suzerainty. The famous conqueror 'Uqbah Ibn Nafi appeared on the African scene in 665 A.D. He laid the foundation of a military cantonment at Qayrawan about a hundred miles to the south of Tunis and ancient Carthage. From Qayrawan he made repeated inroads into the Berber territory. The combined forces of the Berbers and the Romans fought ferociously under the leadership of Kosila but without success. After leading his victorious army across the Atlas, 'Uqbah reached the waters of the Atlantic only to find that there was no land to be conquered. After his death in 683 A.D. the Berbers reoccupied their land, and the Muslim Arabs had to fall back on Barca. The situation became so grave that the Umayyad Caliph 'Abd-al-Malik was forced to despatch a strong army in 693 A.D. under Hassan Ibn Nu'man. Hassan recaptured Qayrawan, occupied Carthage, and after driving out, the Greek and the Roman forces, he turned his attention to the Berbers. They were commanded at this time by their magician queen Kahina who exercised hypnotic powers over her subjects. She died in one of the encounters, and the Berbers gave up all resistance. They were granted peace on the condition that they would supply recruits for the army.

The credit for final pacification of the Berbers goes to Musa Ibn *Nusair*. He was posted as a governor of northwest Africa in 708 A.D. Musa was more than a brilliant general; he was a statesman *par excellence*. By his tactful policy based on a happy compromise of force and friendship, he succeeded where his predecessors had failed. Musa consolidated the Muslim domination in these regions. He directed a series of operations, and pursued his conquests as far as Tangiers. During his viceroyalty north Africa became one of the most important and strategic out-posts of the Islamic empire. Musa conquered not only the territory of the Berbers but also their soul. He appointed preachers to place before them the teachings of Islam. The mass conversion of the Berbers to Islam, and their recruitment in the army gave further momentum to the expansion of the Muslim empire. The stage was set for the conquest of Spain. The Muslims made their *debut* when the call came from the Christians themselves.[2]

Notes

1. The word 'Andalus' is probably derived from 'Vandalicia', the name given by the Vandals to the south of Spain.
2. The reader is advised to see the map of Spain in the book before proceeding further.

Chapter 2

Tariq Lands in Spain

———•—•———

By the end of the 7th century, the Muslims had subdued the whole of northwest Africa except the coastal city of Ceuta. This city commands the entrance to the Iberian peninsula. On clear days the Spanish coast is visible from there. At that time Ceuta was held by Count Julian. We do not know whether the Count was of Gothic descent, or of Berber origin, or whether he was a Greek. All that we know is that he was a Christian, and he held the cities of Tangier and Ceuta on behalf of the Byzantine emperor. The Muslim conquests had reduced the Byzantine empire to such a state of infirmity that the Count (Ar:*Ulyan*), had little hope of effective protection from his own government. The Count was obliged to place himself under the suzerainty of the Gothic kings of Spain. His marriage with a daughter of king Witiza further strengthened his ties with the government of Spain. So long as Witiza lived he supplied the Count with men and money to resist the Muslim armies even after the loss of Tangiers. Witiza's death and Roderick's violent occupation of the throne embittered the Count. He harboured a secret hatred against the usurper. An accident aggravated the matter.

It was a curious custom amongst the Gothic nobles that they sent their children to the imperial court at Toledo where they were schooled in courtly etiquette, and when they grew up, the king arranged their marriage within the nobility. Perhaps, they were kept as hostages in order to restrain the nobility from rebellion. Julian's daughter was amongst the trainees at the court of Roderick. It is alleged that Roderick molested the young maiden forgetting that it was his moral duty to regard her as his own daughter[1]. She wrote to her father about the mishap. The Count rushed to Toledo and brought back his daughter. When Julian was about to leave, Roderick requested him to send a few African hawks for hunting. Julian is said to have replied that he would send such hawks as Roderick had never seen in his life. This was obviously a covert hint to Roderick that he would return to Spain with the Muslim forces to relieve him of his royal duties. The Arab historians, as a rule, attribute the cause of Muslims' expedition into Spain to the foregoing incidence. The modern historians of Europe think that the whole incidence is apocryphal, but they do not give any reason as to why the Muslims set out to conquer Spain. If the alleged seduction of Julian's daughter is false, what else could be his motive in inviting the Muslims to invade Spain? In the circumstances, we can assume that Julian thought of overthrowing the usurper Roderick with the help of the Muslims. Be that as it may, we do not hear anymore of this outraged Helen who 'burnt the topless towers' of Toledo. After his return from Spain, the angry Count visited Musa. He gave him a tantalizing account of Spain — the fertility of her soil, the wealth of her mines, and her sunny climate. He persuaded him to march upon Spain, which he stated, was weak from within. He promised to give all possible help in the enterprise.

Julian was not unknown to Musa. He had defeated the Count

and wrested Tangier from his control. His unexpected appearance as a friend, and his inviting Musa to invade a powerful country inhabited by the Count's own co-religionists must have raised suspicion in his mind. To test his sincerity, Musa proposed that the Count should first invade Spain with his own army. The Count readily agreed. He made an incursion on the Spanish coast about Nov. 709 A.D., and returned with some captives as a proof of his undertaking. Soon after, Musa wrote to the Caliph Walid for his permission. The Caliph authorized him to go ahead, but at the same time, he warned him to be careful, and not to expose the Muslims to the perils of the sea. He ordered that the country should be explored with a small force before undertaking a full-fledged expedition. Acting on the advice of the Caliph, Musa deputed Tarif Ibn Malluk a subordinate commander under him, for conducting a preliminary reconnaissance of the Spanish coast. Julian supplied his boats, and Tarif landed in July, 710 at the small peninsula which has since borne his name — Tarif. He plundered some villages on the coast without any opposition, and returned with a rich booty including some Spanish belles. Musa was satisfied with the result, and he made plans for a regular invasion.

The man whom he commissioned to lead the historic expedition was Tariq Ibn Ziyad a neo-Muslim of Berber origin. A talented freedman of Musa he had rapidly risen to high positions in the army by dint of his bravery and loyalty. At that time he was governor of Tangier. Tariq left for Spain with an army of 7000 Berbers many of whom were probably still Christian[2]. Julian supplied a small flotilla for transporting the army across the narrow straits barely eleven miles apart. In April or May 711 Tariq landed near the rock (Ar:*jabal*) which dominates the Spanish coast like a couchant lion, and is known eversince after his name — *Jabal Tariq* or Gibraltar. Count

Julian accompanied Tariq as his guide. The operation must
have started in the last hours of the night because Tariq is
reported to have offered his pre-dawn (Ar: *fajar*) prayer on the
Spanish soil[3]. After the landing, Tariq moved on to the town of
Carteya, and advancing westward, he fortified his position at
the site of the modern city of Algeciras. When the news of
Tariq's landing reached Roderick he immediately left for
Cordova. In the meantime, Tariq demanded reinforcements from
Musa. He despatched a contigent of 5000 Berbers. The army
consisting of 12000 soldiers arrived at the bank of the Salado
river which enters the Atlantic ocean not far from Trafalgar. In
the meantime, Roderick was converging in the same direction
with a formidable army. Near the lagoon of La Junda, the two
armies were within sight of each other. The memorable
engagement between the Goths and the Muslims began on July
19, 711 A.D. or Ramazan 28, 92 A.H. Tariq is said to have
addressed his soldiers to boost up their morale. He delivered a
long speech which began with a memorable preamble — "Ye
Muslims whither can you flee? The sea is behind you and the
enemy is before you. By Allah only your courage and patience
can now help you." The battle lasted a week. The right and the
left wings of Roderick's army commanded by Witiza's sons
collapsed when they deserted their posts. The centre led by
Roderick himself from his gilt chariot could not hold on, and
its eventual collapse shattered Gothic resistance. The battle ended
in a disasterous rout of the Gothic army. Roderick escaped in
a panic. His sandles were found on the bank but he was never
heard of again. The whole peninsula was now at Tariq's feet.
He was only to advance further to complete the conquest. Like
Julius Caeser, Tariq could legitimately claim with pride —
"Veni, Vedi, Vici" (I came, I saw, I conquered). After the
battle of La Junda, Tariq received orders from Musa to halt his

march and wait for him. Probably Musa did not expect such a rapid victory and he felt jealous of his subordinate. Tactically, it would have been a mistake if Tariq stopped where he was because during the interval the loyalist force could recoup for a second showdown. Tariq pursued his advance in the direction of Toledo, the capital of the Gothic kingdom. On his way he laid seige to Ecija where some columns of Roderick's army had taken shelter. The governor of Ecija was captured and the city capitulated by mutual agreement. On the advice of Julian, Tariq sent out some columns of his soldiers towards other cities.[4]

The capture of Cordova by Mughith al-Rumi is a glowing example of the *esprit de corps* of the Muslim army. The cavalry encamped in a forest near Secunda (Ar:*Shaqandah*) about two miles from the city. Soon after his arrival Mughith dispatched scouts to obtain intelligence about the position of the Gothic army. The advance party came across a shephard who pointed out a breach in the rampart[5]. Mughith decided to take the city by a nocturnal surprise. He crossed the river, and gained the side of the wall where it was broken. A soldier climbed up the wall by taking a bold leap from the top of a nearby tree. With the help of his scarf he pulled up a large number of soldiers. They descended into the sleeping city, surprised the guards, and broke open the gate for their comrades waiting outside. Cordova fell into the hands of the Muslims in Oct. 711 A.D. Toledo offered but little resistance because the Jews opened the gates. Sindered, the Metropolitan of the city (along with members of the Gothic nobility) was already on the road to Rome. Among the Christians who were left behind, there was no spirit to fight. According to the traditional account of the conquest of Spain, an immence booty fell into the hands of Tariq. It included crowns of the former rulers, vases of gold, and a fabulous table belonging to king Solomon. Tariq stayed at Toledo for a short time. After appointing the bishop Oppas, a brother of Witiza as governor of Toledo, he pursued his march towards the northeast, and reached as far as Alcalá de Henares from where he returned to Toledo to receive Musa who had already landed in Spain.

Musa crossed the Straits in June 712 with 18000 Arabs. Ever since Tariq's departure for Spain, Musa had ordered construction of boats, and it was not necessary to depend upon Julian for transporting the army. Soon after his arrival he captured Medina Sidoia, Carmona, Nielba and Beja within a short time. Seville fell after a vigorous seige lasting three months. Some supporters of Roderick had gathered at Merida to organize military action against the invaders. Musa marched upon this city, and encircled it from all sides. The seige of Merida dragged on for several months. The Muslim army had to use mobile towers to attack the ramparts[6]. The city fell into the hands of Musa on June 30, 713. From Merida, Musa proceeded towards Toledo. Tariq had already descended into the valley of the Tagus. He received Musa at Talavera. Their meeting was far from being cordial[7]. Musa is alleged to have reprimanded Tariq, and even whipped him. But soon the two commanders were reconciled, and they proceeded towards Toledo. Tariq placed all the booty before his superior. At Toledo, Musa installed himself in the Gothic palace like a veritable monarch, and had coins issued in his name bearing Arabic and Latin inscriptions[8]. During the whole winter of 713-714 he rested in the city. It was from Toledo that Musa sent a message to the caliph at Damascus giving a full account of the conquest. The message was carried by the "tabi" Ali ibn Rabah and Mughith. When winter was over, Tariq and Musa left for further conquest in the north of Spain. Saragossa (called Caesaraugusta under the Romans) fell after a brief siege sometime in 714 A.D. The "tabi" Hansh al

Sanani who was with the army founded a mosque which was held in great reverence by the Spanish Muslims in the subsequent centuries[9]. Musa pressed on towards Lerida along the Roman highway which connected the city with Barcelona, and beyond the Pyrenees, the French city of Narbonne. From Lerida, Tariq was despatched to reduce the mountainous regions of the north. Fortun the Aragonese chief embraced Islam, and entered into a treaty which guaranteed him full possession of his estate and property. The descendants of this family who came to be known as Bani Qasi exercised a considerable political influence upto the 10th century. Tariq continued his march without much opposition. He occupied Leon, Astorga and Oviedo which brought him to the Bay of Biscay. Meanwhile, Musa reduced Barcelona, and in a whirlwind campaign entered into France. He planned to march through Europe, and to reach Damascus via Constantinople, but he could not carry out this project because he was recalled by the central government.

In the meantime, Musa's son 'Abd al-Aziz was busy in Murcia. This region was held by a clever Gothic governor named Theodomir. He was a vassal of the government of Toledo, and enjoyed a qasi- independent status. He knew that he would not be able to face the invading army. Sometimes, discretion is the better part of valour. Theodomir played a trick on the Muslims. He disguised his women as soldiers, stationed them on the top of his castle, and himself visited the Muslim camp. He told the commander without revealing his identity that he had plenty of soldiers to give a tough fight but would prefer a negotiated peace to avoid bloodshed. 'Abd al-Aziz agreed, and a treaty was signed in Rajab 94 A.H. or April 713. The text of this document has luckily survived. The treaty reads : "In the name of Allah, the Compassionate and the Merciful. Agreement between 'Abd-al-Aziz Ibn Musa Ibn Nusair, and Tudmir ibn

Abdush. The latter receives surety of peace and confirmation of his authority over his subjects and property; that his subjects shall not be killed, shall not be imprisoned, shall not be separated from their children and women; their churches shall not be burned, shall not be deprived of objects therein and they shall not be obstructed in the observance of their religion, subject to surrender of seven towns — Orihuela, Baltana, Alicante, Mula, Villena, Lorca and Ello. Further, he shall not give shelter to any enemy or injure anyone granted peace nor shall withhold any secret information about enemy subject to payment of a tribute of one Dinar per head every year and also four bushels of wheat, four of barley, four measures (qist) of vinegar, honey and oil. The above rates shall be half for the slaves.[10]

After appointing 'Abd al-Aziz as governor general, Musa left for Damascus in 714 A.D. The octogenarian commander crossed the entire coast of north Africa like a victorious Roman general with a long cavalcade of army officers followed by 30,000 prisoners of war and loads of booty piled on wagons and pack animals[11]. As the caliph Al-Walid was seriously ill, orders were issued to Musa that he should enter Damascus as early as possible. The would-be caliph Sulaiman, on the other hand, conveyed instructions that he should delay his entry because he wanted to open his reign with Musa's arrival. But Musa ignored the orders of Sulaiman, and reached Damascus in Feb. 715 A.D., some forty days before Walid died. When Sulaiman came to the throne, he punished Musa for his disobedience. The aged commander and his lieutenant Tariq who had expanded the Ummayad empire by their brilliant exploits, were condemned to live in obscrurity and poverty.

The startling ease of the conquest can be attributed to several factors. Some obvious reasons are the enterprising spirit of the

Muslims, their confidence in their destiny, their valiance, and their tenacity in war, — those very qualities that urged the European empire — builders (Britain, France, Holland, Portugal and Russia) to found colonies in Asia and Africa in the present age. However, other causes cannot be ignored. Spain on the eve of the Muslim conquest was a divided house. The feud between the supporters of the usurper Roderick, and the loyalists precluded a united front against the invaders. The role of Count Julian has been exaggerated, but it cannot be minimised either. He supplied his boats, he acted as a guide and was present at several campaigns. Left to themselves, it is doubtful if the Muslims would have invaded Spain. In fact everything points to their reluctance to cross the Straits as they had very little maritime experience. Moreover, after the conquest of north Africa they had reached the natural frontiers of their expansion. The enemies of Roderick were obviously in conspiracy with Tariq and Musa through Count Julian who acted as their agent and liaison. Exactly at what time the plot to overthrow Roderick was planned, is not difficult to surmise. The sons of Witiza reached the bank of La Junda not as allies but as traitors to stab Roderick in the back. We know that some understanding (if not a formal treaty) was reached between the commanders of the Muslim army and the heirs of Witiza. "When the armies drew near to each other, the princes began to spin the web of their treason; and for this purpose a messenger was sent by them to Tariq informing him how Roderick, who had been a mere menial and servant of their father, had, after his death, usurped the throne; that the princes had by no means relinquished their rights, and that they implored protection and security for themselves. They offered to desert, and to pass over to Tariq with their troops under their command, on the condition that the Arab general would, after subduing the whole of Andalus secure to them their father's possessions amounting to three thousand valuable chosen farms."[12]

The *en mass* desertion of the Jews is another cause of the rapid success of the Muslims. There was a substantial number of Jews in Spain. After the introduction of Christianity, particularly Roman Catholicism under Recared I (586-601 A.D.), their lot became miserable. No Jew was permitted to occupy a public office or to employ slaves. The Gothic king Sisabert (612-620 A.D.) ordered compulsory baptism of the Jews resulting in their migration to north Africa in large numbers. During the reign of king Egica (687-700) the Jews planned a revolt with the help of their brethren across the Straits, but the plot leaked out. Their property was confiscated, and their children were sold out in slavery. The Jews looked upon the Muslims as God-sent deliverers. As they collaborated with the Muslims, the latter placed their trust in them. The cities of Cordova, Granada, and Malaga were left in the charge of the Jews. It was a usual practice says a historian that the Muslim left conquered places in the custody of Jews while the army proceeded forward.[13] "The Jews had much cause to complain of the Christian rule, under which they had been grievously oppressed and plundered. They not unnaturally regarded with favour an invasion headed by Semitic warriors of their own kindred, which promised to avenge them on their oppressors and increase their influence."[14]

Roderick paid for his mistakes in planning and strategy. He got panicky and reached posthaste to check Tariq. He should have given the Muslims a battlefield of his own choice. His greatest mistake was that he brought his whole army on the front leaving no reserves. It was a serious gamble; he should not have placed all his eggs in one basket. His rout came because he had no reserves to give a second battle to the invading Muslims. Roderick made yet another blunder when he gave the command of the right and left wings of his army to those very princes from whom he had usurped their patrimony. By this misplaced trust he exposed his army to double-envelopment and eventual rout and defeat.

We must now turn our attention from the exploits of the conquerors to the fate of the conquered. A few biased historians mostly those belonging to the religious class, bemoan the ruin of Spain (*la perdida de Espana*) caused by the conquest. Those who have made an objective study think otherwise. Dr. J.A. Condé, a Spaniard who was one of the earliest Arabists of his country tells us that the conquest was not such a calamity." The conditions imposed on the conquered nation were such that the people found consolation rather than oppression in the presence of the conquerors; and when they compared their then fate with that which they had previously endured, could not fail to consider the change a fortunate one. The free exercise of their religion, a careful preservation of their churches from all injury, the security of their persons, with the unimpeded enjoyment of their goods and possessions, such were the first returns which they received from their submission to the stranger, and for the tribute (a very moderate one) which they paid to their victors. But there was yet more: the fidelity of the Arabs in maintaining their promises, the equal handed justice which they administered to all classes, without distinction of any kind, secured them the confidence of the people in general, as well as of those who held closer intercourse with them: and not only in these particulars, but also in generosity of mind, and in amenity of manner, and in the hospitality of their customs, the Arab were distinguished above all other people of those times."[15] Several other historians also held the same opinion.

There is no doubt that in some campaigns a few churches used for military purposes were either damaged or destroyed[16] These were isolated instances because the Muslim leaders were quick in controlling lawlessness, arson and pillage. The cities and provinces which submitted voluntarily were treated with consideration and even generosity. The pledges given to Fortun of Aragon, Theodemir of Murcia and the heirs of Witiza were scruplously honoured by the Muslims. As the Christians formed the majority of the population, the conquerors were clever enough not to antagonise them. Here it may be necessary to mention that the Muslims looked upon the Jews and the Christians with respect. They were the People of the Book (*Ahl al Kitab*) with whom they shared God's revelations to the Apostles preceeding the Prophet of Islam[17]. The state felt responsible for protection of their religion, life and property. When the dust of the war settled down, the Christians found that they enjoyed complete autonomy in regard to application of their personal law. They were tried by their own judges — the Christians in accordance with the Gothic code, the Jews in accordance with the Law of Moses. "The Mohammadans here as elsewhere (says Watt) showed an example of tolerance such as never found imitators among those who claim to be of the purer faith. After the conquest those who preferred to remain in the country occupied by the Moors were guaranteed the undisturbted enjoyment of their property and their religion. They were permitted to have their own district governors and judges who administered their own laws"[18]. There were bishops in all the major cities where, "Christian hierarchy, Christian worship, and Christian monasticism, continued practically without interference for something like 200 years after the Muslim conquest; after that the record is comparatively scanty, but even in later years isolated facts point to the continued liberty which the Christians enjoyed"[19]. However, as subjects of the Muslim government they were required to pay the poll tax (Ar. *Jazia*) in lieu of exemption from compulsory military service. The tax was payable at a uniform annual rate of 48 dirhams for the rich, 24 for the middle class and 12 for the labour and manual workers. The tax was collected in instalments at one twelvth of the rate each lunar month by the Christian officials. The poll tax was levied on all able-bodied male adults. The women, the children, the old, the sick, the blind, the beggars and the priests were exempted. As a similar poll tax was paid by the subjects under the Byzantine and the Sasanids of Persia, the Jazia was not new and perhaps was not resented particularly in view of the many exemptions.[20] Toledo continued to be the seat of the metropolitan. As for the Jews, the Muslim rule was a haven of security and an El Dorado of prosperity. Dozy praised the Arabs for "their unbounded tolerance"[21]. How generous the Muslims were to the Gothic nobility is best reflected by the treatment extended to the heirs of Witiza. After the battle of La Junda the three brothers (Almand, Artebas and Rumulu) proceeded to Damascus to ensure fulfilment of the undertaking given by Tariq. The caliph ratified the terms of the treaty. His action was an act of statesmanship because the Gothic princes commanded great respect and were capable of giving trouble to the nascent Muslim state. According to the agreement, Almand the eldest son of Witiza received one thousand villages in western Spain, and he took his residence at Seville; the second was allotted an equal number of villages in the centre of Spain and he settled at Cordova; the third was assigned an estate of his choice round Toledo[22]. Count Julian was confirmed in his post as governor of Ceuta, while bishop Oppas brother of Witiza was appointed as governor of Toledo. We may also add the history of Sara the grand-daughter of Witiza. When here father (Almand) died her nisappropriated her estate. The brave princess sailed for Syria, and had an audience with the caliph Hisham in Demascus. He treated her with respect due to her status, and issued orders that her property be restored to her. In Demascus she married a nobleman Omar al Lakhmi, and returned to Spain. When Omar died she married Isa Ibn Mazahim who was also a Muslim. She had several children from her two husbands, and their descendants flourished during the coming centuries. Some of them followed Christianity and lived as influential leaders of their community, while others adopted Islam. The genealogical tables of Sara's descendants give an interesting picture of relationship between the two communities[23].

So much for the Gothic elite. The conquest proved a boon for the serfs, who were exploited for centuries by the Romans and the Goths. They continued to work in the fields not as bounded labour, but as free tenant — farmers. They were left free to till the land in exchange for a portion of their produce payable to the state. This change, revolutionary as it was, provided an incentive to the farmers and ushered in the marvellous agricultural prosperity of Muslim Spain[24]. While the serfs got freedom from exploitation, the slaves bought their redemption by embracing Islam. The slaves, like the serfs, were nominal Christians. Most of them did not even know the rudiments of Roman Catholicism. The clergy were busy in court intrigues and wordly pursuits. Surprisingly, there were still heathens in Spain. Commenting on this situation an authority on Spanish history says — "The condition of the church was an open scandal. The mass of Latinised Iberians were probably in their hearts almost as much pagan as their ancestors. How could they be expected to resist the influx of a power which showed them a way to freedom, and set them an example of faith; of which goodness and truth seemed to be affirmed by the miracle of victory? In fine, Gothic Spain fell because it deserved to fall"[25]. The mass conversion of the slaves and the serfs was one of the most momentous consequences of the conquest. The Dutch savant R. Dozy expresses himself thus about the impact of Islam on the downtrodden serfs and slaves:" In some respects the Arab conquest was even a benefit to Spain; for it brought about an important social revolution, and put an end to many ills under which the country had groaned for centuries. The power of the privileged classes of the clergy and nobility, was reduced almost to extinction, and since the confiscated land had been divided among a large number of persons, what was practically peasant proprietorship had been instituted. This proved highly beneficial, and was one of the causes of flourshing state of agriculture in Moslem Spain. The conquest had, moreover, ameliorated the condition of the servile classes. Islamism was much more favourable to the emancipation of slaves than was Christianity — as interpreted by the bishops of the Visiogothic dominion. Speaking in God's name, Mohammad had granted permission to slaves to ransom themselves. The enfranchisement of a slave was a good work, and many sins could thereby be expiated. Slavery among the Arabs was, therefore, neither harsh nor permanent. After some years of servitude a slave was often declared free, especially if he had embraced Islamism."[26] Sir Thomas Arnold also writes in the same strain— "The Muhammadans received a warm welcome from the slaves whose condition under the Gothic rule was a very miserable one, and whose knowledge of Christianity was too superficial to have any weight when compared with the liberty and numerous advantages they gained by throwing in their lot with the Muslims"[27].

Muslim Spain wrote the brightest chapter in the history of Medieval Europe. The descendants of the warriors who landed with Tariq promoted a brilliant civilisation at a time when the rest of Europe was shrouded in darkness. All historians are unanimous in their acknowledgement of the unique cultural role of the Spanish Muslims. In an eloquent tribute Stanley Lane — Poole says, "For nearly eight centuries, under her Mohammedan rulers, Spain set to all Europe a shining example of a civilized and enlightened state. Her fertile province, rendered doubly prolific by the industry and engineering skill of her conquerors, bore fruit an hundredfold. Cities innumerable sprang up in the rich valleys of the Guadelquiver and the Guadiana, whose names, and names only still commemorate the vanished glories of their past. Art, literature and science prospered as they prospered nowhere in Europe. Whatsoever makes a kingdom great and prosperous, whatsoever tends to refinement and civilisation was found in Muslim Spain"[28]. As our narrative enfolds itself, the reader will come across cultural glimpses of the period. A fuller account will be found in the second half of the book.

Notes

1. Roderick is alleged to have spotted her when she was bathing in the Tagus. The spot is called 'Bain de la Cava'. Lévi Provençal has given a photo of the place. See photo No. 3 in his Histoire Vol. 1.

2. Gracía Gomez : The article on Moorish Spain, (p. 226) in "The World of Íslam".

3. Al-Marrakeshi: p. 8.

4. Akhbar al Majmu'a: p. 41.

5. Akhbar al Majmu'a: p. 42.

6. Ibid, p. 49.

7. Al Maqqari/Gayangos: Vol. 2, p. 286.

8. L. Provençal Histoire : Vol. 1, pp. 26-27 (p. 27 gives photos of a coin issued by Musa in his name).

9. This mosque is now the chief cathedral of Saragossa.

10. Al-Himyari: Kitab Ar-Rawd, p. 63, and Lévi Provençal: Histoire, Vol. I, p. 33.

11. Al Maqqari;Gayangos, Vol. 1, p. 292.

12. Al Maqqari/Gayangos, vol. I, p. 270. Dr. Emilo Garcia Gomez says — "We must conclude that the Ibero-Roman natives of the Peninsula, not to mention the Jews, could support the weight of the artificial visigothic oligarchy no longer and were only too pleased at the rapid downfall of a structure that they were finding increasingly repugnant. It seems most plausible that they not only helped it on its way, but to this end made treaties before hand." (see The World of Islam, p. 226)

13. Akhbar al majmua, p. 44.

14. H.E. Watt pp. 4-5, Also see Dozy, p. 228.

15. Condé: Vol 1. p. 6

16. Martin Hume in his classic history — "The Spanish people" (London 1901), says "The invaders respected property and life to an extent unheard of in similar wars. p. 68.

17. L. Provençal : Histoire, Vol. 1, p. 73-74.

18. Watts: p. 10.

19. Bernhard and Ellen M. Whishaw, p. 17.

20. About the payment of Jizya, Prof. E.G. Browne has observed that it was "perfectly just arrangement in asmuchas non-Muslim subjects of the caliphs were necessarily exempt both from military services as from the alms [Sadaqat] obligatory or the Prophet's followers". Literary History of Persia, Vol. I, p. 201. Dozy: p. 235.

21. Dozy, pg. 235.

22. Berhard and Ellen M. Whishaw, pp. 46-48.

23. Ibid, pp. 404-413.

24. L. Provençal: L' Espagne Musulmane au Xème Siècle, pp. 160-161.

25. Watt, p. 6.

26. Dozy: p. 236.

27. Arnold: The Preaching of Islam, p. 132.

28. Lane-Poole: Preface to the book: The Moors in Spain.

Chapter 3

Islamic Spain in Search of Stability (714-755)

———•——

The rapid and unexpected conquest of Spain almost dazzled, the conquerors, and they did not know what to do with such a big country thousands of miles away from Damascus, the capital of the empire. Musa left Spain to give a personal account of his achievements to the caliph. Before his departure for the East he appointed his son 'Abd al-Aziz as viceroy, as an interim arrangement. Even though 'Abd al-Aziz had no experience, he proved a good administrator. The fall of the Gothic dynasty had broken up the fabric of the state. 'Abd al-Aziz established order and respect for the new regime. At the same time he completed the work of Taiq and Musa. He reduced Santarem and Coimbra, and consolidated the position of the Muslims in the northwest. He had his father's talent for befriending the people. He married Egilona the widow of Roderick, and allowed her to follow her faith. She continued to worship in her chapel in the residence. The first inter-communal marriage proved successful. She bore him a son named Asim, and for this reason she was called "ummul Asim" (mother of Asim) out of endearment. His remarkable tolerance and personal relations with the Gothic chiefs like Theodomir quietened the Christians into willing submission to the Muslim rule. But some malicious persons were after him. It was noised about that he had turned a Christian, and that he intended to set up his own independent rule. A rumour went around that he was seen wearing a crown made for him at the instance of Egilona. In reality his greatest sin was that his father was Musa who was in the bad books of the government of Damascus. A message was sent from the imperial city to finish him. 'Abd al-Aziz was busy in his dawn prayer when a hired assassin stabbed him to death in March 716.

After his assassination Spain was governed by over twenty viceroys for nearly forty two years. The government of Damascus did not follow a uniform policy in regard to the appointment of viceroys. The Spanish possession was considered an extension of the northwestern African province. Although a viceroy of Spain owed allegiance to the caliph, he was for all intents and purposes, a subordinate of the governor-general of Africa. The latter gave preferential treatment to viceroys with whom he had personal relationship or tribal affinity. This dual control and notoriously frequent changes of Spanish viceroys obstructed the evolution of a uniform policy in administrative matters, led to frequent civil wars, and prevented material and cultural advancement of the country. Many viceroys held office for brief periods, a few even for months. In the circumstances, it is proposed to narrate the main historical events of this chaotic period — (i) the Muslims' expeditions in France, (ii) the origin of tribal feuds, (iii) the revolt of the Berbers stationed in Spain, and (iv) the political confusion caused by the arrival of a fresh contingent of Syrian soldiers.

At the time we are speaking about, France was called Gaul, but to the Arabs it was 'the Great Land' (Ar: *al-ard al-Kabira*).

The southeast of Gaul immediately beyond the Pyrenees belonged to the extinct Gothic dominion of Toledo. This territory was named Septimania because it included seven cities, the biggest being Narbonne on the Mediterranean coast. The Muslims appeared in Septimania in 714-715, but their hold was ephemeral. The subsequent expeditions between 721-732 ended in disastrous failures.[1] A raid was directed by Al-Samh al-Khawlani, the fourth viceroy. He was posted by the caliph Umar II. He was one of the ablest of all the viceroys. At the orders of the caliph he toured the country, and sent to him a report furnishing descriptions of the major cities, rivers, mountains, and the customs of the people. He constructed a mosque at Saragossa, and practically rebuilt the bridge on the Guadalquivir. Al-Samh entered France along the Roman road that connected Barcelona with Narbonne. He captured Narbonne without much resistance, and proceeded towards Toulouse, the capital of the semi-autonomous dukedom of Acquitaine held by a duke named Eudes. The city was about to fall when a chance arrow pierced his throat, and he fell dead from his horse. The encounter at Toulouse took place in June 721 A.D. The Muslims retreated, but Narbonne remained in their hands. Four years after, the next viceroy, 'Anbasa marched into Gaul by the same route. Carcassone, and Nime opened their gates, and 'Anbasa moved deeper into the French territory along the river Rhone. As he advanced, the expedition degenerated into plunder and pillage. The unruly Berbers got out of control, and they committed wonton destructions of abbeys and monastries. Marching rapidly the invading army reached Chalon from where columns were sent-one towards Autun, and the other towards Langres. But in Sept. 725 A.D. 'Anbasa was ambushed, and killed in the mountainous passes while he was returning laden with booty.

Of all the expeditions of the Muslims beyond the Pyrenees, the one led by 'Abd ar-Rahman al-Ghafiqi was the most decisive as well as the most tragic. 'Abd al-Rahman was a seasoned commander of great calibre. He had participated in conquest of Spain. He caught the eye of Al-Samh by his prowness, and virtuous life, and he took him as his deputy. He was present at the battle of Toulouse and had displayed tremendous patience and resourcefulness in bringing back the shattered army after Al-Samh's death. When Anbasa became the viceroy he gave him command of the eastern frontier. 'Abd ar-Rahman wanted to avenge the defeat suffered by the Muslims near the walls of Toulouse. His opportunity came when he himself was appointed as viceroy in 730. A.D. In the summer of 732 he assembled a big army largely of the Berbers at Pamplona. Discarding the route of his predecessors, he crossed the Pyrenees through the pass of Roncesvalles, and triumphantly marched into the French territory. The Muslims flooded the Acquitaine basin. This terrain is almost a plain with but few undulations. Watered by the Garonne, the Dordogne, and the Loire and other tributaries, it is one of the most fertile regions of France famous today for its vineyards and vintage wines. The army and the cavalry moved swiftly towards Bordeaux where many centuries afterwards the French philosopher Montaigne was to serve as a mayor of the city. Eudes tried in vain to stop the invading army from crossing the Dordogne. He was in a great peril because a major part of his realm was already overrun by the Muslims. He approached Charles Martel the leader of the Franks for help. Charles knew about the sweeping victories of the Muslims. A delegation of the Christians had appraised him of the horrors committed by the invaders. He was reported to have replied that it was not easy to stop them as they were spreading like a torrent that uprooted everything that came in the way. He advised them to

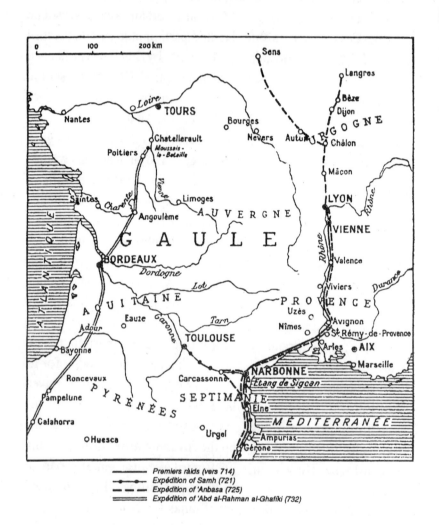

THE EXPÉDITIONS OF MUSLIMS IN GAUL

wait till their hands were full of booty, and disunity broke their ranks. That would be the time (he added) for him to attack and destroy them. However, when Eudes himself visited him, he realized that it was time to act. Charles mustered a huge army of the ferocious German and Teutonic tribes, and moved swiftly to the south. The Muslim army had, in the meantime, captured Poitiers, and was moving towards Tours from where Paris was only one hundred and fifty miles away. The actual site where the two titanic armies collided with each other to decide the fate of Europe is rather uncertain. The French historian L. Provençal has identified the place. According to him the encounter took place about twenty km north of Poiters at a place called today Moussais-la-Bataille[2]. The battle raged for a week from the 25th to 31st Oct. 732 A.D. For a few days the armies were engaged in skirmishes. On the 7th day 'Abd al-Rahman charged with cavalry, but the German warriors wrapped in their wolfskins remained in their position. They stood like a solid wall of ice-so says a monkish chronicle. When the battle was in full swing, Eudes made a detour, and attacked the Muslim camp in the rear. The Berbers abandoned their positions, and ran to safeguard their booty. Indiscipline and disorder broke into the army. While trying to restore order, 'Abd al-Rahman received a lethal blow and died. After his death the army was thoroughly demoralized. The battlefield turned into a slaugherhouse of the Muslims. The bloody drama continued throughout the day. During the night the Muslims retreated. The Christian sources have recorded that the number of the Muslims slain was three hundred thousand which is *prima facie* a gross exaggeration, but there is no doubt that several thousands of them must have perished in the fearful carnage. The Arab historians mournfully call the tragedy 'balat al shuhada' i.e. the Pavement of the martyrs. The astounding victory earned for

Charles the title "Martel" i.e. a hammer, because like a hammer he broke and crushed his enemies on the anvil of Poiters. Apprehending a snare in the quiet withdrawal of the Muslims, Charles, did not persue the defeated enemy, but his soldiers ran into the deserted camps, and appropriated the booty left by them. Instead of returning the booty to the abbeys and monastries, Charles distributed it among his hordes who were as wild and greedy as the Berbers. However, the duke was installed in his fief. The battle of Poiters (also called the battle of Tours) is one of the most decisive encounters in history. If the Muslims had won the battle "the interpretation of the Koran would be taught in the schools of Oxford, and her pulpits might demonstrate to a circumcised people the sanctity and truth of the revelations of Mohamet", says Edward Gibbon in his great history of the Roman Empire. The fear expressed by Gibbon could have come true as several countries of Europe were still pagan. Van Schlegal thought that the "arms of Charles Martel saved the Christian nations of the West from the deadly grasp of all-destroying Islam." Ranke endorsed the opinion of Van Schlegal[3]. The Belgian historian Henry Pierenne thinks the victory of 'Abd ur-Rahman would have resulted in massive destruction only. Gustav LeBon, the French author of the classic "La Civilisation des Arabe", struck a different note when he said that the victory of the Muslims at the battle of Poiters would have contributed a great deal towards civilising the barbaric nations of Europe, — and even enthusiastically adds that under the Muslims there would have been no massacre of St. Bartholomew and no Inquisition.[4] The American Arabist Prof. Hitti would like us to believe that the battle decided nothing as the surging tide of the Muslims' expansion had already lost its momentum, and its rolling back was only a logical result[5].

As Charles did not follow up his brilliant success, the Muslims were left in possession of only Narbonne. For two years there was lull probably because the Muslims were dazed by their defeat. In 734 A.D. Yusuf ibn 'Abd al-Rahman, the governor of Narbonne (who was probably in alliance with Maurant, the duke of Marseille), descended into the Rhone valley. He crossed the river, captured Arles, St. Remy-de-Provence and Avignon. Proceeding along the bank of the Rhone, he carried his vigorous raid as far as Lyon. Four years after (737) the Spanish viceroy 'Uqba bin Hajjaj sent a force for stepping up the operations in France. On this occasion Charles Martel, his brothers, and allies from Lombard took the field. They drove out the Muslims. Charles did not storm Narbonne as he was called upon to check an invasion of the Saxons on the northern boundaries of his dominion. But before he left he destroyed all the places which could afford facilities to the Muslims in their raids. The gates of Nimes were pulled down, its magnificent amphitheatre was set on fire, and many fortifications were levelled to the ground. Narbonne remained in the hands of the Muslims, but its fate too was sealed. At that time Spain was in the grip of serious civil strifes. The Arabs were fighting among themselves; the Berbers were in open revolt; the northern Christians were organising a movement to free the land from the Muslims. The garrison at Narbonne had to depend upon its own resources. Its lines of communications, the vital artery of the army, were cut off. The population of Narbonne was mainly Christian, and when Pepin (the son of Charles Martel) attacked, they opened the gates for him. Narbonne was lost in 751 A.D. We are sure that the Muslims left Narbonne after it fell into the hands of the Franks. "If they had been allowed to settle in southern France they would almost certainly have developed science and art much more rapidly than the Franks."[6] The invasion of France was an exercise in futility as it left no impact of any significance.

Even the most patient reader finds in the internecine feuds of the Arabs, the most disgusting aspect of their otherwise fabulous history. The Arabs belonged to the Semitic stock. They spoke the same language, observed the same customs, and followed a common religion. In reality, they were divided into two mutually antagonistic groups — the Qaisites and the Kelbites. The animosity between these two groups was rooted far into the past before Islam appeared in the Arabian peninsula. The Qaisites (also known as the Mudarites) descended from Ismael, a son of the prophet Abraham. They lived in the north and central Arabia and the coast of the Red sea. Except those Qaisites who lived in the city of Mecca by trade, the rest of them were a nomadic people who wandered with their flocks wherever pasturage was available. The other group — the Kelbites were descendants of Qahtan — the Joktan of the Old Testament. They were also known as the Yemenites after their original home that was Yemen. The Kelbites/Yemenites had attained a high level of culture, and they were also better organized. The two groups were further divided into a plethora of tribes. During the time of the Prophet these tribes were united in one brotherhood. Their mutual rivalries were contained by the four orthodox caliphs, but under the Umayyads the old feuds rose like a pheonix from its ashes. The Qaisites played a leading role in the Arab conquests and expansion. Leaving their inhospitable land, they settled in very large numbers in Mesopotamia. They formed a significant part of the inhabitants of Basra. The members of the Yemenite clan did not lag behind, and migrated to north Syria. The Yemenites were loath to recognize the dominant role of the Qaisites. Thus, the two factions were to face in the new Arab settlements, and always ready to fight for any reason, even a petty one. The poets and wandering minstrels of each side kept alive the memories of the past confrontations and injuries. The early Umayyad rulers did not discriminate between the Qaisites and the Kelbites. When Mu'awiya foisted dynastic rule in Syria by reversing the republican government of early Islam, the Qaisites and the kelbites were equally attached to him. He had a Kelbi wife, the mother of his infamous son and successor — Yazid I. When Yazid died his son ruled only for a few months. His death was followed by a war of succession. There were two contenders in the field — Merwan who depended on the support of the Syrian Yemenites, and his rival 'Abdullah ibn Al-Zubair who had the active sympathies of the Qaisites. The issue was decided at the historic battle of Marj Rahit. Merwan won, and the Qaisites who supported Zubair were utterly routed. Henceforth, the feud between them blazed with greater fury. The Muslim imported these tribal animosities into every land they conquered. From the banks of the Euphrates to the Ebro, the Qaisites and the Yemenites fought relentlessly for domination. In Spain the bloody drama was first enacted by the two Qaisite governors Hudhaifa (728-730) and Al-Haitham (729-730) by their systematic persecution of the Yemenites resulting in the death of several persons belonging to the latter group. For nearly half a century governors/viceroys came and went, but the feuds survived. Before we take up the far reaching effects of the continuous tribal warfare, it will be necessary to turn to the Berbers.

After 'Abd al-Rahman al-Ghafiqi died at the battle of Poiters, 'Abd al-Malik ibn Qatan was appointed as governor. He was found incompetent, and was replaced by Uqba ibn al-Hajjaj. He was just and irreproachable, and worked hard to restore order, but his services were required by the government of

Damascus for suppressing the revolt of the Berbers in north Africa. The rising of the Berbers was so sudden and impetuous that it threatened the very unity of the Umayyad empire. Its vibrations were felt in Spain also. The revolt which erupted in 741 was the outcome of the inequities of the Arab rule. We have already seen how Musa won over their confidence and cooperation by his benevolence. His successors put the clock back. The Arabs behaved like haughty imperialists. Once in the fold of Islam, the Berbers naturally expected to be treated as equals. They found, to their dissappointment, that the Arabs treated them as a subject people whose sole duty was to pay the taxes, and also to supply their hardy young men for the army. There is no doubt that the Arabs imposed unjust taxes on them. There were reports that they carried away their young girls for the pleasure-loving nobles of Syria. They killed their sheep (their important means of livelyhood) to obtain the soft skins of unborn lambs for the fashion - crazy dames and dandies of Syria[7]. These were not the only reasons for their simmering discontent. The Berbers were under the influence of the politico-religious doctrines of the Khariji school according to which anyone could hold the post of caliph on the basis of consensus or election. In their eyes, the Umyyads were impious usurpers who deserved to be deposed. They rallied under a priest-cum-demagogue named Maisara and stormed Tangier in 740. The Arab garrisons were expelled, and after having established themselves firmly in that city they marched upon Qayrawan. Neither 'Uqba, nor Habib ibn 'Abdulla, the commander from Sicily (who too was summoned with his army) succeeded in suppressing the rebellion. Some of the bravest Arabs lost their lives, and in one battle alone, the number of the slain were so great that it came to be known as the Battle of the Nobles, i.e., Ghazwat al-ashraf. When the tragic news reached Hisham, the ruling caliph, he flew into a rage and vowed "By Allah I shall show what the wrath of an Arab is. I shall now despatch an army with its vanguard on their heads and the rear at my end. "He sent an army of his best worriers under the Qaisite generals Kulsum ibn Iyad and Balj ibn Bishr. During the war Balj was besieged at Ceuta along with his Syrian troops from the districts of Damascus, Jordan, Palestine, Emesa, Qinnasrin and Egypt. The blockade was so effective that famine broke out in that city. They exhausted their provisions and were forced to kill and eat the flesh of horses. Balj appealed to the Spanish governor 'Abd al-Malik (he held the post again after Uqba left for north Africa) for permission to land in Spain along with his army. 'Abd al-Malik was a sworn enemy of the Syrians. He turned down the appeal, and even punished those who rushed food to the besieged Syrians.

Very soon circumstances compelled 'Abd al-Malik to seek help of those very people whom he abhorred. At this time the Berbers of Spain also rose against the Arabs. Eversince the conquest, they had been nursing a secret hatred against the Arabs. The Arabs monopolised important civil and military posts. They had settled in the sunny and fertile regions, while the Berbers were thrust into the mountains of the central plateau and the bleak sierras of the north to guard the frontiers. The Berbers were often heard telling the Arabs" we conquered the Andalus, its cities and provinces, faught the Franks. Ours, therefore, is this country and the booty, and not yours". At the battle of Poiters it was this simmering discontent which led to disunity in the fighting forces. When the Berbers found the Arabs suffering defeat after defeat in the home of Berbers, they found the awaited opportunity for sweeping away Arab hegemony from Spain also. The Berbers of Galicia, Merida, Coria elected their leader (imam). They drove out the Arabs

from these regions, and prepared themselves for a direct assault
on Cordova. The aged 'Abd-al-Malik found himself between
the devil and the deep sea. He knew that if the Berbers were
left unchecked, the Arab supremacy would end; he also
apprehended that once the Syrians entered into Spain they would
plot to remove him from power. But after all, he was an Arab.
He invited the Syrians on the condition that they would leave
Spain after the Berber rising was over. Like a drowning man,
Balj clutched at the offer, and he landed in Spain with his three
thousand soldiers. The military operations against the Berbers
were successful. They were finally routed near Gauzalete, a
tributary of the Tagus.

Soon after 'Abd al-Malik asked Balj to leave Spain with his
soldiers. Balj went back on his pledge. Al-Maqqari says 'Balj
and his followers were elated with success, and their nostrils
were swelled with pride.'[8] The Syrians rose against 'Abd-al-
Malik, stormed his residence, dragged him out and executed
him on the bank of the Guadalquivir. Balj installed himself as
governor-general in Sept. 741. His action added fuel to fire.
The sons of Abd-al-Malik rose to avenge the death of their
father. They escaped from Cordova, and organised an agitation
at Saragossa. They enlisted the support of some of the bravest
warriors of the time, as well as some Berbers who were in no
mood to forgive the Syrians. They were defeated, but Balj died
of wounds. The Syrians nominated Thalaba bin Salamah as
governor-general. A civil war again broke out. The Arabs living
in Spain since the time of conquest hated the Syrian intruders;
the Berbers were still thirsting for revenge. The rivals met at
Merida, but again luck was on the side of the Syrians. Thalaba
returned to Cordova with hundreds of prisoners. The author of
Akhbar-al-Majmua has written about the barbarous treatment
of these prisoners many of whom had migrated from Medina

and belonged to the most notable families of the Helpers
(Ansars). They herded them in camps at some distance from
Cordova, and put them on sale as if they were goods and chattles.
old men, women, children were auctioned to the lowest bidder.
A venerable Ansar was knocked down for a dog, another for a
goat.[9]

The people were shocked at this inhuman treatment of the
prisoners. The news reached Damascus, and the government
asserted its authority. A new governor was posted. This was
Abu l-Khattar, a kalbite aristocrat. He arrived in May 743. Abu
l-Khattar immediately released the prisoners and won over the
Berbers by granting them general amnesty. He exiled Thalabah
and his turbulent supporters. He turned his attention to the
settlement of the Syrian soldiers. Acting on the advice of Artebas
(son of Witiza who was now the head of the Christian
community and apparently one of his advisers), he did not
expel the Syrians, but provided them with land to settle
permanently in Spain. The Egyptian division (Ar. jund) was
settled in Beja and Murcia; the contigent from Emessa was
assigned land in Neilba and Seville; the Syrians from Palestine
were settled in Sidonia and Algeciras; those from Damascus
were settled in the District of Elvira, and finally the soliders
from Qinnasrin and Jordon were granted fiefs in Jaen. The new
settlers were allocated a portion of land revenue in lieu of
compulsory military service as and when required.

With all his good intentions Abū l-Khattar was not free from
partiality, and this proved his undoing. He showed favour to
the Yememites, and alienated the Qaisites. It was at the time
that an influential Syrian appeared on the political scene like an
evil genius.

Sumail ibn Hatim was the grandson of the infamous Shimr

who severed the head of Imam Hussain at Kerbala. He fled from Syria, and joined Balj and reached Spain along with him. By his valour and calculated courtesy he won over the Qaisites. He commanded the respect of his group even though he was a drunkard and an agnostic pagan at heart. He was an extremely astute man, and a past master in the policy of divide and rule. Once he called upon Abū l-Khattar and complained about his partiality towards the Yemenites. Both exchanged hot words, and Abū l-Khattar ordered his guards to turn him out. In the scuffle with the guards he received several blows, and his turban fell on one side. As the insulted Qaisite was leaving, a person taunted at him — 'O Abul Joushan why is your turban inclined on one side' Fast came the reply "I shall soon ask my people to set it right." This was obviously a signal for war. Somail lost no time in collecting his partisans for a showdown. He knew that the Qaisites did not enjoy numerical superiority over the Kalbites, but his innate cunning came to aid. He won over the Judhamite chief Thawaba Ibn Salama by dangling the post of governor if he agreed to support him in removing Abu l-Khattar. The offer was too glittering for Thawaba to resist. The two groups fought for supremacy on the bank of the Guadalete in April 745. Abu l-Khattar was defeated and taken prisoner, and Thawaba was declared governor. In October 746 Thawaba died, and Somail manouvered to place Yusuf al Fihri (a grandson of the famous 'Uqbah bin Nafi) in the post of governor general. Yusuf was only a puppet in the hands of Somail. But the civil war was not yet over. The battle of Secunda (747) fought between the Qaisites and the Yemenites was one of the most ghastly bloodsheds since the entry of Tariq into Spain. The combatants fought till their swords broke, and then they resorted to sticks, stones and hand-to-hand scuffles. When the Yemenites showed signs of exhaution, Somail called in the people of Cordova. The rabble of butchers, bakers and shopkeepers fell on the tired Yemenites with their knives and sticks. The final issue was in favour of Somail and Yusuf. Abu l-Khattar ran for life and hid himself in a mill. He was hounded out and despatched, and his chief supporters were executed. The battle of Secunda shattered the Yemenites in the south, but they commanded considerable influence in the northeast. Yusuf posted Somail as governor at Saragossa where he could pursue the vendatta against the Yemenites. Three years after (753-75) an ambitious youth arrived from Cordova to stir up agitation against Somail with the help of the local Yemenites. Somail found himself besieged in the city. He appealed to the Syrians of Jaen and Elvira for help. The Syrians arrived and Somail was freed without much bloodshed.

Along with the Syrians squadrons, there came to Saragossa, some chieftains of the Umayyad family. These Umayyads were on a special mission. They wanted to discuss with Somail a matter of great political importance. A new star was soon to appear on the Spanish sky to restore order in the troubled country.

Notes

1. Regarding the expeditions of the Muslims in France, consult (i) M. Reinaud's Invasion des Sarrazins en France, translated into English by Prof. H.K. Sherwani and published at Lahore in 1964. (ii) L. Provençal: Histoire Vol I, pp. 53-65, and Sir Edward Creasy: Fifteen Decisive Battles of the World (Chapter VII, any edition), and Enan: Decicive Moments: pp. 41-72.

2. L. Provençal: Histoire, Vol. I, pp. 62.

3. Sir E.Creasy: Fifteen Decisive Battles, London,1909,Chapter VII.

4. LeBon: La Civilisation does Arabes, Paris 1884, pp. 325-32.

5. Hitti: History of the Arabs, London, 1953, p. 501.

6. H.A.Davies: An Outline History of the World: Oxford,1957, p.280.

7. Akhbar Majmu'a, p. 66.

8. Al-Maqqari/Gayongos, Vol. 2, p. 42.

9. Akhbar al Majmua, p. 81-82.

Chapter 4

Foundation of the Umayyad Kingdom of Cordova 'Abd ar-Rahman I (756-822)

From the very beginning, the Umayyad caliphs of Damascus were disliked for various reasons. The founder of the Umayyad dynasty, Mu'awiyya ibn abi Sufyan defied the legitimate caliph 'Ali, destroyed the republican form of government, and introduced monarchial absolutionism in Muslim polity by nominating his worthless son Yazid as his successor. The tragedy of Kerbala tarnished the image of the Umayyads which, even their vast intercontinental conquests, failed to rehabilitate. The wordly life of several Umayyads angered the pious Muslims who cherished the ideals of austerity and moral rectitude. The 'Kharji zealots were impatient to overthrow the Umayyads because in their eyes they had no moral legitimacy to rule over the Muslims. The public felt scandalised to see political leadership of the Muslims in the hands of those whose ancestors were the Prophet's worst persecutors. The Yemenites were awaiting an opportunity to avenge their defeat at Marj Rahit. The new converts were unhappy because the state charged jazia from them, even though they had embraced Islam. In

Persia, nationalism was brewing against the domination of the Arabs.

Several parties claimed the right to caliphate, and out of these, the Shias and 'Abbasids, had the largest following. The Shias believed that the imam or leader (both religious and political) of the Muslim ummah should be a descendant of the Prophet's daughter Fatima and her husband 'Ali, the fourth caliph. The Abbasids advanced their claim to caliphate as they were descendants of the house of 'Abbas, an uncle of the Prophet. Later on, the Shias opted in favour of the 'Abbasids. Here, it may be pointed out *en passant* that the Prophet left the choice of leader to the Muslims themselves. He did not recommend any descendant of his, either by a will, a spoken word or even a hint. This is understandable as the Prophet was not a hereditary ruler, and he had no intention to found a dynasty, whether temporal or spiritual.

The 'Abbasid leader at this time was Abu 1 'Abbas a great grandson of the Prophet's uncle 'Abbas. The 'Abbasids carried out extensive propaganda (Ar. da'wa) in their favour. Disguised as merchants, their supporters travelled from place to place preaching hatred against the Umayyads. The chief centre of their activity was Khurasan the northeastern province of Persia. In the reign of Marwan II (744-750) they were so bold that they held a massive rally of two hundred thousand supporters at Merv under the leadership of Abū Muslim, the chief organizer of anti-Umayyad agitation. Nasr bin Sayyar, the governor of Khurasan sent a fervent appeal to Marwan for re-inforcements. His appeal ended with the following celebrated lines pointing out the coming doom of the Umayyads :

"I see amidst the embers the glow of fire, and it
wants but little to burst into a blaze,

And if the wise ones of the people quench it not, its
fuel will be corpses and skulls.
Verily fire is kindled by two sticks, and verily
words are the beginning of warfare.
And I cry in amazement, "Would that I knew whether
the House of Umayya were awake or asleep!"[1]

On the June 9, 747, when the 'Abbasids unfurled a black
flag (symbol of their cause) near Merv, every one could see
that the eclipse of the Umayyads was not very far off. Only
after a few months (Sep. 2, 749) the Abbasids captured the city
of Kufa, and on Nov. 29 Abu l-'Abbas was proclaimed caliph
in the grand mosque. In the final struggle (March 750) Merwan
was defeated at the battle of Zab. He fled to Egypt, but was
caught in a Coptic church and killed. He was the last Umayyad
caliph. The 'Abbasid caliph occupied Damascus. Later on the
new dynasty shifted the capital to Baghdad.

Abu l 'Abbas inaugurated his reign by a virtual genocide of
the Umayyads — an obvious backlash of the tragedy of Kerbala.
The tombs of the Umayyad rulers were desecrated. The leading
princes were hounded out and massacred. A princess was slain
because she refused to divulge the place where the treasures of
her grandfather Hisham were stored. When 'Abbas came to
know that many Umayyads had gone into hiding, he issued a
general amnesty and invited them to a state banquet, and
massacred them in cold blood. Among the luckiest to escape
was 'Abd ar-Rahman, a grandson of Hisham. He made his way
to Spain, and founded the Umayyad kingdom of Cordova to the
perpetual chagrin of the 'Abbasids caliphs of Baghdad. His
dramatic flight from Syria, his narrow escapes, his long travels
through the Libyan sands, his perilous sojourns in north Africa,
and his arrival in Spain, make a throbbing epic.

'Abd ar-Rahman[2] was born in 731. As his father died when he was only six years old, he was brought up by Hisham. He was given a good education befitting a prince of royal blood. He grew up into a tall, sturdy and precociously intelligent youth. A son of Mu'awiya II from his Berber wife, 'Abd ar-Rahman inherited the astuteness of his family, and the tenacity of the Berber. To these inherited qualities he combined the polished urbanity of the cosmopolitan court of Damascus. He was only a youth of twenty summers when the Umayya dynasty vanished from the East. His brother Yahya was captured and killed, and his own life was always in danger. He stole out of Damascus, and retired to a village on the bank of the Euphrates. The spies of 'Abbas scented his whereabouts. One day he was resting in a dark room to give relief to his ailing eyes, when his four years son Sulaiman, and his younger brother came running to him. When he looked out, he saw a company of horsemen galloping towards the house with black flags in their hands. 'Abd ar-Rahman told his sisters of the coming danger, and fled away from the village along with his younger brother. He informed his sisters that he would leave for Palestine if all went well with him. 'Abd ur-Rahman and his brother took shelter in the adjoining woods. Soon he found that the horsemen were still pursuing them. The two brothers ran fast, and plunged into the river. The younger brother was a timid swimmer, and swam back trusting the assurances of safety shouted by the horsemen. He reached the bank, and was slain. 'Abd ur-Rahman swam on and crossed the river. Walking from one village to another he reached the coast of Palestine. His faithful valet Badar found him out. From now onwards Badar became 'Abd ar-Rehman's most trusted confidant, and followed him through all his trials and tears. Before he left Palestine, Salim, a freedman of his sisters, also joined him with some money and jewellery. Salim

had visited Spain during the time of Musa but he had returned
to the East. He was to act as a guide having known all the
routes to north Africa. Passing through the isthmus of Suez, the
three travellers entered Egypt, but 'Abd ar-Rahman could not
remain there very long because the 'Abbasids were gradually
consolidating their position. He had to seek a remoter place for
safety. After years of travelling, he reached Barca. He hoped
that the local governor Ibn Habib who had not yet recognised
the 'Abbasids, would give him protection. But he was
disappointed, because Ibn Habib was planning to declare his
independence, and he had even beheaded some Umayyad
princes. The arrival of 'Abd ar-Rahman upset him, and he laid
a plan to get rid of him. A Jewish astrologer came to his aid,
and he started his westward odyssey once again. He passed into
the land of the Berbers, and again wandered in search of safety.
At last he arrived at the coastal town of Naqur inhabited by the
Berber tribe of Nafza to which his mother belonged.

'Abd ar-Rahman had now enough time to plan his future.
The East was permanently lost to him. He could not think of
settling among the wild Berbers. He saw that his future lay
only in Spain. It was not difficult for him to acquaint himself
with the contemporary political situation in Spain because Naqur
was close to Ceuta which commanded the sea route across the
straits of Gibraltar. The long-drawn-out civil war between the
Qaisites and the Yemenites on one hand, and the Berbers and
the Syrians on the other, had weakened the administration, and
the country was drifting towards chaos. At this hour, a strong
hand was needed to curb civil strifes, and to make a clean
sweep of all the trouble-makers. 'Abd ar-Rahman could depend
on the wholehearted supported of the Syrians, and the many
influential Umayyads from Damascus living in the districts of
Jaen and Elvira. Kindled with hope and fired with ambition, the

young prince wrote a letter to the Umayyad clients. The brief contents of this historic letter are available. 'Abd ar-Rahman began by narrating the fall of the Umayyad dynasty, his own wanderings, the treatment of ibn Habib, and the dire plight of his family members living as exiles and refugees. He told them that he desired to come to Spain, but was afraid of the governor-general Yusuf who would not let him live in peace. He reminded them that being a grandson of caliph Hisham he had a legitimate right to the government of Spain. "It is only from you (the letter said) that I can hope for help, and if you think I stand a chance of success with your support, inform me"[3]. The letter was carried by Badr.

Badr reached Spain in June 754, and sought out the Umayyad clients - 'Obaid Allah, ibn Khalid, and Yusuf ibn Bakhat. In those days clientage meant a sacred bond like blood relationship, and the descendants of a freedman were under an obligation to extend help and hospitality to the descendants of the person who gave them freedom from slavery. These leaders conferred among themselves, and unanimously decided to invite 'Abd ar-Rahman to Spain. Before sending a reply to 'Abd ar-Rahman they thought that it would be prudent to enlist the support of the Qaisite Sumail who was the pivot of contemporary politics of the country. It was for this reason that the Umayyad leaders visited Saragossa along with the Syrian contigents. The pro-Umayyad chiefs were led by Ubaid Allah. As soon as Somail was rescued by the Syrians, the Umayyad clients introduced Badr to him, and explained the purpose of their visit. Somail refused to support the cause of 'Abd ar-Rahman. (A part of the reply he gave 'Ubaid Allah is too dirty to be translated.) The Umayyad leaders returned to Cordova. They were determined to place Spain under 'Abd ar-Rahman. They consulted the Yemenites also. They were most unhappy with the conduct of

Yusuf. After the last confrontation between the Qaisites and the Yemenites, it was agreed that the post of governor-general shall be held by rotation each year by a member of each group, but Yusuf refused to give a chance to the Yemenites. They were ready to espouse any faction which would overthrow Somail and Yusuf from power. They promised to rise to a man in support of the Umayyad pretender. Confident of their success, the Syrian leaders sent a delegation along with Badr to lead 'Abd ar-Rahman to Spain. The delegates were provided with five hundred gold dinars for incidental charges.

'Abd ar-Rahman spent nearly a year in suspense and anxiety. He would frequently visit the coast in the hope of seeing Badr return from his mission. One evening he had finished his sunset prayer when he saw, in the dim twilight, a boat nearing the coast. Badr was so overwhelmed with joy that he lept into the sea without waiting for the boat to anchor. He swam to his master, and imparted the happy tidings. Soon, other delegates led by ibn 'Alqamah also joined. 'Alqamah was introduced to 'Abd ar-Rahman." What is your nickname?", asked 'Abd ar-Rahman. 'Alqamah replied "Abū Ghalib" (father of the conqueror). It is a good omen; we shall conquer", said Abd ar-Rahman[4].

On August 14, 755 'Abd ar-Rahman landed at the Spanish port of Almunecar[5]. He was received by the Syrian leaders — 'Ubaid Allah and Khalid, and conducted to the castle of Torrox situated on the banks of the Xenil. Soon the news of his arrival spread like wild fire, and hundreds of people came to assure him of their readiness to fight under his banner. The time of his arrival was cleverly fixed by his sympathisers as Yusuf and Somail were busy in pacifying the northern frontier in the region of Pamplona. Ummul 'Usman, the wife of Yusuf sent a courier to her husband informing him of 'Abd ar-Rahman's arrival and the mass defection in his favour. Yusuf at once opened negotiations to buy off the young pretender. His secretary ibn Khalid, a converted Goth, visited Torrox, and offered a rich estate on behalf of his master and also the hand of his daughter. The negotiations failed as 'Abd ar-Rahman was not willing to live merely as a rich landlord. Meanwhile, the partisans of 'Abd ar-Rahman increased daily. He rapidly toured the colonies of the Syrians in Jaen, Archidona and Sidonia. In March 756 he entered Seville whose people took an oath of allegiance to him. Thus, without bloodshed the southern districts of Spain acknowledged him as their leader. At Seville a report came that Yusuf was marching towards him from the right bank of the Guadalquivir. 'Abd ar-Rahman left Seville, and proceeded with his army along the opposite bank in order to reach Cordova before Yusuf. It was not long before the two armies lay facing each other with the river between them.

The battle which gave 'Abd ar-Rahman the sceptre of royalty was fought in the plains of Masara very close to Cordova. As the river was in full spate crossing it was hazardous. When the tides began to fall in early May , 756, 'Abd ar-Rahman resorted to an stratagem so typical of the Umayyads. He sent a message to Yusuf intimating his acceptance of the proposals brought by his secretary provided he allowed him to cross the river. Yusuf fell into the trap. As soon as 'Abd ar-Rahman crossed the river, he drew up his army in a battle array. Fighting began on May 15, 756. 'Abd ar-Rahman's cavalry routed the enemy's right wing, but the left wing manned by the Qaisites held out till afternoon. The bravest Qaisites fell on the field. Yusuf and Somail each lost a son, and they fled away in dismay. Wild with joy the Yemenites began to pillage the abandoned camps of Yusuf. A column ransacked his palace, and 'Abd ar-Rahman had to take stern measures to stop their excesses. The Umayyad prince entered Cordova in triumph and occupied the official residence (*dar al-imara*) of the governor-general. The wife and daughter of Yusuf were removed to a safe place, and they were permitted to take with them all their valuables under military escort. 'Abd ar-Rahman was publicly declared *'Amir'* of Muslim Spain at a brief ceremony in the mosque of Cordova. The homeless wanderer became the master of a kingdom. He was barely twenty six at the time.

The victory at the bank of the Guadalquivir gave 'Abd ar-Rahman a dominion, but no security. His position was precarious because he was hemmed in by powerful enemies. The immediate danger came from Yusuf and Somail. They soon gathered their forces for a final bid to oust the insolent Syrian pretender. Yusuf's son Abū Zayd was already moving towards Cordova to join his father. 'Abd ar-Rahman installed 'Ubaid Allah at Cordova as his deputy, and left in pursuit of Yusuf and Somail. Soon after he left, Abū Zayd stormed the city. For a while it seemed that 'Abd ar-Rahman was doomed, but in his darkest hour he never lost his balance. He returned to Cordova like a whirlwind. Abū Zayd ran away, and Cordova was once again in the hands of 'Abd ar-Rahman. Yusuf and Somail soon realised the futility of continued fighting, and they sued for peace. An agreement was reached according to which they recognised 'Abd ar-Rahman as *de jure* ruler of Spain. 'Abd ar-Rahman restored their estates, and permitted them to reside at Cordova. Yusuf agreed to hand over his son as a hostage. He was also under an order not to leave Cordova without permission. However, after two years, Yusuf escaped, and raised a large army at Merida. He intended to occupy Cordova, but on his way he was beaten back by the loyalist governor of Seville. Yusuf ran away to Toledo where he was treacherously assassinated (759-760), and his severed head was transported to Cordova. As for Somail, he was already in prison. One day he was found dead. In all probability, he was strangled to death in the same year.

The death of Yusuf and Somail did not end the woes of 'Abd ar-Rahman. The 'Abbasid caliph Mansur claimed Spain as a legitimate province of his empire. He ordered ibn Mughith, the governor of Africa to annex Spain on his behalf. Mughith was a relative of Yusuf, and he had an obvious interest in the enterprise. He landed (763 A.D.) with a substantial army at Beja, in south Portugal, and unfurled the black flag of the 'Abbasids. Mughith found some supporters even among the Yemenites. Badr was sent to check them, but he had no success. At last, 'Abd ar-Rahman himself took the field. He was trapped by the enemy at Carmona with his contingent of seven hundred soldiers. For two months his fate hung in the balance, but he did not loose his heart. He summoned his soldiers, lighted a fire near the Seville Gate, and threw his scabbard into the flames. This was a traditional signal to his soldiers that they were faced with a grim situation which demanded supreme sacrifice. A few words of courage raised their drooping spirits. Showing unusual courage, 'Abd ar-Rahman made a desperate sortie, and after breaking the siege attacked the 'Abbasid supporters. It was a lucky day for him. Hundreds of enemy soldiers including ibn Mughith lay dead on the battlefield, and the rest fled for life. 'Abd ar-Rahman was not a vindictive person, but he wanted to teach Mansur a lesson. The head of Mughith was cut off, embalmed, wrapped in a black flag along with his order of appointment, and despatched to Mansur through a merchant bound for the East. When Mansur heard about the gruesome parcel, he cried with horror, "Thank Allah that he has placed a sea between me and that devil"[6]. Mansur was often heard praising 'Abd ar-Rahman for his wonderous achievements. One day a lively discussion took place in the presence of his courtiers. The subject was — Who was entitled to be called 'the Falcon of the Quraysh? '(Trained falcons are valued by the Arabs for hunting because of their capacity for flying long distances, their vigilance, and swiftness of attack). Everyone gave his own opinion but Mansur wound up the debate by giving his own verdict. In his estimation the 'Falcon of Quraysh' was the youthful 'Abd ar-Rahman who eluded his enemies, traversed jungles and seas, raised armies, and founded a kingdom in a far off country by his statesmanship, determination and above all by his own efforts.[7]

After the failure of the Abbasid conspiracy, 'Abd ar-Rahman's authority was firmly established, but there was no end to revolts. His army was constantly on the march from one trouble spot to another. Toledo was already simmering with insurgency. After this was suppressed in 764, he turned to the perfidious Yemenites. They had collaborated with him only to overthrow the tyrannical rule of Yusuf. They had no natural liking for 'Abd ar-Rahman. Soon after the battle of Masara, they plotted to remove 'the beardless youth' from Syria. 'Abd ar-Rahman tried to win over the Yemenites and even appointed one of their chiefs — Abū Sabbah, as governor of the important city of Seville, but they did not give up their secret treasonable activities. When ibn Mughith landed in Portugal some of them gave their wholehearted support. 'Abd ar-Rahman watched their designes patiently. As most of his dangerous enemies had been eliminated, he could face the Yemenites from a position of strength. He dismissed Abū Sabbah, but left the door open for an amicable settlement. He invited him for talks. Abū Sabbah arrived with a body of a thousand cavalrymen whom he left at the gate. During the interview he behaved insolently. 'Abd ar-

Rahman scolded him, and to frighten him, he summoned a negress. She entered with a dagger in her hand. Abū Sabbah rushed at her, but was overpowered by the guards and stabbed to death. His murder (whether pre-planned or accidental) unleashed the pent-up fury of the Yemenites. The Yemenite chief Abd al-Ghaffar (a cousin of Abū Sabbah) and Haiyan ibn Mutamis raised an army for direct assault on Cordova. They enlisted the support of some Berbers. 'Abd ar-Rahman by his sheer cleverness won over the Berbers, and when the battle began they deserted *en mass*. Left alone to fight, the Yemenites were routed (774) on the bank of rivulet Bembézar with a fearful carnage. Hundreds of Yemenites perished; the dead were given a mass burial in a trench which could be seen after the lapse of a century. The dream of the Yemenites to capture Spain was shattered. None could foresee at that time that a Yemenite law student of Cordova would confine the tenth descendant of 'Abd ar-Rahman in the golden cage of the royal palace, and himself rule like a *de jure* prince. Such are the vicissitudes of history!

When 'Abd ar-Rahman was dealing with the Yemenites a Berber school master named Shaqya ibn Abdul Wahid was bitten by the political bug. Probably, he had Khariji leanings. His rebellion spread over Coria, Merida and the Guadalajara. Fortunately for 'Abd ar-Rahman, the rebel Berber was killed by his own people sometime in 776. But, 'Abd ar-Rahman had to face the most perilous challenge to his authority from the French king Charlemagne, (the grandson of Charles Martel) who led an expedition into Spain at the invitation of some treacherous Muslim chiefs. The dissident group was headed by the kalbite Sulaiman ibn Yaqzan ibn al-'Arabi the governor of Barcelona, an adventurer named 'Abd ar-Rahman ibn Habib, and Abū Thawr the governor of Heusca. The three conspirators proceeded to Paderborn where they met Charlemagne and forged an alliance to dethrone 'Abd ar-Rahman. Charlemagne undertook to enter Spain, while ibn al-'Arabi agreed to join him with his army. Ibn Habib promised to land with the African Berbers on the eastern coast. The plan so well-conceived was doomed to miscarriage. Ibn Habib landed with his Berber mercenaries at Murcia before Charlemagne appeared in Spain. He suspected the kalbite ibn al-Arabi of treachery. He attacked him and was killed. When Charlemagne arrived in Spain in 778, one of his confederates was already dead. He proceeded towards Saragossa where ibn al-Arabi was waiting for him with his forces in the hope of winning over Hussain ibn Yahya, the governor of the city. But Yahya was not prepared to play second fiddle to ibn al-Arabi. When Charlemagne was preparing to besiege Saragossa, news came that the Saxons had invaded the Rhone valley, and Cologne was about to collapse. Charlemagne hastily wound up the operations. He was so angry that he arrested ibn al-Arabi. In a fit of disillusionment he razed the walls of Pamplona and pillaged the city which was inhabited by the Basques, one of the wildest peoples of northern Spain. On his homeward journey, while crossing through the gorges of Roncesvalles, his rearguard loaded with booty was attacked by the Basques. In a fearful massacre, Charlemagne lost his best paladins, and his proud army was annihilated. The Muslims profited by this chaos. Metruh and Ayshun, the two sons of ibn al-'Arabi succeeded in releasing their father. Two years after (780) 'Abd ar-Rahman himself arrived in the northern region, and captured the city of Saragossa. Ibn al-'Arabi was slain by ibn Yahya in a mosque for his treachery. The danger from France was over, but it left its echoes in the *"Chanson de Roland* (Song of Roland)"*, one of the greatest epics in French literature.

'Abd ar-Rahman was now the undisputed master of his kingdom. What was the territory held by him? It must be made clear to the reader that 'Abd ar-Rahman's authority did not extend over the whole of the Spanish peninsula. A part of the northern territory had been liberated by the Christians, and was permanently held by them before 'Abd at-Rohman's arrival. Already the great divide between Christian Spain and Muslims had taken place. We shall have to look back to find how this happened as it was a very serious development.

When Musa and Tariq left for Damascus, the entire peninsula had been conquered by them, and garrisons had been stationed at all strategic places in the north. After the battle of la Junda, the Gothic Christians submitted to the Muslim rule because they clearly saw that armed resistance would yield no results. Some of their leaders migrated to Rome, while others entered into favourable treaties with the conquerors, and retained their estates. The rest of the people found that their lot was better than under the Gothic rulers. But the patriotic Christians who were not willing to barter their freedom (or submit to the infidel as Watt has put it) took refuge in the inaccessible mountains of the extreme north. They brought with them their religious books, the relics of saints and other ecclesiastical belongings. They chose one Pelayo (Ar. Balayo) son of a Gothic diginatory as their leader. According to Christian sources, he established himself in a village at the Bay of Biscay, and organised a small resistance force. Pelayo and his men could not fight in the open. They organised guerilla attacks against the Berber garrisons. Gradually they became so bold that barely after a few years of Tariq's departure it became necessary to despatch a force under 'Alqamah and the Bishop Oppas to curb their inroads. Pelayo waited for them near the cave of Santa Maria later called Cavadonga, situated about forty miles from the coast at a considerable height. Oppas tried to win over the rebels, but he failed. As the Blessed Mary herself appeared on behalf of the Christians, they believed that their victory was assured. When the Muslim army moved through a narrow pass, Pelayo and his men made a sudden sally. The Muslims were trapped and routed like the Greeks at the pass of Thermopoly, and 'Alqamah was killed. The disasterous defeat is placed in the year 718 when Al-Hur was the governor-general of Spain. A modern historian (Sancho Albornoz) places the event in 721. Whatever the date, the defeat of the Muslims marks the beginning of the long struggle to liberate Spain. The Muslim historians have reported a somewhat different account of the event. They tell us that Pelayo was actually defeated and his men were scattered in the mountain passes where they eked out a miserable life by subsisting on herbs and honey. The Muslims took scant notice of Paleyo and his wandering companions. The Muslim leaders belonged to the warrior class. Born and bred to arms, they lacked the vision to look into the future. Instead of nipping in the bud the movement launched by Pelayo, the Muslims wasted their energies in leading expeditions into France. "Had the Muslims destroyed the last vestiges of Christian power in the moutainous north, the subsequent history of Spain might have been extremely different," — says Prof. Hitti.[8]

Paleyo died in 737 leaving the leadership to his son Fafila. The latter was succeeded by Palayo's son-in-law Alfonso the Catholic (739-757). He was the founder of the tiny Christian kingdom of Asturia in the extreme northwest of Spain. The reign of Alfonso coincided with the mass exodus of the Berbers from their northern settlements when the Berber revolt (reported earlier) broke out in north Africa. Those who remained evacuated their posts in the devastating famine of 750. The Berbers were the sentinels of the northern frontiers. For Alfonso their exodus was a heaven-sent opportunity. He made successive forays and enlarged his small principality by incessant guerilla warfare. He annexed the whole of Galicia by a series of campaigns and even took control of the valley of Duero. The towns of Astorga, Leon, Tuy, Porto, Zamora, Segovia, Amaya, Osma, Salamanca and Avilla fell to his arms. The Berber were driven out to a man. All this happened when a civil war raged between the Qaisites and the Kalbites. In later centuries out of the northern territories arose several Christians states — the kingdoms of Leon, Castile, Navarre and Aragon. The amoeba planted by Pelayo in the craggy heights of the Asturias, grew into the formidable Goliath of Spanish nationalism which the Davids of Cordova could not destroy. When 'Abd ar-Rahman landed in Spain, the Christians had already recovered about one fifth of the country. The peninsula was divided into two parts — the one under the Cresent, and the other under the Cross. The northern boundary line of the territory under the Muslims ran from Coimbra to Pamplona passing through Coria, Talavera, Guadalajara and Tudela. This was not a mutually agreed frontier, but only a line of control flanked on both the sides by a no-man's land, empty and desolate, which afforded a favourite rendezvous for rebels, criminals and spies. There was not much traffic across the border during the days of the early Umayyad rulers. Sometimes, a daring band of monks, Christian pilgrims and merchants (mostly Jews) would cross from one territory to another. Often the border would echo with the clamour of arms when the soldiers would cross from one kingdom to another either as an act of aggression or a punitive reprisal. Whenever a Muslim ruler died, or there was a war of succession, the Christians did not omit to make incursions into the Muslim territory. "The forays of the Christians were a terrible curse to their victims; they were rude, unlettered people and few ·of them could ever read; their manners were on a par with their education; and their fanaticism and cruelty were what might be expected from such uncouth barbarians. Seldom did the soldiery of Leon give quarter to a defenceless foe, and we may look in vain for the fine chivalry and the tolerance of the Arabs; where the latter spared nobly, the rough warriors of Leon and Castile massacred whole garrisons, cities full of inhabitants and those whom they did not slaughter, they made slaves".[9]

When Alfonso died in 757, 'Abd ar-Rahman was fighting for his survival after the battle of Masara. The four successors of Alfonso — Fruela I (757-768), Aurela (768-774), Sila (774-783), and Mauregato (783-789) were contemporary with 'Abd ar-Rahman. He wanted to live at peace with the northern kingdoms as his own future was uncertain, and it was no doubt for this reason that he entered into an armistice with them in June 759. Al-Razi, a later Spanish historian has left details of this treaty between "the noble and very respectable (*al amir al-akram al malik al mu'azzam*) 'Abd ar-Rahman and the monks, the patriarchs and the people of Castile". According to the treaty the Christians undertook to pay a tribute of ten thousand ounces of gold, and equal weight of silver in addition to horses, mules, swords and armour.[10] The impoverished Christians must have felt humiliated by agreeing to what they could hardly fulfil. We are not, therefore, surprised that hostilities broke out in 768. The Muslims suffered a grievous defeat at Pontuvium in Galacia. The Muslim historians are silent on this defeat, and reprisal, if any. Apparently, 'Abd ar-Rahman knew that it was no use to stir up a hornet's nest when his hands were full of serious problems. He was anxious to set his own house in order.[11]

'Abd ar-Rahman's meteoric arrival in Spain was a blessing

for the young Muslim state. He saved it from extinction by halting anarchy. But like a meteor he did not disappear from the political scene as swiftly as he appeared. "He was a political genius of the first order, equal to Octavian Augustius or the younger Pitt in both youth and attainment"[12] says Irving. He laid the foundation of the Umayyad rule in Spain after the eclipse of this dynasty in the East. The western Umayyad kingdom of Cordova lasted for almost two centuries and a half. Most of his successors were remarkable rulers who, by virtue of their achievements in the arts of war and peace, rank with the outstanding rulers of the famous dynasties of Europe. 'Abd ar-Rahman knew the plight of the Umayyads in the East. He felt morally bound to help them. He invited the Umayyads to migrate to Spain. He sent a delegation under the qaḍi Salih al-Hadrami to contact the members of the Umayyad clan and persuade them to settle in Spain. As a result of their efforts many prominent Umayyads and princes of royal blood who were hiding in the East found a haven of refuge in Spain. 'Abd ar-Rahman received them with open arms, provided them with employment, and allocated land for their rehabilitation. These newcomers constituted the hard-core of Umayyad hegemony in Muslim Spain. Only his two sisters declined to leave Syria. They were rich, and the 'Abbasids rulers were kind to them. They regularly exchanged letters and gifts with their brother at the far end of the Mediterranean.

During his long reign of thirty two years he worked hard to consolidate his position. While suppressing numerous revolts, he paid attention to overhauling the administration which had been torn to pieces during the decades of civil wars. He divided his kingdom into provinces, and placed each under a governor (Ar: *Wali*) who was assisted by a high military officer. At the centre, he had a number of advisers who helped him in the discharge of his duties as head of the state. One or two secretaries looked after his correspondence. The judiciary was headed by qaḍis who followed the Syrian imam 'Abd ar-Rahman Al-Awazai in their legal system.[13] He styled himself as *'amir'* of the state, and not the *'amir al-muminin'* (Commander of the faithfuls) out of respect for his powerful enemies, the 'Abbasids of Baghdad. However, he continued the invectives against the house of Abbas in the Friday sermons (Ar:*Khutba*) because of pressure from his relations. Whenever he found time, he toured the kingdom. Towards the middle of his reign he felt the necessity of raising an army. He employed mercenaries from European countries, and the African Berbers. The army was composed of forty thousand soliders. His relations with his non-Muslim subjects were cordial. Sara the granddaughter of Witiza (he had met at Damascus when she came to see his grandfather) was a constant visitor at the palace. He was on friendly terms with the uncles of Sara. As a builder he earned the everlasting gratitude of the Muslims by raising the first congregational mosques (*al-masjid jama*) at Cordova. The city was provided with a new wall. The Gothic residence of the governor was completely rebuilt according to the Syrian taste. The royal palace stood on the bank of the river, and to the west of the mosque. When his presence was not necessary at Cordova he retired with his family to his newly built country palace about three miles form the city. He named it *Rusafa* after a similar suburban palace of his grandfather on the bank of the Euphrates where he passed most of his childhood days.[14] The garden was planted with flora and fauna imported from Syria.

'Abd ar-Rahman was a tall and well built man with frank looks inspite of his having a defective eye. His complexion was fair. He had golden hair which fell in twisted plaits on each side of his face. He was endowed with a robust confidence in his destiny, and possessed almost superhuman courage and power of endurance. He was a shrewd man, and in this respect he resembled Mu'awiya the founder of the Umayyad dynasty. He could be harsh and compromising, relentless and forgiving, as and when necessary. He used force only when his security was at peril, and when a compromise was impossible. He stopped the Yemenites from plundering the palace of Yusuf by telling them philosophically "We should not exterminate our enemies because it is likely that they may become our friends one day"[15] When 'Ubaid Allah his earliest and most influential supporter was suspected of treason, he retailiated by telling his courtiers, "I shall impose on him a punishment worse than death. I shall simply ignore him." He was a deeply religious man and remained a teetotler all his life; women had no attraction for him. He was always dressed in white — a tradition followed by the Umayyad rulers and all Spanish Muslims. He was hospitable, and no one was allowed to leave his palace without taking lunch or supper with him. He visited the sick, and would not hesitate to receive his subjects in order to hear their grievances. He spoke elegant Arabic with a commanding voice.

His last years were clouded by some very sad events. His nephew Mughira was involved (784) in a conspiracy along with Somail's son, and both were executed. His father left Spain in anger, but 'Abd ar-Rahman was good enough to provide him with money so that he could settle in Africa. Even his valet Badr became insolent inspite of the favours showered on him. He was put under house arrest, but later on his impertinence turned so insufferable that he had to be exiled to a border town. 'Abd ar-Rahman became more and more gloomy, aloof and introvert. As he advanced in age he longed for Syria. Once he seriously thought of leading an army to dethrone the 'Abbasids. One day, during a promenade in the garden of the Rusafa, he saw a Syrian palm tree shooting out its branches, and he could not suppress his tears. He expressed his feelings in a short poem which has been preserved by the historians. Overwhelmed with sad nostalgia, he addressed the palm tree thus:

I behold a palm tree in the middle of Rusafa.
Alone in the West, away from the land of palm groves,
I said to it, "You are like me in a foreign land
Far from your relations as I am".
May the morning clouds keep you fresh!
May abundant rains console you for ever!

'Abd ar-Rahman died on Sept 30, 788, and was buried in the funerary garden of the palace.

Notes

1. E.G. Brown : Vol. 1, p. 241.
2. In the kitab al Majmu'a 'Abd ar-Rahman tells the story of his escape in his own words. pp. 89-91.
3. Akhbar Majmu'a : p. 106.
4. Al Maqqari/Gayangos, Vol. 2, p. 65, and also Kitab al Majmu'a, p. 115. See p. 113 for the reply Somail gave to 'Uaid Allah.
5. Provençal , Histoire: Vol. 1, p. 101.
6. Ibn Idhari: Vol. 2, p. 52.
7. Ibn Idhari: Vol. 2, pp. 59-60.
8. Philip Hitti: History of the Arabs: p. 551.
9. Lane - Poole : The Moor in the Spain, p. 119.
10. L. Provençal: Histoire Vol. I, p. 115-116 and Condé: Vol. I, p. 187.
11. At Pontuvium thousands of Muslims were slaughtered. Umar, the youngest son of 'Abd ar-Rahman was arrested, and he was beheaded, on the orders of the christian king. (L. Provençal, Histoire: Vol. I, p. 115).
12. T.B. Irving: p. 3.
13. Awzāi was a most liberal theologian. His liberalism contributed a great deal to the spread of Islam among Christians of Spain — says Prof. Hitti.

He was buried in a simple mosque on the beach outiside Beirut. The mosque still stands. [Hitti: Lebanon in History, London, 1957, pp. 269-271.

14. There is a small village on the site of 'Abd ar-Rahman's Rusafa. It is called Arrizafa. L. Provençal, Vol. 1, p. 136. It is now the property of a Spanish nobleman.

15. Al-Maqqari (Urdu), p. 361.

Chapter 5

Spain Under Hisham I (786-796) and Hakim I (796-822)

' A bd ar-Rahman nominated Hisham as his successor during his life. According to the law of primogeniture, his eldest son Sulaiman had a prior claim to the throne. When 'Abd ar-' Rahman escaped from Syria, Sulaiman was left behind. He was brought to Spain about 764, by a special envoy. Hisham was born in Spain from a Spanish slave girl. Sulaiman was about forty when his father died. Hisham was his junior by ten years. Both the brothers received a good education, but they were poles apart in character, Sulaiman was a happy-go-lucky man with little taste for literature and history of the Arabs. Hisham was a sober prince with attractive manners. Unlike his elder brother who moved with flatterers, Hisham delighted in the company of theologians. It is said that 'Abd ar-Rahman, after subjecting the two brothers to a test, found that Hisham was superior to Sulaiman in mental and moral qualities.

When 'Abd ar-Rahman died, both the brothers were governors — Sulaiman at Toledo, and Hisham at Merida. Only the youngest Abdullah was by the bed-side of his father. Within a week Hisham returned to Cordova, and on October 7, 788 was solemnly declared *"amir"* of Spain. But soon after, his two brothers joined hands to overthrow him. They could not put up a long fight as the most influential military commanders were Hisham's active supporters. They realised the futility of military confrontation, and sued for peace. Sulaiman renounced his claim to the throne. Hisham purchased his estate for a sum of sixty thousand dinars. Sulaiman left for Africa to live among the Berbers. 'Abdulla too followed him and settled at Tangiers. The two brothers remained calm as long as Hisham lived. Several minor revolts disturbed internal peace. Sa'id id ibn al-Hussain Ansari rose at Tortosa with the help of local Yemenites, but the neo-Muslim Musa ibn Forton al-Qasi came to the rescue of Hisham, and the rebellion was put down. A son of Sulaiman ibn Yaqzan ibn al-'Arabi raised the standard of revolt in the northeast, but he was defeated and killed. Some minor military operations reduced the rising of the Berbers in the hills of Ronda.

Peace at home gave Hisham freedom to adopt a forward policy towards the kingdom of Asturia. There were at least three brilliant commanders in the service of Hisham — Yusuf ibn Bukhat, 'Abd al-Wahid and 'Abd al-Karim. The last two were the sons of the famous ibn Mughith who conquered Cordova. They led several expeditions (Ar: *sa'ifa*) in the northwest held by Vermudo I and after him by Alfonso II. In all these expeditions the Muslims were victorious. Between 789 to 795, the Muslims penetrated into Alva and Oviedo. A few years before Hisham died, the Muslims poured into Septimania and reached the wall of Narbonne. The historians have given exaggerrated accounts of the booty which fell into the hands of the Muslims. But these expeditions did not bring any political gain. Except that the northern rulers suffered heavy losses in men and material, the territorial boundaries of the kingdom of Cordova remained what they were when 'Abd ar-Rahman died. The northern kingdom of Asturia was a *fait accompli*, and it was impossible to uproot it.

The state continued to flourish under Hisham. He made no changes in the administrative set-up. He deputed officers of experience to tour the provinces. They gave him reports on the conduct of officials, and those found guilty of misconduct were dismissed. He was particular about the collection of zakat, but imposed no taxes for which there was no religious sanction. He instituted the system of night-watch. He completed the mosque of Cordova, and rebuilt the bridge on the Guadalquivir. Hisham was a saintly man. He attended the prayers five times a day in the mosque. He encouraged the people to pray regularly, and often rewarded those found in the mosque. He would often steal out of his palace at night even in inclement weather on missions of mercy, with food and medicines for the sick and money for the needy. Several anecdotes show the nobility of his soul. When he rebuilt the bridge of Cordova, some cynics spread a rumour that he had done this for his own convenience and personal use. When he heard this he vowed that he would never cross the bridge, and he kept his word.

The fame of this pious king reached the Holy city of Madina where a saintly man was giving lectures on the traditions (hadith) of the Prophet of Islam. He was imam Malik ibn Anas, one of the founders of the Islamic jurisprudence of the Sunni Muslims. Scrupulously clean in dress, abstemious and puritanical, Imam Malik had a deep love for the Prophet, which he shared with the people of Madina. The holy city pulsated with the memories of the Prophet. There was the mosque in which he prayed, the house in which he lived, and the tomb where his holy remains were placed. The city abounded with men who could recall with loving memory what he said, how he conducted himself in public, and the many injunctions he delivered for the guidance of the Muslims. Imam Malik knew personally many sub-companions of the Prophet, and he recorded whatever he learnt about him. The sayings and traditions of the Prophet were compiled by the Imam in a book called 'Muwatta,' which is one of the earliest books on the Prophetic traditions, and forms the basis of the Maliki Jurisprudence. Having lived all his life in Madina, the Imam preferred the practice and usage of the local Muslims to deduction or logical interpretation in legal matters. The Muwatta which embodies over three thousand traditions of the Prophet gave a simple and austere school of Jurisprudence, and was most suitable to early century Muslims. Many Muslims travelled to Madina to learn hadith from Imam Malik. The Spanish Muslims who attended the lectures of the imam were Ziyad ibn 'Abd ar-Rahman, Yahya ibn Mudar, Isa ibn Dinar, ibn Habib, and the famous Berber Yahya ibn Yahya al-Laithi. During their stay at Madina they extolled Hisham's character and piety. The Imam blessed Hisham, and called him a model ruler. These theologians returned with enthusiastic devotion for the Imam, and they narrated to Hisham what the Imam thought of him. Hisham was so much pleased that he became a disciple of Imam Malik and introduced his doctrines among Spanish Muslims replacing the legal system of Awzāi. The 'Muwatta' of Imam Malik was committed to memory, copied and commented upon by generations of theologians. Only judges steeped in Maliki fiqh were appointed in the state judiciary. As all the Muslims in Spain belonged to the Maliki school, the 'Muwatta' was the most revered book after the Quran. Hisham was a devout man and naturally theologians came to occupy a prominent place in the state. They were champions of orthodoxy. It must be said to the credit of the Maliki theologians that they saved Muslim Spain from the disruptive and schismatic doctrines which rent the Muslim East. But except Hisham, the other Umayyad rulers were jealous of their prerogatives, and while they gave the ulema the respect due to them as scholars of theology and law, they did not allow them to interfere in political affairs and governance of the state. Irionically, Hisham's successor had to face the ire of the theologians, and we shall soon see how he assered his temporal authority as the supreme executive of the state.

On April 17th, 796, Hisham died after a brief reign of nine years, and joined his father besides his tomb in the garden of the palace. Before his death, he designated Hakam as his successor overriding the claim of his eldest son. Hakam was unlike his father in all respects. Hisham was gentle, Hakam was an iron man. Hisham was straightforward in his dealings, Hakam could be deceitful if necessary. Hashim pardoned offenders, Hakam left none unpunished. Hashim was abstemious, Hakam drank openly. Hisham lived a simple life, Hakam was fond of ostentation. Finally, Hakam unlike his father surrounded himself with poets and musicians, but kept his distance from theologians. Many circumstances forced him to autocratic, tyrannical and vindictive. The revolt of his uncles, the discontent among the citizens of Cordova, the conspiracies of theologians to dethrone him, the wars on the frontier towns of Merida, Toledo, are some of the major political events of the twenty-six years of his reign. Often one revolt was hardly supressed when another rose like the heads of Hydra. This tall, thin, and olive-skinned king with an aquiline nose never lost his *sang-froid*, and met the most menacing situation with ferocious repression. Hakam resembled many Roman emperors in his high-handed and firm grip over administration. But he deserves the credit due to him; he was a just ruler, and never spared any troublemaker. He consolidated the kingdom, gave it peace and prosperity which ushered in the dawn of Hispano-Muslim culture during the reign of his colourful successor.

Hardly a year after his accession his two uncles Sulaiman and 'Abdullah returned from Africa to claim the crown. 'Abdullah preceded Sulaiman. He reached the northeast frontier, but he was not successful in enlisting any support. In despair he entered into France along with his two sons, and met Charlemagne at Aix-la-Chapelle during the year 797 A.D. The French king did not like to intervene in his favour. 'Abdullah returned to Spain to stir up trouble in the north, but he was expelled by Bahlul a local chief. Disappointed again he entered into Valencia from where he sent feelers for a compromise. Hakam deputed the theologian Yåhya ibn Yahya, and an agreement was reached between the uncle and the nephew. 'Abdullah was permitted to live in Valencia as a vassal of Hakam. The reproachment was cemented by a matrimonial alliance. Hakam gave away his two sisters, Aziza and Salma to the two sons of 'Abdullah. The elder uncle Sulaiman arrived with a contingent of his supporters and made a direct attack on Cordova in 798, but his men could not stand against the better organised army of Hakam. He fled away to Merida where he was taken captive, and killed by a Berber chief. His body was transported to Cordova, and deposited with full honours beside the grave of 'Abd ar-Rahman.

How relentless Hakam could be, is seen in the manner in which he subdued the revolt in Toledo. The citizens of Toledo, both the Christians and the Muslims were a most turbulent people. They were proud of their Gothic/Roman ancestry, and remembered the prestige enjoyed by the city when it was the capital of the Gothic kingdom. Inspite of the great tolerance shown by the Umayyad rulers, the Christians were never reconciled to their position. The neo-Muslims (Ar. Sig: *muwwalad*) joined hands with the Christians, in creating turmoil in the city. Throughout the Muslim rule Toledo remained a boiling cauldron of insurgency. It was the Achilles' heel of Muslim Spain. When Hakam came to the throne Toledo was seething with discontent, and anytime its citizens could stage a massive resistance against the central government. There were at this time two agitators in Toledo. One was 'Ubaid bin Khamir who incited the people to break away form the centre, while other, a neo-Muslim named Gharbib who composed insulting lampoons on Hakam. In this dire situation, Hakam availed of the services of Amrus his loyal governor of Talavera. Amrus was a neo-Muslim of an influential Gothic family. Hakam transferred him to Toledo and gave him *carte blanche* to bring the city to normalcy. Amrus arrived at Toledo, and won over the confidence of the citizens. A major cause of annoyance and frequent riots was the presence of soldiers in the city. Amrus built a new castle on the outskirts of the city, and shifted the army to the new site. When this was done, he asked for more soldiers from the government under the pretext of conducting military operations in the northern borders. The fresh contingents were stationed in the new fort. The 16 years old crown prince 'Abd ar-Rahman who arrived with the army hardly knew what Amrus had in his mind. Amrus invited prominent citizens of Toledo to a state banquet to felicitate the young prince. The guests had to pass through a passage leading to the banquet hall. They reached the end of the passage, where one by one they were beheaded and their bodies thrown into a ditch. The slaughter lasted the best part of the night. As the invitees did not return home anxious enquiries were made about them but none knew their whereabouts. By chance a physician saw fumes reeking with the smell of blood at the back of the fort, and the truth came to light. A pall of gloom hung over Toledo. The people were dazed and paralysed by the ghastly deed. There were lamentations in many houses, but Hakam and Amrus were satisfied that Toledo was a calm city. So long Hakam reigned there was not much trouble in Toledo. This tragedy was known as *waq'at al hufra* i.e. 'Day of the ditch'. The event took place sometime in 807.[1]

Hakam was equally ferocious in handling the rising at Cordova. He was disliked by a body of theologians for his moral laxity. They wanted to see on the throne a puritan like Hisham. They denounced him to the people as a profligate from the pulpits of the mosques. Sometime in May 805, many influential citizens of Cordova, in collaboration with theologians, plotted to remove him, and to place Muhammad ibn Qasim (a grandson of 'Abd ar-Rahman) on the throne. The plot leaked out. Hakam acted swiftly. He arrested the conspirators, and ordered their execution. Among the sixty persons executed there were two uncles of Hakam, and several theologians of renown. For a decade the citizens of Cordova sulked under his autocratic rule. A new trouble arose in a colony across the Guadalquivir. Since the conquest of Spain, the population of Cordova had been increasing steadily, and a new colony had sprung up in the south of the city. The *'rabad'* as it was called, had a mixed population of the Arabs and the neo-Muslims. Most of them were merchants and artisans. They were zealous followers of imam Malik. The theologians had a tremendous hold on them. Yahya ibn Yahya who had run away during the previous riots had since returned and started his religious discourses. Many students daily crossed the bridge to attend his lectures in the mosque of Cordova. These students were vociferous in their condemnation of Hakam. Hakam had correctly sensed that their

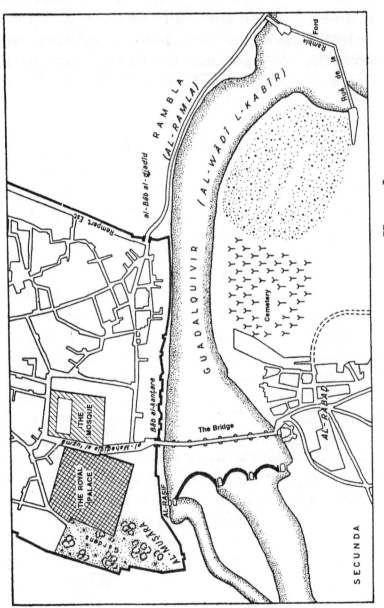

CORDOVA DURING THE REIGN OF HAKAM I

activities against him could start any time. As a precaution, he strengthened the rampart. On the eastern side of the city, he built a new gate (called bāb al-Jadid) from where a road ran along the river to a ford giving additional access to the rabad. The army could reach rabad from two points — the main bridge behind the mosque and the new ford not far from the bridge. Hakam had already raised a powerful mounted guard of five thousand horsemen for the protection of the palace. The new force was made up of some negroes, but mainly of the Christians from European countries. As they could not speak Arabic they were called 'mutes' (Ar: *al Khurs*). Hakam built barracks, and stables for the cavalry, and placed them under the command of Count Rabi son of Teodulfo a local Christian of some influence. The funds for the new force were provided by unlawful taxes (Ar: *magharim*). The burden of the new taxes fell on the merchant community. All these factors, theological and economic, combined to spread dissatisfaction among the people. On March 25, 818 a minor incidence led to a conflagration. A soldier picked up a quarrel with an artisan in rabad and killed him. A cry of revenge rose in the street, and spread over the whole colony. On that day Hakam was hunting in the woods south of rabad. While returning to his palace he was greeted by angry shouts of the infuriated mob. Soon the people marched towards the palace with every weapon in their hands. The army was called in to control the surging crowd, but it was not successful, and Hakam himself came out of the palace with his pretorian guards. In the meantime, 'Ubaid Allah a son of Hakam's uncle (known as *sahib al-sawa'if*) sallied from the New Gate, crossed the ford, and attacked the rioters. The rioting crowds could not withstand the murderous onslaught of the royal cavalry. What followed was a virtual massacre of the people. The soldiers of Hakam entered into the houses, killed the occupants, and burned down their houses. Not even their mosques were spared by the angry army. After three days their leaders were arrested, and three hundred of them were nailed to the stakes. The citizens of rabad rendered homeless, were ordered to leave Spain as Hakam was determined to clear the colony of all demagogues and fanatics. Fifteen thousand men and women sailed from Spain in search of new homes. Many landed in northwest Africa where they were welcomed as they were skilled horticulturists, artisans and builders. Some of them found asylum in Qayrawan where their descendants still live in the locality called 'Madinat al-Andalusiyin'. Their greatest number migrated to the island of Crete via Alexandria under the leadership of an enterprising adventurer named Abū Umar Hafs, a native of Fahs al-Ballut. He founded a kingdom in Crete which lasted till 961 when the island was annexed by Byzantine Rome.

When Hakam came to the throne insurgency loomed all along the borders. Merida was rocked by revolts which endangered the entire western sector. By a series of campaigns Hakam cleared Merida of rebels, and established the Umayyad power as far as Coimbra. In the northeast, the situation was equally confused, as the power of the Umayyads was not yet firmly established in these border areas. In the early days of Hakam's reign the land of the Vascons- the future Navarre, was perpetually threatened by inroads, as there were but few Muslim settlements in this region. The Gothic new converts the Bani Qasi who held this region were only nominally loyal to the government of Cordova. Another Gothic family held Huesca. Saragossa and its environs had already passed into the hands of an agitator named Bahlul. Fortunately Hakam could depend on Amrus whose help was a great factor in rehabilitating his authority. Hakam sent Amrus with full powers to deal with Bahlul. Amrus arrived at Saragossa in 808. Bahul was removed and killed. He carried the war in the land of the Vascons, and remained as governor of the northeastern borders till his death. But neither Amrus, nor Hakam, could save Barcelona. Louis the Pious of France entered this city in 801 after a tight siege for two months. The Franks established a small enclave on the Spanish soil at the foot of the Pyrenees which came to be known as 'Gothic March'. This principality included the towns of Gerone, Cardona, Auson and Manressa. It was a source of perpetual annoyance to the government of Cordova. The loss of Barcelona was a great blow to the prestige of Hakam. Although he had the best generals under him, further attempts to recapture the city proved of no avail. The Franks used Barcelona as a spring-board to expand the Gothic March. In 808-809 Louis attacked Tortosa, but the combined forces of Amrus and the loyal governor of Tortosa, Ubaidun ibn al-Ghamr frustrated the designs of the invaders. In a fierce battle fought near the walls of Tortosa the Franks were routed, and they retired after suffering heavy losses. Sometime in 812 and armistice was concluded between Hakam and the French king for a period of three years. In 815 a war again broke out. Hakam wanted to dislodge the Franks from Barcelona. His cousin 'Ubaid Allah appeared in the plains near the city with a formidable and highly trained cavalry. The Franks suffered a defeat and they died in hundreds, but they held on to the city. Barcelona was lost after having remained in the hands of the Muslims for over eighty years. Hakam must have felt ashamed, but the conquest of the Balearic islands enhanced his prestige. These balmy islands (Mallorca Menorca, Ibiza, and Formentera) remained under Muslim domination upto the thirteenth century. They were centres of trade, agriculture, and celebrated for their fruit gardens. Traces of Muslim influence in these islands can be seen even today.

Although ruthless, Hakam was a good administrator. He had a firm grip over all the organs of the government with the help of an organised system of espionage, which scanned every nook and corner of his kingdom. He gave peace to the country, and firmly established the Umayyad rule even though he had to discard moral principles. He kept the judiciary clean from all pressures. Indeed, if Hakam was afraid of anyone, it was the judiciary. His reign was graced by two eminent judges — Mas'ab, and Muhammad ibn Bashir who were respected for their impartiality. Hakam himself bowed down his head when a qadi decided a suit filed against him by the owner of a slave girl employed in the palace. He heard the witnesses, and asked Hakam to produce the girl before him. Hakam proposed a compromise, and offered double the price for the girl, but the qadi would not agree. He personally went to Hakam, and insisted that either he should send the girl to the court, or accept his resignation. The girl appeared before the qadi, and on hearing her statement he restored her to the legal owner.[2]

We do not know much about his private life. The historians tell us that he left twenty sons and an equal number of daughters. He had several wives but not all of them seem to have borne children. Those found sterile were treated with respect. He encouraged them to undertake works of charity and public welfare. 'Ajab raised a mosque in the western sector of Cordova, and donated her entire income from her country palace (*munayat 'Ajab*) for the maintenance of a poorhouse. Another wife Mut'a allocated funds for construction of a mosque and enlargement of a cemetry called after her — *Maqbarat Mut'a*. Strangely enough, this harsh ruler was very courtly to the fair sex. The man who prided in his swordsmanship fell easy prey to the arrows of Cupid. He has left two fine poems (most of the Muslim rulers of Spain were good poets) bemoaning his utter helplessness when a pretty inmate of his harem got annoyed with him.[3]

Whenever he found time he would leave for hunting excursions in the woods near Cordova. He was fond of polo. He had no taste for theological discussions, but loved music and poetry. He was no hypocrate and made no secret of his love for wine. He was very careful of his personal appearance. A Christian named Jacinto regularly perfumed his beard. He was ready to help the needy. Hassana al-Tamimiya a talented poetess wrote to him against the governor of Elvira who had deprived her of her property. Hakam ordered restoration of her property and also fixed a monthly allowance for her. When his anger was over, he was prepared to forget and forgive. During the course of suppression of riots many theologians lost their lives. Among the prominent survivors was Talut ibn Abd al-Jabbar who had gone into hiding with a Jewish family. When Hakam granted amnesty, Talut was brought before him. Hakam sat on the carpet beside him. Talut was frightened, but Hakam spoke to him kindly. "Tell me Talut", he asked "if your son lives in this palace would he have shown you the same respect as I have now done? Did you ever find me wanting in help? Did I not visit you when you were ill? Did I not come to offer my condolence on the demise of your wife. Did I not walk to the cemetry to attend her burial? But you were after my blood. You insulted me. But I still respect you for your piety. I now forgive you, and assure you of my protection."[4]

Hakam was very proud of having preserved the integrity of his dominion. In a poem of self-appraisal, he sang with diabolical joy :

I have sewed the broken pieces of the earth with my sword

I have been doing this since my early days.
Ask the frontiers of my kingdom if there is any
disturbance there, and if there is such a situation,
I shall put on my armour and.draw out my sword.
Ask the skulls that lie scattered like pieces of broken
gourd.
They will tell you that I spare none, and showed no
hesitation in putting them to the sword.[5]

As years passed, by his pride ended in remorse. Like Macbeth
he saw nemesis hovering over his head. He would summon his
courtiers and entertainers at odd hours in a fit of melancholia
and dismiss them after a while. Already thin, he became still
thinner. Consumed by fever, tormented by hallucinations, and
racked by insominia, he turned to the Quran for spiritual peace.[6]
He remained mentally alert till his end. A fortnight before his
death he called in his ministers, and other high dignitries on the
Eid al-Zuha, and in their presence he nominated his son 'Abd
ar-Rahman as his successor. On May 21, 822, he died and was
laid to rest in cemetery of the royal palace. His last advice to
his son was that he should rule with justice tempered with
strictness.[7]

Notes

1. Ibn Hayyan assigned 181 AD/797, as the date of the event.
2. Akhbar majmu'a: p. 171-12.
3. Here is a free translation of one of his poems :
   Passionate love has turned a ruler into a slave
   If he weeps and complains, he is treated with
   Greater cruelty. Death stares into his face
   The gazalles of the palace have left him to his suffering
   And he has fallen to the ground.
   He who reclined on couches of silk
   Now rubs his cheeks on the dust

When a person falls in love
His fate is nothing but the humility of a slave.
Kitab al majmu'a, p. 182, also Ibn Adhari vol. II, p. 80.

4. Dozy has given full details of this interesting interview, pp. 256-257.

5. Kitab al majmu'a : p. 179-180.

6. Condé : Vol. I, p. 265-266.

7. Provençal: Histoire : Vol. I, p. 191.

Chapter 6

The Dawn of Hispano-Muslim Culture
The reign of 'Abd ar-Rahman II
(822-852)

Toledo born 'Abd ar-Rahman II was thirty years of age when he came to the throne on May 22, 822. Handsome, blue-eyed and golden-haired, 'Abd ar-Rahman was gentle, and affable. He was a cultured man with a solid educational background. He was put in charge of several political missions while he was still a prince. 'Abd ar-Rahman's reign was more peaceful than his father's. There was no pretender to question his title to the throne, except his aged uncle 'Abdullah. He tried to stir up trouble, but he found little support from any quarter. After his death (823), the district of Valencia which he held as a semi-independent vassal was incorporated in the Kingdom, and 'Abd ar-Rahman posted a governor of his choice. Sometime in 822, the Yementies and the Mudarite began to fight and the Tudmir region became a war camp. It all began over a minor issue when a Mudarite plucked the vine-leaves belonging to the other group. The tribal warfare lasted several years and came to a halt in 829. 'Abd ar-Rahman founded the city of Murcia for effective control of this big territory.

These were minor disturbances compared with the massive revolts in Toledo and Merida. The people of the former city remembered the savage repression they had undergone some thirty years back at the hand of Amrus with the tacit consent of Hakam. They took their revenge in the reign of 'Abd ar-Rahman. A blacksmith named Hisham was haunted by the memories of the sufferings of his family and his fellow Toledans. He raised a small band of armed vagabonds who went about destroying the crops and farm-houses. They robbed the travellers who passed through the valley of the Tagus. Soon their activities spread over the district of Santaver. Muhammad ibn Rustum, military commander of the central command chased Hisham and killed him in 831. His death did not end the insurgency which became more organised over the years. The people rallied round another ringleader named ibn Muhajir. Ultimately 'Abd ar-Rahman's brother Walid succeeded in obtaining the submission of the rebels in June 837. The fort at Taledo which was destroyed by the rebels was rebuilt, and a garrison was posted to ensure future security.

The revolt at Merida was much more serious and was fraught with dangerous consequences for the government of Cordova. The insurrection was a joint undertaking of the Christians, the neo-Muslims, and the Berbers. The Christians of Merida were in league with Alfonso II of Galicia, and the French king Louis the Pious. We have an interesting document in the form of a letter sent by the French ruler in reply to a petition for help submitted to him by the Christians of Merida. The letter (dated 828) is a clear proof of the treasonable activities of the Christians. The letter read: We have been informed of your great distress and your suffering at the hands of king 'Abd ar-Rahman. By oppressing you and robbing you of your wealth, he is following his father Abolas who imposed burdens on you forgetting that in this way he turned friends into enemies and loyal subjects into rebels. He is bent upon depriving you of your freedom by imposing all kinds of taxes, and he humiliates you in every way. You have resisted the injustice, barbarianism and greed of your ruler. We have learnt about these matters from different sources. We have, therefore, decided to write to you to console you, and to advise you to remain steadfast in your objective for the defence of your liberty. This barbarian king is your enemy as well as ours, and we propose that we should unite against him. God willing we have decided to send our army to the other side of the Pyrenees next summer for your help. If 'Abd-ar-Rahman and his troops march against you, our army will be there to assist you. We declare that if you decide to throw off his yoke, and cooperate with us, we shall grant you your ancient privileges without delay, and shall not subject you to any tribute. We shall permit you to follow your laws, and we shall treat you as our friends in the defence of our empire"[1]. The two leaders who organised the rebellion were the Berber Mahmud ibn 'Abd al-Jabbar, and the neo-Muslim Sulaiman ibn Martin. The rebels assassinated Marwan al-Jilliqi the governor of Merida in 828. The revolt lasted several years. It was only in 834 after several expeditions (one was led by 'Abd ar-Rahman himself) that the city opened its gates to the royal army. The two rebels fled away. Sulaiman established himself at Santa Cruz near Trujillo, but he was chased and killed. Mahmud appealed to Alfonso to permit him to settle in his kingdom. Alfonso allowed him to settle close to the no-man's land between Porto and Lamego. Mahmud helped his benefactor in his many inroads in the Muslim territory. While Mahmud openly allied with Alfonso, he made secret overtures to 'Abd ar-Rahman for pardon. Suspecting him of double-dealing, Alfonso attacked his fief. Mahmud died in an encounter in May 840, and his family was taken into custody by Alfonso. Mahmud's sister who had a reputation for beauty was coverted to Christianity, and married to a Galacian nobleman. Incidentally, a son from this union became a bishop of the church of Santiago of Compostella, a famous shrine in the northwest corner of the Peninsula[2]. Merida had to be fortified against future forays of the northern Spaniards. 'Abd ar-Rahman built a strong fort with a high rampart at Merida sometime in 835. It stands across the Guadiana and is approached from a bridge. An existing inscription on the wall records the construction of this fort. There is a cistern inside with a covered gallery leading by steps to a reservoir.

Towards the middle of 844 a great calamity befell the people of Seville when the Norman pirates irrupted into the city. These Normans from Scandinavia (the Muslim historians called them '*majus*') first appeared at Lisbon with a formidable flotilla of their fast-moving boats. After several days of plunder they sailed to the south. The governor of Lisbon Wahb Allah ibn Hazm sent an urgent message to 'Abd ar-Rahman who atonce alerted the commanders of all the coastal provinces. In the meantime, the pirates sailed into the Guadalquivir in the direction of Seville. They anchored their boats (Sept. 844) on the island of Menor in the middle of the river famous for stud farms. They massacred the people and did not spare even women, old men, and children. At last they burst into the city which had no protective wall or moat. A mosque was set on fire and the old and the sick who had taken shelter in it, were murdered in cold blood[3]. The fate of these ferocious freebooters was sealed at the plains of Tablada when 'Abd ar-Rahman's three seasoned commanders arrived with their cavalry in Nov. 844[4]. The Normans were routed and many of the survivors disappeared as quickly as they came. A handful of them who remained behind were allowed to settle. They adopted Islam and took to dairy farming. After this tragic occurrence, the state could not afford to neglect the defence of the coast. 'Abd ar-Rahman ordered watch towers to be erected all along the Atlantic coast. The government built a strong navy to protect the coast from the Atlantic to the Mediterranean as well as the Balearic islands. Fortified monasteries (Ar. sig. *ribat*) were set up where volunteers (*mujahideen*) lived a life of austerity, prayer and martial exercises. During an emergency they faught shoulder to shoulder with the regular army. For the first time a rampart was built round the city of Seville. The Normans appeared once again in the reign of his successor in the year 859, and ravaged the eastern coast, but they were repulsed by the Spanish navy.

To befriend the enemy's enemy is one of the cardinal principles of international diplomacy. This is how a balance of power is achieved in international relations. It was precisely this motive which impelled Byzantine Rome to cultivate good relations with Muslim Spain. About this time, the Byzantine emperor was driven into straits from two sides — the 'Abbasids of Baghdad, and the Spanish Muslim buccaneers who lived in the Mediterranean island of Crete. At this time the ruling 'Abbasid caliph was Al-Mu'tasim who succeeded his brother Ma'mun in 833. Under the new caliph the old hostilities with Byzantine Rome broke out when emperor Theophile attacked the fortress of Zapetra. Al-Mu'tasim responded by a swift thrust into Asia Minor (August 838) and laid siege to Amorium. He planned to march upon Constantinople, but he was hampered by conspiracies in his army. The southern sector of the empire was constantly ravaged by the Muslims of Crete. In these circumstances, the Roman emperor looked to Spain for an ally. He sent an envoy to negotiate a treaty of friendship with 'Abd ar-Rahman. The Roman ambassador Kartiyus and his entourage arrived at Cordova sometime in 840. The Roman emperor in his message reminded 'Abd ar-Rahman of the extermination of the Umayyads by the 'Abbasids. He advised 'Abd ar-Rahman to dethrone the usurpers at Baghdad, and take over the 'Abbasid empire on which he had a legitimate claim. The Roman emperor also requested him to hand over the island of Crete. From this message anyone could see that the Roman emperor wanted to exploit the ancestral feud between the Umayyads and the 'Abbasid. 'Abd ar-Rahman gratefully acknowledged the presents, and sent a polite reply, 'Abd ar-Rahman was an intelligent ruler and he could look through the 'advice' given by Theophile. He told the emperor that God alone would decide the claim of the Umayyads. As for Crete, he informed the emperor that the island was not a part of his dominion and that Roman government was free to take any action deemed necessary. The full text of this beautifully drafted letter has been preserved by the great historian ibn Hayyan of Spain. A modern historian thinks that the reply of 'Abd ar-Rahman was a masterpiece of diplomacy (un chef-d' oeuvre de la diplomatie) - polite and non-committal[5]. 'Abd ar-Rahman's reply was carried by Yahya al-Ghazal a brilliant scholar of extraordinary beauty.

Sailing from Mucia, the Spanish delegates reached Constantinople where they were provided accommodation in a marble academy (*akadamiya min marmer*) near the royal palace. Al-Ghazal had several interviews with the Roman emperor, but he declined to prostrate before him as was the custom of the Roman courtiers. At a state banquets he refused to drink. Al-Ghazal was fascinated by the beauty of the vivacious queen Theodora, and the handsome prince Michael. The queen liked his company because he was a master of polite conversation and courtly demeanour. He addressed her in Arabic *"Ya Saiyidati"*. During the course of a tête-a-tête, the queen asked him why the Arabs practised circumcision. His reply was frivolous and rather obscene, but the empress burst into a peal of laughter.[6] When Al-Ghazal left Constantinople, she gave him her neckless of pearls as a gift. Al-Ghazal's poem in which he praised her beauty has been preserved.

I have covered the main events of the reign of 'Abd ar-Rahman. As stated earlier his reign was more peaceful than his father's, but the last two years of his life were clouded by an agitation at Cordova led by a handful of Christian priests and their disciples. This agitation began in 850, continued by fits and starts, and ended in the reign of Muhammad I, 'Abd ar-Rahman's successor. The Dutch orientalist R. Dozy brought to light this interesting event. He drew upon Latin chronicles, but the Muslim historians have said nothing about this agitation.[7] What was actually the ulterior motive of the priests in fermenting hatred against the government? Perhaps it was planned in a limited way to begin with, in order to see if the agitation could spread among all the Christian subjects of 'Abd ar-Rahman, and finally to invite the northern rulers and the Franks to overthrow the Umayyads. Whatever the motive, the event is of much interest and needs to be described in detail.

What was the position of the Christians living in the Umayyad kingdom? We have seen that the Umayyad rulers tolerated Christianity from the very beginning. Many conversions to Islam had no doubt taken place (and often *en mass* at some places), but these were purely voluntary as there was no organised missionary activity. Although the head of the state was always a Muslim, the government never adopted the principle: *Cuius regio eius religio.* "The majority of the converts (says Sir Thomas Arnold) were no doubt won over by the imposing influence of the faith of Islam itself, presented to them as it was with all the glamour of a brilliant civilisation, having a poetry, a philosophy and an art well calculated to attract the reason and dazzle the imagination. While in the lofty chivalry of the Arabs there was free scope for the exhibition of manly prowness and knightly virtues — a career closed to the conqured Spaniards that remained true to the Christian faith."[8] Muslim Spain, it may be frankly stated, was not a secular state, but if a state is secular it does not mean (even in the 20th century) that religious and ethnic minorities would receive a fair deal, and that their life, property and cultural values would be protected. In the letter of the French king quoted above, there is no mention of religious persecution of the Christians. The taxes during the reigns of Hakam and 'Abd ar-Rahman were no doubt rather high, but their rigour was felt by all his subjects. On the whole, the Christians were in a flourishing condition. They were employed in government service, and even in the palace. The posts in the finance department were largely held by them. Cordova, Seville, Toledo, Lisbon, Merida, Saragossa, Granada — in fact all the major cities and even villages had prosperous Christian merchants. They had their churches, and convents, and their chief magistrates decided their cases according to the Christian law.

St. Eulogius, the chief agitator has clearly admitted in his Memorial to the Saints (Memoriale Sanctorum) that the Muslims did not molest the Christians in the exercise of their religion.[9] The mass was held in all the churches, and the Spanish skies echoed with the sound of Christian bells as well as the chant of the meuzzins. Thomas Arnold summing up the position of the Christians in the Umayyad period writes — "Except in the cases of offences against the Muslim religious law, the Christians were tried by their own judges and in accordance with their own law. They were left undisturbed in the exercise of their religion; the sacrifice of the mass was offered with the swinging

of censors, the ringing of the bell, and all other solemnities of
the Catholic ritual; the psalms were chanted in the choir, sermons
preached to the people, and the festivals of the church observed
in the usual manner. They were at one time even allowed to
build new churches. We read also of the founding of several
fresh monasteries in addition to numerous convents both for
monks and nuns that flourished undisturbed by the
Muhammadan rulers. The monks could appear publicly in the
woollen robes of their order and the priest had no need to
conceal the mark of his sacred office, nor at the same time did
their religious profession prevent the Christians from being
entrusted with high offices at court, or serving in the Muslims
armies."[10]

The *fons et origo* of the agitation is attributed by historians
to the rapid arabisation of the Christians. This is the view of
Dozy and other historians. The aristocracy and the middle class
of the Christians were steeped in Muslim culture. Many
Christians gave Arabic names to their children. They admired
Arabic poetry and music, and emulated the Muslims in their
domestic life, and personal habits. Some had their children
circumcised, and some Christians had more than one wife. The
priests frowned at the growing cultural affinity between the
two communities. Probably, they feared that the growing
arabisation was only a step towards conversion to Islam. Alvaro,
a friend of the agitators, who was, ironically, a master of classical
Arabic, laments the impact of Muslim culture on his co-
religionists in the following manner — "Many of my fellow
Christians read the poetry and tales of the Arabs, study the
writings of Muslim theologians and philosophers not to refute
them, but to learn how to express themselves in Arabic with
greater correctness and elegance. Where can one find today a
layman who reads the Latin commentaries on the Holy

Scriptures? Who among them can study the Gospels, the Prophets, the Apostles? All the young Christians noted for their gifts know only the language and literature of the Arabs, read and study with zeal Arabic books and loudly proclaim everywhere that this literature is worthy of admiration. Among thousands of us there is hardly one who can write a passable Latin letter to a friend, but there are innumerable who can express themselves in Arabic and compose poetry in that language with greater art than the Arabs themselves."[11]

There is a great deal of truth in Alvaro's indictment. The number of Latin knowing Christians had dwindled down to such an extent that the Bishop of Seville had to get the Bible translated into Arabic. When Eulogius brought the books of Horace, Juvenal and Virgil from Navarre, very few in the younger generation knew about them. But instead of weaning away the Christians from the cultural influence of the Muslims by peaceful means, a group of hysterical priests fermented communal violence in the city. Their activities were subversive of public peace. These priests had a perverted view of Christianity as preached by the Apostle of Nazareth. In their instinctive hatred for the Muslims they thought that the best way of awakening the conscience of the Christians was to invite persecution and die as martyrs by starting a campaign of vilification of Islam and the Prophet. "They went forth to win the martyr's crown of which the tolerance of their infidel rulers was robbing them- by means of fierce attack on Islam and its founder."[12] The leader of these fanatics was Eulogius, and the centre of their agitation was the church of St. Zoilus in Cordova. Eulogius was a pious priest with a burning faith in his religion. He came from a family noted for its hatred for the Muslims, and Islam. His grandfather was a devout Christian, and whenever he heard the Islamic call for prayer, he would cross, and repeat the words of the Psalmist— "Keep not thy silence, O God hold not thy peace. For, lo, thine enemies make a tumult: and they that hate thee have lifted up the head."[13] Eulogius had two brothers, one was a government employee and the other was a prosperous merchant. He preferred the career of a priest and joined the church of Zoilus where he met the Abbot Spera-in-Deo who "instilled in his mind the life-long and implacable hatred of Islam."[14] The group of fanatics included three young women-Mary, Flora and Leocretia. Mary was a nun from a local convent, while the other two were children of mixed marriages. As often happens in such inter-communal marriages, the father of Flora was indifferent to religion, and when he died, she was brought up as a Christian by her mother. One day Flora absconded from home. Her brother launched a report with the police. She was arrested and produced before a judge. The women confessed that she was not a Muslim, but her brother argued that she had been beguiled by some Christians close to her. The judge restored her to her family. At home she was beaten black and blue by her brother for being the cause of disgrace to the family. The bold girl escaped once again and sought shelter in a Christian home where she met Eulogius. Flora came under the spell of Eulogius, who in addition to being a theologian, was a fine orator. The attraction between the two was mutual. Later on, the pious priest conceived a mystical and Platonic love for the beautiful Flora.[15]

Meanwhile, a priest of the church of St. Acisclus named Perfectus was hanged for very objectionable remarks against Islam. He entered into an argument with a Muslim on religious matters. The discussion began in a cordial manner, but Perfectus turned wild, and used abusive language against Islam and the Prophet. The Muslims took him to a judge but the fanatic priest repeated his remarks. He was hanged on April 18, 850. Even on the scoffold he vomited abusive eloquence on Islam. He was buried in the church of St. Acisclus with great pomp. Soon after Issac, son of a wealthy Cordovan who held the post of Secretary to 'Abd ar-Rahman, left his post and turned a monk. He joined the convent of Tabanos another hotbed of fanaticism in the north of Cordova. Here, in the company of his uncle and aunts (Jeremias and Elizabeth) he fasted, prayed and read the lives of saints which aroused in him a frenzy for self-immolation. One day he visited a qadi and asked him to initiate him into the Islamic faith. While the qadi was busy explaining the fundamentals of Islam, Issac turned upon him with a torrent of abuse. He branded Islam as a tissue of lies, and invited the qadi himself to embrace Christianity if he wanted his salvation. He was tried for his offence and sent to prison. Later the qadi transferred the case to 'Abd ar-Rahman for final orders, recommending that his punishment be reduced as the man seemed to be out of his senses. 'Abd ar-Rahman did not agree and on June 3, 851 Issac was executed. Barely two months after, a French guard of the palace, Sancho by name, who was a disciple of Eulogius, was also hanged for the same offence. On Nov. 24, 851 Flora and Mary set out from the church of St. Acisclus, and appeared before the qadi. After calling her father a pagan, Flora exhausted all her vocabulary in reviling Islam.[16] The qadi was touched by their youth, and asked them to withdraw their remarks and then they would be let off, but the fanatic women redoubled their outbursts. Both of them were sent to prison and on Nov. 24, 852 they were hanged as their activities were dangerous to peace and harmony in the city. Eulogius was in a state of spiritual exaltation at the performance of his disciples. He visited them in their cells before they were executed, and listened the replies (sweet as honey), Flora gave to the qadi during her trial. After Flora was dead, he prophesied that she would attend a nuptial feast with Christ, her bridegroom in heaven.[17]

The main body of the Christians kept aloof from these fanatics but some priests and bishops were alarmed at the growing frenzy for suicide. Reccafred, the Metropolitan convened a synod of bishops at Seville. The meeting was attended by Gomez son of Antonian of the department of finance, but nothing came of it. The agitators and their supporters were blind to all reason. The bishops, loyal to the government, were traitors in their eyes. The agitation continued. Several priests including Saul of the church of St. Acisclus entered into the mosque of Cordova, yelled at the praying Muslims and abused Islam right inside the mosque. They were all arrested and after a proper trial, at which they refused to tender any apology, were executed. Eulogius the leader of the movement was let off from jail. He left Cordova for Pamplona (ostensibly) to meet a friend. On his return he halted at Toledo and tried to incite the local Christians by painting in lurid colours the condition of the Christians of Cordova.

Meanwhile, 'Abd ar-Rahman died and his son Muhammad had to face renewed agitation from Eulogius who returned to Cordova after several years of absence. At this time Leocritia (a child of mixed marriage) ran away from her home. She was given shelter by Anulo sister to Eulogius. The girl was sought out by her parents, and Eulogius was arrested and produced before a qaḍi. He boldly told the qaḍi that he had converted the girl to Christianity at her express request, and would do it again if the qaḍi himself desired. The qaḍi respected Eulogus for his piety, and transferred the case to the Prime Minister. A sympathatic officer who was anxious to save him tried to persuade the fanatic prelate to speak just one word of apology, but he refused. By this time (says Lévi Provençal) the patience of the government was exhausted and Eulogius was executed on March 11, 859. He was buried in the church of Zoilus. Four days after Leocritia also met the same fate. Some fanatics continued to curse and swear at Islam but the movement died out as more and more Christians realised that the fanatic priests were not serving the cause of their religion. The movement cost some thirty precious lives.

But for the energy, the iron will, and the vigilance of Hakam, the Umayyad kingdom would have fallen into decay. Thanks to him,' Abd ar-Rahman inherited a kingdom which was stable and in a flourishing state. The treasury was full of gold and silver. The revenues rose to one million dinars according to ibn Hayyan. 'Abd ar-Rahman had enough funds for maintenance of an army and a navy, regular payments to state functionaries, traditional rewards to courtiers, and for works of public welfare. Agriculture prospered as never before. The state granaries had sufficient buffer stocks of cereals. The districts of Seville, Sidonia and Niebla alone contributed thousands of bushels of wheat and barley in the form of duty to the state. When draughts broke out in 823 and 846, the government faced the situation without much difficulty. On account of all-round prosperity, the historians call his reign 'Aiyam al-arus' i.e. a honeymoon. In any age, culture is the child of prosperity, and peace. 'Abd ar-Rahman's tranquil reign saw the dawn of Hispano-Muslim culture which reached its zenith in the succeeding centuries. This seductive culture, atonce soft and subtle, found expression in all spheres of human activity.

'Abd ar-Rahman modelled the state, court life and etiquette on the 'Abbasid pattern. The coming of the 'Abbasids was a turning point in the history of the Muslim East. While the

Umayyads built an empire spreading over three continents, their successors fostered a universal culture of great charm and glamour. After the transfer of the seat of caliphate from Damascus to Baghdad, Persian and Byzantine influences began to permeate Muslim society and the whole facade of culture. Owners of fabulous wealth (the most colossal the world had yet seen), the caliphs of Baghdad adopted Persian administration, court etiquette, fêtes and festivals, culinary art, dress and music. The 'Abbasid rulers of the golden age (748-847) patronised literature, philosophy, science, arts and crafts at a lavish scale never before known to history. It was a most glorious period of culture and civilization in the history of mankind. "The magnificence of the palaces, mosques, colleges, and official residences, the luxurious appointments, and furnishings of the interior, the gorgeous retinues and equipages, the sumptuous fêtes, the banquets and other gatherings together with the splendour of social life not only in the capital but in all great cities from Cordova to Samarqand surpassed anything of its kind in history".[18] Travellers, merchants and pilgrims brought reports of the spendour of Baghdad to Spain, and 'Abd ar-Rahman succumbed to the influence of 'Abbasid culture. Discarding the traditional animosity between the two dynasties, he opened the windows of his kingdom to cultural breezes from Baghdad. He organized the state after the 'Abbasid pattern. A separate department of Finance (Ar: *Diwan al-Khizana*) was established to look into money matters of the state. The ministers sat in luxurious chambers (Ar: *majlis*) built at the entrance of the palace. He had a seal (Ar: *Khatam*) made with his title engraved on it. The seal was fixed on all letters and orders issued in his name and with his approval. He established a mint (*dar al-sikka*) at Cordova. The mint issued silver and bronze coins. The number of gold coins issued by the mint was perhaps limited because he did not like the treasury to be depleted of the yellow metal. Like the caliphs of Baghdad he established workshops for manufacture of costly silk fabrics required by members of his household. The factory, headed by the master weaver Harith ibn Bazi, prepared silk brocades, carpets, tapestries and hangings. Under 'Abd ar-Rahman the fashion for *"tiraz"* a lustrous fabric embroidered with verses and honorific titles, was introduced for the first time in Spain. He organised urban police, created special officers (Ar. *Sig sahib al suq*) to watch the sale and purchase of consumers goods. Like the caliphs of Baghdad, he kept himself aloof from the people. He was seen by his subjects only when he left the palace to lead a military expedition, or to attend the Friday prayer in the mosque.

Never had the court of a Spanish ruler been so brilliant as it was under 'Abd ar-Rahman. He surrounded himself with a pleiades of poets, men of letters, philosophers, musicians and scientists. He was himself a man of refined tastes, and was fond of reading books. His special interests were music, medicine, philosophy, prosody and astrology. He sent 'Abbas ibn Nasih to the East for collection of books specially translations of Greek and Persian works. The astronomical works from India already translated into Arabic under the title *Sind-Hind* reached Spain and opened the way for study of astrology. His reign saw the first flowering of learning, art and music in Muslim Spain. Among the numerous scholars patronised and handsomely paid by him were: 'Abdullah ibn Shamir the poet and childhood friend of his; Sulaiman al-Shami who visited the East, befriended the two famous poets — Abū Nawas and Abū al-Atahiya and no doubt returned with their works; Sa'id ibn-Faraj the eminent philologist whose love for learning and research in his special field took him to Basra and Kufa; 'Abdullah ibn Bakr, the poet; ibn Habib, the historian; Yahya al-Ghazal, the poet-diplomat;

and 'Abbas ibn Firnas, the scientist. The malikite Yahya ibn Yahya was the chief theologian of the time. He had incited the people of Cordova against his father, but 'Abd ar-Rahman held him in high esteem, and consulted him on important personal matters. Once 'Abd ar-Rahman was on fast when he committed a breach of conduct. He asked Yahya how he should atone for his sin. The stern theologian advised that he should fast for thirty days without a break — a lighter punishment in the form of charity to the poor was not considered enough for the head of state. While patronising these men he did not lose sight of the educational needs of his subjects. He opened schools at several places. In Cordova alone he supported three hundred orphan students.

Ziryab, the musician and *arbiter elegantiarum* was the brightest jewel of the court. His full name was Abu l-Hassan Ali Ibn Nafi, but he was called Ziryab perhaps because of his meladious voice. He was trained in music by the celebrated musician of Baghdad — Ishaq al-Mausili, but he outshone his master. He incurred his jealousy, and was forced to seek his fortune elsewhere. He was in north Africa, when Hakam heard about him, and invited him to Spain. When Hakam died, 'Abd ar-Rahman confirmed his father's invitation. Zaryah landed in Algeciras along with his family. 'Abd ar-Rahman himself left his palace to receive him at the gate of Cordova. He was installed in a splendid mansion, and granted a monthly allowance. Henceforth he became a companion (Ar: *nadim*) of the king. There was no end to gifts for him, and his family. Ziryab was one of the greatest musicians of his time and perhaps one of the greatest composers in the whole history of Spain. He was widely read in history, geography, biography and polite literature. Wit and learning added charm to his conversation, and table-talk. We shall look into his contributions to Hispano-Muslim music in the later part of the book, and for the present, enumerate the many innovations he introduced in the polite society of the Spanish Muslims. He transformed their lifestyle by introducing elegance and a sense of beauty in their daily life. In the opinion of Western historians Ziryab is the Petronius, the Beau Brummell of Spain. He introduced new trends in the dress, coiffure, personal hygiene, laundry, cosmetics, domestic furniture, and culinary art. Before his arrival the Spanish Muslims wore long hair with plaits hanging from the temples. Ziryab introduced a short hair style according to which the hair were parted in the middle and given a circular shape at the forehead. Ziryab prepared a toothpaste, a deodorant, and recommended depilatories of his own making for personal cleanliness. He made a chemical detergent for washing clothes, replacing the use of salt. He taught the art of applying cosmetics to the face. His wives and daughters set new fashions in female coiffure. They were all beauticians and their advice was sought by fashionable people. Zaryab laid down a calendar for clothes according to seasons and prescribed different colours for each season — light silk tunics with vivid colours in spring, white robes from July to September, and quilted gowns with fur linings for the winters. He devised couches or divans of soft leather for relaxation and transformed the designs of domestic furniture[19].

Zaryab imported the culinary art of Baghdad. Readers of the Arabian Nights will recall the sumptuous feasts given by the caliphs of Baghdad, the nobility, the *nouveau riche*, and the merchants like Sindhbad. The proceedings of a Symposium on cooking held in the presence of the 'Abbasid caliph Al-Mustakfi (preserved in the pages of Al-Masudi's *Muruju l-Dhahab* — The Meadows of Gold) throws a flood of light on the art of making exotic dishes.[20] The delicious foods included boiled rice of iridescent colours, meat of kids and partridges, desserts, cookies, lozenges of sweets, pastries, rolls, sandwitches and sauces. A hundred ingredients went into their preparation. The food was garnished in endless ways and scented with suffron, musk, ambergris, marjoram and rosewater. Ziryab introduced this elaborate Baghdadian cuisine into Spain. He himself concocted new delights for the gourmet. The forcemeat balls, and triangular pieces of dough fried in oil were his creations. Thanks to Ziryab the Spanish people enjoyed eating asparagus for the first time. He stopped the practice of all the food being placed before the guests in a pell-mell manner. Henceforth, food was to be served at banquets in several courses one following the other. The initial dish consisted of soup, followed by dishes of assorted meat preparations, desserts of sweet cakes and pastries stuffed with pistachios and almonds. And then came plates overflowing with fruits. This new cuisine became a craze in high society. At Ziryab's suggestion the cups of gold and silver were replaced by tumblers of glass and crystal and the food was served on table covers of fine leather instead of cotton. Ziryab died in 857, an immencely rich man. He was long remembered by civilised society of Muslim Spain. His sons, and three daughters — 'Aliya, Fatima and Humduna carried on the work of their father. They rose in social status, The three sisters were married into top families of Cordova.

Historians give us a peep into the private life of 'Abd in-Rahman. He was a man of varied tastes. Like his father he was fond of hunting in the valley of Guadalquivir. He divided his spare hours between reading and listening music. His interest in astronomy led him into the world of astrology, and he would often consult horoscopes before starting any work. He was a connoisseure of female beauty. The beauties of his seraglio were not merely those who were sexually desirable; they were educated and accomplished in the art of polite conversation.

Names of some of these charmers have been recorded by historians. Tarub, a woman of extraordinary beauty held him in thrall all his life. He wrote love lyrics to her from the battlefield. History is replete with the accounts of the many gifts 'Abd ar-Rahman gave to this proud beauty. Spain was, at this time, a market for de luxe products, and ornaments manufactured in Baghdad. He bought for her rare pieces of jewellery. When a vazir objected to this extravagance, 'Abd ar-Rahman defended his action in the following famous lines of his composition :

Has the Compassionate God (Ar-Rahman)
ever created in the world anything more
beautiful to the eye than a lovely woman.
On her face behold the bloom of the rose
and the jasmine, She is like a garden
full of flowers wonderful! If I were
master of my heart and my eyes I would
make a collar of these for her neck and bosom."[21]

Tarub was an 'Umm ul walad' i.e., a queen who delivered a male child, and, therefore, she ranked higher among the ladies of the harem. There were several queens of the same rank. Mu'ammara the mother of prince Al Mundhir was a pious woman who perpetuated her memory in history by building a cemetery at Cordova at her own expense. Shifa, mother of Al-Mutarrif was celebrated for her beauty, piety and feminine gentleness. She rose in the eyes of her royal spouse when she undertook to suckle (along with her own baby) Muhammad, 'Abd ar-Rahman's successor after his mother died in his infancy. He presented her a famous necklace called 'the dragon' which once belonged to the 'Abbasid queen Zubaida, the wife of Harun al-Rashid. The celebrated ornament was brought to Spain, and 'Abd ar-Rahman purchased it for Shifa for ten thousand gold dinars.[22] He equally doted on the loyal enchantress Fakhr and the three gifted musicians. Fadal, Qalam and 'Alam. Qalam was a scholar of history. She could recite poetry and was a musician with a pleasing voice.[23] 'Abd ar-Rahman built a sumptuous hall where he heard their songs. All his sons and daughters were given a good education. One of 'Abd ar-Rahman's daughters — al-Baha' built a mosque at the Rusafa. She was known for her piety and copied the Quran like an expert caligraphist. The harem was managed by eunuchs as in Byzantine Rome. This custom was adopted by the Abbasid caliph of Baghdad. The eunuchs belonged to various European nationalities. Some of them came from northern regions of Spain. They were imported into Spain after being castrated by the Jews who practically monopolised the trade in these human commodities. Most of them were greedy, servile and unscruplous. Those who were pushing and clever amassed wealth. A typical such slave was 'Abd l-Nasr, who owned a villa in the suburbs of Cordova which he named after himself. This thankless slave played into the hands of Tarub, and plotted to poison 'Abd ar-Rahman to clear the way for succession of her son. A report goes that he contacted a physician named Al-Harrani an immigrant from Iraq who ran a flourishing pharmaceutical business at Cordova. He prepared a poison and sold it to Nasr. When Nasr offered a drink to 'Abd ar-Rahman, he mixed the poison. The loyal Fakhr had already informed her husband about the conspiracy. 'Abd ar-Rahman made excuses, and asked Nasr to drink it in his presence. Nasr could not refuse the royal command. He drank it and died.(850)

'Abd ar-Rahman was the first great builder of the Umayyad dynasty. His many constructions, both civil and military make an impressive list. We have already mentioned about the construction of *rabats* (hospices), the rampart at Seville, and the vast fortress at Merida. Seville was also provided with an elegant mosque. The foundation stone of this mosque (which is now the church of Salvador) is preserved in the local museum. About 825, the citizens of Jaen saw a new and imposing mosque rising in the city. It was a splendid structure with aisles running perpendicular to the mihrab as in the mosque of Cordova. A new city was built at Murcia. The details of this project are not available but it must have cost 'Abd ar-Rahman a colossal sum. Thanks to 'Abd ar-Rahman, Murcia developed into one of the most populous cities of Muslim Spain, and a famous centre of industry and handicrafts. In a later period Murcia was compared to "a house from which a young and beautiful bride would leave for her husband's home bedecked with ornaments and finery."[24] The modern capital of Spain — Madrid (Ar: *Majreet*) was originally built by 'Abd ul-Rahman. It was a modest villages, but he provided it with a rampart and a strong fort for the city's protection. Either he, or his successor constructed a big mosque; which was converted into a church after the city was captured by the Christian. Another important work was the enlargement of the mosque of Cordova. An embarkment was built on the bank of Guadalquivir to protect the city from floods. The road on the rightbank of the river was paved with stones. The royal palace was entirely renovated, and a series of pavalions in glass were built on high terraces commanding a splendid view towards the south. A new irrigation canal was constructed for supply of water to the city by means of metallic pipes. A magnificent marble fountain added beauty to the entrance of the palace. He built baths, watering places for horses and repaired the roads.[25]

Two years after the conspiracy of Nasr, 'Abd ar-Rahman died suddenly during the night of September 22, 852. Was he poisoned? The historians are silent on this point. He was survived by 150 sons, and 50 daughters. He died without nominating his successor, although everybody knew that Muhammad was his favourite son and also the eldest. There are vicissitudes in the lives of men as well as the states. If summer comes, winter is not far behind. After 'Abd ar-Rahman was gone, Muslim Spain was visited by icy winds of sectarian clashes for half a century.

Notes

1. L. Provençal: Histoire Vol. I, pp. 228-229. (Abu l-'Asi was the surname of al-Hakam). [Only a summary of letter of Louis the Pious has been given.]

2. Ibid, p. 210.

3. This mosque was rebuilt and was known as 'masjid al-shuhada'. L. Provençal: Histoire Vol. I. p. 222.

4. Tablada is about 15 km south of Seville. It is now an aerodrome.

5. L. Provençal: Histoire, Vol. I, p. 253. Also see his book, Islam d' Occident, pp. 99-103.

6. L. Provençal: Islam d'Occident p, 93 and p, 106.

7. Dozy, pp. 268-288.

8. Arnold: Preaching of Islam, p. 140. also see L. Provençal: L'Espagne Musulmane au Xème siècle p. 37, and his Histoire Vol. I, p. 233.

9. Arnold: p. 135. The author has quoted the actual words of Eulogius from his Memoriale Sanctorum. Eulogius also writes about churches built during his time.

10. Arnold: p. 135

11. L. Provençal: La Civilisation Arabe en Espagne pp, 108-109; Palencia: Historia, p. 14; Dozy: p, 268; and Arnold pp, 137-138 (Alvaro was a rich Cordovan of Jewish origin. He wrote a biography of Eulogius, the chief of the agitators).

12. Arnold: p. 141.

13. Dozy: p. 273 and p. 274.

14. Ibid.

15. Dozy: pp, 276-277. He has quoted from a highly passionate letter addressed by Euloguis to Flora.

16. I do not like to quote the scurrilous diatribes against Islam and the

Prophet, vomitted by Eulogius, Perfectus, Issac, Flora and others. The reader can read Dozy's Spanish Islam: pp. 268-307, and L. Provençal: Histoire, Vol I, pp. 232-239.

17. Dozy p, 293.

18. H. Farmer: History of Arabian Music, pp. 99-100.

19. Al-Maqqari/Gayangos, Vol. I, pp. 117-120, L. Provençal : Histoire, Vol. I, pp. 269-272, and La civilisation Arabe en Espagne, pp. 63-77. The French historian calls him "un veritable institute de beaute."

20. Arberry : Aspects of Islamic Civilisation, p. 156-164.

21. Ibn Idhari Vol. II, p. 91, and Kitab al majmu'a, pp. 185 to 186.

22. This rare necklace passed on from one owner to another like the famous KohiNoor of the Mughal India. After the fall of the Umayyad dynasty it was purchased by Ma'mun of Toledo. It was inherited by Qadir and fell into the hands of Qadi Jahhaf of Valencia. It was forcibly taken from him by the Cid, and ultimately it reached queen Isabella.

Shifa accompanied 'Abd ur-Rahman when he led an expedition to the northern border. On the return journey, she fell ill and died near Toledo, and was buried there. Muhammad I, who held her in great affection, instructed the local villagers to look after her grave, and granted a modest endowment for its upkeep.

23. Qalam was the mother of Prince Aban.

24. Al Maqqari/Gayangos, Vol. I, p. 69. On the foundation of Madrid. See al-Himyari p. 216.

25. Condé: Vol. 1, p. 274.

Chapter 7

Spain in Turmoil
[The reigns of Muhammad I (852-886), Al-Mundhir (886-888) and 'Abdullah (888-912)]

On the night of 22nd Sept. when 'Abd ar-Rahman died, the citizens of Cordova knew nothing of what was going on in the royal palace. There was a conspiracy to pass on the crown to 'Abdullah, the profligate son of Tarub, the Madame Pompadour of 'Abd ar-Rahman. Only by sheer good luck, Muhammad came to the throne. The historian ibn Qutia has left a haunting picture of the events leading to the accession of Muhammad. They point to the growing power of the European eunuchs (called Slavs) who, if left to themselves, could play the role of king-makers. Immediately, 'Abd ar-Rahman died, the chamber in which his body lay was locked by Sadun and Qasim the two eunuchs who had already opted for 'Abdullah at the behest of Tarub. They consulted their other colleagues to reach a consensus on the candidature of 'Abdullah. They took the advice of Abū l-Mufrih a God-fearing and upright eunuch (a rare person in his fraternity) who had, surprisingly, made a pilgrimage to Mecca. He exercised his influence, and saved the state from a nasty war of succession. Abū l-Mufrih pleaded for Muhammad. He told the conspirators that Muhammad, besides being the eldest son of 'Abd ar-Rahman, was a better candidate for the throne than the irreligious and pleasure-loving 'Abdullah. He warned them that they would be accountable to God for putting Abdullah on the throne. Sadun and Qasim saw reason in his arguments, and the former was deputed to visit Muhammad to announce his accession to the throne. As Muhammad lived across the river, Sadun took the keys of the Bridge Gate and, quietly left the Alacazar avoiding Abdullah who was then in his cups. When Sadun arrived at the residence of Muhammad, the latter asked him the cause of his unexpected appearance. Sadun informed him that his father was dead, and that they had elected him as their king. Muhammad could hardly believe him. He suspected a plot to assassinate him in order to put 'Abdullah on the throne, and begged Sadun to spare his life. He told him that he had no desire for the throne and, if necessary, he would leave Spain to pave the way for Abdullah's succession. Sadun showed him the dead king's ring, and calmed his fears by solemn pledges of loyalty. Disguised as a woman, Muhammad made for the palace, and was ushered in the chamber in which his father died. When the morning sun greeted the Alcazar, the people learnt that they were subjects of a new king.

Like his father, Muhammad was a cultured man of serious temper and peaceful disposition. His critics found him miserly, perhaps, because he avoided unnecessary expenditure from the public funds. He had not much liking for poetry but he was an expert mathematician, and would often inspect all monetary transactions as reflected in the documents. He retained the functionaries of his father's days, but he did not hesitate to inject new blood in the administration. Muhammad's reign saw the emergence into prominence of two Cordova families — the Banu Shuhaid and the Banu Abi 'Abda'. The forefathers of

these two families had participated in the famous battle of Marj
Rahit.[1] They migrated to Spain soon after 'Abd ar-Rahman I
came to power. The kingdom was no doubt, in a sound financial
condition. Muhammad continued his father's beautification of
Cordova. His navy was in a trim condition. He had a large
army and a big cavalry of twenty thousand horsemen. But neither
his parsimony, nor his vigilance saved the kingdom from gradual
dismemberment. His whole life, and public money were spent
in fighting the forces of disunity. From now onwards the neo-
Muslim who outnumbered the old Muslims fought for greater
share in the cake.

His reign opened with a turmoil in Toledo. The people of
this city always rebelled whenever there was a change of ruler
at Cordova. The sparks of discontent were fanned by Eulogius
during his stay at Toledo, on his return from Pamplona. The
Christian were so much enamoured of him that they insisted on
his appointment as the Metropolitan of the city, but Muhammad
could not agree for obvious reasons. Shortly after Muhammad's
accession, they imprisoned the Governor, and refused to release
him unless some detainees at Cordova were freed. The
government had to yield to secure the release of the governor.
The initial success emboldened the rebels, and they marched
upon Calatrava (Ar: *Qal'at Rabh*) situated in the valley of
Guadiana. This assault (853) was so sudden and organized that
the royal garrison found safety in retreat. The rebels destroyed
the rampart, and soon the revolt spread all over the sierra
Morena. At Andujar the army was once again surprised and the
soldiers fled away leaving their arms. The rebels were jubilant
at their success, but also feared a violent reaction from the
government of Cordova. They appealed to Ordono I who had
succeeded Ramiro I in the northern Kingdom of Galacia. He
was a natural enemy of the Umayyads and was interested in

keeping the civil war alive. He placed an army at the disposal of the rebels under the command of Count Gaton one of his most valiant vassals. In June 854 Muhammad himself took the field to restore the authority of the central government. A direct attack on Toledo was not feasible as the rebels had fortified their position. Muhammad conceived of a clever plan (stratagème classique in the words of Lévi Provençal) to beat the enemy[2]. He placed the bulk of his army among the defiles bordering the Guadacelate (a sluggish tributary of the Tagus) and advanced towards the city to lure the rebels to an open fight. This was precisely the terrain on which a century back Balj had crushed the Berbers. The Count attacked the royal troops with a full fury deploying all his soldiers. Muhammad retreated after a mock battle. Throwing all discretion to the winds, the rebels advanced and were trapped among the mountains. The ambushed army fell upon the rebels and their allies under the Count. Thousand of then were slain in the trap laid by Muhammad. The Count himself lost his life. The victors were mad with joy. They erected a rostrum of the severed heads of their dead enemies and held a thanks-giving ceremony at their astounding victory. Peace returned to Toledo for a short period, but under his successor the whole district turned into an autonomous republic.

The neo-Muslims were on the rampage every where. A serious trouble flared up at Merida, the headquarters of the western border. The leader of the insurrection was ibn Marwan al-Jilliqi son of the former governor under 'Abd ar-Rahman. He descended from a Christian family which converted to Islam not very long ago. The rebellion began in 868, but soon ended when the imperial army blockaded the city and the rebels were starved to surrender. Marwan was pardoned, and he was brought to Cordova along with his family. He was given a military assignment, but the haughty man quarrelled with the hajib Hisham ibn Abd al-Aziz, and left Cordova. Once again Merida was up in arms. The position become serious when he joined hands with Alfonso III. Muhammad sent an army under Hisham, but the latter was defeated and taken prisoner. Marwan placed the Cordovan minister into the custody of the Christians. He remained in captivity at Oviedo for two year. His release was obtained on payment of ransom of a hundred thousand dinars. Marwan spread his control over the neighbouring territory, and lived with the authority of a feudal baron with several vassals under him. Ibn Qutia tells us that Marwan and his lieutenants preached a new religion combining the teachings of Christianity and Islam to attract the loyalty of the compatriots of both the faiths. Muhammad watched these developments with impotent rage. Even his two successors-Mandhir and Abdullah could not dislodge Marwan ibn jillaqi and his petty vassals from their position in the whole of the Alqarve region-one half of the present Portugal, and the entire valley of Guadiana. The central government lost control of some of the major cities of the Western sector — Merida, Badajos, Beja, Ocsomba, Huelva and Silves.

The authority of the Umayyads was equally challenged in the north by the descendants of Banu Qasi the Gothic family that converted to Islam at the conquest of Spain. They held the whole of Aragon-roughly the territory between the Spanish March and the valley of the Ebro. They commanded immence prestige among the Christians as well as the Muslims. By and large, the Banu Qasi had been loyal to the government of Cordova. Several of them held important posts, and in exchange for their loyalty, the Umayyad rulers allowed them considerable liberty in internal matters. About the end of 'Abd ar-Rahman's region they began to feather their own nest. By means of gradual annexations they had fortified their position, and when Muhammad came to the throne they were virtuously autonomous. The Qasi Musa II who was contemporary with Muhammad entered upon a career of calculated self-aggrandisement. He was the undisputed master of the region. He defied the Umayyads. He did not hesitate to measure swords with the Count of Barcelona. Alfonso III was his closest ally. He had direct dealings with Charles the Bald of France, and courted his friendship with gifts. Musa was respected and feared all over the northern borders, and was regarded as the 'third king of Spain' - the other two being the Umayyad ruler of Cordova, and the King of Leon.

While the Qasi chief held the cities of Saragossa. Tudela and Huesca, and Marwan ruled independently in the western sector, the position was equally fraught with ominous portents near the imperial capital. The revolt of the neo-Muslim ibn Hafsun in the southeast was the most serious and also the most prolonged. It began with the brigandage of a criminal, and culminated into a rising of the neo-Muslims inhabiting the region. In his early career Omar ibn Hafsun looks like a villain from a novel of cutthroats and convicts. He came from a Gothic family. His father was a gentleman farmer. He lived in his country house near the hilly town of Ronda, and rose to wealth and prosperity by his hard work. Ibn Hafsun was unlike his father. From his early childhood, he was a self-willed boy. He was haughty, bad tempered and quarrelsome. It was usual for him to return home with injuries received in street quarrels. One day he killed a neighbour, and ran away into the woods, and joined a band of desperadoes. Later on, he left secretly for north Africa where he lived as an apprentice to a tailor. Sometime in 850, he returned home, and after a lapse of time, he took to robbery. The mountains of Ronda, are picturesque

and lure tourists even today. They are very precipitous and
serve as haunts of highwaymen. For three years ibn Hafsun
continued to rob the travellers with impunity. At last he was
caught, and brought to Cordova. Muhammad, who had his
father's gentleness, did not send him to the executioner, but
instead, enrolled him in the army along with his band of forty
thieves, trusting that they would give up their evil ways and
turn into faithful citizens. Once again, he picked up a fight with
a local officer, and left for his mountain resort in 884. From
this year he became a self-styled leader of the neo-Muslims,
and the Christians. He established himself at Bobastro, and
built a fortress. Protected by the gorge of Charro in the valley
of Guadalhorce, the fortress of Bobastro was one of the most
awe-inspiring rocky retreats in the southeast of Spain. Many
greedy adventurers, deserted soldiers and turbulent traitors
swelled his ranks. The historian ibn Idhari was not wrong when
called him the leader of pagans, the chief of traitors, and the
protector of those who breed dissensions.[3] He consolidated his
position in the neighbouring villages and towns with the avowed
aim of carving out a small state as a first step towards
overthrowing the government of Cordova. Fortune smiled on
him as the operations directed against him by prince al-Mundhir
had to be wound up on account of the sudden death of
Muhammad. (August 4, 886). The erstwhile leader of
highwaymen turned into a hero and a champion of his race. He
harangued the people with a veritable manifesto like a
communist demagogue: "We have already suffered a long time
with unjust taxes. We have been subjected to numerous
humiliations by the Arabs. I do not want anything for myself
but to avenge the wrongs done to us and to free you from
slavery." His followers increased. He shared the booty with his
soldiers, and decorated the brave with bracelets of gold. He

enlarged his territory by frequent military promenades. He annexed Priego and Iznajar. Jaen was under constant threats. Al-Mundhir who succeeded Muhammad despatched a strong body of cavalry. Iznajar was captured, and the army proceeded to besiege the citadel of Bobastro. On the way, the royal army liquidated the partisans of ibn Hafsun. Finding himself in a perilous situation after the loss of Priego also, he opened negotiations for a peaceful settlement. Mundhir wanted to put an end to blooshed, and he agreed. A document granting certain privileges to ibn Hafsun was prepared. Under the term of agreement ibn Hafsun was required to lay down arms, hand over Bobastro, and take his residence at Cordova. Ibn Hafsun demanded a hundred mules for transporting his effects to the capital city, but the crafty man escaped at night carrying the mules with him. Mundhir was furious at this act of treachery and he vowed to reduce the rebel's nest. But when the siege was in progress, he fell ill. He sent for his brother Abdullah to conduct the operations. Soon after his brother's arrival, Mundhir died on June 29, 888. 'Abdullah found himself in such a hopeless situation that he begged ibn Hafsun to allow the safe conduct of the cortege of his brother to Cordova.

'Abdullah ascended the throne under an evil star. Unstability was writ large on the political firmament. The Umayyad power seemed to be nearing its eclipse. Everywhere, the genie of ethnic hatred was out of the jar. The neo-Muslims were in the ascendant in every part of the kingdom. The western sector was held by ibn Jilliqi and his several vassals. Toledo had opted for a republican form of government. The northeastern frontiers were under the heel of the Banu Qasi and other neo-Muslim chiefs. In the southeast ibn Hafsun was still at large. The kingdom needed an energetic ruler to steer it through the enveloping tempest but 'Abdullah was unfit for the task before him. He was forty-four when he came to the throne. Born of a foreign slave, he had deep blue eyes and golden hair. He was an educated ruler like his predecessors, He was a deeply religious man and read the Quran daily. He was a teetotler; his dress and diet were simple. He was a fluent speaker of chaste Arabic. He liked to meet his subjects, and for the purpose he held an open chart every Friday near the Gate of Justice (bāb al-adal) of the palace. Ibn Idhari has given a whole list of his many virtues. But he was timid, vacillating and suspicious, and lacked confidence in himself. He was able to maintain the figment of his authority by attending to only the pressing dangers. Fortunately, the neo-Muslim rebels were hungry for land. As they had no national consciousness they were not able to forge a united front against the Umayyad authority. This enabled 'Abdullah to carry on the government, sometimes by following a policy of 'divide and rule', and sometimes by an agreement here, and campaign there.

Under 'Abdullah the turmoil spread even to the provinces which had so far remained unaffected by ethnic riots. A few months after Mundhir died, the district of Elvira turned into a theatre of murderous strikes between the Spanish Christians, the neo-Muslims and the Arabs. This district covered the area round the Sierra Elvira, and its main city was Elvira itself. It was predominantly a Christian city even during the time 'Abdullah. It was the oldest cradle of Christianity. The Christians were a wealthy people, and they were also better organised. The conquest caused no disruption to their religious life. They had several churches where the mass was regularly held. Islam had also won some converts, but the Muslims remained in a minority. Although there was no proselytising activity, the number of voluntary conversion increased since the time of 'Abd ar-Rahman II, so much so that the mosque of Elvira (built by Hanash a sub-companion of the Prophet) had to be enlarged.

A number converts were made by Samuel, a disgruntled bishop who was removed from his office by the Christian priests because of his alleged immoralities. The bishop adjured Christianity along with his many followers. As for the Arabs, they were mostly of Syrian origin; they were nearly all descendants of the soldiers who arrived with Balj. Most of them were cultivators. There was not much communication between the various groups. Even frequent inter-communal marriages did not bridge the gulf which divided the Arab settlers and the people of Spanish origin. The Christians and the neo-Muslims disliked the Syrian Muslims whom they found haughty, arrogant and race conscious. The Syrian Arabs were not slow in reciprocating these feelings. It must be said to the credit of the neo-Muslims that they were, by and large, loyal to the government, and made no demonstrations against the arbitrary taxes, even if the Arabs did so. But conditions had changed, and the neo-Muslims were asserting themselves like their compatriots in other parts of the kingdom. Every neo-Muslim of some consequence owned a small principality with a fortified farm house. There was enough combustible material for a flare-up. The proud neo-Muslims applied the spark when they attacked the Arabs, drove them out of their settlements at Montejicar, a town about sixty miles to the north of Granada. They slew Yahya ibn Shaqola an influential Arab chief. This happened in the year 889. The Arabs rallied under a Qaisite leader named Sawwar ibn Hamdun, and a bloody drama of revenge and vendetta was enacted at Elvira and the neighbouring towns and villages in which both the sides suffered heavy losses of life and property. Ibn Hafsun also jumped into the arena on behalf of the neo-Muslims. The government miserably failed in restoring peace, and the ethnic fights went on unabated. Suwwar was killed in an ambuscade. His body was brought to Elvira where the neo-Muslim women — the Amazons of Roman — Gothic origin cut it into bits and even tasted the flesh. The Arabs chose ibn Judi as their leader. This gallant knight was the Casanova of his time. A beautiful face, a lily-white hand, and a lingering glance from a bewitching female turned his head. He offended the people by his tryst with a woman in the house of a Jew. His death broke the unity among the Arabs. One of their groups submitted to the government of Cordova, but the district of Elvira was never peaceful during the region of 'Abdullah.

The germs of ethnic hatred spread to the province of Seville also. Under the Romans, Seville was a city of culture, of joy, song and mirth, as it is even today. In the nineth century the whole province was the most flourishing part of south Spain after the district of Cordova. For the Christians it had the distinction of being one of the episcopal seats of the Catholic church. The descendants of numerous aristocratic Roman and Gothic families and the Muslims lived in amity. Unlike the inflammable rabble led by ibn Hafsun, the prominent families of Serville were merchants, and owners of real estate. The Guadalqivir being navigable, they monopolised sea-borne trade with Africa and the eastern lands. The Arabs lived in their manor-houses mostly in the Ajarafe a region of proverbial luxuriance and fertility in the south of the city of Seville. Those who lived in the city were ship-builders and merchants of olive oil. They rivalled the citizens of Spanish origin in wealth and prosperity. The Spanish Christians, and neo-Muslims were completely arabised even if some families proudly proclaimed their Roman ancestry by retaining their patronyms. Two such Spanish Muslim families were the Banu Angelico and the Banu Savarico who enjoyed great influence by virtue of their wealth. The Arabs were mostly Yemenites. The Banu Hajjaj and the

Banu Khaldun were, at this time, the most prominent families of Saville. The banu Hajjaj were descendants of Sara (Witiza's grand daughter) from her Muslim husbands. The banu Khaldun were also Yemenites whose forefathers from Haḍramaut settled around Seville after conquest. Ibn Khaldun the 14th century historian philosopher hailed from this family. During the time of Abdullah the Banu Khaldun were led by Quraib ibn Usman who was the most ambitious, unscruplous and crooked man of his time. He wanted to the dethrone the Umayyads. This could be done if the neo-Muslims who were loyal to the government were neutralised. Qoraib won over the Banu Hajjaj brothers, 'Abdullah and Ibrahim and fromed a league in collaboration with a Berber highwayman. The Berbers organized raids against the neo-Muslims. All this began in 889 at the active instigation of Qoraib. He carried on insidious propaganda in the provinces of Sidonia and Nielba, and tried to won over Marwan Jilliqi of Portugal. The neo-Muslims felt insecure as the governor was of no help to them. They appealed to 'Abdullah for protection. He authorized them to build a fort at Sant Tirso, a place between Ecija and Seville which was on the route from which the Berbers operated with their gangs. Qoraib and the Banu Hajjaj saw in this, a triumph of the neo-Muslims, and their men attacked the fortress. Abdullah was on the horns of dilemma: He neither wanted offend the Arabs nor to alienate the neo-Muslims. He posted his son the prince Muhammad to investigate the matter. The Yemenite party suspected 'Abdullah for partiality towards the neo-Muslims, and they took to arms, Qoraib seized the castle of Coria, and Abdullah ibn Hajjaj wrested Cormona by a surprise assault. In the meantime, acting on the advice of some of his vazirs, Abdullah committed the greatest blunder of life when he ordered the execution of the neo-Muslim leader Muhammad ibn Ghalib. This heinous crime changed the whole course of events. The neo-Muslims realized that they could not expect any help or protection from the government. They threw themselves into the arms of ibn Hafsun. Riots broke out, and when Ja'd a scion of Arab family was killed by the soldiers of ibn Hafsun, the governor Umayya in a fit of madness instigated the Banu Hajjaj and Qoraib to eliminate the neo-Muslims. In a horrible massare hundreds of the neo-Muslims lost their lives, and some of the wealthiest families were redouced to poverty.

The province of Seville was now shared by the Banu Khaldun and the Banu Hajjaj. The alliance between these two families did not last long. Mutual suspicions embittered their friendship. One day Abdullah received a letter from Khalid brother of Quraib in which he expressed his lack of faith in Ibrahim ibn Hajjaj. By chance this letter (perhaps it was implanted by Abdullah to divide the Banu Hajjaj and the Banu Khaldun) fell into the hand of Ibrahim ibn Hajj. This confirmed his suspicion that the Banu Khaldun were plotting against the Banu Hajjaj. The two brothers, Quraib and Khalid were invited by Ibrahim ibn Hajj at his mansion. During the meal Ibrahim showed them the letter. They blamed each other for breach of trust, and Khalid in a fit anger charged Ibrahim with his daggar. The latter summoned his soldiers, and Quraib and Khalid were done to death. This happened in 899. Ibrahim ibn Hajjaj was now the sole authority in the district of Seville. He applied to 'Abdullah for the grant of a quasi-independent status in return for which he pledged to remit some revenue to the central exchequer. Will-nilly 'Abdullah agreed. Ibrahim set up a brilliant court at Seville with all the trappings of a ruler. He raised his own army, and his own police and judiciary without consulting the legitimate ruler at Cordova. He lived in luxury and donned the princely robe called tiraz. This small province barely 150 miles from Cordova was a haven of prosperity during the time of

Ibrahim ibn Hajjaj. Several poets and musicians added lustre to his court. When he died in 910-911, aged sixty-three, his two sons— 'Abd ar-Rahman and Muhammad divided the province between themselves, the former retaining the city of Seville, and the latter Carmona. Their doom came during the time of 'Abdulla's successor.

Ibn Hafsun took the fullest advantage of the chaotic conditions, and the failure of the government to assert its authority. He was now the most powerful among the rebels of the Spanish group, and virtual master of a sizeable chunk of territory which he continued to enlarge by military adventurism. He seized Jaen, Ecija, Estepa, and Archidona. He carried his arms as far as Algeciras and occupied the fortress after driving out the Berber chief Abū Harb who hăd been loyal to 'Abdullah. Several chiefs like ibn Mastana of Priego were his vassals. Not content with his possession, he planned to take Cordova. This was a time of great danger to the safety of the Kingdom. If Cordova fell, 'Abdullah would be a king without a kingdom. Worst of all 'Abdullah was short of money. The wealth amassed by his grandfather had melted away. The revenues stood at one third of the previous reign because the provinces had stopped their contributions to the central treasury. The soldiers were unpaid, and he had to borrow money to purchase the loyalty of those who were still attached to him. More than once he tried to conciliate ibn Hafsun but he spurned his peace proposals with contempt. When he heard that ibn Hafsun was poised for an attack at Cordova he plucked up courage to face his adversary. He assembled his cavalry in the plains of Secunda with the object of capturing Ecija the nearest stronghold of ibn Hafsun. The army left Cordova on May 15, 891. Ibn Hafsun made a night attack but the archers of 'Abdullah repulsed him. Ibn Hafsun ran towards Polie a fortress about 50 km to the south a Cordova. (On the map of modern Spain it is shown as Aguilar) 'Abdullah's army chased the fugitive and occupied the fortress of Polie. He pushed on towards Bobastro but his army was tired and further operations had to be postponed. Hafsun was not a man to sit quiet. He resolved to wash away the disgrace of his defeat, but he wanted time to chalk out his future plan of action. He sued for peace. Abdullah agreed provided ibn Hafsun sent one of his sons as a hostage. The treacherous rebel sent/only his adopted son, and when the truth came to light, hostilities broke out once again. Surprisingly, ibn Hafsun recaptured (by 892) much of the territory he had lost to 'Abdullah. He became all the more arrogant.

In 889 he formally adopted Christianity along with his wife and children. He took the Christian name of Samuel. From this time, the war between ibn Hafsun and the government assumed a new dimension. It ceased to be an ethnic issue. It was a holy war, a crusade for the Christians and a jihad for the Muslims. Hafsun's conversion to Christianity marks the beginning of his decline. The neo-Muslims who fought under his banner broke away from him as they were deeply attached to Islam. Descendants of serf and slaves of Gothic days they were determined at all cost to "prevent Christianity once again becoming the dominant religion in the fear that if it did so old claims would inevitably revive of which they would be victims."[4] At first ibn Hafsun made no distinction between the Christians and the Muslims but after his conversion, he showed marked preference towards the Christians. All important posts went to them to the exclusion of the Muslims. As a result, serious riots broke out among the followers of the two faiths and ibn Hafsun's bravest neo-Muslims deserted him.

This was the grim political scenario when 'Abdullah died on

16th Oct., 912 after 26 years of inglorious rule leaving his fragmented and bankrupt kingdom to his grandson 'Abd ar-Rahman. The following day, the new sultan received the oath of allegiance at a ceremony held in the "Perfect salon" (al-majils al-kamil) of the Alcazar.

Notes

1. We shall know about these families in later chapters.
2. L. Provençal: Histoire, Vol, I, p. 294.
3. Ibn Idhari: Vol. II, p. 171.
4. Dozy p. 386.

Chapter 8

Caliph 'Abd ar-Rahman III
(Al-Nasir) (912-961)

Born on Jan 7, 891 (22nd Ramazan 277 A.H.), 'Abd ar-Rahman was 22 years of age when he came to the throne. He was an infant of barely three weeks when his father, the prince Muhammad fell a victim to his grandfather's wrath and his younger uncle's conspiracies. His mother was a Christian slave named Muzna. His grandmother was a high born lady-Dona Inigia, a daughter of Fortun Garces of the Banu Qasi family of Aragon. 'Abdullah was her second husband. He called her *'durr'* (Pearl) out of affection. Thus, 'Abd ar-Rahman was more a European than an Asian. He was a youngman of handsome features, with deep blue eyes and golden hair- the typical physical traits of most of the Umayyads of Spain born after Hisham 1. Abdullah had decided during his life time to pass on the throne to 'Abd ar-Rahman, and he took all pains to groom him for kingship. His accession was hailed by all. It was like the appearance of the new moon says ibn 'Abd Rabbihi, a great poet of the time. More than his good looks, 'Abd ar-Rahman had qualities of the heart and the mind which endeared him to all. His charisma lay in his pleasing personality, his engaging manners, his affability and generosity. He was born to rule and

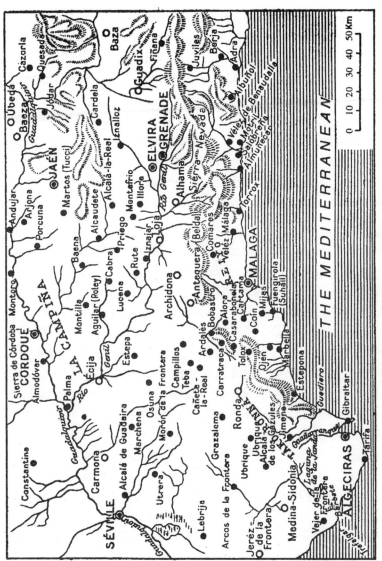

THE SOUTH OF SPAIN IN THE X CENTURY

command, and when he grew in age, his majestic personality inspired reverential awe (*haiba*). He possessed precisely those very qualities which were required of a ruler at this critical juncture in the history of Muslim Spain. The young prince was fearless, energetic, methodical, quick in taking decision, and equally quick in action. Above all he was a born administrator. He did not induct new faces in the executive machinery. Many of the men around him had served his predecessors, but he had the knack of getting work out of them by the force of his personality and leadership. His long reign was one of the most glorious periods in the entire history of Spain-a clear proof of the fact that a state is only a reflection of its leader.

'Abd ar-Rahman had a Herculean task before him. The political horizon was overcast with ominous clouds; the state's economy was in shambles; the authority of the king was limited to the region around Cordova. Armed brigands roamed the countryside and the roads was so unsafe that for seven years no caravans had passed between Cordova and Saragossa. During the last years of his reign 'Abdullah had, no doubt, won over some rebels, but the most powerful of them were still at large. Most of the kingdom, as stated earlier, had been pareclled out by the rebels of Spanish extraction. The northern frontiers were in a state of ferment. At Pechina pirates had set upon a self-governing colony. The kingdom divided within had two enemies outside its frontiers. The rulers of Asturia were becoming more and more aggressive. They looked south for expansion. A historian has eloquently summed upon the dangers from the north. He says, "Their eyes were turned towards the south. Still so poor that, for lack of coinage, they bartered commodities, and taught by their priests to who they were blindly devoted and who they loaded with gifts- that war against the infidels was the surest means of gaining heaven; they would fain seek in wealthy Andalusia the blessings of this world and that of the next. Could Andalusia escape their domination? If she succumbed, terrible would be the faith of the Muslims. Cruel and fanatical, the Leonese gave no quarter, when they captured a town they usually put all inhabitants to the sword. Tolerance such as was accorded by the Moslems to the Christians could not be expected of them. What would become of that brilliant and progressive civilization, at the hand of barbarians who could not read; who had to call in 'saracens' when they wished to measure their fields, and who, when they mentioned a library meant there the Holy Scriptures. It is manifest, therefore,, that task lay before Abd ar-Rahman III at the beginning of his reign was a great and noble one— he had to save not only the country but civilization itself, the difficulties that confronted him were moreover of the most formidable nature. The prince had to subdue his own subjects, as well as to repel on one side the northern barbarians whose insolence increased as the Muslim empire grew weak."[1] Across the straits of Gibralter, the Fatamids held north Africa which they intended to use as a *point d' appui* to uproot the Umayyads from Spain. The crown, passed on to 'Abd ar -Rahman by his grandfather, was in fact a tiara of thorns.

The most urgent task before 'Abd ur-Rahman was to reconsolidate his dominion by eliminating rebels, terrorist and self-styled leaders. Unlike his grandfather, he did not vacillate. He made a determined effort to enforce the rule of law. Time was also on his side. Some of the rebels were already dead, and those alive, like ibn Hafsun, had reached the middle age. The public was disgusted with the long civil strifes which had damaged the economic fabric of the state. There was a genuine desire for peace. Soon after he came to the throne, several rebels voluntaily submitted, and handed over their forts. Those who refused to submit were brought to their knees by swift military action. Ecija, the nearest nest of the rebels opened is gates when Badr, the hajib of 'Abd ar-rahman appeared before the city in Jan 913. After a carefully prepared plan 'Abd ur-Rahman himself took the field. His first campaign which began in March 913 was directed against the rebels in the southeast. Ibn Hudhail of Monteleon was the first neo-Muslim rebel to seek pardon (*aman*) on April 27. He marched into the mountains, and obtained submission of several rebels. Their families were transported to Cordova, and some of them were enrolled in the royal army-a practice 'Abd ur-Rahman consistently followed whenever a rebel chief submitted to his arms. After concluding the mopping up operations in Baza, he moved towards Gaudix, and reached Finana in May 913. The partisans of ibn Hafsun evacuated the hill town after a feeble resistance. 'Abd ur-Rahman penetrated deeper into the valleys and ravines of Sierra Nevada. After subjugating Juviles, he moved further to the south through the rocky terrain and completed his campaign with the occupations of Salobrena on the Mediterranean coast. When he returned to Cordova on July 17, 913 to celebrate Id-al -Zuha, he had the supreme satisfaction of having flushed out rebels and brigands from 66 forts and 30 places of strategic importance. All this was achieved in a period of just four months.

He was now free to pay attention to the province of Seville. The two Banu Hajjaj brothers who we left in the last chapter, quarrelled among themselves. 'Abd ar-Rahman who held the major portion of the province was poisoned by his brother. Family feuds broke their unity. Ahmad ibn Maslama who succeeded 'Abd ar-Rahman ibn Hajjaj, was left alone. While the royal army was knocking at the gate of Seville, he called ibn Hafsun to his aid, but it was of no avail. Finding that the game was up, he handed over (Dec 21,913) Seville to Badr the

military commander of 'Abd ar-Rahman. Muhammad, the lord
of Carmona was isolated and he thought it prudent to hand over
the city to the central government. The dynasty of Banu Hajjaj
faded away leaving only a faint memory of the brilliant court
life of the founder-Ibrahim ibn Hajjaj. The unification of the
state went on steadily and surely. 'Abd ar-Rahman was seldom
vindictive. The Muslims and the Christians who submitted to
him were treated with leniency.

The *en mass* desertion of neo-Muslims as a result of ibn
Hafsun's return to Christianity, the loss of Jaen and Elvira, and
the liquidation of his many allies, lowered his prestige. He
could not hope for any assistance from abroad as 'Abd ar-
Rahman had already destroyed his vessels stationed in a creek
on the coast. Like an eagle with wounded wings, ibn Hafsun
remained most of the time in his eyrie of Bobastro. He was no
more a terror; he was in a state of siege. He was now past the
middle age, and spent most of him time in the church built by
him in the rocks. He died a dejected man in Sept., 917 leaving
his widow Columba, a daughter named Argentea, and four sons-
Ja'far, 'Abd ar-Rahman, Sulaiman and Hafs. Ja'far the eldest
who succeeded his father agreed to pay tribute, but just after
three months of his father's death, he was assassinated by the
Christians as they suspected him of switching over to Islam.
His brother 'Abd ar-Rahman asked for pardon, and he settled
at Cordova where he terminated his days as a caligraphist. The
third brother Sulaiman was killed in an ambush in Feb. 927.
Only Hafs held out at Bobastro. 'Abd ar-Rahman was now in
a strong position, and he resolved to annex this hilly pocket.
The operation Bobastro was conducted by 'Abd ar-Rahman
himself. It is said that he kept fast during the campaign. Bastion
after bastion fell into the hands of the victors. After a siege of
some months Hafs agreed to surrender. The minister ibn Hudair

took possession of the fort, and the white flag of the Umayyads at last fluttered at Baobástro on Jan 17, 928. Hafs was treated with magnanimity. He was allowed to settle at Cordova and was given a post in the army. Columba joined a local onvent, while Argentea was executed for fermenting hatred against the government.

'Abd ar-Rahman had firm grip over the south, but the western sector, and the territory round Toledo remained to be subjugated. At this time the Algarve was held by the descendants of al-Jilliqi and his vassals. The heaquarters of the Jilliqi family was at Badajoz. If it fell into the hands of 'Abd ar-Rahman, the rest of the territory would be easy to capture. On June 5,929 he encamped before the walls of Badajoz after laying waste the suburbs. While the siege was in progress, he reduced Beja, and liquidated the vassals of the Jilliqi family from Ocsonoba, Santa Maria and Silves. 'Abdullah ibn Marwan, the last of the Jilliqi family offered his submission in the middle of 930, and left for Cordova with his family and dependents.

It was now the turn of Toledo. During the stormy days of 'Abdullah, the whole destrict of Toledo had broken away from the centre, and it was administered by leaders chosen by the citizens, some of them belonging to the Banu Qasi family. When 'Abd ar-Rahman resolved to annex Toledo, the district was held by Tha'laba ibn Abdal-warith. He was in alliance with the Christian king of Asturia. Before resorting to arms 'Abd ar-Rahman sent a delegation to the people of Toledo to negotiate a peaceful surrender, but the recalcitrant people were in no mood of reconciliation. For several years they had tasted the joys of liberty. They knew that they had enough men and material for a prolonged blockade. Above all they relied on the natural protection of their city which rose from a rocky bluff and was girdled almost on all the sides by the river Tagus. All their calculations failed before the brilliantly planned campaign of 'Abd ar-Rahman. The campaign began in May 930 When 'Abd ar-Rahman sent a small force under the minister Sa'id al-Mundhir. In July, he himself left Cordova at the head of a large army. He encamped for sometime at the bank of the river Algodor. After reducing Mora, he pushed ahead, and encamped at Chalencas the last halting place on the road to Toledo. 'Abd ar-Rahman knew that the siege would last long. He directed that a mini town be built on the place. Called *Madinat al-Fath* (the City of Victory) it was provided with bazars, shops and houses. After making these arrangements he returned to Cordova. 'Abd ar-Rahman's plan was to starve the citizens. All the approaches to the city were in the hands of the army. Ramiro II of Galicia sent a force to break the siege, but it was badly mauled by the Umayyad army. After two years the stocks of food in the city ran out, and the starving citizens sued for peace. 'Abd ar-Raman again travelled to Toledo to witness formal surrender of the city. Tha'laba appeared in the royal camp, and obtained general amnesty for the citizens. On August 2, 932, 'Abd ar-Rahman rode triumphantly into Toledo. He posted a garrison in the city, and other places of strategic importance. A great function was held to mark the victory, and rewards were given to the soldiers. The capture of Toledo completed the unification of the tattered kingdom of Cordova, inherited by 'Abd ar-Rahman from his grandfather. It took him two decades,, and indeed, it was a miracle. He was now in the prime of his manhood— the fortieth years of his life. He placed each province of his dominion under governors of proved experience and loyalty. Revenues flowed into the coffers of the central government, and the kingdom advanced rapidly towards prosperity.

'Abd ar-Rahman consolidated his position in the Upper
Marches. This was a big territory between the Pyrenees and the
Valley of the Ebro with Saragossa as its capital. The whole
region had been in a state of confusion since the days of 'Abd
ar-Rahman II. It was a playground for the politically ambitious
Banu Qasi. The members of this family were only nominal
Muslims. By nature volatile, restless, and opportunists, they
changed their loyalties as and when they liked. Sometimes they
fought under the Umayyad banner, and sometimes on behalf of
the Christian kingdoms of Galicia and Navarre. Musa the Qasi
we met in the previous chapter was the undisputed master of
the region. He was often at war with the Kingdom of Asturia.
He died in 852 after he was defeated and wounded in a war
with Ordono I. His eldest son Muhammad Lope acknowledged
Ordono as his sovereign. His other brothers— Mutarrif and
Ismail held Tudela and Saragossa. Musa was the last great ruler
of this remarkable family. After his death his descendants were
torn by feuds and thinned by assassinations. Some of them
relapsed into Christianity and left the territory; others migrated
to Cordova and died as Muslims. Their women whom they
gave Christian names entered into Christian harems. After the
fall of the banu Qasi, the Upper March passed into the hands
of Banu Hashim who were descendants of the Arab family of
'Abd ar-Rahman al-Tujibi. Ultimately, Muhammad ibn Hisham
of this family capitulated when 'Abd ar-Rahman besieged the
city of Saragossa. The latter showed his generosity by allowing
him to continue as governor subject to loyalty to the government
of Cordova.

From the very beginning of his reign 'Abd ar-Rahman had
to face two most implacable enemies— the kingdoms of Asturia
and Navarre. The former kingdom was held by Garcia (910-
914) who succeeded Alfonso III. Garcia transferred the capital

from Oviedo to Leon. Henceforth, this principality came to be known as the kingdom of Leon. Before his premature death, Garcia populated and fortified the towns of Osma, Clunia, San Estaban on the right bank of the Douro. These fortress— towns posed a threat to the safety of the kingdom of Cordova, specially during the reign of the ambitious Ordono II (914-924). He understimated the ruler of Cordova, and made several incursions into the western sector. He massacred the Muslims, and carried their woman and children into slavery. They lived in constant fear. Once the citizens of Badajoz were so much frightened that they paid a large sum of money to Ordono with which he built a church in the name of St. Mary. The rebel ibn Jilliqi failed to protect the Muslim. 'Abd ar-Rahman was in a difficult position, and he did not like to open hostilities with his northern neighbours. However, as the rightful sovereign, he felt his moral duty to come to the aid of his subjects. In order to impress upon Ordono that he should not take him for granted, he despatched a small force under his grandfather's general Ahmad ibn Abda. The expedition ended in a disaster. The Muslims were routed (Sept. 4, 917) near the gate of San Esteban and thousands of them perished in the debacle. Ahmad ibn Abda died on the battlefield like a hero. The victors carried away his body and nailed it on the walls of San Esteban beside a pig. 'Abd ar-Rahman could not retaliate at once as Africa claimed his attention. The redoubtable Ordono, fearing a massive reprisal, entered into a defensive alliance with Sancho Garces I of Navarre. Their united forces burst upon the Muslim town of Tudela, revaged the countryside, and burnt the mosque of Valtierra. 'Abd ar-Rahman had to pick up the gaunlet at a great risk because he was still in the midst of unifying his kingdom. He sent his minister Badr to chastise Ordono and hia allies. He left for the frontier in the middle of July 918, and inflicted several defeats on the enemy, but 'Abd ar-Rahman was not satisfied. After two years of brisk preparations, he himself left Cordova on June 5,920 at the head of a large army. He reached Toledo just in four days. From there, he directed his march towards Osma via Guadalajara and Medinaceli. After having pillaged Osma he quickly moved towards the fortress of San Esteban where three years back Ibn 'Abda had met his death. When the Umayyad army reached there, it found the town abandoned. They empty town was pillaged, and its walls and churches were dismantled. A similar fate awaited Clunia. Turning round he reached Tudela. Muhammad Ibn Lope, the last of the Banu Qasi joined with his soldiers. The army penetrated deeper into the territory of Navarre. Sancho suffered defeat after defeat. 'Abd ar-Rahman pushed ahead with the rapidity of a Greek phalanx. After seizing Calahorra he encamped in the valley of Junquera which is one of the most perilous terrains in the extreme north. He was face to face with the wild mountaineers who ancestors had inflicted a murderous defeat on Charlimagne in the not distant valley of Roncevalles. For three months he gave no respite to the enemy. On the 16th August he wound up his camp. He crossed the river Ebro and arrived at Atienza from where he took the road to Cordova. He returned to Cordova in triumph in the month of Sept. with a large number of prisoners of war including one bishop who fought with army of Sancho.

Like his predecessors 'Abd ar-Rahman did not seriously think of permanently occupying the northern territories even after inflicting crushing defeats on the Christian rulers. This attitude is apparently mystifying but it would be interesting to find a definite reason for it. Was it due to the traditional dislike of the Muslims (or to be precise the Arabs of those days) for barren mountains? Perhaps, they realised that it would not be possible to populate the northern regions with the idea of ultimately incorporating them in the Muslim territory. The whole region offered no prospects of economic growth, and the climate, bleak and cold, had no charm for the dwellers in the sunny south. We are inclined to think that the Muslim rulers thought of peaceful co-existence if left alone, but the fierce northern Spaniards fired with a deep-rooted hatred of the Muslims were never in a mood of *entente cordiale,* and friendly cooperation. They were bent upon destroying the Muslim rule. One is struck by their indomitable will never to yield or submit that arose as fresh as ever even after repeated defeats — like some herbs which grow stronger the more they are trodden under the foot. After two years the Christians were again on the war path. Ordono captured Najera, while his ally Sancho attacked Viguera with usual massacres. Once again 'Abd ar-Rahman had to set out to punish the aggressors. Leaving Cordova on the 27th April, 924 (16 muharram 312 A.H.), he took the route through Murcia and Valencia and moved on towards Tudela. On the 10th of July he crossed the Ebro and entered into the territory of Navarre. In the meantime, Ordono died, and Sancho was left without any ally. 'Abd ar-Rahman defeated Sancho in every encounter. The forts of Carcar, Peralta, Falces, Carcastillo which were used by Sancho both for offence and defence fell into the hands of the Umayyad army. 'Abd ar-Rahman entered into the valleys and gorges of the region like a furious tide carrying everything before it. After capturing Lumbier and Lizoain, the road to Pamplona the capital of Navarre was almost clear. Before he reached the gates of the city, the panick-stricken inhabitants had already left. The empty city was plundered and sacked, and its cathedral levelled to the ground. 'Abd ar-Rahman continued his march and reached the fortress of Hurate-Araquil (Sakhrat Qais) which is not even fifty miles from the Bay of Biscay. No attempt was made to occupy any part of Navarre. Obviously, 'Abd ar-Rahman wanted to humiliate Sancho, and not to deprive him of his kingdom. He returned to Cordova at the end of August 924.

For some years there was calm on the frontiers. On the death of Ordono a war of succession broke out in the Kingdom of Leon. This gave 'Abd ar-Rahman enough time to look after domestic affairs. The new king of Leon - Fruela II died of leprosy (925) leaving two sons from his wife Urraca of the Banu Qais family. A civil war broke out in the Kingdom ending in the enthronement of Alfonso IV. He ruled from 925 to 932, and abdicated in favour of his brother Ramiro II. He inaugurated his reign by putting out the eyes of his rivals. Fierce, fanatical and war-like, he opened hostilities with the Kingdom of Cordova without any provocation. He made a surprise attack on the small Muslim town of Madrid, and started upon a career of constant inroads in the Umayyad territory. Throughout his rule (932-950) he gave no peace to 'Abd ar-Rahman. He had the nerve to form a league with Muhammad ibn Hisham, the governor of Saragossa, and the king of Navarre against the kingdom of Cordova. 'Abd ar-Rahman had sensed that trouble was ahead, and in 937, he left for the north. He attacked the kingdom of Leon, and demolished Burgos and many other forts. After this operation he proceeded towards Saragossa to punish the traitor ibn Hisham. The city surrendered after a siege, and ibn Hisham asked for clemency. 'Abd ar-Rahman with his usual generosity pardoned him and reinstated him as governor . He was now free to turn towards Navarre which was held by queen Toda Aznarez as a regent of her son. The queen was so much frightened that she agreed to acknowledge 'Abd ar-Rahman's suzerainty. After two years the clever queen repudiated her submission, and joined hands with Ramiro.

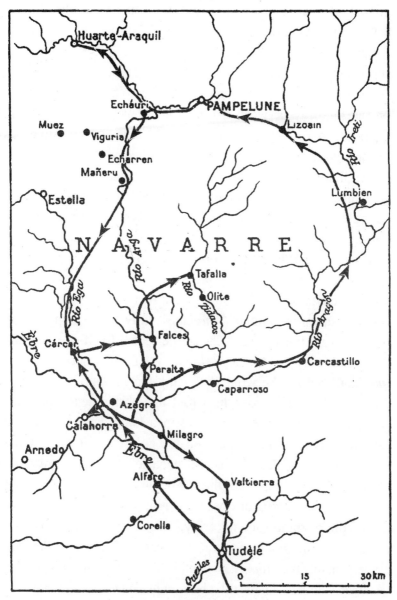

THE CAMPAIGN OF PAMPELONA

The years 939 proved unlucky for 'Abd ar-Rahman. In the middle of that year he invaded Leon to break the alliance between the two northern kingdoms. This expedition was given a pompous title *'ghazwāt al-qudra'* i.e., the campaign of supremacy. At this time, he led the biggest army under his command, but it was doomed to disaster. They army marched on the highway between Cordova and Toledo. After crossing the river Douro, 'Abd ar-Rahman reached the walls of Simancas in the middle of July 939. Ramiro arrived with his army and the auxiliaries furnished by the queen Toda and the Count Fernan Gonzales of Castile. The battle began with skirmishes, and the struggle swayed to and fro for several days. The armies fought during the day and retired to their camps at night. During the course of the battle, Ramiro observed that the wing led by 'Abd ar-Rahman showed signs of lastitude. He made it the target of a massive attack. The Muslims found themselves overwhelmed and ran towards a ditch *"khandaq"* only to be trapped and butchered in thousands. Every soldier cared for his safety, and the proud army of 'Abd ar-Rahman was thrown into confusion like chaff before the wind. The battle dated August 1, 939 or *Shawwal* 11, 327, ended in a rout and a stampede. 'Abd ar-Rahman ran from the camp, and in a hurry he left behind a fabulous copy of the Quran and his gold coat of mail. What was the cause of this disgraceful debacle? The author of *kitab al majmu'a* has reported that 'Abd ar-Rahman gave undue importance to pesons of obscure origin and the foreign slaves in the administration and the army. This discrimination forstered dissatisfaction among the Arab officers, and they had decided among themselves that they would voluntarily suffer a defeat. 'Abd ar-Rahman knew all about this. When he returned to Cordova three hundred officers of the cavalry were hanged on the bank of the Guadalquivir, while a royal herald shouted—

"such is the punishment of those who betrayed Islam and sowed seeds of disunity among the soldiers who fought a holy war.[2]

Henceforth, 'Abd ar-Rahman did not lead any army in person and entrusted the work to his two most faithful commanders— Ahmad ibn Ya'la, and ibn Ghalib. The former was a Berber, and the latter the son of a slave from Carmona. The defeat at Simancas did not disillusion him. He was still at the apogee of his military supremacy supported by a flourishing economy. He continued to depatch punitive expeditions againt the northern states. During the course of an expedition (948-949) the Cordovan army cut through the northwest and reached Ortqueira— the very tip of Spain on the Atlantic Ocean. 'Abd ar-Rahman took effective measure to secure the frontier. He converted Medinaceli into a base from where the armies would fan out with speed into the northern territories. The old forts were rebuilt, and the people were encouraged to settle at the new advance base of the army.

The defeat suffered by 'Abd ar-Rahman at Simancas was as unforeseen as the recognition of his supremacy by the kingdoms of Leon and Navarre. We shall now see how these two states, fanatical in their hatred of their Muslim neighbours, become tributaries of the kingdom of Cordova.

Ramio died in 950, and civil war raged once again in the kingdom of Leon. He had two wives. The first gave birth to his eldest son Ordono III. His second wife was Urraca a daughter of Sancho Garces I and queen Toda Aznárez of Navarre. He had a son from his second wife also. His name was Sancho. The internal politics of the kingdom was further complicated due to unrest in the province of Castile which was aspiring for complete independence under the leadership of the energetic Count Fernan Gonzales. With a view to stopping the emergence of Castile as a separate state, Ramiro arrested the Count and threw him into a dungeon, and confiscated his property. The Count was very popular with his subjects and soon Ramiro had to relent He freed the Count on the condition that he would give away his daughter in marriage to his eldest son Ordono. Thus, the Count was the father-in-law of Ramiro's heir-apparent. In the civil war which broke out after the death of Ramiro, his two sons fought for the throne. The count hated his son-in-law, and supported Sancho. But Ordono won the war, and ruled from 950-955, while his rival Sancho took refuge with his maternal grandmother, the queen Toda of Navarre. Meanwhile, the governors of the Upper Marches continued to make inroad into the territory of Leon. Ordono found himself isolated and completely helpless. He wanted to save his throne at all costs. Towards the end of 955 he sent an embassy to Cordova to negotiate a treaty of peace. Under the terms of the treaty which were negotiated by Muhammad Hussain, and the Jewish minister Hasdai ibn Shaprut on behalf of 'Abd ar-Rahman, Ordono agreed to acknowledge 'Abd ar-Rahman suzerainty. He agreed also to demolish some forts, and to hand over several others to the government of Cordova. After a year Ordono died, but his successor Sancho did not honour the terms of the treaty. 'Abd ar-Rahman's general Ahmad ibn Ya'la attacked Leon, and inflicted a crushing defeat on Sancho. He was already unpopular with his subjects because of his excessive obesity. They knick-named him' the fat 'because he could not ride a horse, and required the support of a person to walk about. He was driven out of his kingdom in 958. Once again he sought the protection of his grandmother Toda. The Kingdom of Leon passed into the hands of Ordono IV.

Queen Toda thought of a plan to restore her Humpty-Dumpty grandson on the throne of Leon with foreign assistance. In her search for help, she turned to 'Abd ar-Rahman who, after all, carried a Vascon's blood in his veins. She had also heard about the clever physicians of Cordova, and begged that she might be allowed to consult some of them. Her envoy arrived at Cordova. 'Abd ar-Rahman seized the opportunity, and sent his Jewish minister Hasdai ibn shaprut to Pamplona for further talks. Hasdai was a physician by profession and also a scholar of Greek, Latin, and the Romance language spoken in the north. He arrived at Pamplona, and by his soft words, he invited the queen to visit Cordova along with her grandson. He assured her that the government of Cordova would give all possible military assistance to place Sancho on the throne of Leon, and also that it was possible to relieve him of his corpulence. In return, she was asked to surrender some forts to the government of Cordova, and also to recognise 'Abd ar-Rahman as her overlord. She agreed to all these conditions. Queen Toda, her grandson Sancho and a large entourage arrived in Cordova in 958. The arrival of a Christian queen in Cordova the capital of a Muslim State, was a memorable day, and a landmark in the history of international diplomacy of the Middle Ages. She was given a red carpet reception at Madinat az-Zahra[3]. Sancho responded to the miraculous treatment administered by the best physicians, and he gained a smart waistline. In due course he was provided with an army, and in 960 he occupied the throne of Leon. Ordono IV ran away and hid himself at Burgos. 'Abd ar-Rahman was now at the pinnacle of his glory. He was master of the whole of the Iberian peninsula, and his word was law from the Bay of Biscay to the Straits of Gibralter. Each year, the rulers of Leon and Navarre as well as the Counts of Barcelona remitted their tribute to the government of Cordova.

'Abd ar-Rahman was also successful in protecting his kingdom from the traditional enemies of his house— the Fatimis of north Africa. The Fatimi challenge was very serious and we may have to look into this matter in some detail. The Fatimis were an offshoot of the Shias who repudiated the first three Caliphs (the *Rashidun*), and believed in the Divine Right of Ali, the Prophet's cousin and son-in-low, and Ali' descendants to rule over and guide the Muslims. The Shias broke away from the main body of Muslims on the succession issue. Later on, the Shias themselves split into several groups on the same issue. The parting of ways came when the 6th imam Ja'far Sadiq, a grandson of imam Hussain died in 965. The Imam had two sons Ismail and Musa. He nominated his eldest son Ismail as his successor, but later on revoked his will, and designated his second son Musa al-Kazim in place of Ismail. Those Shias who recognized Ismail only as the legitimate Imam came to be known as the Ismaili. This was the beginning of the Ismaili faction among the Shias, and the breach continues to this day. The classical Shias (the Ithna ashariyya) have been dominant in Iran since the 16th century when the Saffavid Shah Ismail transformed the Sunni majority into Shias. The Ismailis are scattered in India, Karachi, Hunza and Lebanon and some parts of South Africa. They owe allegiance to their hereditary pontiff. They are, by and large, a community of traders and industrialist. Although busy in 'getting and spending' they do not lay waste their powers. The Ismailis are known for their many philanthropic foundations accruing benefits to peoples of all religions. They do not play any political role today, but it was otherwise in the 10th century. In the whole history of Islam no group was so subversive as the Ismailis. Taking the nomenclature of the 'Fatimis' they established a dynasty in Egypt which they ruled from 909 to 1071 in a sea of Sunni Islam, until it was estinguished by Salah al-Din. The late Agha Khan, had no doubt, in his mind the glorious rule of the Fatimis of Egypt when he preferred to be buried on the bank of the Nile.

Some historians are harsh in their judgment of the Ismaili or Fatimi faction. They look upon this section as an insidious attempt to destroy Islam from within. This is far from being the case, although it cannot be denied that their theology has several very objectional doctrines. Ibn Maymun gave this sect its ideological outlook. The Ismaili doctrine is a curios mixture of metempsychosis, Persian dualism, and deification of Caliph Ali and his descendants. The Quran claims to be a clear book free from mysteries. The Ismaili believed that the verses of the Quran contain an inner (batini) meaning which can be explained only be allegorical interpretation. Numerology was a conspicuous part of the Ismaili theology—specially the number 7 and 12. Their are seven planets, 7 days in a week, 7 cervical ribs, 7 apertures on the face, 12 months in a year and 12 zordical aings — all these have a hidden meaning. Religion was thus reduced to a riddle Its mysteries could be unravelled only by a missionary (dai) of the cult. A disciple to be initiated in the Islamili sect took an oath of secrecy after having undergone nine stages of brain washing. The Ismaili sect was politically motivated. Under its elaborate doctrinaire facade, lay hidden the deep-rooted passion of the Persians to capture power from the Sunni Arabs by espousing the cause of Ali's descendants. Ibn Maymun himself was of Persian origin. His father was a born intriguer. He passed on to his son the doctrine of the incarnation of the Imam. He hoodwinked his disciples by giving them news of foreign lands, but they hardly knew that he obtained his information from his emissaries through carrier pigeons. Ibn Maymun died in the year 874, but his movement was carried forward by his Ismaili spies disguised as merchants and travellers. Their efforts were laurelled with success in north Africa when 'Abū Abdullah a secret missionary arrived there in 893, and captivated the Kutama Berbers by his cleverness and eloquence. He taught the Berbers that the Mahdi's appearance was imminent. After a year of political activity the Berbers of this tribe swarmed under his banner. He established himself at the fortress of Mila in the province of Constantine. When he found that the time was ripe for the Mahdi to appear, he invited 'Ubaid Allah, a descendant of Ibn Maymun from Syria. Travelling stealthily, and after many vicissitudes, Ubaid Allah entered into Qayrawan about the end of 909, and assumed the titles of 'Mahdi' and the 'Commander of the Faithfuls'. As he claimed his descent from Imam Ismail and through him from the Caliph Ali, and Fatima he styled himself as 'Fatimi' to acquire a halo of sanctity. 'Ubaid Allah founded the city of Mahdiya on the north African coast near Qayrawan. Soon he consolidated his position in the northwest, and enlarged his dominion at the expense of the local rulers. By a series of whirlwind campaigns, he annexed much of northwest Africa as far as Tahart. If Morocco fell, the fate of the Umayyads of Spain would be in danger. This was the grim situation in northwest Africa when 'Abd ar-Rahman ascended the throne of Cordova.

The political and intellectual climate in Spain was favourable to the growth of Fatimi ideology. The country was fragmented making the task of an aggressor easy. The Mu'tazili philosophy stared arrogantly in the face of Maliki orthodoxy. The philosopher ibn Massara (883-931) was suspected of being an Ismaili missionary as he taught in an esoteric language which could be interpreted either way. The Fatimi intervention began in a quiet manner during the reign of king Abdullah. A preacher (da'i) named ibn Sarraj arrived in Spain, and carried out propaganda in favour of the Fatimis. Diguised as a harmless holyman, dressed in coarse wool, shod in sandles of twisted grass, and riding a donkey, he travelled all over Spain. He

worked ceaselessly for an alliance between the Banu Qasi and
ibn Hafsun to overthrow the Sunni Umayyads. His efforts failed
but he enticed Ahmad Ibn al-Kitt an Umayyad prince who
descended from Hisham I. The prince was an astrologer-cum-
magician. He hypnotised the people by his tricks. One of his
tricks was that he could pour out water by pressing dry sticks.
He attracted a number of disciples with the help of ibn Sarraj,
and soon he claimed that he was the promised Messiah. He
become so powerful that he organised an army in the Sierra d'
Almadén and declared a holy war against Alfonso III. He was
killed and his head was hung on the wall of Zamora beside a
dead pig. Abdullah, the grandfather of 'Abd ar-Rahman was a
silent spectator of these events, but his grandson did not
minimise the Fatimi peril. He took all possible steps, political
and diplomatic, to protect his kingdom. The Fatimi danger
became more and more menacing. In 917 Ubaid Allah ordered
a massive invasion against the coastal city of Naqur held by
Sā'id II, a scion of a noble Arab family. This family had cordial
relations with the Umayyads of Spain from the time of
Muhammad I. Probably, the Spanish Umayyads had an
emotional attachment for this city. The reader will recall that it
was from this city or near about that the founder of the Kingdom
of Cordova had sailed for Spain. Mohammed was very kind to
this family. Once he paid a heavy ransom for the release of two
princesses of Naqur who were captured by Norman pirates when
they attacked that city in 859. When ibn Habus seized Naqur
on behalf of the Fatimis, the two sons of Sā'id sought refuge
at Malaga. 'Abd ar-Rahman ordered that the two brothers be
treated with hospitality. He invited them to take their residence
at Cordova, but they preferred to stay at Malaga. Later on one
of the two brothers landed at Naqur, executed the Fatimi
governor and occupied the town. 'Abd ar-Rahman conveyed

his felicitations at his astounding success. Impressed by 'Abd ar-Rahman of cordiality, the princes of Naqur placed themselves under his protection. This relationship opened the door for direct intervention into the political affairs of north-west Africa. 'Abd ur-Rahman entered into direct negotiations with several Berber chiefs and obtained possession of Ceuta in 931. He was now able to organize a resistance movement against the Fatimis. With the help of the Berbers friendly to him, 'Abd ar-Rahman established a confederation, and nearly the whole of Mauretania rose as a solid wall against the Fatimis. But they did not give in easily. In 955 some Sicilian ships entered into the port of Almeria on behalf of the Fatimis. This was their first direct intervention on the Spanish soil. The general ibn Ghalib and later ibn Ya'la arrived on the scene with seventy ships and frustrated the designs of the enemy. In retaliation, the African coast was ravaged. Henceforth, Almeria served as a naval bulwark of the Umayyad kingdom. 'Abd ar-Rahman build a powerful navy to guard the coast.

Sometime in the beginning of 892 A.D. the 17th year of his reign 'Abd ar-Rahman added a new jewel to his crown, when he proclaimed himself a Caliph (*khalifa*), and adopted the two titles —Commander of the Faithfuls (*amir al-mu'minin*), and Victorious in Religion (*al-Nasir li-dinillah*). His predecessors had been content with a simple title, — *'amir/sultan/or banu 1-khalaif'* out of respect for Abbasid rulers of Baghdad, who, apart from ruling a vast empire, also held the holy cities of Medina and Mecca. When their power declined, and the Fatimis of Africa assumed the august title of 'commander of the /faithful' 'Abd ar-Rahman saw no reason to deny to himself the dignity and prerogative of a Caliph. Orders to this effect were issued to all departments and provincial governors. The communique said— "we think that our name should be in the double form

of *amir al-mu'minin* and *Nasir-li-diniillah*. These titles should
be used in all documents addressed to us. We feel we are
legitimately entitled to this claim as no other person can rightly
claim or attach it, to his person. For us to deny to ourselves any
longer this obligatory usage would be disinheriting ourselves
from an inherited prerogative. In the circumstances, you should
order that all preachers in the capital of your region use these
titles in all communications addressed to us."[4] By this step he
enhanced his prestige in the eyes of his friends and foes alike.
These two titles appeared on all the buildings constructed during
his reign, the coinage of the time, the flags of the army, and the
royal robes worn by him. But he became inaccessible to the
people. The strict etiquette, and the elaborate ceremonies built
a wall between him and his subjects. He was available only to
trusted courtiers, high digniatories and foreign envoys. They
approached him as if he was a being from another world. They
addressed him with panegyric salutations, and willingly
performed the court ceremonies to bask in the sunshine of his
patronage as he sat on his throne (*sarir*) with a sceptre
(*khaizuran*) in his hand. He was a picture of majesty when he
led his army, dressed in a gold coat of mail, with his sword on
his side, mounting on a chestnut-coloured horse under a canopy
(*mazall*). Gone was the simplicity of 'Umar ibn Khattab, and
'Ali ibn abi Talib!

'Abd ar-Rahman's achievements bordered on the miraculous.
But for him, it would have been impossible to unite Muslim
Spain. His military strength forced the northern kings to become
his vassals. By his efficient administration he endowed the state
with peace after half a century of chaos. His reign marks the
beginning of the golden age of Umayyad Spain. Under his wise
government, Muslim Spain became the richest ṣtate in Western
Europe, and an object of envy to all the countries of the

Mediterranean world. Taxes and contributions, tributes from neighbouring kingdoms, duties from imports and exports, poured wealth into the central treasury. The annual revenues amounted to over six million gold dinars. It was reported that in 951 the state treasury contained gold coins worth twenty million. The travellers spoke in glowing terms about the economic condition of Spain. Ibn Hawqal, the Fatimid spy-traveller, who visited Spain extolled the abundance of all the necessaries of life, the cattle wealth, and the cheap prices of cereals, fruits and vegetables. An epistle from Hasdai ibn Shaprut addressed to the king of Khazars (an independent state to the north of the Black Sea inhabited by the Jews) gives a vivd picture of the prosperity of Spain under 'Abd ar-Rahman. As Hasdai was an eminent man of his time, his evidence is of much historical value. He wrote: "Spain which is under the sovereignty of 'Abd ar-Rahman (to whom God be propitious) is rich, abounding in rivers, springs and acqeducts, a land of corn, oil and wine, of fruits and all manners of delicacies; it has pleasure gardens and orchards. Fruit trees of every kind including the trees on which the silkworm feed, we have great abundance. There are found among us mountain veins of silver, gold, copper, iron, tin, lead, sulpher, porphyry, marble and crystal... Merchants congregate in it, and traffickers from the ends of the earth, from Egypt and adjacent countries bring spices, precious stones and splendid wares... Our king has collected a large treasure of silver, gold ar.d precious things and valuables such as no king has collected, kings of the earth to whom his magnificence and power are known bring gifts, conciliating his favours. All these gifts pass through my hands, and I am charged with making of gifts in return.[5] The agricultural prosperity during the reign of 'Abd ar-Rahman is further attested by a curious book— The Calendar of Cordova, which enumerates the month wise activities of the farmers and horticulturists. Yet another evidence is afforded by the list of opulent presents given to 'Abd ar-Rahman by ibn Shuhaid (a rich aristocrat) as a mark of his affection for his sovereign. The formidable list includes— four hundred thousand mithqals of minted gold, four hundred pounds of gold bullion, three hundred sacks of pure silver, twelve pounds of Indian aloes, one hundred ounces of musk, five hundred ounces of ambergris, ten qintars of pure white sugar, thirty pieces of embroidered silk, thirty pieces of silk brocade, four thousand pounds of spun silk, one thousand pounds of raw silk, one hundred dressing gowns, forty eunuchs, twenty female slaves all bedecked in jewellery, eighty mules for use of attendants, one hundred mares for the cavalry, fifteen horses of the best Arabian breed fully caprisoned, one hundred thousand swords, an equal number of arrows, eight hundred suits of armour, one hundred prayer carpets, skins of samur, and last of all a village with cultivable land part of which provided high grade wood.[6]

During the second part of his reign, Spain commanded great prestige in the Mediterranean world. 'Abd ar-Rahman arbitrated between the fighting northern rulers; his navy sailed from one end of Mediterranean to the other; and his army won brilliant victories over his rivals. Several foreign rulers were, therefore, constrained to court his favour and friendship. The emperor Constantine VII of Byzantine Rome, king Otto I of Germany, the French King, and the Counts of Provençe and Tuscany sent their missions to Cordova. After 'Abd ar-Rahman II there were no diplomatic exchanges between Constantinople and Cordova. His two successors Muhammad and Abdullah did not enjoy any prestige in the international world, because the world worships the rising sun, and not a falling star. The first Byzantine envoy arrived in Cordova in 947, and in response 'Abd ar-

Rahman sent the Catholic priest Hisham ibn Huddail with gifts for the emperor. Two years after, another envoy came from there. The historian ibn Hayyan has left a picturesque account of the arrival and reception of the Byzantine diplomat. The ambassador was received at Pechina in the month of August by high Cordovan officials. The arrival of the mission at the imperial city was marked by a grand parade to honour the guest. The foreign diginatories were accommodated in the Munyat Nasr, the palatial residence of prince al-Hakam. Every possible precaution was taken to ensure the security of the envoy and his entourage. On 8th Sept., 'Abd ar-Rahman formally received the ambassador in the Majlis al-Zahir which was furnished with rich carpets, curtains and tapestries of silk and brocade. The Caliph sat on his throne surrounded by his sons and ministers. According to the programme of the ceremony the inaugural speech of welcome was delivered by the qaḍi Mudhir al-Balluti a famous orator of his time. After his moving speech was over, the envoy presented a letter from the Byzantine emperor. The letter with a list of gifts were placed in an ornamental casket of silver. Continuing his narrative, ibn Hayyan says that the letter was inscribed in Greek in gold letters with two golden seals, one bearing the image of Jesus Christ and the other of the emperor himself. The preamble of the missive read— "From the Christian Emperor Constantine, the august Roman, to the magnificent, illustrious and noble 'Abd ar-Rahman, the caliph of the Arabs of Spain— may God prolong his life". The many gifts from the Emperor included an illustrated botanical work of Dioscorides. This book was rendered into Arabic by the monk Nicholas and Hasdai ibn Shaprut. There were repeated exchanges of diplomatic missions between Spain and Germany. Before 'Abd ar-Rahman came to the throne piracy was on the increase in the Mediterranean. The Drakes and

Hawkins of Spanish origin had set up a small colony at Frxinetum, a place about on hundred km to the east of Marseille. They plundered the neigbouring countries of Provençe, Switzerland and northern Italy. The German emperor, Otto sent an ambassador to Cordova with a letter in which he blamed the Spanish government for the activities of the pirates. 'Abd ar-Rahman replied in 950 denying the hand of his government. Otto again sent an envoy—Jean the abbot of Gorze in Lorraine. The abbot and his companions were lodged in a comfortable villa near the Church of St. Martin where they could attend the Sunday service. According to the diplomatic usage of the time, the contents of the message were communicated to 'Abd ar-Rahman preceding a formal reception. He found that the message was outrageous in tone, and he refused to receive the German ambassador. The obstinate abbot stayed on for three years enjoying the hospitality of the Spanish government. Ultimately, 'Abd ar-Rahman took the initiative, and sent Recemundo the bishop of Cordova to Germany. He met the German king (955) at Frankfort to put matters straight. On his return 'Abd ar-Rahman gave a formal audience to Jean at an impressive ceremony, and extended his hand as a jesture of good will to the abbot who had dared to defy him in his own kingdom.

'Abd ar-Rahman had a penchant for building. During the greater part of his reign he lived at the *al-qasr* (Alcazar) on the bank of the river. The *al-qasr* was the official residence of his predecessors also. The *al-qasr* was built on a vast area enclosed by a high wall with five gates. The main gate called *'the bab al-sudda'* stood on the esplanade i.e. the *rassif* as it was called, which ran parallel to the river. It was a splendid structure built on a lofty pedestal. Inside this gate was the Secretariat and chambers of the ministers and other high officials. 'Abd ar-Rahman demolished several portions of the palace, and built new galleried halls and pavilions. The details of the several additions made by 'Abd ar-Rahman have been given by the historian ibn Bushkuwal. We do not know how they looked like, but their poetic names— the Beloved (al-ma'shuq), the Felicitation (al-mubarak), the House of Joy (Qasr as Surur), the Crown (al-Taj) are sufficiently symbolic of their sumptuous beauty. Beyond the royal palace were the vast gardens. 'Abd ar-Rahman had a special foundness for building villas among sylvan surroundings. He built several such villas. The most celebrated was the villa of Munyat al-na'ura (the Villa of the Water Wheels) situated about five km from the city. This royal retreat was placed in the midst of a garden of exotic beauty, and was irrigated by hydraulic machines. 'Abd ar-Rahman constructed several forts to safeguard his kingdom. They do not exist now, but the foundation stones of some of them are still intact. The great mosque at Tarragona was completely restored in 960/349 A.H. The Arabic inscription commemorating this work is still embedded in the ancient wall of the mosque now a cathedral.[7] An existing inscription dated 333 A.H. recalls the construction of a dockyard at Tortosa.[8]

Sometime in Nov. 936 'Abd ar-Rahman started the most ambitious architectural project of his life costing more than half a million gold dinars. This was the construction of the mini-city-cum palace of Madinat al-Zahra about five km northwest of the metropolitan city of Cordova. The new city was named after Zahra, a favourite wife of the Caliph. The lay-out of the city, the design of the palace and other structures within the complex were prepared by the architect Maslama ibn 'Abdullah under the supervision of prince al-Hakam. The historians of Muslim Spain have left revealing statistics about this project. We are told that twelve thousand men-engineers, masons, decorators and labourers took a decade to complete the work. Four thousand camels, ten thousand mules were hired for transporting building material to the site. Ja'far al-Iskandari, the contractor supplied stones and marble. On an average six thousand dressed stones were used daily. White, black, green and pink marble and onyx were brought from the quarries in Almeria, Malaga and Tunisia. The city was connected with Cordova by a newly constructed road. Built on the southern spur of Sierra Morena (called in those days the *Jabal al-'Arus* or the Bride's mountain), the Madinat al-zahra was a terraced city like the Hanging Gardens of Babylonia. The royal palace was at the top; the middle terrace was reserved for gardens and artificial lakes; the last terrace housed government offices, villas of important diginatories and a very elegant mosque.[9] No eyewitness description of the palace at the top has come down to us. We learn that a gallery led to the main portal. At the entrance a statue of Zahra greeted the visitors. We get only tantalising glimpses of this architectural extravaganza mainly from the evidence. gleaned by al-Maqqari from the books available to him. Like all palaces it was, no doubt, an enchanting conglomeration of receptions halls, loggias, belvederes and boudoirs. One of the splendid halls in the complex was the *Qasr Khilafat* which was perhaps meant for receptions. Its ceiling and walls were embellished with panels of crystal, ivory and ebony studded with precious stones. It had eight doors on each side flanked with pillars of marble and crystal. A basin of quicksilver in the centre lighted up the hall during a reception. The rich hangings and carpets completed the décor. The historians also give us a peep into another apartment called *Mu'nis*: In the middle of this hall there was a basin in which water fell from golden statues of a loin, an antelope, a crocodile, an eagle, and a duck. All these were wrought in the royal factory (*dar al-sina'a*) of Cordova. The palace commanded a beautiful view of the valley, but Zahra's aesthetic sense was hurt at the sight of the distant dark hills. One day the witty woman told the Caliph with blandishments, "Sir do you see this beautiful slave of yours in the lap of a black negro" The Caliph understood her remark, and ordered that the hills be planted with almond and fig trees. The garden and lakes of the palace were fed by means of lead pipes connected to a reservoir which received its supply of water from an acquaduct newly built for the purpose. A tiger of gigantic sieze with golden eyes poured water through its mouth into the vast reservoir. There was an aviary of rare birds, several aquariums and even a small zoo. Al-Maqqari adds, "We might go to a great length if we were to enumerate all the beauties natural and artificial contained within the precincts of Zahara palace— the running waters, the luxuriant gardens, the stately buildings for the household guards, the magnificent palaces for the reception of functionaries of the state, the throng of soldiers, pages, eununchs, slaves of all nations and religions, sumptuously attired in robes of silk and brocade moving to and fro through its broad streets, or the crowds of judges, Khatibs, theologians and poets walking with becoming gravity through the magnificent halls, spacious ante-room and ample courts of the palace[10]."

Such a vast palace naturally employed an army of domestics. Many guarded the palace, while others served in different capacities. The black slaves ('abid) carried exotic names — Gaiety (Bishar) Moon (Badar), Hyacinth (Yaqut) etc. The blue-eyed and fair-complexioned slaves came from Navarre, Lombard, France and Bulgaria. The white slaves were imported into Spain by the Jews who were the chief slave dealers in the Middle ages. Since the 9th century the Jews of Narbonne were in the vanguard of sea-borne trade in the Mediterranean world. The geographer ibn Khuradadhbeh has narrated the commercial activities of the Jewish merchants. The Jews (he says) who speak Arabic, Persian, Greek, Frankish and Spanish, and Salvonic languages, travel from west to east and from east to west by land and sea. From the west they bring eunuchs, slave-girls, brocades, casor-skins and swords.[11"] They captured young boys and brought them to Verdun in France where they were emasculated by an operation which was often fatal. From Verdun they imported their human wares to Pechina for sale. As they were caught young , they picked up colloquial Arabic, and nearly always grew up as Muslim like the Janissaries of Ottoman Turkey. Thousands of these eunuchs from Europe called *'Saqaliba'* served in the caliphal palace as porters, guards, messengers, attendants and butlers. They were required to wear thin veils while performing their duties inside the harem. They were provided with uniforms according to their rank and service. They were fed at state expense. We are told that thousands of pounds of meat, poultry, fish and twelve thousand loaves were daily supplied to them from the royal kitchen. They were placed under a senior officer of their own race who was officially designated as *'al-fatayani al-kabirani,'* who was responsible for their disciplined behaviour and etiquette. The personal staff of the caliph was exclusively composed of these foreign eunuchs. Some the chief officers were, the Chef de la Cuisine (Sahib al-*Matbakh*) the Superintendent of constructions (*Sahib al-bunyan*), the Master of Royal Stables (*Sahib al-khail*), Postmaster (*Sahib al-burud*), the Master Falconer (*Sahib al- bayazira*), the Master Goldsmith (*Sahib al-sagha*), the Master of Wardrobe (*Sahib al-tiraz*). In addition to eunuchs there were thousands of females slaves, most of them being prisoners of war. Under 'Abd ar-Rahman they numbered six thousand and three hundred.

These female slaves were employed in the service of the wives and daughters of the Caliph or to look after younger children. It would be preposterous to suppose that he shared conjugal life with, them, although nothing prevented him taking a fancy to beautiful slave. If she bore him a child she ceased to be as slave, but if she became mother of a male child she was called 'umm al walad." The luckiest slave was the one who became mother of the first male child. She was addressed as 'Saiyada Kubra' i.e. the Grand Lady such as Marjanah, the concubine who gave birth to prince al-Hakam, the successor of 'Abd ar-Rahman. The Caliph spent his private hours in the company of his wives and young children. Throughout the day he was busy with state affairs. At night he was host to poets, men of letters and musician. His closest associates were the famous cultured aristocrats of the time - 'Abd al-Malik ibn Jahwar, Abul Qasim Lubb, ibn Shuhaid and Ismail ibn Badr. Even these informal gathering were marked by strict etiquette. Perhaps, the only person who took liberties with him was his blind buffoon, ibn Imran with whom he often exchanged repartees. Occasionally, he would discard his polished Arabic, and break into the Romance dialect, but he was always conscious of his dignity.

As the caliph, he was the temporal as well as religious head of his people, but in his latter capacity he allowed all his subject to worship the Supreme Being according to their beliefs. The Muslim theologian were his subordinates because he was head of the state, but they gave him no trouble. He respected them for their learning and piety, and invited them to all state functions. Sometimes, he would not mind being snubbed by them for his extravagance, and his omission in performance of religious duties. He pocketed the insults like an errant school boy, and never retaliated. One day he was waxing eloquent on the magnificence of the al-Zahra palace. He meant to say-" *si monumentum requiris, circumspice*." He received appreciative response from his courtiers, but the austere qadi Mundhir al al-balluti who was also present, took him to task for squandering public money on personal vanities. The qadi wept, and quoted verse 32 of Sura XLIII of the Quran. 'Abd ar-Rahman listened quietly, and regretted his extravagance. On another occasion, the same qadi upbraided him when he appeared in the mosque for his Friday prayer after an absence of some weeks as he was busy with work relating to construction of Madinat al-Zahra. 'Abd ar-Rahman again listened to the qadi's fulminations. Soon after, the prince al-Hakam asked 'Abd ar-Rahman if would like to dismiss the qadi and appoint another person in his place. The generous Caliph replied, 'I would rather disinherit you, but I will not dismiss the learned qadi, who is a source of blessing to all. So long he is alive, I will pray on Fridays behind him[12].

His non-Muslim subjects lived happily. The Christians were suspected of disloyalty during the reign of Abdullah because of the agitation launched by ibn Hafsun, but during 'Abd ar-Rahman's rule they were no more under a cloud. Several Christian served as diplomats— Hisham ibn Hudhail, Asbagh ibn Abdullah and Recemudo Rabi ibn Zaid. The state made no distinction on grounds of faith. Al-Khushani (d-970) who wrote short biographical sketches of the judges of Cordova narrates an interesting case of the equitable treatment of the Christians. A Christian chieftain submitted to the government and settled at Cordova. He had a Muslim concubine who applied to the qadi for being relieved of her bondage. Her plea was that she was a Muslim and belonged to free parents. The Prime Minister Hajib ibn Badr informed the judge that the Christian chieftain had submitted on the basis of a solemn pact and could not be deprived of his possessions. While he told the qadi that he had no intention to interfere with the ends of justice, he emphasised that it was their duty to treat the Christians with equity and consideration[13]. Jean the abbot of Gorze who spend three years at Cordova expressed satisfaction at the condition of the Christians. The abbot says the Christians were free to practise their religion. A local priest even told him that the Muslim respected those Christians who strictly observed the teachings of their religion[14]. One of the greatest Jews of all time was in the service of 'Abd ar-Rahman. This was the physician-cum-diplomat who negotiated the treaty with queen Toda of Navarre. He ascertained the conditions of the Jews from every envoy who visited Cordova. He used his high position to improve the condition of the Jews who lived beyond the shores of Spain — particularly those who lived in the south of France. He boldly approached the government of Byzantine Rome to stop persecuting of the Jews. He made great contributions to the advancement of Hebrew studies, and to this day the Jews gratefully remember this great man of their faith in the service of a Muslim sovereign[15].

We witness the extraordinary brilliance of his reign in some of the brightest luminaries of Hispano-Muslim culture who rose under his patronage, and some of them continued to shed their light in the reign of al-Hakam. The galaxy includes the historian ibn Qutia, the geographer-cum-historian Mosa al-Razi, the pantheist philosopher, ibn Masarra, the scholarly grammarian Abū Ali al-Qali, the biographer al-Khushani, the astronomer-cum-mathematician Maslama ibn Qasim, the jurist and orator qaḍi, Mundhir al-Balluti, the master of prosody az-Zubaidi, the physician and surgeon Zahravi, and the linguist Hasdai ibn Shaprut. Classical poetry with new themes was born during his reign. It was a poetry pregnant with the fresh air of Spanish valleys and meadows, and the perfume of flowers. Poetry flew from mouth to mouth. Friends exchanged verses with bouquets of flowers. Ismail ibn Badr sent verses of his own composition to the Caliph. In one of these poems he extolled the beautiful looks of this sovereign- his radiant forehead, his ruddy complexion, his silver smiles and his crescent-shaped whiskers lined as if with a pen dipped in musk[16]. Ibn Jawahar set the fashion of composing short poems expressing joy at the sight of flowers. In a poem of this genre, Ibn Jahwar sings:

> I sent to you a fresh narcissus (narjus)
> having the colour of a lover in anguish;
> smelling the perfumed breath of a tryst,
> depicting his paleness at the beloved's avoidance[17].

The taste for poetry spread among the educated people. Writing poetry was the hall-mark of a cultured Spanish Muslim. Even the ascetic kill-joy theologian was not free from the influence of the Muse. The qadi Mundhir al-Balluti who snubbed the caliph, was adept at replying questions in poetry. Possessing a fine sense of humour, he would make an extempore poem when asked to reply in the verse form. One day he was asked to explain the reason as to why a maiden grows red, and the lover pale yellow. Out came his reply:

> The maiden's face grows red because her eyes
> and sword-like glances draw blood from the lover's heart;
> The lover turns pale when the beloved leaves him
> like the setting sun which leaves a trail of afterglow[18].

'Abd ar-Rahman was one of those Heaven-sent men who appear in a nation's life in the times of great crisis. Year after year he worked hard to consolidate his kingdom, and to make it the cynasure of the neighbouring eyes as a seat of great civilization at a time when the whole of western Europe was sunk in sloth and ignorance. His miracle having been accomplished, it was time to rest from his labours. On Oct. 15,961 the great Caliph died aged seventy after a reign of nearly half a century. He was buried in the royal cemetery at the Alcazar. The funeral prayer was led by the saintly qaḍi Mundhir. After his death they found in his private papers a diary in which he had recorded that during his whole life, he enjoyed life only for fourteen days without any mental worry[19]. 'Abd ar-Rahman is no doubt one of the most resplendent personalities in Spanish history. The modern Spaniards gratefully remember him, and it is, no doubt, in recognition of his great services, his tolerance, and the prosperity of his reign, that the Spanish government celebrated the millennium of his caliphate in the year 1930[20]. We may end the account of his glorious rule by quoting the tribute paid to him by Dozy. 'Of all the Umayyad princes (says the Dutch historian) 'Abd ar-Rahman was unquestionably the greatest. His achievements approached the miraculous. He found the country a prey to anarchy and civil war, rent by factions, parcelled out among a hundred petty chiefs of diverse races, exposed to incessant raids by the Christians of north and on the point of being absorbed by the Leonese or the Fatimids of Africa. Despite innumerable obstacles he saved Andalusia from herself, as well as from foreign domination. He had raised her to a nobler and mightier position than she had ever before attained. He had won for her peace and prosperity at home, and consideration and respect abroad. He found the public treasury in a lamentable state of depletion, he left it overflowing. ... The state of the country harmonised with prosperity of the public treasury. Agriculture, manufactures, commerce, the arts and the sciences all flourished. The traveller's eyes were gladdened on all side by well-cultivated fields,

irrigated upon scientific principles, so that what seemed the
most sterile soil was rendered fertile. He was struck, too, by the
perfect order, which, thanks to a vigilant police, reigned in
even the least accessible districts. He marvelled at the cheapness
of commodities (the most delicious fruit could be bought for
next to nothing), at the prevalent spruceness of attire, and
especially at a universal standard of well-being which permitted
everyone, with scarcely an exception, to ride a mule instead of
journeying on foot. Many different manufactures enriched
Cordova, Almeria, and other towns. Commerce was so highly
developed that, according to the report of the Inspector General
of Customs, the import and export duties provided the larger
part of the national revenue... 'Abd ar-Rahman's power became
truly formidable. A splendid navy enabled him to dispute the
mastery of the Mediterranean with the Fatimids, and secured
him the possession of Ceuta, the key of Mauritania. A numerous
and well-desciplied army- perhaps the finest in the world in
those days— gave him a marked preponderance over the
Christians of the North. The proudest monarchs sought his
alliance. The Byzantine Emperor, the rulers of Germany, Italy,
and France, sent embassies to his Court... Such achievement as
these were unquestionably great, but what strikes the student of
this brilliant reign with astonishment and admiration is not so
much the edifice as the architect— the force of that
comprehensive intellect which nothing eluded and which showed
itself a no less admirable master of the minutest details than of
the most exalted conceptions. This subtle and sagacious man,
who by his alliance virtually established a balance of power,
and who in his wide tolerance calls to his councils men of
another religion, is a pattern ruler of modern times, rather than
a medieval Khalif[21].

Notes

1. Dozy: pp. 414-415.
2. L. Provençal: Histoire, Vol. II, p. 59. Kitab al-Majmu'a pp, 203-204.
3. The Jews were overjoyed at the remarkable diplomatic success of Hasdai ibn Shaprut. This is how a Jewish poet praised him "Bow down, O ye mountains to Judah's Chief. Let laughter burst from your lips. Let the waste-lands and forests burst with song... Without sword or arrows, but by the mere words of his mouth, he hath taken by storm the fenced cities of the devourers of the accursed flesh."
   (Dozy: p. 403)
   Ibn 'Abd Rabbini recalled the visit of the queen Toda, in his Iqd al-Farid, in lines 432 and 433 of the Arjuza relating to 'Abd ar-Rahman.
4. Provençal: Histoire, vol II, pp. 112-113, and ibn Idhari, vol II, p. 198.
5. E.N. Adler: The Jewish Travellers, pp. 26-27.
6. Al-Maqqari/Gayangos: vol ii . pp. 151-152, and L. Provençal: Histoire, vol. II, pp. 142-143.
7. The Photos [plates XX, XVII] of these inscriptions can be seen in Provençal: Histoire, vol. II.
8. Ibid.
9. The mosque at Madinat al-Zahra was a miniature of the Cordovan Jama masjid. It was made of marble and onyx. Three hundred masons, 200 carpenters, and 500 labourers worked on the site. The roof of the prayer hall rested on five rows of columns. Its spacious courtyard had a basin for ablution and a fountain in the centre of the basin. Its minaret reached a height of 40 cubits. During the excavations carried out by Felix Herández the main elements of the mosque have been identified. The Spanish government proposes to rebuild the mosque.
10. Al-Maqqari/ Gayangos, vol I. 238.
11. Bernard Lewis: The Arabs in History, p. 90.
12. Al-Maqqari, (Urdu Trans), p. 300.
13. Al-Khushani: p. 107.
14. Arnold: p. 135.
15. Cecil Roth: History of the Jews, New York, 1965 p. 159.
16. Akhbar Majuma: p. 215 and p. 208.
17. Ibid.
18. Nykl: P. 34.
19. Al-Maqqari/Gayangos, vol II p. 147.
20. Provençal: L Espagne Musulmane au xeme siecle, P 196.
21. Dozy: pp. 445-447. (This is a long passage and has been shortened).

Chapter 9

The Reign of Caliph al-Hakam al-Mustansir Billah (961-1008)

———•—•———

Spain in the 10th century was dominated by two rulers of colossal eminence — the Caliph 'Abd ar-Rahman al-Nasir, and his son al-Hakam. He was nominated by his father during his life. From his early childhood, al-Hakam was placed under good tutors who initiated him into the world of books and learning. When he grew to manhood, his father associated him in all the major decisions of the government, and often took his opinion before taking any action. When he came to the throne, he was already a mature person of considerable experience. Hakam's reign was very peaceful with hardly any factions, and life flowed smoothly throughout the length and breadth of his kingdom. The robust economy bequeathed to him by his father continued to flourish, and Spain shone with greater brilliance. The wealth of Spain at this period was immense. It was partly derived from mining, but the chief sources were agriculture and commerce. Hakam undertook great irrigation projects at Granada, Murcia, Valencia, and Aragon. Big reservoir were built, and every kind of fruit and vegetable was cultivated according to the nature of the soil. The urban centres gave birth to a prosperous middle class of civil servants, teachers, traders and manufacturers. Hakam's name is inseparably connected with Hispano-Muslim culture, especially the grand mosque of Cordova which he enlarged with magnificent ornamentations. The careful attention with which he embellished the mosque, and his love and patronage of art and literature are sufficient to perpetuate his memory. Hakam possessed most of the qualities of his father, but he was not energetic like him because of his feeble health. Nevertheless, he kept a watchful eye on all state matters, and never sank into self-complacency. He issued orders to all state governors to be careful in the discharge of their duties, He would set out on inspection tours, and at least once he visited the dockyards to inspect the navy.

Soon after his coronation, he took prompt action to ensure that the treaties between his father and the northern states were implemented in letter and spirit. It came to his knowledge that Sancho refused to hand over the forts specified in the treaty with his father. When he was reminded to surrender the forts, he came out with all sorts of excuses. In the meantime, events took an unexpected turn. Count Fernan Gonzalez drove out Ordono IV from Castile. The unlucky Ordona entered into the Muslim territory. He met ibn Ghalib, the commander of the upper Marches at Medinaceli, and asked him to arrange an audience with the Caliph al-Hakam. As his cousin had recovered the kingdom of Leon with the help of 'Abd ar-Rahman, he hoped that he too might occupy the throne of Leon with the help of al-Hakam. Here was an opportunity for the government of Cordova to bring Sancho to his knees. Ibn Ghalib conducted Ordono to Cordova. They reached the capital on April 8, 962. The uninvited guest was given a grand reception. He was received by Walid Ibn Khaizaran, the judge of the Christian community and Obaidallah ibn Qasim, the Metropolitan of Cordova, and was presented a guard of honour. Soon after his arrival, he desired to be conducted to the tomb of 'Abd ar-Rahman. He fell down and prayed at the grave of 'Abd ar-Rahman in the garden of the al-Qasr. From there he was taken to the Villa of the Water Wheels (Munayat Na'urah) where he stayed with the his twenty attending nobles. Two days after al-Hakam granted him an audience in the Madinat al-Zahra. Clad in a white tunic and a cloak, Ordono rode to the main gate of the palace followed by his noblemen on foot. He passed through the main gate between, rows of armed guards in glittering uniforms. He was received by the admiral ibn Tumlus. He was led to a waiting chamber, and on a signal from the audience hall, was conducted into the hall which was already packed with liveried servants, the Saqaliba, the ministers and other high officials. Hakam sat on a throne of gold, and in front of him at a distance, was a silver chair for the honoured guest. Ordono took off his cap, and advanced towards the Caliph in all humility, knelt before him, and kissed the offered hand. The splendour of the hall and the rich furnishings dazzled Ordono who was not accustomed to such sights. When al-Hakam saw that he had settled down, he broke the ice by expressing his delight at his unexpected appearance at Cordova. Walid ibn Khizuran acted as interpreter. The verbatim report of the conversation between al-Hakam and Ordono has been preserved by a historian[1]. Encouraged by the words of welcome, Ordono rose from his seat, walked towards the throne, and kissing the carpet said, "I am the slave of the Commander of the Faithfuls, and recognise you as my sovereign. I have come to you with high hopes of your magnanimity." Then he related how his cousin Sancho had deprived him of his kingdom with the help of the government of Cordova on the basis of a treaty which he had no intention to honour. He assured al-Hakam that he would surrender all the forts if he was installed on the throne of Leon.

As a guarantee he was prepared to leave his son Garcia as a hostage. Everything was finally settled, and al-Hakam agreed to place his army at his disposal under the command of ibn Ghalib. Al-Hakam also constituted an advisory council composed of bishops of Cordova and Seville to advise Ordono on political affairs. At the end of the reception, Ja'far the Slav brought presents for the guest which included a tunic of gold set with pearls, and a cap of matching beauty.

News travelled fast even in those days when there were no intercommunication systems such as we have today. Sancho came to know of Ordono's activities at the court of al-Hakam, and he saw a storm gathering round his throne. A frightened Sancho sent a powerful delegation of barons and bishops to Cordova. They gave promises of speedy surrender of forts if Sancho was allowed to rule in his kingdom. Ordono was still at Cordova when he came to know of the arrival of the delegates sent by his rival. He found all his hopes shattered to the ground, and he died (962) of frustration and shock. His rival gone, Sancho once again threw his pledges to the winds. He concluded an alliance with the Counts of Barcelona and others. Al-Hakam was forced to take the field. Accordingly, he led an expedition in 963. He besieged San Esteban on the bank of the Douro. The Count Fernan Gonzales hastened to sue for peace. On the other fronts opened against Sancho, the Cordovan commanders Yahya ibn Muhammad al-Tujibi and ibn Ghalib inflicted defeat after defeat on his allies. The forts stipulated in Sancho's treaty with 'Abd ar-Rahman were forcibly occupied, and garrisons were stationed as a mark of their occupation. Some of the forts were extensively repaired. The remains of a grand fort at Gormaz which dominated a vast plain, and a fragment of inscription have survived to this day.

About the year 966, Sancho was poisoned by one of his noblemen. As his son was a small boy, his sister— the nun Elvira acted as a regent of her nephew. The nobility were averse to domination of a female, and the kingdom of Leon broke into several unites, each under a Count. They entered into direct negotiations with the government of Cordova, and pledged to become vassals of Hakam. During the following years, several embassies poured into Cordova, representing Count Borell II of Barcelona, Count Fernán Lainez of Salamanca, Count Garcia Fernandez of Castile, count Fernando Ansurez of Monzon, Gonzalo of Galicia, Elvira the regent, and Sancho Garces II, the king of Navarre. All these delegates were lavishly entertained and they returned home with gifts[2]. Al-Hakam showed the warmest regards to the mother of count Rodrigo Velazquez the doyen of the Galician nobility. He gave a grand reception in her honour, and each member of her entourage was loaded with presents. Before her departure, al-Hakam gave her a palfrey with a saddle of gold mounted on brocade. Between 972-974, ambassadors arrived once again from Constantinople and Germany. Except some minor disturances here and there, the kingdom of Cordova thrived in peace. He had no fear of the Fatimis, as the days of their expansion were over. They retired to Egypt, and the local chiefs of northwest Africa transferred their allegiance to the Caliph of Cordova, through military operations conducted by ibn Ghalib. The white flag of the Umayyads flew on the towers of Ceuta and Tangier, and like his father, he was master of the whole Iberian peninsula. Al-Hakam had now enough time to devote to cultural pursuits.

Hakam was a prince of literary taste, and was found of reading. He had a passion for books. He was the greatest bibliophile of Europe of his time. The books were imported from the Muslim East. The eighth and the nineth centuries had seen a marvellous intellectual efflorescence in the East under the magnificent patronage of the 'Abbasid Caliphs. Their capital Baghdad was a centre of culture 'paralleling Athens as its philosophic, Rome as its juridical, and Jerusalem as its religious centre[3]. The 'Abbasid Caliphs—Mansur, Harun al-Rashid, and Ma'mūn were great lovers of learning. During their glorious reigns the scientific and philosophical writings of the Greeks were rendered into Arabic often at fantastic costs. Within the course of century and a half (750-900), the writings of Aristotle, Plato, the neo-Platonic thinkers, the medical works of Galen, Hippocrates , Dioscorides, the mathematical books of Ptolemy Euclid, and Apollonious were available in Arabic in addition to some literary and astronomical works from Persian and Sanskrit[4]. The period of translations was followed by original contributions by a host of universal minds. No department of human thought was left out. Mankind had never seen before a mass production of books on history, literature (poetry and fiction), bibliography, biography, metaphysics, ethics, political science, medicine, surgery, botany, agriculture, optics, opthalmology, arithmetic, geometry, algebra, chemistry, pharmacology, lexicography, philology, grammer, music, jurisprudence, and various Quranic disciplines. Many books ran into encyclopaedias. In the words of the great American historian of science, Prof. George Sarton "the most valuable of all, the most original and most pregnant were written in Arabic; from the second half of the 9th century to the end of the 11th century, Arabic was the most progressive language of mankind. During the period anyone wishing to be well informed, up-to-date had to study Arabic (a large number of non-Arabic speaking people did so) even as now anyone who wants to further intellectual advance must begin by mastering one of the great western languages"[5]. Al-Hakam wanted to put Cordova on the intellectual map of the world as a rival of Baghdad. He appointed his agents in Alexandria, Baghdad, Basra, Damascus, and Musal for purchase of books. They ransacked the book markets and brought books to Cordova. Some authors, learning of al-Hakam's love for books, sent their works direct to him and earned rewards. This is how the monumental work of Abū al-Farraj Isphani, the *Kitab al-Aghani* (Book of Songs) which now runs into more than twenty volumes, reached Spain. The Caliph sent him a reward of one thousand dinars. Al-Hakam's library contained four hundred thousand volumes— the greatest single collection of books in Europe. The library was housed in the Madinat al-Zahra. The catalogue of the books ran into forty volumes. The entries were made subject-wise. Each catalogue had three columns giving the name of the author, his short biography, and a brief note on its contents. A host of copyists caligraphists, decorators, illuminators and book binders worked in the library. The staff included two female attendants—Lubna and Fatima[6].

Al-Hakkam opened twenty seven seminaries for the general public specially for the weaker sections. The mosque of Cordova was already a famous seat of learning where hundreds of students attended lectures on literature, grammer, and religious subjects. Ibn Hajari, a later historian (d 1194) says that during the time of the Umayyads "students flocked from all parts of the world to learn the sciences of which Cordova was the most noble repository[7]." Historians have preserved the names of some of the eminent scholars who lectured in the mosque of Cordova during the reign of al-Hakam. Ibn Qutia taught grammer and history, al-Zubaidi lectured on lexicography, Abū Ali al-Qali on literature, Abū Bakr ibn Mu'aiya on law, and Muhammad ibn al-'Udhri on medicine. Through his enlightened patronage, easy availability of books, and educational tours, Muslim Spain in the 10th century, enjoyed a high percentage of literacy which led Dozy to acknowledge that in Andalusia everyone could read and write while in Europe persons in the most exalted position —unless they belong to the clergy—remained illiterate[8]. The portals of learning were open to all. Praising al-Hakam for initiating one of the most brilliant epochs in intellectual history, the French thinker Renan says, "The taste for science and literature fostered in the 10th century in this privileged corner of the world was based on tolerance of which modern times hardly offer any example. Christians, Jews, and Muslims spoke the same language, chanted the same songs, participated in the same literary and scientific studies. All the barriers which separated the various people were knocked down; all worked in building a common civilization. The academies of Cordova, Granada, Toledo, Seville, Jativa, Valencia, Jaen, Murcia, Malaga and Velez became active centres of philosophical studies"[9]. For the this cultural glory the prime credit goes to 'Abd ar-Rahman II, 'Abd ar-Rahman al-Nasir, and al-Hakam who were the greatest promoters al learning among the Umayyad rulers of Spain.

His personal life was clean. Throughout his life he remained a teetotler. He was gentle, benevolent and regular in his daily devotions. He was the *beau ideal* of a ruler in the eyes of his subjects; Unfortunately, his health was fragile. Two renowned physicians—Ahmad ibn Yunus and his brother Umar were always in his service. In 974 he was attacked by a serious illness and was confined to bed for several months. During the illness he abolished some taxes, and also freed a number of slaves[10]. He enlarged the mosque, and endowed it with decorations which captivate the visitors even today. He had but few women in his life. When he came to the throne he had no issues. Soon after a son was born, but it died after a few years. The same wife gave birth to his second son Hisham. She was a beautiful blonde from Navarre. Her name was Aurora (meaning: the dawn), and for this reason she was given a Arabic equivalent name—Subh. She was the first lady of the kingdom, and was addressed as 'Saiyida Kubra.' But al-Hakam called her by a masculine name of 'Ja'far' because she sometimes dressed herself like an ephebe a la baghdadian fashion.

On Feb. 5, 976 Hakam nominated his 11 years son Hisham as his heir apparent at a grand ceremony. He took oaths of loyalty to the teenage prince from all the ministers. Eight months after, he fell ill and passed away in the arms of his two favourite eunuchs (Slavs)— Fa'ik al-Nizami, and Jawdhar during the night of Oct. 1, 976.

While discussing the fate of dynasties and the dangers to their existence, ibn Khaldun has stated what usually happened if a king died leaving a minor son to the throne[11]. In this situation, a clever minister took control of the government by initiating the boy-king into a life of ease and indolence. He would 'advise' him that a king's duty is to sit on the throne, and to receive homage from his courtiers. Gradually, the minister would rob him of his prerogatives, take control of the finance and the army. Ultimately, the legitimate king would be reduced to a mere puppet, and the clever minister ruled as a virtual monarch. Slowly, he would pave the way for inheritance of the throne by his own son. In the following chapter, we shall see what happened to the golden-haired and blue-eyed minor left by al-Hakam.

Notes

1. Al-Maqqari/Gayangos, Vol II, pp 163-165. A frequent visitor to Spain saw the reception of Ordono IV being enacted by a television crew and actors. See the article 'When the Moors Ruled Spain. (published in the National Geography of July 1988.)

2.　Provençal: Hostire, vol. II, pp 181.

3.　Hitti: Makers of Arab History: p. 93

4.　O'Leary: How Greek Science passed to the Arabs. This book gives a full account of translations made into Arabic.

5.　Sarton: vol. I, p. 17.

6.　Macabe: p. 188.

7.　al-Maqqari/Gayangos: Vol I, p.30.

8.　Dozy: p. 455.

9.　Renan: pp. 4-5.

10.　He freed all the slaves of his father. One of these was Raḍhia, also named Najm. She married the Slav Labib. After her marriage she left for Syria, and Egypt, and performed the haj with her husband. She returned home, and died in 1032. She was a scholarly woman. (Ibn Bushkuwal, Vol II, p. 693)

11.　Ibn Khaldun, The Muqaddimah, Vol I. pp. 377-378.

Chapter 10

The Dictatorship of Abi 'Amir al-Mansur and his son 'Abd al-Malik al-Muzaffar (976-1008)

The pious Caliph al-Hakam must have died with the satisfaction that his minor son Hisham, the child of his old age whom he and the sultana Subh had brought up tenderly, would be trained by the Prime Minister hajib al-Mushafi, and the minister Abi 'Amir, in the affairs of the state, and that after he came of age he would reign in peace. Al-Hakam miscalculated by reposing his trust in Abi 'Amir who, of all the ministers, was the most ambitious and also the most competent. He aspired to rule the kingdom with all the powers of a legitimate sultan. The task before him was not easy. There were many hurdles before him. The legitimate ruler though a minor was alive; the Arab aristocracy could not tolerate a Yemenite ruling over them; the new aristocracy of the rich merchants and the European Slavs constituted a powerful lobby in favour of the Umayyads. He had also two formidable rivals— the Prime Minister Ja'far Ibn Usman al-Mushafi, and ibn Ghalib, the brave commander of the northern borders who were known for their unflinching loyalty to the Umayyads. But for Abi 'Amir nothing was difficult. By his craftiness he overcame all the difficulties that came in his way.

Abi 'Amir was an Arab of Yemenite extraction. His ancestor 'Abd al-Malik was one of the few Arabs who landed in Spain with Tariq. In recognition of his services, he was given a piece of land at Torrox near Algeciras. His descendants gave up military service, and distinguished themselves as lawyers. Abi 'Amir was born in June, 938, during the reign of 'Abd ar-Rahman al-Nasir. He came to Cordova for higher education, and attended the lectures of some of the most renowned scholars of the time. He specialised in literature, law and rhetoric. Even while he was a student he cherished high ambitions. He was dominated by the *idée fixe* of capturing the state. Ibn Marrakashi has narrated an interesting anecdote in this connection. One day Abi 'Amir was in the company of his fellow students. They found him lost in thoughts. All of a sudden he woke up from his reverie, and asked his friends what posts they would like to hold if he became the head of the state. They did not take him seriously. Still, one student replied that he would like to be appointed as a judge at Malaga where he would eat the local figs to his heart's content. The other wished to be appointed as an inspector of the Market. The third thought that Abi 'Amir had gone megalomaniac. He called him a braggart, but added that if his wishful thinking proved to be true, he would like to be paraded through the streets with his face smeared with honey[1]. There is no doubt that Abi 'Amir was a gifted man. He was hard working, full of pluck and had confidence in his destiny. His polished manners attracted the people, but they did not know that his pleasing exterior (and he was a handsome man) was only a masquerade. He was armed with a deadly weapon— the art of flattery which melted every heart, and rendered every opponent vulnerable. When flattery failed, he resorted to his innate cunning with Machiavellian finesse.

Abi 'Amir started his career as a writer of a petitions and legal documents. He set up a small office not very far from the palace. His mastery of language, his perfect drafting, and knowledge of legal matters, attracted the notice of the chief Justice— Muhammad ibn al-Salim, and he introduced him to the Prime Minister al-Mushafi. At that time the sultana Subh required the services of an honest man with a good educational background to supervise the property of her son 'Abd ar-Rahman. Out of the several candidates recommended by al-Mushafi, Abi 'Amir was selected, and he was appointed on a pay of fifteen dinars per month. This job opened for him the Keatsian 'magic casements' of good luck. He got promotion after promotion by dint of his merits. Within a short period he was appointed Master of the Mint. We can read his name on the coins issued in 356 A.H.[2]. Abi 'Amir took the fullest advantage of his position to win friends, and to influence people. Muhammad ibn Aflah, a client of al-Hakam was in dire need of money for the marriage of his daughter. Abi 'Amir readily advanced money from the mint. An obliged ibn Aflah used to say, "I love Abi 'Amir with all my heart, and if he orders me to rebel against the Caliph, I would do so[3]". The ladies of the harem were charmed by the promising young official, and when he presented a big silver model of the royal palace to Sultana Subh, he became the talk of everyone in the royal household. Perhaps, he was free to visit the *sanctum sanctorum* of the palace— the innermost part of the harem. Al-Hakam once told one of his confidents, "By what clever means this young boy has captivated my ladies! I shower the most gorgeous gifts of the world on them, but they do not appreciate. Is he a magician, or a civil servant. I am not satisfied in my mind about the public money in his hands.⁴" The Caliph was not wrong in suspecting the *bona fides* of Abi 'Amir. His rapid rise had aroused the jealousy of some of the courtiers, and they missed no opportunity to poison his ears against the young upstart. One day he summoned Abi 'Amir for a scrutiny of the accounts. Abi 'Amir knew that the cash in the treasury was less than what the account books revealed. He ran to the minister ibn Hudair and asked him to advance some money. In this way he made up the deficit. When the Caliph found no discrepancy in the accounts 'Abi 'Amir rose in his eyes. Henceforth, nothing stood in the way of his promotions. In 968 he was put in charge of the estates which had no owners. After sometime he was posted as a judge at Seville. In July 970 he was brought back to Cordova and given charge of the property of Hisham, the second son of al-Hakam. By this time he had earned enough money, and he built a villa at Rusafa where, no doubt, he gave grand parties to top echelons of the government to enhance his prestige.

Al-Hakam had great trust in Abi 'Amir. He posted him to north Africa on a a confidential mission. The Fatimid tide (as state above) had swept back to Egypt, and their danger to Spain was over. But al-Hakam wanted to neutralizes their influence because they still had some supporters in that region. Fot this purpose he had posted ibn Ghalib with instructions to win over the ruling Idrisi princes. Large sums of money were placed at his disposal, and he was told to spend the money lavishly in order to enlist their friendship. He transferred Abi 'Amir to Morocco as an assistant to ibn Ghalib, but actually he was under instructions to keep a watch on the money spent by the former. It was rather a delicate assignment but Abi 'Amir did his job with intelligence. Both the officers were eminently successful in their mission. Ibn Ghalib returned to Cordova

with the Idrisi princes he had won over to the cause of the
Umayyads. Al-Hakam received them with great affection. He
was equally happy that Abi 'Amir had acted discreetly without
giving rise to suspicions in the mind of ibn Ghalib. His posting
in Africa added a new dimension to his experience. He
familiarised himself with the local conditions in northwest
Africa, the sociology of the Berbers, and above all the
organization of the imperial army.

One month after his return to Cordova, Hakam died. He was
hardly buried when there was a conspiracy to put Mughira, a
brother of al-Hakam, on the throne[5]. The conspiracy was hatched
by the rich and powerful Slav eunuchs — Fa'ik al-Nizami, the
Master of the Wardrobe, and Jawdhar, the Grand Falconer.
They were not only knaves, but also fools. They tried to take
al-Mushafi into confidence, and by this action they brought
their doom. Al-Mushafi preferred Hisham who being a minor
would be more pliable than the 27 year old Mughira. After
consulting Abi 'Amir it was decided to eliminate Mughira. Abi
'amir was assigned the unholy job. He agreed willingly, and
taking a strong body of soldiers with him he proceeded to be
mansion of Mughira. After the building was cardonned off, Abi
'Amir went in, told Mughira of his brother's death and the
succession of his nephew to the throne. Mughira gave a frank
reply. He regretted that his brother was dead, and saw nothing
wrong in Hisham occupying the throne. Abi 'Amir was
impressed by his reply, and he saw no reason to dye his hands
with the blood of an innocent man. But al-Mushafi had no
scruples. He ordered that the deed must be done otherwise
none of them would be safe. Abi 'Amir was still at the residence
of Mughir, when the second order of al-Mushafi reached him.
He showed the orders to Mughira and left the hall. After he
was out, the soldiers entered the hall, and strangled Mughira to

death before the eyes of the ladies of the harem. Next morning Hisham was crowned with the usual ceremonies. He assumed the title of *al-Mu'aiyad billa*-the Recipient of Allah's help. Al-Mushafi and Abi 'Amir worked together to undermine the influence of the Saqaliba i.e. the Europena slaves or eunuchs. They were put under surveillance, and their movement was restricted. The gate they often passed through when they entered the palace was walled up. They felt that they were being humiliated. Jawdhar resigned, and Fa'ik al-Nizami left Cordova, and settled in the Balearic Island.

The history of the reign of Hisham is an epic of the gradual ascendancy of Abi 'Amir till be became the virtual dictator of Muslim Spain, dreaded alike by foes and friends. Hisham lived in the Madinat al-zahra with his mother the sultana Subh. When he grew up to manhood, he had already lost the will to rule. He preferred to live in his golden cage, while Abi 'Amir ruled in his name. Abi 'Amir worked with a calculated plan, and took every move like a master chess-player. He checkmated all his opponents. After making the Slavs ineffective, he plotted to remove al-Mushafi from his path. It was a difficult task because al-Mushafi belonged to an influential Berber family distinguished for learning. His father Usman was one of the teachers of al-Hakam. Al-Mushafi himself was steeped in classical literature. He possessed a natural talent for poetry, and a passion for beautiful singing girls. Many of his poems have come down to us. These poems indicate that he was "a deeply cultured aesthete.[6]" He started his career as al-Hakam's secretary, and later on he was posted as governor of Majorca island. From there he returned to Cordova as the Prime Minister of the Kingdom— the highest rank to which a man could rise under the Umayyad monarchy. He lived at al-Mushafiya one of the most beautiful villas of the 10th century Cordova. Unfortunately, he had many enemies. There were complaints of nepotism against him. His three sons, and nephews held high posts under the government. Al-Mushafi was not suited to the high office held by him. He was a man who could carry out orders of a superior, but had no initiative of his own. He often depended on Abi 'Amir, and nearly always acted on his advice. But if he dreaded anyone it was ibn Ghalib the commander of the frontier. He felt disgruntled that he should take orders from a mediocre parvenu heading the bureaucracy at Cordova. Abi 'Amir exploited their mutual dislike to his advantage. He knew that in his struggle with al-Mushafi, ibn Ghalib's support would be necessary. He urged upon al-Mushafi that ibn Ghalib deserved to be rewarded for his brilliant military services. The sultana Subh also agreed, and ibn Ghalib was decorated with the title "dhu l-wizaratain" i.e. holder of double honour both civil and military. Al-Mushafi was too simple a person to look through the game the Cordovan Iago -Abi 'Amir was playing. Ibn Ghalib felt himself obliged to Abi 'Amir for the new feather in his cap. When they met at Madrid during a campaign in 977, the two leaders came closer, and they reached a secret understanding to remove al-Mushafi. Ibn Ghalib wrote to al-Mushafi that the success of the campaign was entirely due to Abi 'Amir, and he recommended that he should be appointed as Prefect of the city (*Sahib al-Madina*) of Cordova. The letter from ibn Ghalib reached Cordova before Abi 'Amir's return to the city. This post was held by a son of al-Mushafi, and it had to be vacated for Abi 'Amir. It was no doubt an insult for the aging al-Mushafi, but he had to swallow the bitter pill as he had no guts to assert his authority. The new post gave Abi 'Amir complete control of the city. He acted with vigour and justice, and removed corruption and bribery rampant under al-Mushafi's son. He made the police conscious of their duties. He enforced the rule of law with an iron-hand, and became the hero of the people. He was already popular among the employees of the palace. Al-Mushafi felt crestfallen when he found that Abi 'Amir was stealing a march over him by his cleverness and duplicity.

Al-Mushafi was not a man to give in easily. He thought of coming to terms with ibn Ghalib in order to isolate abi 'Amir. He wrote to ibn Ghalib proposing marriage of his son with Asma, ibn Ghalib's daughter. Surprisingly, ibn Ghalib agreed, and a contract setting out the terms of the proposed marriage were drawn up. Abi 'Amir saw his plans crumbling before him. He moved heaven and earth to stop the marriage. A spate of letters reached ibn Ghalib warning him of the matrimonial alliance. Abi 'Amir also wrote to him not to fall into a trap laid to destroy him. To please ibn Ghalib, Abi 'Amir offered himself for the hand of Asma. Ibn Ghalib cancelled the contract, and conveyed his acceptance of Abi 'Amir as his prospective son-in-law. The sultana gave her approval to the proposed marriage of her protégé with Asma who united in her a cultured intellect and fascinating beauty — in the words of Dozy. Early in 978, the marriage was celebrated with great ostentation.

Abi 'Amir was now in a formidable position. He made a sudden swoop on al-Mushafi with the tacit consent of the sultana. On March 26, 978, al-Mushafi and his sons were arrested on charges of corruption. His villa was auctioned, and the properties of his sons were confiscated. Abi 'Amir showed no humane feelings for the aged hajib who had provided him with employment when as a young man he struggled for livelihood. A committee was appointed to look into the charges against him, but it was a mere mockery. Al-Mushafi wrote a poem from the prison which began with the line—" I, admit I am wrong but where is *al-'ufou wal karam* i.e. pardon and magnanimity." The heartless man replied, "when my soul is angry, kindness is ruled out even if all the Arabs and the non-Arabs plead for you." Al-Mushafi languished in prison for five long years. He longed for death, and it did come one day in 983. He was perhaps poisoned under the orders of Abi 'Amir. His body was not handed over to his relations. Muhammad ibn Ismail, the secretary to Abi 'Amir has left touching details of the funeral of the man who used to move through the streets of Cordova with a glittering cavalcade of attendants. He recalled how one day he had to wade through a crowd, just to put in a petition into his hands. Ismail found the dead body of Al-Mushafi covered with an ordinary piece of cloth. The body was placed on a broken door for the ritual washing. It was carried by him and the imam for the funeral service, and deposited in an unknown place[7].

Already before al-Mushafi died, Abi 'Amir was the prime Minister of the kingdom of Cordova. The greatest families living in the city were either in his pay, or dreaded the consequences of opposing him. However, in 979 about the time when al-Mushafi was disgraced some persons joined hands to replace Hisham by Ubaid Allah, a grandson of 'Abd ar-Rahman al-Nasir. The conspirators included several supporters of al-Mushafi, the Slav ibn Jawdhar, Qadi Abd al- Malik son of qadi Mundhir, and the poet Yusuf al-Ramadi. Ibn Jawdhar undertook to assassinate Hisham. As he was a former employee he was allowed entrance in the palace, and also granted permission to see Hisham. He was about to stab him when a servant caught him. The conspiracy failed. 'Ubaid Allah and the qadi were hanged in front of the palace as warning to others. Probably, ibn Jawdhar also met the same fate. Yusuf al-Ramadi was exiled to Saragossa. On his return he lived in complete isolation. Abi 'Amir saw in this incidence, the hand of disgruntled theologians.

He apprehended that they might stage a more organised opposition against him; he was anxious to forestall that situation. At this time the Maliki theologians were in an angry mood on account of the growing influence of philosophy. For a clever politician this was opportune time to exploit the situation. Why not win over the theologians by posing as a champion of orthodoxy? He banned the study of philosophy. He ordered that the library of al-Hakam be purged of all books which fostered free thought. The qadi Dhakwan and qadi Zubaidi were deputed to weed out all books obnoxious to the clerics. The books were either thrown in a well in the Madinat al-Zahra, or committed to flames. This act of vandalism was followed by a flattering attitude towards the theologians. He paid them greater respect, and invited them to state functions. On their part they held him in great esteem when they came to know that he had transcribed a copy of the Quran in his own hand. A greater cause of their happiness was the enlargement of the mosque of Cordova. In this way Abi 'Amir was able to silence the ulamas.

After destroying the Slavs and al-Mushafi, Abi 'Amir plotted to overthrow ibn Ghalib. He had already raised a formidable army. Once he held a review of his troop in the plains outside Cordova, and it was reported that the infantry was composed of six hundred thousand men, and a cavalry of one hundred thousand horsemen. During his stay in north Africa he had seen the fighting qualities of the Berbers of the High Atlas. Hundreds of them were imported into Spain to join the army. They were equipped with the finest arms. Economic distress and lack of even ordinary amenities of life forced the Christians of the northern states to seek employment in the Cordova army. The new army units were not constituted on ethnic lines as was hitherto the practice. The Arabs, the Berbers and northern recuits were all mixed up in the new formations. The soldiers were

paid well. The Christians were allowed Sunday as a holiday. A
Christian chronicler— the monk of Silos has written that in
disputes between the Muslims and the Christians Abi 'Amir
favoured the latter[8]. The new army was entirely subservient to
him. It was the tool of his authority at home and abroad.

While al-Mushafi was languishing in prison, a conflict arose
between Abi 'Amir and his father-in-law in Ghalib. He was the
greatest military commander (qaid) of his time. Like Abi 'Amir
he too was a man of humble origin. A freedman of 'Abd ar-
Rahman al-Nasir, ibn Ghalib had a along career of distinguished
service in the army. Except for a short period of duty in
northwest Africa, he spent his whole career on the borders. In
946, he built Medinaceli, a deserted village into the military
headquarters of the border which kept a watchful eye on the
northern kingdoms. Being near the borders he had direct contacts
with the rulers of Leon and Navarre, but he was always loyal
to the Umayyads. He was the idol of the army under his
command. As a loyalist he was opposed to the continued
seclusion of ibn Hisham. He suspected the military reforms of
Abi 'Amir and his growing hold on the army. In the middle of
July 981 the two leaders met at Atienza which is 40 km west
of Medinaceli. After a hearty entertainment they indulged in
mutual accusations, and drew swords. Abi 'Amir jumped down
from a tower and escaped without much injuries. This encounter
was a sequel to a war between them. Ibn Ghalib summoned the
Leonese to his side. He fought with reckless bravery. Wearing
a gold helmet and a red scarf, he spurred his steed through the
melee. The horse stumbled, and he fell down. The pointed part
of the saddle pierced through his chest killing him on the spot.
His head was cut off, and brought to Cordova, and was displayed
before his daughter Asma. A faithful wife, she faced the tragedy
with astonishing composture as ibn Ghalib was painted in her

eyes as a traitor and an ally of the Christians. The former law student of Cordova was now the *de jure* ruler of Muslim Spain. There was none to challenge his authority. As he was victorious in destroying his enemies he adopted the title of "al-Mansur". It is by this title that he is known in history, legends and literature.

The only person who could remove him from the political scene was Hisham, but he was a mere puppet. Hisham was born in 965. He lived at Madinat al-Zahra with his mother, the sultana Subh. During his childhood he was put under several tutors. Ahmad al-Zubaidi, one of the greatest scholars of his time, was his tutor for many years. He found that Hisham was a keen student. About the time Abi 'Amir assumed the title of al-Mansur, he was already an adult, but he showed no desire to take over control of the government. He would have found many supporters including top military commanders only if he raised his little finger to overthrow the yoke of Abi 'Amir[9]. Why was he satisfied with his gild-cage existence? An answer to his question is not difficult to find. The possibility that he had exhausted his manly vitality by premature indulgence in the company of eunuchs and slave-girls of the palace cannot be ruled out. Probably, the sultana saw (or heard about) her adolescent son sporting with the tangled locks of the palace nymphs. But she kept her eyes closed hoping that time would awaken in him a sense of his responsibilities. This is only one side of the matter. Was Hisham's mental growth slow or retarded? Was he destitute of intelligence? There is no evidence that he was born with infantile abnormality. There was a similar case in the history of Mughal India. The emperor Akbar was a minor when his father died. He was taught and trained by Bairam Khan, and when he came of age he took the government in his own hands. Abi 'Amir did not act like a loyal regent. His sole aim was to usurp all power in his hands, and to pass on the kingdom to his son. Perhaps, it was constantly dinned into him that kingship was not a bed of roses, and that the unruffled life he led in the palace was much better than the task of ruling a turbulent people. There is not doubt that in his early youth Hisham developed an escapist attitude to life which rendered him incapable to steer the ship of his kingdom. We can only infer from Abi 'Amir's actions that be had a hand a in destroying Hisham's individuality and power of free volition by keeping him confined in the al-Zahara palace.

The sultana Subh depended upon Abi 'Amir for the safety of her only son. In fact, two attempts were made on his life. Of all the officials of the kingdom she had the fullest trust in him, and did not mind his arrogating to himself some of the privileges of royalty. The people who were jealous of Abi 'Amir spread the rumours that the sultana was his *belle amie*. Some wrote satires, and some indulged in ribald jokes[10]. There is no categorical evidence to support these insinuations. There is no doubt that Abi 'Amir flattered here, danced attendance upon her, but it is doubtful if he had any liaison with her. He honoured here, and expected others to give her the respect due to her as the princess-mother (*al-Saiyida al-walida*) of Hisham. On her part, the sultana patiently watched the gradual concentration of power in the hands of Abi 'Amir. At last she could not bear it any longer, and in 996 when Hisham was nearly thirty years of age, she made an attempt to oust Abi 'Amir with the help of her brother Ra'ik who was a slave like her and had been brought up by al-Hakam as his own son. The state treasury was still at Madinat al-Zahra. She removed large quantities of gold in a hundred jars sealed with honey for distributions among her agents and helpers[11]. This could not escape the vigilant eyes of the spies of Abi 'Amir who reported to him about everything that happened in the palace. Subh's attempt at *coup d' etat* failed. The matter ended as quietly as it began. To ensure tranquillity in the city., Abi 'Amir took out a grand procession headed by Hisham in the full regalia of a Caliph— high turban on his head and a sceptre in hand. The people were delighted to see that their Caliph was, after all, alive. As for the sultana, she must have realised that like her son, she too was a captive in the palace. Henceforth, she resigned to her fate. Three years later (999) she died a disillusioned woman, leaving her only son to a cruel world.

The northern rulers posed a perpetual threat to the kingdom of Cordova. They never missed any opportunity to make devastating inroads into the Muslim territory. They broke solemn pledges, and harboured rebels. Soon after al-Hakam died, their armies crossed the frontiers, and Abi 'Amir was commissioned by al-Mushafi to drive them out. The states of Leon, and Navarre, and the counts of Barcelona gave no peace, and the Cordovan armies were often in state of either alert, or mobilization. Towards the end of the 10th century they became ambitious, and fired by religious zeal, they made repeated attacks with the sole objective of biting off some portion of the Muslim territory. Abi 'Amir with all his faults (and crimes too) was no warmonger, and wanted to live in peace without any interference from across the borders. As they had no respect for inter-state obligations, he was obliged to undertake many expeditions— nearly 52 in all, which the Muslim historians gleefully call holy wars against the northern Christian states. There was nothing holy or religious about these wars. They were all punitive expeditions. He had no intention to wipe out Christianity from the northern regions. Abi 'Amir had two Christian wives, while his army was full of Christian soldiers. Within the Muslim territory the Christians lived in peace. His objectives were,

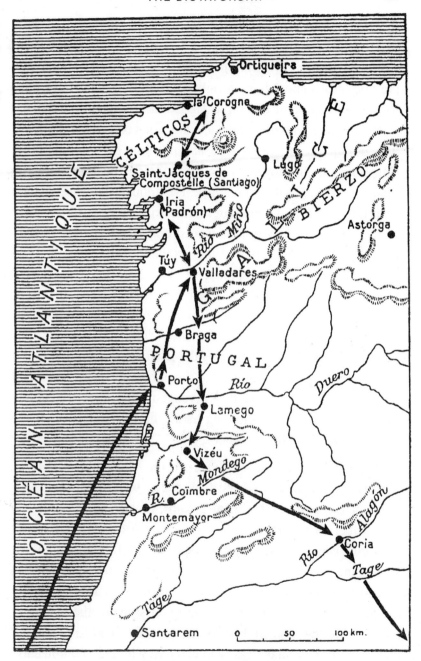

THE CAMPAIGN OF SANTIGO

therefore, purely political and secular. He wanted to destroy their military capacity to wage a war against the kingdom of Cordova. In our own time many highly civilised nations who are vociferous about human rights and moral values have gone to war with the same objective. He led these expeditions usually in the summer months and they did not take very long, as it was not in his interest to be absent from the capital. From Barcelona in the northeast, to Santiago in the northwest, no Spanish city was safe from attack. He flooded the whole region with his Berber and Christian mercenaries. The period of most of the northern campaigns is placed between 981-997. In 981, he sacked Zamora, in 983 he attacked Simancas, in 985 Sepulveda, in 985 Barcelona, in 987 Coimbra and in 997 Santiago. These wars left in their trail massive destruction of forts and religious places. Their worst legacy was the feelings of rancour on both the sides which darkened the relations between followers of the two faiths in times to come. The evil that men do, lives after them, and the good they do, is entombed with them. In order to take their revenge for the arson at Santiago (to be narrated in the following para), the Christians forgot the tolerance of the Muslim rulers.

The 48th expedition which earned for Abi 'Amir al-Mansur the everlasting hatred of the Christians, was directed against Santiago de compostella (Shant Yaqub), situated in the northwest of the Iberian peninsula about 50 km from the Atlantic coast. This city was a centre of pilgrimage for the Roman Catholics. According to legends, the cathedral at Santiago was the burial place of St. James. Al-Mansur left Cordova on July 3, 997 at the head of a powerful cavalry. On the first leg of the march he reached Merida, and from there, he took the road to Coria. At this place his Christian vassals joined him with their contingents. The combined army took the direction of Vizeu. Braving hills and rivers, he arrived at Valladares. At Porto he halted for sometime. Soon ships arrived from Alcacer do sol (Qasr abi Danis) near modern Lisbon bringing infantry, archers, provisions, and military stores. Al-Mansur continued the march, crossed the Mino river without opposition, and entered into the most dangerous terrain of the northwest surrounded by a wilderness of high rocks on all sides. Even the guides were at a loss to point out the route to Santiago and the sappers had to cut the woods to build roads. The army arrived in the town of Pardon and on August 10, Santiago was within sight. When he entered the city it was all deserted; there was none to defend either the city or the shrine of Santiago. The basilica was set on fire. Only the tomb of St. James was left untouched. Al-Mansur found a monk at the tomb. He asked him what he was doing there. The monk replied that he was a devotee of the saint. Al-Mansur told him to go on with his worship, and instructed his soldiers that no harm be done to the monk. After a week's stay at Santiago, he resumed his march, and reached Coruna on the Atlantic coast where no Muslim (says a historian) had so far set his foot. At this spot he wound up the camp, and began his journey back to Cordova. He arrived at Braga, crossed the Douro and at Lamego he parted company with his Christian allies after having lavished them with gifts. (Al-Maqqari has given a long list of the gifts.) A report says that al-Mansur brought the bells of the church to Cordova, and had them melted and shaped into lamps for the mosque of Cordova. The myopic generalissimo did not know that a time would come when the Christians would be able to settle old scores. When Cordova fell into the hands of the Christians in the 13th century, the lamps were carried by the Muslim captives to the church of Santiago[12]. The matter did not end just there. To avenge the burning of the shrine at Santiago, the Christians destroyed every Muslim cemetery and tomb, and razed or converted into a church every mosque in Spain— even their holiest, the one at Saragossa which enshrined the mortal remains of Hanash al-Sanani a sub-companion of the Prophet. So complete was the destruction that in Spain where Muslims lived for eight centuries there is not a single tomb of any Muslim sage, savant or sovereign on the Spanish soil. Out of the hundreds of mosques (in Spain and Portugal) not one has survived in its original shape.

For twenty years al-Mansur bestrode like a colossus. He was the most dreaded man both at home and abroad. The northern states were his tributaries, while at home, none could speak a word against him. He rose to this position by sheer craftiness. He was Machiavelli's "The Prince" in action. But he was very hard-working, and at the height of his power, he would sleep very little at night. He was a man of phenomenal energy, and never spared himself. When a velet named Sho'ala asked him why he kept awake the best part of the night, his reply was characteristic of the man — "O Sho'ala when the subjects are asleep a ruler should not. If I sleep, my subjects in this big city would never rest[13]." History books are full of stories of his generosity and justice. His 'bleeder' asked him to intervene in a law suit against him, but he refused, and told him that the matter was in the hands of qaḍi who alone was competent to decided the suit[14]. He was a strict disciplinarian, but he had no scruples when his own safety was concerned. When his son Abdullah rebelled against him, he did not demure to have him executed, and his severed head was shown to Hisham as a proof of his loyalty. He enlarged the mosque of Cordova, and built several bridges on the Xenil, and a new one at Guadalquivir. Inspite of his preoccupations, he snatched some moments of relaxation. He loved poetry, and invited poets and men of letters. Sometimes he would listen the songs of his *prima donna*—

Unsul Qulub (Joy of Hearts), or short stories from his story-teller. He was fond of flowers, and took bath with rose water. After his marriage with Asma, he began the construction of a grand palace. Begun in 979, the palace was ready for occupation in 981. The palace stood on the bank of the river a few kms to the east of the bridge. The rest of the life he lived in the marbled splendour of this palace which was called al-Zahira., He surrounded himself with all the luxuries and *objects d' art* befitting the royalty. When ibn Sa'id of Baghdad was in Cordova, al-Mansur invited him to the Zahira palace. He received him in a hall crowded with courtiers. In the centre of the hall, the guest from the East saw an aquarium topped with statues of females, and its inside bottom studded with pearls[15]. The only occupant of the aquarium was a live snake. His receptions were planned to display his wealth, specially to foreign visitors. Once he received a mission at the Zahira palace in a pavilion overlooking a lake planted with lilies. Already before the guests arrived, small pieces of gold and silver were placed inside the flowers. When the guests arrived, servants entered into the lake and gathered the pieces of gold. The "harvest" was placed before the guests and the host[16]. Al-Mansur transferred the treasury and the mint to his palace. All important dignitaries were asked to take their residence in the mansions built near the palace. In fact Madina al-Zahira grew into a small city. Hisham continued to live at Madinat al-Zahra. Its importance was dimmed as it was no more the residence of a Caliph, but a prisoner. The gorgeous palace wore a deserted look. The Alcazar on the bank of the river was already decaying. Hisham lived in a small apartment of Madinat al-Zahra, but sometimes he shifted to the Alcazar. Al-Mansur gave prosperity to the people, but the peace in the state was only the silence of a cemetery.

The year 1002 saw his last military expedition when he was already sixty years of age. He left Cordova, but never returned either alive of dead. Not many details are known about this expedition except that he arrived at Burgos after passing through Calatanazor and Canales. At Burgos he committed yet another act of sacrilege at the monastry of St. Milan. During the campaign he fell ill, and his condition became so serious that he had to be carried on a canopied stretcher. After a painful journey of 14 days (says ibn Bassam), he was brought to Medinaceli[17]. As his condition deteriorated, he summoned his eldest son 'Abd al-Malik to his bedside and gave him advice on political matters. The advice he gave to his son-a veritable manifesto, shows that he must have retained his consciousness upto his last breath. He died on August 11, 1002 — the 27th of Ramazan, 392 A.H. According to his will he was buried in the Alcazar of Medinaceli in a simple cotton sheet which was woven under the supervision of his three daughters, each named after the flowers he loved — Bahar, Narjis, and Banafsah. He carried it with him on his military missions as his ambition was to die fighting for the defence of the frontiers. His grave was marked by a stone with the following epitaph:-

> His relics will tell you the history of his life,
> And you will see him face to face;
> Time will not beget the like of him
> Nor the one like him to guard the borders of Spain[18].

A Christian chronicler viewed his death differently. He wrote — "In 1002, died Almanzor, and was hurried in hell."

Leaving his brother to perform the last rites of his father, 'Abd al-Malik hastened to Cordova. The news of his death spread all over Muslim Spain. Cordova was plunged in mourning. Inside the palace, the ladies tore away their glittering costumes and jewellery, and put on mourning clothes of coarse material. Perhaps, the Umayyads and the Slavs who wore the mask of loyalty to al-Mansur, saw in his death, the return of their better days. They were soon disappointed. The regency imposed by al-Mansur was inherited by his son without any bloodshed. The imbecile Hisham transferred to him all his prerogatives. His message which was drafted on his behalf by Nizam a lady employee of the chancellery, removed all doubts and speculations.

Al-Mansur had groomed 'Abd al-Malik as his successor. Even as he lay dying, he gave him detailed instructions about conducting the state. While the son wept, the father went on with his sermon. He told him that he was leaving behind a prosperous state; the treasury was overflowing with gold; the granaries were full; the depots were full of all the requirements of the army; the Arab aristocracy has been paralysed. He told him that he would have smooth sailing if he acted on his advice. He emphasised friendly relations with all officials particularly the army commanders. Regarding Hisham he stressed that he should be shown all honours due to him, but he should be completely isolated from all public duties.

'Abd al-Malik followed the path chalked out by his father. He was brave, conscientious and cultured, but he lacked his father's craftiness so necessary for success in politics. He was intelligent enough to please all. He reduced some taxes, and ordered that none should be imprisoned for life. He paid stipends to poets, and patronised such hangers—on as the astrologers. A lover of chess, he rewarded master chess-players. He did not hesitate to look after the taverns set up by his father for the Christian armymen. He visited holymen to earn their blessings. Like his father, he was forced to chastise the northern Spaniards for their aggressive activities. Sancho Garcia and his allies were beaten in 1007. His victory was celebrated with great fervour at Cordova, and he adopted the title of *"al-Muzaffar"* i.e, the Victorious. Sometimes, he arbitrated between the northern kings. When a quarrel broke out between Sancho Garcia and the king of Leon, both solicited his help in solving the dispute, and 'Abd al-Malik despatched Asbagh ibn Nabil the leader of the Christian community, to arbitrate between them.

Under 'Abd al-Malik, some notorious Slavs regained their lost position. Within a very short time they formed a grand aristocracy (*fata kabir*) of their own class. Their leader (or rather the ringleader) was Wadih, the commander of the middle frontier. At Cordova they were represented by Tarafa. The other Slavs were Zuhair, Khairan, and Mujahid of Murcia, Almeria, Denia and the Balearic islands. They were all waiting for an opportunity to strike.

During the brief period of only 7 years 'Abd al-Malik was in power, Muslim Spain was at the peak of material prosperity. Public functions and parades were held at Cordova as before. A great function marked the arrival of an envoy of Raimond Borell III of Barcelona. The last ambassador to arrive represented the Roman emperor Basil II. He came to negotiate the ransom of some prisoners of war. 'Abd al-Malik was fond of display. On several occasions, specially when he led an army, he marched through the streets of Cordova like a real monarch on a richly caprisoned horse of the best breed. He was seen clad in a mail of gold with a hamlet laid with diamonds and a flamboyant rubi in the middle. As wealth flowed in, love of finery and luxurious living became a passion with the people of Cordova and other major cities. The Zahira palace was a scene of frequent fêtes and glittering receptions which Hisham often attended with ladis of the harem. It was a time of plenty, of joy and affluence. But under the placid surface a violent storm was slowly building up. It broke out when 'Abd al-Malik died prematurely at the age of 33 on Oct. 20, 1008: *Après moi le déluge*.

Notes

1. Al-Marrakashi, pp. 18-19.
2. Miles : Vol 1 p 68 and also the photos in vol II.
3. Al-Maqqari/Gayangos, vol II, p 179.
4. Ibn Idhari, Vol II. p. 252.
5. The Caliph Abd ar-Rahman left eleven sons from his several wives. Mughira was perhaps the youngest. His mother named Mushtaq build a mosque at Cordova. The inscription relating to the mosque has survived.
6. Nyki: p 51.
7. Ibn Idhari: Vol. II, pp.280-281.
8. Provençal: Histoire, vol II, p. 249.
9. A poet of pro-Umayyad sympathies has left the following lines: O sons of Omayyas! Where are your full moons, your stars, your constellations? Where were your lions when the usurper seized your empire. (Al-Maqqari/ Gayangos, vol. I p. 197).
10. A poet wrote these lines: The Domesday is near as corruption is rampant. The Caliph is an immature youth, while his mother is frisking. (ibn Idhari: Vol II, PP 380. Dozy: p. 488).
11. Al-Maqqari/Gayangos, vol II, p. 186 and ibn Bassam Vol IV, pp. 52-53.
12. Al-Maqqari/Gayangos, Vol II, pp 196, Dr. Titus Burkhardt says that al-Mansur destroyed the abbey because it was the assembly point for the crusade against Spanish Islam. (See his 'Moorish Culture of Spain, p 12) Even so, there was no justification to bring down a holy shrine. As regards the bells of Santiago, both the stories seem to be apocryphal and were written in a spirit of bravado, by the Muslim historians. Bernhard and Ellen Whishaw have stated (pp. 170-170) that the accounts of taking of Santiago are contradictory. They have also cited an instance of Al-Mansur's respect, (p. 173) for a defeated foe. In 995, he took prisoner Garcia Fernandez the Count of Castile. He was badly wonded and died on May 25, 995. Al-Mansur ordered that the body of the king be placed

in a well-carved coffin, and wrapped in a beautiful covering of scarlet and gold with fine perfumes, and be handed over to the Christians who came to receive the body.

13. Ibn Idhari: Vol, II, p. 398.

14. Al-Maqqari/Gayangos, vol II, p. 207, also p, 240, on the tragic end of his eldest son 'Abdullah.

15. Al-Maqqair Gayangos, vol. II, p. 204 and 243.

16. Al-Maqqair Gayangos, vol. II, p. 204 and 243.

17. Ibn Bassam, IV P.55. Medinaceli or Madinat Salim was built by a Berber named Salim. It was a fairly large town with a formidable fort built by the caliph 'Abd ar-Rahman. The town is almost in the middle of the railway between Madrid and Saragossa. Provençal has given a photo of the minaret of a mosque now part of a church at Medinaceli (see his Histoire, vol II, p. IX).

18. Ibn Idhari, Vol II, P 401. (In the original Arabic the word "jazira" is used for Spain).

Chapter 11

The Decay and Fall of the Kingdom of Cordova

---·•·---

Usually, kingdoms and empires take a long time to die out. Before they crumble in the dust, they are eaten up by a long and wasting disease. The social and political microbes invade every vein and vital system of the state. By slow degrees they go into a coma and die. The fall of the kingdom of Cordova, on the other hand, came suddenly like the tragic end of a person who only yesterday was in the pink of health. The regency of al-Mansur and his son al-Muzaffar (whatever their faults) was a continuance of the *siècle d'or* ushered by the Caliph al-Nasir. The brief regency of al-Muzaffar is known in history as the time of honeymoon (*ayam al- 'aras*) which follows an auspicious marriage. Within just two decades after his death, the kingdom of Cordova faded out for ever:

Although al-Mansur preferred al-Muzaffar, he actually doted on 'Abd ar-Rahman his younger son, he affectionately called by the diminutive name of "Sanchol" after his maternal grandfather — Sancho Garces II of Navarre. Sancho's daughter Abarca converted to Islam, and took the name 'Abda after her marriage with al-Mansur[1]. Sanchol (Ar. *Sanjool*) was born in

984. From his early childhood he was treated as a pampered child. He was given the tile of a vazir while he was in his early teens. When al-Mansur gave a reception to his father-in-law on his state visit to Cordova (Sept. 4, 992) the boy was gorgeously dressed like a prince. Sancho paid homage to his own grandson by kissing his feet! Sanchol grew up into a shallow, and a vainglorious youth. His father had no illusions about him, and it was for this reason that on his deathbed he had advised al-Mazaffar to take special care of his younger brother[2]. Sanchol was a youth with no character and self-respect. He freely moved with buffons, ballerinas and musicians of easy virtue. He was a shameless libertine with heretical leanings. When he heard a muezzin chanting the call of prayer, he would sometimes remark jestingly "How I wish he called the people to a drinking party." He was on familiar terms with Hisham and address him as his "maternal uncle," because like Hisham's mother, his mother too, was a Basque from Navarre.

Sanchol had no sense of realities. At this time Cordova was heading towards a bloody revolution. There was a growing opposition to the family of al-Mansur, and the people wanted a change. The self-complacent Sanchol did not know that he was sitting on a powder keg. He invited his own doom by his several acts. He obtained Hisham's orders for conferring on him the honorific title of "al-Ma'mum." His megalomania had no end. One day he asked Hisham to nominate him as his successor. At that time Hisham was already forty. He had no desire to take over the government into this own hands, and was content with his voluntary retirement. He passed his days in prayer and fasting. Sometimes he would visit the Zahira palace to attend a house-warming party. On such an occasion, the roads were closely guarded, and he rode out shrouded in his clothes so as not to be seen by the public. He had developed a taste for collecting religious and antiquarian relics. He was mere wax in the hands of everybody. As he had no child of his own, he readily agreed to the audacious request of Sanchol. The Secretary of State—Ahmad ibn Burd was ordered to draw up an Instrument of Succession. The full text of this historic document (which is a masterpiece of draftsmanship for its clear and precise language) is available in the history of Al-Maqqari. The document began with a preamble which stated that the Caliph Hisham, finding that his end was near, had decided without pressure, but with his free will, and also for the good of the people, to appoint Abū l-Motrif 'Abd ar-Rahman, son of al-Mansur Abi 'Amir Muhammad, as his successor. The document added that Sanchol belonged to a noble Qahtan family, member of which was destined to rule over the Muslims. Besides, the nobility of birth, he possessed the qualities of a good ruler. The document was signed in the month of Nov. 1008. On Jan. 13, 1009, a glittering ceremony was held at the Zahira palace, to celebrate the occasion. Cordova was illuminated with lights.

The northern states got the wind of political developments at Cordova, and without any provocation, they opened hostilities. Their raids forced Sanchol to set out from Cordova to punish them. He had hardly reached Toledo, when a revolution broke out in the capital. The Umayyads who had been nursing their grudge against Al-Mansur and his family, rallied under the leadership of Muhammad ibn Hisham ibn 'Abd al-Jabbar, a great grandson of Caliph 'Abd ar-Rahman. Even al-Dhalfa, the mother of al-Muzaffar aided the revolutionaries with money because she suspected that Sanchol had poisoned her son. A crowd of rioters gathered outside the Alcazar, where Hisham had shifted to pass the winter. Another crowd attacked the city jail and released the convicts. Hisham got nervous and ordered that the gates of the palace be closed, while he himself climbed on the terrace with the Quran in his hand to pacify the people. The mob became all the more restive, and in despair Hisham left the terrace. In the meantime, a gang of vagabonds who supported ibn Jabbar scaled the walls and entered into the palace. The royal guards were under strict orders not use their arms even under provocation. The hired desperadoes of ibn Jabbar spread consternation in the palace. Hisham realised that the best course to avoid bloodshed was to abdicate in favour of ibn Jabbar. He sent a message to him, and an Instrument of Abdication was hastily drawn up. Ibn Jabbar occupied the palace and an announcement was made in the mosque of Cordova in Feb. 1009. Ibn Jabbar adopted the title of "Mahdi." While this was going on an angry mob forced its way in the Zahira palace and it was plundered under the very eyes of the guards. The treasure amassed by al-Mansur and al-Muzaffar—gold, silver, rare jewellery, precious stones, furnishings, carpets, vases all fell into the hands of the looters. They dismantled the palace and removed its marble and ornamental doors. What was left, was committed to flames. Every house in Cordova had its share of the plundered wealth. Many curios reached the markets of Baghdad[4].

The news of the revolution reached Sanchol, and he decided to return to Cordova. The qadi ibn Dhakwan who was with him advised against returning to Cordova, and warned him that his action would lead to a civil war, but Sanchol was adamant. He lefts for Cordova in the company of Count Carrión. He arrived at Manzil Hani, a halting place only two days journey from Cordova when he was arrested along with the Count. He was produced before al-Mahdi who treated him in the most humiliating manner. Sanchol had no doubt that he would be executed. He released his hand from the cord that bound him, and pulled out a dagger to stab himself, but a soldier rushed forward and stabbed him to death. Thus ended the family rule of al-Mansur. The fall of the Umayyads was not far off. The Banu "Amir fell, but like the blind Samson they brought the whole fabric of the empire," Says Amir Ali[5]. The ensuing two decades saw a sanguinary race for the throne. The Umayyads, the Berbers, the Slavs fought for supremacy. Each faction propped up its own candidate, and Cordova turned into a theatre of bloody scenes in which actor after actor appeared wielding the sword and dying by the sword. Ibn Hayyan, the Thucydides of the Caliphate period of Spain who was at this time in his twenties, has minutely described the *tableau vivant* of the events he saw with his own eyes.

Mahdi proved no better than Sanchol. He was cruel and pleasure loving. He had a mania for music. Nothing less than an orchestra of a hundred lutes would please his ears. He had no political sense. He dismissed the Berbers, and to add insult to injury, he forbade them from keeping arms, and a Berber colony near Rusafa was plundered . By these actions he incurred the hatred of the Berbers, and they never forgave him. In his heart of hearts, Mahdi wanted to remove Hisham from his path, but he had not the courage to kill him. He resorted to a fraud. Just then it was reported to him that a Christian who exactly looked like Hisham had died. He obtained the cadaver of the dead man from the cemetery. It was passed for the body of Hisham, and given a ceremonial burial, while the living Hisham was transferred elsewhere. The Umayyad pretenders most of whom were Mahdi's cousins and closest relations did not believe that Hisham was dead. The leader of the crop of claimants to the throne was Sulaiman the aged son of Caliph 'Abd ar-Rahman al-Nasir. Mahdi ordered his arrest but his supporters rallied under his son named Hisham. The retrenched Berbers joined

hands with them. A frightened Mahdi released Sulaiman, but
Hishm was not satisfied because he wanted the throne for his
father. The Berbers who were eager for quick results took to
the streets, and began to pillage and burn shops. Mahdi drove
out the Berber ringleaders, and ordered execution of Sulaiman
and Hisham. But the Berbers were determined to place an
Umayyad of their choice on the throne. At this time, they were
led by their clever and calculating general Zawai bin Ziri .
Their choice fell upon another Sulaiman a great-grandson of
Caliph al-Nasir. In their search for allies they turned to Sancho
Garcia, the Count of Castile for help. When their envoy went
to see him, they were surprised to find that an embassy from
Mahdi was already there. Disunity among the Muslims had
brought them to such a stage that they begged for help from the
state which was a satellite of the kingdom of Cordova. Sancho
opted for the Berbers in return for some forts along the river
Dourro. His demand was accepted in principle, and the Berbers
and their Christian allies marched upon Cordova. A fierce battle
was fought at Kantish about 25 km north of the city. Nearly six
thousand Cordovans perished in this battle. Mahdi was defeated.
He was averse to predominance of the Berbers, and be sent a
message through qadi Dhakwan that he was prepared to resign
provided Hisham was restored to the throne. The Berbers replied
to the qadi, "Yesterday Hisham was dead, and a funeral was
held. How can he be alive today." The talks failed. Sulaiman
was declared caliph with the title of *al-Musta 'in billah* in the
mosque of Cordova, on Nov. 8, 1009. Mahdi sought asylum at
Toledo.

At this time Wadi, the Slav commander of the northern
frontier (one of the shameless rascals of the time) jumped into
the political arena. He wanted to wipe out the ascendancy of
the Berbers. He travelled to Catalonia and negotiated an alliance

with count Raimound of Barcelona and his brother count Ermengaud of Urgel. He tempted them with offers of gold, wine, victuals, and generous pay to their soldiers. They agreed to place their soldiers at this disposal. The two counts gathered their soldiers at Medinaceli where al-Mansur lay buried. They entered into the city not as allies, but as conquerors. Their first action was to convert the mosque of the Alcazar into a church by sprinkling it with wine[6]. The joint armies of Mahdi, Waḍi, and the two Counts left for Cordova. Once again a fierce engagement took place at El Vacar (Aqabat al Baqr) in the plains of Cordova on May 22, 1010. The Berbers were routed. Zawi ibn Ziri and Sulaiman fled away, leaving the Catalans to pillage the city. The notorious Mahdi once again occupied the precarious throne. Waḍi was now the recognised leaders of the villainous Slav faction. He was a rogue thirsty for power. He had no love for Mahdi. His objective was to defeat the Berbers by espousing the cause of Mahdi. Soon he pulled off his mask of loyalty, and started secret conspiracies to remove Mahdi. By his tacit encouragement, a movement was launched for restoration of the Caliph Hisham. The people marched through the streets shouting slogans in favour of Hisham. Waḍi managed to get him released, and one day he was conducted to the coronation hall. While the ceremony was in progress, Mahdi burst into the hall. There was an altercation between Hisham and Mahdi, the former blamed the latter for causing suffering to the people. The brief drama ended in the murder of Mahdi by a Slav who was a friend of Waḍi. Mahdi had seized the throne by one conspiracy, and now by another conspiracy against him he lost his head as well as the crown. The happened on July 23, 1010.

Hisham's restoration was a belated step. He was now about 45 years of age. He had lost the desire to rule. He appointed

Waḍi as his Prime Minister, and left all matters in his hands. But the path was not smooth for this king-maker. The presence of the Berber hordes was a nightmare to him. News were coming that they were consolidating their position in the predominantly Berber districts of Malaga and Algeciras. Day by day, he found that his position was becoming critical. In the meantime, Sancho Garcia asked for formal surrender of the forts. He promised that he would not open hostilities, and as part of a fresh deal, Waḍi handed over two hundred forts, particularly San Estevan, Clunia, Osma and Gormaz, over which the white Umayyad flag had been fluttering for nearly a century. Waḍi was also short of money as the treasury was practically empty. When his soldiers clamoured for pay, he sold a part of the library of al-Hakam without any qualms of conscience. The public resentment was mounting against him. Persistent rains and floods rendered thousands of citizens without a roof. Soon an epidemic broke out. The prices were shooting up. Waḍi was so much disillusioned that he wanted to run away. But before he could do this his enemies ripped his body with sabres. After he was gone the field was open for the Berbers to step in.

During the second decade of the 11th century events moved with the inevitability of a Greek tragedy. The Umayyad kingdom was living on borrowed time. It was already falling apart as the local governors— Arab, Berber, and the Slav were poised for complete independence. The Berbers pitchforked Sulaiman once again into the royal seat. His coming back was a great calamity. It was during his brief reign that the caliph Hisham disappeared from the political scene. Clio is silent about his ultimate end. Some historians have stated that he slipped out of Spain, and died in the East in poverty and obscurity. The 14th century historian ibn Khatib wrote that Hisham was strangled to death on May 18, 1013 at the instance of Sulaiman. A victim of heartless selfishness, Hisham is one of the most pathetic figures in all history. Sulaiman had no control over the Berbers. They were burning with revenge for the cruelties and humiliations they had suffered at the hands of Mahdi, the Slavs, and the jeering mobs of Cordova. The murder of a nephew of their leader Zawai ibn Ziri brought their hatred to a head. Blind alike to beauty and culture, they entered into Cordova like demons of destruction. They plundered the Madinat al-Zahra, and set it on fire in Nov. 1010. In a few days the most magnificent palace in Europe was reduced to debris. They spread terror in other parts of the city. The rich colonies of Cordova were their favourite targets. Blood flowed into the streets littered with corpses. Many aristocratic families and eminent jurists, perished in the holocaust let loose by the Berbers. The pious historian ibn Farid was murdered in his own house, and his body was found in such a stage of decomposition that it had to be buried without a wrapping. The house in which ibn Hazm lived in the fashionable colony of Balat Mughit was looted and destroyed. He has lamented the ruin of his home and the sack of Cordova in a memorable passage in his Tawk al-Hamama[7]. He was at Jativa when a visitor from Cordova informed him that his villa with its ornamented halls, patios and boudoirs had been reduced to a howling wilderness. Ibn Shuhaid gave vent to his grief in an elegy on the havoc wrought by the Berbers. Except for the Berbers to whom he was their 'imam', Sulaiman was a *bete noire* to all others. They looked upon him as a stooge of the Berbers, a silent spectator of the sack and plunder of Cordova, and a criminal responsible for the regicide of Hisham. In order to get rid of him they invited an outsider.

This new evil star was Ali ibn Hammud of Ceuta. He entered into Cordova with his army in July, 1016. He killed Sulaiman, and made confusion worse confounded. Ibn Hammud failed to restore order in the torn city. On March 22, 1018, he was found laying in a pool of blood. The horrible deed was done by his own servant with pro-Ummayd sympathies.

After him several kings followed one another from the throne to the mortuary. The Slav Khairan contrived to place on throne a great-grandson of al-Nasir. On his accession on April, 29, 1018, he took the title of al-Murtada. He did not like to play into the hands of Khairan, and he lost both his life and throne. Seeing no hope for himself in the troubled politics of Cordova, Khairan left for Almeria to set up a small kingdom of his own. There was no dearth of aspirants to the throne even though a sword of Damocles hung over it. The family members of ibn Hammud fought for the throne causing widespread violence. Ultimately, some Cordovans decided to elect an Umayyad from among the descendants of Caliph 'Abd ar-Rahman al-Nasir. They had a meeting in the mosque of Cordova. Three candidates were in the zone of selection— Sulaiman son of 'Abd ar-Rahman IV (al-Murtaḍa), 'Abd ar-Rahman a brother of the infamous Mahdi, and Muhammad al-Iraqi. The meeting was in progress when the brother of Mahdi entered into the mosque with his supporters. The frightened assembly offered the throne to him. He assumed the title of 'al-Mustazir bilah'. He appointed a good team of ministers which included ibn Hazm and ibn Shuhaid. They were all men of culture with little experience of politics and administration. Muslim Spain at this hour needed a ruthless king like Hakam I. 'Abd ar-Rahman went the way of his predecessors. He became unpopular when he introduced new taxes to pay for his guards. A vagabond grandson of 'Abd ar-Rahman who had considerable influence among the working class stirred up agitation against him. A violent mob assaulted the palace (the old Alcazar), the guards were massacred and even the ladies of the harem were molested. The Caliph who had gone into hiding in the chimney of the bath was caught and murdered in cold blood on Jan. 17, 1024.

The new Caliph Muhammad al-Mustakfi was a patron of the rowdy middle class, and a glutton with a Falstaffian waist. He celebrated his accession to the kingdom (not more than a small district) by killing his enemies. Ibn Hazm was put in prison, and ibn Shuhaid sought safety in Malaga. In order to placate the working class with whose support he had come to power he appointed a weaver as his Prime Minister. This action triggered a revolt against him, and finding himself in danger, he slipped out of the city (May, 1025) disguised as dansuese. On his way towards the north, he was poisoned. He left behind at Cordova his daughter — the poetess Wallada.

Cordova was without a ruler for several months. The Umayyad kingdom had definitely broken up into small bits. The new rulers were looking after their new princedoms. The dowager Cordova robbed of her dominion was left to fend for herself. Some heads of families who had so far remained impotent spectators of the tragic scene came forward under the leadership of a rich and influential Cordovan named ibn Jahwar. They stirred into activity when the kingdom of Cordova was in the agony of death. They still fondly hoped that the restoration of the Umayyads would furnish a rallying cry for the people to unite. But they did not know that the Ummayd stock was almost exhausted. Many Umayyads had died during the periodic purges carried out by al-Mansur, and those who remained, destroyed themselves by fighting in the wars of succession. Far away in Alpuente, there lived the elder brother of 'Abd ar-Rahman al-Murtada. They appointed him as Caliph in absentia. The people waited for the new ruler for a long time. At last he appeared on Dec. 18, 1029. He came riding on an ordinary horse and dressed like a commoner. The initial impression so unfavourable, was confirmed when he took a weaver as his minister. There was perfect understanding between the two. Hisham gave him full liberty to run the government of the moth-eaten territory of Cordova. In return, his minister Hakam provided his master with all the joys of life—music, dance, delicacies and endless number of cups in bowers of myrtles. Those who put him on the throne soon realised that Hisham was not a person who could lead a forlon cause, and they decided to remove him. On a cold day in Dec. 1031 he was ejected from the palace. The miserable man and his wives walked bare-footed on the bridge which connected the palace with a door in the western wall of the mosque of Cordova[8]. They were stationed in an old and cheerless vault but were provided with light and meal. Hisham's life was spared only after he agreed to resign. Soon he was removed to a fort from where he escaped, and reached Lerida in the far north. He lived as a guest of Sulaiman ibn Hud who had already broken away from the kingdom of Cordova, and founded an independent state of his own. Sometime in 1036, Hishm III died, unwept and usung. Such was the end of the kingdom of Cordova: *sic transit gloria mundi*.

Notes

1.   Al-Manur's second wife of Christian origin was Teresa. The facts leading to this marriage may be narrated briefly. In 982, as a result of a war of succession in Leon, Ramiro III who was unpopular with the barons was driven out by Vermudo II. The new king was crowned at the church of Santiago. As his position was not secure, he asked for help from al-Mansur. In exchange for annual tribute, al-Mansur stationed a small force at Leon for the protection of Vermudo. After sometime, the Cordovan troops were expelled on account of their alleged misconduct. Al-Mansur took this action as a breach of faith, and invaded Leon. Vermudo suffered several defeats, and sued for peace. As a condition for peace he agreed to give his daughter in marriage to al-Mansur. She was conducted to Cordova by Leonese nobles, and the marriage took place

in 993. After his death, 'Abd al-Malik allowed her to return to Leon. She became a nun, and died in April 1039 when the House of al-Mansur had already disappeared. (Provençal: Histoire, Vol. II, pp. 235 and 243).

2. Ibn Bassam: vol. IV, p. 57.

3. Al-Maqqari/Gayangos, vol. II, pp. 223-224.

4. A holyman foretold the ruin of Zahira palace in the following couplet:-

    O palace of the king, every house contributed to thine ornamentation; Thou shall afford material for every house. (Al-Maqqari/Gayangos, vol. II, p. 245). There are no remains of the Al-Zahira palace, and no attempt has been made to locate the site.

5. Amir Ali: p, 526.

6. Provençal: Histoire, vol II, p. 313.

7. Tawk al-Hamama: pp. 180-181.

8. The bridge has long disappeared but the door in still intact.

Chapter 12

The Kingdoms of the "Muluk at-Tawā'if and the Fall of Toledo

——————•·•——————

Muslim Spain broke up into thirty five or more small units after the fall of the Umayyad kingdom of Cordova. The Arabs, the Berbers, and the Slavs tore up the kingdom limb by limb like hungry vultures feeding on a carcass. The centrifugal forces kept in check by the Caliph 'Abd ar-Rahman and his successors burst out with a fury. A minister here, and a military governor there, a clever judge, and an unscrupulous upstart rose into power, and plunged the state into territorial anarchy. The old hatred between the Arabs and the Berbers revived once again[1]. The Berbers held the whole of the southeast — Malaga, Algecira, Granada, Carmona, Ronda and Moron. The Slavs grabbed Valencia. Murcia , Almeria, Denia and the Balearic Islands. The Arabs established themselves at Cordova, Seville, Saragossa. Toledo was grabbed by an Arabised family of distant Berber origin. In the west, which included much of the southern Portugal. the Banu al-Aftas, a family of the Berbers set up their kingdom. Some of the new kingdoms were so small that their territories did not extend beyond a few fortified towns and their suburbs. During this period of anarchy and blood—drenched feuds, only the strongest survived; the bigger states forcibly seized the weaker neighbours. As years went by, the kingdom of Seville occupied Nielba, Huelva, Arcos, Ronda, Cordova, Moron and Meretola. The biggest states which emerged out of the ashes of the Umayyad kingdom were, Saragossa of Banu Hud, Seville of Banu 'abbad, Toledo of Banu Dhinnon, and Badajoz of Banu al-Aftas. The rulers of these principalities assumed pompous titles, they struted in tiraz robes, walked on dainty carpets, carried jewelled arms, and struck their own coinage like the Umayyads[2]. Although frequently involved in inter-state wars, these small kingdoms were museums of culture. Their rulers held glamourous courts, built palaces and pleasure gardens, and collected books on literature, history and philosophy. Literary men, artists, interior decorators, musicians and freethinkers congregated in their courts. Some of the greatest names in Hispano-Muslim culture flourished during this period of political anarchy, which is why European authors compare it to Renaissance Italy of the 15th century[3]. Most of them were highly cultured persons versed in books and literature. Al-Muzaffar the ruler of Badajoz (d.1068) was a great bibliophile of his time. He was the author of an encyclopaedia of history, anecdotes, songs and poetry. This book ran into 40 volumes. Abdullah of Granada has left his memoirs which have been printed in Spanish and French. Abū Ja'far al-Muqtadir of Saragossa who ruled till 1081, was a brilliant mathematician of his time. Mujahid of Denia cultivated the art of 'qirat' i.e, recitation of the Quran. Al-Mu'tamid, the colourful ruler of the kingdom of Seville was one of the greatest names in Arabic literature whose poems portraying the trysts, the triumphs and the tragedies of his life, are still widely read and enjoyed all over the Arab world.

A list of the leading muluk at-tawā'if is appended at the end of this book. This period of 60 years of so, presents (in the words of L. Provençal) "a picture of constant turmoils, opposing interests, rivalries and perpetual disputes through which it is not possible to trace a guiding thread[4]." In the circumstances, it is proposed to give a brief account of the important kingdoms of this most confused period before all of them were absorbed by the Berber conquerors from northwest Africa.

After the formal dissolution of the Caliphate in Dec 1031, the leading citizen of Cordova decided to hand over the administration of the city to ibn Jahwar who was respected by the public for his honesty and good morals. Ibn Jahwar established a republic, and he governed the district of Cordova with the help of a team of advisers. He was impartial in his dealings. Whenever he was asked for a favour, he referred the person concerned to the senate. A deeply religious man, he was a true servant of the people. He lived in his own house, and assumed no honorific title, and acquired no privileges. He restored the rule of law, and dismissed the Berbers involved in acts of violence He adopted several measures to improve the economy. The trade flouished, and the prices of articles of daily consumption fell to a reasonable limit. The localities which lay in ruin due to the last civil war were rebuilt. Under his wise administration, the people got a welcome respite from two decades of turmoils. But Cordova though shorn of its former glory was still a coveted mistress in the eyes of her neighbours. The princes of Seville and Toledo wanted to grab it, and in June 1075 they actually went to war to possess the city. Al-Ma'mun of Toledo nearly succeeded, but he died near the walls of the city. Ultimately, al-Mu'tamid annexed it to his kingdom with the help of his Christian mercenaries.

When Cordova was rocked by wars of succession, Granada together with Jaen, and Malaga broke away from the centre.

Founded by the Berber Zawai ibn Ziri, it was one the earliest independent states to come into existence even before the funeral of the Umayyad kingdom of Cordova. Ziri gifted the state to his nephew Habus. He adopted the titles of *hajib sayaf al-Dawlah*. He died in 1038, leaving the small kingdom (which embraced the towns of Elvira, the newly founded city near Granada, Cabra and Jaen) to his son Badis. An object of hatred for the Arabs, and the Slavs, Badis came under the influence of the talented Jew Rabi Samuel ha Levi. This one-eyed Jew was a reputed scholar of Arabic, Hebrew and a noted mathematician of his time. Badis took him as his minister, and the state of Granada rose to unrivalled prosperity thanks to his efforts. He was the most respect Jew of his time, and even the present day Jews still remember him[5]. After his death, he son Yusuf stepped into his place. He was the unworthy son of a worthy father. By his narrow-mindedness, he vitiated the peaceful atmosphere of this beautiful territory. He took full control of the administration, and infested the state with Jewish spies. He oppressed the Muslims, so much that they were reduced to the position of hewers of wood and drawers of water. Even the meat market was not left in their hands. He scoffed at Islam and ridiculed the Quran. As the Jews were economically better off, and also in a predominant position numerically, Yusuf plotted to carve out a Jewish state. Many complaint wore made to Badis, but he was never sober and took no action. In the meantime, a learned alfaqih named Abū Isḥaq of Elvira incited the Muslims against Yusuf by exposing his designs. He composed a poem on the subject which was recited at public gatherings. This poem is a vituperative attack on Yusuf, his arrogance, his ostentatious life-style, and his animosity towards the Muslims. As Badis remained unmoved, the Muslims broke into a riot (Dec 1066) in which a large number of the Jews lost their lives. Yusuf hid himself in a coal celler. He was dragged out and despatched. Badis ruled till 1073. After the death of Badis one of his sons ruled Granada, and another held Malaga. They were swept away by African conquerors about whom we shall speak in the next chapter.

The princedom of Banu Al-Aftas was one of the biggest states that emerged out of the broken kingdom of the Umayyads. It was a coastal state situated south of the Tagus, and was composed of several important fortified towns — Coimbra, Lamego, Viseu, Evora, Badajoz, Lisbon, Cintara Casceres, Trujillo, and Santarem. The entire region was known as 'Algharb' i.e. the west. During the twilight of the Umayyads, the governor of the region Sabur by name broke away from the centre sometime in 1019. After him four rulers held the region — Abdullah, Muzaffar, Yaha, and Omar al-Mutawakil. The Banu al-Aftas were never on happy terms with the kingdoms of Seville and Toledo, and were isolated. This made their position insecure. The Christians took full advantage of this situation. Muzzaffar conferred the administrations of Coimbra on a Christian named Rando who defected and joined hands with the king of Leon[6]. In 1054 Fernando of Castile seized Viseu and Lemego. In the next year Muzaffar saved his kingdom by agreeing to pay a yearly tribute to him. The treaty gave him time to pursue his literary tastes, and to complete the "Muzaffari" his celebrated encyclopaedia of which not a page has survived. Omar al-Mutawakkil was the last ruler of this dynasty. He was not very rich, but he enjoyed the company of poets and musicians. He invited them to his palace — the famous Badi (The wonderful), where the three brothers of the celebrated Banu al-Qabturnuh family were frequent visitors. He took as his secretary the poet ibn 'Abdun of Evora who wrote the famous elegy 'al-basama' on the fall of the al-Aftas dynasty. This elegy has given him a permanent niche in Hispano-Arabic literature. Omar was the last prince of this clan.

Sarogossa had the distinction of being the headquarters of the upper frontier of the Umayyad kingdom. It would be recalled that the caliph 'Abd ar-Rahman al-Nasir appointed Hisham al-Tujibi as a governor of this military district. His descendants continued to hold the post. After the fall of the Umayyads, the governor of Lerida Abū Aiyub Sulaiman of the Banu Hud family seized Saragossa and created an independent state comprising Lerida, Tortosa, and Calatayud. Like his contemporaries he took the title of *al-Mustain*. The last Umayyad caliph Hisham III spent his last days under his protection. Under the Banu Hud the kingdom enjoyed three decades of prosperity. The territory was fertile and was famous for its farms and orchards. It had sweet water sources, and like Valencia its climate was so salubrious and its air so dust-free that the people stored cereals and fruits for years. Al-Mustain died in 1046. He son Abū Ja'far al-muqtadir ruled till 1081. He was a cultivated man, and a noted mathematician and author of a book on the subject. He built several beautiful palaces. Two of these palaces were famous during his life— *dar as-surus* (The Abode of Joy), and the *al-Ja'faria*. The latter palace has been reconstructed by the Spanish government, but not many tourists visit it because of its distance from Madrid. The court of his son and successor—Yusuf al-Mu'tamin who ruled till 1085 was a sanctuary of needy poets and exiled scholars. The famous Christian knight the Cid lived as his guest after he was turned out by king Alfonso. The rulers of Saragossa had no religious prejudices. The famous Jew Abū I Fadl served as minister to the banu Hud rulers. There were several monasteries and churches in the kingdom. We have a report that a bishop resided Saragossa from 1040-1063[7].

The Banu 'Abbad kingdom of Seville was the biggest territory held by any Arab family. The Babu 'Abbad were Syrian Yemenites from Emessa. The ancestor of this family came to Spain with Balj, and settled at Tocina in the vicinity of Seville. The kingdom of Seville was carved out by Abū 1-Qasim who came from a family of jurists. Like ibn Jahwar he started his political career as he head of a republic with Zubaidi, the tutor of Hisham II, as one of his advisors. He cleared the district of all pretenders to the caliphate, by his diplomacy. As he was one of the wealthiest men of Spain at this time, it was not difficult for him to establish his personal rule with the power of the dinar. Working on the pretence that Hisham was alive and under his protection, he consolidated his position. Abū 1-Qasim died in 1042. His two successors— the cruel sensualist al-Mu'tadid and the dreamer-poet al-Mu'tamid (1069-1091) extended the kingdom by armed encroachments. The Banu 'abbad rulers considered themselves leaders of the Arab party. During the rule of Al-Mu'tamid, the kingdom owned some of the most fertile regions on both sides of the Guadalquivir stretching from Silves to the borders of Valencia. The whole kingdom was dotted with orchard of citrus fruits, figs, almonds, and olive trees. The fertility of the plain Asharaf which covered meanly 40 miles of greenery was proverbial. Seville, the capital of the kingdom was a rival of Cordova. It was a city of poets, musicians, men of learning. "Seville is a young bride, her husband is 'Abbad (i.e. Mu'tamid), her diadem is Asharaf, and the river her neckless"- sang a poet in rapturous praise of the city. It was a delight to walk through its streets. The white-washed houses looked "like stars in a sky of olive groves." Al-Mu'tamid built numerous villas with formal gardens. As the 'world was too much' with the rulers of Seville, it is doubtful if they raised any great mosques, but the number of palaces ran into dozens His cultural pastimes carried him from palace to palace. The people of Seville led a joyous life. The islands in the river were pleasure spots for holiday makers, wine flowed at gondola parties, and gatherings of court poets, musicians and dancers.

Such was the social and political scenario of Muslim Spain after the collapse of the kingdom of Cordova. Let us now see what was happening in Christian Spain. In 1035 Fernando ascended the throne of Castile which was now an independent state. By his marriage with a princess of Leon, he became king of both Castile and Leon. The long wars between these two warring states came to an end— at least during the his reign. The Christians were now united and powerful, and in a better position to avenge the humiliating defeats they had so long suffered. They had already recovered the many forts they had ceded to 'Abd ar Rahman Al-Nasir. The balance of power went into their hands. The Muslim states consumed their energies in mutual' warfare and hedonistic pursuits. Their fragmented economy rendered them incapable to mobilise their resources. They also lacked' the war-like spirit and religious enthusiasm of the Christians[8]. The 11th century in Spain "presents a unique spectacle of the struggle between the Christian North and the Muslim South; the struggle of rude, primitive mountaineers of mixed, predominately Indo—European stock, against the highly cultured dwellers of fertile vegas, predominately *Semitic-Hamitic* stock. So long as the latter were united under an-Nasir and later under al-Mansur, they were able constantly to terrorise the North, by summer and winter razzias against them. When these expeditions stopped after the death of al-Muzaffar ibn Abi 'Amir in 1008, and violent internecine struggles destroyed the unity of the Cordovan Caliphate, situation was reversed[9]." Fernando took advantage of the disunity among the Andalusian princes and he opened a new chapter of Christian expansion towards the South. He had already grabbed some territory of the kingdom of Badajoz in 1054. Ten years after (1064) he occupied Coimbra, and all Muslim settlements between the Douro and the Mondego were ruthlessly liquidated by him. He withheld his sword only when al-Muzaffar agreed to pay a tribute. By a series of vigorous campaigns he brought all the Andalusian petty rulers to their knees. His arms were successful everywhere. He attacked the kingdom of Saragossa and annexed several forts. He moved into the kingdom of Toledo, and forced al-Ma'mun to acknowledge his suzerainty. Alone and isolated al-Ma'mun agreed, and to purchase future safety he parted with enormous quantities of gold and jewellery. Even al-Mu'tadid of Seville was not safe from the surging tide of his expansionist adventures. Al-Mutadid fought his co-religionists like a lion and gloated over the skulls of his fallen foes. A heartless tyrant, he eliminated his enemies with gruesome reality. Those who left Seville to escape his wrath were killed by his agents. A muezzin who left for Toledo was slain there, and a blind scholar who settled at Mecca was poisoned by men of his secret service. He killed the Berber chiefs of Ronda, Moron, and Jerez by suffocation in the tepidarium of his baths. But this man had not the courage to challenge Fernando when he irrupted into his territory with fire and sword. He visited his camp, offered rich presents and begged him to spare his kingdom. The wheel of fortune had taken a full round. Only half a century after al-Mansur's death, the Muslim states became tributaries of the northern kingdoms. How vulnerable was Muslim Spain during the middle of the 11th century is seen from the heart-rending cruelties the Muslims had to face when the border town of Barbastro in the north-east fell into the hands of the Christians. This town largely Muslim in population, was situated at the foot of the Pyrenees. It was stormed by the Normans crusaders under the command of Gilaume de Montreuil, a standard-bearer of Pope Alexander II. The historian ibn Hayyan has given harrowing details running into pages, of the barbarities of the Normans. They committed every conceivable crime-torture, indiscrimination massacre, and rape of Muslim women before their husbands and parents[10]. A large number of helpless Muslims were taken captive, and transported to France. But the greatest tragedy was yet to come.

When the Umayyads fell, a military commander named Ismail al-Zhafir ibn Dhinnun opted for independence sometime in 1035-36, and founded the kingdom of Toledo. It was a sizeable kingdom. It was bordered in the east by the Slav kingdom of Valencia and Denia; on the west its boundries touched the kingdom of Badajoz; on the north it was flanked by the kingdom of Saragossa, and in the south lay the kingdom of Seville. In addition to Toledo which was the capital of the kingdom, it included the towns of Madrid, Hucet, Cuenca and Uncles, and Calatrava. This region had always been in a state of unrest. We have seen that the Umayyad rulers had to take military action to crush repeated revolts often with great severity. Most of the inhabitant were arabised Christians called the "Mozarabes." They were a proud people of Gothic/Roman ancestry. Inspite of the tolerant Muslim rule, the mozarabes looked to the north for deliverance.

After al-Zhafir died, the kingdom was inherited by his son Yahya, who, according to the usage of the time, took the title of *al-Ma'mun*. His long reign (1044-75) was a period of unprecedented prosperity. The kingdom was celebrated for its wheat which was of such a high quality that it remained unspoiled for years. It was also famous for in-lay work in metals, specially swords with ornamental hilts—an industry that has

endured to this day. The mosque schools were in no way inferior
to similar institutions in other parts of Muslim Spain. Poetry
did not flourish here, but the kingdom boasted of many
intellectuals in the 11th century. Toledo, and to a lesser degree
Madrid, were centres of astronomic and mathematical studies.
Like his other contemporaries, al-Ma'mun was a cultivated
tyrant. He was immensely rich, and he beautified his kingdom
with botanical gardens and palaces. Ibn Bassal, a great botanist
of his time, laid out gardens for him. The Alcazar at Toledo
where al-Ma'mun lived was a marvel of engineering and
architecture. One of its wonders was a pavilion in the middle
of a lake. By means of hydraulic devices, the water from the
lake was carried to the top of the pavilion from where it fell
down in sheets. At night, when al-Ma'mun relaxed in the light
of tapers, the sight of shimmering water was enchanting to see.
Once, a most sumptuous function was held in the Alcazar. The
occasion was the circumcision ceremony of his grandson.
Ma'mun squandered vast sums on the celebrations which became
proverbial for elegance and luxury both in Spain and in the
East under the name "the fêtes of Dhu 1-nun (*idhar dhu 1-
nuni*)". The floors was covered with Persian carpets. The ornate
doors were hung with silk curtains embroidered with inscriptions
in the praise of the prince. The garden was decorated with
vases sculptured with birds and bushes. The reception was held
in a hall with frescoes along the walls depicting pastoral scenes.
The guests were served with the choicest cuisine (which included
meat of birds and vension) on plates of silver. Perfumes from
crystal containers were sprinkled on the invitees. Many servants
in flowing robes fanned the guests. Aromatic woods were burnt
in censors of precious metals, while wine (nabiḍ) and orchestral
music added warmth to the royal banquet[11]. All this magnificence
was like the glow preceding the sunset!

Fernando died in Dec. 1065, and the Christian kingdom was torn to pieces, as it happened everywhere in the Middle Ages, when a king died after dividing his realm among his children. He was survived by three sons and a daughter. Alfonso was his favourite son and he was assigned Leon; Sancho, the eldest was given Castile; Garcia received north Portugal, and Zamora went to the share of his daughter Urracha. A war broke out among the brothers. Alfonso was imprisoned, but through the intercession of his sister, he was exiled to the court of al-Ma'mun, her father's vassal. Ma'mun received him with warm hospitality. He was housed in a mansion near the river Tagus. He stayed at Toledo for full nine months. When his brother died in Oct., 1072, he returned to Leon. Ma'mun escorted him to the frontier and the two departed with promises of friendship and mutual esteem. Alfonso occupied the throne of his father. During his exile, he had seen the wealth that flowed in kingdom of his guest and he resolved to annex the kingdom. He had quietly familiarised himself with the topography of the city of Toledo and obtained many secrets by eavesdropping on the courtiers[12]. On his return, Alfonso the 6th in the line of the dynasty, directed a relentless policy of pushing his frontiers to the south, forgetting the hospitality he had enjoyed as a guest of Al-Ma'mun. Under him, the movement to liberate Spain from the Muslims (which came to be known as Reconquesta) gathered a further momentum because he excelled his father both in astuteness and the crusading spirit.

Al-Ma'mun died in June, 1075 at a ripe old age. The new ruler, his grandson Qadir was an effeminate child of the seraglio. He was incapable to rule in that age of violence, perfidy, and survival of the fittest. Hardly two months after his accession he had to face many problems, and when he instigated the assassination of ibn Hadid, his grandfather's trusted minister, his subjects became hostile. Qadir appealed to Alfonso for help without knowing that he was stepping into the spider's web. Alfonso demanded forts and gold in return. Qadir met his every demand, but when his sources dwindled, he taxed his subjects. They resented his taking help from the Christian king. They rose against him, drove him out and invited Omar al-Mutawakkil of Badajoz. With the help of Alfonso, Qadir expelled Omar, and returned to his dominion. Meanwhile, conditions were changing fast in the city. Qadir had totally lost the sympathies of his subjects, while the local Christians—the mozarabes were in secret communication with Alfonso. Qadir's days were numbered as he was no match to Alfonso who was a brilliant soldier as well as a clever politician. He struck a baragain with the stupid Qadir by which he undertook to place him on the throne of Valencia if he handed over the city of Toledo. Alfonso besieged the city under the pretence of protecting Qadir. The city was starved into submission. No Muslim ruler came to the aid of Toledo. On May 6, 1085, Alfonso entered into the city through the gate of Visagra which stands to this day as a national monument of Spain. Barely two months after (July, 1085) when he was away, the Christians assembled at the Jama Masjid of the city for converting it into a church. At that time the Muslims were busy in their liturgical prayer which was being conducted by a faqih named al-Maghami. After the prayer was over, he asked his disciples to recite the Quran. When the recitation was over, he prostrated, raised his head, and left the mosque in tears. The loss of Toledo gave rise to gloomy premonitions of the shape of things in store for the Muslims. The Hispano-Arabic Muse poured her anguish in many elegies— some of the finest in Arabic literature. The Muslims were seized with death-wish. The poet Abū Muhammad al-Assal administered a warning to the Muslims:

Ride on your horses, men of Andalus,
to live here is sheer folly.
Clothes get torn at the sides,
but our country has been ripped at the centre.

The poet was right. Toledo was almost in the centre of the Spanish peninsula, and its loss opened the flood-gates of further invasions from the north. After the collapse of the Umayyad kingdom of Cordova, the fall of Taledo was the most ominous and catatrophic event in the history of Spanish Muslims. This was the first milestone of their gradual decline.

Notes

1. This natural hatred (an-nafara at-tabiyya) is articulated by the poet As-Sumaisir of Elvira in the following lines:-

   I saw Adam in a dream and said to him
   "Father of mankind, they say that the
   Berbers are your descendants". He replied
   "If that were true, Eve would stand divorced."

2. The poet ibn Sharaf (d. 1067) mocked at the high-sounding titles of these petty rulers in the following famous couplet:

   What makes me feel humiliated in Spain
   is the use of the titles: Mu'tasim and Mu'tadid.
   These princely titles are not suitable to them.
   They are like a cat that by blowing itself up
   imitated a lion.

3. Nichalson: Literary History of the Arabs, p 414.

4. Ency. of Islam (New Edition) article on al-Andalus.

5. Abū Ahmad al-Munfatil, a local poet who was obliged to the rabbi Samuel has left a qasida on his Jewish patron. It is composed in a highly hyperbolic and blasphemous language. "There is none like him (says the poet) either in the East of the west." He is superior to al men as gold is to copper. Munfatil advised the Muslims that they should kiss his hands instead of the Kaba. He ended by adding that he was at heart a Jew, and practised his faith in secrecy.

   Ibn Bassam, vol, II p. 267.

6.   Peries: p. 274.

7.   Bernhard and Ellen whishaw: p 238.

8.   Dozy: p. 654

9.   Nykl: p. 69

10. Al-Maqqaris/Gayangos: vol II, pp. 265-267. Dozy: p. 658.

11. Provençal: Islam d' Occident pp. 119-120.

12. Ibid. pp. 117-118.

Chapter 13

Muslim Spain under the Rulers of Northwest Africa

After the annexation of Toledo, Alfonso became hold and arrogant He considered himself invincible. He held the Muslim princes in utter contempt. When Hasam ad-Dawla, a prince of Albarracin visited him with presents to court his favour, he found him playing with his pet monkey. He told the Muslim prince scornfully, "Take away this monkey for thy gifts[1]." There is no doubt that Alfonso was the most powerful ruler of Spain having undisputed sway over Leon and Castile, while all the Muslim princes were his vassals. Their courts were full of his spies. Most of the Muslim princes had Christians in their armies, and it was not unlikely that some of them kept him informed of what went on in the territory held by them. A greedy Alfonso 'crushed the treasuries of the Muslim kinglets as in a wine-press till they poured forth gold[2]. His soldiers and mercenaries were active everywhere. In Valencia, he had planted a colony of his soldiers under Alvare Fanez with the object of protecting Qadir from the Banu Hud rulers of Saragossa. These soldiers were a gang of criminals who committed every crime for money.

They raped women, murdered children, and would not hesitate to sell a Muslim prisoner for a jar of wine, a loaf of bread and a pound of fish. "If a prisoner was unable to pay ransom, they would cut out his tongue, put out his eyes, and cause him to be torn to pieces by mastiffs." says Dozy. At Aledo, which was an strategic fortress, he had installed Gracia Ximenez with a small cavalry which posed a constant threat to Almeria. When for some reason, a l-Mu'tamid failed to remit the annual tribute on time, Alfonso sent a delegation of armed men headed by a Jew in 1082. The envoy used threatening language, and behaved so insolently that al-Mu'tamid ordered his execution. His action angered Alfonso, and he vowed by the Trinity that he would lay waste the infidel's dominion with warriors as numerous as the hair on his head[3]. He kept his words, and in a swift campaign he ransacked the kingdom of Seville. As if this was not enough, he asked al-Mu'tamid to evacuate one of his palaces near Madinat al-Zahra for his wife who was pregnant, and needed the healthy climate of Seville. He further demanded that arrangements be made for the delivery to take place in the mosque of Cordova[4]. Al-Mutamid was at the end of his tether. This was the darkest hour in the history of Muslim Spain since the conquest. By fighting among themselves, the Muslims had opened the Pandora's box, and their only hope lay in getting foreign help. In this desperate situation, al-Mu'tamid thought of calling to his aid the 'murabitun' ruler of northwest Africa. He discussed the matter with his son and other advisors. They expressed apprehension that the 'murabitun' ruler might try to occupy Spain. But Mu'tamid replied that he did not want to be cursed by future generations for handing over Spain to the Christians. He also told them that if the worst came to the worst, be would rather be a camel-driver in Africa than a swineherd in Castile. The die was cast. Al-Mu'tamid wrote to the rulers of Badajoz, Granada and Malaga. All of them agreed to the proposal. The qadis of these kingdoms assembled at Seville for further discussions, and it was decided to send a delegation under the leadership of the minister ibn Zaidun to seek the support of Yusuf Tashufin, the ruler of a vast Berber empire in the northwest Africa.

While the petty princelings of Muslim Spain were fighting among themselves, a great Berber empire had already arisen on the African continent. The Berbers who controlled the northwest Africa were known as the *'Murabitun.'* The European historians call them 'Almoravids'. The word is derived from the Arabic noun*'al-Murabit'* which means a pious man who lived in a *ribat* or monastery. He dedicated himself to prayer and austerity, and kept himself ready to take part as a volunteer (mujahid) in a holy war for the defence of faith. They were also known as the *'multhathamun'* or the people of the veil,' because most of them covered the lower part of their faces, like the Tourages of today, as a protection from the hot winds of the Sahara. The emergence of the murabitun/Almoravids is rooted in a religious movement which started in the middle of the 11th century. Initially reformist and missionary, the movement acquired a definite political colour, and ultimately resulted in the installation of a dynasty— a usual feature of Muslim polity of those days.

The movement began in a modest way. In the early part of the 11th century, a Berber chief of the Sanhaja tribe named Yahya bin Ibrahim who was returning from a pilgrimage to Mecca, broke his journey at Qayrawan. He was in search of a teacher who could accompany him for missionary work among the Berbers of the western Sahara who were still pagans. He found his man in Abdullah bin Yasin a professor theology and law, known for his learning and piety. The two arrived in the land of the Berbers. Soon after his arrival ibn Yasin threw himself ardently in his task. He built a monastery (ribat) on an island in the river Senegal. His most devoted disciples were the two Berber brothers— Yahya and Abū Bakr who belonged to the influential Lamtunah tribe. Many Berbers who were still pagan, and those who had only a passing acquaintance with Islamic teachings, came under the spell of the new teachers. The 'Murabitun' emerged as upholders of a simple and austere Islam. There was no place for music, no value of poetry, and no room for philosophy in their mental make-up. When Yahya died in 1059, his brother continued his mission. He gave the movement its political direction and destiny. He united the Berbers in one solid brotherhood. From the western Sahara they fanned out all over the Atlas region. Abū Bakr married Zainab the beautiful and intelligent widow of a local chief. This marriage added to his prestige. Abū Bakr died in 1088, but before his death he handed over the command of the movement to his cousin Yusuf Tashufin. He returned to the western Sahara after divorcing Zainab who found a new husband in Tashufin. He is one of the greatest figures in the history of north Africa. Yusuf Tashufin is the real founder of the first ever Berber empire in history stretching from Ghana to the coast of north Africa. Although rough in exterior, he was gentle in manners, and generous to all. He lived a simple and virtuous life. He was a fearless warrior, and was always ready to serve the cause of the Muslims. The delegation of Spanish Muslims led by ibn Zaidun met Yusuf Tashufin at the capital city of Marrakesh. They gave him an account of the political situation in Spain, appealed for his intervention for the sake of his Muslim brothers. Yusuf consulted his lawyers and theologians. They authorized him by a religious decree (fatwa) to give military help to the Spanish Muslims in their hour of need.

Yusuf bin Tashufin sailed for Spain with an army of 20 thousand soldiers— the pick of his fighting force. A hundred boats were pressed into service for transporting the army. Tashufin landed at Algeciras on June 30, 1086. The Spanish Muslims gave him a tumultuous welcome. The small town of Algeciras became instinct with life. Several markets and stores were set up to meet the requirement of the quests. After a brief halt, Tashufin left for Seville. Al-Mu'tamid rode out to receive him with a body of hundred cavaliers and state dignitaries. Very soon brisk preparations were made to give battle to Alfonso. 'Abdullah of Granada, and Temim of Malaga Joined with their contingents. 'Mu'tasim of Almeria despatched his cavalry but he could not appear in person because of the siege of Aledo. After a week of preparations, the combined forces marched towards Badajoz. At this time Alfonso was sitting with his army at the gates of Saragossa. When the news of Tashufin's landing reached him, he wound up the siege, and took the direction of Badajoz. The two armies were encamped in front of each other in Oct. 1086 at a place called Zallaqa by the Muslim historian, and Sarajas by the Christians. It is situated beyond the river Guadiana at a distance of about 20 km north of Badajoz. As Yusuf was going to fight a jihad, he sent a message to Alfonso offering him three alternatives—Islam, tribute or war. Alfonso sent him an indignant rejoinder in which he stated that the Muslim rulers were his vassals and that he was fully prepared to punish his enemies. Yusuf, a man of few words, wrote back— 'what will happen thou shalt see[5]'. Alfonso was a clever fighter. He intended to launched a surprise attack, and in order to keep the Muslims in a state of suspense, he opened talks for fixing a day for the battle. He sent a message saying that Friday was a Muslim Sabbath, and Sunday being a holiday for the Christians, he suggested Saturday for the fighting.

Yusuf agreed to the proposal. Al-Mu'tamid suspected that Alfonso was playing a *ruse de guerre*, and he was right, because soon his scouts brought the news that the enemy was getting ready to attack. Alfonso stormed the vanguard led by al-Mu'tamid. The Sevillian ruler fought gallantly, but soon his defence began to collapse. When Alfonso penetrated deeper, Tashufin threw in his negro and Berber squadrons. The thunderous sound of drums (tabl), and the sight of camels frightened the cavalry of Alfonso, and it broke into confusion. At that very time a large part of Tashufin's army wheeled around, and attacked Alfonso in the rear. His proud army was sandwiched and in a fearful carnage, he lost the flower of his fighting force. A negro soldier spotted him, and dealt such a powerful sword thrust that the weapon cut through the horse and reached his thing. Alfonso ran away leaving heaps of the dead and the wounded. The news of the victory was conveyed by al-Mu'tamid to his son Rashid by trained pigeons[6]. Yusuf intended to carry the war into Alfonso's territory but an urgent business called him to Africa. Before he left Spain, he posted an army of three thousand soldiers under the command of al-Mu'tamid.

After Tashufin left, Alfonso resumed his military operations in the southeast. Although he wound up his operations in Saragossa and Valencia, he began to harass other Muslim states. The ruler of Murcia, ibn Rashiq was incapable of self-defence and it seemed that Murcia would fall in the lap of Alfonso like a ripe apple. Al-Mutamid ordered his son Razi to attack the Christian, but he pretended illness. He gave the command to another son, but he was beaten back. It was clear to all that the Spanish Muslims were utterly demoralised by indolence and disunity. Once again theologians and notables from Murcia, flocked to the court of Tashufin and made fervent appeals for his help. He landed again in Spain in 1088. According to an agreed programme it was decided to liquidate the siege of Aledo. The princes of Almeria, Murcia, and Granada joined with their forces. Alfonso vacated the town after setting it on fire. During the second visit Tashufin got disgusted at the malicious back-biting and mutual jealousies of the Andalusian princes and left in despair. He visited Spain again after a year when he learnt, to his amazement, that 'Abdullah of Granada had entered into an alliance with Alfonso. 'Abdullah had already incurred the displeasure of his subjects. On the orders of Tashufin he was arrested and packed off to Morocco. Yusuf asked the other princes to join him in the war against the Christian but he found no response from them.

During his earlier visits Tashufin had seen the luxurious life led by the Andalusian princes. A puritan to the heart, he put on clothes of coarse cotton and lived on frugal meal. He felt hurt at their wasteful expenditure on magnificent palaces, their sartorial splendour, and the armies of liveried slaves. He had no doubt heard about their musical soireés, their ambrosial cuisine, and *champêtres* in pleasure gardens in the company of dancers, licentious poets, and freethinkers. At first he had no intention to annex Spain to his empire. After the battle of Zallaqa he had refused to take his share of the booty on the ground that he had come to help the princes for the sake of Islamic brotherhood. By and by, he came to realise that the Andalusian princes were a worthless lot. He used to say, "I came to Spain to deliver the land from the Christians, but I have found that the Andalusian princes are indolent, cowardly, with no war-like spirit. They fight among themselves, and are fond of drinking, singing girls, and amusements[7]." His convictions were confirmed by the theologians. They told him that the princes had no moral legitimacy to rule, and it was necessary to remove them. They jointly issued a decree authorizing Tashufin to dismiss all the princes. The decree (fatwa) specified the names of the princes. Even Rumaykiyya was accused of pushing her husband into a life of indolence. Armed with this authority, Tashufin orders his valiant general — Ibn Abū Bakr to start operations to dethrone all the Andalusian princes, and replace them by governors from the armed personnel. By a series of campaigns all the muluk at-tawā'if were removed during the course of next few years. In March 1090 Cordova was occupied. Ma'mun, the son of al-Mutamid died fighting. In May, Carmona was taken. The greatest resistance came from al-Mutamid himself. Proud of his Arab lineage, he had been aspiring to become master of the whole of south Spain. His dream seemed to go up in smoke, but he would not yield without striking a blow. He begged Alfonso for help forgetting that only yesterday he had fought him. The Christian ruler responded quickly, and sent a force under Alvar Fanez but it was intercepted on the way. In the meantime, the Almoravids burnt the fleet, and surrounded Seville on all sides. Al-Mu'tamid fought gallantly, and his son Rashid died fighting. The Almoravids reached the walls of the palace. For a moment Al-Mu'tamid thought of ending his life, but he desisted from committing suicide. On 9 Sep. 1091, he laid down arms on the advice of his family and other relations. Al-Mutamid was taken into custody by the Almoravid commander, and he was transported to Tangier along with his family[8]. When the boat carrying him left the quay, there were loud lamentations, and women tore their veils. The poet ibn Labbana (d. at Majorca in 1113) who was an admirer of al-Mu'tamid wrote a memorable poem. The capture of Seville hastened the reduction of the Almeria, Murcia and Denia. In 1094 the southwest was cleared of the Banu al-Aftas, and the fortified cities of Santarem, Badajoz, Evora and Lisbon fell into the hands of the Almoravid. Only Valencia and Saragossa remained unconquered for some years.

The coastal territory of Valencia (which comprised the towns of Orihuela, Alpuente, Cabra etc) faced many vicissitudes as it was mercilessly exploited by Alfonso, the princes of Saragossa, and the Cid campeador. Founded by two Slavs— Mubarak and Muzaffar (who wore big ear rings), the kingdom of Valencia passed into the hands of 'Abd al-Aziz, a son of Sanchol. He styled himself as al-Mansur although he was without even an iota of his grandfather's capabilities. He ruled from 1001-1065. Thereafter it became a protectorate of al-Ma'mun of Toledo. After his death, his worthless son Qadir was placed there by Alfonso in exchange for Toledo. The presence of Christian troops for which a daily subsidy was paid by Qadir made him unpopular, and his subjects rose against him under the leadership of qaḍi ibn Jahhaf. Qadir was assassinated and his body was paraded through streets. The qaḍi set up a republic which lasted for three years from 1092-1094. In 1094, the famous Christian warrior— the Cid appeared at the gates of Valencia like a thunderbolt.

Born, Rodrigo Riaz (in 1045) of a noble family from Burgos, he is knows as Cid in all history. A man of prodigious size and strength, a fearless warrior, the Cid is regarded by the Spaniards as the very epitome of valiance and chivalry. Many legends, ballads and epics celebrate his heroism. The English poet Robert Southey, and the French dramatist Corneille took him as a subject for their literary works. However, the historical Cid was a different person. Except for his family life, he was in no way different from the contemporary Muslim princes. He was greedy and his love for Mammon turned him into a professional condottiere. He would sell his sword to the highest bidder, like

some modern journalists who for the sake of money employ
their pen to espouse any cause. His one ambition was to own
a kingdom. He had not the ghost of a chance in the Christian
territory because of his hostile relations which Alfonso, but
Muslim Spain held out a promise because of widespread
instability[9]. He entered into the service of Maqtadir the ruler of
Saragossa as commander of his Christian mercenaries. Muqtadir
died in 1081 after dividing his kingdom between his two sons.
He gave Saragossa to M'tamin and Denia, Tortosa and Lerida
to al-Mundhir. Soon the two brothers began to fight. Al-Mundhir
sought the help of Sancho Ramirez the king of Aragon and
Count Ramon Berenguer of Barcelona. The Cid fought on the
side of Mu'tamin. He defeated them near the walls of Lerida,
and returned to Saragossa with booty. Mu'tamin loaded him
with gifts. From that day he was addressed as 'Ya Saiyadi' by
his Muslim patrons and collaborators. (The title 'Cid' in Spanish
comes from the Arabic word *'Saiyadi'* meaning a leader). The
Cid was hand in glove with Mu'tamin who wanted Valencia
for himself. He gave his tacit approval to the Cid to invade
Valencia with his Christian soldiers under his command. It was
agreed that the Cid would keep the booty to himself, and hand
over Valencia to Mu'tamin. This never happened because the
Cid was a traitor to his friends and foes alike. He erupted into
Valencia. After carrying out extensive pillage and arson in the
suburbs, he besieged the city in July 1093[10]. Although the
Almoravids had control of Murcia they were not in position to
come to the relief of Valencia. During the siege which lasted
for about two years, the citizens had to face untold suffering.
The Valencian historian ibn Alqama (1036-1116) has left an
eye-witness account of the dire suffering of the people. The Cid
cut off all roads, and the supply of food became limited. The
price of wheat rose by leaps and bounds, and when the stocks

ran out the people dropped dead in the streets from starvation. Many subsisted on hides and skins of animals, barks of trees and dead bodies. At last negotiation were opened and on June 15, 1094, the Cid marched into the city[11]. He siezed the jewellery of Qadir from ibn Jahhaf. The supporters of the qadi were cast into prison and tortured to death. Many of them along with ibn Jahaf were burnt alive. The qadi showed remarkable perseverance when he was placed in a pit full of wood. As the flames rose to his face the qadi invoked the name of Allah and perished in the fire. The Cid summoned the citizens and consoled them with the promise that he would rule with justice. He told them that he was not like Muslim princes who passed their time in the company of drankards and dancing girls. He told them that he had allotted two days in a week (Monday and Thursday) to hear public grievances. But his subsequent conduct belied his professions. The main mosque was converted into a cathedral in the name of St. Mary[12]. The Cid's ambition to become the ruler of an independent kingdom was at last fulfilled, thanks to disunity among the Muslims. Half arabised, he set up his court imitating the life-style of his Muslim neighbours. He brought his wife Ximena and his children to Valencia. He dreamt of conquering the whole of Muslim Spain. He was often heard saying. "One Roderick lost the kingdom and another will reconquer.[13]" But his hopes were dashed to the ground. He suffered defeat after defeat at the hands of the Almoravids who had consolidated their position, and were in a better position to throw him out. In one of the encounters he lost his son. This tragedy told upon his health, and he died on July 10, 1099. His wife held out for two years. In the meantime, the Almoravids were closing in from all directions. She appealed to Alfonso for help, but she received no response. The situation became critical and she abandoned Valencia after the garrison under her had committed largescale arson. She took with her the mortal remains of her husband and settled in Castile. The Almoravid general Mazdali occupied Valencia in April May 1102[14].

Yusuf Tashufin died in 1106. His son Ali succeeded to the empire which was so vast that thousands of mosques in the maghrib and Spain echoed with his name in the Friday sermons. He confided the government of Spain to his brother Tamim. His first task was to stem the tide of continuous eruptions from the north. He won a singular victory at Uncle (1108) by defeating the combined forces of Alfonso, the ruler of Aragon and Count Ramon of Barcelona. Two years after (may 31, 1110), the Almoravids annexed Saragossa and the Banu Hud rule came to an end. Ibn e Tifelwit was placed as governor. By the conquest of the Balrearic islands, they became master of the whole of Spanish territory except the district of Toledo. The Muslims still held nearly half of the Iberian peninsula, but their hold was weak. The empire was too big, and Muslim Spain was tied to the Almoravid north Africa only by a fragile thread.

Muslim Spain was no more an independent state, It was a province of the Berber empire directly ruled from Marrakesh through a governor who had his headquarters at Cordova and later at Seville. The Almoravids gave a uniform administrations to the province by removing the petty rulers who could hardly be called patriotic. The Almoravids were fresh from the Sahara, but they found a ready-made civil machinery. They employed the officials of the dethroned rulers. Some of the most brilliant bureaucrats (Abu1-Qasim ibn Jadd, ibn Qabturna, ibn 'Abdun, and ibn Khisal) left Spain to take up service at Marrakesh. They advised him on matters relating to Spain. Fiercely orthodox in religious matters, the Almoravids were against all innovations in religious beliefs. On the advice of qadi ibn Hamdin, the *Ihya ulum al-din* of imam Ghazali was banned, and its copies were committed to flames. The Christians came under a cloud, and the possibility of many of them leaving the Muslim territory for safer palaces in the northern states cannot be ruled out . The conversion of mosques by Alfonso VI and the Cid, invited reprisals against the Christian places of worship. They were also suspected of treasonable activities. In a fit of popular fury the Muslim dismantled a church at Granada. The Jews of Lucena were required to pay additional taxes. But there was no systematic persecution of the non-Muslims, and their rights were respected. We may cite one interesting incidence in this context. In May 1128, Ali dismissed Abū Umar Inalu, a grandson of Tashufin on charges made against him by the mozarebes i.e. the non-Muslims of Granada. The charges were established by a court of law. The culprit Inalu was sentenced to imprisonment, and he was also forced to make adequate compensations[15]. The Almoravids employed them on civil jobs, and did not even hesitate to recruit them in the army. One of their generals was the famous Catalan Reverter whom the Arabs called 'Reuburtair'. The taxes levied on the Spanish subjects were less than under the previous regime of the petty princelings. The presence of Almoravid troops on the frontier gave the Spanish Muslims a sense of security. Muslim Spain began to recoup, and her economy began to flourish. Trade and commerce prospered, and the people returned to *joie de viver* of olden days. Literary activities continued unabated though music was considered a forbidden pleasure. A new prosodical poetry in the form of muwashshah — the songs of love, wine and spring were composed by Andalusian poets under the very nose of orthodoxy. Ibn Khafaja and ibn Zaqqaq the poets of nature, ibn Baqi and ibn Quzman composers of zijals, Abū Salt Omayya the versatile scholar of history, philosophy, medicine and musicology, and the philosopher ibn Bajja lived in the Almoravid period. The Almoravid period also saw the compilation of the monumental anthology of prose and poetry by the famous Portuguese, ibn Bassam. If the Almoravids gave peace to Muslim Spain they received a lot in return. They found a complete civilization in Spain, and they came under its spell. They imported artisans, carftmen, architects, gardeners and botanists to beautify the cities of their empire particularly Marrakesh and Fez. Even Andalusian brides reached north Africa. In due course north African cities of the maghrib blossomed into centres of Hispano-Muslim culture. From the 11th century Andalusian culture began to permeate north African cities, and this process continued in the succeeding centuries. Several features of Hispano-Muslim inspiration influenced Almoravid architecture. The mosques built during this period at Algiers and Tilimsan were only replicas of the great mosque of Cordova, both in design and decoration.

After a rule of some sixty years in Africa and Spain the Almoravid dynasty fell with catastrophic suddeness. In the reign of Ali ibn Tashufin, the murabitun/Almoravid empire began to show signs of their coming collapse. Ali was a deeply religions man. He passed his days and nights in fasting and prayers, and left the government tin the hands of his wife Qamar. She, along with other Berber ladies of influential families interfered in administrative matters, and the top posts were filled at their recommendations. The Berber women have always been fond of freedom. Even today they divorce their husbands as quickly as the marry. There was none to curb their freedom. The social conditions became so degenerate that according to al-Marrakeshi, the females of Lamtuna and Mussufa tribes patronised highwaymen, wine merchants and dregs of society. It is alleged that the sudden exposure of the nomadic Berbers to wealth and the soft Andalusian culture corrupted their morals and they lost both their piety and their war-like spirit. These allegations seem to be rather exaggerated because al-Marrakeshi wrote his history under the succeeding dynasty. The prime reason was political. The tribes who resented the domination of the Sinhaja clan under the murabitun/Almoravids, united to overthrown them. This rivalry took a religious shape, and expressed itself in the rise of the *Muwahhids*, or the Almohads.

The *Muwahhid* dynasty also came into existence as the result of a theological and reformist movement. We perceive an almost identical pattern in the rise and progress of the two movements which shook the northwest of Africa in the 11th and 12 centuries. Both the movements were inspired by religious enthusiasts. The founder of each movement passed on the leadership to his most trusted disciple, who in turn gave it a political direction by installing a dynastic rule. The *Muwahhid* movement was started by Muhammad ibn Tumart, a Berber of the Hargha tribe. A man of humble origin, he was born about 1081 among the cave-dwelling Berbers in an obscure village in the Atlas region. In his youth he went to Cordova for studies. After a year, he left for Almeria from where he boarded a vessel bound for Alexandria. It was there that he met the famous Spanish scholar Abū Bakr of Tortosa who exercised much influence on his mental and spiritual outlook. After his pilgrimage to the Holy cities of Mecca and Madina, he journeyed to Baghdad to study hadith, theology and philosophy. He was enrolled at the Nizamiyya university. After completing his studies, and bubbling with new ideas, he returned to northwest Africa, and settled at the small village of Mallala near Bougie where he attracted many disciples by his piety and moving oratory. He found his greatest supporters among the Masmuda tribe. It is not possible to trace the whole career of this remarkable man who is still revered from Tangier to Timbakto. The word *'Muwahhid'* which means a unitarian, is a pointer to the teachings of ibn Tumart. There in nothing original in his teachings because most of what he propounded was already in the air. He was against a literal interpretation of the Quran. This view according to him led to anthropomorphic conception of God which is basically against the teachings of Islam. He denounced taqlid, and ruled out speculative analogy (qiyas'aqli) , and impressed upon his followers to derive inspiration from the consensus of the companions of the Prophet (*ijma al-sahaba*) in all legal matters. He advocated a return to early century Islam of pure monotheism, austere living, honesty in all walks of life, and strict spiritual discipline. As the bedrock of his teachings was belief in the Unity of God (tawhid), his supporters came to known as *'al-Muwahhidun.'* The European historians call them 'Almohads'. In due course, ibn Tumart declared that he was the Infailable Imam (*imam al-Ma'sum*) who was ordered by God to remove the Almoravids. He whipped up a hysteria against the Almoravids whom he denounced as heretics. His followers increased by a geometric progression when the Berbers opposed to the Sinhajas' domination joined his movement. During the course of his activities, he came across a youngman named 'Abd al-Mu'min who was planning to go to the East for higher studies. He belonged to the powerful Zanata clan. Ibn Tumart prevailed upon him, by his hypnotic eloquence, to cancel his programme, and to join him in his missionary work. "The learning for which you are gong to the East (said ibn Tumart to him), you will find in the West." This historic meeting between ibn Tumart and Abd al-Mu'min took place in the year 1117 near Mallala. 'Abd al-Mu'min became his disciple. As his follower increased, the ruling dynasty was alarmed, and action was taken to suppress it. Ibn Tumart died in 1130 after having nominated 'Abd al-Mu'min as his successor. Under him the Muwahhidins, took to guerilla warfare to remove the Almoravids. Thousands of the supporters of the Almoravids perished in the wars with he Almohads.

The Almoravid ruler Ali (1106-1143) fond himself in a dangerous situation. At home the dynasty was under a tightening siege, while in Spain its position was threatened by grave perils from the Christian states of Leon and Castile. He recalled his son Tashufin ibn Ali from Spain to help him in containing the activities of the Almohads. So long as he lived he was able to hold them in check. After his death Tashufin was not able to protect the dynasty from the fast gliding avalanche of sabotage. There was no end to their defeats and slaughter. They lost their best fighters and generals—including the loyal Reverter. One by one they lost their stronholds—Tilimsan, Ceuta, Tangier, Fez, Aghmat, and Marrakesh. The last Almoravid ruler Ishaq bin Ali was executed inspite of his tearful appeals for mercy. By 1150, the Almoravid dynasty was a thing of the past. 'Abd al-Mu'min adopted the exalted title of *'amir al-Mu'minin'* after wading through a pool of blood. Such is the ethics of struggle for political power. The history of these two movements is a classic example of exploitation of religion for political ends.

After the recall of Tashufin ibn Ali, Spain, once again, relapsed into fragmentation as a result of Andalusian nationalism which had been simmering for sometime. The Almoravid officials were chased out of Spain. Once again, influential chiefs, and adventures grabbed whatever territory they could by military coups. Valencia and Murcia were occupied by ibn Sa'd Mardanish'; ibn Hamdin, the qadi of Cordova proclaimed himself 'amir al-Muslimin' with the help of the king of Castile, while other chiefs held Malaga, Granada, Cadiz, and the Balrearic islands. The south of Portugal was shared by ibn Wazir, and ibn Qasi, and their minions. The latter was a notorious charlatan who concealed his political ambitions by claiming that he was a disciple of the famous sufi 'Arif of Almeria. From his headquarters at Mertola he declared that he was the Promised Messiah. In short there ware as many chieftains as the number of cities according to the sarcastic remark of a historian. They were rulers only in name as they were either satellites of Alfonso VII or his allies. They were a bunch of selfish men with no feeling of patriotism, no sense of realities, and no code of morality. Ibn Sa'd Mardanish, a warrior of Gothic/Roman origin was openly in alliance with the kings of Castile, Aragon, and the Counts of Barcelona, and had treaties with the republics of Pisa and Genoa[16]. He robbed the people to pay for his Christian mercenaries, and even opened drinking clubs for them. He dressed like the Spanish Christians, and used gold crockery. A shameless debauchee, he used to sleep with several women wrapped in a single bed-sheet (*lihaf*) and took liberties with the plump Hassan who served him drinks. He created havoc by grabbing Jaen, and Carmona. The consequences of this moral degradation and political anarchy (the second *'fitna'* called by the historians) were disastrous. As weakness invites aggression, the Muslims rulers became easy targets of their strong neighbours. The territory under the Muslims began to shrink like a pricked ballon. The Almoravid hold in the far northeast was already weak, and the first casualty was Saragossa during the twilight days of this dynasty. The Christian pressure on the kingdom of Saragossa had ben mounting for a long time. There was a substantial number of the Christians in the civilian population as well as in the army. Not all of them were loyal to their rulers. Attempts were made to proselytise the Muslims. A Christian monk from France came to win over the Muslims to Christianity but without any success. Moreover, the whole region was politically isolated, and its doom was certain. Saragossa was captured on Dec 19, 1118 (Ramazan 4, 512 A.H.) and incorporated in the kingdom of Aragon. Between 1148-49, Count Roman of Berenguer IV of Catalonia annexed Tortosa, Fraga and Lerida. In this way the Muslims lost the whole of the Ebro basin. The land beyond the Spanish Extremadura as far as Lisbon in the west and Silves in the south, was an abiding thorn in the side of the Muslim possessions. If the Christians had been united at that time, they would have wiped away all the Muslim states and claimed the whole of Spain for the Cross instead of waiting until the end of the 15th century. It was in this political environment that the Almohads came to power in the northwest Africa. Muslim Spain was like a patient hanging on to mortality by a fragile thread, but the Almohads prolonged its life by a century.

The Almohads had to fight for several yeas to establish their authority in the Muslim territory of Spain. The Almoravid admiral ibn Maymun went over to 'Abd al-Mu'min, and handed over Cadiz to him. An Almohad army attacked the fiefdoms of ibn Qasi, and his vassals[17]. Nielba, Beja, Badajoz Mertola were seized, while between 1154 and 1157, Seville, Granada and Almeria were snatched from the Almoravids. 'Abd al-Mu'min was so busy in his country that he visited Spain only once. He came to Gibraltar and left after giving instructions. A year after (1163) he died to joined his mentor in the cemetery at Tinmallal.

His two successors— Abū Yusuf (1163-1164) and Abū Yaqub (1184-1199) were the most remarkable rulers of the Almohad dynasty. The former came to Spain to liquidate ibn Mardanish. After his defeat, Ibn Mardanish died in 1172. His son Hilal received a property in Africa and left after giving his sister in marriage to Abū Yusuf. After staying in Spain for nearly five years he returned to Marrakesh. In 1184 we find him again in Spain on hearing the devastating raids of Alfonso Enriques and his captains in the western sector, leading to the loss of Evora, Trujillo, and Caceres. The historian Sahib as-Salat has described the *modus operandi* of the raids against Muslim towns. As they had no equipment for a frontal attack, they arrived as plunderers. Usually they chose moonless and stormy nights for their operations. They arrived with ladders to scale the walls and to see the security arrangements. Their men descended into the town, surprised the guards, slew the sentinels, while at the same time they shouted watch-words of the security-man to lull the sleeping citizens into the belief that the night was not yet over[18]. The operations of 1184 ended in a tragedy. Abū Yusuf received a fatal shot from the crossbow, and he died (july 29, 1184) near the walls of Evora. His successor Abu Yaqub brought the body of his father to Seville. Soon after he returned to Marrakesh to occupy the throne. For five years he was so busy that he did not bother about Spain, because the very existence of the Almohad dynasty was at the stake when their territory in Africa came under a vigorous naval attack by Ali bin Ghaniya of the Majorca island. The banu Ghaniya were notorious pirates, and the struggle between this family and the Muwahhidin/Almohads lasted for half a century. The long wars with the Banu Ghaniya drained their energy and resources. In Spain, the Portuguese and the Castilian relentlessly pursued their crusade against the Muslims. Sancho I of Portugal laid siege to Silves (Ar. Shilb) in Sept. 1189 with the help of the crusaders who were getting ready to go to Palestine. After three months the city (famous for its scenic beauty and the polished Arabic of its citizens), was lost. At the same time, Alfonso VIII was making repeated raids with usual damages to crops and gardens. Abū Yaqub led two expeditions against the enemy in 1190 and 1191. He attacked Torres Novas and Tomar. The siege had to be raised for want of enough food and an epidemic that broke out in the camp. In the counter-offensive of 1191, Abū Yaqub recaptured Silves. He paid special attention to the defence of the frontiers. But Alfonso VIII of Leon gave him no peace, and in 1195 he landed in Spain with a numerous army to punish the aggressor. A most memorable battle was fought in the plains of Alarcos on Thursdays of Sah'ban 8, 591/ July 18, 1195. It was a disaster for Alfonso. Thousands of Castilian solders perished in the battle, and many thousands were taken into captivity. A captive was sold for a dirham, a sword for half a dirham and a horse for five says al-Maqqari[19]. The relics of the defeated army ran towards Calatrava. Next year (Nov. 1196) Yaqub entered the valley of the Tagus, and marching through Trujillo reached near Talaveria. Taking a turn he crossed into the vega of Toledo, and arrived at he very gate of the city. Toledo was about to fall into the hands of the Muslims when the mother of Alfonso, his wives and daughters came begging with tears to spare the city. Abū Yaqub was moved to compassion, and he granted their appeal, and sent them away with gifts[20]. Had Yaqub any political sense and taken advantage of the situation, the history of Spain would have been different.

The reign of these two rulers saw a blossoming of architecture poetry and philosophy. Their courts were adorned with thinkers and physicians like ibn Tufial, ibn Rushd and ibn Zuhr. Both the rulers were admirable builders. The architecture of the Muwahhidin/Almohad, on both sides of the straits is massive, proportionate, austere and sober. The only surviving specimen of their religious architecture in Spain is the tower of the great mosque of Seville built by Abū Yaqub. The architect Ahmad

ibn Basoh started the work and it was completed it in 1184.
The mosque which had 17 aisles, is now one of the largest
Gothic cathedrals. Its original shape has entirely vanished except
the tower rising to a height of 260 feet. The Giralda (the name
given to it by the Christians) with its glittering whiteness is one
of the great landmarks of Seville visible from a distance. From
the top of the tower one gets breath-laking view of the sprawling
city for miles. Square in shape with identical windows flanked
with panels of trellis work, the tower is a picture of soaring
grace. The top of the tower is reached by a ramp. Higher above
the platforms where ends the Muslim part of the tower, are two
storeys (100 feet in height) which were added after the tower
was turned into a belfray. The Almohad rulers fell in love with
Seville, and made it the headquarters of their Spanish dominion.
They spent immense sums on heautying the banks of the river
with elegant buildings near the renovated bridge of boats. They
provided an aqueduct for supply of fresh water to Seville. Two
wharfs with flight of steps were added to facilitate foreign trade
specially export of olive oil for which Seville was famous.
More than civil, it was the military architecture that claimed
the attention of the Almohad rulers, because of constant threat
to the security to their territory. Their military architecture is
represented by remains of several defence structures at Caceres,
Trujillo, Badajoz, Ecija and Seville. The bent gates, the
polygonal towers, and secret posterns are the chief features of
their military architecture. The ruins of the fort at Alcala de
Guadaira, about 20 km from Seville are still majestic in
appearance. This fort was known as the key to Seville. Built on
a high plateau with a massive wall, it is flanked with square
towers from where the defendants could look for miles in all
directions[21]. Another significant example in Seville is the Torre
do Oro (Tower of Gold) This tower was once a part of the

defensive system of Seville, and stands in solitary grandeur without any connecting walls. This remarkable tower multi-sided in shape has vaulted galleries inside, while the exterior carries band of blind windows. The upper story is crowned with crenellations in pyramidical form. The sophisticated unbanisation of northwest Africa which began under the Almoravids continued more vigorously under the Muwahhidin rulers as more and more Spanish Muslim architects, engineers and artisans were imported by them to beautify their cities. The Spanish historian Shaqandi was, no doubt, justified when he claimed that without Spain, Africa would have never been heard of. Some of the finest mosques still be seen in various parts of Morocco were built by the Spanish Muslims for their Muwahhidin masters. The great kutubiyya mosque at Marrakesh, and the Jama Masjid at Tinamallal were planned and designed by architects and craftmen from Spain. The famous Spanish engineer al-hajj Ya'ish of Malaga installed a mechanically operated prayer chamber (maqsura) in the kutubiyya mosque for the king. This marvel of engineering was operated by pulleys, weights and counter weights. The lift rose up as soon as the sovereign stepped into it, and reverted to its position after he left.

In the reign of Muhammad al-Nasir (1199-1213), the successor of Abū Yaqub, the Spanish Christians got ready to avenge their defeat at Alarcos. About this time, a great religious revival had taken place among the Christians. Roman Catholicism had blossomed into a number of militant organizations— the knight Templers, the Hospitallars, the order of Santiago, and the Order of Calatrava. On the political level, the rulers of Leon, Castile, and Catalonia patched up their old feuds as a result of ceaseless efforts of the archbishop Rodrigo Ximenez. He toured Germany, France, and Italy and returned with volunteers. Like Pope Urban II who inaugurated (Nov, 1095) the first Crusade at Clermont, Pope innocent III declared a Crusade against the Spanish Muslims. Led by Alfonso, they ravaged the territories under the Crescent with appalling atrocities. Nasir saw war clouds gathering thick on the frontiers, and he left for Spain with one of the biggest armies that ever crossed the Staits of Gibraltar. A most fateful encounter took place on July 17, 1212. The battle of Iqab or Las Navas de Tolosa was fought about seventy miles east of Cordova. It was a day of calamity for the Muslims. On the very eve of the battle there were differences among the commanders. The Andalusians claimed that they knew the Christian method of warfare, and insisted on their own tactics, but Nasir brushed aside their advice. Within the army there were many soldiers who grumbled that they had not been paid their pay and advances. Their treasonable designs and half hearted will to fight sealed the outcome of the battle. Still Nasir fought with superb courage. "The battle (say Watts) raged furiously all day, and for time the issue was in doubt. The Christians were on the point of giving way to the vastly superior force of the infidels. The Templers, and knights of Calatrava, who were in front, were overborne and destroyed. King Alfonso himself who showed here, as before, a better soldier than a general, was in despair, and calling out to Archbishop Rodrigo, "Let us die here prelate," made ready to throw himself into the enemy's ranks. The Archbishop, however, to whom the chief glory of the day belongs was a cooler head, and himself fighting in the van restored the battle. The Andalusians were first to flee. Entangled among the rocks and woods, fighting on the ground least suited to their tactics, the very numbers of the enemy were a hindrance to their rallying and impediments to their fight.[22]" The Muslims were simply routed, and thousands of them died on the battledfields. The battle was followed by their massacre, and the burning and conversion of their mosques. In their brutal lust for reconquest the victors overran Ubeda and Baeza and got a permanent foothold on the bank of the Guadalquivir. The northern Christians were on the march, and nothing could stop them. Henceforth, the Muslims fought with their back to the wall as they had lost military supremacy.

The disastrous defeat at Las Navas de Tolosa heralded the decadence of the muwahhid/Almohad empire in Span. Stricken with grief and shame, Nasir died in Dec. 1214[23]. After his death the wars of succession between his silly sons and selfish brothers, hastened their decline, and final disappearance from the African scene. Hie brother al-Ma'mun who was governor-general of Spain left Africa to claim the throne: His departure (1230) led to a general rising against the muwahhidin as had happened after the fall of the Almoravids. In the absence of a strong hand, the small territory left in the hands of the Muslims once again spilt up. With the help of the map in this book, the reader will be able to identify the dimensions of the territory left to the Muslims. Even this small enclave was in a state of confusion as if it had been hit by a tornado. The general public must have been demoralized by uncertainly and repeated defects. Three chiefs of Spanish origin parcelled out the tottering kingdom among themselves. The lion's share was grabbed by ibn Hud who became the lord of Murcia, Denia, and Jativa, and nearly the whole of Andalusia, south of the Gaudalqivir. He recognised the sovereignty of the Abbasid caliph al-Mustansir, and in 1212 the caliph's envoy arrived to invest him with the title of 'amir' of Andalusia. Valencia was occupied by Zayyan of Banu Mardanish group, while ibn Ahmar founded the kingdom of Granada. Each of thee chieftains had the qualities of leadership and experience in arms, but they did not confederate to forge a defensive bulwark against the flood of terrorist aggressions from their Christian neighbours. They were unable to rise above their suicidal feuds. No thought of collective security, no instinct for self preservation, and no ideal of self-respect prompted them to form a bond of union. A similar situation prevails today among the Arabic speaking states, and no one should be surprised if they are bullied by the big powers and beaten by their minions.

Ibn Hud belonged to the family of rulers of Saragossa. He must have been a man of some influence because within a short period he became master of the biggest chunk of territory in the south of Andalusia. But his efforts to save the wreckage of Muslim Spain were rendered unsuccessful by his rival ibn Ahmar of Granada. The defeat of Las Navas de Tolosa had destroyed the prestige of the Muslims. Soon after their victory, the Christians burst into the western sector, and occupied Merida and Badajoz. These losses exposed the entire region south of the Sierra Morena to attack and infiltration. About this time a significant development took place in the north. With the accession of Ferdinand III, Castile and Leon united (1234) for ever. Ferdinand III the grandson (of Alfonso VIII) was the Christian al-Mansur of the 13th century. He had before him a glorious opportunity to destroy a divided house. He struck at the very heart of the Muslim territory— he besieged Cordova. There was no hope of help from outside. North Africa was in the throes of a dynastic revolution; Valencia was nearing collapse; and Al-Ahmar pursued his career of self-aggrandisement with the support of Ferdinand. Ibn Hud could hardly muster enough force to face Ferdinand on the battlefield. After the collapse of a tower in the south of Cordova, the Christians just walked into the city. Cordova fell on June 29, 1236. The terms of surrender specified that the Muslims shall have full rights to their property, freedom of religion and the undisturbed use of their mosques. The solemn pledges given by Ferdinand were honoured more in breach than fulfilment. Soon after the surrender, the Muslims were expelled from the city where they had lived for more than five centuries. The great mosque of Cordova was converted into a church. Cordova lost its former glory for ever. The only object of interest which attracts tourists from all over the world is the great Umayyad mosque which retains much of its beauty even though it has been modified for Christian worship. This is the only surviving relic of her greatest past.

After the capture of Cordova, Ferdinand tried his arms against Jaen. This beautiful town celebrated for its silk industry was the frontier outpost of the newly-founded kingdom of Granada held by al-Ahmar. Unable to defend the city, he sued for peace. The Christian sources tell us that ibn Ahmar himself visited Ferdinand and offered to serve as his vassal. A treaty of friendship was signed between them under the terms of which ibn Ahmar agreed to pay tribute and also to place a contingent of his cavalry at the disposal of Ferdinand when required. Not long before ibn Ahmar was summoned to render service to his master. Ferdinand was bent upon annexing as much territory as it was possible from the hand of the Muslims. His next target was Seville. The whole region was in a state of turmoil which facilitated Ferdinand in his operations. Ibn Hud had already been assassinated in Almeria in 1237. There were also many traitors who were willing to make a gracious offer of some more towns. After taking Cantillana, Carmona and Alcala del Rio, the road to Seville was open before him. The city was defend by a council of some notable citizens, one of them being ibn Khaldun, the ancestor of the historian philosopher of the same name. It was a fight between a giant and the lilliputians.

Ferdinand encircled the city from the sea and the land. Al-Ahmar joined with his cavalry under the terms of his treaty. On his advice, the bridge of boats built by the Muwahhidin ruler Abū Yaqub was destroyed. This bridge was the only link by which Seville received its supply of food from Asharafe. The beleaguered city was starved into submission after a stage of nearly 17 months. The massive enceinte six km in length with 116 towers was of no avail[24]. On Dec 22, 1248, Ferdinand rode into the city at the head of a great procession of his commanders, and bishops who carried an image of the Virgin Mary. Immediately after the surrender the grand Jama masjid of Seville was "purged of the filthiness of Mohammadan impiety"[25]. The Muslims were ordered to leave Seville. Al-Ahmar returned to Granada. He had, after all, saved his kingdom.

The Muslims were at the mercy of the rulers of Castile and Aragon, who, it seems, had divided the mission of reconquest among themselves. While Ferdinand was tearing away bit by bit of the Muslim territory, another brave king was committing similar depradations in eastern Andalusia. King Jaime of Aragon, the son of Pedro II who had played a magnificent role at the battle of Los Navas, launched a naval attack with a hundred vessels against the Balrearic islands. These islands fell into his hands in 1230 after inflicting a murderous defeat on the defendants. The governor Yahya was taken prisoner, and tortured to death. Sometime in April May 1235, Jaime laid siege to Valencia. The Aragonese army advanced from all sides burning towns and helmets, and destroying orchards and gardens. The ruling prince Zayyan ibn Mardanish implored the help of Abu Zakariya, the sultan of Tunis, but his fleet came late, On Sept 28, 1238, they opened the gates to Jaime. In 1243, he annexed Murcia and Denia. The defeat of the Muslims was not just loss of territory. Everywhere they were targets of rapine, and slaughter by the victors. Those who survived the sword were exiled. Towards the middle the 13th century, only the small kingdom of Granada was all that was left in the hands of the Muslims. The story of the rise and fall of this kingdom, which, surprisingly lasted two centuries and a half, shall be the topic of the next chapter.

Notes

1. Pérès: p. 241.
2. Dozy: p, 690.
3. Ibid p, 693.
4. Al-Himyari: pp. 104-105.
5. Al-Maqqari/Gayangos, vol II p. 282 & also p, 284
6. Ibn Khatib: Ihata, vol II pp. 79-80 for the full text of the message.
7. Al-Marrakashi, p. 114. (Arabic edition)
8. From Tangier, Al-Mu'tamid and his family were taken to Meknes and then to Aghmat. He passed his days in misery. His daughters walked bare-footed, and spun wool for a living. His wife lost her health in the dusty wilderness of Aghmat. She was put under treatment of ibn Zohar but he failed to cure her. After two year of exile she died of grief, and was buried at Aghmat. In Dec.. 1095 Al-Mu'tamid followed her to the grave. He composed some of his finest poems during his exile.

   Zaida, the widow of al-Mu'tamid's son Ma'mun, was so much dejected by the family tragedies that she ran away along with her children. She crossed the Sierra Morena, and took refuge in the territory of Alfonso. He converted her to Roman Catholicism, and took her as his concubine.

   It has not been possible to trace the lineage of Zaida. Perhaps, she was originally a Christian or the child of a mixed marriage. There was such a mingling of blood among the Spanish Christians, the Slavs and the Arabs, that many children born of such marriages had no particular attachment to any religion. There are many such instances. One of these deserves to be mentioned. Mujahid the Slav ruler of Denia had a son from a Christian wife. She fell into the hands of pirates of Sardinia along with her son named Ali. Ali was ransomed on payment of a considerable sum, but his mother refused to return. Ali was brought up as a Christian by his mother. Throughout his life he preferred the Christians. When Ali succeeded his father, he placed all the churches of his kingdom and the Balearic Islands under the bishop of Barcelona. A daughter of Mujahid was the mother of al- Mu'tamid, and another daughter was married to 'Abd al-Aziz of Valencia the son of Sanchol.

(Pérès: pp. 274-275 and 284. Provençal: Islam d' Occident; pp. 139-148 and Bernhard and Ellen Whishow; pp. 238-239.

9. Writing about the Cid, H.E. Watts says, "It was the source of every cavalier of broken fortunes in that day to go forth to plunder the infidel — a resource not only not condemned by the public opinion but held to be worthy of every man of good descent and a high independent spirit." (Watt: p, 81)

10. Provençal: Islam d' Occident pp. 177-181.

11. Ibid.

12. Ibid.

13. Watts: p. 88.

14. Provençal: Islam d' Occident, pp. 155-285 give a masterly narration of the occupation of Valencia by the Cid, and its recovery by the Almoravids.

15. Ency. of the Islam (N.Ed) Article on Gharnata.

16. Some historians suppose that his name is arabised from Roman name Mardonious. For his career and character, see ibn Khatib: Ahata, vol II pp. 86-87.

17. Ibn Qasi allied with the Almohads to get rid of the Almoravids. But the treacherous man conspired with the Christians of Coimbra to overthrow the Almohads. He lost the trust of his disciples, and they killed him with the very lance he had received as a gift from his Christian allies.

18. Al-Maqqari/gayangos vol II, p. 522 note No: 1.

19. Ibid. p. 322. Alacros (Ar. al-arak) is near the present Campo de Calatrava and is now-a-days called Santa Maria de Alarcos.

20. Al-Maqqari/Gayangos, Vol II p. 322.

21. G. Marcais: Manuel d' art Musulman, Vol I p 358. Bernhard and Ellen in their 'Arabic Spain' (p. 303) have described the Alcala de Guadaria in these words: "One only needs to see the castle to understand why it was so, for it lies high above the Roman road from Cordova to Seville, with a sheer fall of some hundred feet to the river on two sides and of the two gates giving on the keep one is protected by a deep moat, and the other is approached by a narrow path which runs for a quarter of a

mile beneath the ramparts, while the gate itself commands a sudden turn and such a deep incline directly before it, that an attack from that side could have been resisted by a couple of men in doorway of the tower."

22. Watts: pp 115-116. al-Himyari: pp 164-165, and al-Maqqari/gayangos, vol. II, p. 323.

23. It was Nasir who in 1213 received a request from king John of England (who signed the famous Magna Carta) offering to put his country as a tributary under him, and also to embrace Islam. Hitti: History of the Arabs, p. 549.

24. The city wall survived the Christian recongquest and was demolish in 1861,—only a small portion is still left.

25. Bernhard and Ellen: p. 331. These are the words of the historian Zuniga author of Anales de Sevilla (1795)

Chapter 14

The Rise and Decay of the Kingdom of Granada

One evening in May 1237, a cavalier was seen riding towards the city of Granada. He appeared to be in his early forties. He looked an ordinary man in every aspect. The man wore no silk'robe, but only an old tunic of cheap material open at both ends. When he entered the city, the sun had already set, and even its last glow was dying. Just then, he heard the chant of the muezzin from the tower of a nearby mosque, calling the faithfuls for the sunset prayer. The man entered the mosque, and found that the people were ready for the congregational prayer, but the imam who was to conduct the prayer was nowhere to be seen. A certain sheikh, named Muhammad al-Basti who perhaps knew him, gently pushed him towards the mihrab of the mosque to lead the service. The man recited the sur Nasr of the Quran in first part of the prayer. After the service was over, he left for the castle on the nearby hill, in the light of tapers. This man was Muhammad al-Ahmar, the founder of the kingdom of Granada.

At the time of conquest of Spain, several famous families of the Ansars (those who invited the Prophet to Madina to preach the teachings of Islam) migrated to Spain. Many of them settled in the southeast of the peninsula— the Bani Ja'd in Seville, the Bani Qasim in Valencia (Where a village named Benicasim still keeps alive their memory), and the Bani Nasr who made Archidona their new home. The Bani Nasr family rose to prominence in the 13th century. They were direct descendants of Sa'd bin 'Obaidah one the Prophet's most illustrious companions. They lived on their farms, and were wealthy and much respected by their neighbours. The chief of this clan was Muhammad ibn Yusuf al-Ahmar who carved out the kingdom of Granada, the subject of this chapter. It was a small strip of coastal territory on the Mediterranean running from Almeria to Gibraltar, and included the sunny beach now called Costa del Sol. About 200 km long, its width (not more than 50 km) was bounded by the Serrania of Ronda and Elvira. The kingdom embraced some of the most picturesque and fertile regions of Spain. The fertile vega west of the city was irrigated by Xenil which received its waters from the snowy peaks of Sierra Navada (Ar: Jabal Shulair). The Kingdom also owned the peninsula's highest peak— the 11,420 feet high Mulhacen. Apart from the vega and some other plains, most of the kingdom was mountainous, but the hardy people who had inherited centuries of skill in agriculture turned the hills into cultivable spots by terraced farming. The kingdom abounded in minerals, valuable herbs, and forests. Although the Nasrite kingdom was insignificant compared to the Umayyad kingdom of Cordova, it was destined to as great a splendour. It had all the resources and wealth of an empire[1]. Inspite of its small size, it was able to weather the political pressures and military assaults of its powerful neighbours (the kingdoms of Castile and Aragon) for two centuries and a half, before its final eclipse.

We do not know much about the early life of al-Ahmar[2]. he

was born in 1195 at Arjuna, about 20 miles from Jaen. He came to the limelight in 1231 when he occupied the local fort. Within a year he took Jaen. By his bravery, and active support of his many relations particularly the Bani Ashqilula, he brought under his banner, the people of Gaudix (Wadi Ash) and the adjoining villages and towns. In 1237, he took by a bloodless coup the prestigious city of Granada (as already narrated) which became the capital of his principality. But he was not left in peace by Ferdinand who was bent upon stripping the Muslims of their possessions. The year 1246 was ominous for al-Ahmar, when Ferdinand assailed Jaen with a powerful forces. The invading troops destroyed alive-groves, fruit -gardens, stole away cattle, and captured the civilians both male and female. Al-Ahmar realised the risk to the kingdom if the issue was decided on the battlefield. After a brief skirmish, he purchased peace with dishonour by signing a treaty under which he parted with Jaen— "the silken Samarkand," of Muslim Spain. He accepted him as his superior, and also agreed to pay a fixed tribute. He further pledged to give military assistance to Ferdinand. By this last provision in the treaty, he isolated Seville. We have already seen that al-Ahmar joined Ferdinand with his cavalry when the latter attacked Seville. Al-Ahmar remained a most faithful ally of Ferdinand. When he died in 1252, al-Ahmar sent a condolence message to his successor. The body of the Christian ruler, wrapped in a cloth of Muslim manufacture, was laid to rest, and wax candles were placed at his grave by noblemen from Granada, while a hundred soldiers saluted the departed king[3].

Al-Ahmar planted not only a new kingdom on the Spanish soil amidst the most unfavourable circumstances, but he also strengthened its roots enabling it to stand for a long time against the most violent storms. He proved a great administrator, and

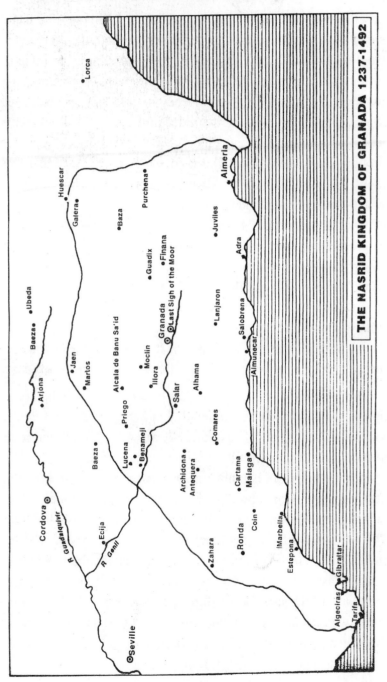

THE NASRID KINGDOM OF GRANADA 1237-1492

Lorca

Huescar
Galera
Purchena
Almeria
Baza
Juviles
Ubeda
Guadix   Finana
Baeza   Last Sigh of the Moor
Arjona   Granada
Adra
Jaen   Lanjaron
Alcala de Banu Sa'id   Salobrena
Martos   Moclin   Almunecar
Priego   Illora
Baeza   Salar
Lucena   Alhama
Benameji   Comares
Cordova   Archidona
R Guadalquivir   Antequera
Ecija   Cartama
R Genil   Coin   Malaga
Ronda   Marbella
Zahara   Estepona
Gibraltar
Seville   Algeciras   Tarifa

organised his kingdom from top to bottom. Although he had a small council of ministers, he personally looked into all matters. Coming from a family of wealthy cultivators, he gave impetus to agriculture which made the kingdom famous for abundant harvests. He issued his own currency in gold and silver. On the top of one of the hills, he started building the Alhamra castle which was expanded and embellished by his successors. He brought the water of the Darro to the Alhamra by means of tubes fed by a dike. The Alhamra castle was a big complex which housed his residence, the chancellery, and a small body of soldiers to enforce peace in the city. He built several forts to protect the frontiers. His personal life was exemplary. He was pious and abstemious[4]. He lived in patriarchal simplicity and could be seen mending his own sandles. He was a father to his subjects, and was easily accessible to them on every Friday. The full text of the epitaph in classical Arabic preserved by ibn Khatib, glorifies the king for his many virtues, although there is no trace of his grave. Al-Ahmar died from an accident.

The prosperous kingdom founded by al-Ahmar was inherited by his handsome son Muhammad II in Sept. 1272 who reigned for thirty years from 1272-1302. He was a scholarly man fond of theology, law and philosophy and a master of Spanish. His deep knowledge of Islamic jurisprudence earned for him the title 'al-faqih'. Immediately after coming to the throne he had to face the rebellion of his father's allies— the Bano Ashqillula. The members of this powerful clan were governors of Malaga and Gaudix. This insurrection was so serious that he had to call in the Castilian army. The Spanish army arrived under the command of Infante Don Fillip and Don Nuno de Lara. The rebels were routed at Antequera in 1273. A.D. The subsequent conduct of the Castilians made Muhammad realise that they intended to perpetuate sedition in the kingdom[5]. Acting on the dying advice of his father, he turned to north Africa for help. The Merinid sultans of Africa proved that they were friends in need only if they had some gains in sight. Muhammad virtually pawned Algeciras to the ruling sultan 'Abd al-Haq in return for his military help. Henceforth, the Africans formed a sizeable section of the armed forces of the kings of Granada. 'Abd al-Haq visited the kingdom several times. In one engagement (August or Sept. 1275) the Spaniards were defeated, and their general Nuno Gonzales was killed. But inspite of foreign help, taken at a great risk the kingdom of Granada could not effectively check Christians infiltrations. The Christian were angry at the growing military collaboration between Granada and the Merinid rulers. They attacked Tarifa from the land and the sea, under the leadership of a valiant warrior named Alfonso Perez de Guzman. After bitter fighting, Tarifa was seized in 1292. This was the first territorial loss of the kingdom after the death of its founder. After Muhammad II who died in April 1302, the kingdom was ruled by two kings — Muhammad III (1302-1309) and Nasr (1309-1314) . The latter's reign was far from being tranquil. A prince of royal blood forced him to abdicate. Nasr left for Gaudix and died in 1322.

With the accession of the fifth Nasarite ruler — Abū -I-Walid Ismāil (1314-1325) the crown passed to the descendants of the brother of al-Ahmar. The new ruler was one of the most remarkable members of the Banu Nasr Dynasty. The kingdom rose to great heights of prosperity during the reign of this wise and energetic ruler. The Banu Ashqitula who raised many internal problems had already left for Morocco, and at least one major cause of sedition was over when Ismail ascended the throne. He retrieved Algeciras from the clutches of the Merinid sultan. In 1319. Don Juan and Don Pedro, the guardians of Alfonso XI of Castile launched a major offensive without any provocation. The Pope granted the tithes of all the Spanish churches to cover the expense of the crusade. Ismail was a man of peace. He sent a message to the Christian commander that he would give twenty loads of money if he withdrew. The commander replied that nothing would deter him from his objective to sieze the capital of the kingdom. Thinking that the bait was not enough, Ismail sent another message enhancing the offer. Still the commander repeated the same haughty reply, and even put the envoy into prison[6]. This convinced the Granadine ruler that issue would have to be solved not by the word but by the sword. The Muslim archers attacked the invaders under Sheikh al-Ghuzat Abū Sa'id Usman. The Christians were routed at Alicun situated in the defiles of sierra Elvira. The two commanders — Don Juan and Don Pedro died in action. This brilliant victory took place on June 26, 1319. The booty which fell into the hand of the victors was so much that its sale in the markets of Granada lasted half the year. Ismail followed up his victory by recapturing Huescar, Orce and Galera. The Muslims penetrated deeper into the Christian territory, and assaulted Baeza with naptha ball which shattered the wall of the town, and forced defendant to surrender. On the 10th Rajab 725 June 1325, he marched upon Martos barely twenty miles to the south of Jaen, and captured the town after a sanguinary battle. He did not pursue his in march, but returned to Granada on the 24th Rajab. His entry in the capital was marked by public festivities. The streets through which he passed were hung with silk and brocade, and the air was filled with the smell of perfumes. On the 26th Rajab, he was assassinated at the instigation of his cousin. It is said that the assassin was standing with a dagger hidden in his sleeve, and when the sultan was about to enter into the palace he rushed forward and plunged the dagger in his neck. Ismail was an able administrator, and a valiant soldier with qualities of leadership. He was a teetotaller and was regular in the performance of his religious duties. He must have been influenced by his mother Fatima who survived him. She was the pride of the harem, and much respected for intelligence, piety and all the ornaments of her sex. Ismail's death was lamented by all as he was a true servant of his people.

Isma'il's minor son Muhammad IV succeed him to the throne. The administration was run by the efficient Prime Minister, ibn Mahruq. He knew no peace during the eight years of his rule on account of rivalry between the Prime Minsiter and the army commander ibn Abi -ula. One day he was returning to his palace after inspecting a border fort when he was surprised and killed in August 1333. The kingdom was inherited by his brother.

Abū I-Hajjaj Yusuf was sixteen years of age when he mounted the throne in 1333. He ruled for twenty years. He was an amitious person, and wanted to recapture *Tarifa* from the hands of the Christians. Accordingly, preparations were made on a grand scale. The Merinid sultan Abū I-Hassan was invited to join the undertaking. The Christian king Alfonso XI of Castile called to his aid the kings of Aragon and Portugal. The battle for Tarifa fought on Oct. 30, 1340 ended in a disastrous defeat of the Muslims. It was yet another Las Navas de Tolosa for them. Thousands of them died on the bank of the Salado river. Abū I-Hassan ran way and sought safety in Morocco, and a crest-fallen Yusuf returned to Granada. The panic among the Muslims encouraged Alfonso to grab the fortress towns of Alcala la Real, Priego, and Benameji. The triumphant Alfonso sent news of his victory to Pope Benedict with trophies of the battle— Muslim captives and captured flags. Two years after, Alfonso appeared at the gates of Algeciras, the birth pace of Abi 'Amir al-Manusr. This place was of immense strategic importance as it commanded the sea route to Ceuta. In good weather, a boat took three hours to land on the north African coast. The siege of Algeciras was a calculated move by the Spaniards of Castile. Their intention was to cut off the kingdom of Granada from trade and military relations with northwest Africa. The siege of Algeciras (August, 1342) attracted valiant knights and crusaders from abroad. The Earls of Derby and Salisbury from England, the comte do Faix and his brother Bernal from France arrived with their knights. The king of Navarre reached with his soldiers and generous supplies of wine and bacon. Even Chaucer's Squire in the Canterbury Tales participated in the celebrated siege which lasted twenty months. The Muslim archers and their naptha balls failed to break the obstinate siege. On March 27 1344, the Muslims surrendered the city, and left *en mass*. A truce for ten years was signed, but it was broken in 1350 on the plea that the ruler of Granada had failed to pay homage to the king of Castile. The Christians encamped before Gibraltar, but plague carried away their king, and the siege was raised.

During the period of peace, Yusuf devoted his attention to the welfare of his subjects. He introduced a number of social and religious reforms for the moral and material uplift of the people. He opened schools in many parts of his realm with a uniform curriculum. He regularised the collection of Zakat, and its distribution among the needy, specially the orphans and the widows. He restricted women from visiting the mosques unless chaperoned by male relations. A code of conduct prescribed that after the prayer all males should remain in their seats until all women had left. He banned the burials of dead bodies in shrouds of silk and other rich tissues, and the hiring of professional mourners. Some boisterous people celebrated the Eids on the streets by throwing oranges and other fruits on the passers-by while young boys and girls danced in the streets in

merry festivity. An ordinance banned all such celebrations. He
ordered that a mosque be built in every village with twelve
families, and the funds from zakat be utilised for this purpose.
He enjoined moderation in expenditure on domestic festivities
like the birth of a child and the marriage feast of walima. He
forbade amputation of the arm of a thief on the first offence. In
1349, he built a big madrassa at Granada, of which the prayer
hall and the marble slab of the inscription on the facade have
survived. He is also remembered for his many additions to the
Alhamra. The inscriptions on the walls of the palace proclaim
these additions. The monumental gate at the Alhamra called the
Bab al-Sharia (the Gate of the Esplanade) was built by him in
Rabi I, 749. The surviving inscription (*amara bi-bina'i hadha'l
bab al-musamma bi-babil sharia* etc) on the gate tells the story
of its construction[7]. This wise, humane and handsome ruler died
from an assassin's dagger on the Eid al fitr (Oct 18, 1354)
when he was praying in the grand mosque of Granada. In the
evening he was laid to rest in the Alhamra. He was the third
ruler to have been murdered in cold blood. It is obvious that the
kingdom was full of insidious pretenders bent upon capturing
the throne by violence.

The sixteen years old Muhammad V who bore the title of
al-Ghani billah, was like his father in all respects. The first six
years of his reign passed in harmony, and the state prospered,
chiefly due to the statesmanship of his Prime Minister Hajib
ibn Rizwan. But a palace intrigue obliged him to flee from his
kingdom in 760/1359. The details of this coup recorded by his
secretary ibn Khatib, show how dangerous it was to sit on the
throne of Granada. His stepmother Maryam and his stepbrother
Ismail lived in a mansion near the Alhamra. She was a crafty
woman possessing great wealth which she had misappropriated
after the death of her husband. She took into confidence her

son-in-law and hatched a plot in favour of her son, the prince Islam'il. On the night of 28 the Ramazan 760 (August 1359) when Muhammad was sleeping in the Generalife, the conspirators took advantage of a breach in the wall of the Alhamra, then undergoing repair, and sneaked into the palace by means of ladders. They occupied the palace while another group attacked the house of the Prime Minister Ibn Rizwan and slew him along with his family. Muhammad fled away to Gaudix, and from there he reached the coast, and took a vessel (Nov, 1359) for Africa. He lived as a state guest of the Merinid sultan Abū Salim. Ibn Khatib followed his royal master.

Isma'il II did not enjoy the fruits of the power he had usurped. Scarcely after six months a revolt swept him away, and Muhammad VI seized the throne. Cruel and blood thirsty, he eliminated his rivals with inhuman atrocities. In the meantime the fugitive sultan Muhammad V landed in Spain (August 1361) with African squadrons provided by the Merinid sultan. Finding that the game was up, he ran away to Seville to seek the aid of Pedre the Cruel. He carried with him a fabulous collection of jewels among which was a ruby now a part of the crown of the British rulers[8]. Pedro received him and his entourage with fair words, and lodged them in a palace. What happened next is described by Watts." Then learning of the rich jewels which they possessed, Pedro sent a party of armed men, who seized the persons of the /Red king and his attendants, and relieved them of their jewels and money. The king of Granada was despoiled of his even of raiments, and then meanly clad, was led out into the plain adjoining the city and mounted upon an ass, and with him thirty-six of his Moors, who were then severally done to death, on the pretence of having betrayed king Pedro in his war with Aragon.[9]"

The second reign of Muhammad V started in March 1362 and lasted about thirty years. Family quarrels and disorders continued to distract his attention. He was at peace with king Pedro, and even gave him (at his request) military assistance when the Castilian monarch nearly lost Cordova to a rebel brother. He followed the humane traditions of his father. He built a hospital (maristan) at Granada. The hospital was an elegant building surrounded with avenues of trees with a *jet d'eau* in its courtyard. The water-spouts in the form of two seated lions of the central basin have been refixed in the Alhamra. The hospital does not exist any more, but its plan has been preserved. From this we learn that porches with pointed arches ran along the sides of the courtyard on the ground floor. The second floor rested on wooden lintels. The entrance to the hospital was through an arch gate which was richly ornamented and topped by an arcade. The rooms opened into the courtyard with windows which were either single or geminated[10]. Industry and agriculture poured wealth into the kingdom. Merchants from Syraia Egypt, Africa, Italy and Armenia jostled in the markets of the kingdom making it the common country of all nations[11]. Several poets, thinkers, historian and jurists graced his reign. The celebrated scholar Lisan ad-din was his minister. The philosopher-historian ibn Khaldun visited Granada during his time and lived as an honoured guest. The kingdom was at the meridian of its glory and prosperity. His death was followed by a period of rapid decline. The final twilight was slowly creeping across the small Muslim enclave. Let us have a parting glimpse of the kingdom and the life of its people.

The kingdom of Granada was a miniature of the Caliphate of Cordova in al its aspects—its administration, the hierarchy of state official, the sources of its revenue and its military organization. The rulers were all-powerful. They styled themselves as "Commander of the Faithfuls" and other high sounding titles. The Granadine rulers, like the Umayyads of Cordova had a chief Minister (Hajib) and a council of ministers. A secretary (*kitab al-sirr*) was in charge of the correspondence, and its was he who drafted all treaties, messages, and administrative orders. The final orders were signed by the ruler himself. The state was divided into several small districts with administrative headquarters at Almeria, Gaudix, Ronda, Baza and Malaga. The posts of Governors were held by princes of royal family or chiefs of prominent families. The financial matters were taken care of by an officer called *wakil* — according to the testimony of ibn Khaldun[12]. The judiciary functioned without interference from the executive. There was a qaḍi in every major town. In addition to deciding civil case, the qaḍi performed some ex-officio functions such as performance of marriage ceremonies, and the administration of waqf properties and management of zakat funds. When ibn Battutah was in Malaga, he saw the local qaḍi raising funds for ransom of some Muslim captives in the custody of the neighbouring countries[13]. The police department was headed by an officer called the '*Sahib al Madina*' and the '*muhtasib*' watched the working of the markets. The state derived its revenues mainly from land-tax, and excise duties on imports. It seems that the people paid their taxes cheerfully[14]. An officer carrying the designation of '*mustakhlas*' managed the personal property of the ruler[15]. The frontiers of the kingdom were defended by numerous forts and no strategic spot on the borders was left undefended. Some border forts like those at Zahara, Gibraltar, Antequera, Alhama, Moclin, Baza have found a place in the Spanish ballads. The security of the borders was constantly reviewed. The old forts were repaired and new ones built. Muhammad V built twenty forts on the borders, and completely renovated the fort at Archidona at a cost of twenty thousand dinars[16]. The forts were built on the crest of a high rock. They had massive walls with watch towers made of stone and carried vaulted chambers at the ground level. In addition to facilities for storage of provisions and arsenals, barracks for the soldiers, a continuous supply of water was ensured by means of underground channels and pipes. A foray into the kingdom was not easy as the borders bristled with awe-inspiring forts remains of which can still be seen. "It was the strength of fortifications combined with their local position which frequently enabled a slender garrison in these place to laugh, to scorn all the efforts of the proudest Castilian armies.[17]" The kingdom maintained a fairly large army, both foot and cavalry, drawn from the Berbers, the Arabs as well as volunteers. The 'Sheikh al-ghauzāt' was the commander of the army. The soldiers were armed with cross-bows, lances, shields and scimitars. The cavalry was the backbone of the army. A good horse was the battle tank of warfare. The dexterity of the cavaliers of Granada is portrayed in the Spanish ballads. If the fight took place in the plains, the cavalry was irresistible. In a book entitled 'Khilat al-fursan' (The Ornament of Cavaliers) written by Ibn Huḍail in 1400, there is a full account of the qualities of the horse, the saddlery, and the proper use of arms when riding a horse. The Muslims of Granada knew the use of gun powder, but it seems that they did not build heavy canons to utilise its destructive power, and contented themselves with only throwing naptha balls at their enemies. The coastal waters were defended by a modest navy. Under Muhammad V. The navy was the biggest the kingdom ever had, but it was no match to the navy of Aragon and Catalonia.

Though small in size, the kingdom of Granada was one of the most affluent states of the Mediterranean world. Its prosperity

(the envy of its northern neighbours) was based on a judicious exploitation of its natural resources both mineral and agricultural. The entire kingdom was dotted with farms, orchards, wine-yards, mulberry and olive plantations. The land was irrigated by numerous canals which distributed the waters of the Xenil and the Darro. Neither distance, not rocky terrain stood in the way of their irrigation projects[18]. The Granadine vega (al-fahs) which stretched as far as Loja (Ar. Lawsha) was the granary of the kingdom. Irrigated by canals, the vega yielded year after year bumper crops of the finest wheat. Numerous water-mills — one hundred and thirty around Granada only converted wheat into flour[19]. The kingdom was in fact a cornucopia of grain, fruits and flowers. The markets were full of fruits throughout the year. Ibn Buttutah was amazed when he saw a heap of grapes being sold in a fruit market of Malaga for a mere piece of silver. He relished the ruby-coloured pomegranates, the figs and almonds of Granada[20]. The exploitation of agricultural resources went hand in hand with working of the mines. The kingdom was rich in gold, silver, copper, iron and lead. Exquisite marble, jasper, alabaster were found in abundance. The influx of refugees from the territories siezed by the Christians brought diverse skills which gave considerable impetus to industry. Malaga. Almeria and Granada were the chief centres of organized industry employing hundred of workers. The manufactures embraced cotton textiles, curtains, domestic utensils, glassware, leather goods, gilded ceramics, cutting and shaping of precious stones for ornaments, swords and ornamental daggers, carpets and articles of luxury. Ibn Khaldun, praised the people Granada for their efficiency in making musical instruments, carpets, well-planned houses, metal works and pottery[21]. Malaga had a flourishing export trade for its golden pottery. The kingdom of Granada was proud of its silk industry.

Except Iraq, no country could compete with the silks of Granada[22]. The silk industry brought affluence to many families. Silks of different colours with gold borders (washy) were known in Europe under the names 'alvici' and 'albeci'[23]. Malaga and Almeria were the emporiums of foreign trade in silk and pottery. The dry figs of Malaga reached as far as India[24]. The Florentines, the Genoese had their mercantile establishments at these ports. The merchants of the kingdom were known for their honest dealings. "The reputation of the citizens for trustworthiness was such that their bare word was relied on than a written contract is now among us.[25]"

Granada was one of the most beautiful cities of Spain even before the Nasarites came to power. In his risala or epistle, the historian Abū 1-Walid Shaqundi (d. 1231) wrote that 'Granada is the Damascus of Andalus. It is a delight of the eye, and a place of contemplation of the soul[26]. As the capital of the kingdom, it achieved its greatest glory under the Nasarite dynasty. The city had a population of about two hundred thousand citizens. Ibn Buttutah was captivated by the beauty of the city. "Granada, (says the great traveller) is the metropolis of Andalusia and the bride of its cities. Its environs have not their equal in any country of the world. They extend for the space of forty miles, and are traversed by the celebrated river of Shannil (Xenil) and many other streams. Around it on every side are orchards, gardens, flowery meads, noble buildings and vineyards. One of the most beautiful places there is 'Ayn ad-dama' (The fountain of Tears) which is a hill covered with gardens and orchards and has no parallel in any other country[27]. The wealthy nobility, high officials and prosperous merchants owned stately villas with gardens, fountains and kiosks. The bank of Xenil was carpeted with villas. Ibn Khatib himself lived in a villa in Ayn ad-Dama. In his history Granada he has

quoted the verses engraved on the kiosk of his villa[28]. A poet
found Granada a city without a peer— a beautiful bride whose
dower would cover Egypts, Syria and Iraq. Several bridges
spanned the river. They must have been of attractive designs
because ibn Khatib likens them to 'silver bangles on the ankles
of a maiden.' Like all Andalusian cities, Granada was encircled
by a rampart. The Berber ruler and provided a rampart which
surrounded the old city (al-qasaba al-qadim). Under the Nasarite
dynasty the population of the city increased, and the rampart
had to be extended to cover the new colony. The walled city
was crowded, and its streets were narrow, and many houses so
small that they looked like swallows' nests. These are the
observations of Thomas Munzer, a German traveller who visited
the city just two years after it was annexed by the Christians.
The houses (says Munzer) were clean inside and were decorated
with pictures. Each house had two pipes one for the supply of
drinking water, and the other for sewage[29]. The houses of the
rich who preferred to live in the walled city were, no doubt big
with dwelling halls and alcoves for relaxation as seen in a few
very old houses even today. The bigger house were built round
a courtyard (sahan) with a fountain in the middle or an orange
tree or both. The courtyard was the lung of the house which
provided the inmates with cool and perfumed air. A house in
Granada was modest in appearance and it gave no inkling of
the little paradise within. The entrance door opened into a dark
passage before one reached the patio with creepers on the four
walls and flower pots around the fountain. Many houses had an
ornate casement (Ar. al-shimasa, Sp: ajimes) which opened on
the street. After the Muslims left Granada, the city was gradually
transformed but it is possible to locate some of its old landmarks.
One of the famous localities was the Rabad al-Bayyazin (named
after migrants from Beza). This locality is now called Albaycin,

and it has retained much of its oriental flavour with palm trees and cypresses reaching the roof tops. The locality Ayn ad-dama , close to the city has been corrupted into adinamar[30]. It was a much frequented spot during the time of the Spanish aristocrat Pascual de Gayangos who translated some sections of al-Maqqari's Naf at-tib into English[31]. The site of the main market of Granada for de lux articles — the al-Qaisurya is still called Alcaiceria. Facing the chief mosque (now the cathedral) stood the madrasa built by Yusuf I. Not far was the street for second-hand garments now called el-zacatin (Ar. al-Saqqatin). Proceeding westward one could reach the famous gate — bab al-ramla. The plaza before this gate is no more but its memory has been preserved by the site called today Bibarramla[32]. Granada was a city of mosques — more than two hundred according to Manzer[33]. The biggest mosque according to him had nine rows of columns with 130 arches. In one mosque which he visited when the night prayer was in progress he saw a candelabra with a hundred candles[34]. There were numerous inns (*fundaq*) for travellers in all the major cities of the kingdom. The site of one inn is now occupied by the Corral de Carbon which has retained some of its old features. Manzer found that the Muslims of Granada were 'clean beyond imagination[35]. Water was available in plenty in all homes. There were hundreds of public baths. The architectural glory of Granada was the Alhamra palace whose beauty defies time. This will be described in the chapter on Hispano-Muslim architecture.

Frequent wars on the borders, and internal disturbances did not prevent the people of Granada from intellectual pursuits. Education was widely diffused among the people of all the classes. There were mosque schools all over the kingdom. The curriculum included the Quranic sciences, law, mathematics, geometry, botany medicine, classical literature, and history. A student acquired higher learning from specialists in each field. The teachers issued *ijaza* to their students after completion of their studies. The texts of some certificates or diplomas of graduation are found in the historical works of ibn Khatib. Written in a florid style, the *ijaza* ended with a prayer for intellectual advancement of the pupil while giving him permission to teach and comment upon the books taught to him. Travel was a part of education. Love for learning urged scholars to visit distant lands. We may cite a typical example of one such scholar. Muhammad ibn 'Abd ar-Rahman al-Lakhami who rose to the post of Prime Minister to Muhammad III, began his educational career as a humble student of Quranic studies at Ronda where he was born. While he was still young he left for the East in 683, and after staying at Mecca for the month of Ramazan, he went to Madina, and joined a caravan of hajis returning to Damnascus. He visited Baghdad, Jerusalem, Cairo, Tunis, before the returned home in 687 A.H. During his travels he attended lectures of nearly a hundred scholars including two women. He owned a big library, and kept an open house. The foods served at his dinner parties were proverbial for excellence[36]. Scholars and bibliophiles like him were not rare in the kingdom of Granada. As for the teachers, they were dedicated to their profession, and were free from pedantry and greed for worldly gains. Education was not a means of placement against jobs, but a dedication for self-enlightenment and service to others. Ahmad 'Abd al-Noor (died 702 A.H.) an eccentric scholars of logic and mathematics at Gaudix, was once asked about the cause of his failure in worldly matters. He replied," I am like a candle that burns itself out in order to spread light around it.[37]" Scores of scholars poets, physicians, botanists historians, and philosopher flourished in the kingdom of Granada. Regretably, their works have perished.

After the fall of Granada a pious priest in his desire to wean the Muslims from all cultural influences of their Islamic background, committed a bonfire of nearly a hundred thousand books. From this incidence we can get a rough idea of the books produced in the kingdom of Granada at a time when the printing press was yet to be invented. "The kingdom of Granada (says Prof. Nykl) gives proof of the remarkable vitality and tenacity of the Muslim spirit represented by powerful minds whose literary works close, in a glorious and dignified manner, the Muslim domination in Spain.[38]"

The kingdom of Granada carried within its polity, the seeds of its own decay. We have already observed how the caliphate of Cordova fell because of the ethnic disputes between the Arabs, the Berbers and the European Slavs. The kingdom of Granada was likewise sapped by factions led by chieftains of powerful families and a host of pretenders to the throne. The descendants of Ismail, the brother of al-Ahmar, the Zegris who belonged to family of the former rulers of Granada, and a crowd of brothers, cousins, and nephews — all offsprings of bigamous marriages, stood armed in a queue for the throne. The African volunteers also fished in troubled waters. The Bani Siraj, an influential Arab family added to the existing confusion[1]. These powerful families were in fact political parties, and they were prepared to go to any extent in order to place on the throne of Granada a king of their choice. In their mad scramble for the crown, all ethical considerations were thrown to the winds. A son rebelled against his father, a brother against his brother, and a nephew against his uncle. The administration was rotting from within due to mutual jealousies, intriques, and backbiting. A typical instance is the enmity between the qadi al-Nubahi, and ibn Khatib leading to the tragic death of the latter on false charges of heresy.

Muhammad V died in 1391, after 30 years of reign. He was the last rose of the high summer. After his death the kingdom passed through a period of disturbances and intriques, as a result of which kings appeared and vanished like shadows in a marionette show. Each palace coup in Granada was followed by a Christian raid, and each time the kingdom lost a slice of its territory. Muhammad V was succeeded by his son Yusuf II. He was poisoned in Oct 1392 at the instigation of the king of Fez. His younger brother Muhammad VII occupied the throne and exiled his elder brother Yusuf to Salobrena. It was probably during his reign that the kingdom lost the strategic town of Zahara. Soon after he seriously fell sick. He wanted to pass on the throne to his son before his death, and this could be done after eliminating the elder brother. He sent a message to the commandant of Saloberna to finish Yusuf. When the messenger arrived, Yusuf was playing chess reclining on cushions of silk. His opponent was the commandant himself with whom he was on friendly terms. When the message was read out to him, he asked for permission to finish the game. While the game dragged on, another messenger arrive from the capital announcing that the nobles had nominated him as their king. Walking on streets strewn with flowers, the new king entered into the Alhamra palace to fill the throne floating on stormy waves[39]. Yusuf III was a man of pacific nature. He sent an embassy to Castile for negotiating a treaty of peace. A truce was concluded for a period of two years. After the expiry of the truce, the Castilians attacked and wrested the fortress town of Antiquera. Yusuf died in Nov. 1417 leaving the shaky throne to his son Muhammad VIII commonly known as the left-handed.' He offended the official by his haughtiness, and was forced to abdicate as a result of the seditious activities of the Banu Siraj[40]. He left for Tunis. After sometime, he returned to the capital only to be expelled again. The throne passed on to another claimant— Yusuf IV a son of Muhammad VI in 1431. After a few months Muhammad VIII recovered the kingdom for the third time. His restoration proved ominous. Between 1435-1438, the Christians annexed Jimena, Helma and Huescar — all strategic places. Muhammad VIII was deposed by his nephew. The Banu Siraj held a meeting, and put Abū 1-Nasr Sa'd on the throne in 1454. The frequent changes of the rulers in Granada gave the Castilians an opportunity to open a battlefield of their choice. They attacked Gibraltar under the command of the Duke of Madina Sidonia, one of the most brilliant soldiers Spain has produced. The loss of Gibraltar (Aug. 20 1462) was a major tragedy for the Muslims. The kingdom of Granada was cut off from Muslim north Africa; it was left helpless. After the loss of Archidona, another fortress town, Sa'd used for peace. He acknowledged Enrique IV of Castile as his superior, and pledged to pay annual tribute of twelve thousand gold dinars. After Sa'd died in 1464 the kingdom of Granada survived for only four decades.

Notes

1. Prescot: Ferdinand & Isabella, Vol. I, p. 222.
2. Ibn Khatib, Ihata, vol II, p. 59-66 give a short biographical sketch of al-Ahmar.
3. Bernhard a & Ellen, pages 340-342.
4. Ibn Khatib: Ihta, vol. II, pp. 66-67.
5. Dr. Condé has made a startling revelations in this connection. It seems that Muhammad was a guest of the Spanish king. During the visit the Spanish queen entreated him to grant a truce for one year to the rebels. Muhammad naturally suspect the intentions of the neighbours (Condé; vol. III, p, 172.
6. Al-Maqqari/Gayanagos, vol II, note 24 at p. 536.
7. Provençal: Islam d' Occident, p. 55.

8. Watts: pp. 203-204 and John A. Crow: Spain, the Root and the flower, New York, 1963, p. 109.

9. Ibid.

10. H. Terrasse: Ency of Islam (N.Ed.) article on Gharnata, p. 1316.

11. Condé: vol III, p. 292.

12. Ibn Khaldun: the Maqqadimah, vol. II, p. 18.

13. Ibn Battuta, p. 315.

14. Ibn Khatib: Ihata, vol. I, p. 34.

15. Ibn Khatib has given a short biography of Abū Ali ibn Hudba who was an honest manager of the royal properties. He built baths, toilets, dug wells and planted trees. (Ibn Khatib Ihata vol. I. p. 263).

16. Ibn Khatib, Ihata, vol II, p, 30.

17. Prescot: Ferinand & Isabella vol I, p, 276.

18. Mr. Thomas Abercrombie of the National Geographic visited the hilly Alpujarras, the mountains to the south of Granada. He found remains of a canal built by the Muslims used till recently. See his article: When the Moors Ruled Spain (July 1988).

19. Ibn Khatib, Ihata, vol. I page 34. (The opening chapters of this work are a mine of information on agriculture, gardens, mines and some social aspects of the kingdom of Granada).

20. Ibn Buttutah, p. 314

21. Ibn Khaldun; the Muqqadimah, vol II p 349-350

22. Ibn Khatib: Ihata vol I p 15

23. Ency of Islam (N.E.), article on 'Malaka', and also Provençal: La Civilization Arabe in Espagne," p, 128.

24. Al-Maqqari/Gayangos : vol. I, p. 49.

25. Prescott: Ferdinand and Isabella Vol. I, p. 224. The ambassador of the emperor Frederic III, on his passage to the Court of Lisbon, in the middle of the fifteen century contrasts the superior cultivation as well as general civilization of Granada, at this period, with that of other countries of Europe through which he had travelled.

26. Al-Maqqari/Gayangos Vol. I, p. 49.

27. Ibn Buttutah, p. 315. He was in Andalusia in the reign of sultan Yusuf I. He could not see him because of the sultan's illness, but the sultan's mother sent some gifts to ibn Buttutah.

28. Ibn Khatib: Ihata, vol. I, pp. 28-29.

29. J.B. Trend: Spain from the South, p 154. Also see Don Torres Balbas: Los Edificious Hispano-Musulmanes, published in Revista del Instituto Egipcio de Estudious Islamicos, (Madrid, 1953), pp. 117-121.

30. Al-Maqqari/Gayangos, Vol I, p. 349.

31. His grandson the Madrid based Rafael de Gayangoes is carrying on the work of his illustrious grandfather by promoting cultural exchanges between Spain and Morocco.

32. Like the Umayyad Cordova, the city of Granada was served by several gates. A gate which carried the figure of a lion was called bab al-asad. A famous gate was called bab al-bunud — the gate of Flags There was a gate of Potters (bab al-fakhkharin), a Gate of Tanners (bab-aldbbaghin), a gate of Antimony (bab al-Kuhl) a gate of Perfumes (bab al-attarin). And finally the gate of Elvira (bal albira) now called Porte d' Elvira.

33. J.B. Trend: pp. 153-154.

34. Ibid.

35. Ibid.

36. Ibn Khatib: Ihata, vol II, pp. 279-301 give a long biographical note on this remarkable son of Granada, and his tragic death.

37. Ibn Khatib: Ihata, vol I, p. 82.

38. Nykl: p. 101.

39. Condé, Vol. III. pp. 302-303.

40. Bernhard & Ellen are of the view that the Banu Siraj (the Abenserranges of European authors) were descendant of the Gothic princess Sara from her Muslim husbands. (Arabic Spain: p 407). This seems to be doubtful.

Chapter 15

The Fall of the Kingdom of Granada

About the end of the 15th century, the Christian offensive assumed a determined resolve to wipe away the kingdom of Granada. The task was facilitated by the union of the Kingdoms of Castile and Aragon, This is how it happened. When king Juan II of Aragon died (Jan. 1479) the crown devolved on Ferdinand, who, while he was still a prince, had married Isabella the sister of Enrique of Castile. On the death of Enrique, she was nominated as his successor, and the two monarchies were united. The marriage of this handsome couple is an event of singular importance in the history of the Spanish nation. They were the founders of a united Spain. The country was blessed with a fresh vigour, and a restless spirit for new enterprises. After having settled the affairs of their joint dominion, they turned their eyes to the small territory over which the crescent still shone even though with a dim light. Both considered that it was their duty to Heaven to put an end to the last vestige of Muslim rule in Spain. In fact one of the conditions of Ferdinand's marriage with his beautiful espouse was that he would continue to fight against the Moors. They waited for an opportunity to strike the meditated blow. The pretext was given by the Muslims themselves[1].

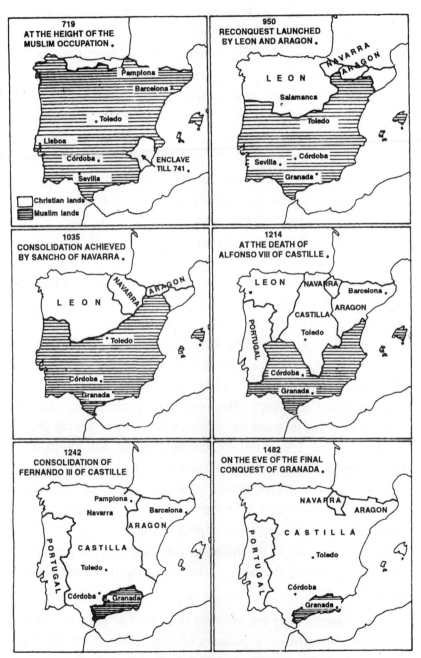

Step by Step Rise and Fall of Muslim Spain

While Ferdinand and Isabella ruled over the united kingdom of Castile, Sa'd's son Abū l-Hasan Ali sat on the throne of Granada. Hassan Ali felt ashamed of the territorial losses suffered by the Muslims during the reigns of his predecessors, and he wanted to wash away the shame by recovering the forts and towns wrested by the Christians. He made strenuous preparations for this purpose. Al-Maqqari tells us that Hassan Ali raised a fresh army which he inspected from a bedecked rostrum specially built for the ceremony held outside the main gate of the Alhamra. He felt angry when Ferdinand sent an ambassador demanding the cusomary tribute. Hassan Ali is alleged to have replied. "Tell your sovereign that the kings who paid tribute are no more. The mints of Granada no longer coin gold but steel blades." This undiplomatic reply was followed by an inroad into the Christian territory. On the night of Dec. 26 1481, he surprised the border town of Zahara which not long ago was a part of the kingdom of Granada. Zahara is situated about twenty miles west of Ronda on the present road that leads towards Seville via Moron. Nowadays, tourists from cold countries of Europe often visit this pictureque and sunny town which has retained its oriental aroma. Very few of them know that the attack on Zahara by Hassan Ali marks the beginning of a long crusade against the kingdom of Granada. The war lasted a decade during which the Muslims fought for every inch of their mother land until (according to the eloquent words of the American, Washington Irving) "the crescent that symbol of heathenish abomination was cast into the dust, and the blessed cross, the tree of our redemption erected in its stead.²"

The Christians did not offer the other cheek. They retaliated by a surprise attack on Alhama (Ar: al-Hammah) under the command of Rodrigo Ponce of Leon. It was one of the most beautiful towns of the kingdom of Granada famous for its hot springs. The sick from al over the kingdom came here for medicinal bath. On the night of Feb. 28 1482, a small part of infiltrators ascended the battlements, killed the sentinels, and opened the gates for the army. Unshaken by the sudden attack, the Muslims put up a fierce residence. The streets were barricated with timber. The soldiers and the civilians fought from the windows, the balconies and roofs of their houses. The deadly contest lasted throughout the day. The streets were choked with the mangled bodies of the dead citizens. At last they lost all hope, and laid down their arms. The town was plundered. The Muslims who sought shelter in a mosque were either put to the sword, or dragged into captivity. The news of the disaster cast a gloom over Granada, and on March 5, Hassan Ali arrived at the spot with is cavalry. After a fierce contest, he succeeded in penetrating into the fortress, but the timely arrival of troops under the command of the Duke of Medina Sidonia, changed the fortune of the battle. Hassan Ali raised the camp and returned to Granada. An immense booty fell into the hands of the victors. In May, Ferdinand himself arrived at Alhama with a brilliant retinue of priests and nobles to see the conversion of mosques into churches. The principle mosque was dedicated to Santa Maria de la Encarnacion. The pious queen donated a covering for its altar, embroidered with her own hands.

Encourage by the success of his daring stroke, Ferdinand put on his armour for further exploits. The queen issued orders to district officials for sending troops. Early in July 1481. Ferdinand encamped near Loja (Losha), the birth place of ibn Khatib. Situated on the Xenil, Loja was encircled on all sides by hills which gave it natural protection against the strongest armies. The fortress town was commanded by Ali Attar, a vetern soldier versed in the wiles and tactics of mountain warfare. His well-planned attacks and surprises with his light cavalry frustrated the invaders. The expedition ended in a disastrous failure. Ferdinand lost the flower his army, and decided to retire.

At his perilous hour, a revolution broke to a in the kingdom of Granada. Hassan Ali had two wives— a Muslim and a Christian. He showed more favour to the latter, and this made Ayesha his Muslim wife jealous of her rival. Her son Abū 'Abdullah (usually called Boabdil by the Spanish historians) was the eldest son of Hassan Ali. He suspected that the young prince might create trouble in the state, and he had him imprisoned in a tower of the Alhamra. Ayesha, his mother contrived his release with the help of her *fammes de chamber* and a civil strife broke out in the city. Hassan Ali left Granada, and took refuge with his brother Abdullah al-Zagahal who was governor of Malaga. The kingdom had now two kings — Abū 'Abdullah and Hassan Ali, at a time when an implacable enemy was near at hand. The political situation was in such a deplorable state that a reconciliation between the father and the son was ruled out. The whole administration was divided into pro-Abdullah and pro-Hassan Ali factions. It seemed that the leaders of the kingdom were prepared to lose everything— their honour, liberty, and the sanctity of their homes and religious places, rather than to unite and face the enemy knocking at the gate. They sowed disunity and harvested destruction.

For the Christians this was the most favourable time to avenge the check they had suffered at Loja. They launched a massive attack on Malaga through the mountainous regions north of the city. The leaders of this enterprise were Don Alonso de Cardenas, the grand master of St. James, Don Pedro Henriques, the adelento of Andalusia Juann de Silva, count of Cifuentes, Don Alonso de Aguilar and the marquise of Cadiz. They were brilliant commanders of great experience to whom warfare was a child's play. Headed by Don Aguilar, they marched into the Muslim territory on March 19, 1483, burning and destroying vineyards and plantations. Forcing their way they entered into the mountain passes from different directions. Soon, the valiant al-Zaghal appeared on the scene. In one decisive encounter he allowed the invaders to penetrate deeper into the mountains and when they reached an open glen, he took them unawares. Many lost their lives, while the rest shaken, and tired retraced their steps to reached the route by which they had come. Zaghal chased them through the enveloping darkness. He had lighted fires on the hill to keep a watch on the retreating soldiery. Throughout the night he attacked them by arrows, and large pieces of rocks were rolled down from the top of the hills. Hundreds of soldiers perished in the mountain passes. The remaining soldiers, tired, hungry and wounded, took to their heels. The Count of Cifuentes and Don Pedro de Silva were captured. The marquise of Cadiz had a miraculous escape, but his brother along with thirty commanders of the order of St. James died in the calamity[3].

Zaghal's name was on the lips of everyone in the city of Granada. Abū 'Abdullah grew jealous of his growing popularity, and he thought of boosting his image in the eyes of the people by some singular acts of glory. As Ali Attar, the valiant defender of Loja was his father-in law, Abū 'Abdullah was sure of success with his help. Collecting a large army, he led an expedition in April 1483 against Lucena with the object of carrying his offensive deeper into the plains of Cordova. As he passed through the bab ilbiria, he broke his lance by an accident. This was taken as an ill omen by his advisors, but discarding their advice, he continued his march. The Count of Cabra set out to check the invader. While marching towards Lucena the Muslim

infantry had collected a large booty, and in their anxiety to
preserve it, they took to their heels at the very first encounter
leaving the cavalry to face the enemy. The cavalry could not
stand very long. The arrival of more troops under Don Alonso
de Aguilar turned the tables against the Muslims, and when a
fatal lance struck Ali Attar, they were totally disheartened. There
was confusion in their ranks, and the cavalry melted away in
the ensuring slaughter. Some fifty warriors who formed a
protective ring round Abū 'Abdullah lost their lives, and he
was left alone. His charger was already tired, and leaving it, he
went into hidding among the bushes. But the soldiers of the
Count pursued him and he was arrested. Abū 'Abdullah was
bold enough to reveal his identity. There was frenzied joy at his
arrest among the Christians, but gloom and frustration in
Granada at the humiliating incident. His Royal Highness, the
Prince Abū Abdullah was conducted to Cordova where
Ferdinand received him with courtesy. Hassan Ali returned to
Granada to fill the empty throne, and Zaghal remained at Malaga.

Hassan Ali was the last person to bother himself for a
recalcitrant son, but his wife Ayesha was the unhappiest women
in Granada. She sent envoys to the Spanish court to negotiate
release of Abū 'Abdullah. The advisors of Ferdinand were
divided on the issue. Some advocated his indefinite incarceration,
but others thought that his release would prolong the civil war,
and hastened the fall of the kingdom. Ferdinand who was a
crafty politician — he was one of the heroes of Machiavelli,
opted for the latter suggestion[4]. Abū 'Abdullah was released
only after he agreed to the terms of his captor. Under these
conditions he was (1) granted truce for two years; (ii) he was
to free all prisoners of war: (iii) he was to pay 12 thousand
dinars every years; (iv) he was to allow the Christian troops to
pass through his territory for the propose of carrying war against

his father, and (v) to hand over his son as a hostage. In August 1483, the required hostage was delivered to Ferdinand, and Abū 'Abdullah was set free. "Thus did the unhappy prince barter away his honour and his country's freedom for the possession of immediate, but most precarious sovereignty" — says Prescott[5]. Abu 'Abdullah entered into the Albaycin locality of Granada at midnight in Sept. 1483 when his father reposed in the Alhamra. Once again there was confusion in the state. The Christians broke the truce with impunity, and started their attacks. In Oct./Nov. the marquise of Cadiz took Zahara by a surprise assault. In June 1494, they reduced Alora, Cartama and Coin in quick succession. Ferdinand's army was now using heavy artillery. He had invited engineers from France, Germany and Italy who manufactured canons capable of discharging stones, iron balls and incendiary material. These canons called 'lombord' proved most effective in breaking the massive fortifications of the kingdom of Granada. With the help of this new artillery, the Christians were able to reduce Ronda one of the bulwarks of the kingdom. Neither its situation among the most rugged and awe-inspiring terrain, nor the bravery of its hardy Berber warriors was of any avail against the havoc let loose by the canons. Ronda capitulated on May 20, 1485.

The loss of forts and the continuous turmoil in the city of Granada affected the health of Hassan Ali, and he abdicated in favour of his brother al-Zahgal. The theologians of Granada repudiated Abū 'Abdullah's right to the throne. Abū 'Abdullah and Zaghal never came to any agreement; the former held the city of Granada, and the latter, Baza, Malaga and Almeria. In May 1486 the enemy launched his second assault on Loja. The duke of Cabra and the marquise of Cadiz led the attack with a powerful army of the Spanish soldiers as well as many volunteers from France, Switzerland and England. The Earl of Rivers a close relative of Henry VII of England played a conspicuous role in the crusade against Loja. Abū 'Abdullah hastily collected a small army but he could not challenge the Christian forces backed by the devastating power of the canons, and ever increasing reinforcements. The vanguard of his army was massacred, and those who escaped ran into the town. The Muslim cavalry had little space for manoeuvre after the stone bridge connecting the town was destroyed by the invading army. The city was under heavy fire from all sides. Its ramparts crumbled, the house were in flames and the people were dying under the debris of falling roofs. The British Earl lost his front teeth, and Abū 'Abdullah received a gash on his head. As he feared that he might be captured again, he decided to lay down arms. Under a treaty the Muslims were required to evacuate Loja, and Abū 'Abdullah pledged to recognise Ferdinand as his suzerain after the subjugation of the territory held by his uncle. By this treaty Abū 'Abdullah drove the last nail in the coffin of the kingdom. Ferdinand followed up his victory by storming the forts of Illora— 'the right eye' of the Moors. After his abdication, Hassan Ali had retired to this fort. Before the Christians occupied it, he left the fort to lay his bones at Almunecar. Soon after, the Muslims lost Moclin known as the shield of Granada. These conquests brought the enemy within easy distance from the heart of the kingdom— the city of Granada. Ferdinand allowed Abū 'Abdullah to enjoy life for a few years more in the Elysium of the Alhamra. His first objective was to destroy al-Zaghal before laying his hands on Abū 'Abdullah.

The offensive against Malaga is one the most memorable events of the crusade against the kingdom of Granada. Ferdinand set out from Cordova on April 7, 1487 with the biggest army he had so far deployed. It was composed of twelve thousand cavalry and forty thousand infantry. He had under him the most fearless and faithful commanders from the Spanish nobility whose descendants living today are held in great honour. After marching through mountains and swollen streams, he encamped at Velez (Ar. Ballash) on April 17,1487. This small town was famous for its magnificent mosque (ibn Buttutah prayed here), and its orchards. Being near the coast, it provided easy access to Malaga. Zaghal made a night attack on the advancing army, but it ended in failure. Muslims fought with the courage of despair because the little town was key to the defence of Malaga. On one occasion Ferdinand nearly fell into their hands. But Velez was doomed as it was blockaded from all sides; and the people short of provision, clamoured for peace. Rizwan, the commander of Velez had treated the Count Cifuentes with generosity during his captivity, and the two had a soldier's esteem for each other[6]. The terms of surrender were settled through him, and Velez was handed over to Ferdinand on April 27, 1487. The fall of Velez sealed the fate of Malaga.

Malaga (Ar. *Malaqa*) was on of the most beautiful and populous cities of Muslim Spain. It was a natural harbour from where, silk, lustre pottery, and dry fruits were exported to foreign countries. Malaga was frequented by merchants from all countries of the Mediterranean, specially the mercantile republics of Italy. The main city (alqasaba) was encircled by a massive rampart with several gates, two facing the sea. At one end of the city near the coast, the fort of Gibralfaro stood like a sentinel on a rocky height. The fort was connected to the city by a passage some remains of which are still extent. The main mosque of Malaga (now the cathedral) was a copy of the mosque of Cordova with a roofed sanctuary resting on five rows of pillars. Ibn Battutah saw this mosque. He has reported that its spacious courtyard was of unrivalled beauty with tall orange trees. A portion of the suburbs of Malaga which sloped towards the sea presented a charming landscape with gardens, vineyards and orchards of almonds, figs and pomegranates. Malaga was a city of Joy, like Seville. Wealth flowed into the city, as most its people were engaged in trade[7].

Ferdinand was still at Velez when rumours reached him that the merchant community was in favour of capitulation without bloodshed. He deputed the marquise of Cadiz to negotiate with the commander of Malaga whose name as given in the Spanish Chronicles was — Hamet al-Zaghri. He was renowned for his valour and integrity. He declined to accept the proposal for surrender. Ferdinand raised the camp at Velez and reached the outskirts of Malaga in May 1487. His plan was to blockade the city. For this purpose, he had to lead his army through a valley at the periphery of the city. He despatched a body of Galician troops under the grand master of St. James. The Galicians are tough fighters. (Incidentally, the late General Franco was a Galician) After a fierce fight, the defendants were overpowered. The invading army advanced through the pass like lava, and surrounded the city. They speedily fortified their encampment with bulwarks and trenches. A fleet was stationed at the harbour under the Catalan noblemen Requesens. The canons went into action. Undaunted by incessant cannonade, the Muslims sallied forth from their fortifications every night and day. The war raged on the land and the sea. The Muslims fought with superb courage which surprised even their enemy. "Who does not marvel (says Pulgar, Secretary to Ferdinand, and author of' Reyes Catholicos) at the bold heart of these infidels in battle, their prompt obedience to their chiefs, their dexterity in the wiles of war, their patience under privation and undaunted perseverance in their purposes[8]." The siege of Malaga lasted several months and the people died of hunger and exhaustion.

While the Muslims shed their blood, Abū 'Abdullah remained unmoved. He sent felicitations to Ferdinand at his victory with caskets of perfumes and costly silks for him and the queen. A body of cavalry sent from Gaudix for relief of Malaga was intercepted by his soldiers. On the other hand, the army of Ferdinand derived Fresh strength from reinforcements. The Duke of Medina Sidonia arrived in person with men and money. The situations became so hopeless, that voluntary surrender was the only alternative left to the citizens. A deputation led by an influential merchant (named Ali Dordux) went forth to the Christian camp to negotiate the terms of surrender. But Ferdinand refused to receive the delegates[9]. They were told that the people shall have to surrender on terms and conditions which he as a conqueror would dictate to them. On August 18, 1487 (Shaban 27, 892) Ferdinand entered Malaga in a triumphal procession. Conquered Malaga was treated in the most unchivalrous manner. The central mosque described above was converted into a church. The valiant commander Hamet al-Zeghri was arrested at Gibralfero. When questioned as to why he did not surrender earlier, he replied "Because I was commissioned to defend the place to the last extremite, and if I had been properly supported. I would have died sooner than surrender now'[10]. He was put in chain for his Spartan reply, and thrown into a dungeon. A most dreadful fate awaited the citizens of Malaga, the Muslims as well as the Jews. They were condemned to slavery, and later ordered to ransom themselves. In this clever manner the Catholic sovereign robbed the people of their wealth and jewellery. Fifty of the most beautiful maidens were sent as presents to the Queen of Naples, thirty to the queen of Portugal and many were distributed among the ladies of the court[11]. Ferdinand sent one hundred prisoners to the Pope Innocent VIII, who paraded them in the streets of Rome, and forced them into Christianity. Writing about the fate of the citizens of Malaga., Prescott says —"One cannot, at this day read the melancholy details of their story without feelings of horror and indignation. It is impossible to vindicate the dreadful sentence passed on the unfortunate people for a display of heroism which would have excited admiration in every generous bosom[12]."

After the loss of Malaga and the nearby places, al-Zaghal was left with Baza, Gaudix and Almeria. In the middle of 1489, Ferdinand set out to subjugate Baza with a galaxy of his most brilliant cavaliers. The defeat at Malaga and the inhuman treatment of its citizens did not break the spirit of the Muslims, and they were in no mood to hand over the city without striking a blow. The historian-philosopher ibn Khaldun says that a dynasty or state nearing its doom shows some sign of resilience before it is estinguished like a burning wick the flame of which leaps up brilliantly a moment before it goes out[13]." This is illustrated by the events narrated above, and those that follow. The Muslims rose to face the challenge even though the odds were heavily against them. They raised an army of several thousand warriors from funds raised by the sale of ornaments donated by patriotic women like "dames of ancient Carthage" in the words of Prescott[14]. The command of the army was given to Cidi Yahya, a close relation of al-Zaghal. The first encounter was a calamity for the Spaniards. The army was thrown into disorder, and Ferdinand thought of raising the camp, but for the advice of the queen. The greatest hurdle before his army was the thick forest in the suburbs of Baza held by the Muslims. It was necessary to dislodge the Muslims from the forest. Skirmishes and hand-to-hand fights proved unsuccessful because the tangled vegetation gave advantage to the defendants for ambush and surprise attacks. Ferdinand ordered that the woods be cleared. He deployed an army of seven thousand men on this task. A deep trench was dug on the levelled ground, and the water of nearby stream were diverted into it. At the same time a long trench was dug at the rear of the city completing its encirclement. Such discipline as now was never seen in the Christian camp. Peter Martyr, the Italian priest who was present at the siege of Baza, saw in the disciplined harmony a model of Plato's Republic. But still the victory was not in sight. The Christian camp was being thinned by disease and many soldiers murmured against the continuing siege. It was felt that Isabella's presence would enliven the falling spirits of the soldiers She came on Nov. 17, 1489 in all her splendour, 'surrounded by a choir of nymphs as if to celebrate the nuptials of her child[15]. Her appearance in the forward area infused a new spirit among the soldiers. Accompanied by Ferdinand she inspected the troops. She was determined on the conquest of Baza. She had a already pawned her jewellery to the merchants of Barcelona and Valencia. But the army did not achieve any brilliant success. Skirmishes and forays continued with loss of life on both the sides. Soon the combatants realised that a negotiated settlement was the best course to end the war. The initiative came from the Muslims. Cidi Yahya visited the Christian camp, and met Ferdinand and Isabella. Ferdinand used al his diplomacy and his art of dissimulation to win over the young commander. The queen showered paternal kindness on him. She was so much impressed by his graceful manners and polite address that she proposed to take him in her service. Yahya fell a prey to their soft words. He returned to Zaghal and reported that it was fruitless to resist the Christians. Zaghal bowed to the inevitable. On Dec. 4 1489, the Spanish monarch occupied Baza, and soon after the cities of Gaudix and Almeria. Zaghal was allotted a small estate in the valley of Andaraz. He did not like to live in humiliation as a vassal of Ferdinand, and after selling his estate left Spain in 1490 for Oran.

After Zagal's defeat nothing remained in the hands of the Muslims except the city of Granada and its suburbs held by Abū 'Abdullah. He had rebelled against his father, stabbed his uncle in the back in the hope that he would be secure under the protection of his powerful ally. He was soon disappointed. After the campaign against Baza, Ferdinand threw away his mark of hypocracy, and communicated formal orders to Abū 'Abdullah to vacate Granada. He would have, in all probability, agreed to hand over Granada, if he had been his own master. At this time, the whole of Granada was in an angry mood. The people looked upon him as a traitor responsible for the ignominious defeat of Zeghal, and calamities they saw written on the wall. The idol of the people at this time was Musa ibn Ghassan, a valiant knight whose prowess and patriotism shed a lustre on the last days of Granada. Washington Irving in his 'Conquest of Granada', has drawn a pen- portrait of Musa. " He was of royal lineage, of a proud and generous nature and a form combining manly strength and beauty. None could excel him in the management of the horse, and dexterous use of all kinds of weapons. His gracefulness and skill in the tourney was a theme of praise among the Moorish dames: and his prowess in the field had made him a terror of the enemy.[16]" Musa and his small group of men of like calibre (Naim, Abdul Kerim, and Muhammad ibn Zaid) were against surrender. They preferred to die fighting beneath the walls of their beloved city. Finding himself powerless in the face of surging enthusiasm of these officers and their supporters in the public, Abū 'Abdullah sent a reply to Ferdinand asking him to wait till the public opinion became favourable. Ferdinand was not prepared to wait as he was anxious to put an end to the crusade which had already dragged on for several years. From his experience at Malaga, he had learnt that the best way to reduce a city was to starve its citizens. He adopted the same strategy at Granada. He spent the spring and autumn of 1490 in desolating the vega by fire and sword. This vast expanse of land, famous in history and romance for its fertility, was laid waste. His troops torched villages, uprooted fruit trees and vines and destroyed the harvest. By this scorched earth policy, he turned the vega into a scene of desolation[17]. In April 1491, he appeared in the suburbs of Granada with a powerful army. The last campaign of the crusade had begun.

On the orders of Musa, the gates of city were opened. Every day and night the Muslim cavalry went froth to fight the besieging army. The Christians and the Muslims fought with indomitable courage and both sides performed feats of bravery. The French ambassador marvelled at the bravery of the Muslims[18]. Thousands of them perished in the defence of Granada. In the words of the Chronicler Bernaldez 'there was not a lance that was not dyed in the blood of the indidel[19]. The marvellous defence of Granada by the Muslims was like the last flicker of the candle. While they fought alone, Ferdinand had the moral and material support of the entire Christendum The crusade against the infidels of Granada attracted men from all parts of Europe— gallant knight in quest of fresh laurels, adventurers greedy for the wealth of the cities, and pious soldiers anxious for blessings of the Hereafter. Ferdianad was getting impatient to terminate the gruelling crusade. He converted the camp into a mini city with streets, houses and stables. It was called 'Santa Fe' or the Holy city' to reminds his soldiers that they were fighting a holy war. In the meantime, the beleaguered city began to suffer from famine as winter had set in, and the passes were covered with snow, making it impossible to obtain even modest supplies of food. In despair, 'Abdullah sent his minister Abdul Qasim 'Abd al Malik to negotiate terms of surrender. The Christians were represented by Ferdinand de Zafra and Gonsalvo de Cordova who knew Arabic. The secret meetings took place in the present village of Churriana. After long and repeated meeting, 'Abd al Malik returned with a draft of the treaty.

The historian al-Maqqari has faithfully preserved the conditions of the fateful treaty. Briefly, the conditions were; that the war should end within two months; the Muslims shall be secure in person, they shall have unrestricted enjoyment of all their property both moveable and immoveable; each side shall release the prisoners of war without ransom, the Muslims shall have compete freedom of conscience and worship; their mosques and religious places shall remain intact; the muezzin shall not be interrupted in the azan; the Muslims wishing to adopt Christianity shall be allowed some days to reconsider their decision after expiry of which they shall be questioned by a court of law consisting of one Muslim and one Christian, and if he should refuse to return to Islam, he shall have the freedom to follows the new faith; in the case of a Christian willing to embrace Islam, he shall not be forced to relinquish it; Under the terms of the treaty, the Christians were forbidden to enter the mosques, to drink from or wash clothes from the fountains owned by the Muslims. It was further agreed that the Muslims shall not be required to pay taxes more than what they paid to their kings, and that they shall not be forced to serve in the army. The treaty also allowed the Muslims to have their own markets and slaughter houses. By another clause they were to enjoy full libterty to observe their customs, manners, and to dress, and use their language. The treaty also gave them the right to be judged by their own judges according to the laws of

Islam. The treaty also contained a pledge by Ferdinand and Isabella to observe its provisions[20]. The pledge read — "We ensure, promise, and swear by or faith and royal word that we shall observe and made observed everything herein contained, everything and every part, now and hereafter, now and for ever.[21]"

When these terms of the treaty were presented to 'Abdullah the only person who voiced his disapproval was Musa ibn Ghassan. He told Abū 'Abdullah in the presence of the assembly of his advisors with a prophetic sense of the future happenings: "Do not believe that the Christians will be faithful to the promises they make you. Will the king who hath led them to conquest be as generous a victor as he is a fortunate enemy? Be certain he will not. Do not deceive yourselves; these Christians are thirsting for our blood, and they will sufficiently appease their desire for that sacrifice. Death is the least of the evils that menace you; more fearful are the torments and humiliations which our inimical fortune is preparing for us; the plunder and sack of our houses, the desecration of our mosques, the outrage and degradation of our wives and daughters; wrongs of every kind; unjust demands; oppressive enactment; cruel intolerance; and the burning pile of the bigot on which these infidel will not fail to consume our miserable bodies. All these things we shall see with our eyes; those will see them that is to say those who now fear the honourable death I propose for myself—by Allah, I will not see them.[22]" They listened in gloomy silence . In disgust, Musa left the hall. He returned home, and after putting on his armour rode out of the Gate of Elvira. The treaty was signed on Nov. 25 1491.

On the morning of Jan. 2, 1492 (2nd Rabi I 897 A.H.) Abū 'Abdullah rode out from the Alhamra palace. He met Ferdinand on the bank of the Xenil. He got down from his horse to pay homage to Ferdinand, now that he was his subject, and handed over the keys of the Alhamra, saying "these are thine, since Allah so wills. Use they success with generosity." In reply, the Christian monarch spoke some words of consolation. Abū 'Abdullah moved on to pay his respects to Isabella who handed over to him his son who had been a hostage since his release from captivity. In a short while, he was seen ascending the Alpujjaras on his way to his new home. His family, and whatever goods, if any, he was allowed to take, had already been transported on mules. On the way he checked his horse to have a last glimpse of the Alhamra before it would be out of sight. He heaved a sigh, and tears welled into his eyes at the thought of losing his prestige and partimony. While he was wiping his tears, his mother Ayesha who was travelling with him chided him thus," Your are weeping like a child for what you failed to defend like a man." This rocky height at Padul is called to this day by the Spaniards — *el ultimo suspiro del Moro*, or 'the last sigh of the Moor.'

Soon after he left, the Christian troops entered the city to the sound of trumpets. The big silver cross which was borne before Ferdinand throughout the war was planted on the tower of the Alhamra by the grand bishop of Avila — Hernando de Talavera. The flags of St. James, Castile and Aragon were unfurled amidst shouts and slogans of victory. A distance away, Ferdinand and Isabella, their courtiers, and military commander knelt down in gratitude for the successful termination of the crusade[23]. The priests sang — To Deum Laudamus! Thus ended Muslim rule in Spain. By the conquest of Granada, the defeat of Roderick at the bank of the Gaudalete was finally avenged at the bank of the Xenil. The struggle for reconquest started by Pelayo and his handful of supporters at the Bay of Biscay, seven centuries back, was brought to a glorious cosummation by Ferdinand and Isabella. It was indeed a marvellous achievement, the glorious fulfilment of a great yearning. The fame of the great victory was blazed throughout Christendom. The event was celebrated by a mass at St. Peters where public rejoicings lasted several days. At Naples they enacted plays in which the Prophet of Islam was insulted. A thanks-giving ceremony was also held at St. Paul's Cathedral in London[24]. The Spanish people keep alive the memory of the crusade by annual fiestas and mock battles.

The rest of Abū 'Abdullah's life is not pleasant telling. He languished in the valley of Porchenna for a year or so. Every effort was made to induce him to embrace Roman Catholicism, but without any success. Sometime in 1493, like his uncle, he too sold his estate, and boarded a boat at the port of Adra for north Africa. He landed at Melila, and settled at Fez along with his family. He entered into the service of the reigning Merinid sultan Mulay Ahmad. He served as a commander, and took part in several battles. It was destined that this Spanish prince who lost his own crown, should lay down his life in preserving the kingdom of another prince. He died fighting for the Merinid ruler in 1533, and was buried outside the *bāb al-Shari'a* in the city of Fez. His descendants fell on evil days. After a century they were seen begging their way through life.

The fall of the kingdom of Granada marks the end of Muslim rule in Spain, but the story of the Spanish Muslms is not yet over. There were thousands of Muslims in the erstwhile kingdom of Granada as well as in Valencia, Murcia and other part of Spain who for one reason or the other, had remained behind. They differed in language and customs; they dressed differently, they had different names;, they had their own laws of marriage divorce and inheritance, they had different food habits. In short they followed a different pattern of life. How to treat this seemingly unassimilable element of the Spanish population? For more than a century, this was one of the most vexed questions of Spain's domestic policy. When the French king Francis I who was a prisoner of Charles V (successor of Ferdinand) and the story of the conquest of Granada was narrated to him, he is said to have exclaimed," And these Musulmans? They were not driven out. Then everything is still to be done[25]." We shall now see how Catholic Spain solved this problem.

Notes

1. We have now reached a stage when Muslim sources on subsequent history are very limited. Ibn Khatib died in1317, and ibn Khaldun in 1406. As usual, the main Arabic source is al-Maqqari who mostly depended on a small booklet entitled 'Tuhfat al 'Asr fi'naqida' Dawlat bani Nasr'. On the other hand western historian, are useful. They went direct to the Christian chronicles of Pulgar, Bernaldez, Mendoza, Carvajal, Peter Martyr, and many others. For this chapter and those that follow, I have depended on the masterly works of Prescott and H.C. Lea. I have also utilized Washington Irving's Conquest of Granada and Condé's History of the Dominion of the Arabs in Spain where necessary, in addition to numerous articles in the Ency. of Islam (New Edition).

2. Washington Irving: The Conquest of Granada. p. 3.

3. Pescott: Ferdinand and Isabella, vol I, pp. 261-269 and Washington Irving: pp. 49-56, describe the numerous encounters in the mountain passes.

4. Machiavelli: The Prince. (Eng. Trans by George Bull, London 1980) pp 119-120. Machiavelli is full of praise for Ferdinand for his pious cruelly in chasing out the Moors from the kingdom of Granada

5. Prescott: Ferdinand & Isabella Vol I pp 273-274 Condé, pp 357-358, and Washington Irwing, p 81 Abdullah's son was handed over to Martin de Alarcon, a high official with instructions to treat the boy with every possible care.

6. Condé, vol III p 373, Irving p 188. The Muslim commander was called Reduan/Rodovan in Christian chronicles. These are only modified forms of 'Rizwān' a popular Muslim name all over the Muslim world.

7. On descriptions of Malaga, consult Al-Himyari, pp. 312-315, ibn Battutah pp 314-315, and Ency. Of Islam article 'Malaka.'

8. Presacott: Ferdinand & Isabella, vol I p,307 & p 309. Pulgar also praises the chivalry of the Muslims. While the war was going on, a Muslim came across a number Spanish children who had wandered from their homes. The brave Knight touched their backs with his lance saying, "Get Ye gone to your mothers," "An example of magnanimity" says the curate of Los Palacios, "truly wonderful in a heathen, and which might have reflected credit on a Christian hidalgo."

9. Ibid.

10. Prescott; Ferdinand & Isabella vol. I p. 311-312.

11. Ibid.

12. Ibid.

13. Ibn Khaldun: The Muqqadimah, Vol. II p. 118.

14. Prescott; Ferdinand and Isabella Vol. II, p. 326. The entire chapter XIV (pp. 315-333) relates to the conquest of Baza which according to the author was "one of the most precious jewels in the diadem of Granada."

15. Ibid, p. 327.

16. W. Irving: p. 280.

17. Prescott: Ferdinand & Isabella, Vol. I, p. 336.

18. Irving: 316

19. Prescott Ferdinand & Isabella, Vol. I p. 340.

20. Al-Maqqari/Gayangos, vol. II pp 388-389. The treaty had 37 clauses

21. Louis Bertrand: The History of Spain, London, 1952, p. 147.

22. Condé: Vol. III pp. 397-398, Irving: p. 321.

23. Christopher Columbus was among the spectators. He recorded in his Diario, "This present year of 1492 on the second day of the month of January, I saw the Moorish king come out to the gate of the city, and kiss the Royal Hands of Your Highnesses." (The Muslim World of January, 1993, p. 4 of the article — "Inter-religious conflict and Columbus" by Rogers A Johnson.

24. Prescott: Ferdinand & Isabella Vol. I, pp. 346-347. Lord Bacon, the famous essayist himself attended the service.

25. Louis Bertrand; p. 147.

Chapter 16

Bearing the Cross

————•·•————

After the crusade against Granada was over, Ferdinand handed over the conquered territory to civil and military administration. In the last week of May 1492, he and his queen left on a tour of their kingdom. At this time, and even long afterwards, there existed in Spain a well-organised ecclesiastical order side by side with the civil administration. The Roman Catholic clergy — priests, prelates, friars and cardinals, constituted an *imperium in imperio* professing allegiance only to the Pope at Rome. During the crusade, the church had played a leading role. The priests bearing crosses in their hands, were present at every campaign to uphold the morale of the army. They were unhappy at the presence of the large number of the Muslim and the Jews in the country. They believed that Spain belonged to only those who professed the Roman Catholic faith. The first axe fell on the Jews. Hardly three months after the annexation of Granada, an edict was issued by the Spanish sovereigns on March 30, 1492, ordering the Jews to leave the country. The fact that two Jews (Abraham and Isacc) had provided money to the Catholic rulers for their war with Granada was of no consequence in their eyes. The Jews offered a sum of thirty thousands ducats to propitiate the king, but the heartless priest Torquemada who was head of the Inquisition burst into the royal chamber and shouted "Judas Iscariot sold his master for thirty pieces of silver. Your Highness would sell him again for thirty thousand". He flung the crucifix before the royal couple and left[1]. They did not react to the rude behaviour of the priest. Isabella could not go against the fanatic Torquemada as he had been her confessor during her youthful days. The edict was enforced and thousand of the Jews, despoiled of their wealth, left for Muslim north Africa. Most of them settled in Morocco. Some reached Naples, others migrated to Turkey where one could come across Spanish speaking Jews till recently. After the Jews were gone, the clergy turned to the Muslims.

A steady exit of the Muslims had already began. Many notable families of Granada and passed into the cities of northwest Africa. Sometime in 1492, it was reported that all member of the famous Banu Sirraj family had left. This indicates that the Muslims were not sure of their safety under their new masters. For sometime they lived in peace. The travel book of Munzer who was in Granada two years after the crusade gives no indication of the persecution of the Muslims. Not along after a movement for conversion of the Muslims began at Granada. The head of the clergy at this time was Archbishop Hernado de Talavera who was also the confessor to Isabella. He was a kindly soul. He respected the Muslim; he used to say about them: "They aught to adopt our faith, and we aught to adopt their morals[2]." Unlike other priests, he believed that conversion to Christianity should be done through peaceful means. He and some of his colleagues, learnt Arabic to expound the teaching of Christianity to the Muslims. By his ceaseless efforts and offer of gifts, he succeeded in wining over some converts. The progress was slow, and many priests desired that drastic measures be adopted to accelerate the pace of conversion.

The leader of this group was Cardinal Ximenes, the Archbishop of Toledo. He arrived at Granada with the approval of Ferdinand to help Talavera in his missionary work. Soon after he reached Granada, he summoned some leading Muslims, and explained to them the teachings of Christianity. He liberally distributed gifts among them. The number of the Muslims wishing to abjure Islam increased so much that on one day (Dec. 18, 1499) about four thousand Muslims were said to have presented themselves for mass baptismal.

The thinking element among the Muslims were alarmed at this mass defection, and they vigorously exercised their influence to prevent it. Ximenes was angry at their interference with his activities. He had their leader named Zaghri arrested. He was so much tortured that he gave up his religion to escape painful death. Ximenes hated both Islam and the Arabic language. He collected Arabic books and had them burnt. "Neither splendour of outward garniture, nor intrinsic merit of composition could atone for the taint of heresy in the eyes of the stern inquisitor," says Prescott. The bonfire of books celebrated by Ximenes destroyed no less than a hundred thousands books. The intolerant policy of Ximenes caused unrest and resentment among the Muslims. Some Christians, no doubt disapproved of the activities of Ximenes, but the bigoted priest silenced them with these words—" a tamer policy might, indeed suit temporal matters, but not those in which the interest of the souls were at stake: that the believer if he could not be drawn should be driven into the way of salvation and that it was no time to stay hand when the ruins of Mohametism were tottering to their foundation[3]." The cardinal proceeded with his work with greater resolution because he had the tacit connivance of the government. The Muslims patiently bore his oppression, but one day an incident led to a riot. A girl was being dragged for baptismal against her

will through the Albaysin locality. Some Muslims came forward
to release her. This led to a dispute and a scuffle. A section of
infuriated mob surrounded the house of the Cardinal and if he
had not been well-protected, he would not have escaped alive
as the Albaysin was still thickly populated by the Muslims
inspite of voluntary exodus to Africa. Count Tendilla the military
governor rushed to the spot with his troops along with Talavera.
By their conciliatory attitude they won over the mob, and peace
was restored in the disturbed locality. The Muslims who were
held responsible for the riot were handed over to the
administration, and four of them were executed.

A government anxious for the safety of its religious minorities
should have tried and punished Ximenes who was the real villain
of the piece. We are told that Ferdinand was unhappy when the
news of the riot reached him at Seville where he normally
resided. He summoned Ximenes and demanded his explanation.
The bold Cardinal went to Seville. He admitted his responsibility
for the riot, but also assured Ferdinand that what he was doing
was in the best interest of the Christian faith. It seems that the
king was satisfied with the Cardinal's reply because he returned
to Granada and worked with greater enthusiasm. The number
of converts increased so much that even the meek Talavera was
full of praise for the Cardinal. Said Talavera, "Ximenes has
achieved greater triumphs than Ferdinand and Isabella: since
they conquered the soil but he had gained the souls of Granada[4]".

While the Muslims of Granada were sulking with rage, events
were taking a different shape in the Alpujarras. This mountainous
region is one of the most picturesque in Spain. It lies to the
southeast of the snow-covered Sierra Nevada, and stretches to
the shore of the Mediterranean. The whole terrain is broken
into ragged hills , ravines and frightening chasms which make

the journey into the interior both difficult and risky. For this reason, it remained one of the least explored regions of Spain. It has been opened to tourists only in the last few decades when some roads were built. But even now one has to either walk or to ride to reach the interior of the Alpujarras. There are several beautiful valleys— Padul, Bexnar, Lanjaran, Cardiar, Ugijar, Cadavar etc. Many small towns with Árabic names (Almocita, Bubion, and Mecina Alfahar, to cite a few) are dotted all over the Alpujarras. In these delightful valleys, "the Moorish peasant had exhausted the elaborate culture which in the palmy days of his nation was unrivalled in Europe[5]." The Muslim farmers had cut terraces on the rocks, and planted them with vines and fruit trees. The Alpujarras was the home of a sturdy people mostly of Berber origin who were proud of their faith. When they heard about the tortures and forceful conversions going on in Granada, they feared that a similar fate might befall them also. They decided to throw off the yoke of government which had gone back on its pledges. The Alpujarras was up in arms. Angry mobs broke into violence and killed the Christians and the new converts. Count Tendilla deputed Gonsalvez de Cordova and Alonso de Aquilar to suppress the insurgents. When the latter died fighting, and the mob fury remained unabetted, Ferdinand himself appeared on the scene in March 1500 with a massive force. The insurgents were routed at every place. The Spanish army took full revenge for the reverse suffered by it at the initial stage. At Andarax a mosque where women and children had taken shelter was blown up with gun powder[6]. At Belfique all men were put to death, and women carried away in slavery. The entire population of Guejar and Nijar was enslaved and children below eleven were distributed among the Chrisitans[7]. By the end of April, 1500 the revolt was completely suppressed. The Muslims were forced to pay a fine of fifty thousand ducats.

The mosques in the Alpujarras were pulled down, and the entire region was flooded with priests for missionary work. By the middle of Jan. 1501, some ten thousand Muslims of Seron, Tijola and nearby places were baptised and nearly the whole population of Gaudix and Almeria abjured Islam. To hasten the process of conversion, Ferdinand passed the edict of Feb. 12,1502 by which the Muslims were ordered to either embrace Christianity or leave the country by 30th April. But after the expiry of the date, the conditions regarding exile were made so stringent that few could dare to leave the country. The avowed aim of the government was that the Muslims should remain in Spain, but only after conversion to Christianity[8]. By the middle of the 15th century, most if not all of the Muslims of the former kingdom of Granada had turned Christian. But except some who embraced Christianity (their number was very small) the rest of them were at heart devout Muslim. They were called 'Moriscos' or little Moors. After baptismal, they took Spanish names, but they secretly adhered to the teachings of Islam. They attended the mass, but on returning home, they prayed as Muslims, fasted in the month of Ramazan, and read the Quran behind closed doors. In their secret profession of Islam which they loved, while outwardly conforming to the rites of a religion forced on them, lies the pathos, the poignancy of their suffering. It is a rather unique phenomenon and proves the tenacity of Islam to survive in a ruthless environment.[9] As the Moriscos had taken baptismal (even if under compulsion), but secretly practised the rites of Islam, they were looked upon as heretics. This brought them within the purview of the Holy Inquisition — the fearful tribunal for punishment of the heretics.

So far we were concerned with the Muslims who lived in the kingdom of Granada. We may now have to see what was happening to the Muslims who lived in other parts of Spain. As the Christian reconquest advanced, the Muslims left Spain in a large numbers. In the middle of the 13th century, there were hardly any Muslims left around the Gaudalquivir. Cities, and town and whole villages were cleared of them . However, there were pockets of the Muslims in Valencia, Murica although their number is not exactly known. In many villages in Valencia and Murica they were perhaps in a majority. There were sizeable pockets in Albarracin. Tueral, suburbs of Saragossa and even in Navarre. They were known as the mudéjares' They were vassals of the big landlords on whose estates they worked, and resided in their ghettos called 'morerias.' They were, by and large, farmers, artisans, builders— the educated intelligentcia was very much thinned by mass migration to Africa. The 'mudéjares' were granted protection by their landlords and even allowed freedom of worship much to the annoyance of the clergy. The mudéjares were loyal to their masters, and also to the government They willingly helped the government in times of need. In 1283, Pedro relied on these Muslims to check the invasion of Philippe le Hardi[10]. In 1385 they supplied their quota of levies raised at Murcia for war with Potugal. They kept up relations with their brothers-in-faith living in the kingdom of Granada, and never stabbed in the back of Castile and Aragon if they went to war with the Muslim kingdom. The 'mudajare' Muslims were indispensable to the state. A proverb current in those days said, "mientras mas Moro mas ganancia" i.e. the more the Moors, the more the profit[11]. They were the only dependable source of income to the government and the clergy because they paid their taxes willingly even if they were overtaxed. In the words of the historian Henry Charles Lea." It was on their industry, moreover, that the prosperity of the land reposed. None of the resources of the State were more relied upon than the revenues which they furnished. They were virtually indispensable to the nobles on whose lands they were settled for they were most skilful in agriculture and unwearied in labour. They carried these characteristics in every department of industry, science and art. As physicians they ranked with the Jews, and when, in 1345 the prior of the order of Santiago built the church of Nuestra Senora de Ucles, we are told that he assembled Moorish masters, and good Christian stone masons who erected the structure. They were equally skilled in marine architecture, and the Catalan power in the Mediterranean was largely due to their labours. The wonderful system of irrigation by which they converted Valencia into the garden of Europe still exists, with is elaborate and equitable allotments of waters. They introduced the culture of sugar, silk cotton rice and many valuable products and not a spot of available ground was left untitled by their indefatigable industry. The Mohometan law which prescribed labour as a religious duty was fully obeyed, and every member of a family contributed his share of work to the common support... They were temperate and frugal; they married early, the girls at eleven and the boys at twelve without fear of the future, for a bed and ten libras or ducats were considered sufficient dowery. There were no beggars among them for they took affectionate care of their own poor and and orphans; they settled all quarrels among themselves and held it unlawful to prosecute each other before a Christian tribunal. In Short, they constituted the most desirable population that any land could possess, and we shall have occasion to note hereafter the curious perversity with which these good qualities were converted into accusations against them by their Christian persecutors[12]."

Some Christian rulers patronised Muslim learning, employed architects and craftsmen. They admired refinement of the Muslims and listened their music and learnt from them the courtly respect for the fair sex, a salient feature of medieval chivalry. "But these good relations decreased (says the modern Spanish historian Altamira) in proportion as the territory under the Muslims decreased.[13]" Below the surface of this outward cordiality, there lurked a deep-rooted hatred for the pagans. The church felt scandalised at the sight of the Muslim pockets in the midst of the Christians. The clergy, as stated earlier, had a tremendous influence over the rulers, and it was easy for them to fan the smouldering embers of hatred into a blaze of violent fanaticism against the Muslims. One of the earliest examples is furnished by an incidence following the conquest of Toledo by Alfonso VI who styled himself.' imperador de los dos cultos' or Emperor of two religions. At the time of the surrender, he had pledged that the Muslims shall be free to practise their religion. But soon after Archbishop Bernard made a surprise attack on the principal mosque with the help of troops, and converted it into a church. Alfonso who was away, hastened to Toledo. He wanted to punish the guilty and to return the mosque to the Muslims. But the Muslims, seeing their helplessness, implored him to pardon the offenders, and they also declined to receive back the mosque. Their argument was that to punish the guilty would mean that they would suffer the consequences of stored-up resentment after the king was no more. Alfonso must have been delighted at the conciliatory attitude of the Muslims because he conferred a rare honour on their spokesman. "Among the sculptured figures adorning the chancel of alter in the church is one of the Moor Abū Wahid, the mudéjare alfaqi or savant who was spokesmen for the Muslims when they urged the king Alfonso VI not to inflict punishment on the despoilers of the mosque[14]."

After the battle of Las Navas de Tolosa, Alfonso IX advanced toward Ubeda where seventy thousand Muslims offered to become his vassals on payment of ransom of a million doblas. The king was ready ot accept the offer, but the clergy led by Rodrigo of Toledo, and Arnaud of Narbonne forced him to reject the offer, and the "Moors were all massacred except such as were reserved a slaves.[15]" The Spanish rulers were under constant pressure from the clergy and the Popes to expel the mudéjare Muslims. From the 14th century onwards a number of measures were taken to humiliate the Muslims and to demoralize them. Even the pleadings of the sympathetic landlords for protection of the mudéjare Muslims were of no avail.

How helpless were the landlords in protecting the Muslims is proved by the agrarian revolt known as 'Germania' which broke out in Aragon in 1520. This was a rising of the poor Spaniards against the oppressions of the landlords. The mudéjare Muslims kept aloof from the rebels, and remained attached to the landlords. They even supplied men to root out the rebellion. The rising was over in 1522 but he leaders of the movement did not forgive the Muslims and unleashed a vendetta against them. They initiated forcible conversion of the mudéjare Muslims. Valencia saw the first outburst on July 4, 1521, when a Franciscan monk appeared brandishing a crucifix and shouting, "Long live the faith of Christ, and war to the Saracens.[16]" The wandering bandits called 'Agermanados' took the law in their hands and spread all over the province destroying the property of the Muslims and forcing them ot embrace Christianity. These wandering fanatics let loose a veritable inferno over the Muslims. At Jativa, Alcoy and many other places, the residential colonies of the Muslims were burnt and many families perished in flames. At Gandia and Oliva they were driven into church amidst shouts of "Death to the Moors", "Dogs be baptised". The mosques were converted into churches, and the pictures of Christ and the Virgin were fixed on the doors.

About twenty thousand Muslims fled away to Africa inspite of the assurances of their landlord[17].

Forcible conversion of the Muslims continued unabated under Charles V who came to the throne in 1518. He was Charles I at home, but emperor Charles V as head of the Holy Roman Empire. It was neither holy, nor a Roman empire, but Charles as emperor was the champion of the Catholic Church. He believed that the political stability of a state could be achieved only if all the subjects profess only one religion. He was opposed to all innovations and schism in the Church. He banned the activities of Martin Luther. He could not view with equanimity that many of has subjects followed the teachings of a religion other than Roman Catholicism. He had before him the example of Ferdinand, Isabella, and Ximenes who had, at least, outwrdly converted the Muslims of Granada and Castile to Roman Catholicism. He wanted to stimulate the conversion of all the mudéjare Muslims of Aragon. There was, however, a technical difficulty in taking harsh measures because at the time of his accession he had taken an oath to protect all his subjects. He wanted to be relieved ot that pledge. He put pressure on Pope Clement VII to grant him freedom from the pledge through the Duke of Sesa his ambassador at the papal court. On May 12, 1524 an obliging Pope issued the historic brief which absolved Charles from all censures and penalties of perjury. The brief expressed grief that many subjects of Charles were 'Moor with whom the faithful cannot hold intercourse without danger.' The document authorised the emperor to adopt all measures for conversion of the Muslims, and in case of their obstinacy to stick to their faith, they either be exiled or put under perpetual slavery. On the basis of this papal permission, Charles issued the memorable Edict of Nov. 25, 1525 which required the Muslims to give up Islam, and embrace Roman Catholicism.

Those who wanted to adhere to their religion were to leave Spain — the mudéjares of Valencia by the 31st Dec., 1525, and those of Aragon and Catalonia by the 31st Jan., 1526. The Edict further laid down that those who wanted to leave Spain should obtain their passport at Cuenca, and take ships at the port of Coruna via valladolid and Madrid. The port of embarkment in the far north, and the route were intentionally prescribed because the journey to Coruna was long and hazardous. This was done because the government wanted the Muslims to convert to Christianity, and not to leave the country. This is clear from yet another condition by which they were forbidden to sell their property, while the Christians were prohibited to purchase any property or article put up for sale by the Muslims. As a result of this Edict serious riots broke out at Almonacir and Castillo de Maria (near Saragossa) and in the Sierra de Espadan. The Muslims rose under a leader named Selim Almanzo, but they were overpowered by the military. The leaders were strangled, the pulpits were broken, and the copies of the Quran were burnt. During these riots hundreds of mudéjare Muslims lost their lives. The Spaniards slew old men and women, looted property which was sold for thousands of ducats. In this way says H.C. Lea, the Muslims of Valencia and Aragon were 'compelled to submit to the Gospel[18]. Like the Muslims of the former kingdom of Granada, they adopted only Christian names, but remained impervious to the teachings of Christianity. They were advised by their theologians that is was a sin to follow a religion thrust upon them, but it was perfectly lawful to practise their religion in secrecy. After the incidents described above all the Muslims were called Moriscos. As they followed Islam in secrecy, while posing as Christians, they were heretics, in the eyes of the clergy, and the Holy Inquisition took upon itself the responsibility to turn them into true

Christians by trial and torture. To what extent the government and the Inquisition were successful remains to be seen.

The Holy Inquisition was a Roman Catholic institution created in the 13th century in Italy to make inquiries into cases of heresy, and all beliefs and practices which contravened the dogmas of the church. As this tribunal is known to all students of history, I give here such facts only as are relevant to the present context. (The reader can pursue the subject in the three-volumed "History of the Inquistion", by the American H.C. Lea. It is a classic on the subject written after a study of original documents rarely available to a historian). The Inquisition was established in Spain by Pope Gregory IX, but it was given a permanent footing in Spain by the appointment in 1483 of Tomas de Torquemada as the Inquisitor General for Castile and Aragon. When Musa Ibn Ghassan in his parting speech at the Alhamra, warned the gathering of the prosecutions which the Muslims would have to undergo after Granada surrendered, he was no doubt, aware of the working of the Inquisition. Like the tentacles of an octopus, the tribunals of the Inquisition were spread all over Spain. Its officials were recruited from the clergy. They formed the spiritual militia of pious priests of high rank who were strict followers of Jesus Christ because they wanted to keep his faith free from all schisms. The Inquisition worked with the utmost secrecy. A suspected heretic was arrested by the spies of the Inquisition, and put in prison. After his arrest, he simply disappeared from the earth, and no one knew his whereabouts. He was allowed to defend himself, but he had to choose his counsel from the list supplied by the judges. During the trial, the prisoner was not considered innocent because the mere fact of his arrest was regarded as a sufficient proof of his guilt[19]. The prisoner was made to confess, and subjected to barbarous tortures. (Some of these instruments of torture are displayed in a museum at Toledo). Those found guilty were punished according to the nature of their offence. In lighter offences, they were required to undergo certain penances for their reformation or to put on special dress of yellow colour called sanbenito to be worn in public. The Inquisition could also impose heavy fines, confiscation of property and life imprisonment in a dungeon. If a prisoner refused to recant, he was relaxed i.e. he was burned alive at a ceremony called 'auto de fe' or an act of faith[20].

The case of a Morisco women named Maria Gomez who secretly followed Islam gives an insight into the practical working of the Inquisition[21]. She was a native of Daimiel, and was arrested on May I, 1540 on the basis of evidence which was being collected since 1538. The judges read out to her the information which established that she was a practising Muslim. She hesitated in making her confession. On June 8, She was taken to the torture chamber, and stripped. She confessed, and was sentenced to life imprisonment. After three years, the jailer testified that she was a penitent, and she was released on the condition that she would hear the mass on all Sundays and confess on Christmas, Easter and Pentecost. But her woes were not over. In 1559, she was again arrested for being a relapsed impenitent. It was reported that she had killed a lamb in the Muslim manner, changed her sanbenito for normal dress, and was irregular in attending the mass. It was further alleged that she proposed to marry her son within the prohibited relationship, and that she often uttered the word 'Allah'. The Judges ordered that she be tortured to extract a confession of her guilt. Her legs and feet were tied and she was placed on a frame called the escalera, and water was poured into her throat. The women shrieked with pain, but she did not make any confession. The judges gave their verdict. She was put under house arrest for four months with permission to come out only on Sunday for attending the Church. She was required to fast on Fridays, to the chant four paters and Aves. "Now all this was (says Lea) the every day routine of the inquisition, and there is small cause for surprise if the Moriscos were confirmed more and more in their abhorence of a faith propagated after this fashion[22]."

Notes

1. Prescott: Ferdinand & Isabella, Vol. I, p. 368. This historian has devoted the entire chapter No: XVII on the expulsion of the Jews and their dreadful sufferings.
2. H.C. Lea: p. 7 (Harnando di Talarvera was the same priest who planted the Cross on the Alhamra).
3. Presoctt: Ferdinand & Isabella, Vol III, p. 371 and pp. 376-378.
4. Ibid
5. Prescott: History of the Reign of Philip II, Vol III, p. 5,
6, 7 & 8. H.C. Lea: Moriscos of Spain, pp. 38-39.
7. Ibid.,
8. H.C. Lea: pp 44-45. Some of these condition were absurd and cruel. They were ordered to sail only from the bay Biscay. They were not to go to Turkey or Egypt of any country near Spain. All children, male over fourteen and female over twelve were to remain behind.
9. Just as Islam has survived in the Central Asian Republics and even in eastern Russia, in the face of regimentation and suppression imposed by the bandits and bigoted atheists of Moscow.
10. H.C. Lea: p. 5-7 and p. 57.
11. Ibid
12. Ibid
13-14. Altamira: p. 134 and p. 146.
15. H.C. Lea: p. 4.
16-17. H.C. Lea: 63-68 for full details.
18. H.C. Lea: pp. 82-95.
19. Ibid p. 111-113. Thanks to Protugal, the Holy Inquisition was introduced in Goa also.
20,21-22. H.C. Lea: The entire chapter no. V is relevant in this connection. The case of Maria Gomez, will be found at pages 114-117.

Chapter 17

The War of Liberation

———•◆•———

We shall take up the activities of the Inquisition later on, and in the meantime, revert to Granada where 'the experiment was pushed to the uttermost of how far the endurance of a population could be tried by oppression and wrong of every kind[1]'. In 1556, Charles abdicated in favour of his son Philip II. He had inherited from his father his hatred of non-Catholics. From the very outset. he was determined 'never to rule over heretics' — whether they were Protestants in Flanders, or the Moriscos in Spain. In the early years of his reign he was too much occupied with foreign affairs. Nevertheless he passed a few irritating laws which gave ample premonitions of the fate that awaited the Moriscos. The Moriscos of Granada employed Negroes in their homes and on their farms. As they were inclined to Islam, it was feared that the number of the Muslims might increase. A law was passed in 1560 prohibiting the employment of Negroes. By another law passed three years later the Moriscos were forbidden to posses arms. These were a prelude to an ordinance which worsened the situation, and forced the Moriscos to fight for their liberation. The apostasy of the Moriscos, or to be more precise, the constancy with which they secretly adhered to Islam, was a source of great annoyance to the clergy. Everyone knew that they conformed only outwardly to such Catholic practices as were unavoidable. In all other respects, they were different from the old Christian. An attempt was made during the reign of Charles to do away with all the customs and rites which gave them a distinct individuality, by passing the Edict of Dec. 7 1526. However this was not enforced strictly as the Moriscos paid eighty thousand ducats to Charles, and also agreed to pay a special tax (known as farda) in lieu of permission to use their language and dress[2]. Philip was not prepared to grant any such permission.

Don Pedro Guerro, the Archbishop of Granada submitted a memorial to the government in which he cited numerous facts to prove that the Moriscos had made a mockery of religion by taking baptismal while they continued to be heretics at heart. The memorial alleged that they attended church only to escape being fined; on days of Christian festivals they stayed at home; they observed weekly holiday on Friday instead of Sunday. The report also said that they frequently washed themselves daily — even on chilly days: their children were baptised for show only and they washed off the traces of baptisms, and on returning home they gave Islamic names to their children; the male children were secretly circumcised; they had memorized certain prayers to pass off as Christian. At the time of marriage the couple appeared in church in Christian robes borrowed from neighbours, but on returning home, the marriage was solemnised according to Islamic rites, and the nuptials were celebrated with zamras and leilas, the traditional Muslim dances[3]. Before submitting his memorial, the Archbishop had visited Rome, and discussed the matter with Pope Pius IV. The holy pontiff reprimanded the Spanish government on their slackness in converting the Moriscos as true Christians. Don Pedro's memorial could not, therefore, be ignored. Philip appointed a commission to study the matter and to submit its recommendations. The commission was headed by Diego de Espinosa who was Philip's evil genius' in the words of Lea.

The commission recommended that the Moriscos should be forcibly disassociated from all those influences which had their roots in their history and the faith of Islam. They should be compelled to stop speaking Arabic, and all the documents in Arabic be translated into Spanish. All books in Arabic should be deposited with Deza , the head of the local office. The Moriscos were given three years to learn Spanish. They should be required to put on the national dress of the Christians and their women should go without the veil. Their marriages should be conducted in public in the Christian manner, and they should keep the doors of their houses open during the marriage ceremony. They should be forced to stop frequent bathing and washing, and all the baths public and private, should be demolished[4]. These recommendation were accepted by Philip and incorporated (on Nov. 17, 1566) in a royal Pragmatica which for 'cruelty and absurdity, has scarcely a parallel in history[5]. On Jan. 1, 1567 on which day the Spanish government celebrated every years, the capture of Granada, the officials of the government took out a procession to the great public square— the bab all-bonat where the provision of the fateful order were read out before a gathering of the Moriscos. Similar announcements were made at other places also. To begin with, all the baths were to pulled down immediately, and the children between three and fifteen were to be placed in schools run by the priests for being taught Christian theology in Spanish.

We can imagine the effect of this barbarous law on the helpless Moriscos. Everywhere in the former kingdom of Granada it was received with feelings of anger, anguish and resentment. They decided to make a representation to the President of Castile, and an elderly Moriscos was chosen to explain the impracticability of the law. He argued that a particular dress involved no religious considerations, that if their women covered their faces, modestry was the obvious reason, that their songs were equally harmless, that the use of Arabic had nothing to do with religion since it was spoken by many Christians outside Spain, and that bathing was a part of cleanliness. All these arguments feel on deaf ears. The president replied that the law was just and holy and could not be repealed as His Majesty estimated the salvation of a single soul as of greater price than all the revenues he drew from the Moriscos[6]. The Moriscos sent a direct appeal to the emperor. A noblemen named Don Juan Henriquez of Baza who had a strong sympathy for the Moriscos proceeded to Madrid, and obtained an audience with Philip. He received a rebuff in return. Phillip told him, "What I have done in this matter has been done by the advice of wise and conscientious men *(hombres de ciencia y concienca)* who have given me to understand that it was my duty[7]." Henriquez did not give up his efforts. He saw Espinosa the influential minister of Philip. The minister expressed his amazement that he should espouse the couse of the Moriscos, and bluntly told him that the law shall be enforced[8]. The Moriscos did their best to solve the matter peacefully, but the stern attitude of the government and the clergy left no room for negotiations, and much against their wishes, they took to arms. Aben Farax, a dyer by profession, took upon himself the task of raising a small force to attack the city of Granada. The Holy Thursday in the month of April (when the Christian would be busy in religious ceremonies) was fixed for the contemplated attack. In the meantime, an impassioned appeal was despatched to the sultan of Morocco for help. By accident this appeal (in the from of a traditional Arabic poem) fell into the hands of Mondejar, the governor of Granada. It was composed by one Muhammad bin Daud[9]. Mondejar had it translated into Spanish, and despatched it to Philip. This poem confirmed the rumours, already current of the impending revolt of the Moriscos. Mondejar at once strengthen the garrison, and freely distributed arms to the Christians. The Moriscos suspected of conspiracy were put in prison. Aben Farax was already in the Alpujarras rousing the people to rise against the government[10]. The revolutionary spirit spread all over this mountainous region inhabited by a people known for their reckless bravery, and in Dec. 1568, it developed into a war of liberation. In order to make the movement a success, the Moriscos needed an authoritative leader to serve as a symbol of inspiration. The long-forgotten name of the Umayyad dynasty, builders of the glorious Caliphate of Cordova, flashed across their minds in this dark hour of their destiny. There lived at Albaysin a young man known by his Spanish name— don Fernand de Valor, who descended from the Umayyads. He escaped from Granada, and took shelter in the Alpujarras. The Moriscos acclaimed him as their ruler, and he was solemnly crowned at Andarax as Mulay Muhammad Abū Omeya, Lord of Andalusia and Granada. Thus a parallel government was set up in the Alpujarras. Omeya toured the sierras rousing the people to revert of the faith of Islam. At several places, the Moriscos turned violent. The greedy tax-collectors, the spies of the Inquisition who were mostly priests were the target of mob fury. The revolutionaries destroyed the newly-built churches, broke the crosses and killed the priests, in the most barbarous manner. An Augustine priest was thrown in a cauldron of boiling oil. At another place, a priest was raised up by means of a pulley to a certain height and allowed to fall on the ground repeatedly, till he died. Even the children of mixed marriages were not spared.

Once again, the Alpujarras was aflame with one of the cruelest wars in history. On Jan. 2, 1569, Mondejar set out with his army leaving Granada in the charge of his son, Count of Tendilla. A large number of troops were quartered on the Moriscos of the Albaysin "where they freely indulged in the usual habits of military license". The complaints made to the Count were replied with haughty rebukes[11]. Taking his route through the valley of Lecrin, Mondejar halted at Padual to refresh his troops before reaching the gorge of Tablate which commanded the entrance into the region. There was a bridge across the frightful chasm which the Moriscos had destroyed leaving only such a flimsy support as would enable only one daring man to cross at a time. The soldiers were frightened at the thought of crossing the shattered bridge but a brave Fransiscan monk named Christovel of Molina, invoking the name of Jesus, and balancing himself with a crucifix in one hand and a sword in the other, succeeded in reaching the other side[12]. The bridge was repaired and Mandejar was able to transport his army. The Moriscos had fortified their position near the pass of Alfajarali beyond which lay Bubion, the capital of the district. It was a ruggesd terrain, suitable for querilla warfare. Aben Omeya intended to lure the Spaniards in the labyrinthine hills. As soon as they entered into the pass, the Moriscos made a sudden sally like a swarm of angry hornets and charge their enemy with musket balls, stones and arrows dipped in poison. (The poison was extracted from wolfsbane which grew wild in the Alpujarras) But the Moriscos could not hold on against the superior might of Mondejar's army, and they ran away as swiftly as they had emerged from their ambush. In this campaign as well as those that followed the fight was between two unequals. They were ill-equipped to fight in heavy snow and bitter cold. The route was open for the victorious Spaniards to march upon Bubion where the Moriscos had left their treasures of bullion, jewellery and fine silk fabrics. The town was practically defenceless. The Spanish army took as much booty as they could carry, and committed the rest to flames. Mondejar protected the Moriscos women, as his policy was to leave the door ajar for reconciliation. There was no question of winding up the campaign to start negotiations. The next target of the army was Jubiles. The Moriscos offered no resistance, still the town was plundered when it was occupied on Jan. 18, 1569. Some two thousand women and three hundred men were taken into captivity. The men were huddled into a camp, and the females were accommodated in a church. At night a Spanish soldier tried to molest a Moriscos girl. Her lover who was disguised as a women saw all this. The enraged Othello drew his scimitar to avenge the wrong done to his Desdamona. Soon a wild cry rose that there were soldiers disguised as women among the captives. In a fit of blind fury, the Spanish soldiers attacked the camp. The butchery lasted the whole night. "It was not till the morning light showed the pavement swimming in gore, and the corpses of the helpless victims lying in heaps on one another, that the appetite for blood was satisfied."[13] Mondejar was angry at this barbarity, and those found guilty were hanged. Meanwhile, Abū Omeya had taken shelter at Paterna with his six thousand volunteers. Mondejar attacked Paterna, and once again the Moriscos were routed. The residence of Abū Omeya was plundered, but he escaped leaving his mother and sisters who were granted protection by Mondejar.

The Spanish army encountered tough resistant from the Moriscos at Las Guajaras when he assaulted this fortress on the 5th February. The fortress stood on a precipitous hill between Salobrena and Valez-Malaga. The Moriscos garrison, even though it was not well armed, was in an advantageous position

because they could roll down big pieces of rocks on the enemy.
The initial assault cost Mondejar eight hundred soldiers. The
Moriscos commander al-Zamar, was not fighting a battle, but
only taking as much revenge as possible. He had no hope of
defeating Mondejar, and he slipped out at night. "On the next
day, when the Spanish general prepared to renew the assault,
great was his astominshment to find that the enemy had
vanished, except only a few wretched beings incapable of
making resistance. All the evil passions of Mondejar's nature
had been roused by the obstinate defence of the place and the
lives it cost him. In the heat of his wrath he ordered the helpless
garrison to be put to the sword. No prayer for mercy was heeded,
no regard was had to age or to sex. All were put down in the
presence of the general who is even said to have stimulated the
faltering soldier to go though their bloody work[14]." El-Zamar
was hotly pursued. He wandered from hill to hill carrying his
little daughter in his arms. Broken with hunger and fatique, he
fell into the hand of his hunters. He was sent to Granada where
his body was torn to pieces with red hot pincers[15]. The spies of
Mondejar reported that Aben Omeya had taken refuge at Mecina
in the house of his relation Aben Aboo, but Omeya escaped
again. Aben Aboo was questioned as to the whereabouts of
Omeya. When he was tortured, he replied," I may die, but my
friends will live." Taking him for head, the Spaniards left with
booty and prisoners.

The rising of the Moriscos was so widespread and alarming
that the Spanish government had posted two vetern generals to
wipe out the revolutionaries. While Mondejar was chasing
Omeya, another commander — Los Velez, was fighting the
Moriscos in the eastern sector of the Alpujarras. In this region,
the Moriscos freedom fighters were so active that Almeria was
under constant threat. The marquise of Los Velez was a haughty

person, and known for his implacable hatred of the Moriscos. They called him, "Devil of an iron chief[16]." The bloodthirsty marquise routed the Moriscos in several campaigns. At Filix he massacred women and children in thousands. Those who took shelter in bushes were dragged out and slaughtered. Many men and women with infants in their arms plunged headlong into the gorges rather than fall in the hands of their enemies." The cruelties committed by the troops, says one of the army who chronicled its achievements, "were such as the pen refused to record. I myself saw the corpse of a Moriscos women covered with wounds stretch on the ground with six of her children lying dead around her. She had succeeded in protecting a seventh, still an infant with her body and through the lances which pierced her had passed through her clothes, it had marvellously escaped any injury. It was clinging," he continues," to its dead mother's bosom, from which it drew milk that was mingled with blood. I carried it away and saved it.[17]" The greedy soldiers stripped dead women of their ornaments. At Ohanez, the victory was celebrated with great religious fervour. A fête of the Purification of the Virgin was held and a procession was taken out headed by the marquise. The cavalcade included valiant knights, priests, and Christian women rescued from captivity of the Moriscos. All carried white tapers and chanted To Deum. When the religious ceremonies were over, secular festivities were begun by the wild soldiery under Los Velez. The Moriscos women, many of them young and beautiful were delivered to the lust of the soldiers, and the camp turned into a carnival of debauchery which lasted a fortnight[18].

There was also no end to outrages committed by the brutal and licentious troops under the command of Mondejar. A tragic incidence added fuel to the raging flames. When the revolt began in the Alpujarras, one hundred and fifty Moriscos were imprisoned. The father and brother of Omeya were among the prisoners. Early in march 1569, a false alarm was raised that Omeya was about to lead an assault to liberate them. No assault took place, but the rumour sealed the fate of the prisoners. Shouting their favourite war-cry- 'saint Iago,' the soldiers stormed the prison at midnight, and fell upon the unarmed citizens. The historian Prescott had described the ensuring dance of death. He compares the foul deed to the September massacres of the French Revolution, and blames and government for its inability ot provide adequate security of thc Moriscos[19]. A cry of revenge rose in the Alpujarras. Aben Omeya sent his brother Abdullah to Constantinople ot implore the help of Turkey. Although the Turkish government did not like to intervene, it allowed volunteers to join the cause of the Spanish Muslims. With more recruits under his command, Omeya staged his guerilla warfare on a larger territory. Neither Mondejar, nor Los Velez were in a position to suppress the freedom movement launched by the Moriscos. They carried the war to the very walls of Granada. There were no signs that the war in the Alpujarras and other places would end soon. We are told that there was no collaboration between Mondejar and the Marquise. Their approach to the problem was different. While both were ruthless, Mondejar believed in an open-door policy. From time to time, he communicated with Omeya, but the marquise wanted to pursue the war to the bitter end. He was proud of the slaughter of the Moriscos — at Filix he had killed seven hundred Moriscos with the loss of only a small number of his soldiers. He saw no need of a peaceful settlement, as he had the backing of high officials of the government. All of them carried a campaign of calumny against Mondejar. Philip replaced him by his own illegitimate brother—the famous Don John of Austria.

Don John arrived at Granada on April 12, 1569., A war

council was held and it was decided that before starting the operations, the Albaysin which was thickly populated by the Moriscos should first be cleared of them. Philip's approval was obtained. On the morning of the day fixed for the purpose, the Moriscos between the age of ten and sixty were ordered to assemble at parish churches. The women were to remain for sometime to dispose of their assets. Marmol Carvajal was an eye witness of the exodus. Bound by cords like a gang of criminals or galley-slaves, the Moriscos moved out of the city of their birth in an orderly manner. The heartless government did not provide any facilities on their doleful journey to their new destination into the interior of Castile. Many of them died of grief and exhaustion, or were slain, robbed or sold as slaves by the very soldiers who escorted them[20]. Over three thousand men, and a considerably larger number of women were evacuated from Granada. We are not informed about the children.

While the Albaysin was being emptied of the Moriscos a serious faction broke out among them. Omeya became unpopular because of his dictatorial manners, and even offended the Turkish volunteers and others who had come from distant lands to help the Moriscos. His love for Zahara, a seductive ballerina and lute-player resulted in his alienation from a commander who was related to her. Some leaders opposed to him plotted to remove him. On the night of Oct. 23rd, a body of Turkish soldiers and Moriscos surprised him in his home at Lanjaron. He was torn from the arms of Zahara, and strangled to death. Aben Aboo, mentioned earlier was elected as their leader by the revolutionaries. He was a man of a different cast. He was a fearless warrior with a commanding personality. He was devoted to his mission without any personal ambition. Under his leadership, the liberation movement spread over a larger area. News were reaching Philip that his generals were haunted by the fear that the whole of coastal region between Almeria and Malaga might slip out of their hands, and if that happened about half of the former kingdom of Granada would be resuscitated. The emperor ordered that new armies be raised and the pay of the soldiers be enhanced. On Oct. 19 he issued two momentus edicts. One ediet granted 'campo franco' to the soldiers, by which they could retain with them whatever they plundered during the war. By the second edict he ordered that the war should be prosecuted with 'fuego y á sangre' — fire and blood[21]. It must be said to the credit of Don John that he carried out the orders of his royal brother, both in letter and spirit. According to the plan of the first campaign, the capture of Galera and the valley of Almanzora was of paramount importance if the eastern sector was to be protected from the attacks of the Moriscos. On Dec. 29, 1569, Don John took the field. Passing through Gaudix with thousands of soldiers and heavy artillery, Don John was in front of Galera on Jan. 19, 1570. The town was situated in one of the wildest regions with hills rising to perpendicular heights. After surveying the town, Don John ordered that canons to be stationed on three sides of the town. By Jan. 24, sufficient breaches were made in the wall inspite of fierce resistance put up by the Moriscos. They had erected barricades on the terraced streets, and every house was like a fortress with loopholes through which they showered arrows and rocks. The Moriscos Women (Prescott calls them heroines) fought side by side with men. They tended the sick and fought hand to hand with the Spanish soldiers. A stout Moriscos woman named Zarzamodonia despatched several soldiers before she herself succumbed to the wounds[22]. The Spanish army, inspite of superiority in numbers and equipment, reeled and faltered. Don John ordered that a mine with forty barrels of gun powder be planted close to the walls. An order and signal from the commander, and the mines exploded. The houses from where the Moriscos defended their faith and liberty crashed down burying hundred of them under the debris. But they showed no sign of defeat. Don John saw his officers and soldiers dying before him, and he ordered a retreat. A born leader of men, he consoled his battered army. "The infidels shall pay dear (he told his soldiers) for the Christian blood they have spilt this day. The next assault will place Galera in our power, and every soul within its walls— man, woman and child, shall be put to the sword. Not one shall be spared.[23]" Like the Roman Scipio who destroyed Carthage, he told his soldiers that every house shall be razed to the ground and the soil shall be sown with salt. On Feb. 7 the mines exploded once again, and a veritable inferno was let loose on the Moriscos. When the smoke cleared, the Spanish soldiers sprange up from their trenches to complete the bloody drama.

The' storming of Galera was one of the most frightful encounters between the Moriscos and the Spanish army. Prescott has described the entire campaign- the theatre of the battle, the disposition of the combating forces, the equipment used by them, the valiance of the defendants, and the vengeance of the victors. He has devoted page after page to the dreadful fight at Galera and his style of writing reminds me of Edward Gibbon. I cannot resist the temptation to quote form his work the account of the subsequent assault on Galera, the only one in English known to me. "It was a deadly struggle calling out—as close personal contest is sure to do— the fiercest passions of the combatants. No quarters was given; none was asked. The Spaniard was nerved by the confidence of victory, the Moriscos by the energy of despair. Both fought like men who knew that on the issue of this conflict depended the fate of Galera. Again the war-cries of the two religions rose above the din of the battle, as the one party invoked their military apostle, and the other called on Mahomet. It was the same war -cry which for more than eight centuries had sounded over hill and valley in unhappy Spain. These were its dying notes, soon to expire with the exile or extermination of the conquered race.

"The conflict was at length terminated by the arrival of a fresh body of troops on the field with Padilla. That chief had attacked the town by the same avenue as before; everywhere he had met with the same spirit of resistance. But the means of successful resistance were gone. Many of the house on the streets had been laid in ruins by the fire of the artillery. Such as still held out were defended by men armed with no better weapons than stones and arrows. One after another, most of them were stormed and fired by the Spaniards; and those within were put to the sword or perished in flames. "It fared no better with the defenders of the barricades. Galled by the volleys of the Christians, against whom their own rude missiles did comparatively little execution, they were driven from one position to another; as each redoubt was successively carried, a shout of triumph went up from the victors which fell cheerfully on the ears of their countrymen on the heights; and when Padilla and his veterns burst on the scene of action, it decided the fortunes of the day.

"There was still a detachment of Turks, whose ammunition had not been exhausted, and who were maintaing a disparate struggle with a body of Spanish infantry, in which the latter had been driven back to the very verge of the precipice. But the appearance of their friends under Padilla gave the Spaniards new heart; and Turks and Moriscos, overwhelmed alike by the superiority of the numbers and of the weapons of their antagonist, gave way in all directions. Some fled down the long avenues which led from the summit of the rock. They were hotly pursued by the Spaniards. Others threw themselves into the houses, and prepared to make a last defence. The Spaniards scrambled along the terraces, letting themselves down from one level to another by means of the Moorish ladders used for that purpose. They hewed openings in the wooden roofs of the buildings through which they fired on those within. The helpless Moriscos, driven out by pitiless volleys sought refuge in the street. But the fierce hunters were there, waiting their miserable game, which they shot down without mercy— men, women and children none were spared. Yet they did not fall unavenged; and the corpse of many a Spaniard might be seen stretched on the bloody pavement lying side by side with that of his Muslim enemy.

"More than one instance is recorded of the desparate courage to which the women as well as the men were roused in their extremity. A Moriscos girl whose father had perished in the first assault in the Gardens, after firing her dwelling is said to have dragged her two little brothers along with one hand, and wielding a scimitar with the other to have rushed against the foe, by whom they are speedily cut to pieces. Another instance is told of a man who aftering killing his wife and two daughters, sallied forth, and calling out," There is nothing more to loss; let us die together," threw himself madly into the thick of the enemy. Some fell by their weapons other by those of their friends, preferring to receive death by any hand but those of the Spaniards.

"Some two thousand Moriscos were huddled together in a square not far form the gate where a strong body of Castilian infantry cut off the means of escape. Spent with toil and loss of blood, without ammunition, without arms, or with such only as were too much battered or broken for service, the wretched fugitives would have made some terms with their pursuers who now closed darkly around them. But the stag at bay might as easily have made terms with his hunters and the fierce hounds that were already on his haunches. Their prayers were answered by volley after volley, until not a man was left alive.

"More than four hundred women and children were gathered together without the walls, and the soldiers mindful of the value of such a booty, were willing to spare their lives. This was remarked by Don John, and no sooner did he observe their symptoms of lenity in the troops, than the flinty-hearted chief rebuked their remissness, and sternly reminded them of the orders of the day. He even sent the halberdiers of his guards and the cavaliers about his person to assist the soldiers in their bloody work; while he sat a calm spectator, on his horse as immovable as a marble statue, and as insensible to the agonizing screams of his victims and their heart-breaking prayers for mercy.

"While this was going without the town, the work of death was no less active within. Every square and enclosure that had afforded a temporary refuge to the fugitives was heaped with the bodies of the slain. Blood ran down from the kennels like water after a heavy shower. The dwellings were fired, some by the conquerors, others by the inmates, who threw themselves madly into the flames rather than fall into the hands of their enemies. The gathering shadows of evening— for the fight had lasted nearly nine hours were dispelled by the light of the conglagration, which threw an ominous glare for a league over the country proclaiming far and wide the downfall of Galera[24]." Except women and children below twelve years, all the rest of the adults— Turks, Africans Moriscos were mercilessly slaughtered. It would not be easy, even in that age of blood, (say Prescott: p. 93) to find a parallel to so wholesale and indiscriminate massacre. The town was destroyed, the houses were razed to the ground and the soil was strewed with salt.

After the fall of Galera, Philip ordered Don John to deport all the Moriscos from every city, and hamlet of the former kingdom of Granada, into the interior of the peninsula. These orders were issued on Feb. 24, 1570, and the deportment was completed towards the close of the year. The Moriscos of Granada, Ronda, Gaudix, Malaga, and other places were gathered in local churches. Their farms and houses were taken over by the government, but they were permitted to carry with them money and necessary personal effects. The government ensured their personal safety and convenience en route to their new destinations. They were formed into companies of 1500 each in such a manner that families were not disrupted. The Moriscos were settled in different parts of the country— Estremadura and Andalusia and even far-flung Galicia. Don John himself supervised the operation with his usual energy. For once, he was moved to pity at the plight of the exiles. In a letter dated Nov., 5 1570 despatched from Gaudix to his friend Ruy Gomez, he wrote," the number sent away from this district alone has been very large, and it has been done with a thousand soldiers. The last party was sent off that day and was the most unfortunate affairs in the world, for there was such a tempest of wind, rain and snow that the mother will lose her daughter on the road, the the wife her husband and the widow her infant. It cannot be denied he adds that the depopulation of a kingdom is the most pitiful thing that can be imagined[25]."

Don John's next attack at Seron cost him six hundred soldiers.

This small town was defended by El-Habaqui with such energy that the Spanish soldiers ran way in a panic. Don John had a providential escape, but his tutor Quixada died of fatal injuries. The Spanish soldier were getting demoralised, and desertions were becoming frequent. Although a large number of the Moriscos had laid down their arms, the Alpujarras was far from being calm. He was anxious for early termination of hostilities, and saw negotiation as the only alternative to a long war. He wrote to Philip and obtained his permission to open talks with the Moriscos leader Aben aboo. He made overtures also to El-Habaqui, the deputy of Aben Aboo. The Moriscos commander himself came for an interview with Don John. He prostrated before Don John and asked for general pardon on behalf of his people. As a mark of reconciliation he drew his sword and presented it to Don John. The Christian commander raised him from the ground, returned the sword and asked him to use it for the service of the king. But such was the bankruptcy of the Spanish government that it did not restore the *status que ante bellum*, by repealing the law that had caused so much bloodshed; it was ready to grant amnesty to those who would stop fighting within twenty days. Aben Aboo came to know that el-Habaqui had negotiated *suo motu* and sacrificed the interests of his people. When he came to see Aben Aboo the latter had him arrested and strangled to death for his treachery. Don John sent Hernan Valle de Palacios to Aben Aboo for talks. The Christian envoy met Aben aboo and placed before him the so-called liberal terms of the peace-treaty. Aben Aboo declined the offer and replied, "I shall not attempt to prevent any of my subjects from submitting that prefer to do so. While I have a single shirt (camisa) to wear. I shall not follow their example. Though no other man should hold out in the Alpujarras, I would rather live and die a Muslim than possess all the favours which king Philip may heap upon me. At no time, and in no manner, will I ever consent to place myself in his power.[26]" Aben Aboo gave the command to his brother El-Galipe. (el-Galipe seems to be the Spainish from of al-Ghalib) The war was fought with usual savagery. Don John and his troops entered into the heart of the Alpujarras spreading death and desolation in their wake. The Moriscos homes were sacked, and those who took refuge in caverns were smoked to death. Aben Aboo escaped by a secret route, but his wife and daughters died of suffocation. Those Moriscos who were caught alive were butchered as Philip had already announced a reward of twenty ducats for every head of a Moriscos. By the end of 1570, the war of liberation was almost over and Don John left for Madrid. But Aben Aboo was still alive and he had to be finished to prevent a fresh outbreak of revolution. The Inquisitor General Deza entered into a conspiracy to murder Aben Aboo. He took the help of a criminal named Gonzalo el Xenis. Deza promised to give him life pension, and freedom for his wife and daughter from slavery if he brought Aben Aboo dead or alive. Prescott has given full details of this plot. The traitor el-Xenis met Aben Aboo, and charged his guard with his armed men. In the ensuing scuffle Aben Aboo fought bravely, but El-Xenis struck him with his musket and he fell down and died. His body was transported on a mule and delivered to Deza. The head of Aben Aboo was struck off, and hung over the gate that led to the Alpujarras with an inscription— 'The is the head of the traitor Aben Aboo. Anyone who removes it will be put to death' (In the original Spanish, the order read — *Esta es la cabeza del traidor de Abenabo. Nadie la quite so pena de muerte.*) The rest of the body was given to children who dragged it through the streets and ultimately it was thrown into flames[27]. Such was the tragic end of Aben Aboo. To the Spaniards of those days he was a barbarian infidel, but in an enlightened age he should be honoured as a martyr who laid down his life for the right to liberty of faith. The bold reply he gave to Don John's emissary shows the spirit that moved Aben Aboo. It is a pity that he is not remembered today.

After the war, the Draconian edict of 1569 was enfored with a vengeance, and the Moriscos were delivered to the hounds of the Holy Inquisition. The spies of the Inquisition and even bigoted old Christians kept a watchful eye on their movement and activities. They lived under a content fear of arrest and trial. In each town and parish an officer was appointed to visit every Moriscos home once every fortnight. Every Moriscos was registered, and he was prohibited form changing his residence without special permission. No Moriscos was allowed to visit Granada. If found within ten leagues of the city, his punishment was death. Some of the most conspicuous rites and daily practices which roused suspision against the Moriscos were— abstinence from pork and wine, refusal to eat meat of dead animals, marriage among cousins, circumcision of male children, fasting in the month of Ramazan, performance of ritual washing, use of henna by the females and wrapping dead bodies in white linen before burial. Possession of the Quran was the most heinous crime. The punishment for possessing the Quran or writing in Arabic was a hundred stripes and four years in the galley. The presence of a Christian midwife was compulsory at the time of delivery in a Moriscos family. They were required to keep the doors of their houses open for inspection. Their songs and fêtes were banned. The Christians who protected the Moriscos were liable to prosecution. Hentry Charles Lea, the American historian who has been my guide through these pages, has collected statistics from the proceedings of the Inquisition and other relevant records, of the trials, punishments and burnings of the Moriscos Muslims who refused to give up their faith. It will be too lengthy to take extracts from the statistical data compiled by him. But the plight of the Moriscos is best reflected by cases of very trivial offences which came up before the Inquisition. We may cite some to show what happens in a society in which religious tolerance and humans feelings are mere empty words. In 1575, Garci Rodriques was tried because he unwittingly expressed the opinion that in the war with Granada a certain military officer was saved by a soldier and not by invoking the Blessed Mary. He was forced to put on penitential dress. A certain Diego Herrez received a hundred lashes because he objected to disrespectful language against the Prophet. Alonso de Soria was tortured and fined because during a discussion he had said that confession before a priest was meaningless because real confession and accountability for one's sins would come after one's death. Isabel, a young Moriscos girl employed in a Christian family was tried because in a quarrel she cursed the Christians and also admitted that she followed a different code of Law. In 1587 Bartolome Sanchez was punished with three years in the galleys for frequent washing and cleanliness. The Inquisition did not pity even old women. Isabella Zacim, ninety year old woman was paraded through the streets on an ass and fined ten ducats, her crime being that she possessed a copy of the Quran[28]. These daily prosecutions widened the gulf between the Christians and the Moriscos, and deepened their aversion for Roman Catholicism. The remarks of Cervantes in his colloquio de los Perros (The Dialogue between Dogs) reflect the attitude of the educated Spaniard towards the Moriscos. He says regretfully, "the Moriscos are multiplying because they all marry; they neither join the army nor take to celibacy; they spend little, and hoard their earnings; they are consuming Spain like a slow fever[29]." But some sensible

Christians like Pedraza a canon of the cathedral of Granada who was contemporary with the war in the Alpujarras, held different views. He found that the Moriscos had few idle persons among them; they were a moral people honest in their dealings, the most charitable to the poor and that it was only the avarice of the judges and cruelty of the officials that had rendered them hostile to religion[30]."

Notes

1. H.C. Lea: p. 213 and p. 217.
2. Ibid.
3. Prescott: Philip II, vol. II, pp. 8-9, H.C. Lea: pp. 213-24.
4. Prescott, Phillip II, vol. III, pp. 10-11 and H.C.Lea: pp. 228-230.
5. Ibid.
6. Presoctt, Philip II, Vol. III, p. 13.
7. Ibid.
8. Ibid.
9. H.C.. Lea translated this poem from Spanish into English. It will be found at the end of this book.
10. In correct Arabic Aben Farrax would be ibn Farraj.
11. Prescott: Phillip II, p. 26.
12. H.C. Lea: Moriscos, p. 241 and Prescott: Philip II, pp. 27-28.
13. Prescott: Philip II, p. 34, and H.C. Lea, p. 74.
14. Prescott: Philip II Vol. III pp 38-39 The crime of el Zamar was that he had fought too bravely for the independence of his nation" says Prescott.
15. Ibid.
16. Prescott: Philip II, vol. III, pp. 41-46 give a detailed account of the cold-blooded massacres of the Moriscos at Fillix, Ohaez, and other places, committed by the soldiers under the command of the maquis Los Velez. The Arabic knowing Moriscos called him, Ibliz arrez al Hadid — Devil, an iron-headed chief." as stated by Marmal Carvajal in his "Historia del rebelion y Castigo de los Morscos del Reyno de Granada". The book appeared in 1600 at Malaga, and was reprinted in 1797 at Madrid. It was this edition which Prescott used in the preparation of his account of the war between the Moriscos and the Spanish Government. See also also Lea: Moriscos, pp. 41-45 on Los Velez.

17. Ibid.

18. Ibid.

19. Prescott: Philip II, Vol. II, p. 45-48.

20. H.C. Lea: pp. 250-251. Prescott: vol. III, pp. 64-65.

21. H.C. Lea: p. 253.

22. Prescott: Philip II, Vol. III, p. 83, p. 87 and p. 89. The author says that the Moriscos women had formed a military organization of their own for the defence of the town.

23. Ibid.

24. Prescott: Philip II, Vol. III, p. 91-93.

25. H.C. Lea: p. 260.

26. Prescott: Philip II Vol. III, P 104. The reply of Aben Aboo is based on the information furnished by Marmol Carvajal. He has quoted the actual words of Marmol from his 'Rebellion de Granada.

27. Prescott: Philip II, Vol. III, pp. 110-111 and H.C. Lea: pp. 261-262.

28. H.C.. Lea: pp. 98, 106-107, 109, 128-129, 131-133, and 161.

29. Ibid, pp. 209-210.

30. Ibid, p. 213.

Chapter 18

The Expulsion of the Moriscos

———·•·———

D uring the last decade of his reign Philip was busy with
foreign affairs. From his cabinet room in the Escurial at
Madrid, he guided the destiny of his vast dominions. He was
the most dreaded (and perhaps the most hated) ruler of his time
because of his haughtiness, boundless ambition and unrelenting
aversion to non-Catholics. His hands were full of many
problems. Netherlands was in ferment. The rising power of the
Ottoman Turks in the Mediterranean posed a great threat to his
Italian possessions. The position was further complicated as it
was constantly dinned into his ears that the Turks intended to
invade Spain. Philip formed the Holy League with Venice and
the papacy, and Don John fresh from his victory over the
Moriscos was placed in charge of the navy. The Turks were
defeated at Lepanto in the Gulf of Corinth, and Spain was
secure from the Turkish peril. Philip pursued a forward policy.
He forcibly annexed Portugal. He sought the hand of queen
Elizabeth I of England to convert the British people to Roman
Catholicism. Count de Feria, his envoy at the Court of England
proposed to her on behalf of his master. The wily queen rejected
his suit. He decided to dethrone the heretic queen to glorify the
holy faith. He sent a formidable Armada under the Duke of

Medina Sidonia, but the naval adventure ended in a shameful defeat. He tried to seize the French crown, but failed. In the midst of these political adventures he was constantly haunted by the problem of the Moriscos. The war in the Alpujarras was over, and the Moriscos had been scattered into the interior, but they were still on the Spanish soil. Several measures were thought of to solve the problem of this heretic sect. Garcia de Loaysa, the Archbishop of Toledo suggested that the Moriscos be allowed to marry only in old Christian families to ensure their gradual integration, but this was objected to as the Moriscos were infidels. Some suggested that they should be allowed to follow their faith n lieu of crushing taxes so that in due course they would realise their error, and embrace Roman Catholicism. In 1581, a suggestion emanated from the Duke of Alva and others that the Moriscos be put on ships and drowned in the sea. The Archbishop Ribera proposed that all able-bodied Moriscos be deported to mines in the Indies. The most drastic proposal was put forward by Fray Bleda, author of the 'Defensio Fidei.' Bleda was one of the most eminent theologians of his time. He urged that all the Moriscos be massacred in a single day as a warning to all heretics[1]. Philip did not decide which measure to adopt. He died on Sept. 13, 1598 after a most horrible illness.

"God has given me so many dominions, has not given me a son to govern them" — these were the dying words of Philip II [2]. His successor, Philip III proved that the last words of his father were not inappropriate. Instead of shouldering the responsibilities of his office, he transferred these to his favourite courtier— the Duke of Lerma of Denia. For a period of some twenty years this noblemen was the real ruler of Spain. The Duke was a bitter enemy of the Moriscos, and once had given his written opinion (Feb. 2, 1599) that the Moriscos between the ages of fifteen and sixty were Muslim at heart, and each of them deserved to be slain[3]. Before his fall in 1618, the Duke of Lerma, in collaboration with Archbishop Ribera solved the problem of the Moriscos for ever. Ribera was a very pious and a learned theologian of his time, and an energetic missionary of his faith. He had worked hard for years among the Moriscos, but his experiences had convinced him that they obstinately clung to their faith, and were Christians only in name. He submitted a memorial to Philip III at the end of 1601 in which he built up a strong cases for their expulsion. He reminded Philip that he had told his father that the defeat of the Spanish Armada sent to remove the British queen, was a warning from God that his own kingdom should first be purified before fighting heretics in distant lands. He quoted from the Bible to prove that it was the King's duty to wipe out the enemies of God[4]. The Moriscos, he added deserved to be killed, but it would be an act of grace and charity if they were exiled from the country. The king, the Duke of Lerma, and Fray Gaspar de Cordova thanked Ribera for hia advice, but the government did not take any action as there was a great fear of intervention from France on behalf of the Moriscos.

The Moriscos of Granada and the Alpujarras took up arms twice, but their movement was ruthlessly suppressed. The Moriscos of Valencia and Murcia were left untouched when those of Granada were exiled and scattered in distant parts of Spain. But they continued to suffer at the hands of the Inquisition. The deep-rooted hatred against them is illustrated by what H.C. Lea calls a 'curious custom' described by an eye witness. It has been related that whenever a Morisco was to be executed he was asked whether he desired to die as a Christian or as a Moor i.e. a Muslim. "In the former case he was hanged in the market ; in the latter case he was taken to a spot outside the wall, known as the Rambla, where he was stoned to death and afterwards burnt according to the command of God for idolators (Deutt. XVII. 5). To escape this they usually professed Christianity with great zeal and then on the gallows invoked Mahomet. The populace were prepare for this and to ensure the execution of the divine command they stood with stones in their hands and as soon as the word Mahomet was uttered they sent a volley like a hailstorm which not only killed the culprit but broke not a few Christian heads. Next morning not a stone could be found on the ground where the previous evening they had lain by the thousand — all were carried off during the night and treaured as the relics of a maryr[5]." In these circumstance the Moriscos of Valencia made a bid to over throw the Spanish government, and to set up an independent state of their own where they could live freely and also practise their faith. They could not hope for any help from the Muslims of northwest Africa. They were in the throes of demoralising wars, while the Turkish navy was cripped at the battle of Lepanto. Miguel Alami, an influential Morisco leader contacted a French intelligence officer named Pasqual de S. Étienne. The French spy took Alami to Hentry IV of France and laid before him a plan of action. The Moriscos leader informed the French monarch that he would be able to raise a force of sixty thousand men, and if the French landed at Denia, Valencia would fall and the Spaniards would take to their heels. The plan impressed Henry, and he referred the matter to Marshal Duke of La Force. The Duke suggested that a simultaneous attack on Coruna would facilitate the undertaking. S.Etienne was sent to place the matter before queen Elizabeth I. He discussed the matter with a secretary of the queen who encouraged him. The conspiracy leaked out due to the treachery of one of the collaborators. In the meantime, the English queen died and the new monarch showed no interest in the enterprise. It is also probable that some information regarding the plot ws cnveyed to the Spanish government by king James I. S.Ètienne and Alami were executed[6].

After these events, the Spanish government realised that the problem of the Moriscos was getting internationalised, and it was, therefore, dangerous to keep them in the country any longer. After long deliberations in which the clergy played a decisive role, an edict was passed on Sept. 22, 1609 ordering the Moriscos to leave Spain for northwest Africa[7]. Ribera was thc moving spirit in urging the government to take this castastrophic decision. He felt immencely relieved. His thoughts and feelings are expressed in his historic sermon of Sept. 27, 1609 in which the scholarly theologian injected the magic of his eloquence. He justified the orders of expulsion of the Moriscos by citings from the scriptures which according to him prohibited intercourse with infidels and hereties. He told his audience that the Moriscos had sought help of the Turks, and the time was not far when the Turkish fleet would move near the Spanish shores. He drew a lurid picture of the time when the Spanish Christians would be slain, and throughout Spain the name of Muhammad would be invoked, and that of Christ blasphemed. It was this eventuality that the emperor had thought of the only remedy which was so divine and humane that it would draw the admiration of the whole world. He reminded his audience that he had lived and worked among the Moriscos for forty years and seen their heresies. After they were gone, the churches, now full of dragons and wild beasts, would be filled with angels and seraphim[8]. The Spanish government posted five commissioners one each at the ports of Valencia, Alicante, Denia, Vinaroz, Valencia and Tortosa. The decision was welcomed by all the Moriscos. They made demonstrations at one or two places, but they were easily overpowered by the Spanish military. At one place (Muela de Cortes) three thousand Moriscos were slaughtered — perhaps their last mass killing on the Spanish soil[9]. Everywhere else they heaved a sigh of relief from the long sufferings they and their forefathers had patiently borne. Happily, they got ready to pack up. The land says H.C. Lea became a universal fair[10]. The Moriscos were seen selling their household goods at throwaway prices. The eager customers bought for a song, Moorish silks, laces, embroideries, gold and silver brocades. Escorted by military guards they tracked their way to the ports of embarkment with provisions and goods they could easily carry with them. At Alicante they arrived singing and chanting hyms of gratitude to Allah for their deliverance. When a Muslim/Moriscos theologian was asked why they werę happy at leaving Spain, he replied that they were going to the lands where they would be free to follow their ancestral faith. The children of mixed marriages posed a great problem and there were long debates on the .subject. Ultimately, it was decided that children under six whose fathers were old Christians were to stay back with the Morisco mother. However, if the father was a Morisco and his mother a Christian the former was to leave the country after giving the custody of the child of the mother. Many Moriscos lost their children when pious Christian stole them from camps to save their souls. Dona Isabel, wife of the viceroy of Valencia employed her servants to steal the children of the Moriscos[11]. The vessels for their transport were provided by the Spanish government. The first group of exiles sailed form Denia on Oct. 2 1609. The deportment of the Moriscos was completed in about three years. Murcia was the last province to be cleared of the Moriscos in 1614.

The Spanish historians have given different estimates about the number of exiled Moriscos. Among the modern historians,

Lafuente assumed a figure of one million, while Janer cut in down to ninety thousand. Danvila based his estimates on official records and reached a figure of half a million. We do not know if all the records have survived. The Muslims were constantly leaving Spain. With every thrust of reconquest a sizeable number passed into north Africa particularly after the battle of Las Navas. The process of voluntary migration was hastened soon after Ferdinand and Isabella planted the Cross on the Alhamra. In all thousands of Muslims must have left before their final deportment in the 17th century. For this reason, the number of those expelled has been variously estimated from half a million to as high as three million. While the exact number of Muslims who left Spain will remain unknown, it is not difficult to picture the suffering of the those who were uprooted from their homes in the first decade of the 17th century. On their *via dolorsa* to the ports of embarkment, they were robbed and even murdered. The bodies of the dead Moriscos were seen littered on the roads. The rapacious commissioners made the Moriscos pay for the supply of water, and even for their rest under the shade of trees[12]. Some twenty thousand Moriscos of Aragon entered into France though the Pyrennes. Their journey was so arduous that many of them perished from exhaustion. France refused to take them, and they returned to Spain thinned by death and disease. Some succeeded in reaching Marsilles after bribing the French officials and from there they hired boats for Africa. By the middle of the 17th century, the Muslims were completely combed out of Spain. Perhaps, the last Muslim to be tried on the Spanish soil was Lazaro Fernandez alis Mustafa who refused to abjure Islam, and was burned alive at the auto de fe of June 30, 1680, at Madird[13].

The exiled Muslims landed at Oran from where they spread out all over northwest Africa (Morroco and Algeria) in the hope of finding 'fresh woods and pastures new.' At first they were looked upon with suspicion. They were strangers in the land where they had come to seek safety. Many of them did not know Arabic which made intercourse difficult. They were maltreated and robbed and their women were kidnapped by local Muslims. Gradually, they settled down in Tunis, Fez, Sale, Rabat, Tetuan and Tangier. Many took to piracy and sailed the seas in their corsairs to revenge themselves on the Spaniards. Others joined the army of the Moroccan Sultan. Some went to work in the mines in the Sahara. Many descendants of these Spanish exiles lead a prosperous life today— particularly those living on the Atlantic shore. Although they have been completely absorbed in the social life around them, some can be recognised even today by their names which are Arabic with Spanish surnames such as — Palamino, Peres, Moreno, Lopez, Torres etc. They have retained their music which they call *'al-ghina al-andalus'* or *'Kalam Gharnata'*, after the land of its origin. In their cuisine, the interior decoration and planning of their homes they have remained essentially Andalusian. In cultured homes, they still wash hands with rose water after meals, as did their forefathers in the salons of their Spanish homes. Several handicrafts have a distinct Hispano-Arabic stamp. Their males are often monogamous and their women are admitted with respect into family discussions. A number of eminent leaders, doctors of theology and men of letters trace their descent from the Muslims who were exiled from Spain. Some families even retain the sad memorabilia of the tragedy faced by their ancestors, — these are the keys of the houses left by them under the cerulean skies of Spain.

The expulsion of the Muslims was welcomed by contemporary politicians, leaders of church and literary men. Fray Bleda thought that their expulsion was the greatest event in history after the resurrection of Christ[14]. The historian Guadalajara was so jubilant that he prophesied that Spain would recover Jerusalem, and shatter the Muslim power[15]. The poet Lope de Vega welcomed the just order for liquidating the last remants of the Muslims. Cervantes in his Don Quixote justified the expulsion as the country could no longer shelter the snake in its bosom[16]. Later on liberal historians (Janer and Lafuente) concluded that the deportment of the Moriscos spelled disaster for the country even though it was politically necessary. The Moriscos in their opinion, were a thrifty, hard-working people, and agriculture, agro-industry and many handicrafts depended on their labour and skill. The average Spaniard, on the other hand, was an indolent dreamer (recall the proverb 'building castles in Spain), and being a hidalgo, i.e a gentlemen, he despised manual labour. It was a well-known fact that no Spaniard of those day brought up his children to learn the virtue of honest labour. Most of them sought a job in the army, failing which they entered the service of the Church. A Spaniard with a number of daughters felt himself responsible for marriage of only one daughter, and the rest were placed in a convent. Thus, a great section of population was employed in unproductive work. The Moriscos, by virtue of their industry and skill in several fields, formed an important segment of the labour force, and a reliable source of income to the state. They were not a burden on Spanish economy, but enriched it by their labour and regular payment of all government dues. Already Spain was suffering from exhaustion owing to the wars of Philip II. Her economic decadence continued on account of reckless extravagance of Philip III. The treasury was empty and the army was unpaid. The emigration to the American colonies thinned her population. The mass of her nationals were made up of wealthy courtiers, swashbuckling army officers, priests and nuns and gentlemen beggars. The sudden exodus of the industrious Moriscos hastened her economic decay. Many rich and flourishing villages were depopulated. Vast lands in Valencia and Andalusia where the Moriscos grew wheat, rice and sugar-can languished into decay. A large number of Moriscos from Granada had settled in La Mancha and set up a booming silk industry. It went to piece after they left. The noblemen whose prosperity depended on their Moriscos tenants were brought to the brink of ruin and the state had to advance loans to save them from sinking into poverty.. The cattle wealth dwindled down. At one time it was reported that at some places Spanish people subsisted on herbs of the fields which they shared with the herbovirous cattle[17]. Lane-Poole has truly said that by driving out the Muslims, the Spaniard killed their golden goose[18]. Don Palencia, a modern historian of Spain and a authority on the Muslim period laments that the expulsion of the Moriscos resulted in the decadence of agriculture and industry and de-population[19].

Spain did not flow with milk and manna after the Muslims faded out from her soil, but their mass exodus conferred on her a great spiritual blessing, i.e. the complete unifomity of faith of all the Spaniards. The Jews were driven out, the Muslims were expelled, and the Protestants were crushed. The sacred duty of the Spaniards to exterminate all non-Roman Catholic faiths, was at last fulfilled. The crusading spirit carried the Spaniards across seas and oceans. Armed with the Bible and the bullet, the Roman Catholics founded colonies on three continents of the globe. They gave to mankind one of the three international languages of the world. The story of these great achievements is beyond the scope of this book. But wherever the Spaniard and the Portuguese went — whether soldier or sailor or the priest, they carried a deep-rooted hostility towards the Muslims and their faith. How they treated the Muslims they found in the Philipines , Sri Lanka, Lakhshadeep and Maldive islands and Goa, is known to all students of history. The city of Matamoros (on the Gulf of Mexico) which in Spanish means 'Moors-Slayer' speaks for itself. The Portuguese Albuquerque even planned to starve Egypt by digging a canal to divert the waters of the Nile into the Red Sea. One of his ambition was to seize the Holy city of Madina as a ransom for Jerusalem. In 1510, when Albuquerque captured Goa which was the port of the Muslim kingdom of Bijapur in the Deccan, he exterminated the Muslim population. But times have since changed. All over the world men are realising that religious tolerance is as vital to them as the very food they take. The present day Spaniard is more religious than other Roman Catholics, but he is no more under the baneful influence of priests like Ximenes and Ribera. The modern Spaniards are also proud of their Muslim heritage.

During the current century, Spain has producd several eminent scholars whose contributions have enlarged our knowledge of Hispano-Muslim history and culture. There are departments of Arabic studies at the universities of Madrid, Valencia, Barcelona and Granada. Spain also hosts conferences to promote study of her Muslim past. The Spanish government takes almost motherly care of the remaining monuments of the Muslims. Gradually, Spain has opened its doors to the Muslims. The late General Franco did not hesitate to recruit Muslims from Morocco during the civil war. Friendship with the Muslim states has grown beyond all expectations. Several heads of states from the Arab world have visited Spain from time to time. The Saudis have invaded Spain peacefully with their petro-dollars . They swarm into Spain for sight-seeing and investments. For the first time mosques have come up on the Spainish soil with Saudi money. There is a mosque at Marbella on the Mediterranean coast and the call for prayer (*Azan*) is heard five times a day after a lapse of centuries. Another mosque was formally opened in 1998 at Gibraltar. In one of the most prestigeous localities of Madrid, can be seen the splendid building of the Islamic Cultural Centre and an elegant mosque, built at an immense cost by His Majesty king Fahad, the present ruler of Saudi Arabia. There are reports that more mosques are in the process of construction in Andalusia. We hope that relations between Spain and the Muslim world will grow more and more in this millennium. God bless Spain!

Notes

1. H.C.. Lea: For all these and other atrocious proposals, read pp. 293-297. About Bleda's Book 'Defensio Fidei.' Lea says — "I have met with few books more calculated to excite horror and detestation than the Defensio Fidei. Christianity as there presented is a religion of ruthless cruelty, eager to inflict the most pitiless wrongs on the defenceless. Moloch has usurped the place of Christ, and the bloody sacrifice of those of different faith is the most acceptable offering to their creator. The most deplorable feature is that the learned author has incontrovertible authority to all his hideous conclusion — utterance of the Fathers, decrees of councils, decretals of Popes and the decision of the most eminent theologians" (p 298)

    H.C. Lea has described the last days of Philip II. "Consumed by gout strangled with asthma for almost two months, he lay nearly motionless and with but enough of life to render him capable of suffering. Covered with tumours and abscesses, which when opened and continued to discharge till the stench in the death-chamber could not be overcome by the strongest perfumes the long-drawn agony was greater than any of his executioners had invented for the torture chamber. Yet his bearing through all this showed the sincerity of conviction which had inspired the most ruthless of his acts." (p 304)

2. G.Davies: The Golden Century Spain, p. 230.

3. H.C. Lea: p. 306, gives Lerma's complete programme of elimination of the Moriscos/Muslim from Spain.

4. H.C. Lea: p. 307-308.

5. Ibid, p. 211.

6. H.C. Lea: pp 286-288. Lea has given full details of the plot, and the reasons why it failed.

7. Ibid., pp. 320-321.

8. Ibid., p. 325.

9. H.C Lea: p 334

10. Ibid., p. 328.

11. Ibid., pp. 322-324 for further details regarding the plight of the Moriscos children.

12. H.C.Lea: p. 339.

13. Ibid., p. 391. Mr. Merle Severy, the Assistant Editor of the National Geographic Magazine is also a good historian. He has compared the consequences of the fall of the Spanish Muslims with the fall of the Ottoman Turks in the Balkans, in his article — "Suleyman the Magnificent" which appeared in Nov., 1987 issue of the magazine. He writes — "Neighbours gathered like vultures around 'the sickman of Europe". But in the twilight of an empire that would endure 600 years, a score of nations emerged from its cosmopolitan umbrella, they had preserved their languages, religions, cultures. Thus the Ottoman experience differed from that of "Purified" Spain where no muezzin's call or Arabic was heard. (p. 600)

14. H.C. Lea: p. 366.

15. Ibid., p. 366,

16. Cervantes: Don Quixote : Trans. by Charles Jarvis, London Chapter LTV p, 653.

17, 18 & 19.
    Palencia: Historia, p. 121; H.C. Lea: pp. 366-401 and Lane-Poole: p. 280. Chapter XI of Lea's Morisco gives a detailed account of the results of expulsion.

Part II
Hispano-Muslim Culture

Chapter 19

Administration and Economy

From the 9th century onwards, the Muslim World from the borders of China in the East, to Saragossa in Spain, was a single cultural entity. Even though empires rose and fell, and independent dynasties emerged after breaking away from political centres (Madina under the pious caliphs, Damascus under the Umayyads, and Baghdad under the Abbasids), the cultural complexion remained unchanged. A Spanish Muslim visiting north Africa and the near East did not find himself in a *terra incognita*. He moved about in a familiar world. Although he met ethnically different peoples — the ruddy Berbers, the fair Egyptians, the stalwart Arabs, the dark negroes, the fine-featured Syrians, the radiant Turks, the robust Tartars, the magnificent Afghans, and the handsome Persians, he found them following the same way of life. He heard them speaking the same *lingua franca*, composing the same type of poetry, enjoying the same music, and having complete identity in mental and moral outlook with only marginal differences, here and there on account of local colour. The Arabic language and the Islamic faith wove them into one vast cultural tapestry. Again, the Spanish pilgrim would have noticed that the very administration of these countries was not different from that of his own homeland. Even the nomenclature of the officials and their duties were already known to him. In this connection it may be stated that soon after the conquests were over, the Islamised Arabs quickly organised their vast dominions and established a uniform system of administration. This has surprised the historians because the Arabs were fresh from their desert homes, and they could hardly visualise the problems which were likely to arise in governing the far-flung territories. They took over the existing Byzantine and Persian systems, and moulded it according to the requirements of their faith and peculiar needs. In this process, they evolved an efficient system of administration, which had no doubt many defects, but surprisingly, worked without many changes for centuries. Prof. Husiaini has rightly said 'If the Muslims conquered and maintained a large part of the then known world, it was not an accident or aimless activity. There was a well-thought system in all that they accomplished, a system all the details of which were carefully planned and precisely executed.'[1]

As Muslim Spain was a part of the Islamic world, the Spanish Muslims imported every manifestation of their civilization and culture from the East — their poetry, prosody, grammar, music, personal law, and even their administrative system. The principles of government, the rules of taxation, the secretarial arrangements, and the judicial system, were exactly the same as in the other Muslim states. But the reader may be frankly told that our knowledge about the administration of the Spanish Muslims is rather limited due to several reasons. Many records have perished, and those available furnish scanty information on the subject. We have but few copies of the executive orders passed by the Muslim rulers; these are embedded in historical writings. The historians took rapturous delight in recording lengthy narratives of the military campaigns, the wars of successions, the internal revolts, the splendour of court life, and even the amours of the rulers. No writer has left any treatise exclusively devoted to the administrative machinery and its actual working. The most important sources are the historical works of ibn Idhari, al-Maqqari, and ibn Khaldun, and some biographical writings. Even with the help of these works, it is possible to reconstruct only an outline of the governmental system. This task has been admirably performed by the French orientalist the late Lévi Provençal, Piecing together the scattered information, he has described the main features of the administrative system of the Umayyad period. His contribution is important because the Umayyad system of administration was adopted by the subsequent rulers, and it persisted till the end of the 15th century with only slight changes.

During the period following the conquest, Spain was governed by viceroys (Ar. Sig : *Wāli*) like any other province of the Umayyad empire. Although some viceroys were able administrators, it was not possible for them to consolidate the nascent Muslim state of Spain for three major reasons — the tribal feuds among the newcomers, the frequent changes of viceroys, and the distance from Damascus, the capital of the empire. If 'Abd ar-Rahman had not migrated to Spain, it is doubtful if the Muslims would have continued to hold on for a long time. 'Abd ar-Rahman laid the foundation of a new state as well as an efficient administration which was developed by his successors into the most centralised bureaucracy of Europe. The administration installed by him was not his creation. It was a replica of the Syrian tradition to which Abbasid features were added by 'Abd ar-Rahman II. A passage in al-Maqqari's book lays down the policies and principles observed by the Umayyads of Spain. It is a veritable manifesto of monarchical rule. He says — 'It is generally known that the strength and stability of their empire consisted principally in the policy planned by the princess — the magnificence and splendour of their courts, the reverential awe with which they inspired their subjects, the inexorable vigour with which they chastised every aggressor on their rights, the impartiality of their judgements, their anxious solicitude in the observance of civil laws, their regard and attention to the learned whose opinion they respected and followed, and calling them to their sittings and admitting them to their councils[2].

The 12th century ibn 'Abdun almost repeated the same views about an ideal prince. The ruler, in his opinion, was the pivot of body politics, the centre of a circle on whom depended the stability of the state. The wise men should guide him, correct his abberrations, by impressing upon him that kingdoms are ruined by the mistakes of rulers. Muslim rule in Spain from the restoration of the Umayyads to the fall of the Nasarite kingdom of Granada, may be characterized as monarchical dictatorship. Force was the basis of the state as in all Muslim and non-Muslim states of the Middle Ages. This was perhaps necessary, because Spain was not composed of a homogeneous people. It was a conglomeration of diverse ethnical and religious groups — the restless Arabs, the inflammable Berbers, the wily Gothic and Roman converts to Islam, the unreliable Jews, and the Christians who detested the Muslims. These diverse elements could be kept under control only by a strong ruler. Under such a system the people had no share in the governance of the state. The duties of citizens were to be loyal to their ruler at all time, to pay their taxes, and observe all the laws of the state without any protest. However, every citizen was free to address petitions to the ruler expressing his grievances against state officials. Several rulers held open court on specified days. If he considered necessary, he issued immediate orders on the petitions presented to him. Under a weak ruler, the pent-up dissatisfaction found expression in anti-government activities throwing to the winds all feelings of patriotism and humanity. We have seen what happened during the reign of 'Abdullah, the grandfather of 'Abd ur-Rahman III.

The monarchy was an institution of inheritance. Although a ruler was generally succeeded by his eldest son, the law of primogeniture was not strictly observed. Quite often, a sultan rejected his eldest son, and nominated his successor from amongst his other male issues during his lifetime. This gave rise to the system of 'bait' or oath-taking. The ruler took an oath of loyalty to his nominee, from all top ranking officials. Soon after a ruler ascended the throne, he too took an oath of allegiance from the princes of the royal blood, his ministers and secretaries. The oath-taking ceremony was a glittering spectacle like that of an elected head of today. As in all centralised depotisms, the sultan was the nucleus of the administration. In his capacity as the head of his realm, he appointed and dismissed all functionaries, he supervised the receipts and expenditure of the state, he directed the foreign policy, he was the supreme commander of the armed forces, and he was also the last court of appeal. In short, his word was law. Every Muslim ruler believed: *l'état, c'ést moi.*

At the same time, it was physically impossible for him to look after the business of the government all by himself. For the sake of his personal convenience, he delegated such powers and functions as he deemed necessary, to his trusted confidents and men of experience. He placed each branch of administration under the charge of a minister (*wazir*) who took an oath of loyalty before he took charge of his office. There were separate ministers for finance, official correspondance, redress of public grievances, and supervision of the borders.[3] The body of ministers constituted the cabinet (*mushâwara*). The ministers belonged to aristocratic Arab and Berber families, but capable men from the middle class could rise to the highest post by merit or manoeuvre. Abi 'Amir was not the only ranker — there were many others like him in the army as well as in the civil service. The wazirs were the tools who implemented the orders of their sovereign. A separate building was assigned to them in the royal palace, where they sat, as in the eastern Muslim lands, on cushions and carpets. One of the ministers acted as *'hajib'*. He was the liaison between the sultan and the rest of the ministers. The word 'hajib' means a door-keeper, and this gives a clue to his duties. He looked after the protocol matters, and ensured that those who came to see the sultan knew proper etiquette and court manners. In addition, the 'hajib' could be required to perform any other duties assigned to him. Under the Umayyads we come across many instances of a hajib leading the army. A hajib or any minister who acted as a military commander was generally recognised by the pompous title of *'du'l-wizaratain'* i.e., holder of two titles, the pen (*qalm*) and the sword (*saif*). A hajib acted as the representative of the sultan when the latter left the capital on a military mission.

The sultan was also assisted by secretaries (Ar. Sig: *Katib*) who enjoyed almost a ministerial rank. The Secretary in charge of official correspondence was called *'Katib ar-rasail'*. He drafted executive orders, and treaties. A Secretary in Muslim Spain (as in the eastern states governed by the Muslims) sat in front of the sultan, like a stenographer of today, and jotted down his verbal instructions.[4] He prepared a draft, and after approval the document was sealed with a signet bearing the sultan's name. The sealing of official correspondence was introduced in the East by Mu'awiya, the founding-father of the Umayyad dynasty.

It is said that he sent a letter to an official instructing him to pay the bearer a sum of one hundred thousand dirhams, but the letter was opened and the figure was altered to read two hundred thousand. The fraud came to light, and the practice of sealing official correspondence was introduced.[5] The seal was fixed with red clay mixed with water. The document was folded and glued on both sides and sealed again before being despatched.[6] That this practice was observed in Spain also cannot be ruled out. 'Abd al-Hamid, the renowned Secretary of the eastern Umayyads (who died in 751) wrote an epistle to his fellow secretaries aspiring for proficiency in the performance of their duties. The historian ibn Khaldun has preserved the text of this valuable document.[7] The secretary in charge of correspondence was required to be a master of elegant style of composition (Sahib al insha) in Arabic. He was expected to be a scholar of literature, history and biography, a man of polished manners, and one who would not let out state secrets. These qualifications were fulfilled by many eminent secretaries of Muslim Spain. History is full of their names. Perhaps the last secretary was ibn Khatib of Granada, whose official correspondence in polished Arabic gives evidence of his command of language and literature. The number of secretaries varied from ruler to ruler. Under 'Abd ar-Rahman III, we hear of four secretaries each with distinct responsibilities. Jahwar ibn 'Abda was in charge of correspondence relating to internal matters; Isa Futais drafted the caliph's correspondence with the provincial governors; 'Abd ar-Rahman Az-zajjali prepared treaties with vassal states; and Muhammad ibn Hudair drafted replies on petitions from the Caliph's subjects.[8] The copies of final orders were reproduced by block printing, and despatched to the departments concerned.[9]

Our knowledge of the financial system of Muslim Spain is piecemeal and insufficient. We know that there was a Bureau of Finance (Ar. *diwan*) headed by an official of ministerial rank designated as *'Sahib al Ashghal.'* He shouldered great responsibilities as he maintained an account of the receipts and expenditure of the state. Al-Maqqari says 'all necks lowered before him, all hands were stretched out to him, and he kept the provinces in awe by means of his overseers.[10] The main sources of revenue were, the land tax, the tributes from vassal states, taxes on mineral products, excise duties on imports and exports, the poll-tax (*jazia*) payable by non-Muslims, and the compulsory 'zakat' Islam's levy on the rich for the support of the less privileged section of the society. The land-tax varied according to the nature of the soil. When the time of harvesting arrived, the divisional officers (Ar. sig: *'Amil*) visited the farms to estimate the quantity of produce and to fix the quantum of tax.[11] The tax was recovered both in cash and kind. After keeping some of the produce in reserve stocks, the rest was sold in the open market, and the proceeds were credited to the government treasury—*the Khazinat al Makhzan*. The rate of poll-tax paid by the Jews and the Christians has already been stated in an earlier part of the book. The revenue on this account could not have been very substantial, as more than half of the non-Muslims were exempted. The perishable goods, and articles like books, ornaments for the brides were free from excise duty. On other commercial goods, the rate of duty varied from 3% to 15% during the Umayyad period.[12] The revenues of some Umayyad rulers are known to us. 'Abd ar-Rahman II had a revenue of one million dinars, but under his two immediate successors, particularly 'Abdullah, the revenues dwindled down because of civil wars. When 'Abd ar-Rahman al-Nasir consolidated the state, the revenues increased and stood at twenty million gold dinars and an enormous sum of silver dirhams. He had also an income of 765000 dinars from his personal property (*mustakhlas*). It is said that he left five million gold dinars in the treasury.[13] The moneys were divided in three parts — one was used for defence, the other for civil constructions, and the rest was kept as a saving.[14] In addition to lawful taxes, some Spanish rulers resorted to illegal taxation (*magharim*) whenever there was a deficiency of funds. Hakam I raised money by illegal means to finance his corps of foreign mercenaries. 'Abd ar-Rahman II also needed money for his many projects, and personal extravagance, and once the treasury officer refused to release money from the public funds. But conditions improved under the two caliphs—'Abd ar-Rahman III and Hakam II, and the dictator Abi'Amir. 'Abd ar-Rahman abolished taxes contrary to the sunnah imposed by his predecessors. Some relief from taxation was granted by Hisham II and al-Muzaffar also. The rulers of the small kingdoms which emerged after the fall of Umayyads, were notorious for imposing illegal exactions. The philosopher ibn Hazm expressed his anguish at their heartlessness on this account. The department of finance employed non-Muslims. If we are to believe ibn Sa'id, the post of *Sahib al-ashghal* was held by either a Jew or a Christian.[15] Some Jewish tax-collectors under the finance department were notorious for their harshness.[16]

The Muslims were required to pay a tax called 'zakat' at a scheduled rate. All personal wealth—real estate, income from trade came within the purview of zakat tax. The moneys received on this account were kept in a separate treasury—the *bait al mal*, which was under the custody of a judge. The moneys in the *bait al mal*, and all incomes from waqf (endowments) were utilized for welfare schemes to support the needy, the orphans, the widows, to ransom prisoners, and to help students and teachers. The bait al mal could advance loans to honest persons for trade. Qadi Sulaiman bin Aswad a famous grudge of Cordova advanced a loan to a certain person, but his action was not considered objectionable.[17]

The monetary system of Muslim Spain was based on metallic currency. From the very beginning of Muslim rule, all public and private transactions were made in currency — dinars and dirhams. Hispano-Muslim numismatics is a subject of much interest, but it is full of many problems which would require lengthy discussion. The subject has been studies by several experts — Dr. J. Condé, Codera, Antonio Vives in the last century. Prof. G. Miles in the present century, is one of the very few specialists in this field. His studies relate to the coinage of the Umayyads, and the mulūk at-tawā'if, and are based on the coins in possession of the Hispanic Society of America.[18] Writing a history of the coinage of the entire Muslim period would be a stupendous task, and will involve a scrutiny of all the coins available in the society mentioned above, as well as in the museums of Spain.

For their elegance and perfection of engravings, the coins of Muslim Spain are the collectors' pride. The bilingual dinars in gold issued in 98 A.H. (when Spain was governed by viceryos) are the earliest specimens of Hispano-Muslim coinage. They carry a Latin legend on one side, and the Kalima on the other. Sometime in 102, A.H., the bilingual coins were replaced by coins stamped with only Arabic inscriptions — the complete *'bismillah'* on one side and *'la illaha illallah wahdaho'* on the obverse side. The coins issued by 'Abd ar-Rahman I, and his successors upto the caliph 'Abd ar-Rahan were largely in silver. The earliest dirham of this category belongs to the year 146 A.H. These dirhams usually weighed 2.60 grams. The weight kept on decreasing, and under 'Abdullah, it dwindled down to a mere 2.14 grams—a clear indication of the turmoil in his reign, and consequential rise in the price of silver.

The establishment of the caliphate by 'Abd ar-Rahman al-Nasir marks the definite minting of gold dinars — one-half, one-third, add one-quarter; all were made of pure gold. The full dinar weighed more than 4 grams. The coins of the caliphate period are splendid in design, and finish. There is a uniformity in the inscriptions. All the coins upto the end of Hisham III, the last Umayyad rulers bear the name and title of the ruler on one side and *'la illaha la sharikala'* on the other side. Sometimes, the name of the officer-in-charge of the mint (*Sahib al-sikka*) was also punched on the coin. There are many coins which bear the name of Abi 'Amir who held that post in the beginning of his career. The coins were minted at Cordova, and the sub-mint at Madinat az-Zahra. They were struck with dies and punches. The coins of the Umayyad period, specially of the caliphate, are conspicuous for their beauty and complexity of ornamental engravings. They were invariably circular in shape with linear and beaded margins, and carried an endless variety of symbols and ornaments — fleur-de-lis, pomegranates, vine-like scrolls, and floral flourishes. Their epigraphy is kufic, and in no way different from the coins of the eastern Umayyads.

The mulūk aṭ-ṭawā'if, the Almohad, and the rulers of the Granada had their own coins. They were of different shapes and sizes. The coins of the kingdom of Granada were perfect in design, and their metallic content was pure. The coins of this period bear the motto of the Nasarite sultans — *walla ho ghalib illa allah*, the name of the sultan, and a verse from the Quran usually verse 200 of Sura III.

We know about the judiciary of Muslim Spain more than any other aspects of their administration — thanks to the vivid life — sketches of the judges left by biographers like ibn Fardi, al-Khushani, ibn Bushkuwal, and ibn Khatib. It has been stated earlier that the sultan was the last court of appeal, but he enjoyed this position by courtesy. The judiciary in Muslim Spain was entirely in the hands of the judges who worked independently, and whose decisions were final. There was a judge (*qadi*) in every district and major town. The judge at Cordova was designated 'Judge of the community' (*qadi al jamat*), but it seems that he was not the head of the judiciary. He held the rank of a minister and was often addressed as '*al-wazir al-qadi.*' He was conspicuous by his presence at all state functions. Many anecdotes prove that the executive respected the judges, and allowed them to function without interference. In an earlier chapter, an example has been given of the manner in which the qadi Mus'ab bin Imran asserted his authority, and Hakam I had to eat humble pie. Mus'ab did not care if a defendant happened to be an influential person. There is an interesting case recorded by al-Khushani in his "Biographies of the Judges of Cordova". The story goes that al-Abbas al-Marwāni, a courtier encroached upon a farm belonging to two minor orphans. When they came of age, they filed a suit against al-Marwani. The qadi sent a message asking him to vacate the encroachment, but al-Marwani refused, and instead, went straight to Hakam I, and begged him to decide the case as head of the state. Hakam asked the qadi to refer the case to him. The qadi did not oblige him, and gave his own judgement in favour of the orphans, and soon after informed Hakam that he had given his verdict according to what was right and just. Al-Marwāni requested Hakam to quash the judgement of the qadi. Hakam was incensed at the man's audacity, and sent him away saying — 'Unfortunate is the man who receives a blow from the pen of the qadi.'[19]

The judiciary was manned by pious ulemas, and it is in this sphere that they found a congenial outlet for their learning. A God-fearing judge was constantly haunted by the fear that any wrong or partisan judgement by him might deprive him of Allah's mercy in his after-life. Al-Khushani has given instances of learned persons who declined to accept the post of a qaḍi because of this apprehension. A qaḍi considered his appointment as a trust from God. The qaḍi Muhajir bin Naufal was a man of such a clean conscience that he did not like people to go to a court of law for their disputes. However, when a case came up before him, he gave a lecture on moral values to the parties concerned. With tears in his yes, he would point out to the litigants that man was accountable to God for all his actions, and dire punishment awaited those who transgressed His commandments. It is said that his anguish softened the hearts of the litigants, and they reached a compromise in his presence. A qaḍi decided a case as early as possible. Justice was never delayed. There were no long postponements, and no stamp or court duties. The contending parties were given full freedom to cross-examine witnesses, and also to see the documents relating to the suit. The qaḍi usually held his court in a corner of the mosque, but he could summon the parties at his residence particularly when a case involved settlement by compromise. We have interesting details of a divorce case settled by qaḍi Sa'id bin Sulaiman. There is a ring of sincerity in the manner of narration, and this incidence is worth quoting as it is of much sociological interest. One day says Nasir, the narrator, that he visited the qaḍi to deliver his share of the harvest. He found him sitting with his assistant and a couple. After greeting, the qaḍi introduced Nasir to those present, saying, "Here is the man who, by the grace of Allah, feeds me and my family." Then turning to Nasir, he asked him about the harvest. The qaḍi was happy to learn that the harvest was plentiful. The qaḍi thanked Allah for His bounty, and then turned to the couple. The man said to the qaḍi, 'Sir, you order this woman to return home with me.' The woman flung herself on the floor, and began to cry. She told the qadi that she would not move one step with her husband, and that if she was forced, she would commit suicide. When the qaḍi heard these words he was agitated, and he asked his assistant what he thought of the matter. He replied that if there was nothing to prove that the man was mistreating her, then she should be forced to go with him unless, she pays some compensation to him. When the husband heard these words he said, 'By Allah she is poor and has no money on her.' The qaḍi who had been thinking about the case, interposed, and asked the man if he would accept suitable indemnity and release her. "In that case I would with pleasure," replied the man. The qaḍi turned to Nasir, his tenant-farmer, and asked him, 'Have you brought some provisions with you as my share?' He replied, "I have brought with me one measure of wheat and two measures of barley." The qaḍi made some mental calculations on his fingers, and turned to the husband, "Look, I have enough food to last this season. You can take the produce, and let your wife go in peace." The man replied that he would gladly accept the offer, provided the produce was delivered at his door. The qaḍi was surprised at his mean mentality. He went inside his house, and returned with a piece of woollen cloth. Handing it over to the man, he said, "This cloth was spun in my house, and I was to use it in the coming winter, but for the present I can part with it. You sell it, and utilise the proceeds for transporting the provisions." The man readily took the cloth, the stock of wheat and barley, and let his wife free.[20]

The qaḍi would also allow a culprit, what we now call 'the benefit of doubt.' We have an instance recorded by al-Khushani. One day an inspector (*muhtasib*) produced a man before qaḍi Ahmad bin Mukhald (one of the greatest scholars of Islamic jurisprudence) on a charge of drunkeness. The qaḍi asked his secretary to smell the man. He confirmed that the man had drunk wine. The qaḍi was not satisfied, and asked another man to smell the culprit. The second man replied that the culprit smelt of something, but he was not sure whether it was wine or anything else. The qaḍi released the man on the basis of doubtful evidence.[21]

The qaḍi was primarily a civil judge. He tried cases relating to wills (*wasaya*), divorce (*atlaq*), inheritence and division of property (*mawarith and qisam*). He was also the custodian of *waqf* property, and the public funds like the *zakat* and *ushar*. The Quran, the Hadith, and the *'muwatta'* of iman Malik were the basis of civil law and human rights. In actual practice, there was no bar to a judge exercising his discretion within the framework of the fundamental teachings of the faith. In complex case, the qadi invited the opinion (*fatwa*) of a jurisconsult (*mufti*). The rulings of many judges were preserved in registers (*diwans*) which constituted the juridical archives of the state for consultation and reference. Several such collections are extent today. One such authoritative collection is the *'Diwan al ahkam āl kubra'* of the famous jurist Abu l-Asbagh ibn Sahl (d. 1093) of Jaen. This contains many important judgements on diverse matters — disputes between boatmen and shepherds, permission to build a new church at Cordova, encroachment by the Christians of land belonging to a Muslim graveyard, reduction of agricultural rent in favour of farmers whose crops had been destroyed by heavy rains, and a criminal suit against a bootlegger.[22] Apart from their legal worth, these court decisions open a window on the social life of the age. A collection of fatwas of Ibn Rushd Rushd's grandfather is stated to be in the National Library at Paris.[23] During the early centuries, classical Malikism insisted on *taqlid*, the basic doctrine of this school.

However, as time went on the Maliki fiqh had to draw upon other schools of jurisprudence to meet new challenges resulting from the growth of agriculture, and commercialism in urban areas.

For the trial of criminal suits, there was a separate department known as the *'Shurta'* which was headed by an officer who carried the designation of *'sahib al shurta.'* He was the most dreaded officer of the state because of his vast powers. He was competent to impose any punishment on the offenders—fine, imprisonment, confiscation of property, amputation, and execution. The capital punishment was carried out after final approval of the sultan. The peace and harmony in the city depended upon him, and his other associates—*the sahib al-Madina,* and the *sahib al-mazalim.* The specific duties of the last two officers are not clear. They, no doubt, kept a watch on day-to- day law and order. The sahib al-mazalim dealt with complaints of high-handedness and corruption of civil servants *(ahl al maratib as-sultaniya)* — it was somewhat like ombudsman of today. The administration of the markets and commercial centres fell under the crime branch. For this purpose the state appointed a *'muhtasib'* in all the major cities. He protected the cosnumers from commercial fraudulence. He patrolled the markets with his sub-inspector *(amil),* and punished the shop-keepers who did not indicate the prices of goods sold by them. He inspected the weights and measures. He also ensured that the goods were sold at prices fixed by the government. On a tip-off, he rounded up offenders, and imposed suitable punishment on the spot. The *'muhtasib'* was also a censor of public morality. One of his duties was to see that no one drank in public. He was competent to round up persons found indulging in rowdy behaviour on the roads. The duties of the *'muhtasib'* were laid down for their guidance in books of censorship *(hisba)* which were taught as part of the criminal law of the state. Several such books have survived—one by ibn Abdun of Seville, and the other by ibn Saqati of Malaga. The book by ibn 'Abdun who flourished in the 11th century has been rendered in French by L.Provençal.[24] Ibn 'Abdun was a cynic who saw no virtue in men. He held that all bachelors, merchants, hawkers, ferry men, tax-collectors were cheats and rakes. For this reason his book has to be utilised with care as it abounds in sweeping generalizations.

No ruler could entirely depend on the loyalty of his subjects with an olive-branch in his hand. The royal throne was not a bed of roses. Dangers beset the ruler on all sides. The assassin's dagger, the intrigues of his nobles and his own relations kept him in a state of perpetual vigil. The northern Christian states were a source of constant threat to the security of the borders. In these circumstances, the army was the only steel framework which protected the golden throne of the rulers from revolts and aggressions. During the formative period, the kingdom of Cordova depended upon soldiers supplied by the military districts *(kura mujannada)* of Malaga, Jaen, Beja, Murcia, Elvira and Sidona where the Syrian Arabs were granted fiefs in lieu of military service.[25] The Berbers had their own settlements, and they too were under a similar obligation. This system could not be depended upon for a long time, as its main flaw was that the soldiers could not report at short notice. Besides, it would affect agricultural production. From this realisation, arose the need to maintain a regular fighting force. The first Umayyad ruler 'Abd ar-Rahman was obliged to raise an army of the Berbers, and his grandson Hakam recruited foreign mercenaries from European countries. The latter had a standing force of seven thousand foreigners. They were stationed in barracks near Cordova, and could be mobilised without much delay in times of emergency. The rulers after Hakam kept formidable armies, and earmarked a big slice of their revenues for defence purposes. In addition to these regularly paid soldiers (*murtaziqa*), the state inducted into the army volunteers also who received a fixed monthly allowance during the period of their service. The historians have left absorbing details about mobilisation of troops, their formations, weapons, and tactics. On the Friday preceding the departure of troops, a ceremony was held in the mosque of Cordova where flags were distributed to the commanding officers. After this Flags ceremony (called *'aqad al-alwiya*), the army, both foot and cavalry, assembled for a grand parade (*buruz*) at the spacious parade grounds of *Fahs as-suradiq* in the neighbourhood of Cordova.[26] The parade lasted several weeks, and it was attended by the sultan and enthusiastic spectators. It was organised by an officer—the *sahib al'ard* who was presumably the pay-master general of the army. The army during the caliphate period was divided into battalions of 5000 each, under the command of an *'amir'* who was easily recognised by his grand flag (*raya*); each battalion was made up of five contingents of 1000 soldiers each under a *'qaid'* who carried a flag called *'alam'*; each contingent comprised five companies of 200 soldiers under a *'naqib'* who had his own flag — the *liwa*; each company had five units of forty soldiers under an officer called *'arif'* who carried a 'band' in his hand; the last officer in the military hierarchy was the *'nazir'* with a group of eight soldiers under his supervision.[27] The army had four wings—the vanguard (muqaddama), the right wing (*maimanah*), the centre (*qalb*), and the rear-guard (*Saqa*). The soldiers were armed with a lance (*rumh*), a shield (*daraqa*) and a javelin. The shields were made of skins of antelope. The soldiers wore coat of arms, breasplates, and protective helmets. The army carried catapults (*majāniq*) for throwing rocks on the enemy. Every army, had a group of men who were trained in detection of breaches and vulnerable points in the fort of enemy. These men (naqqabun) carried battering rams with them for siege warfare. The army moved on the sound of drums (tabl). An army on the march with its different formations, the infantry, the cavalry, the archers, the forest of flags fluttering in the air, followed by hundreds of mules and wagons loaded with provisions and camping equipment, all moving to the thunderous sound of drums was an awesome spectacle.

The Spanish writer Abū Bakr of Tortosa (d. 1120) has given a theory of warfare in his famous book — The Light of Kings (Siraj al-Mulūk). He has warned that an armed conflict should be resorted to only when it is inevitable. A war is a game of deception. (How true it is even in our more civilised world!) An ambush followed by a surprise attack on the enemy is the surest way to victory. The commander should be bold and courageous with a long experience in fighting. He should be fully conversant with the capability of the army under him. He should carefully plan his strategy before giving a battle to the enemy. As for the actual technique of fighting, he says that the best order of the army is to place the infantry (rijal) in front; the infantry should be armed with long lances, javelins and swords and should be stationed in rows (safūs); the but of the lance should rest on the ground, and its point in the direction of the enemy, while leaning on the left, and with their shields held aloft. Behind the infantry, there should be a second formation for archers only. Their arrows should be powerful enough to pierce the armour of the enemy soldiers. When the battle starts, the infantry should remain in its position, while the archers should discharge their arrows. When the enemy comes near, the infantry should go into action. While the infantry and the archers destroy the left and the right wings of the opposing army, the cavalry should jump into the battle and inflict on the enemy 'what Allah wills'.[28] Before fighting began, it was not uncommon to have a trial of strength between champions of each side. We have a complete description of such a duel in the history of al-Maqqari[29]. The hilly terrain required a different method of warfare. The Muslims of Granada were masters of mountain warfare. In such encounters they adopted the tactics known as 'al kar w al far' or strike and run. In this way, they lured the enemy deeper into a defile before a massive attack from all sides.

From the 9th century, the Mediterranean which the Romans proudly called 'mare nostrum' (our sea) was in fact a Muslim lake. From the shores of Spain to Tyre, they had a firm control of the sea. In the early years, the Spanish Muslims had no navy worth the name. After the unexpected irruption of the Norman pirates into the south of Spain, and the havoc caused by them, the then sultan of Cordova 'Abd ar-Rahman realised the vulnerability of the kingdom to naval attacks. He was the first ruler of Muslim Spain to take up the task of building a powerful navy. The navy *(ustul)* continued to expand, and under the later Umayyads Spain was the unchallenged naval power in the western Mediterranean. 'Abd ar-Rahman III had to defend his kingdom from the Fatimis who owned a formidable navy. During his reign the Spanish navy boasted of two hundred ships.[30] In several naval battles, the navy of 'Abd ar-Rahman proved its mettle. Admiral ibn Rumahis was the commander of the navy at that time. The European navy was nothing in comparison with the Umayyad navy in striking power and size. The Muslim fleet pounced upon European boats as a lion upon its prey — says ibn Khaldun.[31] The navy under Abi 'Amir al-Mansur was equally powerful. When he attacked Santiago, a part of his army, and arsenal were transported in military vessels from

Qasr Abi Danis (Alcacer do Sal in Portugal) to Porto on the Galician coast. There was no European navy on the Atlantic to intercept it. After the fall of the Umayyads, their navy was divided by the mulūk aṭ-ṭawā'if among themselves. Perhaps, the major share was siezed by al-Mu'tasim of Almeria, and Mujahid of Denia. The latter was a Slav who made his name as the prince of Andalusian buccaneers of his time. With the help of his navy, he became the virtual master of the islands of western Mediterranean. He even conquered the island of Sardinia. The Almoravids and the Almohads organized their navy on the lines of the Umayyads. The latter owned a navy of one hundred vessels.[32] The kingdom of Granada was very small in area, but it had to look after a long coast from Gibraltar to Almeria. Its navy was small, but it was enough for its requirements. Muhammad V paid special attention to the navy.[33] The Granadine navy constantly patrolled the coast—says ibn Khatib. The navy in Muslim Spain was commanded by a captain (qaid) who was in charge of all the vessels, the stores and the combatants. He was assisted by another officer (rais) who was responsible for the movement and manoeuvre of the ships. There were several shipyards (dar as-sina'a)—the Alcacer do Sol, Silves, and Santa Maria on the Atlantic, Gibraltar and Algeciras on the southern coast, and Almeria, Denia and Tortosa on the Mediterranean coast, during the various periods of the history of the Spanish Muslims. The international maritime vocabulary of today has several words of Arabic origin—admiral, cable, barque, shallop, arsenal, and monsoon.[34] These are eloquent proofs of the naval supremacy of the Muslims in the olden days. Nowadays, the Arabic-speaking states have no control of the waters even at their door-steps! Such is the punishment for their disunity.

Our knowledge of provincial administration of Muslim Spain is limited and sketchy. Upto the decline of the Umayyads, the

Muslim territory was divided into administrative units (Ar. sig: kura). Each district was placed under a governor *(wali)*. A garrison commanded by a military officer of high rank *(qaid)* was stationed, in the chief town of the district. The governor was provided, or he himself recruited, the necessary staff for collection of taxes, and administration of justice. It was not uncommon for a local aristocrat to head the district. This arrangement proved harmful to the state. The number of districts is not exactly known. Al-Razi placed their number at thirtyseven. He. was a geographer, and so was Idrisi according to whom there were twenty-six districts in Muslim Spain. A district was named after its chief town. The most important district was Cordova which included the Fahs al Ballut (plateau of Oaks) in the north, and the fertile plain called 'qanbaniya' (modern Campina). This district was protected by the advance military fort of Ghafiq—the present Belalcazar. Beyond this plain were the small districts of Cabra and Ecija. Adjoining the district of Cordova, there were the fertile districts of Carmona, Seville, and Nielba. Further west were the districts of Ocsconba, Silves, which together correspond to the Algarve region of modern Portugal. The other western districts were Merida, Badajoz, Santarem, and Lisbon. The south had several districts of importance—Meron, Sidonia, Algeciras, Tacaronna and Ronda. To the east lay the districts of Malaga and Elvira. The Sharq al-Andalus was composed of two districts on the Mediterranean coast from north to south—the Tudmir with Murcia as its provincial headquarter, and Valencia which touched the delta of the Ebro. The territory beyond the Sierra Morena formed the district of Toledo with Santaver and Ucles as its chief towns. It is probable that the Blearic islands formed a single district. On the borders, there were three important districts called the Marches *(thughur)* — the Superior *(al a'lá)*, the middle *(al awsat)*, and the Lower *(al adná)*, with their headquarters at Saragossa, Toledo, and Merida. These military districts were placed under commanders *(qaid)* of approved loyalty and experience in arms. Muslim Spain began to shrink after the fall of the Umayyads. As the Christians advanced into the Muslim territory, district after district was lost. It seems probable that those that remained in the hands of the Muslims retained their original names.

The forgoing paras give the salient features of the Umayyad system of administration. The subsequent dynasties adopted this system. Even the northern Christian states borrowed some aspects of the Muslim administration. Their Zalmedinas, alcaldes, the almojaifes, the nadires, the almotacenes, the amines, the zabacequias, are only modified Arabic designations of officers, — the sahib al-madina, the qadi, the mushrif, the nazir, the muhtasib, the amin, and the sahib as-saqiya. The Arabic 'al-wazir' has been debased into Spanish 'alguacil' meaning a public officer.[35] In the Spanish army of today a lieutenant is still called 'alferez' which is only the Arabic 'alfaris' meaning a cavalier.[36] Even Arabic names for taxes passed into Spanish during the Middle Ages. The influence is seen even in the coinage. Some Christian rulers like Alfonso VII, Alfonso VIII, and the duke Raman Berenguer of Barcelona used Arabic inscriptions on their coins to enhance their prestige. The coins issued under Alfonso VIII of Leon and Castile (1158-1214) bore the inscription 'Amir al-qatulaqin' i.e., the 'commander of the Catholics.' There is a coin which was issued at Toledo in the year 1220 according to this Arabic inscription. Imitating the Muslim 'kalima', this unique coin carries the Catholic affirmation of Trinity — the Father, the son, and the Holy Ghost, and also a prayer, 'He who believes and is baptised shall be saved.'[37]

The economy of Muslim Spain thrived on agriculture, industry and trade. Agriculture was the backbone of the economy. It may be relevant to mention that agricultural activity was given a religious sanction by the Quran. There is also a hadith of the Prophet cited by Anas b. Malik which says that if a Muslim plants a tree and sows a field which benefit human beings, cattle and birds, his action will count as charity. The erudite and humane scholar of Islamic studies — Prof. Seyyed Hussain Nasr of Iran does not exaggerate when he says that 'the variety of climate and geographical conditions which made up dar al-Islam, and the vast experience inherited by the Muslims, incited them, from the beginning, to seek and intensify agricultural activity.'[38] The agricultural system of the Spanish Muslims was organised on the basis of proprietorship and sharing of the produce. There were big landlords who cultivated their land with the help of hired labour. Some of the greatest families who rose to political eminence belonged to the landed aristocracy — the Banu Hajjaj, the Banu Khaldun, and the Banu al-Ahmar. Many owners rented out their land on the basis of a written agreement. There were many holdings owned by the former serfs of the Gothic days. They were all tillers of the soil under the Goths, but the Muslims made them masters of their land. This measure motivated the serfs to produce more as they were emotionally attached to the land placed under their ownership. Many Arab families from the East were allotted land in return for military service. The newcomers particularly those from Syria and Egypt were inheritors of the agricultural methods of their countries. As they came without wives, they married the local women, and this fusion resulted in the formation of colonies of farmers. This was also an important factor in promoting agricultural growth. The geography of Spain was yet another contributory factor. The Spanish peninsula, as we all know, consists of a central plateau — the Meseta which rises to a height of about two thousand feet above sea level. This is suitable only for pastoral farming and herding. The rest of the peninsula held by the Muslims embraced the Ebro basin in the northeast, the coastal region from the south of Barcelona to Algeciras, the valley of Guadalquivir, the plains of Valencia, the territories watered by the Xenil, the Atlantic coast from Lisbon to Cadiz, and the Balearic islands. These regions were most suitable for cultivation.

There was no dearth of water for irrigation. The Guadalquivir, the Tagus, the Ebro, the Guadiana, and their tributaries flowed through the Muslim territory. The Muslims established an elaborate system of irrigation which transformed the country into a paradise of cornfields, meadows, and orchards. They irrigated the land by artificial methods to supplement rain water — wells, canals, and hydraulic machines. They knew where to look for sub-soil water. When they found that there was not enough water in a well, they dug three or four wells very close to it, and connected it with subterranean channels with the other wells. In this way the water was transferred to a well from which the required quantity of water was not previously available. Numerous canals (qanat) criss-crossed the plains of Valencia, Murcia, and the kingdom of Granada. Sometimes canals were dug through solid rocks to feed the terraced farms. Hydraulic machines were installed for raising water from the rivers. An ordinary machine was pulled by mules, like the Persian wheel, but the larger ones were run by water currents. A 'na'urah' as it was called consisted of a gigantic wheel of iron with scoops which transferred water to the canals. Most of these were installed at Seville, Valencia, Saragossa, Toledo and Murcia. These could be seen at many places even till the beginning of the 20th century. The supply of water to the farmers was regulated by the government. A special officer — the 'sahib *as-saqiya'* supervised the supply of water. The disputes over supply of water were settled by a tribunal the *'wakalat as-Saqiya'* which met at the gate of the local mosque under a qadi. This tribunal functions in Spain even today, and it meets at the church gate. The legal terminology of the court is largely Arabic even today. The irrigation system was so good (say Sir John Glubb) that the sound of running water in Spain is called "Moorish music".[40]

An almanac — the Calendar of Cordova, compiled in the year 961 by Arib in collaboration with Bishop Rabi bih Zaid, gives a peep into the monthwise activities of the farmers, — ploughing, sowing, planting, harvesting, picking of fruits, and flowers. The Calendar shows that the farmers and gardeners planned their work on the basis of the Gregorian months, but followed the Islamic calendar for festivals and religious ceremonies. In January, the farmers fixed trellises for the vines, harvested sugar-cane, and prepared syrup of lemons; in February, suffron bulbs were planted, while women were employed to look after the silkworms which would be ready for hatching the next month; in March, sugar-cane was planted. In this month the farmers were issued warnings against the likely invasion of the locusts. In the month of April, they planted cucumbers, jasmine, and rice; May, was the harvesting time for cereals including wheat. In July grapes were ready for being gathered; in September and October, purple violets and pomegranates were plucked; in November, they collected chestnuts, and flowers of saffron. Soon the winter season came, and the farmers rested for a while.[41]

Wheat, rice, sugar-cane, olives and cotton were the major crops during the Muslim rule. The country was self-sufficient in food production, and even if sometimes famine broke out, food was not imported as the state maintained stocks to meet such a situation. Wheat was the staple food of the people; the lower middle class consumed barley and maize. Ibn al-Awwam of Seville, an authority on scientific farming has discussed in several chapters of his book all matters relating to cultivation of wheat and other cereals — the preparation of soil, selection of seeds, irrigation of the fields, the protection of crops from pests, harvesting, and storage. The chief wheat producing region was nearly the whole of the eastern coast. Toledo and the adjoining suburbs were renowned for the best wheat because it could be preserved for years without being contaminated on account of local conditions. Hundreds of mills, both wind-mills and water-mills converted wheat into flour. Ibn al-Awwam recommended that flour made in mills run by water currents was the finest. Not far from the bridge at Cordova can still be seen remains of a flour mill of the Ummayad period. Rice (Ar:aruzz, Sp:arroz, Fr: riz) was sown mostly in Valencia and Murcia in February and March, and transplated in May. Olive oil (Ar: Az-zait, Sp: aceite) being the main cooking medium, there was extensive cultivation of olives in the vega of Granada, the Alpujarras, the Fahs al-Ballut, and the suburbs of Seville. The Asharfe (Ar: Ash-Sharaf) near Seville was a world of olive plantations and sunny meadows. It may be recalled that the geographer Idrisi placed the whole of south Spain in the Iqlim az-zaitun, or the region of olives. Another important crop was sugar-cane for which the soil of Valencia was particularly suitable. Cotton was an equally important crop. The Spanish cotton was pronounced superior to Egyptian cotton. The province of Elvira, and the territory watered by the Xenil were famous for cultivation of cotton. A learned historian tells us that the Muslims introduced rice, sugar-cane, cotton and suffron in Spain.[42] All the green vegetables and spices were grown in plenty both on big fields and in private gardens. Muslim Spain was a land of fruits, flowers, and aromatic herbs. The whole year was a 'season of mellow fruitfulness.' Grapes, figs, pomegranates, peaches, cherries, apricots, apples, pears, water-melons were grown almost everywhere. The entire south of the peninsula from Silves to Murcia was clothed with orchards, vine-yards, and mulberry plantations. Almonecar was famous for bananas, Seville for oranges, and Cintra for unusually big melons. Malaga figs were favourite of every household. During his stay at Malaga, the author Shaqundi (d. 1231) travelled a distance of three days, and saw fig trees on his whole journey.[43] A variety of fig called 'quti' was in great demand for its sweetness and flavour. There were vast groves of palm-trees at Elche. The island of Mallorca produced the best almonds used for making desserts. Flowers, medicinal plants, fragrant herbs, saffron, cumin, coriander, and henna were cultivated in many part of Spain. There was a great demand for many flowers like the jasmine and the roses which were used for perfume-making, and for supplying rose water for bathing. Suffron was cultivated at Toledo, Granada, and Valencia. The Spanish saffron (Ar:az-zafaran, Sp: azafran) is still famous all over the world, and it is greatly prized by perfumers and confectioners. Spain was rich in forest wealth, specially the oak and yew trees. The wood of these and other trees was used for making charcoal for domestic cooking, and for making masts of ships. Esparto was in great demand for making baskets, and it was grown at many places in the south-east.

The sub-soil of Spain was rich in metalliferous wealth. The Spanish mines yielded gold, silver, copper, iron and mercury. The sands of the river Darro (which was called 'Nahr Falum) yielded the purest gold. The yellow metal was also mined at Elvira. The finest silver came from Murcia, Elvira, Alhama and

Beja. In the north of Cordova, there was a famous mine of mercury which the geographer Idrisi visited and saw its working. The mine employed a thousand workers. They worked in gangs. One gang descended into the pit and extracted the material; the other transported wood for heating, and the third produced pure mercury with the help of ovens.[44] The mining of iron revived during the Muslim rule. Almeria, Toledo and Constantina were the centres of iron mines. There was also a lead mine at Cabra. Copper was obtained chiefly from the mines of Almeria. The district of Ocsonoba in the Algarve produced tin, alum and sulphate of iron. The rock salt mined at the coast of Cadiz was a source of flourishing business. The quarries met the demands of jewellers and builders. Saragossa was famous for gems, Lorca for lapis-lazuli, Malaga for hyacinths, Almeria for rubies, Granada for onyx, and Macael for marble.

The industry of Muslim Spain may be divided into two categories — one provided articles of daily use, and the other *de lux* products for the wealthy class. In the former category may be included manufacture of leather goods, paper, household utensils, ceramics, and miscellaneous metallic articles. Spanish leather industry flourished in the major towns throughout the Muslim period. These were, probably, located outside the cities, and only finished leather was brought for sale in the 'shops. It seems that most of the shops selling leather were located at the city gates. This is proved by the fact that there was a Gate of Tanners (*bab al dabaghin*) at Granada, and also one at Toledo. Of all the places, the leather made at Cordova was the best, and its fame reached beyond Spain. The words 'Cordovan' and 'Cordwainer', used respectively for leather and a shoemaker in Medieval Europe, are derived from the name of the city famous for its leather.[45] The Muslims were expert in decorating leather by filling gold leaf into sunken designs, a craft for which Morocco is famous.

The Oxford Dictionary of Paper-Making says that the word 'ream' is the oldest word in paper making technology.[46] The Latins knew this word in the form of 'rizma', before it passed into English as 'ream! The word is derived from the Arabic 'rismah' meaning a bundle. This etymological survival is a proof of the fact that paper manufacture was introduced in Spain by the Muslim[s,47] We do not exactly know when the first paper mills were started in Spain. However, it is certain that paper was being made in abundance in the 10th century. This is attested by the Arabic manuscripts dating from the 10th century in the Escurial. It is probable that paper manufacture started earlier, perhaps, during the reign of 'Abd ar-Rahman II. Valencia and Jativa (Ar. Shatiba) were the main centres of paper industry. A certain quality of paper is known even today as 'Shatibi' in Morocco. Cotton and linen were used in making paper. Europe is indebted to Spanish Muslims for paper manufacturer.

There was a booming metallic industry. Cordova, Toledo, Seville, Medinaceli, Albacet, Murcia and Almeria were famous for manufacture of weapons, utensils, ornaments and caskets, lamps, chandeliers, waterspouts in the shape of animals, incense-burners, crockery and ornamental beds. The sultania factory of arms was located at Cordova during the caliphate period. It produced helmets swords, spears, breastplates, bows and arrows. No specimens of the arms of this period are extent, but from descriptions of arms in the poetry (of the Umayyad and the mūluk at tawāif periods) we learn that the helmets were ornamented with borders of silver stars and studs. We do not have the specimen of arms made during the two periods. Only some swords and daggers made at Granada are kept in the museums. The marquise of Vilaseca whose ancestor captured Abū Abdullah at the battle of Lucena, and the marquis of Campo

Mosque Lamp from Granada

Tejar (a descendant of a certain prince Yahya), and several other nobles have left swords belonging to the Granada period.[48] Some of these belong to Abū Abdullah, the last ruler of Granada. But the blade of the sword attributed to it is a latter addition. The swords and daggers of the Granada period (there are about a dozen of them) bear the usual Arabic inscription *'la ghalib illallah'* in coloured damascene on the handles studded with pieces of ivory. A helmet attributed to Abū 'Abdullah is decorated with gold filigree, and it is considered a work of marvellous craftsmanship. The sword-making industry flourished at Toledo and Albacete after these cities were lost by the Muslims. Pascual de Gayangos came across a dagger in London which was made at Albacete in 1705 with an inscription in Arabic inscription meaning 'I shall kill your enemies with the help of Allah.'[49] A Morisco craftsman named Julian del Rei was famous for sword-making: his trade mark was a dog.[50] Even today, Toledo is famous for sword-making. Bronze and copper were extensively used for making articles of daily use. The museum at Madrid has a unique suspension lamp in bronze belonging to a mosque of Granada. This is a pretty piece of four balls of varying sizes put one above the other in a pyramidical order. The lower part consists of two chambers — a bigger one in octagonal shape followed by a smaller one for the wick. The entire surface is perforated with delicate floral designs. An inscription reads that the lamp was made at the orders of Muhammad III in 705.[51] Gold and silver were used for making numerous articles for rich patrons, — statuettes, caskets, cutlery and jewellery. Several *objects d'art* were made in silver. The reader will recall the silver model of the palace of Madinat az-Zahra presented by al-Mansur to the sultana Subh. It was so heavy that it was brought to the palace by two men. The treasuries of Spanish churches own silver caskets of exquisite workmanship. The cathedral of Gerona has a fine silver box with palmett scrolls. The inscription says that it was made by the orders of Hakam II for his son Hisham II.[52] Gold and silver ornaments were made at Cordova, Seville and Granada, but very few specimens have survived. The museums and private collections have some gold ornaments — mostly necklesses, earrings and bracelets in filigree work. Most of them belong to the 14th century. It seem that the goldsmiths of Granada were masters in the technique of making ornaments of polychrome enamels.

The Muslim peoples of the Middle Ages produced some of the finest pottery. Alleppo, Fustat (old Cairo), Sultanabad in the East, and Madinat az-Zahra, Malaga in Spain were the greatest centres of pottery. The Andalusian master potters made an infinite variety of vessels of different shapes, designs and colours. They made plates, jugs, vases, ewers, bowls, flasks, lamps, ornamental bottles and tiles in white, green, red, turquoise blue, lapis-blue and golden iridescence. Some of their pottery is considered second only to the Chinese pottery of the Ming period. The art of lustre pottery was imported by the Spanish Muslims from the East. In making lustre pottery, a design is drawn on glazed surface, and it is fixed by firing in smoke. This process involves use of metallic salts which leaves an iridescent sheen on the pot. The earliest examples of this type of pottery were found during excavations at the Madinat az-Zahra.[53] These finds have not been thoroughly studied, but opinions are divided as the whether these ceramics (mostly pots, bowls, plates with figures of birds and animals) were of local make, or imported. There is, however, ample evidence to show that the art of lustre pottery was known in Spain in the later centuries. The 12th century geographer Idrisi has mentioned Calatyaud *(Qalat Aiyub)* as a centre of ceramics. But it is likely that the art of lustre pottery was known much earlier. The observant eyes of ibn Buttutah did not fail to admire the fruits of the potter's wheel displayed in the markets of Malaga. The kingdom of Granada saw the golden age of ceramics. We have several specimens of the pottery of the 14th century Granada and Malaga, which are the pride of museums and private collections. The most spectacular are the several storage vases which were unearthed from a tower of the Alhamra. A magnificent vase at the archeological museum of Granada is 4 feet and 3 inches in height. It has a band of inscriptions in the middle of its circumference, a pair of gazelles in the upper half, with blue, gold and creamy arabesques all over the body which give this 'foster child of silence and slow time', a look of harmony and serenity, even though one of its handles is missing. Hanover, an authority on ceramics thinks that this and other such vases are 'one of the immortal works of ancient craftsmen'.[54] After the conquest of Valencia, some families of potters remained there, and James I of Aragon allowed them to carry on their craft on payment of a tax.[55] These mudéjare potters preserved the technique of gold faience in traditional motifs — geometrical patterns, running deers, birds, and even the coat of arms of their patrons. Many plates and dished made by these annoymous masters are found in the Louvre and museums of Spain. The Italians imported drug-jars painted in lustre from Spain. Some experts are of the opinion that the art of lustre pottery reached Italy through Spain.[56] Ceramics tiles were in great vogue in Spain from the 10th century. The manufacture of tiles was an offshoot of lustre pottery. The ceramic tiles (Ar: Zellij, and Sp: azulejos) were used in decorating floor, and the lower parts of walls. The manufacture of tiles reached its greatest perfection in the 14th century. We find them on the walls of many halls of the Alhamra. They are of such a consummate workmanship that their colours (blue, green, brown and white) have not dimmed with the passage of time. They are square in shape with arabesque ornamentation. Each tile had an independent design, but many could be dovetailed to form a bigger tile or panel. In the museum of Madrid, there is a splendid plaque with a border inscription along its rectangular shape which reads that it was made during the reign of sultan Yusuf Hajjaj.[57] The rest of its space is a veritable garden with birds perched on vines in their natural growth. Even today houses in Spain and Portugal are decorated with ceramic tiles. In Seville a person who owns a house with no tiles is considered poor by his neighbours, and they often say, "non ava casa azulejos", or "his house has no tiles."[58]

In his epistle on the merits of the people of Spain, ibn Hazm has compared his countrymen to the Chinese in the perfection of their craftmanship. This quality is distictly perceptible from the many ivory works of the Andalusians. The Spanish word for ivory-marfil, comes from the Arabic 'anab al-fil'. As there were no elephants in Spain, it is almost certain that ivory was brought by merchants from Africa. Pieces of ivory were used for manufacture of articles for rich persons. The 10th and the 11th centuries were famous for ivory works — caskets, hilts of daggers and swords, chessboards, needles and also for decorating doors and windows. The greatest work in ivory ever executed in Muslim Spain was the celebrated pulpit (mimbar) of the mosque of Cordova commissioned by Hakam II. The pulpit does not exist anymore, but more than a dozen ivory boxes and caskets have luckily survived. These are preserved in Victoria and Albert Museum, the Louvre, the Hispanic Society of America, and several museum and monasteries of Spain. Most of the existing caskets were made for 'Abd ar-Rahman III, and the succeeding Umayyads, and the members of the al-Mansur

Moorish Ivory Casket of the 11th Century in the Cathedral of Pamplona

family. A description of each piece of ivory will occupy much space. We may be content with general features of the caskets. These caskets are either cylindrical or rectangular with dome-shaped and prismatic lids. Migeon, the French authority on Muslim art, says that 'in the ingenius composition of the themes of astonishing variety, they present the most charming fantasy.'[59] Almost all the caskets have bands of kufic inscriptions praising Allah, and blessing the owner. The carvings mostly in relief, depict hunting scenes, musicians with instruments in their hands, mounted warriors, and fights with animals. The decorative scenes are placed in medallions surrounded with birds, deers, elephants, and mythical figures like the sphinx and the griffons. A casket gives the name of the craftsman — Muhammad ibn Zayyan.

The textile industries — cotton, woollen and silk, provided employment to hundreds of people. The cotton industry produced all kinds of plain and printed cloth and bed sheets. Wool for clothes and rugs were available in abundance. Davies says that the merino sheep famous for their wool were introduced in Spain by the Moors.[60] Most of the wool went into the making of rugs. Idrisi praised the carpets made at Chinchilla and Cuenca. But the pride of textile industry was silk and silken goods. The Muslims of Spain were masters in producing silk. The mulberry plantations for raising silkworms grew in Elvira, Malaga, Gaudix, Finana, Jaen and the valleys of the Alpujarras. In the district of Jaen, which was known as 'Jayyan al-harir' or Jaen the silken, three thousand helmets were covered with mulberry trees for silk production.[61] Silk production on a large scale began under the patronage of 'Abd ar-Rahman II, and the influence of Ziryab who introduced Abbasid dress fashions at the court. The first looms for spinning silk were set up at Cordova from where the industry spread to Seville, Saragossa, Valencia and other cities. In Almeria, at one time, twelve

Gold Dinar of 'Abdur Rahman al-Nasir

thousand weavers were engaged in manufacture of silk textiles. It seem that silk cloth was within the reach of most of the people. Al-Maqqari has mentioned different qualities of Hispam-Muslim silk textiles — the *tiraz, dibaj, 'atabi, hulul, al-jurjani,* and *isqalatun.* The *tiraz* was the costliest fabric as it was made exclusively for the royal family and the *beau monde.* A piece of tiraz was a thing of beauty, a veritable mosaic in silk, with inscriptions giving the rank of the wearer, words of praise, prayers and verses. The silk fabrics carried the usual designs— figures of birds, leaves, geometric designs, star-shaped polygons and scrolls. They were all woven, and not printed. Some rich fabrics were woven with silver and gold threads for wealthy patrons. Many fragments of Hispano-Muslim silks are found in several museums. Most of them were used for altars—the church authorities took the Arabic inscriptions as decorative patterns. They are fine in texture, and their usual colours are green, brown, black for background, and cream, red, brown, blue and white for designs. The most celebrated piece of *tiraz* belongs to Hisham II. This was found in a casket at the altar of the church of San Estaban (in the province of Soria) and is now kept in the museum at Madrid. This piece of tiraz has octagonal medallions, and figures of lions, birds, and quadrapeds. An inscription reads, "In the name of God the Merciful and the compassionate. His favours and benedictions be upon the caliph and imam Abdullah Hisham."[62] The silk industry continued to flourish even after the fall of the Umayyads. Even the orthodox Almoravids were fascinated by Andalusian silks. The silk industry had its second golden age in the kingdom of Granada. Says ibn Khatib, "Granada is proud of silk production, and the industry is a source of employment and income."[63] The brocades of Almeria were prized by the ladies of Granada. Silk fabric made in the kingdom reached the Christians of Castile and Aragon. The rare pieces of silks and brocades of Almeria/ Granada show the decorative patterns reminiscent of the ceramic tiles seen on the walls of the Alhamra.

Muslim Spain carried on vigorous foreign trade with north Africa, Egypt and Constantinople. The Byzantum merchants purchased Andalusian products and resold them to India and central Asia. The Jews and the Christian were equal partners in trade and commerce.

Notes

1. H.A.Q. Husaini: Arab Administration, p. 245. Unfortunately, the author has written very little on administration of Muslim Spain.
2 Al-Maqqari/Gayangos. Vol. I, p. 98.
3 Ibn Khaldun: The Muqqadama, Vol. II, p. 12.
4. Ibn Khaldun: The Muqqadama Vol. II, pp. 26-27.
5 Husaini: pp. 84-85.
6. Ibn Khaldun: The Muqqadama, Vol. II, p. 26.
7. Ibid, pp. 29-31.
8. Ibn Idhari, Vol, II, p. 220

9. Hitti: History of the Arabs, p. 564

10. Al-Maqqari, Vol. I, p. 104

11. Imamudin: Economic History, p. 372

12. Ibid, p. 383

13. Ibn Khaldun: The Muqqadama, Vol. I, p. 365.

14. Ibn Idhari, Vol. II, p. 241

15. L. Provençal: L'Espagne Musulmane au Xème Siècle, p. 69.

16. Imamuddin: p. 372, and p. 383.

17. Al-khushani: p. 102.

18. G. Miles: Tee coinage of the Umayyads of Spain, New York, 1950. For a general survey of the coinage of the Umayyad period, see pp. 20-110, of Vol. I. The second volume contains photos of the many coins representing all periods of the kingdom of Cordova.

19. Al Khushani: pp. 25-26.

20. Al-Khushani, pp. 63-64.

21. Ibid, p. 112.

22. L. Provençal. L'espagne Musulmane au Xème Siècle, pp. 80-84, and Pérès, p. 367.

23. Renan: p. 10.

24. Under the title— Seville Musulmane au debut du XII Siècle, Paris, 1948.

25. L. Provençal: L'Espagne Musulmane au Xème Siècle, p. 129.

26. L. Provençal: L'espagne musulmane au Xème Siècle, pp. 141-142.

27. L. Provençal: L'espagne musulmane au Xème Siècle, pp. 141-142.

28. L. Provençal: L'Espagne Musulmane au Xème Siècle, pp. 146-147,

29. Al-Maqqari/Gayangos, Vol. II, p. 211-212.

30,31&32.

    Ibn Khaldun: The Muqqadamah, Vol, II, pp. 40-43.

33. Ibn Khatib: Ihata, Vol. II, p. 30.

34. Arnold and Guilaume: The Legacy of Islam, p. 30.

35. L. Provençal: L'Espage Musulmane au Xème Siècle, pp, 98-99, and p. 167.

36. L. Provençal: La civilisation Arabe en Espagne, p. 123.

37. Journal of the American Oriental Society No. 103.3 of 1983, pp, 513-514 give the full text of the Arabic inscriptions on this coin.

38. S.H. Nasr: Islamic Science, p. 209 & p. 218.

39. Ibn al-Awwam: Vol. I, p. 103.

40. Sir John Glubb: The Course of Empire, London, 1965, p. 79.

41. L. Provençal: L'Espagne Musulmane au Xème Siècle, pp. 172-173.

42. Don Palencia: Historia, p. 137.

43. Al-Maqqari/Gayangos, Vol. I, p. 49.

44. Al-Himyari: p. 15.

45. Arnold & Guillume: Legacy of Islam, p. 15.

46. Dictionary of Paper and Paper-making, Oxford, p. 223.

47. Arnold and Guillaume: Legacy of Islam, p. 145.

48. G. Migeon: Manuel d'art Musulman vol. I, pp. 414-418, and also: pp. 350-358. Migeon has published many phatos of the swords, daggers and helmets of the Granada period.

49. Al-Maqqari/Gayangos: Vol. I, p. 593, note: 49.

50. R.T. Davies: p. 68.

51. G.Migeon: Vol. I, p. 386.

52. Diamond: p. 156. and G. Migeon: Vol. II, p. 18. The casket was made by two craftsmen, named Tarif and Badi whose names are inscribed in it.

53. G. Migeon: Vol. II, p. 242.

54. Warren E. Cox: p. 334.

55. G. Migeon: Vol. II, pp. 242-273 give a good survey of Hispano-Muslim ceramics, with many photos.

56. Warren E Cox: p. 325.

57. G. Migeon: Vol. II, pp. 248-249. The author has given a photo of this plaque.

58. Warren E. Cox: p. 320.

59. G. Migeon: vol. I, p. 344.

60. Davies: p. 18.

61. Al-Himyari, p. 80.

62. G. Migeon: Vol. II, pp. 321-322.

63. Ibn Khatib: Ihata, Vol. I, p. 15.

Chapter 20

Urban Centres

———·———

"Certain Spanish scholars (says Prof. Hitti, the American historian) lament the break in the Christian tradition as Islamic rule sandwiched in between medieval and modern times. The fact remains, however, that Spain under Islam reached economic and cultural heights unattained before".[1] An important impact of Muslim rule in Spain was the phenominal growth of urban centres. The process of urbanization had been going on under previous regimes, but it received fresh impetus on a much larger scale during the Muslim rule. The Muslims built only a few towns — Murcia for political reasons, Madinaceli for strategic, Algeciras for military purposes, and Madinat as-Zahra for the pleasure and prestige of the first Caliph. But almost all the old cities of Roman/Gothic days survived, expanded and prospered. Even many retained their old Roman names — Corduba, Hispali, Caesaraugust, Valentia, Toledum, which were slightly Arabised into Qurtuba, Ishbiliya, Sarqust, Balansiya and Tulaitula. The most teeming cities/towns during the various period of the Muslim rule were — Almeria, Archidona, Granada, Badajoz, Baza, Beja, Carmona, Cordoba, Coimbra, Denia, Ecija, Fraga, Gaudix, Huesca, Jativa, Lisbon, Jaen, Lorca, Malaga, Murcia, Neilba, Orihuela, Saragossa, Seville, Silves, Toledo, Valencia and Ubeda.[2]

These towns did not flourish in isolation. They were connected by roads, several dating from the Roman days, but kept in good repair for movement of troops and public transport. The eastern geographer Istikhari (d. 934) has enumberated fourteen main roads and highways during the reign of caliph 'Abd ar-Rahman. The roads radiated from Cordova in all the directions. One of the longest highways started from Cordova, passed through many cities and rural settlements, and reached Saragossa via Tudela, and ended at Lerida. A road joined Cordova with Toledo and Guadalajara. Militarily, this was an important highway because most of the expeditions against local rebels and the northern kingdoms marched on this route. A road connected Cordova to Coria, Merida and Beja. An important road for tourists and merchants passed through the valley of Guadalquivir towards Seville and Carmona. Cordova was also connected to Valencia, Murcia and Tortosa. Al-Mansur led his army (May, 985) along this great highway when he attacked Catalonia. A number of small roads of commercial importance sprouted from Ecija to Moron, Ecija to Archidona, Pechina to Malaga, and Gibraltar to Madina Sidonia. The ports of Almeria, Almunecar and Algeciras were connected by a road mostly used by merchants and travellers. A road started from Cordova and reached Ghafiq, the capital of fahs al-Ballut, and from there it took a turn and ended at Nielba.[3] This was perhaps one of the longest roads built by the Muslims. There were also smaller roads which connected a big town to rural settlement, but their list will be long. All the roads had halting places (Ar. sig: *manzil*) with inns for rest. The people travelled in groups with adequate means of defence. The highways were patrolled by police for the safety of travellers, but there was no certainty that the roads would be free from robbers and freebooters. After the fall of the Umayyads, travelling became risky. During the

Almohad rule, the roads were safe for travellers; Ibn Jubayr's journey to Mecca from his home in Granada which he left after the sunset for Tarifa, passed without any untoward happening. But in the kingdom of Granada, the travellers were not always safe. On his journey from Ronda to Marbella, ibn Buttutah had to travel on a rough road, and nearly escaped being killed by a party of Christian pirates.[4] Many journeys took several days. From Cordova to Carmona, the journey was completed in four days. A traveller took six days to reach Toledo, thirteen to Saragossa, and Fourteen to reach Neilba.

Muslim cities in the Middle Ages were walled settlements, some rectangular, and others manysided depending upon the size of the population. (Baghdad of al-Mansur was an exception as it was circular). Almost all the major cities had ramparts with watchtowers, some had even moats, and secret gates. The nucleus of an urban centre, whether big or small, was the "madina" proper with a big mosque in the centre from where streets fanned out in different directions. This was the usual pattern of an Andalusian urban centre. A town was divided into sectors. The citizens of each sector (rabad) in big cities like Cordova led an autonomous life, and could carry on their daily activities without having to visit the main city unless absolutely necessary. The main throughfares were wide, but the cobbled streets leading to houses were so narrow that two persons could hardly walk side by side. Many congested localities have retained this feature even today. The narrow lanes turned and twisted, and emerged into plazas with a fountain in the middle. The towns like Ronda built on rocky terrain had stepped streets. The bigger towns had centres of industry, mosques, churches, bazars, baths (hammam), hotels (funduq), and flourishing markets (suq). The shops were stocked with goods from all parts of the known world. The big cities hummed with trade.

"In Seville one could buy even a bird's milk" — so ran a lively proverb.[5] Most of the shops were clustered round the main mosque, and formed a tangled conglomeration of narrow winding lanes. The artisans were organised into corporations. As in all cities of Muslim East, so also in Spain, shops of similar articles were located in one part of the street which often derived its name from the merchandise sold there, for example, the 'suq al-attarin' (the Market of Perfumers) where all sorts of beauty creams, powders, and perfumes were sold. There were streets of goldsmiths, parchment makkers (raqqaq), paper (kaghaz), booksellers (kutubi), money-changers (ṣairafi) and tailers (al-khaiyat). (There is still a lane in Cordova called 'Alfayates' which was once the street of tailors.) At some places weekly markets and fairs were held every Thursday. In addition to these ordinary markets, the bigger cities had special markets for sale of jewellery, silks, brocades, and articles of luxury. A *qaisariya* (the name for such a market) was better organized, and well-protected as their owners were rich merchants. These markets were entered through a main gate which opened into a rectangular plaza with flower-beds and a fountain in the centre.[6] The shops were located in galleries around the plaza. An officer designated as *'amin'* looked after the management of these exclusive shopping centres. The petty shopkeepers had tented booths. Most of the eatables — fried fish, roasted mutton, pastries of cheese (called mujabbanat) were sold there. They advertised their goods by shouting lustily. Some Christian hawkers loudly swore by the Prophet to attract Muslim customers. There were also numerous bakeries in every town, as the people liked oven-fresh bread.

The geographical dictionary of al-Himyari reveals that there was a jama masjid in almost all the cities and towns of Muslim Spain. Many of these were spacious and beautiful. The jama masjids of Ecija, Jaen, Algeciras, Malaga, and Tortosa had five aisles each. There were churches in all the cities. There were six churches inside the city of Cordova, and equal number outside. The church at Ecija stood close to the local jama masjid.[7] The Christian owned monasteries and Churches almost everywhere. The Jews had their synagogues. Their main place of worship in Cordova was very near the royal palace. This synagogue has been restored by the Spanish government.The major cities were encircled by long stretches of lush green fields, meadows, orange groves, mulberry plantations, forests of oak and yew, pleasure gardens and orchards of figs and other fruits. Murcia was known as the 'bustan' (garden), and Valencia the 'bouquet' (mutayyab) of Spain. Seville was situated in a small paradise of Axarafe which was covered with green fields, figs and olive trees for miles. Lorca was surrounded by grape vines. A hill near Cordova was adorned with rose gardens, and it was known as 'jabal al-ward' i.e., the hill of roses. Toledo was famous for its forest of oaks. The south of Portugal from Lisbon to Silves was famous for fruit gardens, specially of apples. The houses were continuously white-washed — a practice faithfully followed by the present day people of Spain. An exiled prince of Valencia recalled the glimpse of the white villas seen through the swaying trees on a breezy day. In a distich, he compared Valencia to a beautiful maiden who tries to conceal her white bosoms with a green robe when surprised by an intruder.[8]

Cordova, the metropolis under the Umayyads was known as 'the bride of Andalus'. The city was in a ruinous state at the time of the conquest. Its wall was broken at many places, and its only bridge had been destroyed by floods. The city expanded and prospered under the Muslims. They endowed it with new contours, ethos and culture giving it a unique place in Medieval

Europe. Muslim Cordova had a soul, an individuality, and a distinctive aroma of its own. Once a citizen of Cordova visited Toledo to see a friend, and the latter cried with joy, "Come near me that I may inhale the scent of Cordova from your dress."[9] Cordova was an ancient city with a long history. The Pheonicians called it 'karttuba' which means a good city.[10] Under the Romans and the Goths it was a small provincial town with a brisk trade, but famous for being the birth place of great Romans such as Seneca. A great tragedy befell in Cordova when in 45 B.C. Julius Caesar destroyed nearly half of the town and massacred thousands of its citizens for supporting the sons of his rival Pompey. The most glorious epoch in the history of the city opened after the Arab conquest. The Muslim established their capital at Cordova, and not at Toledo. They chose Cordova for the obvious reason that it was close to northwest Africa, the nearest outpost under the crescent. Perhaps, they liked its situation also. Nestled in the lap of the Guadalquivir, protected by the Sierra de Cordova (the Jabal al'arūs), the city is situated in one of the most fertile regions of Spain.

The new comers did not arrive in an alarmingly large number. We cannot imagine that the twenty thousand Berbers and Arabs who arrived with Tariq and Musa settled only at Cordova. Still, the population increased, particularly from the time of Hakam and during the reigns of his immediate successors. Scholars, merchants from the East, and European mercenaries made Cordova their home. The Muslims, no doubt, multiplied faster, but we cannot rule out the postulate that people from the adjoining districts flocked to Cordova to seek employment dazzled by its glamour as the seat of government and trade. We see the same process in developing countries today. When Cordova grew in size, it embraced twentyone colonies (Ar.

sig:*rabad*). The historians have left the names of these new colonies, but except Rusafa, it is not possible to identify their exact site. The biggest expansion took place towards the west (al jānib al-gharbi) with nine colonies: 1. Rabad Khawānit ar-Raihani; 2. R.ar-raqqaqin; 3. R.Masjid al-Kahf; 4. R. Balāt Mughith where ibn Hazm lived; 5. R. Masjid ash-Shifa, named after the beautiful wife of 'Abd ar-Rahman II; 6. R. Hammām al-ilbiri; 7 R. Masjid Masrur; 8. R.ar-rawza; 9. R. as-sajn al-Qadim. There were seven colonies in the east (al jānib ash-sharqi) - 1. R. Shubullār; 2. R. Furn Birril. This colony was very thickly populated. (In 972, a street in Furn Birril was found too narrow for the procession of Hakam II.) 3. R. al-burj; (4) R. Munyat Abdullah; 5. R. Munyat al-Mughira, named after Mughira, a son of Hakm I; 6. R. Zāhira; 7. R.al-Madina al-Atiqa. The northern sector had only three colonies — 1. Rabad bab al-Yahud, the Jewish quarter of the city; 2. R. Masjid Umm Salam, named after the sister of Hakam I who had built a cemetery in the neighbourhood; (3) R. ar-Rusafa. Beyond the south bank of the river, there were only two colonies — 1. R. Shaqunda which under the Romans was known as Secunda. The governor al-Samh founded the first Muslim cemetery — the famous Maqbarat al-Rabad; 2. R. Munyat 'Ajab, named after a concubine of Hakam I. Cordova was enclosed by a massive wall some remains of which have defied the brunt of time. The traffic passed through several gates. The Bridge Gate (bāb al-qantara) was almost at the back of the grand mosque. It opened on the bridge resting on sixteen arches. The bridge was a famous landmark of the city. It is still in use, and is constantly repaired by the Spanish government. The 'bāb al-hadid' (The Iron Gate) stood on the eastern wall. It was also called 'bāb Tulaitula (The Gate of Toledo). All traffic to and from Toledo passed through this gate. On the extreme north,

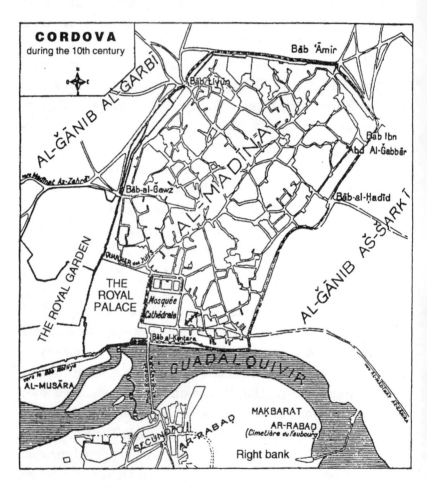

Cordova during the Caliphate

was the 'bāb ʿAmir al -Qurashi. When ibn Hazam lived in the walled city, he passed through this gate to attend the lectures of his tutor, the Shaikh ibn Yazid al-Misri who lived in Rusafa. The 'bab al-Jawz; on the western side of the wall, was one of the most important gates because it marked the starting point of the road to Badajoz. The site of this gate is now called Almodovar. The Gate of Seville was also on the western side of the rampart, but the general public called it 'bab al'attarin (The Gate of Perfumers).[11]

The Cordova of today is not what it was during the Muslim period as it has undergone many changes. The old landmarks of the city's Islamic past have disappeared. However, history helps us to visualise (without romanticizing) some old features of the city, and the life of the people. A visitor coming to Cordova for trade or for higher education in the tenth century, — say from the south, entered the municipal limits of the city in the colony of Shaqunda (Secunda). He passed the historic cemetery of Banu Marwan, and reached the bank of the Guadalquivir. After crossing the bridge, he entered amid the sights and sounds of the city i.e., the madina. On his left, he could see the royal palace glittering in the sun with its towers, monumental gates and elegant outer galleries. Exactly before him loomed the minaret of the mosque of Cordova. Within minutes, he found himself on the 'mahajja alʿUẓmā — the grand road between the western wall of the mosque and the royal palace. Presumably, there was a plaza at the southern end of this road, and from there the road branched off to the west along the bank. This road was called 'rasif' which led to the boundary walls of the vast gardens of the royal palace. The main gate of the palace built on a high pedestal, known as 'bab as-sudda' faced the river. If the visitor moved to the east, taking the road behind the qibla wall of the mosque, he could reach the famous qaisariya, the hub of the city's shopping centre for articles of luxury. He had three options to enter the mosque. He could walk along the 'mahajja al-uẓmā,' and enter the mosque through the doors on his right. He would have found the gate of the mosque after walking the whole length of the mosque. He could also get entrance into the mosque through any of the doors on the western wall. His third option was to enter the mosque through one of the doors on the eastern wall built by al-Mansur. Let us assume that the visitor entered the mosque through the main gate on the north flanked by the magnificent minaret installed by 'Abd ar-Rahman III. He traversed the courtyard of the mosque with its fountains and basins of water, and found himself into the vast prayer hall — a vertitable forest of columns. Groups of eager youngmen could be seen around a venerable looking scholar lecturing on literature, hadith, law, and theology. Outside the mosque, the life was different. Cordova was a noisy city. One could hear all sorts of noises — the clutter of horses on which the wealthy rode, the cries of vendours hawking their wares, the greetings in Arabic, Hebrew and the Romance dialect, the public announcements by heralds about the arrival of foreign ambassadors, the coming military parade, or the victorious return of the army from a campaign. The visitors were equally assailed by the inviting smell of roasted meat, the heady smell of perfume wafted by the rustling robes of a passer-by, and the soothing smell of luscious fruits piled in shops. Like Baghdad and Constantinople, Cordova was a cosmopolitan city where one could meet men of different faiths and climes, Merchants and jewellers from Syria, Iraq, Yemen, jostled with traders from Cairo, northwestern countries, and even far away Azerbijan. On the open plazas, one could see crowds of men around street-singers, magicians, storey-tellers, and quacks selling talismans and aphrodisiacs, — the usual sights seen on the streets of Morocco of today. The street performers, no doubt, included the tricksters mentioned by ibn Hazm. They kept the spectators spell bound by their many tricks such as stabbing a man with a knife without hurting him.[12] (This was possible because the blade slipped into the handle).

Through the city's labyrinthine lanes one could reach the Gate of Perfumers (bāb al 'attarin) a favourite rendezvous for ladies who came here from all parts of the city to purchase cosmetics. Here, at the Gate of Perfumers, the young poet Yusuf ibn Harun Ar-Ramadi experienced the first pangs of love when he was struck by the beauty of the slave girl Khalwa, the subject of his lyrical serenades. Ibn Hazm has narrated the incidence, and the courtly manner of the poet who was a gentleman of polite address, and not an eve-teasing Romeo of today. Yusuf followed her quietly when she left the Gate of Perfumers and headed towards the bridge for her home in Shaqunda. When she looked backed, and found that she was being followed, she stopped, and confronted Yusuf with the stern question: "Why do you walk behind me?" Yusuf poured out his soul, but the girl snubbed him. "Give up all thought about me, and do not expose me to shame. You shall never get what you want," said the girl. The agitated Yusuf replied, "I shall be happy if I only look at you." The girl replied, "That is permitted". Probably she lifted her veil, and exposed the poet to the full bloom on her face. Yusuf asked, "My lady are you a free woman or a slave?" "I am a slave," replied the girl. "And what is your name?" asked Yusuf. "My name is Khalwa, and if you want more information, you may easily know what is in the Seventh Heaven, but no reply to your further questions." The terse reply must have convinced Yusuf that he had no chance of a romance with her, but he put his last question, "My lady can I see you again?" The girl, who wanted to get rid of him replied, "Where you saw me today, the same hour, every Friday." Then she added, "Will you now let me go." Yusuf replied, "You can go under God's protection." She crossed the bridge, but often looked back to see that she was not being followed by the stranger. She was soon out of sight. Yusuf made several trips to the Gate of Perfumers, but the girl who had taken his heart away, never reappeared.[13]

Under the Umayyad caliphs, Cordova was the biggest and the most populous city of western Europe. At that time Paris was a small village, London a stackade fighting for its existence against Viking invaders, and Moscow was slumbering its sleep of ages. The citizens were known for their etiquette, love of poetry, excellent cuisine, the art of polite conversation, and passion for books. "Cordova, says a historian, is the capital of Andalus, the residence of the caliphs; it is a populous city inhabited by the Arabs of the noblest families in the land (both Muslim and non-Muslim) who are distinguished by the elegance of their manners, the superiority of their mind, and wit, and the opulence and exquisite taste and display in their meals, drink, dress and houses."[14] The city had 213077 houses belonging to the general public, 60300 mansions of the rich, 84433 shops both big and small. Hundreds of mosques raised their minarets towards the skies, and several hundred baths served the people known for their cleanliness. The above figures have been left by ibn Hayyan who saw Cordova in the city's golden prime.[15] We do not now the exact number of its citizens. Taking a minimum of four persons as the average size of a family, it would seem that the population of Cordova was nearly a million, a colossal size for a city in the Middle Ages. The late L. Provençal has cut down the figure to half a million.[16] Economically, the citizens were divided into two major groups, the aristrocrats (khasa) and the general public (al'umma). The former class comprised the big landlords, the commercial tycoons, the civil and military officials, the men of letters, and the educated intelligentcia. Most of them lived in stately villas on the periphery of the city. Those belonging to old families were proud of their wealth and blue blood like the Romans. They had many traits in common with the Romans, — ambitiousness, bravery, love of learning and eloquence, respect for law, and fondness for display of their wealth. Some of the most aristocratic families of Cordova during the various periods of the city's history, were, — Banu Hudair, Banu Burd, Banu Fuṭais, Banu Rushd, Banu Abi Khisal, Banu Siraj, Banu Shuhaid, Banu Abi 'Abda, Banu Mughith, Banu Jahwar, Banu Yannaq, Banu Hamdon and many others. They were known for their wealth, learning, military service, and political influence. The politically conscious families were power-hungry, and many of them engaged themselves in subversive activities if the ruler was weak. Below the aristocracy came the 'umma, the middle class of shopkeepers and sem-literate artisans. The lowest class comprised hawkers, butchers, bakers etc. They were a most turbulent people, and they had to be kept in check in a city which was already bursting at the seams. The caliph 'Abd ar-Rahman had sensed the coming troubles, and he beefed up the police administration (shurta) by creating an additional post.[17] Al-Mansur exercised strict vigilance to enforce law and order in the city. When the revolution came after fall of the al-Mansur family, the notorious al-Mahdi found his greatest supporters among the butchers, the coal merchants, and sweepers of the city. It is said that the Almohad sultan Yaqūb al-Mansur once asked a former governor, to give his opinion about the people of Cordova, He replied, "They are like a camel which cries whether you increase the load or lessen it."[18]

We are informed by writers that Cordova was a clean city. It is difficult to believe that there were no stinking slums in the localities where dyers and leather-makers carried on their trade. But it is certain that the city had underground sewage centuries before any city in Europe.[19] The main roads were wide and even paved with stones. After sunset, Cordova was a *ville lumière*, and a pedestrian could walk for miles in the light of lamps. The American Arabist, Prof. T.B. Irving, says that Cordova was the first city of Europe to have street lighting.[20] A typical house in Cordova in the walled city was structurally introverted. It had an uninviting appearance from the outside, and gave no impression of the luxurious interior. It was closed on all the sides to protect the privacy of the family. The entrance gate was always shut, and it had a knocker in the shape of hand — the hand of Fatima (considered a good omen) and is seen in many houses even today. A visitor entered the house through a dark passage, and found himself in the patio which was open to the sky. The patio with a basis of water and sweet-smelling herbs allowed fresh air in the living rooms built around it. The latticed windows ensured proper ventilation. In aristocratic homes, the patio was resplendent with marble, and the interior apartments were cooled by fountains jetting cascades into basins of water. On the top-most storey, there used to be a belvedere (manzarah) where ladies retired to enjoy a panoramic view of the city.[21] Some houses had a weather cock at the top, like they have even today in Seville and other Spanish cities in the south. There is no doubt that there were curtains on the doors, tapestries on the walls, carpets on the floor, and cushioned divans arranged along the walls as in the homes of the rich Moroccans and Algerians of today who have inherited much of their culture from the Spanish Muslims. Some houses had furniture of ivory and costly woods. The rooms and salons of the wealthy were

lit by perfumed candles. All this refinement was seen in Cordova
at a time when "the dwellings of the rulers of Germany, France,
and England, which were scarcely better than stables."[22]

The fame of Cordova reached beyond the Pyrennes. The
Saxon poetess Hroswitha (d. 1002) sang the praises of the city.
For her Cordova was 'the ornament of the world, renowned for
its charms specially the seven streams of knowledge.[23] Cordova
was the intellectual Centre of Europe from the middle of the
9th Century to the end of the 12th century. The city's writers,
historians, poets, orators, physicians and botanists were too
numerous to be mentioned. Cordova was a seat of learning, a
city of libraries, and an emporium of books. Hakam II was not
the only connoisseur of books. Even the poor had a thirst for
collecting books, and many would sacrifice personal comforts
and save money to buy books. The rich Cordovans vied with
one another in building personal collections. A personal library
was a prestige symbol of men of culture and influence. Their
private libraries were open to scholars. The qadi Abul Mutrif of
Cordova (d. 1011) owned a splendid library. He had six full-
time scribes, and whenever any scholar wanted a book, the
generous qadi had it copied for him, free of charge. Cordova
had a booming book bazar. Al-Maqqari has described a scene
at a bookshop where a scholar of modest means and a wealthy
collector competed for the purchase of a book. The scholar Al-
Hadhrami was in search of a book. Luckily, he found it and
offered to buy it, but an elegantly dressed customer offered a
higher price. Time after time, the wealthy customer outbid him
until the price exceeded his purchasing power. Hadhrami told
him that he was prepared to withdraw if he was really in need
of the book. The latter told him that he was fond of collecting
books for his library, following the example of other notable
citizens. As there was still some space on his shelves for a

neatly written and handsomely bound volume, he wanted to buy it, and its price was of no consequence to him.[24] Even after the fall of the Umayyads, Cordova remained the chief market for books. The philosopher, ibn Rushd, when comparing Cordova with Seville is reported to have remarked, "It is a fact known to all that if a scholar died at Seville, his library was brought to Cordova for sale, and if a musician died at Cordova, his musical instruments were put on sale in Seville."[25] Adam Meź has lamented the dearth of books and libraries in countries of Medieval Europe. Some of the biggest libraries in Europe contained only a few hundred books, and these were on religious matters only.[26] When Cordrova was full of books a famous monastery in Catalonia had 192 books only. Stanley Lane-Poale tells us that even up to the 18th century, Madrid had no public library.[27]

Cordova had also its dark side. The wealthy Cordovans, to whatever race they belonged, were arrogant and ambitious. Their love for gain, and personal aggrandisement led to intriques. The proletariat class was restless and inflammable. They were always ready to take to arms at the behest of selfish political leaders, because a major disturbance in the city brought looted wealth in their homes. The unruly Berber soldiery, recruited by al-Mansur, prowled about like hungry wolves. No citizen was safe from them during the twilight days of the kingdom of Cordova. Inspite of opportunities for intellectual enlightenment, the common man was steeped in superstitions of the primitive man, — belief in the evil eye, use of talismans; they would make loud lamentations at funerals; many had faith in horoscopes and divination, and some even practised black magic. Overcrowding resulted in several social abuses — such as we see today the world over. Robberies were a daily occurrence in the city. The nigh-watch and capital punishment to offenders,

proved inadequate in arresting burglary. The presence of
hundreds of slave girls undermined the moral fabric of society,
and destroyed domestic peace. Some instances from ibn Hazm's
Tawq al-Hamamah are very revealing in this respect. A man
jumped from a high wall to prove that a certain abducted slave
girl was actually owned by him. A religious man cut the size
of his beard to make himself acceptable to a slave girl, only to
find that she preferred his brother. A prince of royal blood
(Taliq who was a first class poet) stabbed his father out of
jealousy and landed himself in prison. A youngman fell in love
with his brother's slave girl, and lost his senses when his brother
refused to part with her. And lastly, a fellow student of ibn
Hazm turned lunatic because his mother would not permit him
to marry a slave girl.[28] The possibility of some slave girls being
involved in immoral traffic cannot be ruled out. Al-Saqati, has
left a report on the subject. He has narrated an incidence which
throws a lurid light on growing indecencies in Cordovan society
of later days. As he was a censor of public morality (muhtasib),
we have no reason to doubt him. A man from Granada (says
Saqati) who flourished in the 11th century) came to Cordova to
purchase an attractive female slave. He bought a woman of his
liking. He mounted his prized possession on a mule with a
splendid saddle of brocade, and left for Granada. His servant
pulled the mule. When he came near Granada, he left her in the
charge of his servant, and himself went forth to find a suitable
accommodation for her. On the way, the woman saw a man
who sold cages for birds. He was once a dissolute person, but
in his declining years he had repented, and lived alone in his
workshop. As she passed by the shop, the woman recognised
him, and greeted him with the remark, "You old debauchee.
Are you still alive?" The man looked up, and said, "Oh, is it
you. Have you returned?" Now the servant heard all this, and

reported to his master. The man was upset, and he asked one of his friends to meet the cage-maker to ascertain the truth of the matter. His friend met the cage-maker who told him that the woman led an immoral life. He regretted that he had made a blunder in buying a slave girl of loose character. In the meantime, the woman had sensed that her purchaser wanted to get rid of her. The brazen hussy suggested to him to take her to Almeria where he would be able to sell her at a higher price[29]. Nor was a procuress wanting in the city of Cordova. During the time of ibn Hazm, young women were put on guard against the activities of women who visited homes such as soothsayers, professional mourners, and hairdressers.[30] The secret trade went on even under the strict Almohad rule. The poet J'affer ibn Sa'id composed a ten line poem describing such women who 'could mingle fire with water'. However, these social abuses were not rampant. On the whole, the Cordovans were a deeply religious people. They respected the law (shari'ah) and upheld the doctrines of imam Malik ibn Anas. At Cordova arose the conception of chaste love under the influence of the writings of Da'ud Isphani. Later, ibn Hazm systematised this concept into his 'Book of Love,' the famous Tawq al. Hamamah. After a century and half, this idealised love would inspire the early Provençal poets of France, and Italy.

At the height of its greatness in the 10th century, Cordova was like Constantinople in every respect. Like that great Byzantine city, Cordova was a centre of learning, philosophy, and the medical sciences, a conservatory of music and musical theorists and performing artist both vocal and instrumental. Like that city, Cordova was frequested by merchants of all nations, and visited by foreign missions. The citizens of Cordova, like those of Constantinople, were hungry for the pleasures of life, and like Constantinople, Cordova too had a lower class of turbulent people. By the middle of the XII century, Cordova lost much of its beauty. Several years of anarchy, brigandage, rapine and arsons comitted by the Berbers ruined the city for ever. The great palaces were deserted, and many aristocratic colonies on the bank of the Guadalquivir were either damaged or abandoned by their owners. The unkept gardens were haunts of idlers or lovers like ibn Zaidun, in search of solitude. The Banu jahwar tried to rebuild the ruined parts of the city, but the damage was so colossal that it needed all the treasures of Hakam II to rebuild the city. Al-Mu'tamid of Seville did nothing to arrest the decay, and even the Almoravids and Almohads neglected the city. Slowly, Cordova languished into decay. Only the poets and historians wept at its departed glory. In fact, the glory of Cordova departed after the demise of the Umayyad dynasty. When His Catholic Majesty Ferdinand III of Castile seized the city in June, 1236, the 'bride of Andalus' was only an old widow of vanished charms.

Notes

1. P. Hitti: Makers of Arab History, p. 71.
2. For a complete lists, see Al-Himyari.
3. On the roads in Muslim Spain, see L. Provençal: L'Espagne Musulmane au Xème Siècle, pp. 180-181.
4. Ibn Buttutah: pp. 313-314.
5. Al-Maqqari/Gayangos, Vol. I, p. 57.
6. L. Provençal: L'Espagne Musulmane au Xème Siècle, p. 188.
7. Al-Himyari: p. 44.
8. Al-Maqqari/Gayangos; Vol. I, p. 66.
9. Ibid, p. 31.
10. Some authors believe that the word 'Cordova' is of Iberian origin.
11. L. Provençal: L'Espagne Musulmane au Xème Siècle, pp. 204-205, and Al-Maqqair/Gayangos, vol. I, pp. 206-207, give full details of the colonies and gates of the city of Cordova.

12. Ibn Hazm: Kitab al-Milal, Vol. III, p. 286.

13. Ibn Hazm: Tawq al-Hamama. pp. 52-53.

14. Al-Maqqari/Gayangos, Vol. I, p. 505.

15. L. Provençal: L'Espage Musulmane au Xème Siècle, p. 207.

16. Ibid, p. 232.

17. L. Provençal: L'Espagne Musulmane au Xeme Siecle, pp. 232-233.

18. L. Provençal: Ibid.

19. McCabe: p.54.

20. T.B. Irving: Falcon of Spain, p. 101. (This book is a nice biography of the founder of the Umayyad Kingdom of Cordova, — ʿAbd ar-Rahman.

21. Ibn Hazm, Tawaq al Hamama, pp. 209-210. Ibn Hazm has lamented the destruction of his beautiful mansion in a long passage, p. 180.

22. Dr. W. Draper; Intellectual Development of Europe, Vol. II. This is quotation from Dr. Drapers's book. On pages 30-35 he has given an evocative descriptions of the culture and civilization of the Spanish Muslims.

    Many poets praised Cordova in their poems. One poet sang :
    Do not talk to me of Baghdad.
    Do not narrate the glories
    Of Persia and China,
    As Cordova, is peerless.

23. L. Provençal: L'Espagne Musulmane au Xeme Siecle, p. 225, and Hitti: Islam and the World, Princeton, 1962, p. 171.

24. Al-Maqqari/Gayangos, Vol. I, pp. 139-140.

25. Ibid, p. 42.

26. Adam Mez: p. 172.

27. John A, Crow: The Root and the Flower, New York, 1963, p. 56 and Lane-Poale: preface, p. IX.

28. Ibn Hazm: All these instances will be found in the Tawq al-Hamama: pp. 91, 201 etc.

29. L. Provençal: L'Espagne Musulmane au Xeme Siecle, p. 193.

30. Ibn Hazm: Tawq al Hamama, p. 74.

Chapter 21

Architecture of Islamic Spain

———·•·———

The Spanish rulers were remarkable builders, but it is unfortunate that almost all their buildings — mosques, palaces, pleasure-gardens, bridges, hospitals have disappeared. Time-worn ramparts, towers, bastions, gates, irrigational devices, and numerous inscriptions commemorating foundations of chateaux forts, are scattered all over Spain south of Toledo, like the jewels of a broken crown. The palaces raised by the Umayyads exist no more. The site of the Alcazar (al-qasr) on the bank of the Guadalquivir where most of the Umayyad rulers lived and were buried, is now occupied by the bishop's residence with no trace of its existence let alone its former glory. The Madinat az-Zahra (described earlier) was destroyed and sacked by the Berbers in 410/1010. After Ferdinand conquered Cordova, the ruined site of Madinat az-Zahra was handed over to the Municipal council. It was excavated for stones for building palaces, convents and bridges. It was further pillaged by the monks of St. Jerome for their monastery in 1408. During the subsequent centuries, the site remained a heap of ghostly rubble with trees growing here and there. Early in this century the site was surveyed by archeologists. The excavations started in 1911 by the Spanish archeologist Ricardo Velazquez have continued from time to time. These excavations have unearthed pillars, capitals with acanthus leaves, hundreds of ceramics, fragments of mosaic floor, and the walls of what was once a grand reception hall. Some marble pilasters are inscribed with the names of the carvers — Badr, Nasr, and Tariq who worked on the site. In 1944, the Spanish government reconstructed a reception hall, but none can restore a flower if its sepals and petals have been scattered by the wind. Only a few monuments of the Muslim period have survived in a fairly good condition. These are: the Umayyad mosque at Cordova, the minaret of the Almohad mosque at Seville, the Alhamra, the pleasure-garden of Generalife at Granada, and scanty remains of the Aljaferia palace at Saragossa. Tourists from all over the world who visit the south of Spain for its mild climate and sunny skies, make it a point to inhale the enchantment of the Alhamra, and to feast their eyes on the austere beauty of the mosque at Cordova. In addition to these monuments, many forts of the Muslim period stand out in varied degrees of preservation, of which the Castle of Bano at Jaen is the best example.

A period-wise study of Muslim architecture in Spain would require a book. However, some features of this architecture may be stated. Broadly speaking, the early Spanish Muslim architecture was a transplant of the Syrian tradition. Even the early designs and decorations were of Syrian origin. After the passage of time, the Spanish Muslims worked according to their own aesthetic sense. The Andalusian architects did not raise buildings with majestic domes and round minarets like the Mughals of India and the Ottoman Turks. Their civil architecture carried round pillars, and a variety of arches — the horseshoe, the semicircular, and the polylobbed. Their minarets were not cylindrical, but almost always square in shape. The roofs of small domes rested on intersecting arches of great precision. A sound knowledge of geometry imparted serene symmetry to Hispano-Muslim architecture. For decorating the surface, they used polychrome mosaic coating and arabesques of an infinite variety which 'neither the camera, nor the brush, nor pen can reflect with fidelity the effect obtained by the Moorish masters of the Middle ages.¹' These feature are found in the Umayyad buildings. The Almoravids and the Almohads borrowed some features of Umayyad architecture, but being puritans, they did not insist upon ornamentation. In the Nasarite Granada which saw the second blossoming of Hispano-Muslim culture, the architecture became delicate and even voluptuous with new features — the elaborate stalactite pendants, ceramic tiles, and highly bold and refined calligraphy which is easier to read than the austere kufic inscriptions of the Umayyad mosque.

The mosque at Cordova is the supreme pearl of the Umayyad architecture. It stands very close to the Guadalquivir. It is a vast rectangle measuring 585 ft by 410 ft, and covers an area of 26,5000 square feet making it the third largest mosque of the Arab world in the Middle Ages, and the biggest ever built in Spain. Indeed, the mosque is so huge that the cathedral built in its midst by Charles V is almost engulfed by it. The mosque is enclosed by a high wall rising to a height of 35 feet including the crenellations which give it the appearance of a fort from outside. The outer walls have projecting bays at intervals and several ornate gates. The main entrance of the mosque is at the north wall, and the other gates on the eastern and western sides remain closed. The main gate of the mosque is now known as the Gate of Pardon, but this is not the original entrance. It is a new one built on the site of the old gate after the mosque was converted into a church. Inside the mosque, the visitor is greeted by tall orange trees, and swaying palms. This is the courtyard (sahan) of the mosque. They call it the Courtyard of Oranges —

Patio de los Naranjos. The courtyard is nearly one-third of the aggregate area of the mosque. There were arcades all round the courtyard *(sahan)*. The rest of the space — the southern portion (towards the qibla) is covered by the immense sanctuary *(maqsūra)* which the visitors enter through an arch which is on the axis of the main entrance to the mosque i.e., the Gate of Pardon. All other approaches to the hall of prayer have been walled up. This has robbed the mosque of much of its beauty. The reader can imagine how the grand mosques of Delhi and Lahore would look like if all the arches of the hall of prayer are closed by masonary, and only the middle arch is left open for entrance. Leaving the colonnade of orange trees in the courtyard, the visitor enters into a forest of columns joined together by rows of arches which seem like interlacing branches of trees. There are pillars and pillars of marble, jasper, porphyry, alabaster with breathtaking vistas in all directions except where the view is obstructed by the church in the middle of the hall of prayer. The pillars —9 feet high are cylindrical with smooth and glowing surface. A few pillars have flutings like the Greek Corinthian columns; This suggests that the pillars were excavated from Roman monuments in Africa, and installed in the mosque after necessary treatment. The aisles run perpendicular to the qibla wall. Incidentally, the qibla of the mosque is not exactly oriented towards Mecca. How this mistake occurred, none can say. Once it was suggested that the whole structure be dismantled and built *de novo*, but the theologians intervened and the matter was dropped.

Several historians have recorded a detailed structural history of the mosque. The surviving inscriptions also confirm what the historians have written. We are told that a Roman temple stood here.[2] The Christians destroyed the temple, built a church which they dedicated to St.. Vincent. When the Muslims arrived

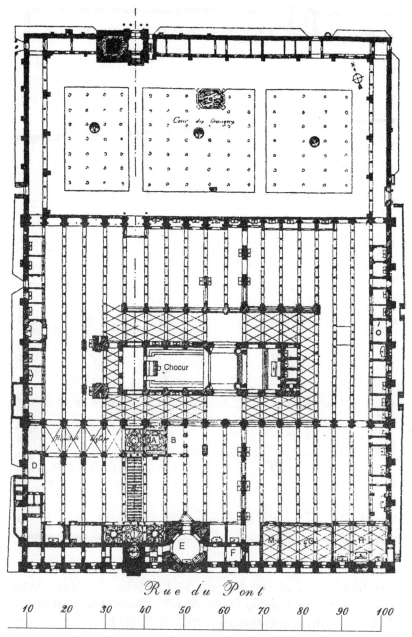

Cour des Orangers

Chocur

D

E

F

M

The Mosque after its conversion into a Church.
The Cathedral of Charles V is shown in the middle.

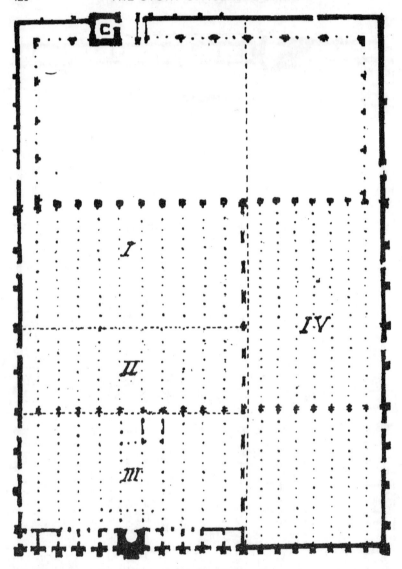

Building stages of the Mosque of Cordoba: I. Under 'Abd ar-Rahman I and Hisham I (785-796); II. Under 'Abd ar-Rahman II (848); III. Under al-Hakam II (962-965); IV. Under al-Mansur (987-990).

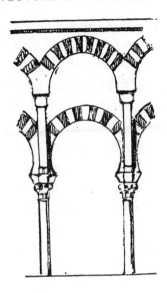

The arrangement of arches the prayer hall of the mosque.

in Spain they occupied half of the church under a treaty, leaving the other half to the Christians. It is said that the Muslims and the Christians worshipped in their respective portions during the period Spain was ruled by viceroys. Some ramshakle additions were made by them but the mosque remained incommodious. When 'Abd ar-Rahman I established an independent kingdom, he felt the need for erecting a new mosque like those he had seen in Syria. He approached the Christians for selling the portion held by them. After prolonged negotiations, they agreed to sell their portion for a sum of eighty thousand dinars. The Christians also obtained permission to build new churches. Two years before his death when he had almost pacified the new kingdom, he ordered construction of the mosque. The work began in 785-786. A.D. and when it was nearing completion, he died. His son Hisham completed the work, added a minaret at the main gate, installed basins in the courtyard, and built galleries *(saqifa)* for women. The original mosque of 'Abd ar-Rahman/Hisham had eleven aisles of ten arcades each having twelve arches. This is the oldest part of the mosque, and can be easily identified by any observer. It was 241 feet by 221 feet in dimension.[3] The roof was supported by pillars joined by horseshoe arches. The builders (some of them must have come from Syria) were faced with the problem of carrying the roof of the mosque to its present height. They struck upon a plan which is one of the original features of the mosque not to be found in any country. The horseshoe arches were superimposed by rows of round arches arising from pilasters resting on capitals. Some authors have suggested that the scheme was borrowed from the Roman acquaducts. Creswell who has studied the subject in depth has brushed aside this suggestion.[4] Be that as it may, this novel scheme of arcades raised the roof of the mosque to a reasonable height. The arches were composed of stone voussoirs alternating with red bricks fixed edgewise. These voussoirs have imparted warmth to the design. Many of them are now painted white and red.

Early in the 9th century, the Muslim population increased, and it was felt necessary to enlarge the mosque. 'Abd ar-Rahman II added (833 A.D.) eight rows of columns towards the south, and a new qibla wall was provided by removing the earlier one. More additions followed under his successors. Muhammad installed a gate on the western side. An inscription on the tympanum of the arche gives the date of its construction. The next sultan 'Abdullah built a covered passage connecting the mosque to the palace. In March 958, 'Abd ar-Rahman III ordered strengthening of the facade of the northern wall. An existing inscription recalls this repair. The old minaret of Hisham was pulled down, a magnificent one was built in its place. The geographer Idrisi saw this minaret, and he has left its description. The square tower rose to a height of 73 cubits. Two independent staircases led to a domed kiosk at the top. The minaret was crowned with three balls (which Idrisi calls apples — *tuffahat)* made of silver and gold. Decorative panels in mosaic ran on the four sides pierced with ornamental windows at regular intervals. Moralès who saw the tower in 1572 (before it was destroyed by an earthquake) admired its wonderful symmetry.[5]

The second enlargement of the mosque was undertaken in 961 under Hakam II. Again, the necessity arose on account of the increasing number of the faithfuls. Hakam added eleven more aisles. The qibla wall was once again perforated. The addition was made under Tamlih, Ahmad bin Nasr, and Khalid bin Hisham whose names appear in gold inscriptions on the mihrab. It is said that the plan was drawn by Hakam himself in consultations with his architects, and that he was, sometimes, seen working at the site. This enlargement, and beautification of the mosque was completed in 965 A.D. The mihrab, the facade of the wall in which it is fitted, the long enclosure in front of the qibla wall, and the ceiling constitute the most sumptuous part of the mosque. The mihrab is enclosed in a rectangular frame of decorative motifs. The Byzantine emperor Nicephorus Phocas (963-989) sent several bags of polychrome cubes at the express request of Hakam. But except for the material, there is nothing Byzantine in the decorative work because the local artisans had already mastered the technique, and worked independently according to their own tastes and traditions. On the vertex of the mihrab, the 23rd verse of Sur Hashr of the Quran in kufic characters can be read to this day. The inscription begins with 'bismillah; and starting with 'ho wallazi la illaha illaho', it ends at "am a yushrakun." — all in one straight line. An opening in the form of a horseshoe arch leads into a seven-sided grotto made in stucco in the form of a lustrous shell. The acoustics of this niche were so good that the faithfuls even in the last row could hear the voice of the imam during the prayer. The niche is framed in a wall of incredible beauty with a frieze at the top and flanked with small columns of veined marble resting on pedestals. The arches in the sanctuary have curling loops of rich decorations. Once again, the builders were faced with yet another problem. They were required to give a semi-circular ceiling to the square space formed by the supporting walls in front of the mihrab. Geometry came to their aid, and an original improvision was created by giving an octagonal vaulting of intersecting arches to the dome. Actually, the architects built cinquefoils across the corners on a heavy cornice line. Rising from the cornice there were clusters of small columns or shafts from which ribs fanned out on both sides, and intersecting others formed an eight-petalled flower of consummate beauty in the centre of the ceiling. The beauty of the mihrab, the ceiling of the dome, and the maqsūra, lies in their gorgeous ornamentations. Calvert ranks this decorative work with the art of Greece and Japan. While the decorations in Greek art are symmetrical and restrained, and vivacious in the art of Japan, the ornamentations of the Muslim masters who worked on the mosque, are characterised by supreme elegance. In their abstract ornamental motifs and an almost unlimited variety and complexity of designs — geometric figures, stylized leaves and petals, the Spanish Muslims had hardly any equal. In fact, they excelled the contemporary Byzantine artisans in this field. Calvert quotes the views of an Italian antiquarian Edmondo de Amicis on the beauty of this part of the mosque when the Umayyad art was at its peak, and without a parallel in contemporary west. "It is a dazzling gleam of crystals of a thousand colours, a network of arabesques which puzzle the mind, and a complication of bas-reliefs, gildings, ornaments, minutiae of design and colouring of a delicay, grace and perfection sufficient to drive the most patient painter distracted. It is impossible to retain any of the pretentious work in the mind. You might turn a hundred times to look at it, and it would seem to you in thinking it over, a mingling of blue, red, green, gilded and luminous paints, a very delicate embroidery changing continually with the greatest rapidity, both of design and colouring. Only from the firey and indefatigable imagination of the Arabs could such a perfect miracle of art emanate."[6]

Hakam II dismantled the covered passage built by 'Abdullah, and replaced it by an elegant arch which spanned the street of mahajja al-uzmā, and joined the palace. The third and the final enlargement which gave the mosque, its present dimensions was made by al-Mansur sometime in 987 A.D. Again, the reason was the mushrooming of the population. The mosque could not be extended in the direction of the qibla (i.e. towards the south) because the Guadalquiver was very near. On the west stood the palace, therefore, the extnesion was possible only towards the east. Al-Mansūr added eight aisles in that direction, by dismantling the eastern wall. The previous arrangement of the arches, their shape and design were maintained giving the new addition a unity with the rest of the hall of prayer. A corresponding enlargement was made to the courtyard of the mosque. After the final addition, the mosque had 19 aisles in the prayer hall, but the mihrab of Hakam in the qibla wall was no more in the middle. Don Torres Balabas, a modern authority on Islamic architecture of his country thinks that the addition made by al-Mansūr lacks the richness of decorations. However, it cannot be denied that the gates on the eastern wall are of classic beauty, — simple, and serene.

Hakam installed four magnificent basins of water for ablution. These were hewn out of rocks, and transported to the mosque by specially built wagons. The basins were connected with tubes which brought water from the neighbouring mountains. Hakam also provided a pulpit *(mimber)* made of rare woods, and studded with mother-of-pearl, ivory and nails of gold and silver. Over a hundred employees — cleaners, lamp-lighters and muezzins, served in the mosque. After the sunset a hundred chandliers (Ar. sig: *Suraiya*) and lamps *(misbah)* illuminated the mosque. During the month of Ramazan, and on every Fridays, aloes *('ud)* was burned in silver censors. The Quran which according to a tradition belonged to the third caliph Usman was placed in the niche of the mihrab on a shelf made of costly wood. It was exposed to the general public on Fridays.

After Cordova was wrested from the hands of the Muslims, the mosque was ceremoniously converted into a church, and then followed its systematic disfigurement. The floor of the prayer hall was shorn of marble, and a new floor was laid with the result that the bases of the columns became invisible. Several chapels were built along the walls, and several doors were walled up. In 1523, a cathedral was built right in the heart of the prayer hall. When Charles V saw the transformation, he chided the clergy in these words, — "If I had known what you intended to build, I would not have given the permission. What you have built could be built anywhere, but what you have spoiled, the like of it does not exist in any part of the world." Yet these changes have not destroyed the prevailing character or spirit of the mosque resulting from the purity of its conception, the rhythm of its design, and its structural symmetry. The Spanish archaeologist Amados de los Rios admits this very eloquently.[8] Perhaps, it is on account of its essentially Islamic character that the Spanish people of today call it 'Mezquita-

Aljama' (the jama masjid), although it is a cathedral dedicated to the Virgin of Assumption where Christian worship is held regularly.

The sixty years of the mulūk at ṭawāif period were barren of great monuments. These refined and pleasure loving princes squandered their wealth on country palaces (munyat), poets, dancers, perfumed wines, and books. In their architecture, they faithfully followed the Umayyad traditions. They were, no doubt, good imitators, but lacking the wealth of the Umayyads, they often used cheaper materials like plaster, bricks and wood, but not much of marble or other precious stones. How true was ibn Khaldun when he said that refinement in crafts is determined by the demands made by wealth. However, the want of architectural grandeur was compensated by giving scenic beauty to their numerous palaces by installing fountains, running water-courses in the living apartments, and sweet-smelling herbs (myrtle and jasamine) in the patios, and paintings on the walls. The number of palaces built by these princes ran into dozens. The gorgeous palaces (with exotic names) built by al-Muʿtamid of Seville, al-Mutawakkil of Badajos, al-Ma'mun of Toledo, the princes of Malaga and Almeria exist only in the pages of history. The architecture of this period is best represented by the remains of the Aljaferia palace of al-Muqtadir of Saragossa. Located on the outskirts of the city, the Aljaferia faced many transformations after the conquest. What is now left is a series of salons, and the remains of a mosque. The sculptured arches and capitals of the Aljaferia are of wonderful construction. "The capitals are generally twice as high as they are wide, the volutes curl over like rams' horns, acanthus is palmetized and made to tip over like the serpent hoods." Cordovan arches are mere child's play compared with the rococo arches of the Aljaferia, says an authority.[9] Realising its beauty, the government of Spain has been restoring this palace of 'extraordinary originality and decorative profusion.'[10]

The Almoravids whose flaming enthusiasm and rugged energy gave a new lease of life to the dying Muslim rule, were a nomadic people without any cultural traditions. Naturally, they had to employ Andalusian architects to beautify their cities with mosques and palaces and gardens. In this way, the Umayyad architectural features, both structural and ornamental went over to northwest Africa. The Andalusian craftsmen introduced the polyfoil arches and the horseshoe-shaped mihrabs. In Spain, the Almoravids did not raise any buildings of significance. Their successors, the Almohads were also patrons of Andalusian architects and artisans. Their reign is famous for several constructions, both civil and military, but most of the works were carried out in their African dominion. Massive and symmetrical mosques, tall square minarets, and city gates which look like triumphal arches of the Romans, adorn the cities of northwest Africa. In Spain, the Almohads constructed the Jama masjid at Seville, and numerous fortifications. These have been described in a previous chapter.

The Islamic culture, as pointed earlier, saw its last summer in the kingdom of Granada. The architecture of this period inherited certain definite traditions from the past. The horseshoe, and semicircular arches seen in the Umayyad buildings dominated both the secular and religious architecture of the Granada period, but the pillars are slender and are often ringed. Ceramic tiles, stucco work (made from gypsum and finely powdered alabaster), the beehive pendents are some of the main features of the Granadine architecture which give an impression of luxury and delicacy as against the strength and vitality of the Umayyad architecture. The architecture of the kingdom of

Cordova is symbolic of majestic beauty *(jalal)*, while that of the kingdom of Granada breathes of sensuous refinement *(jamal)*. The Alhamra, and the garden palace of Generalif *(janat al'Arif)* are the most important monuments of the Nasarite dynasty.

The Alhamra is the swan-song of the Islamic architecture of Spain. The Alhamra stands on the narrow plateau of Sabika rising above the river Darro with the snow-covered Sierra Nevada in the background. This situation has given the palace a unique place among the monuments of the world. The Alhamra is also unique in another respect. While other palaces from Damascus to the coast of west Africa built by Muslim world during the Middle Ages have faded away, the Alhamra alone has survived the tooth of time. This is the only surviving example of a royal residence. The vast complex looks like a colossal ship anchored between the mountains and the plains — an apt description of its situation by Don Torres Balabas. When al-Ahmar occupied the city (May 1238) he resided for sometime in the Zirid alcasaba, but soon after he started the construction of the Alhamra palace. His successors enlarged the palace according to their need and taste. The successive enlargements were made in a rather haphazard manner with the result that the whole complex looks like a conglomeration of galleries, courts and apartments, even though some courts have axial alignments. However, taken as a whole, it is a palace of crystalline beauty. After the fall of Granada, Ferdinand took special care of the Alhamra, but under his successors, it was abandoned to neglect and even plunder. Charles V disfigured it by building a massive structure in the Renaissance style which is wholly incongruous, and looks like a 'brick among lace pillows!'[1] For a long time it was used as stables for donkeys, and lodgings for gypsies. Its floors were dug out for suspected treasures. An earthquake destroyed its several portions. About the middle of 19th century,

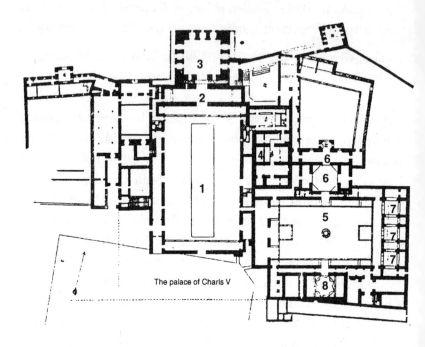

The palace of Charls V

(1) The Court of Alberca
(2) The Hall of Alberca
(3) The Hall of Ambassadors
(4) The Royal Baths
(5) Court of Lions
(6) Hall of Two Sisters
(7) The Hall of Kings/Justice
(8) The Hall of Abencerrajes

A map of Alhamra

the Spanish government awoke from its apathy, thanks to the publicity given by Washington Irving through his 'Tales from the Alhamra' and restoration work was undertaken by eminent architects and engineers. The Spanish government is now taking all possible steps to preserve this enchanting monument which even today looks like a palace straight from the pages of the Arabian Nights. Its porticos, walls and ceilings glow with their pristine brilliance. If Abu Abdullah, the last ruler of Granada comes back from his grave, he would be able to recognize the remaining halls and courts of his ancestral palace.

The Alhamra, like the Taj Mahal at Agra, is one of the most photographed monuments of the world. Like the Taj Mahal, it is enchanting in moonlight. A full description of the palace would need a separate book. In fact literature on the Alhamra is growing fast. For the purpose of this book, a short description of this great monument will suffice. The exterior of the Alhamra with its square towers and its embattlements gives no indication of the Sleeping Beauty inside. Some of the most celebrated portions of the Alhamra are, the Court of Myrtles (also called the Court of Alberca), the Hall of Ambassadors, the Court of Lions, the Hall of the Abencerrages, the Hall of Justice, the Hall of Two Sisters, and the royal baths[12]. All these courts and halls are interlinked so that one can pass from one wing to another through corridors and connecting chambers. The Court of Alberca is a sanctum of serenity. Built by sultan Yusuf I, it is a rectangle measuring 140 feet in length and nearly half as wide with a big pond in the middle. The long sides are pierced with doors of great beauty and symmetry on the ground floor, and twin windows on the first floor. The Hall of Ambassadors which occupies the floor of a bastion is a superb hall with bay windows which give a breathtaking view of the mountains and the vega — a perfect place for the Nasarite sultans to receive their ministers and foreign ambassadors. The Court of Lions is one of the most celebrated portions of the Alhamra. This oblong court is enclosed on all sides by galleries supported by a hundred columns joined by graceful arches. It was built during the reign of Muhammad V. The arrangement of the columns, some paired and some isolated shows a rare and tantalising subtlety. Here, the architecture melts into music — say Henri Terrase, the French authority on Hispano Muslim architecture of the period. A domed pavalion projects into the Court on two sides. Two paths intersect at right angles, and at the centre where the paths meet, there is circular fountain supported by twelve small and rather achaic cubs sprouting water. Not long ago, there were two basins, one above the other, but the upper basin has since been removed. Perhaps it was too heavy for the seven hundred years old cubs! Along the rim of the basin runs an inscription praising its beauty. The empty spaces were covered with flower-beds as the whole Court was planned as an interior garden. The Hall of Abencerrages is a perfect square of great elegance. According to a tradition some chieftains of the Banu Siraj were murdered in this hall. The hall has fine trellised windows, and a splendid ceiling which looks "like a vast pomegranate shedding its ruby drops.[13] The Hall of Justice is an immense gallery of heavily ornamented arches fashioned like homeycombs. There is a small picture gallery showing human figures in Arab dress.[14] These paintings, perhaps of the Nasarite sultans are painted on stucco in lively and vivid colours. Nearby is the Hall of Two Sisters. It is an architect's tribute to female beauty as it was the queens's sitting room. An inscription in this delicious boudoir sings, 'The stars would gladly descend from their orbits to live in this hall instead of the heaven." Another inscription on the top of a twin window repeats the last line of verse 64 of Sur Yusuf of the Quran which translated in English would mean,

'God is the best to take care of, and he is the most Merciful'. The royal baths prove the efficiency of the engineers of those days in installing hot and cold baths. There are alcoves for rest and relaxation. The light filters through star-shaped ventilators without annoying the bathers when they rested on divans and listened to the musicians performing in the galleries above.

The Granadine builders planned like architects but finished like master jewellers. The walls, the ceilings, the arches, the alcoves and windows flash like diamonds with prismatic radiance. 'The Alhamra is the supreme example of monumental decoration in Muslim Spain in its final stage,' Says Henre Terrasse.[15] Owen Jones in his classic book on ornamentation has enunciated certain principles for decoration which impart everlasting glory to artchitecture. The first principle in his aesthetic criteria is to decorate construction, but never to construct decoration. 'True beauty in architecture (say Jones) results from that repose which the mind feels when the eye, the intellect, and the affections are satisfied from the absence of any want'. The Moors (by which he means the Spanish Muslims) observed this rule and reached the summit of perfection.[16] The Alhamra, he adds, is perfect like the Parthenon in Greek art. All ornamentations in Alhamra are harmonious. The lines emerge from a parent stem, and any motif, however, distant, can be traced to its original branch and root. The decorations are always opulent, refined and almost bewildering in their variety. Dadoes, vines, palmettes, rosettes, polygonal stars, simulated colonnades cover the walls with a precision and play of light and line which impart individuality to each panel. Then there are the pendants (maqarnas) which hang from the arches, corners, and cupolas like stalactites defying the law of gravity. Last but not the least are the Arabic scrolls—poems, and prayers in elegant cursive style. The calligraphy of the inscriptions on the walls of the Alhamra is beautiful and easy to read. The motto of the kings of Granada, - walla ho ghalib illallah' (God alone is the Victor) is emblazoned on every wall and window of the palace. Several poems engraved on the walls were composed by ibn Zamrak. Another element of decoration is the flowing and splashing water. Whether in the pool as in the Court of Alberca, or the numerous cascades and channels right inside the palace, water was seen everywhere in the Alhamra.[17] It helped to convey a sense of repose and coolness, and more significantly, by its mirror effect, a feeling of openness and breadth to spaces. In conjunction with the light of the sun during the day, and the moon and the stars, as well as the hanging lamps at night, it created enchanting patterns and shadows, fluid and kaleidoscopic. Much of this fantasy can be experienced even today by visitors to the Alhamra. As a matter of fact it is difficult to describe the beauty of this peerless triumph of Hispano—Muslim art—the lacework on its capitals, the grace of the arcaded galleries, the endless variety of geometric patterns in red, carmine, gold, royal blue, violet, apple green, orange and brown colours, and the atmosphere of refinement and luxury of its courts and boudoirs. There is something illusive in the strange and hallucinating beauty of this fairy palace. The German traveller Thomas Munzer who was lucky to see the Alhamra just two years after it was vacated by Abū Abdullah, was dazzled by its beauty. "I do not believe (he wrote) that anything like it is to be found in Europe, seeing that everything is no magnificent, so majestic, and so exquisitely worked: that neither he who contemplates it can free himself of the idea that he is not in a paradise, neither would it be possible for me to give an exact account of what I beheld.[18] The poet ibn Zamrak a native of Granada whose poems adorn the wall of the Alhamra sang :-

Sabika is the crown of Granada's brow,
And the Alhamra, the central ruby of its crown.[19]

Notes

1. Albert Calvert: The Moorish Remain in Spain, Preface, p. X.
2. Hitti: History of the Arabs, p. 594.
3. Creswell: p. 225.
4. Ibid, p. 228.
5. G. Marcais: Vol. 1, p. 395.
6. Albert Calvert: p. 189. See also G. LeBon: pp. 325-326.
7. L. Provençal: L'Espagne Musulmane au Xème Siècle, p. 197 and G. Marcais: Vol. I, p. 229.
8. It would be interesting to hear Amados de los Rios on this point. He says, "Neither the sumptuous Christian fabric that today rises in the midst of these countless columns, nor the treasures of art lavished upon it by the celebrated artists of the sixteenth century who erected it, nor the interminable series of chapels of every epoch resting against the walls of the mosque that disfigure it, nor the clumsy angles that seem to suspend their flights to shed glory over the Dine Service; nor the words of the Evangelist sounding from the seat of the Holy Spirit, can dispell in the slightest degree, the majestry of these wandering shades that in vain seek in the sanctuary, the sacred volume whose leaves according to tradition were enamelled with the blood of the caliph Usman martyr of the faith. A world of souveniers here enthralls the mind of the traveller as he gazes with a feeling of sorrow upon the profanations — works dedicated by the intolerant and yet sincere faith of our ancestors, impelled by the desire of banishing for ever from that spot consecrated to the law of Jesus, the spirit of Muhammad and the ghost of his slaves that haunts it and will haunt it while it exists. For inspite of multiliations it has endured, and the changes it has indergone, there is impressed upon it by a superior ineradicable law, the seal of art that inspired it, and the character of the people by whom it was planned and executed." (Calvert: p. 184).
9. Rafiq Ali Jairazbhoy: Outline of Islamic Architecture, p. 91.
10. Ency. of Islam (N. Ed.), article on 'Al-Andalus'.
11. Thomas Abercrombie: When the Moor Ruled Spain. This article will be found in the National Geographic, of July, 1988. p. 110. Marcais: Vol. I, p. 229.

12. These names have been endowed by European authors. There is no mention in the Arabic works. In fact these is no contemparary description of the palace. Ibn Buttuta would have described it, but he fell ill and returned home without caring to visit it.

13. Jairazbhoy: p. 104.

14. G. Marcais: Vol. II, p. 547. The author thinks that the paintings were drawn by mudejar artists.

15. Ency. of Islam (N.Ed.), article on 'Gharnata', p. 1019.

16. Owen Jones: The Grammar of Ornament, pp. 66-74. This book was published in 1856, and was hailed as a classic on the subject. It has been printed several times. I have consulted the edition of 1986, published by Portland House, New York. The first chapter of this splendid book deals with the author's aesthetic philosophy of ornamentation.

17. Regarding the plumbing system of the Alhamra, the reader will be astonished to know that it has remained intact to this day. During the several centuries only a few pipes have been replaced. Built on the slope of a hill, the entire system works on gravity.

18. J.B. Trend: Spain from the South. P. 154. The author has translated several pages from the original Latin travelogue. Munzer was remarkably free from religious prejudices, but it seems that he succumbed to bazar gossip. He says that the ladies entered into the baths without clothes, and that there was a secret window through which the king watched the ladies as they took their bath. He has also added that the king threw an apple to the lady with whom he intended to spend the night.

19. M.R. Nykl : p. 367.

Chapter 22

Learning and Literature in Islamic Spain

Spain under the Muslims was a world in itself. It was one of the great ages of man. The chief glory of Muslim Spain was the people's thirst for knowledge. The literary and intellectual history of this luminous epoch began in the reign of Hisham I, when Spanish scholars began their visits to Madina to learn the Prophetic traditions from imam Malik. Hisham's reign was the seeding time of the efflorescence which came later. How eager and serious these scholars were in their pursuit of knowledge, is shown by a story about Yahya ibn Yahya the doyen of the learned men of his time. It is said that the imam was holding a class when a cry arose that an elephant was passing through the street, and all the students rushed out to see the animal. The young Yahya remained glued to his seat. When the imam asked him to go out and see the elephant as there were none to be found in Spain, Yahya replied, 'I left my country to see you, and obtain knowledge from you, and not to see an elephant'.[1] The imam was so much pleased with his reply that he used to call him, 'the wiseman of Spain'. Hisham's grandson ʿAbd ar-Rahman II ushered in a period of secular studies so that the two streams of knowledge (theological and secular) flowed side by side. Hundred of Spanish scholars travelled to the Eastern centres of learning. They were, no doubt, motivated by the famous hadith of the Prophet, — Seek knowledge even if you have to travel to China.' The books produced in the East reached Spain fast, as the Spanish scholars (and also merchants and other travellers) returned home laden with books on every subject under the sun. Ibn Ghalib (d. 1044) found that the Spanish Muslims were like the Indians in their love of learning, and like the Greeks in their knowledge of the physical and natural sciences. By the time Hakam, the bibliophile came to the throne, literacy had definitely reached the masses. Dozy would make us believe that in Muslim Spain everybody could read and write. Nicholson has endorsed the views of Dozy.[2] Perhaps, they exaggerated. But there is no doubt, that Spain during the Muslim rule attained a high level of literacy that was unprecedented in history of the Iberian peninsula. Indeed, in the widespread literacy among the people, the civilization of Spanish Muslims surpassed Athens of Pericles. This was a great achievement which the rulers of Europe upto the 18th century could not claim on behalf of their countries. Herein, lies the role of Muslim Spain so much praised by European historians and orientalists. We all know that the early Middle Ages were a period of darkness in Europe. After the closure of the Greek schools by the Roman emperor Justinian in 529. A.D., Europe entered into a period of intellectual penumbra. During this period from the 9th to the 13th century; Muslim Spain was the only country in western Europe to keep burning the flame of learning. What in Spain was regarded as enlightenment, was magic and communion with the evil in the West. Love of learning was regarded as a vice of the pagan Muslims. 'The legends and mystery plays of the Middle ages were not unfrequently based upon crime of apostasy — generally to Muhammadanism[3].'

Surprisingly, this marvellous development in the field of literacy, did not result from any organised system of education directly under the supervision of the government. There was no education minister, and no educational advisor to the government. Some Muslim rulers like ʿAbd ar-Rahman III, and Hakam II did set up schools. One school, presumably, in the kingdom of Granada had an inscription on its porch which shows the priority assigned to learning in the society of Spanish Muslims. It read, "the world is sustained by four things, the learning of the wise, the justice of the great, the prayers of the righeous, and the valour of the brave".[4] However, there was no university like the Nizamiya of Baghdad, and the al-Azhar of Cairo. The whole system of education thrived on private teachers who were paid by the state, but mostly by the students themselves. Facilities for primary education were available in the mosque schools in the villages and towns. For graduate studies, the students came to the major cities — Cordova, Seville, Toledo, Saragossa, Granada, Malaga and Valencia. It is possible to prepare a short list of the most eminent scholars, poets and thinkers, who passed out from these mosque schools. The doors of knowledge were open to all, and not to a particular section of society as in other previous civilisations. When a student completed his studies, he was awarded an 'ijaza' by his teacher. This conferred on him the right (haqq al-riwaya) to teach the subjects/books learnt under the tutor. The classes were held in mosques, but many teachers taught at their own homes. The tuition fee was not very high. Ibn Bassam tells us that in the 10th century a private teacher charged 20 dirhams for a short course of grammar, and 1000 dirhams for a complete course.[5] Higher learning was imparted by specialists in their respective fields. Take the case of ibn Hazm who had a separate tutor for each discipline. Al-Azdi taught him grammar, lexicography and dialectics, Abu'l Khiyār taught him Islamic jurisprudence (fiqh), and Abū Sa'id al Ja'fari, classical poetry. Another teacher initiated him into hadith literature, while he attended the lectures of Abū Abdullah al-Hassan on philosophy.[6] The curriculum was the same as in other Muslim lands. It was divided into two parts — the *Ulum al naqliyā*, and the *Ulum al'aqliyyā*. The former included theology, the Quranic exegesis, hadith, grammar, law, literature; the latter covered geometry, algebra, commercial arithmatic, botany, medicine and philosophy. The education of a student began with study of Arabic which opened for him the world of learning. This is revealed by a statement of the qaḍi Abū Bakr al-Arabi (1076-1148) quoted by ibn Khaldun. The learned Spanish judge emphasised the study of poetry which he called the archives of the Arabs. A thorough mastery (according to him) of the Arabic language provided the basis of advanced studies. This system of education seems to have been followed from the 10th century if not earlier, and it was later adopted in the academic circles of the kingdom of Granada. Ibn Khaldun who respected the Andalusians for their mental sharpness, has also praised their curriculam in these wonds —" as for the Spaniards, their varied curriculum with its great amount of instruction in poetry, composition and Arabic philology gave them from their early years on, a habit providing for a better acquiantance with the Arabic language'.[7] A 12th century document gives a comprehensive list of text books on different subjects. This list *(fahrasa)* was compiled by the learned scholar ibn Khayar (1108-1179) of Cordova, and was published by the Spanish orientalist Julian Ribera, at Saragossa towards the end of the 19th century.[8]

Arabic was the medium of instruction. Before the Muslims arrived in Spain, Latin was the official language, and the people spoke a Romance dialect. After the conquest, classical Latin retired to the cloister, and its place was filled by Arabic. However, the converted Muslims and others continued to speak the local language during the earlier centuries. An interaction of Romance language with Arabic and *vice versa*, was inevitable. Many Arabic words passed into Romance language, while Arabic absorbed some Romance words. Out of this linguistic fusion, spoken Arabic developed at least three dialects — the eastern (spoken in Valencia), the southern (spoken in Seville, Cordova and Granada), and the northern which was current in Aragon including the region around Toledo. The Spanish Muslims of Iberian origin had difficulties in pronouncing some letters of Arabic alphabet particularly, the letters qaf' and 'Ayn.' Some speakers would drop 'ayn' altogether. For example instead of 'ya ashiqayn' (o you lovers), they would speak 'ya shiqayn'. The Arabic letters of similar sounds were also difficult for them to distinguish. However, the classical Arabic, the vehicle of learning and literature, remained homogeneous in all parts of the country. The Arabs were proud of their language. A proverb was current among them in those days which said that God bestowed His wisdom on three organs of the human body — the hands of the Chinese, the brain of the Greeks, and the tongue of the Arabs. Out of this classical Arabic, its polished periods, and rhymed prose grew up the flower of Hispano-Arabic literature. The Arabic language was so flexible, and so luxuriant was its vocabulary, that it could be used with ease and clarity in expressing subtle emotions, scientific truths, philosophical dissertations, and legal matters.

Out of the immense output of books on almost all the subjects, only a very small fraction has survived. The reader will recall the wonton destructions of books and libraries by the wild Berbers. In the 15th century Archbishop Ximenez burned thousands of books, "to annihilate the record of seven centuries

of Muhammadan culture in a single day[9]." The mass distruction
of books is one of the greatest tragedies of Muslim History.
What little is left is now preserved in the Escurial at Madrid.
The catalogue of the thousands of manuscripts (many of which
belong to the library of Mulai Zaidan captured by the Spaniards
during the reign of Philip III) has not been completed as yet
although three scholars were put on the job—Michael Casiri in
the 18th century, Derenbourg in the 19th, and Lévi Provençal
in the 20th century.[10] In addition to the library at the Escurial,
there are private collections in northwest Africa. One of the
most famous libraries in Morocco is owned by the humanist
and theologian. Abdul Hayy al-Katani. It was from his library
that L. Provençal borrowed the manuscript of *kitab ar-Rawd al-
Mitar of al-Himyari,* and published it with a French translation
from Leiden in 1938. Some valuable manuscripts are kept in
the libraries in U.K., Paris, Rome, and Istanbul. From time to
time, some manuscripts are printed, but a vast field lies ahead
of scholars. In the circumstances, what follows is not a history
of literature of the Spanish Muslims, but only a distilled account
of some of the important landmarks in the eight centuries of
their intellectual endeavour.[11]

A through study of grammar and philology was a *sine qua
non* of entry into the world of letters. It would not be an
exaggeration to say that without the Quran there would have
been no systematic study of Arabic grammar. In order to
appreciate the pristine purity and musical flow of its majestic
prose, as well as to ensure faultless pronunciation of the Divine
Word, it was necessary to make a scientific study of the structure
of the language. Not long after the Prophet, two schools of
grammar were founded, one at Basra, and the other at Kufa.
Space does not permit to write here about the achievements of
these two schools, but it may be emphasised that the Eastern

Muslims had already laid down the principles of grammar, and rules of prosody, before similar studies were undertaken in Spain. The Spanish Muslims worked on the labours of the Eastern scholars. Grammar and philology were important part of curriculum of advanced studies. Ibn Sa'id says,' the various systems or schools into which the science of grammar has been divided are by them (the Andalusians) preserved with the greatest care, and with so much attention as the different schools of divinity and jurisprudence are kept in the East. Every literary man, whatever may be the nature of his studies, must needs be a grammarian in order that he may penetrate the subtleties of the language and appreciate the merits of good composition; for if he be not perfectly conversant with the rules of grammar it will be in vain for him to seek distinction and ...he will be continuously exposed to the venomous shafts of criticism'[12]. Equally important was the science of lexicography. Both these subjects are boring to us, but to the scholars of the old world they were of supreme importance, and more so for all the writers — even the poets, and the philosophers.

An Eastern Muslim from Armenia introduced the Spanish Muslims to the subtleties of grammar and the study of lexicography. Abū Ali al-Qali (901-967) migrated to Spain, and settled at Cordova as a teacher of these two subjects. He attracted many disciples, two of them being ibn Quttiya (d. 977) and al-Zubaidi. The former has left a valuable work on grammar—the *kitab al-afāl* (the Book of verbs). He was a direct descendant of the Gothic princess Sara' and this is a proof of the rapid arabization of the families of Spanish origin. Zubaidi outshone his master. Born at Seville, in 928, he came from a Syrian family, and died at Cordova in 989. He was a master of three subjects — grammar, lexicography and prosody. His work on grammar — the *al-Wāḍih* (The Clear Treatise) gave him a permanent place in the field. Ibn Khalikan called him the ablest grammarian, and the most learned philologist of his age. A copy of his *al-Wāḍih* is preserved in the Escurial. His *kitab al-Istidrak* dealing with words and their forms was published at Rome in 1890.[13] Zubaidi also abridged the kitab al-ʿAyn of Khalil, the great authority on Arabic prosody. Numerous grammarians and lexicographers flourished from the 10th century onwards as the level of literacy went up. Ahmad ibn Iban (d. 939) composed a notable work entitled 'The Book of the Learned', which is a dictionary in one hundred chapters on nouns leaving nothing from the sky to the smallest particle.[14] The 11th century was made conspicuous by the great Ali ibn Ahmed ibn Sida of Murcia. Born blind to a blind father, ibn Sidah was a prodigy of gigantic talent and industry. His monumental dictionary in seventeen volumes (called *Mukhassas*) has been printed at Cairo. Heywood considers this dictionary a miracle of hard work[15]. Dr. Johnson's dictionary of the English language is a minature compared to the work of this blind lexicographer of Spain. In Sidah died at Denia in 1066 aged sixty. Ibn As-Sid al-Batalyawsi (from Badajos, the present frontier town between Portugal and Spain) was a great encyclopaedist of his time. Born at Silves in 1062, he died at Valencia in July 1127. He wrote an interesting work on the right use of letters which create confusion in writing on account of similarity of their sounds. His class was crowded with students because of his method of teaching which was clear, intelligible, and full of quotations by which he illustrated his lecture. Nearly contemporary with al-Batalyawsi, was Abū Ali Shalūbini (1166-1247) a native of Salobrena, a famous town on the Mediterranean coast. He was a great grammarian of his time and, had numerous students. There is a joke which is worth mentioning in the context of his mastery of grammar. One day a student came to

see him, and he sent in his card on which he wrote, 'Abū
Ommaya is at the gate'. For some reason, the grammarian did
not like to be disturbed. He sent back the card. The student
looked at it, and left because by a simple diacritical amendment
made by the master, the card read, 'I sent him away'.[16] The
13th and the 14th centuries were graced by two eminent
grammarians whose works are still current in the Arabic speaking
world. They ware ibn Malik (1203-1274) of Jaen, and Abū
Hayyan (1256-134) of Granada. The former is the author of the
famous resumé of Arabic grammar in the form of a poem in
1000 verses called the *'Alfiya'* which is memorized by students
learning Arabic from Nigeria to Damascus; it is a prescribed
text book in Arabic schools in India and Malaysia. The Berber
Abū Hayyan was one of the most renowned sons of the kingdom
of Granada. He was a brilliant scholar of grammar, tafseer, and
qirat, and above all he was a linguist. Out of his sixty works
atleast fifteen are stated to be extant. He wrote on Turkish,
Persian, Coptic and Ethiopian grammar. The book on Turkish
grammar has been printed. He knew by heart the books of
Sibawayhi the great eastern philologist. One of his most valuable
books is his *'Manhaj al-salik'*, which presents, 'a miniature
bibliography of grammatical science and a panorama of thought
on some of its most difficult problems on which the opinions
of hundreds of grammarians, Quran readers, lexicographers are
cited."[17] A much travelled man, he was gentle in manners, and
never got annoyed. The study of grammar did not dry up his
sense of humour, and love of beautiful things. He was a fine
poet. He could be witty as shown in the following lines
composed on a man putting on a woollen dress :

O you clad in pretty wool,
you have no sense of propriety.

you are proud of wool that only yesterday
was worn by a sheep, and today by a he-goat.

Not many prose writings of a purely literary character are
extant today. The available prose works in the form of complete
books can be counted on fingers. Most of the prose writings
comprise personal letters, sermons, dialogues, short essays and
'maqamat (assemblies). The last literary genre of theatrical
elements was popularised in the East by Badi 'ul-zaman al-
Hamdani (968-1008) and Hariri (1054-1122). It found eager
imitators in Spain throughout the Muslim rule. The Andalusians
modelled their Arabic prose on the eastern pattern. The famous
Umayyad Secretary Abdul Hamid, and the prose-writer Jahiz
had their disciples in Spain also. The rhymed prose (Saj) also
appeared in Spain. This style, even though, it was rhetorical,
and extremely artificial abounding in puns, alliterations, was
considered the hallmark of literary culture. This is not to say
that prose writings in easy, fluent style were entirely lacking.

The middle of the 10th century opens with the 'Unique
Neckless' (al-Iqd al-Farid) a major work of prose strewn with
poems. The author was ibn 'Abd Rabbihi, the poet laureate of
the caliph 'Abd ar-Rahman. The 'Iqd al-Farid is one of the
greatest books of polite literature in Arabic. It has been printed
over and over again. (The recent edition printed at Beirut is the
most attractive. In fact this city has published hundreds of
literary, historical and theological works of Arabic, of an
international standard in the printing and binding technology.)
The 'Iqd' is still read and enjoyed, although the critics jealous
of the author condemned it as 'a garland of garlic.' It is in fact,
the tour de force of a literary craftsman. Reading it, is like
loitering in a vast picture gallery full of portraits of eminent
men, and glittering frescoes of social life. It enfolds a panorama

of the cultural life of the Arabic speaking world of the East but not much about Spain. This lively book is divided into twenty-five chapters of rather unequal length, and each chapter is named after a precious stone. The subjects chapter-wise are: (1) The duties of a ruler, (2) the art of strategy, (3) generosity and gifts (4) diplomatic relations, (5) the art of addressing the rulers, (6) learning *('ilm wa adab)*, (7) wisdom in proverbs, (8) the fickleness of the world, (9) elegies and funerals, (10) genealogy of the Arabs, (11) the speech of the Beduins, (12) the art of polite conversation (13) examples from the speeches of famous men, (14) the duties of secretaries, (15) this chapter contains the famous epic poem on the military exploits of caliph 'Abd ar-Rahman, (16) Ziyad, Al-Hajjaj, and the celebrated Bermaki family of Persia, (17) battles of the Arabs, (18) & (19) deal with prosody and poetry, (20) music and musical instruments, (21) women, and their diverse qualities, (22) misers and cheats, (23) animals, medicines and sorcery, (24) food and drinks, (25) Jokes and anecdotes. Prose writings of this type, mainly for entertainment were written throughout the Muslim rule. A contemporary of ibn 'Abd Rabbini, the grammarian Abū Ali al Qali has left a book entitled *'kitab al-amali* (The Book of Dictations). This is an anthology of poetry of the ancient Arabs, and anecdotes concerning poets, and famous proverbs. An important literary work was composed by Abū Bakr of Tortosa, a famous city during the Muslim rule, about a hundred miles south of Barcelona. Abū Bakr (b. 1059) studied at Saragossa, and later at Seville, went on a pilgrimage in 1083, and died at Alexandria in April, 1131. He is known for his book — *Siraj al-mulūk* (The Lamp of Princes). The title is expressive of its contents (A translation in Spainish by Alarcòn Santòn was published at Madrid in 1930). Elsewhere, his views on the art of warfare have been cited. But Abū Bakr was essentially an ascetic, wedded to voluntary poverty. He was endowed with a fine poetic sensitivity, which we shall refer to later. His philosophy of life is summed up in his well-known saying, — 'When two advantages are before you, one of this world, and the other spiritual, get hold of the latter, and you will obtain both'.[18]

The philosopher ibn Hazm (d, 1064) was a writer of prose of incomparable elegance. His Tawq al Hamama (The Ring of the Dove) written by him in 1027, when he was in exile at Almeria, is one of the few masterpieces of Hispano-Arabic literature to have been translated in all the major languages of Europe. In this book he has narrated the romantic episodes of men and women known to him, in order to illustrate his theory of courtly love. In the society of Spanish Muslims, lovemaking was a secret affair, and the lovers had to converse with their eyes to avoid criticism. In a fine passage, ibn Hazm has classified the meaningful glances exchanged by them with the expertise of a choreographer. 'After verbal allusions, (says the author) when once the lover's advance has been accepted, and an accord established, the next step consists in hinting with the glances which play an honourable part in this phase, and achieve remarkable results. By means of a glance the lover can be dismissed, admitted, promised, threatened, upbraided, cheered, commanded, forbidden; a glance will lash the ignoble, and give warning of the presence of enemies and watchers; a glance may convey laughter and sorrow, ask a question, and make a response, refuse and give — in short, each of these various moods and intentions has its own particular kind of glance which cannot be precisely realised except by occular demonstration'. And then the author gives a whole repertory of the oculer signals. 'To make a signal with the corner of the eyes is to forbid the lover; to droop the eye is an indication of consent; to prolong the gaze is a sign of suffering and distress; to break off the gaze is a mark of relief; to make signs of closing the eyes is an indication of threat. To turn the pupil of the eye in a certain direction and then to turn it back swiftly, calls attention to the presence of a person so indicated. A clandestine signal with the corner of both eyes is a question; to turn the pupil rapidly from the middle of the eye to the interior angle is a demonstration of refusal; to flutter the pupil of both eyes this way and that is a general prohibition.'[19]

Another name famous both for his poetry and prose was the Cordovan ibn Shuhaid (992-1035). Ibn Hazm was his closest friend. 'One imagines them (says Prof. García Goméz) as two youths dressed in white, conversing among the white porticos of Cordova, devotees of swans, and lovers of the blonde women who were the erotic ideals of the Umayyads in Spain.'[20] Both of them were writers of independent thinking. They rejected their teachers, condemned the teaching methods, and detested bookish traditions in literature. Both were of the view that a writer, whether a poet or a prose writer is born, not made. Slavish imitation does not produce great literature. The art of writing (bayan) is a gift from God. Ibn Shuhaid wrote prose satires against grammarians and promotors of bookish culture. His fame rests on his Risala al-Tawābi wa-z-zawābi which the American Arabist Prof. J.T. Monroe has published with an introduction under the title 'The Treatise of Familiar Spirits and Demons' (Berkeley, 1971). This is an account of a mental journey (a sort of Divine Comedy predating Dante, in the opinion of Prof. García Goméz) through the underworld — a valley of genies where he meets and converses with the spirits of great personalities in Arabic literature-the poets imru' al. qays, Abū Tammām, Abū Nuwas, al-Mutanabbi, al-Jahiz, and the prose writer Abd al Hamid. Unfortunately, ibn Shuhaid did not live

long. He died at the age of 43 after a long illness which he bore
with Stoic courage. He wrote his own eptitaph, and was buried
in the famous garden of Khair al-Zajjali by the side of the great
Cordovan aristocrat Abū Marwan al-Zajjali who was the owner
of the garden. Before his death, he left a code of personal
cleanliness for literary men. He advised them that they should
take care of their dress, keep their teeth and nails clean, and
regularly use perfumes to enlive their imaginative faculties.

Another writer of fine prose comparatively free from verbal
conceits, was ibn Jubayr, a scholar of Valencia, and author of
a Travel Diary *(Rihla)* which is one the great prose works, and
perhaps the only travelogue of importance written in Spain.
Luckily, this book has survived and is available in English
translation. The genesis of this book is interesting. Ibn Jubayr
(b. 1145) was secretary to the Almohad governor of Granada.
One day the governor summoned him for some official work.
On his arrival, he was offered to drink against his most fervent
excuses. Later, the governor regretted his mistake, and to please
him, he poured seven handful of gold dinars in his taylisan. Ibn
Jubayr was so much overwhelmed by remorse that he utilised
the money for a pilgrimage to the Holy Cities to atone for his
sin of drinking wine. He left Granada in 1183, and returned
home in May 1185. His travel diary written in elegant and
musical prose reads like a modern travel book — vivid and
sparkling. Ibn Khatib in his lengthy note on ibn Jubayr has
quoted his several epigrams of practical wisdom, but no writing
of ibn Jubayr can surpass his travel book which abounds with
vignettes of life seen by him. He was a master of descriptive
prose.

But the craze for rhymed prose lasted till the end of the
Muslim rule. Most of the prose works were written by scholarly

secretaries either for pleasure, or in their official capacity. To the latter category belong the official communiqués drafted by them as the head of the Chancellary *(diwan al-insha')*. The anthology of ibn Bassam contains many such pieces of prose writings of great beauty and elegance. The Banu Burd family of Cordova in the early 11th century enjoyed great reputation as prose writers. Abū Hafs Ahmad ibn Burd (d. 1027 at Saragossa) was the famous draftsman of the Instrument of Abdication of Hisham II in favour of Sanchol. He wrote in a fluent style free from pedantic expressions. His grandson ibn Burd al-asghar (d. 1054) was an equally fine prose writer. We are indebted to ibn Bassam for preserving his essays *(risalat)*. He was a master of the dramatic effect such as shown in his dialogue between the pen and the sword *(saif w'al-qalm)*. The pen is proud of its importance because the Quran has extolled it as a source of all knowledge; the pen claims that it removes the darkness of ignorance; the orders of kings are put in black and white with the help of a pen, and unlike the sword it never rusts. The sword asserts that it is the symbol of royal authority; it dispells lawlessness, reduces forts, and life shudders at its very sight. The debate goes on covering several pages. There was no end to prose writers under the Almoravids and the Amohads. Several prose writers flourished in the kingdom of Granada. We may mention some outstanding names. Ibn Khisal served the Almoravids. He was a master of ornate prose. Another writer was al-Mawa'ini (d. 1168). He was secretary to the Almohad ruler Abū Yaqub. His book on various topics (similies, ambiguous sentences, ironic expressions, and history of the Umayyads and the Abassids) entitled *"Rayhan al-albāb"* is preserved in a library at Madrid. The most famous prose writer of the kingdom of Granada was ibn Khatib. He wrote fine prose, bejewelled with eloquent phrases. His official correspondence, some of which has survived is estimated as marvel of literary Arabic.

The *'maqamāt'* (assemblies) were composed by many Spanish writers soon after they appeared in the East., Some critics believe that ibn Shuhaid referred to earlier, was inspired by the muqamāt. The Andalusian *muqamāt,* more or less, observed the traditions of eastern muqamat both in concept and style. Their vogue increased in the 12th century, and persisted till the 14th century. Many maqamāt have been published and translated in Spanish by F.de la Granja, an authority on the subject.

History and geography were also part of literature. Many historians combined facts with fiction. They were in the habit of interweaving in their historical narrations, anecdotes, and poems, to make their works spicy, and the reader has to be on his guard all the time if he wants to reach the truth. Some mixed history with theology. The earliest historian ibn Habib (793-854) falls in this category. The subsequent historians were less prone to romanticising. The great historians belonging to the al-Razi family — Musa al-Razi, Ahmad al-Razi, and Isa al-Razi who flourished during the 8th and the 10th centuries were free from this malady. Their writings have not survived, but there are ample quotations from their books in the histories complied by later historians. Ibn Qutiyya is perhaps the first Spanish Muslim whose complete work has come down to us. His Tarikh *iftitah al-Andalus* (History of the Conquest of Spain) shows what a good narrator of history he was. This book as well as the anonymous work — Akhbar *al-majmu'ā*, are the best works of the early history of Muslim Spain. In the 10th century and the subsequent periods, a great mass of histories were written in Spain. The greatest historian (and the greatest in Europe during his time) was ibn Hayyan (987-1070) who saw the kingdom of Cordova at its zenith, and also its fall and disruption. His sixty-volume history is lost. Three volumes of another book — *kitāb al muqtabis* relating to the reigns of ʿAbd ar-Rahman II, 'Abdullah, ʿAbd ar-Rahman III and Hakam II have survived, and have been published. Ibn Hayyan was a painstaking narrator of events in a fluent and perspicuous prose. He is also a reliable historian who writes neither with favour nor malice, — an example to some modern historians who write history subjectively. Several good historians flourished in the 11th and the 12th centuries. We may mention ibn Humaidi (1029-1095), ibn Sahib as-Salāt (d. 1184), and Abū Bakr ibn al-Abbār (1199-1238). Ibn al-Abbar's books — *kitab Hullah al-Siyarā*, *kitab al-Takmila*, and *Tuhfat al-qādim* have ensured his position among the scholarly historians and geographers of Spain. The Dutch historian, R. Dozy attached great value to the writings of ibn al-Abbār. From the pen of ibn Saʿid al-Maghrabi (1214-1274) came the famous book *Al-Maghrib fi Hulā' l Maghrib*. Biography was cultivated by ibn Saʿid and many other writers. Several works in this field have been published. Al-Khushani compiled vivid biographical sketches of the famous judges of Cordova in his *Kitab Qudat Qurtaba*. Zubaidi wrote his *Tabaqāt al Nahawiyin* which gives life stories of famous grammarians. Al Faradi (d. 1013) presented a biography of great scholars, entitled *'Tarikh'Ulema al-Andalus*. His work in this field was taken up by ibn Bushkawal (1101-1183); he was of Gothic origin, —Bushkuwal is the arabised form of Pascual. He is known for his *Kitab al-Ṣilah*. In the 13th century, the Murcian Al Ḍabbi wrote his *Bughyat al multamis fi Rijal ahl al Andalus*. More biographies appeared in the following centuries. But it is doubtful if the Spanish Muslims produced any biographer of the stature of the eastern, ibn Khallikan whose

Wafayāt al'ayān, is counted among the greatest works of its kind in world literature. To him we owe much about the lives of many Spanish Muslims. The last historian was the scholar, philosopher and man of letters — ibn Khatib al-Salmani of Granada known by his honorific title of "Lisan ud din'. He was born at the beautiful town of Loja, on Nov. 15, 1313. His father was a cultivated courtier who lost his life at the battle of Tarifa. Ibn Khatib received education in all the subjects taught in the academic circles of Granada, — literature, poetry, history, philosophy and medicine. He entered into the service of sultan Abū l-Hajjaj Yusuf Isma'il. After his death, his successor Muhammad V took him in his service as his secretary. When the sultan was dethroned, ibn Khatib followed him to northwest Africa where he met ibn Khaldun. On the restoration of Muhammad v, he returned to Granada in April, 1362. He continued to serve the sultan, but his enemies accused him of heretic leanings, and he was forced to leave his beloved city (1371). He took refuge at the court of sultan 'Abd al-Aziz of Tlemsen. His enemies headed by the qaḍi al-Nubahi, and ibn Khatib's own perfidious pupil ibn Zamrak (since appointed Chief Minister in his place), set up a commission to look into the charges of heresy against him. Muhammad asked for repatriation of ibn Khatiab, but the ruler of Tlemsen refused. After 'Abd al-Aziz died, ibn Khatib was imprisoned. In the meantime, the commission continued with examination of the case, but before it reached any conclusions, hired murderers, strangled him to death in May/June 1375. This great aristocrat of Granada was a versatile scholar distinguished for his writings in almost every field. Many of his works have have been printed. The students of history will always be grateful to him for his historical writings, — the *kitāb Ihata fi Tarikh Ghurnata, Kitab A'mal a'lam* and *al-Lamhāt al-badriyya fi'l-dawalat an-nastiriyya.* If these books were lost, our knowledge of the political, social and cultural history of the kingdom of Granada would have remained incomplete.

Islam awakened interest in the study of geography. The Quran lays down in a majestic language that the phenomena of nature — the sun, the moon, the starry heavens, the night following the day, the rhythmic changes of seasons, the life-giving rain, the fruits and cereals, are all signs of God's bounty. The Quran urges men to travel and see God's wonderful world. During the Middle Ages, a wander-lust seized the Muslims. Travellers, traders, and scholars moved from country to country braving the perils of travel on sea and land. From Spain to Korea, from Timbucto to Siberia, there was hardly any country they did not visit. The sea lanes of the world — the Mediterranean, the Arabian Sea, the Red Sea, the Indian Ocean and the waters of the far East were under their control, long before the Portuguese and the Dutch appeared on the scene. The obligation to perform the haj pilgrimage also promoted foreign travel. All these factors contributed to production of geographical literature. The necessity to determine the direction of Mecca towards which all the Muslims turn for daily prayers fostered interest in mathematical geography. Those who travelled by the sea carried with them the miners' compass and quadrants and astrolabes to locate ports and countries. When Vasco da Gama, on his search for a sea-route to India reached the eastern cost of Africa, a Muslim seaman named Abdul Majid came to his help. The veteran sailor supplied Vasco da Gama with maps showing the route to India.

The Spanish geographers worked on the patterns laid down in the East. Strictly following the old Greek/Persian concept, they divided the inhabited world into seven climes, — iqlim.

The geographical literature (except travel books) was modelled in the form of a dictionary in alphabetical order. They recorded comprehensive information about each country, — the climate, the physical features, the situation in terms of longitude and latitude, the mineral resources, the flora and fauna, the arteries of trade and traffic, the rivers and ports, the handicrafts, and the social customs of the people. In this way, physical, economic and social geography were all combined to form a fascinating panorama of each country.

Spain's earliest geographer was al-Warrāq of Guadalajara who lived during 904-973, but his work, now lost, was utilised by succeeding authors. The celebrated historian Ahmad al-Razi was a geographer also. He gave a description of Spain as an introduction to his history. This description was rendered into Portuguese under the orders of king Denis of Portugal (1279-1325) with the help of some Muslims one of whom was a certain Muhammad. Pascual de Gayangos rendered it into Spanish in 1852. The original Arabic work of Razi was a milestone, and served as a valuable guide to later geographers A peculiar feature of his geographical study was that he divided Spain into two parts — western and eastern, according to the direction of winds and flow of rivers. The rivers of western Spain join the Atlantic, and the westerly winds bring rain, while in the eastern half, the rivers flow towards the east, and the winds also blew in that direction. Razi's division remains unchallenged. During the 11th and 12th centuries, three eminent geographers appeared in the field, — al-Mazini, al-Bakri, and al-Idrisi. Abū Hamid al-Mazini (1080-1169) hailed from Granada. He travelled all over north Africa, Syria, Iraq, and spent years in Hungry and the eastern Russia. He has left an account of his travels and observations in his *Tahfatu l-albab* which was published by the French orientalist Gabriel Ferrand in 1925. The book contains descriptions of the wonders of the animal kingdom on land and sea, and even fossils. Abā Obaid al-Bakri came from a noble family of Huelva where his grandfather was governor under the Banu 'Amir rule. The family left for Cordova when it was held by Jahwar. Al-Bakri spent most of his life at the court of al-Mu'tasim of Almeria and died there in 1094. He left several books on geography which included a voluminous dictionary entitled, '*Kitāb al-mujam al-kabir*' which is lost. In another book on the subject — The Book of Roads and Regions *(Kitab al masālik w'al mamālik)*, he collected elaborate information about north Africa and Russia. A fragment of this book was translated in French by Baron de Slane in 1857. Al-Bakri was quoted copiously by later geographers as a respected authority on the country of his birth, of which he was very proud. In an oft-quoted passage he compares Spain to 'Syria for the purity of air and sweetness of water, to Yemen for mildness of climate, to India for aromatic herbs, to China for mines and precious stones, and Aden for its coastal advantages.'[21] He was aware of the Canaries islands in the Atlantic (Bahr al-Zulumat) and perhaps Britain (Britaniya) also in the far north. The greatest geographer of Muslim Spain (and one of the greatest of all time) was Sharif Idrisi who received his education in Cordova, and spent all his life (if not actually travelling) in Sicily at the court of the Norman king Roger II (1011-1154) and his successor William (1154-1166). He was a geographer-cum-cartographer. Roger commissioned him to prepare a silver planisphere showing the known world. Idrisi also wrote for his patron his famous book 'Enjoyment of those who want to travel distant lands/'*Nuzhatu al-mushtāq fi ikhtirāq al-afāq*. This book contained seventy maps, ten for each of the seven climes. Some of the maps were coloured. Idrisi travelled a lot before writing his book. He located the

source of the Nile, calculated the circumference of the world.[22]
The *Nuzhatu l--mushtāq* (also called the Book of Roger or
Kitab Rujar) is a work of invaluable help for a study of 12th
century Spain. He has described from his personal observation,
almost every aspect of the physical and economic geography of
Spain, its cities, rivers, mines, ports, agricultural produce,
manufactures, buildings and churches, and even the character
of the people. Unfortunately, we do not know much about the
author, and his life remains a mystery. The Italians have a great
respect for Idrisi. An abridgement of his book was published at
Rome by the Medici Press as far back as 1592, followed by an
Italian translation in 1600. The complete manuscripts of the
original book of Idrisi are available in several libraries. A critical
edition of his book running into several volumes is being printed
at Naples by an international group of specialists. Idrisi died in
1165, perhaps in Sicily, but after him no geographer of his
stature appeared in Muslim Spain, although travel diaries
continued to be written. A reference has already been made to
ibn Jubyr, the author of a famous travelogue. On his homeward
journey he visited Baghdad, Damascus, and passed through the
Latin Kingdom of Crusaders. Ibn Jubayr halted at Sicly from
December 1184 to March 1185, and visited several cities. At
that time the Muslims had already lost Sicily to the Normans,
but they continued to live as a religious minority. The island
was ruled by William II at the time of his arrival. He has
painted a pleasing picture of the deep impact of the Muslims on
the social life of the Christians. He writes that the king spoke
and wrote in Arabic, and dressed himself like the Muslim kings
in robes embroidered with Arabic inscriptions. He employed
Muslim astrologers, and physicians. His harem was full of
Muslim women, and black guards, and eunuchs looked after
the security of his palace. His dress was tailored and embroidered

by a Muslim. The Christian ladies walked veiled in the streets. They applied kohal to their eyes, henna to their fingers, wore gilt slippers, and dressed in silk brocade after the fashion of the Muslim ladies. But below this outward amity, he found many instances (he has cited these) which put him in doubt about the future of the Muslim community of the island. Ibn Jubayr was an intelligent observer, and time proved that he was right. Islam was ultimately wiped out of the island leaving a faint memory of its cultural life which inspired Iqbal in our time to compose his famous poem (Saqlia) when he sailed across the Mediterranean. Several books were written by authors who lived in the kingdom of Granada, but their canvas was limited to their country and northwest Africa. Some wrote about their travels in the form of maqamāt. Ibn Khatib himself wrote accounts of his journeys on both sides of the Straits of Gibraltar. When the great globe-trotter, ibn Buttutah wanted to dictate an account of his travels, he found his amanuensis in ibn Juzayy, a famous scholar of Granada. We are, therefore, indebted to a Spanish Muslim for preserving one of the greatest travelogues of all time, — the Rihla ibn Buttutah. It may not be out of place to mention that the sailors' guides known as portolani in the Middle ages which were prepared by the Jews of Aragon and Catalonia, were in fact based on the writings of Arab geographers.[23]

The prose literature of the Spanish Muslims included a considerable mass of books on theology and law (fiqh). Their theological works were the result of life-long dedication and arduous journeys to distant centres of Islamic learning. Their studies covered a wide range of subjects viz. commenties on the Quran, the hadith, the Muwatta of imam Malik, jurisprudence, biographies of the Prophet, and his companions, and the art of recitation of the Quran. The authors who composed works on these subjects were men of piety who lived and worked for promotion of true Islamic spirit among the Muslims. They did not hanker after loaves and fishes of official recognition, and only a few of them came near the cesspool of politics. The earliest theologians were the three jurists -ibn Dinar, ibn Habib and Yaha al-Laithi. The first was known as *faqih* (the savant), the second as *'alim* (scholar), and the third as the *'aqil* (wiseman) of Andalus. They were followed by a legion of experts in the field of theology, Quranic exegesis, and law. Baqi bin Mukhalad (817-889), and Qasim bin Asbgh (861-951) were the most famous scholars of their time. Baqi lived for many years in the East. He studied at Mecca, Madina, Damascus, Basra, Baghdad, Kufa, and Cairo. At Baghdad he is reported to have met imam Hanbal. His thirst for collecting hadith carried him to Khurrassan. On his return to Spain, he wrote an exposition of the Quran, and also prepared a compilation of hadith according to different subjects in an alphabetical order. Ibn Hazm used to call him 'the imam Bukhari' of Spain. Baqi was opposed to taqlid, and was rather eclectic in his jurisdical outlook. The Maliki theologians were opposed to him, but the sultan Muhammad saw nothing objectionable in his writings, and took him under his protection. Soon after, the erudite Cordovan 'Abd al-Barr (d. 1071) came to the forefront. A famous jurist of his time, he served as a judge at Cordova, Seville, Denia, Lisbon, and Jativa. Al-Barr wrote biographies of the Prophet's Companions, and the founders of the three schools of jurisprudence, — Abū Hanifa, imam Malik, and imam Shafi'i. Several books of this great scholar have been printed at Cairo. Almost contemporary with him were ibn Hazm, (994-1064), Abū l-Walid al Baji (1012-1081), Usman ibn Sa'id al Deni. Ibn Hazm has earned everlasting fame as Europe's first writer on comparative religion. We shall write about him in detail in the next chapter. Abū l-Walid left for the orient when he was very young, and returned home after thirteen years of studies. He served as a judge at Almeria. When he was at Saragossa, the ruling prince al-Muqtadir ibn Hud asked him to give a reply to a monk who came from France to convert him to Christianity. The manuscript of his reply is available at the Escurial, and it has been translated and published by Prof. D.M. Dunlop.[24] Al-Beji advised the monk that if one Sura of the Quran reached his ears, it would suffice to enlighten his heart and soul, and lead him to the most perfect way of life. Usman ibn Sa'id (d. 1053) was an authority on the seven styles of reciting the Quran. We may like to mention some of the most eminent scholars in field of theology after the fall of the kingdom of Cordova and thereafter. Ibn Khisal al-Ghafiqi (1078) wrote a biography of the Prophet. Abū Bakr ibn al-Arabi (1076-1149) compiled the traditions of Tirmidhi, commented on ibn Hisham's biography of the Prophet, and also wrote on marriage a book entitled, *'Faraiḍ al Nikh.'* Abū l. abbas Iqlisi (d. 1155) prepared a compendium of hadith based on Sahih of Muslim and Bukhari. The famous judge ibn'Ayad (1083-1148) wrote on the theories underlying the collection and compilation of hadith literature. Ibn 'Ayad is the author of the celebrated biography of the Prophet — *Kitab as-Shifa* which has survived, and is used extensively even today. Innumberable theologians appeared in the following centuries. Out of the massive host, Abū Abdullah al-Qurtibi (d. 1212), Abū Hayyan (1256-1344), Abu Ishaq Shatibi (d. 1388), and ibn 'Asim (1359-1426), have found a permanent niche for themselves. Al-Qurtibi was a scholar of profound learning. Pious and ascetic, he spent his time in reading prayer and meditation, Al-Qurtibi left Spain for the East, and died at Cairo. He wrote many books, but his *magnum* opus was his rich and comprehensive commentary on the Quran-*al-Jami li-ahkam al-Quran.* Al-Qurtibi was a maliki theologian, but he held independent views in many respects — for example he was of the opinion that an imam who leads the prayers can he teenager provided he can recite the Quran faultlessly. This book has been published and is greatly valued even today. Abū Hayyan, the 14th century grammarian of Granada was also the author of a commentary of the Quran entitled *'al-Bahr al-Muhit'* which runs into eight volumes and has been published several times. This is an important reference book for scholars and students in understanding the grammer of the Quran. Shatibi of Granada was a rationalist theologian of his time. His *al-Muwafaqat fi'usaul as-Shariah* is a milestone in religious thought. He looked upon Islam as a way of life, and the Shariah a comprehensive code covering all the activities of man. The Quran is totality of the Shari'ah, and the code enshrined therein protects the life, property and rights of man. It also regulates man's life as an individual and also as a member of society, and promotes a healthy society as well as a happy home. The *'muwafaqat'* of Shatibi has been printed again and again for its rationalistic approach and clear thinking. The city of Granada also gave birth to ibn'Asim (1359-1426) who was a great theologian. He is honoured to this day as the author of *"Tohfa Asimyya"* in which he embodied the basic aspects of maliki fiqh in 1698 verses. It is a prescribed text book for beginners of hadith studies all over to Muslim world.

The output of poetry during the Muslim rule was simply immence. The Spanish rulers, whatever their faults, were cultivated gentlemen who liberally rewarded poets and men of letters. They invited them to their private parties as well as public functions. A really talented poet was a friend and a boon companion *(nadim)* of his patron. Many poets were on the payroll of the rulers. Al-Mansur paid atleast forty poets from the state treasury. His entourage included ibn Darraj, the greatest panegyrist of his time. Many poets rose from anonymity to eminence, from poverty to prosperity. Once a poet visited al-Mu'tamid of Seville, and recited his poems. He was so much pleased that he rewarded him with one thousand dinars. It so happened that at that time al-Mu'tamid had before him a small statue of a camel inlaid with precious stones. The poet eyed the curio, and said to him, 'Sir, you have loaded me with so much money. Now give me also a camel to carry it: 'Al-Mu'tamid understood his remark, and parted with the statuette. Such instances of generosity to the poets are numerous in the history of the time. The most interesting, is the story of a village lavandière who became a queen by virtue of her skill in improvising verses. She was ar-Rumaikiya, a slave girl who used to wash clothes on the bank of the Guadalquivir, near the meadow known as the 'Silver field.' Once al-Mu'tamid, and his elderly poet friend ibn 'Ammar (who came from a poor family and rose from rages to riches) lingered on the bank, quoting poetry. In those days, adding a verse to half-a-verse was a favourite pastime of the poets. Seeing the ripples on the river, al-Mu'tamid improvised the following line :

Behold! The breeze has spun a coat of mail on the river. He asked ibn 'Ammar to add an appropriate second line. He was pondering over the matter, when a girl who happened to pass close to them added the second line :

What a shield would it be if it was frozen!

Al-Mu'tamid was astonished at the quick response of the stranger. On a closer look he found that she was also beautiful. Later on he married her. He named her I'timad. Theirs was the most successful marriage at first sight.

The taste for poetry was shared by all. The prince, the peasant, and even the artisans were devoted to the Muse. The contagion affected even the pious scholars. A qaḍi used to say 'Nothing pleases me so much as a handsome face and a beautiful verse.' Out of the innumerable poets who flourished in Muslim Spain, the most famous were: Yahya al-Ghazal (772-864) the diplomat who visited Constantinople; ibn Hani (d. 973) the licentious lover of Greek philosophy; Mundhir ibn Sa'id al-Balluti the great jurist and orator; ibn ʿAbd Rabbihi the court poet of caliph ʿAbd ar-Rahman; ibn Darraj (958-135) the cultured aristocrat of Cordova, Yusuf ar-Ramadi the court poet of Hakam II; At-Taliq(961-1009) the passionate grandson of caliph'Abd ar-Rahman, and ibn Zaidun (1003-1071) the lover of princess Wallada. All these poets were steeped in the classical tradition. After the fall of Umayyad dynasty, the succeeding centuries saw an almost endemic passion for poetry. Literature and poetry suffered no set back even though Spain was bedevilled by political anarchy. Shaqandi (d. 1231) says that under the mulūk aṭ-ṭawa'if, 'the cause of science and literature, instead of losing, gained considerably'. The most important poets upto the end of the 12th century were ibn Hazm, al-Muʿtamid, ibn ʿAmmar (d. 1031), ibn Labbana (d. 1113), ibn 'Abdun (d. 1134), ibn al-Abbar (d. 1041), ibn Zaqqaq (d. 1134), ibn Khafaja (d. 1139), ibn Quzman (d. 1160) and ibn Sahl (d. 1251). The kingdom of Granada had a host of poets. The most outstanding were ibn Khatib (d. 1374), ibn Khatima (d. 1369) and ibn Zamrak (d. 1393). The poems of all these and other Andalusian poets are available in literary histories, anthologies, and diwans i.e. their collected poetical works. Some anthologies are the treasure troves of Hispano-arabic poetry A few of these deserve to be mentioned: (i) *ibn Bassam's Dhakhira fi mahasin ahlil jazira*, (ii) ibn Khaqan's Qalaid al-'iqyan and Matmah al-nfus, (iii) Al-Himyari's *Al-Badi fi wasf ar-rabie*, (iv) ibn Dihya's *al-*

Mutrib, (v) ibn *Said's Rayāt āl-mubarrizin*, and (vi) ibn Khatib's Jayash at-tawshih. Most of these anthologies are available in print.

Arabic poetry of Spain is a bouquet of many flowers. It comprises songs of wine *(khamriyat)*, poetry of mysticism and moral counsels *(zuhd wa mawāiz)*, love lyrics *(ghazal)*, elegy *(marathi)* and satire *(hija)*. The Andalusians use all the metres current in the East, and systematised by the famous prosodist Khalil Ahmad. The most popular was rajaz (the oldest metre out of which evolved rhymed prose), the *kamil* (perfect), the *wafir* (ample), the *tawil* (long), the *khafif* (light), the *basit* (wide), and many others. Rhyme was the soul of poetry. The Spanish poets would not think of blank verse, like Milton of England who centuries afterwards, justified its use in his Paradise Lost by condemning rhyme as the 'jingling sound of like endings.' The numerous metres and endless rhymes endowed the Andalusian poetry with some of its many characteristics, — its thunderous eloquence, its lilting tone, its sad and soothing music. Writing poetry even for the most talented poet was like walking on a tight rope. The poet had to conform to the rules of prosody, and also to enrich his vocabulary before he stepped into the realm of the Muse. The influence of classical poetry, both pre-islamic (the *muallaqat*), and the new poetry nurtured at the courts of Damascus and Baghdad, had a great impact on the Andalusian poets. The qasida (ode), the chief delight and *tour de force* of eastern poets, found admirers as well as imitators in Spain. A good deal of Arabic poetry was, therefore, bound to be pompous, artificial, and a mere jugglery of far-fetched conceits, and hackneyed metaphors. The beloved's eyes are like the gazelle's, her stature is slim like the willow (ban), and her lips are cornelians, the bosoms are pointed arrows, the generosity of poet's patron is like a perennial river, and the five fingers of his hand are like its tributaries. However, when the entire Hispano—Arabic poetry is sifted, we are left with a considerable mass of pretty pieces which spring from the poet's heart. Prof. A.N. Nykl, an authority on the Arabic poetry of Spain says, 'For the Arabs, more so than for the Hindus, Persians, Greeks or Romans, language was an instrument of incomparable flamelike brilliancy. Its mastery in prose and especially in poetry, required a most powerful memory coupled with an uncanny elasticity of thought. Often it degenerated into a mere mental game, but rarely was it entirely dissociated from intensity and depth of feeling.'[25] Prof. García Goméz (of Madrid University, who is the doyen of the Spanish Arabists) likens Arabic poetry to delicate arabesques and verbal Alhamras[26]. Many figures of speech found in Andalusian poetry are startling in their originality and pictorial effect. The poet Abū l. ʿAbbas of Tudela (d. 1126) describes a brass lion discharging water from its mouth into a pool:

> Behold the lion of the firmament;
> from its mouth issues forth the Milky way.

Or hear ibn Ash-Shabuni, who describes a maiden dressed in a red robe:

> Walking slowly —
> A gleaming moon,
> Her glances have drawn
> My lifeblood.
> And with her glances
> She has dyed
> The red robe (she wears).

Or see the pleasing picture of the ripples on a river with branches overhanging on it:

The breeze has written many a scroll on the river
For the boughs to lean over, and read.

One day al-Mu'tamid was reading, when the sun fell on his book. A moon-like maiden (perhaps her name was Qamar) stood before him to ward off the sun's rays. The prince-poet broke into a four-line verse quoted by al-Marrakeshi:

She stood with her full stature
Between me and the sun.
I swear only the moon (qamar)
Can eclipse the sun.

The poet Al A'ma at-Tutili has condensed the beauty of his beloved in just four lines :

Smiling like the pearls,
Unfolding the moon,
Time cannot grasp her beauty
Yet my heart has enclosed it.

The 11th century poet al-Sumaisir describes the mosquitos in a short poem:

The mosquitos are sucking my blood —
sweet like wine to them.
How merry they are!
Happily, they sing on their lute — my body,
And like the musicians, pluck
The chords of my veins.

A legend current in Spain said that at the time of creation of the world, Spain asked God for a sunny sky, plenty of fruits, and beautiful women. These wishes were granted, but the fourth - a good government was denied by God because that would make Spain a Heaven on the earth. For the Muslims, Spain was a Paradise *(Jannat al dunya)*. Ibn Khafaja, who was known as *'jannan'*. i.e., a gardener because of his love of nature, sang with rapture;

> O people of Andalus,
> God has bestowed on you his many bounties—
> Rivers, brooks, and shady trees
> Not to be seen elsewhere.

and again :

> Andalus is a veritable Paradise
> Of lovely sights and perfumed breeze.
> her mornings are radiant like sparking teeth

> And her evenings like the scarlet lips.
> When the breeze blows
> Spreading fragrance around
> I cry with ecstasy — 'Ah Andalus!

A great deal of Spanish poetry was inspired by the beauties of nature — the rivers, the clouds, the tempests, the mountains, the starry skies, the moonlit meadows, the trees, the flowers, and the song of birds. Prof. Nicholson finds in the Spanish Arabic poetry 'an almost modern sensibility to the beauty of nature!'[27] The Anadalusian poets described nature as they saw her. Nature was to them an attractive arrangement of form, colour and sound. They had an innocent, child-like joy for her, a purely aesthetic delight, free from supernaturalism and metaphysical philosophising. The feeling for nature is also expressed in short and musical poems (called *nawariyāt*) composed in the late caliphate period. This genre appeared in the East, and became a favourite with the Spanish poets. A hundred figures of speech were improvised to describe the flowers, their colours and perfume. The flower as a subject of poetry and prose imparted enchantment to Andalusian literature

- says H. Pérès.[28] We have many instances of these flower-songs. The qaḍi of Seville (grandfather of al-Mu'tamid) was one of the best composers of nawariyāt. This is how he describes the jasmine flowers in his two poems quoted below:

> Oh jasmine flowers, you outshine others
> In your white glory and perfume.
> On the boughs, you look like
> Silver coins on green silk.

> Behold the wild jasmine on the boughs
> Refreshed by showers of summer clouds.
> Yellow hyacinths glistening
> On emerald twigs in the midday sun.

We have many descriptions of gardens in Andalusian poetry, and there are also many poems on natural and atmospheric phenomena. The song of birds, the nightingale and the dove moved poets to compose verses. Abū l. Hassan, a poet of Seville contemporary with al-Mu'tamid wrote a touching poem which ends on a serene and meditative mood :

> My heart aches with melancholy
> At the cooling of the dove from the far river island
> Pistachio coloured is its collar.
> Its breast is lapis-luzali,
> The rainbow colours adorn its neck,
> and brown are the tips of its plummage,
> Golden lids crown its ruby eyes,
> The break is dyed black.
> Resting its head on its wings,
> on the throne of boughs it sat.
> It saw my tears and was frightened.
> Stretching itself on the green boughs,
> It flew away taking away my heart.

O where has it flown?
None will say.[29]

The philosophy of *carp diem* so dear to Omar Khayyam is
a recurring theme of Andalusian poetry. Eat, drink, and be
merry as the future is uncertain. Spanish poetry abounds in
bacchanalian songs. Instances of this type of poetry will take
several pages. A typical instance relates to the three brothers,
— Abū Muhammad, Abū Bakr, and Ali Hassan who belonged
to the highly cultured family of Banu Qabturnah of Iberian
origin. The brothers served as secretaries at the court of al-
Mutawakkil of Badajoz. Their poetry is permeated with fine-
feeling and pleasing Epicurean spirit, according to Prof. Nykl.[30]
Once, the three brothers spent a pleasant night at Al-Badi' (The
Wonderful) palace. They drank all night, and slept among the
flower-beds. Abū Muhammad was the first to wake up. He
addressed his two brothers who were still sleeping, with the
following couplet :

Dear brothers! The morning's face has appeared
The day's light has sent the night into hiding.
Let us sip the morning cup, and enjoy the pleasures of
today.
None knows what the evning has in store for us.

The other brother Abū Bakr opened his yes, and looking around
addressed the third brother :

O brother arise. The languorous zephyr
Has arrived in the garden laden with cool wine.
The flowers embrace like friends in love,
Sleep not, enjoy the pleasures before you
Ere we sink in a long sleep under the earth.

Soon the third brother also woke up, and he addressed his two
brothers quoting the following lines :

> My brothers, leave all accusations.
> Arise, and let us finish the stock of our wine.
> Make most of time's inadvertence.
> Today is the day of drinking, and tomorrow of
> apology.[31]

No Andalusian poet has portrayed better than Al-Mu'tamid,
the feeling of nostalgia for the time spent in pleasure and
dalliance. In his early youth, he was posted as governor of
Silves (about 1053), and Abū Bakr ibn 'Ammar who was himself
a poet, was sent along with him. Silves (Shilb) in Portugal is
known for its scenic beauty. During those days its hills were
clothed with fruit gardens and orchards of apples. Its valleys
had rich pasturage and magnificent woods. It was inhabited
mostly by the Arabs of Yemenite origin who spoke pure Arabic,
and were known for their hospitality and love of poetry. Even
a farmer would lay aside his plough, and rattle out extempore
verses. Al-Mu'tamid spent the most joyous and impressionable
years of his life in this valley[32]. When he inherited the kingdom
of Seville from his father, he posted his friend ibn 'Ammar as
governor of Silves perhaps .because he (ibn 'Ammar) was a
native of Estombar near the town. In a poem addressed to ibn
'Ammar, al-Mu'tamid recalls, with a delicate and fine felicity,
the days of joy and festivity spent by him at the Castle of
Verandahs (Qasr ash-Sharājib) :

> Convey my felicitations, O Abū Bakr
> To the pleasant spots of Silves, and ask them if they
> remember me.
> Greet the alcazar of Verandahs on behalf of a youth
> Who pines for its halls (sculptured) with lions

And maidens charming.
What nights I spent in the company of maidens
Of plump hips and slim waist.
Their radiant beauty and bewitching glances pierced
my heart.
I remember the nights spent in playful mirth on the
river bank.
At times she would offer cups of wine with kisses.
She would play on her lute and thrill me
And I heard the clash of swords.
And last of all, she would let her robe fall.
And I saw her in all her splendour.
She stood before me
Like a freshly unfolded bud.

Beauty, pleasure and youth do not last long. Every summer is
followed by winter. Al-Mu'tamid was dethroned by the
Almoravids, and transported to Aghmat in the foothills of the
Atlas south of Marakesh. He lived in poverty with his wife and
daughters, and wrote touching poems on his life of misery and
privations. On the day of Id al fitr, the sight of his daughters
moved him to tears, and he poured out in a poem the sorrow
that was eating into his body and soul. His wife died, and soon
he followed her, and was buried beside her. Before his death,
he wrote his own epitaph — a masterpiece of poignant poetry
which began with the following lines *(matla)*:

Grave of a foreigner *(qabar al gharib)* may the rains
of Heaven refresh thee!
Thou hast, indeed, truimphantly received
The mortal remains of ibn 'Abbad.

The dominant theme of Andalusian poetry was love. The
whole gamut of lovers' psychology — the joy of stolen meetings,

the anguish of farewell, the agony of separation, the indifference and coquetry of the beloved, — all these are the themes of hundreds of love poems. Although, the poetry of languorous sensuality (some of which remind us of the paintings of Sir Alma Tadema) was not entirely nonexistent, the Hispano-Arabic love poetry was, on the whole, free from stark frankness. Even ibn Quzman, the lecherous poet of the 12th century rarely transgressed the limit of descency. A significant point to be noted, in this connection, is that Andalusian poetry is characterised by fine sentiments of chivalry, devotion and sincerity. Love was a cult of loyalty, and the lover was a slave ('abd) of the beloved. He pocketed insults, submitted to reproaches, and patiently listened the accusations of his beloved. In addition to utter submissiveness, love enjoined absolute fidelity, undying affection, and patience. The lover was morally bound to guard his beloved against slander and tale-bearing. This attitude was the result of the social values of the age. Among the Spanish Muslims, love-making was a risky affair. Islam offered a complete code of sexual behaviour and hygiene. It looks upon mixing of the sexes as a step towards lewd misbehaviour leading to breaking up of domestic life. For this reason, the Spanish Muslim society offered limited opportunities for romantic attachment. The reserve between the sexes transformed the very ideal of love. Love became synonymous with idealised devotion. The biological urge sublimated into a chivalrous cult of distant worship, mute admiration, and silent suffering. Rarely, it would turn into morbid melancholy with obvious pathological symptoms, viz. insomnia, anaemia, neurasthenia, anorexia, resulting in premature death. He who loved, remained chaste, and died was considered a martyr. As romantic friendship was frowned upon by guardians of public morality, (parents and religious leachers), the lovers adopted a secret strategy to circumvent publicity. In the preliminary stages, love was expressed by words, glances and riddles, quotations from poetry and followed by exchange of valentines and locks of hair in perfumed capsules. The lovers proceeded with caution because they were afraid of persons who could destroy their love. These were, the watcher/observer *(raqib)*, the jealous *(hasid)*, the moralist *('adil)*, and the defamer *(nammam)*. Such, in short, were the main features of the love-game, and the stock-in-trade of Arabic poetry, which in the opinion of Nicholson anticipate medieval chivalry.[33] Here is ibn Zaidun signing a charter of submissiveness to Wallada :

> Disdain me, I shall bear,
> Postpone, You will find me patient.
> Be haughty, I shall be all humility.
> Turn back, I shall follow.
> Speak, I shall listen,
> Order, I shall obey.

It is really a *cri du coeúr* when the poetess Amat al-Aziz makes the following complaint :

> My glances have wounded your heart.
> Your glances have wounded my cheeks.
> Wound for wound, the scores are settled.
> But why wound me by avoiding me.

The mystic Abū Bakr of Tortosa (author of Siraj al mulūk) expresses his chaste love *(hubb al-muruwwa)* in the following charming lines:

> Often I look at the sky wistfully,
> Hoping that I might see the very star
> You too might be looking at.
>
> I greet every passing caravan from distant lands

Hoping to meet someone who brought
The fragrance of your breath.

I stand facing the breeze
Hoping that it might
bring news about you.

I walk along the road aimlessly
Hoping that I might hear
Someone pronounce your name.

I look at every passerby
Hoping that I might have a glimpse
Of your face.

Here is a touching poem in which the poet ibn Hazm expresses a lover's joy when he sees the things belonging to his beloved:

I am forbidden to draw near
To my mistress dear;
She persevered most cruelly
To abandon me.

Some garment wherein she dressed,
something she caressed —
To gaze of these, all else denied,
I was satisfied.

So likewise Prophet Jocob, who
Came with guidance true,
And over Joseph many years
Shed such bitter tears.

Until the sorrow struck him blind,
Scenting on the wind
His tunic, hailed him with delight
and regained his sight.[34]

ʿAl-Mu ʿtamid could not bear separation from his wife Iʾtimad. From the battlefield, he sent her the following message of love, perhaps through a carrier pigeon :

> Absent from my eyes
> Enshrined in my heart
> Greetings numberless from a painful heart.
> Greetings from the eyes deprived of sleep.
> You have enslaved my soul that was so restless,
> And made it submissive to you.
> How I wish to be near you?
> Keep thou the pledge of love between us.
> Even though far from you,
> I have sealed this message
> With your sweet name — Iʿtimad.

Ummal Hanna, daughter of a qaḍi of Almeria who lived in the 12th century, expresses her feelings on receipt of a love-letter:

> A letter from beloved says —
> He would be coming.
> My eyes began to shed tears.
> Excess of joy *(sarrūr)*
> And contentment *(musarrat)*
> provoked the tears.
> O eyes! It is habitual with you
> to weep with joy *(farah)*
> As well as sorrow *(ahzan).*
> greet him with joy
> When he arrives.
> Leave tears
> For the night of separation.[35]

The following lines depict the helplessness of a lover who cannot finish his *billet doux* because of the torrent of tears flowing from his eyes:

> I wrote a letter to my love.
> She sent me a reply thereto
> That stilled the agitation of
> my heart, then stirred it anew.

> I watered every word I penned
> with tears o'erflowing from my eyes
> As lovers will, who intend
> In love no treacherous surprise.

> And still the tears flowed down apace,
> And washed the careful lines away:
> O wicked waters, to efface
> The lovely things I strove to say!

> Behold when fresh I set my pen
> Then tears have made my writing plain,
> But as I come to close, Oh! then
> The script is vanished in their rain.[36]

Here is a fine pictures of a maiden who leaves her lover after a friendly meeting:

> As she withdrew, the lissom maid,
> This way and that she gently swayed
> As a marcissus 'neath the trees
> Swings on its stems before the breeze.

> Deep in his heart the lover hears
> The pendents hanging from her ears
> Ring out a tender melody:
> 'I love thee tenderly: Lov'st thou me?.

There was no dearth of reflective poetry. The passing away of youth, the fleeting nature of life's pleasures, the instability of man's destiny, simple living, humility, contentment, and the brotherhood of mankind, were favourite themes of many poets. The physician Abū Bakr ibn Zuhr (d. 1198) saw his image in a mirror, but he could not recognise it. The mirror, however, revealed the truth:

> I looked at the polished mirror
> My eyes did not believe what they saw—
> An old man not known to me.
> But I recalled having seen him in his youth.
> I asked, 'Where is the one who I saw but yesterday,
> O tell me where he has vanished'?
> The mirror laughed and replied—
> 'The one you do not recognise, is already here.'

Abū Ishaq of Elviria (d. 1066) looked upon the world as an inn where men come and go; the pleasures of the world are meaningless, as all things come to an end. He warned the rich that they should not strut about in fine clothes because fate can reduce their garments to rags. When he was asked to build a pretty house for himself, he replied:

> I am happy in my own hut.
> Were it not for the winter's rain,
> The summer's heat,
> The fear of thieves,
> The need to store food,
> And a curtain for privacy,
> I would have preferred to live —
> In a spider's web.

Abū l-Qasim of Granada (d. 1345) who was buried at the famous cemetery near bāb al-Ilbira, composed short poems embodying great wisdom, for example the following:

Knowledge is beauty *(husn)*
and Ornament.
Ignorance is ugliness
and evil.

Prosperity commands respect
And poverty is disgrace and death.

All men are organs of one body,
Some are heads, some eyes.
This is the only truth I know
There is no doubt about it.[37]

The Andalusians composed a great deal of religious poetry,
— hyms in praise of God, poems in honour (sena) of the Prophet,
and poems explaining certain aspects of the teachings of Islam.
Earlier we have seen that ibn Asim of Granada wrote a poem
on the basic teachings of Maliki school. Long before him, a
Cordovan named Yahya al-Qurtubi (1098-1172) composed a
poem of winning sweetness setting out the teachings of Islam
— profession of the unity of God, prayer, ablution, fasting,
alms-giving and pilgrimage. The poem is written in rhyming
couplets in 18 parts. It was composed for being learnt by heart
by children, and for this reason it is entitled 'Urjuzat al-
Wildan'[38]. One of the finest poems composed in honour of the
Prophet was by ibn Jubayr when he saw the lights of the city
of Madina from afar. This long poem, throbbing with a highly
educated Spaniard's love for the Prophet, has been preserved
by ibn Khatib.[39] It is still recited by the pilgrims when they see
the minarets of the Prophet's mosque from a distance. Ibn Khatib
himself wrote the following lines on the Prophet.[40]

The Verses of the Holy Book have praised you — so
how
Could my eulogy possibly praise your greatness.

Many elegies on personal sorrows and political losses, were composed by several poets. In the latter category two deserve to be mentioned, the one by ibn ʿAbdun, and the other by Abū l-Baqa. The former was minister of Omar al-Mutawakkil of Badajoz. This elegy is known as 'Abduniya', and it mourns the fall of the Banu Muzaffar dynasty and their misfortunes after the Almoravids removed them from power. Ibn ʿAbdun was a native of Evora (in the present day Portugal), and he was in the service of Omar. He was a scholar with a remarkable memory; he knew the Kitab al-Aghani by heart. Deep feelings and historical erudition, are the main features of this elegy. The historical part of the poem was elucidated by ibn Badrun of Silves to facilitate its appreciation. The elegy begins with a preamble describing the fate of kings and empires, — Darius, Alexander, the Sassanids, the Greek rulers, the Umayyads and the Abbasids, before lamenting the tragic end of Omar and his two sons. Abū l-Baqa who lived in the 13th century was born at Ronda at an uncertain date. At the time he wrote the elegy, the Muslims had lost Cordova, Seville, Jativa, and Jaen, and their future was bleak. Like the ʿAbduniya,' this elegy too begins with introductory couplets about the fall of great kingdoms from their pinnacles of power and glory. This great elegy is composed in basit metre and consist of 52 verses rhyming in nūn. This is how he laments at the fate of the Muslims of Spain :

> Islam has been struck by a disaster
> For which no consolation is adequate.
> So serious it is that the hills
> Of Uhud and Thahlan have felt the shock.
> A curse has smitten the Muslims
> The provinces under Islam are now desolate,
> and beyond any hope of recovery.

Ask Valencia about the fate of Murcia.
And what has happened to Jativa. And where is Jaen?
Where is Cordova, the seat of learning
Home of eminent scholars?
And where is Seville, and its joys
On its river full of sweet waters?
These were the pillars on which
Stood the edifice of Spain.
How can a building stand

If its pillars are gone?
Like fond lovers, they weep at the fall
of the pure faith of Islam,
They weep over for the dwellings now
desotate, and occupied by pagans.
The churches stand arrogantly in place of mosques.
Where bells are ringing and crosses are standing

The mihrabs weep though made of hard stone.
The pulpits bitterly cry though made of wood.

Before this regrettably short account of Andalusian poetry is
brought to a close, we may have to look into the new strophic
poetry which appeared in Spain in the form of the muwashashaha
and the zajal. This new poetry is the glory of Andalusian
literature even as the Alhamra is in the domain of architecture.
There is a vast critical literature on the subject, mostly in
Spanish, French and German, but not much in English. The
structure, the prosody, the thematic contents, the history of the
two genres, the likely music in which they were sung, and their
possible influence on the French poetry, have been discussed in
learned monographs in several European languages. More and
more books on the subjects continue to appear at Madrid, Paris,
Oxford, Palermo, the U.S.A., and Latin America. The whole

subject is monopolised by the specialists, and the layman feels lost as in a labyrinth. 'I propose to give a peep into this complicated subject as briefly as possible.

The term 'muwashshaha' is derived from the word 'wishah' which stands for a long belt of brocade with stripes of pearls, and gems of different colours which was worn diagonally on the chest and tied at the waist by aristocratic ladies. The word 'muwashshaha' aptly describes the different forms of stanzas and different rhymes of each stanza. This new poetry, was, perhaps, a reaction against the qasida type of classical poetry which had a fixed rhyming scheme, viz. aa, ba, ca, da, etc. The muwashshaha poetry was invented about the middle of the 9th century by the blind poet Maqqadm ibn Mua'afa who lived at Cabra, a small town about 30 miles to the south of Cordova. Some scholars have suggested that Maqqadam took for his model, the current folk songs in the Romance dialect spoken by the Christians, and the converted Muslims. The basic scheme of the stanzas of a typical muwashshah is — aa, bbaa, ccaa etc. Yet another feature of many of the muwashshaha was the tail piece called 'kharja', which was of crucial importance as it added the finishing gloss to the poem. Ibn Sana al-Mulk (an Egyptian authority of the 13th century, who was also the author of *Dar al-tirāz,* one of the fundamental works on the subject) calls the 'kharja', the spice of the muwashshah, its salt and sugar, its musk and emergris.[41] The *Kharja* was introduced for the sake of fun *(sukhf),* and it had an erotic appeal. It was usually put in the mouth of a boy, or a woman in love or a drunkard. The entire poem was composed in classical Arabic, but the kharja if there was one, it was mostly in spoken Arabic, and sometimes even in the romance dialect. The other genre i.e., the zajal was introduced a century later by the philosopher ibn Bajja. There is a slight difference between these two sister genres. Unlike the muwashshaha, the zajal was composed in spoken Arabic. The usual pattern of a zajal was aa bbba, ccca. A muwashshaha had several stanzas, but a zajal was shorter. Some zajals look like Shakespearan sonnets in the number of their lines. The stanzas of a zajal are divided in three parts — the *markaz*, the *asghan*, and the *simt*. Take the following extract form a zajal composed by Ibn Quzman:

> Haqqa khulla, tubtum: Allah kan yatefíkum! (a)
> Sa-tarau da'n-nawwar ey sharab yasqikum! (a)
>
> Ya behar, yā narjas, lakumu 'r-ruh ta'shaq (b)
> Ente amlah w'amlah,w'et arshaq wa arshaq. (b)
> Hubbukum yaqtulni;in qatalni bi-l-haqq (b)
> kulla yawm min qabri as-salam nuqrikum! (a)
>
> Repent, O you drankards. It would be right to do so.
> God will reward you.
> See the flowers,
> What a wine they offer to drink!
>
> O behār, O narcissus. My soul craves for you.
> Grow more and more in your grace and splendour.
> My love for you kills me. If it really kills me,
> I shall give you my greetings from the grave.

In the above zajal, the two introductory lines (aa) would be called *markaz* or *matla*, the next three lines (bbb) would be the *asghan*, and the last line which rhymes with the first line will be the *simt*. The zajals and the muwashshahas were songs of wine and love. They were sung in solo to the accompaniment of a lute and a tamborine, but the last line (the smit) was sung in chorus[42]. Ibn Khaldun, an avowed classicist liked these poems because of 'their sweetness, artistic language and internal rhymes'[43]. When ibn Tifelwit, the Almoravid governor of

Saragossa heard a zajal sung by a musician and composed by ibn Bajja, he was so much moved, that he tore his robe out of excitement, and cried, "How thrilling — ma atrabahu." The spontaneous language, and lilting music of a zajal gave a thrilling experience to the audience, particularly a zajal of short lines such as the one below composed by ibn Qazzāz :

"Badru tamm,	Full moon,
shamsu duha	Mid-day sun.
Gusnu naqa	Bough on a sandhill.
Misku shamm	Fragrant like musk.
Ma atamm	How perfect!
Ma auḍaha	How shining!
Ma auraqa	How flowing!
Ma ashamm	How fragrant."
La jaram	No doubt that
Man lamahā	He who sees her
Qad ashiqa	Falls in love:
Qad haram!	With her only.

This strophic poetry was cultivated for centuries. The Almoravid and Almohad periods were the springtime of the muwashshahas and zajals. A list of the poets who composed these poems would be too long. Those who earned everlasting fame were ibn al-Qazzaz, ibn Baqi (d. 1145), Abū Bakr al-Abyad, Abū l-Abbas Tutili, ibn Zuhr, ibn Sahl, ibn Khatib, and ibn Zamrak. The high-priest of the zajals (imam al-Zajjalin) was the poet ibn Guzman who lived during the Almoravid rule. Born at Cordova about 1086, he moved in the cities of Seville, Granada, Malaga and Valencia, charming his wealthy patrons with his poems during nights of full moon and glittering stars. His blue eyes, and a red beard betrayed his probable descent from a German/Gothic family. Fond of old and expensive wines (thanks to the money advanced by his patrons), this bard of 'passion and mirth' desired to be buried in a vineyard. Nothing delighted him more than a pretty face and yellow wine (*wajhan melih wa sharaban asfar*). He committed every hateful vice, and was arrested several times, for his impiety, but every time his patrons came to his rescue. During his old age, he repented and died in Oct. 1160. He composed many zajals, but only 150 have survived and have been published by Don García Gomez. The first translation in English of about 50 zajals was made by Prof. A.R.Nykl. Their theme is wine, earthly love, spring, musical parties, frolics of gay youths and dandies, and pretty women. He was the happiest of men in the company of cultured friends of easy virtue. His poetry reflects the decadent society of the upper class whose members had no thought of the dark days ahead, but Prof. García Goméz considers him one of the best poets of the Middle Ages in any language.[44]

The ultimate literary manifestation of the Spanish Muslims is to be found in Renaissance Spanish written in the Arabic script. This strange literature is known as aljamiado, — from the Arabic *al-ajamiyya*. The main objective of this literature was obviously to keep the Morisco families informed about the basic teachings of Islam so that they could practise their religion in secrecy. Hundreds of aljamiado texts are available in the libraries of Spain, particularly at Madrid. Once a whole library of aljamiado literature was found hidden in the house of a Morisco who lived at Al Monacid in Aragon region. After the owner left for Africa, the house collapsed, and the books came to light. Several scholars have worked on the aljamiado books, and thanks to their efforts, it is now possible to read and understand this literature. It is no more a museum piece. It has opened the way to a study of the social life of the Moriscos, and their firm faith in Islam. During the last four decades, interest in aljamiado literature has grown, and as usual, most of the scholars hail from Spain. Among the notable names in aljamiado literature are, Isa ben Chebir of Segovia, Juan Peres/ Ibrahim Taibili of Alcala de Henares, Muhammad Rabadan of Rueda de jalon. Ben Chebir wrote on Muslim law and hadith; Juan Pérès wrote against Christianity; Rabadan composed poetry. Much of the aljamiado literature is annonymous perhaps because the authors wanted to keep their names secret from considerations of personal safety. That was why an annonymous poet composed the 'Poema de Yusuf' on the basis of Sura XII of the Quran. This remarkable poem written in stanzas of four lines each, narrates the life of the Prophet Joseph (Yusuf). The poetry of the Moriscos shows that they had not forgotten the zajjal strophy. They wrote poems extolling the Prophet of Islam viz. *almadha de al annabi* Mohammad. The aljamiado literature recalls the Quranic stories of Solomon, Moses, Jesus, the Prophet of Islam and his companions. The other subjects are: the miracle of the moon, the ascension of the Prophet, the convertion of caliph Omar to Islam, the golden deeds of caliph Ali, the battle of Yarmuk, the exploits of Alexander, the conquest of Spain and other historical events. Many books contain prayers, details of rituals for birth, marriage and funerals, and other obligations under the Muslim personal law. Even popular superstitions, magic formulas, and charms have found a place in the aljamiado books.

For reasons already stated in Part I of the book, very small number of Moriscos could read and write Arabic. In their desperate struggle to keep close contact with their religion, they translated the Quran in aljamiado as well as in Spanish in Latin characters. Many copies of the aljamiado Quran (a good number are fragmentary) are available in public libraries of Spain, but mostly in Madrid. The Provincial Library at Toledo

(Biblioteca Publico provincial de Toledo) has a unique Quran written in elegant and accurate Spanish in the Latin script. This remarkable copy (No. T. 235) runs into 347 folios. The Toledo copy was made from an already existing translation. The name of the translator is not known, but he must have been a Morisco with sound knowledge both of Spanish, and Arabic. It seems to have been borrowed by the scribe of the present copy at Toledo. The manuscript carries notations based on tafsir (commentries of the Quran) in three languages — Spanish, Arabic and adjamiado. The value of the copy of the Quran lies in these trilingual notes or explanations. The translator took every possible care to ensure precise pronounciation of the sacred text by indicating correct phonetic value of Arabic letters that have no equivalents in Spanish alphabet. The work involved a lot of painstaking dedication as the scribe took four months to copy it. In a small paragraph at the end of the Quran, the scribe writes : 'The great Quran *(al Quran al Azim)* was finished on the 5th of Rabi al-Awwal, which was Tuesday by Christian reckoning *(hisab al Nasara)*, the 11th July, 1606. May Allah forgive who copied, and him who recites it, and him who acts according to it, and the whole community of Muslims *(al-muslimeen al ajmaeen)*. Amen. O Lord of all World *(ya rab al Alameen)*![45] We imagine the pious Morisco Muslim doing his work quietly, perhaps, at night, in a corner of his home in a ghetto (moreria) under the light of a candle. The year 1606 in which it was copied is significant. Barely three years after, the Moriscos were ordered to leave Spain.

Notes

1. Al-Maqqari/Gayangos, Vol. II, p. 102. He has given names of 350 Spanish scholars who visited the East on educational tours.

2 .Nicholson: Literary History of the Arabs, p. 419. Dozy: p. 455.

3. John owen: Skeptics of the Italian Renaissance, p. 69.

4. Hitti: History of the Arabs, p. 563.

5. Ibn Bassam: Zakhira, Vol. I, (I), p. 198)

6. Ency. of Islam (N. Ed.), article on 'ibn Hazm.'

7. Ibn Khaldun: The Muqaddimah, Vol. III, pp. 303-304.

8. Ency. of Islam (N. Ed.), article on 'ibn Khayr, also Péres: chapter II.

9. Nicholson: p. 435.

10. Casiri, M: Bibliotheca arabico-hispana Escurialensis, Madrid, 1760. Derenbourg, H : Les manuscripts arabes de l'Escurial, Paris, 1884. Levi Provençal: Les manuscripts arabes de l'Escurial, Paris, 1928.

11. Noteworthy attempts have been made in this direction by Don Palencia in his Historia de la Literatura Arábigo-Espanola, The Arab scholar Ihsan Abbas has advanced the subject (in his Tarikh al-adab al-Andalusi). But a comprehensive work will appear only after more material is available in print. Let us wait.

12. Ãl-Maqqari/Gayangos, Vol. I, p. 142.

13. John Heywood: Arabic Lexicography, p. 64. This Zubaidi was one of the tutors of Hisham II. He was a poet of distinction with mystic tendencies. He believed in the brotherhood of man. In a poem he sang, "The earth is the same wherever you go. All men are brothers and neighbours'. (Nykl: p. 47)

14. Palencia: Literatura Arábigo-Espanola:, p. 140.

15. J. Heyword: p. 114.

16. Nykl: p.324.

17. Ency. of Islam (N. Ed), article on Abū Hayyan. (p. 126).

18. Ibn Khalikan: Vol. II, p. 666. Palencia: Literature Arábigo-Espanola, p. 130.

19. ibn Hazm: Tawq, p. 68. The entire chapter is entitled 'On Hinting with the eyes'.

20. B. Lewis: The World of Islam, p. 230.

21. Al-Himyari: p. 5.

22. Kimble: p. 56. The circumference given by Idrisī is very near the correct figure, says Kimble.

23. Beven and Singer: The Legacy of Israel pp. 226-228.

24. Journal of the American Oriental Society (103.3 of 1963), Prof. Dunlop's translation was published in 1952 in Al-Andalus, a learned journal of Spain on Andalusian subjects.

25. A.R. Nykl: pp. 226-227.
26. Palencia: Historia de la Literatura Arábigo-Espanola, p. 44.
27. Nicholson: Literary History of the Arabs, p. 416.
28. Pérès: p. 187.
29. Palencia: Literatura Arábigo-Espanola, p. 74.
30. Nykl: p. 173.
31. Ibn Khatib: Ihata, vol. I, pp. 340-341.
32. Prof. Nykl visited Silves. His observations would be found interesting in the present context : 'The present-day visitor of the valley, which is surrounded by a chain of low hills, as he goes during the spring through the castle, built of local red stone on a hill above the river, can understand the nostalgia which permeated Al-Mu'tamid's verses. Though in 1940 the war in Europe was raging, here, among the almond blossoms (amendoeiras), in the quiet valley, and under the azure sky, there was an atmosphere of peace and beauty, which invited the pilgrim to recite the king's verses while standing on the wall of the ruined castle, then undergoing repairs. The only discordant note came from the three square towers filled with sullen convicts, who were asking for cigarettes which the pilgrim did not have: the former dwelling of Muslim princes was now used as a jail!

Here began, in happiness, a poet-king's life, which was destined to end on the bleak African landscape, in misery of a cruel captivity. The Portuguese convicts wondered why a wanderer from foreign lands, paying no attention to their stupid jeers, recited in Arabic what to him seemed to be the summing up of the peregrination on earth of a noble, deep-feeling soul — the song of his youth, and the elegy he composed shortly before his death. (A.R. Nykl: p. 135).
33. Nicholson: p, 416.
34. Arberry: The Ring of the Dove, p. 185.
35. H. Pèrés: p. 416.
36. Translation A.J. Arberry: The Ring of the Dove, p. 72.
37. Ibn Khatib: Ihata, vol. I, p. 322.
38. This beautiful poem has been published in the Islamic Quarterly, London, in Jan-June, 1972, with a translation in English by R.Y. Ebied and M.J.L. Young. (pp. 15-33). The author has a copy of the Arabic poem as well as translation.
39. Ibn Khatib: Ihata, vol. II, pp. 171-172. It begins with the following lines:

Seeing the lights at night, I said to myself, 'Lo! The Lamp of Guidance is shining bright.'

40. Annemarie Schimmel: 'And Muhamamd is His Messenger,' printed at Lahore, 1987. (p. 177). She has also translated a beautiful poem of the Spanish poetess Sa'duna Umm Sa'd (d. 1242) in which she passionately longs to kiss an image of the Prophet's sandals to earn blessings in her life after death.

41. S.M. Stern: Hispano-Arabic Strophic Poetry, Oxford, 1974. (pp. 158-160).

42. L. Provençal: Islam du Occident, p. 285.

43. Ibn Khaldun: The Muqaddima, vol, III, p. 454. He has written a long article on the Spanish muwashshhahs and zajal. (pp. 440-465) For the above poem, see Nykl: p. 392, and also the Muqaddima (p. 441). For the zajal of Ibn Quzman see Nykl: p. 296.

44. A.R. Nykl: pp. 266-331. Also, see the learned article of Prof-García Goméz in 'The World of Islam', referred to in the bibliography.

45. Consuelo López-Morillas: 'Trilingual' marginal notes (Arabic Aljamiado, and Spanish) in a Morisco Manuscript from Toledo." Published in the Journal of the American Oriental Society: Vol. 103/No. 3/July-Sept. 1983, pp. 495-504.

Also Chapter XIV: :Literatura aljamiado, in Palencia: Literature Arábigo-Espanola.

Chapter 23

The Study of Science and Medicine in Islamic Spain

———————

The Muslim society in the Middle Ages was basically religious. The philosophers and freethinkers were sometimes looked upon with suspicion, and they were even persecuted, but there was no confrontation between science and religion. 'It is noteworthy, says Sidgwick, that there was no hostility between science and the Mohammadan Church.'[1] From the 10th to the 12th century, — the period of zenith in scientific studies, the Muslim East produced great scientists: Al-Razi and ibn Sina in medicine, Omar Khayyam in astronomy, Al-Khawarizmi and Al-Battani in algebra and trigonometry, Al-Jahiz in zoology, Al-Kindi and Al-Haytham in optics, are some of the greatest names in the history of science. Their value lies both in theory and practice and in this respect they excelled the Greeks. The Arabic-speaking scientists advanced Greek theories and enriched them by investigation, analysis and experimentation. The contributions of the Spanish Muslims in science seem to be modest except in the field of medicine. Very few of their scientific writings have been published. The case of ibn Firnas (d. 888) illustrates this point. This brilliant man flourished during

the reign of ʿAbd ar-Rahman II, He was an astronomer, a
meteorologist, and a musicologist. He designed and constructed
a metronome. He believed that man could fly, and actually
made a successful attempt. Attaching wings to his body, he
flew to a considerable height. He produced glass from sand. He
constructed a planetarium for study of stars, and atmospheric
phenomena. But no book about this remarkable man has come
down to us. By the 10th century, the scientific works from the
East reached Spain. These texts promoted the study of
mathematics, astronomy and medicine. From the 11th to the
13th century, Muslim Spain saw the golden age of science.
Many scholars of science graced these discipline but it is to be
regretted that the manuscripts relating to mathematics,
astronomy, natural sciences, and medicine in the Library of
Escurial have not seen the light of the day. These have to be
studied and evaluated before we are able to get a full picture of
the contributions of the Spanish Muslims in scientific subjects.
Even the Spanish scholars who are in the vanguard of Hispano-
Muslim studies have not evinced much interest in science beyond
writing a few books on medicine and metallurgy.

One of the earliest scientists (after ibn Firnas) was Muslim
Abū Obaida (d. 907). He was an astronomer-cum-astrologer
with heretic views. He was accused of praying with his face
towards Jerusalem. They also made fun of his theory that
the earth was round, and was encircled by the sky.[2] Spain's
first astronomer-cum-mathematician was the Madrid born
Maslama bin Ahmad who died at Cordova in 1004. He was
honoured as the imam (leader) by his contemporary
mathematicians. Maslama edited the planetary tables *(zij)* of
Al-Khawarizimi, and what is more significant, he rendered them
into Arabic. This work was to prove of much importance in
Europe, as we shall see later. He prepared a commentary on

Ptolemy's Planisphaerium, and also wrote a treatise on commercial arithmetic *(muamālāt)*. He was also a chemist of repute. In one of his books he described the method of making mercuric oxide.[3] The Arabic encyclopaedia of rationalistic thought and scientific spirit — the *Risalat Ikhwan al-Safa,* was introduced in Spain through his efforts. His work was carried forward by his several students of whom ibn Samah outshone the rest. Ibn Samah lived at Granada when Muslim Spain had already broken up. He died in 1035. He was a genius in all the branches of mathematic. He wrote books on commercial arithmetics, mental calculus *(hisab al-hawai)*, and the nature of numbers. He was a critical student of Euclid, and the Indian astronomy of the school of Siddhanta. He wrote two books on astrolabe, one in the form of a dialogue on the right use of this instrument. His contemporary Ahmad al-Safar (d. 1034) also wrote on mathematical instruments. In the same century flourished 'Abd ar-Rahman bin Isma'il who was so famous for his knowledge of geometry that he was known as Euclid of Spain.[4] He was also a profound student of the philosophy of Aristotle.

Spain's greatest astronomer and mathematician flourished during the rule of the muluk at-tawa'if. This was Abū Ishaq al-Zarqali (1029-1087) who became famous in Europe as Arzachel. He was a tireless worker, and made 400 experiments to determine the apogee of the sun. Prof. G. Sarton says about him that 'he was the first to prove explicitly the motion of the solar apogee with reference to the stars; according to his measurement it amount to 12.04" per year (the real value being 11.8")'.[5] He was the first to calculate the length of the Mediterranean which according to modern calculations is almost correct.[6] He was a great authority of his time on construction of astrolabe. This was a useful instrument in the Middle Ages, but has now been replaced by the telescope, the sextant, and the theodolite. Astolabe was used in finding the height of stars, the depth of wells, and the distance between two places. Al-Zarqali made a multipurpose astrolabe which he named — *safihah*. He was also an expert in making water clocks. He installed a big water clock at Toledo where he spent most of his life. The waterclock was built on the bank of the Tagus not far from the Gate of Tanners. The whole structure consisted of two basins in which water was released on the night of the crescent moon. Every night and day water flowed into the basins in specific quantities through underground tubes and the level rose with the rising moon. When the moon was full, the basins were also full to the brim. With the waning of the moon, the water level began to fall gradually. After the fail of Toledo the water clock was dismantled by a Jew who wanted to know the secret of its working, but could not repair the damage.[7] Two more scientists need to be mentioned. Abū Ishaq Al-Butruji lived in the second half of the 12th century. He came to be known as Alpetrogius in Europe. He was a pupil of the philosopher ibn Tufail. Al-Butruji believed that the celestial spheres revolve around different axes, and produce a spiral movement which he termed, *'harka lawlabiya'*. Only one book of this scientist has survived — the *Kitab fi l'Haya*. It has been translated into English, and was published at Berkeley in 1952 by M. Scott and Carmody.[8] The other scientist, Jabir ibn Aflah (Gerber filus Affloe of Latin Europe), was critical of Ptolemaic system. He wrote books on spherical and plane trigonometry.[9]

The philosopher ibn Bajja was also a physicist of distinction. He was interested in the motion of bodies. He maintained that the natural motion of a body in a medium should be determined by substracting the accidental retardation caused by the density of the medium, from the essential velocity which the body would have if falling in void. Galileo in his Piscan Dialogue had given the formula: V=P-M, in which 'V" represents the speed or velocity, and 'P', the motive power measured by the specific gravity of the mobile body, and 'M', the resisting medium. Thus, the formula given by the great Italian was known to ibn Bajja long before. This sensational revelation was made in a learned research article by Earnest A. Moody.[10] Ibn Bajja was the last important scientist of Muslim Spain. After him, mathematics and geometry were, no doubt, studied by numerous scholars, but they did not proceed beyond what they gathered from Euclid and Al-Khawarizimi. The passion for poetry, the reverence for Maliki theology, and the awesome hold of Aristotalian metaphysics held the Spanish Muslims in virtual thraldom. Astronomy degenerated into astrology, and mathematics into mysticism. Subsequent scholars attached superstitious value to numerals. They made magic squares, and collected amiable numbers, and wrote on the erotic values of numbers — 240 and 284. There were many good mathematicians in the kingdom of Granada. The 'Taljis' of Al-Bana of Granada, a renowned mathematician is still taught in the university of Fez.[11] A 16th century astronomoer from a Hispano-Muslim family — Muhammad al-Maghribi was a respected authority of his time. He has left a book on eclipses, a manuscript of which is preserved at Leyden.[12]

After the poets and the historians, the physicians formed the largest number of specialists. In fact many philosophers were also famous as physicians — ibn Sina, and Al-Razi in the East, and ibn Zuhr, ibn Tufail, and ibn Rushd in Spain. It would be necessary to know some basic facts about the Arabian system of medicine, before we meet the Spanish physicians. This system which still thrives in many parts of the Muslim world (in India, it is known as the Greek/Unani system) is different from the modern allopathy even through the latter is a child of the former, but parted company when Louis Pasture discovered that diseases are cased by germs which invade the human body through air, water, food and other sources. The Arabian system was based on two concepts — the Theory of Humours, and the Doctrine of Temperaments. According to the first concept, there are four humours *(akhlāt araba'a)* — the blood, phlegm, yellow bile and black bile[13]. The humours reside in different organs of the human body — the blood in liver, the yellow bile in gall bladder, and the black bile in spleen. The phelgm which has no special location is formed by the residue rejected after digestion. The humours are produced by the conversion of food into chyle. The chyle is carried to the liver where it undergoes a second digestion resulting in yellow bile. Black bile, and the blood. The humours are present in a state of natural equilibrium and when this is disturbed, a person falls sick. Every patient has his own temperament *(mizaj)* which is natural to him. He can be either bilious (hot and dry), melancholic (cold and dry), phelgmatic (cold and moist), and sanguine (hot and moist). This concept was borne in mind before a physician began the treatment of a patient. In addition, he kept in view the ancestry of the patient, the seasonal changes, the domestic environment, the food he took, and the water he drank. The famous physician, Abū Marwan ibn Zuhr of Seville (d. 1161) was once asked to cure a patient of dropsy. He insisted on checking the water he drank, and looking into the pitcher, he found a frog at the bottom.[14] The physicians examined also the urine of the patients. As blood contained all the humours, phlebatomy was a popular treatment along with drugs. A clever physician like Abū l-Ala Zuhr administered medicines with the weakest potency *(fi awwal al darajat al-ūla)* and increased gradually depending upon the intensity of affliction.

Like a patient's temperament, drugs were also found to have their own properties, and the physican recommended a medicine which would neutralise the preponderance, or the lack of the particular humour which, according to his diagnosis, was the cause of illness. The physicians obtained their medicines from the three kingdoms, — botanical, the mineral, and the animal. Ibn Juljul of Cordova (a physician of Hisham II) wrote in his *materia medica:* "God has created the means of restoring health to the body of man by disseminating them in the plants which cover the earth, the quadrupeds that move on it, the fishes that swim in water, the birds that fly through the air, and the minerals that lie hidden in the bowels of the earth, and permitting that these should be appropriated to the cure of diseases as a proof of His extreme mercy and kindness".[15] Some physicians treated their patients with some medicines of miraculous potency (called *nawādir*) which perhaps were known only to them.

The Eastern system of medicine outlined above reached Spain. It may not be incorrect to say that the early physicians of Spain were either the Jews or foreigners from the East who settled in Spain. We know the names of several physicians who arrived in Spain in the reign of 'Abd ar-Rahman II. Regular studies in medicine must have begun during the reign of 'Abd ar-rahman III, if not earlier. His most famous physician was the Jew Hasdal ibn Shaprut we met in an earlier chapter. An important event of his reign was the translation of the Materia Medica of Dioscurides. This book was already known in the East, and a translation had reached Spain along with other medical literature. Sometime in 948, the Byzantine emperor sent an illustrated copy of the work of Dioscurides as a gift. The work was rendered into Arabic by a board of scholars, — the monk Nicholas, Hasdai ibn Shaprut, Muhammad the botanist, and a Sicilian named Abū Abdullah who knew Greek. A physician brought Abū Jazzar's *Zad al-Musafir* (Provision of the Traveller), a great work on therapautics which fostered interest in the medical science. From the 10th century onwards, several important books were written by the Spanish physicians. 'Arib ibn s'ad, the author of the Calendar of Cordova was an outstanding authority on gynaecology, hygiene of pregnant women, and the care of the infants. On obstetrics he has left a book entitled '*Khalq al-Janin* (creation of Embryo), a copy of which is preserved in the Escurial.[16] Another notable physician, Ishaq ibn Haitham was an authority on poisons and laxatives.[17]

The golden age of Hispano-Muslim medicine began in the 10th century, and lasted for some three centuries. Spain's famous medical men whose writings revolutionised the science of medicine in medieval Europe, flourished in this period. The 10th and the 11th centuries were dominated by a host of physicians. Among them were Muhammad bin 'Abdun, 'Abul Qasim Zahravi (936-1010), ibn Wafid (998-1074), the members of Banu Zuihr family are the most illustrous names. Zahravi (known in Latin Europe as *Abulcasis*) was the author of a medical encyclopaedia, — the famous *Kitab at-Tasrif*. The book comprises thirty sections giving an exhaustive account of each disease, its symptoms, cures, and instructions regarding diet for patients. The methods of preparing drugs by distillation and sublimation etc are also given in this book. The author deals with surgery in a separate chapter, dually illustrated with drawings of some surgical instruments — scalpels, scrapers, forceps, hooks etc. He describes some of the operations he could perform, and discusses the quality of threads required for stitching incisions and wounds. Zahravi wrote on cauterization, stypics, obstetrics, lithotomy, surgical treatment of the diseases of eyes, ears and teeth. He was also expert in crushing stones in the bladder. Muhammad ibn 'Abdun, was one of the physicians who attended Hisham II. He left for the East in 938, visited Basra, and saw the working of the hospitals in Cairo. He returned home in 981, and entered into the service of Hakam II. He had numerous students many of them rose to fame after him. Ibn Juljul was one of his pupils. Ibn Wafid (998-1074), the minister of Dhunnun of Toledo, and a student of Zahravi was a scholar of the works of Aristotle and Galen. After twenty years of study and experiements, he wrote a book (*Kitab fi-l-adwiya*) in which he gave properties, and reactions, of medicines. He came to be known in Europe as Abenguefit. His book was translated into Latin by Gerar of Cremona — there are also translations in Hebrew and Catalan, and a part of the original Arabic is stated to be extant. Inspite of his vast knowledge, he came to realise the importance of nature-cure. He relied on the minimum use of medicines, and prescribed simple remedies, avoiding compound drugs as far as possible. In ordinary ailments, he cured his patients by a judicious regulation of diet.[18] Yet another physician was Muhammad Al-Tamimi who lived in the 11th century. His treatise on diagnosis is available in the Escurial.[19]

The Banu Zuhr was one of the most remarkable families of Muslim Spain. The members of this family spanned two centuries, from the middle of the 11th century to the first decade of the 13th. This family came from Arabia and settled at Jativa in the 10th century. The first member of the Banu Zuhr to come into prominence was Abū Marwan who studied medicine at Cairo and Baghdad, and after his return to Spain, settled at Denia, and died there in 1078. He was a household name during his time as he was more of practitioner than an author. He was known for his unorthodox views, particularly his opposition to hot baths which according to him, upset the humours. His son Abū l-'Ala Zuhr outshone him. He started his education in hadith at the grand mosque of Cordova, but switched on to literature. He was so much charmed by the 'maqamat' that he corresponded with the celebrated al-Hariri of Basra, Ultimately, medicine claimed him, and he made a name in the profession both as a practitioner and also as an author. He died at Cordova in 1130 of gastric ulcer, and his bodied was carried to Seville for burial. Henceforth, all members of this family were natives of Seville. Abu l-Ala Zuhr was very skillful in his diagnosis. He felt the pulse, examined the unrine of the patient, and prescribed treatment without questioning the patient. He wrote several books, but it seems that none of these has survived. He was very famous in medieval Latin world and was known by several Latinized names viz. Aboali, Abuleli, Ebilule, Abulelizor, and Albuleizor. The second leading light of the Banu Zuhr family was Abū Marwan 'Abd al-Malik, the son of Abu l-'Ala zuhr. He too was born at Seville in 1092, and died there in 1161. He was initiated into medical studies by his father after a through education in literature and law. He acquired extraordinary skill in therapeutics and performed wonderful cures. His fame attracted the notice of the Almohad ruler Yaqūb al-Mansur who took him as his personal physician. Ibn Usabia, the historian of Arabian medicine has recorded some anecdotes which give a lively glimpse of this great physician. One anecdoate has already been mentioned. The other is equally interesting. Ibn Usabia has narrated that once the Almohad ruler needed a purgative, but he would not take any drug. Ibn Zuhr plucked some fresh grapes from a vine which had already been fed with water mixed with a strong purgative. Ibn Zuhr presented the grapes to the royal patient who was relived of his pain after taking ten grapes.[20] Marwan was not very fond of figs. One day he predicted that his colleague al-Fār would die of convulsions because he ate too many figs, the other predicted that he (Zuhr) would die of an abscess because he did not eat enough figs. Both the predictions came true.[21] Out of half a dozen books attributed to Abū Marwan by the historian ibn Usabia, some have survived. Two of these were taught as text books: *Taysir fi'l-muddawt wa'l-tadbir* (Manuel of Treatments and Cures), and the Book of Foods. He was an authority on purgatives, diseases of the kidney, and leprosy. Some of the special features which distinguished his Taysir (it was translated into Latin by Paravicus at Venice in 1280) are his descriptions of mediastinal tumours, pericardial abscesses, intestinal erosions, paralysis of the pharynx, and inflammation in the ears. He has discussed artificial feeding thorugh rectum. His description of the itch-mite has made him a pioneer in the field of parasitology. A pious physician, he believed that relief from illness comes only if God wills it. His grandson Abū Bakr (1110-1198) was an erudite scholar of many disciplies. He learnt the Quran by heart, studied Arabic literature, hadith, and the teachings of Imam Malik, and composed beautiful muwashshat. He wrote an opthalmology, but the treatise has been lost. The Almohad ruler took him in his service, but a certain minister who was jealous of his learning and influence, had him poisoned. His son Abū Muhammad bin Zuhr was educated by him. Like his father, he too was poisoned at Sale in 1205. This budding physician was the last of the Banu Zuhr family. Several ladies of this family were experienced gynecologists.

Some philosophers of the 12th century were also famous physicians. The Jew ibn Maymun (Maimonides) was a Cordovan by birth. Born in 1136, he left Spain, and entered into the service of sultan Salahuddin. He is known for his 'Aphorism'. a great work in the science of medicine. Ibn Rushd is the author of a work which is one of the milestones in medical history, — the *Kulliyat fi tib*. The Kulliyat of ibn Rushd deals with all aspects of medical science — anatomy, physiology, materia medica, diagnosis, therapeutics, and hygiene. He described the function of the retina, and asserted that no one can be afflicted twice by small-pox.[22] Ibn Rushd's friend, the philosopher ibn Tufail was also a renowned physician of his time, but he seems to have left no book on the subject.

There were many physicians in the kingdom of Granada, but none of the stature of ibn Khatib and ibn Khatima. Ibn Khatib wrote a treatise on plague in which he asserted that the dreaded disease spread by contagion. The existence of contagion (he said) is proved by experience and observation, and other trustworthy sources such as use of utensils of persons suffering from the disease. The seaports where persons arrive form distant lands are also carriers of plague[23]. A similar observation was also made by ibn Khatima when plague broke out in Almeria in 1348. Ibn Khatima's work in the original Arabic is preserved in the Escurial. The findings of ibn Khatib and ibn Khatima have drawn words of praise for their boldness and originality from historians of medieval science.

Closely allied to the science of medicine is pharmacology, which in turn is related to botany. The numerous books produced on these two subjects were based on research and personal observations involving long travels both inside and outside of Spain. The most outstanding specialists in these fields were, ibn Bajja, ibn Baitar, ibn Bassal, Abū l-Khayr, and ibn al-Awwam. The versatile ibn Bajja was deeply interested in botany. A small treatise on the subject was brought to light by the Spanish scholar Miguel Asin. In this book, ibn Bajja classified plants on the basis of their habitat, anatomy and physiology. He divided the plants into several groups — plants having roots, and without roots, independent plants, parasites, terrestrial, aquatic, marshy, plants from hot and temperate climates, seasonal plants, perennials, plants with leaves and without leaves, nutritive plants, and medicinal plants, and harmful plants. He seems to have knowledge of sexual reproduction of plants specially the palm and the fig trees[24]. Medieval Spain's greatest pharmacist-cum-botanist was ibn Baitar (d. 1248) of Malaga. He was initiated into botanical studies by the famous herbalist of Seville — Abū l-Abbas al-Nabatati with whom he collected plants and herbs in the suburbs of Seville. He left Spain on a study tour when he was twenty years of age, travelled all over north Africa, Asia Minor and Greece. While he was in Egypt he was appointed chief botanist to the government. He left Cairo for Damascus to continue his research, and died there while experimenting with a poisonous herb. Ibn Baitar has left two monumental works in the filed of botany and pharmacology: the *Jami al-Mufradat*, and the *kitab al-Mughni*. The first book, fruit of his arduous research, is a descriptive encyclopaedia of 1400 plants, and the second is a *materia medica* arranged according to the organs of the body. Ibn Usabiya, the author of biographies of great physicians — the Tabaqāt al-Atiba, was his student and disciple. Prof. Browne thinks that Ibn Baitar was a worthy successor of Dioscorides.

The earliest book on agronomy was written by the great physician-surgeon Abū l-Qasim Zahravi. A compendium on the subject entitled *'Mukhtasar kitab al filaha'* was discovered not long ago by the French orientalist, H. Piérès. The science of horticulture had its greatest fruitation between the 12th and the 13th centuries. Seville, Toledo, Granada and Cordova were the centres of these studies. Besides ibn Wafid already mentioned, there were several others in the fields of botany and horticulture. One of greatest botanists of the time — Ibrahim ibn Bassal was in the service of Al-Ma'mun of Toledo. After long and repeated travels to distant lands, he returned to Spain via Sicily, and wrote his book — *diwan al-filaha*, for his patron. Its abridged form was rendered in old Spanish and was reprinted in 1955. Prof. Colin regards the work of ibn Bassal, the most objective and original of all Hispano-Arabic specialists. Before the fall of Toledo, ibn Bassal, left for Seville, and died in 1105. At Seville, he must have met Muhammad bin Hajjaj, and ibn al-Awwam, and perhaps even ibn Tighnari, because Seville at the time was the rendezvous of famous botanists. In an important work — the *kitab al-filah*, Abū khayr of Seville wrote on many aspects of agriculture — the influence of the moon on the crops, a calendar of the growth of trees - the olive trees, the fig trees, and the vines; growing of vegetables, aromatic plants; cash crops like flax, cotton and sugar-cane; layering, pruning, grafting; animals which destroy crops such as rodents and reptiles; and conservation of fruits.[25] Equally important is Zakariyya ibn 'Awwam of Seville, a master in the fields of agriculture, agronomy and veterniary. The Book of Agriculture *(Kitab al-fillaha)* is a painstaking compilation from the work of his predecessors (the Greeks as well as the Arabs), and supplemented by his own experience. The work is divided in 35 chapters, and covers all the aspects in a systematic manner[26]. He discusses the nature of soil, the selection of seeds, the methods of irrigation, the use of fertilizers. There are chapters on cultivation of rice, wheat, sugar-cane, date-palm, citrus fruits, figs, peaches, bananas, and dozens of vegetables. There are also chapters on olives, cotton, flax, and spices, fruit preservation, distillation of syrups, and rose-water, and growing flowers and fruits out of season and fruits of different tastes and colours from a single plant by grafting. A chapter gives the method of imprinting floral designs on apples. Full attention has been given to storage of cereals, and protection of plants from pests. The last chapters of the book deal with poultry farming, honeybees, domestic birds, and some animals particularly the horse. A horse of good breed was the cadillac of the Spanish Muslims. Most people travelled on donkeys, but for the rich a horse with a fancy saddle was a must for short visits. A Spanish gentleman was expected to be an expert equestrian. Ibn al-Awwam could, not, therefore, ignore the diseases of the horse. He deals with the subject in detail, prescribes remedies for every disease, and even describes surgical operations.

Botany and agronomy were deligently studied in the kingdom of Granada. This was necessary for the continuous agricultural prosperity of the kingdom, and the proper maintenance of the innumerable gardens and orchards that brocaded this small Paradise of Spain. In the 14th century, the most famous botanists were Abū Usman of Almeria, and ibn Luyun (d. 1349). We shall speak about the latter when writing about the gardens of Muslim Spain.

Notes

1. Sidgwick & Tyler: p. 165.
2. Ibn Sa'id of Toledo: Tabaqat al-umam, pp. 111-113. He has quoted a poem of ibn Rabbihi, in which the poet mocked at the views of Abū Obaida.
3. G. Sarton: p. 668.
4. Ibn Sa'id: p. 117, also Palencia: Literatura Arábigo-Espanola, p. 84.
5. G. Sarton: p. 758.
6. Kimble: p. 63.
7. Al-Maqqari/Gayangos: Vol. I, pp. 81-82.
8. Ency. of Islam (New Ed.) article on Al-Butruji.
9. Palencia: Historia Literature Arábigo-Espanola: pp. 285-286.
10. The article, 'Galileo and Avempace', published in 'Roots of Scientific Thought', edited by P.P. Wiener and Aaron Noland, New York, 1957.

11. Palencia: Literatura Arábigo-Espanola, pp. 282-287, give an excellent summary of famous mathematicians and scientists.

12. Ibid.

13. Browne: Arabian Medicine, pp. 119-122.

14 Maqqari/Gayangos: Vol. II, Appx: A (part V). This appendix contains extracts from Abi 'Usabiya's 'Lives of Physicians' relating to the famous physicians of Spain.

15. Ibid.

16. Palencia : Literatura Arábigo-Espanola, pp. 289-290.

17. 'Ibid.

18. Ibn Sa'id. Tabaqqat, p. 139.

19. Palencia: Literatura Arábigo-Espanola, pp. 290-291.

20. Al-Maqqari/Gayangos: vol. II, Appendix A(I).

21. Ibid.

22. Hitti: Makers of Arab History, p. 228.

23. Arnold & Guillaume: Legacy of Islam, p. 340 - 341.

24. The Islamic Culture (Hyderabad), July 1942, pp. 373-374.

25. Ency. of Islam (N. Ed.), article on 'Abū Khayr' by H. Pérès, who examined the book which is still in the manuscript form.

26. Ibn al-'Awwam' Kitab al-filah. (Urdu trans. in two volumes by Syed Muhammad Hashim, Azamgarh, 1927. It was translated into French by M Mullet is 1867.

Chapter 24

Philosophy and Sufism

Yaqūb Al-Kindi was probably the first philosopher to write in Arabic. He praised philosophy as the noblest of all human activity! In his *'Risala fi al-flasafah'*, he defined philosophy as the 'knowledge of the reality of things'.[1] Al-Kindi lived in the first half of the 9th century, but in Spain philosophy had a rather late beginning. The scholars of the early Umayyad rule were absorbed more in theology, poetry and mathematics. When 'Abd ar-Rahman II built a cultural bridge between Spain and the Muslim East, scholars brought new books and new ideas. By slow degrees philosophy found a number of devotees. The liberal regimes of 'Abd ar-Rahman III, and Hakam II were congenial to philosophical studies. A further stimulus was given by scholars like Maslama of Madrid, and Al-Kirmani of Cordova who imported the Epistles of the Brothers of Purity *(Risalāt Ikhwan al-safa)*, a society of Basra dedicated to promotion of science and philosophy.[2] Although the authors of these essays were not irreligious, they made bold assertions which could be conducive to free thought. In nearly 52 essays they discussed every aspect of philosophy-epistemology, metaphysics, psychology, politics, ethics, and theology. We distinctly observe the dawn of philosophy in Spain in the early decades of the

10th century. This is clear from the *Tabaqāt al-Umam* of ibn Sa'id of Toledo. One of the earliest of thinkers was Abū Usman bin Fathun of Saragossa. He wrote an introductory treatise entitled 'The Tree of Knowledge *(Shajarāt al-hikam)* during the time of al-Mansur. The author was imprisoned, and on his release, he sought asylum in Sicily.

Two brilliant stars shone at Cordova in the firmament of philosphy - ibn Massara and ibn Hazm. Both belonged to families of Iberian origin whose forefathers converted to Islam in the early days of the Muslim rule. Ibn Massara was born during the reign of Muhammad I. His father was a virtuous man who followed Mutazilism, a school of Islamic theology with rational leanings. He injected these doctrines in the mind of his son. The Mutazilites while believing in one Eternal God held many views which were rather offensive to the orthodox Maliki theologians. Their basic idea was that theology should be subjected to rational enquiry. They believed that the Quran did not pre-exist, but was revealed in time. The miracle of the Quran was not its diction, but in its unparalleled message. God, they said, was so transcendental that whatever we say about Him limits him. Therefore, we should not say what He is, but what He is not. We should not attribute any qualities to Him such as Omnipotence, Beauty, Will etc. The Heaven and Hell do not exist at present, but would be created by God on the Last Day of Accountability. They did not believe in physical ascension of the Prophet to Heaven; they rejected all miracles, repudiated all saints, and scoffed at mysticism. Most of these ideas had their origin in the philosphy preached by the Ikhwān al-safa. Out of this Mutazili philosophy-cum-theology, grew the Muslims' interest in philosophy. In fact Mutazili thought was itself a child of liaison between Islamic teachings and Greek/ neo-Platonic philosophy. Ibn Masarra was already in love with speculative theology when his father died. He left Spain for the East when it was noised about that he had Mutazili leanings. He returned during the reign of 'Abd ar-Rahman III, and retired among the mountains of Sierra Morena with a small group of his disciples who were taught in an esoteric, double-meaning langauge like the Ismaili/batini teachers. Ascetic life, prayer, and fasting ruined his health, and he died in 931 A.D. honoured for his piety, if not for his doctrines. Ibn Masarra's books have been lost, but a gifted Arabist of Spain-Asian Palacios has tried to reconstruct his philosophy from other sources.[3] In a nutshell, his philosophy was a mixture of Islamic teachings, neo-Platonic doctrines, and perhaps some teachings of Empedocles. The human body is composed of two opposite elements, the body and the soul. The flesh is the inheritor of all hatreds and discords, while the soul is a purely ethereal element, and part of the Universal Soul. The human body is the prison of the soul from which it can obtain its freedom only by a life of prayer, voluntary poverty, and silent meditation. We hear Plotinus of Alexandria speaking through ibn Masarra of Cordova. The study of philosophy is an aid to freedom of the soul, as it illuminates the mind, and the soul from the contaminating influence of the body.

Encyclopaedic as a scholar and prolific as a writer, ibn-Hazm is one of the intellectual giants of Spain. The Spanish government has installed his statue at Cordova (and also that of another famous Muslim Cordovan — ibn Rushd) to honour this great thinker and writer of elegant prose. He belonged to an aristocratic family known for their wealth, political influence, and perhaps beauty also. His father was a minister of Al-Mansur and his son. Ibn Hazm grew up in an atmosphere of learning and refined luxury. He received a good education from several learned teachers. His earliest teachers were women who taught him the Quran, poetry and calligraphy. In his youth, he was placed under several teachers of hadith, law, literature, philology and philosophy. His family fell on evil days after the fall of the Bani 'Amir family. His father was dismissed, and he died an unhappy man in June 1012. When the Berbers broke into violence, and sacked Cordova, his father's palatial house was reduced to ashes. The Hazm family was persecuted, and the young scholar was forced to take refuge in Almeria in July 1013. Ibn Hazm hoped that the restoration of the Umayyads would unite Muslim Spain. When 'Abd ar-Rahman IV was entrhoned, he returned to Cordova and served as his minister. In 1922 he had to leave Cordova once again. He was in Jativa when a letter reached him from a friend asking him to write a book on love. He complied with his request and wrote his famous Tawq al-Hamma during the sad days of his exile. Ibn Hazm returned to Cordova and served 'Abd ar-Rahman V, but when the latter was assassinated, he lost all hope of a united Umayyad state. He returned to his ancestral estate at Huelva, and died a lonely man in 1064. Although ibn Hazm lived in the most tragic times, still he was able to write many books. If we are to believe his son Abū Rafi, ibn Hazm left 400 books running into 80 thousand leaves, but the extent works of the author can be counted on fingers. His printed works are *Tawq al-Hamama* on love, the *Jamharāt ansāb al'arab* on genealogy of the Arab families, the *Kitāb al-Ihkam fi usūl al-ahkām* on jurisprudence, the *Kitāb al-Milal wa l-Nihal* on Islamic sects and comparative religion, and the *Kitāb al-Akhtaq*. The last book shows the many facets of the character of a highly sensitive soul. Ibn Hazm was a fine critic as shown by his *Risala fi fadail ahl al-Andalus* in which he tried to establish the superiority of the Spanish men of letters. This epistle, slightly chauvinistic, has been quoted at length by al-Maqqari, and has been printed by Prof. García Goméz of Madrid University under the title - Elogio del Islam Espanol.

Ibn Hazm was a queer mixture of rationalism and extreme orthodoxy. He rejected mythological legends such as the one according to which the earth rested on the back of a fish, the fish on the horn of a cow, the cow on a stone, and the stone on the shoulders of an angel[4]. He believed that the earth was spherical (like the authors of the Ikhwan al-safa) and quotes a verse from the Quran in support of his view.[5] Ibn Hazm did not build any school of philosophy, but he was a thinker in his own way. Dr. Omar Farrukh the noted Arab scholar says about him that, 'the problem of, of time, and space which confronted Kant (d. 1804) so often in his Critique of Pure Reason, had busied ibn Hazm in the same way. It is astonishing that the Muslim theologian had tackled this problem in the same spirit of objectivity seven and a half centuries before the German philsopher.' Proceeding further, the learned doctor adds 'ibn Hazm does not agree with Heraclitus that the world is in constant flow, nor with the Eleatics that motion is non-exestent. In keeping with the general trend of his thoughts he affirms that space and time are limited, and they are like all other things, created by God. In the same way, he maintained that atoms are divisible, but it is in the power of God to do everything, and to this power of His, infinite divisibility of an atom is no exception'[6]. But he would not give reason a free hand. Reason and logic, he maintained were unable to pronounce value judgements. Reason has its limitations. It is here that religion helps man.

In his theology and jurisdical thinking, ibn Hazm differed from all the current schools of law, particularly the Hanifi fiqh. He could hardly visualise that this school of fiqh would, one day, be the most dominant among the Muslims of the world. Ibn Hazm rejected some sources of jurisprudence such as intuition, *(ilham)*, interpretation *(tawil)*, hearsay *(khabar)*. He was the chief exponent of the Zahiri school of theology. This school had its origin in the East, and it was founded by Dawud ibn Ali (b. 817) as a reaction against allegorical interpretation of the Quran. The Zahiris insisted on outer meaning of the Divine Word, and rejected analogy *(qiyas)*. But ibn Hazm was liberal enough to support *ijma* based on the consensus of the companions of the Prophet. Ibn Hazm defended the legal rights of women laid down in the Quran. He had liberal views about zakat tax, and advocated that cereals (other than wheat and barley), fruits and vegetables, and plants used for textiles, should be exempted form the tax.[7] His interest in theology led him to the study of religions. His *Kitab al-Milal Wa l-Nahal* deals with various schools of philosophy, religions and some Muslim sects. In his criticism of the New Testament he 'pointed out difficulties in the biblical narratives which disturbed no other mind till the rise of higher criticism in the 16th century'.[8] He denied Trinity, and considered the divinity of Christ as untenable. He revered him as one of the Prophets of God, and had firm faith in his miraculous birth. He made fun of the Mutazilis who by denying God's attributes reduced His power to that of bugs, fleas and worms. Ibn Hazm wrote like a pleader arguing in a court of law, and did not hesitate in making digs at his opponents. After sifting the teachings of all religions and philosophers (even atheism) this great Muslim of Gothic/Roman parentage came to the conclusion that Islam is God's true guidance for man, the Quran the word of God, and the Prophet the best model for character building.

Ibn Hazm's Ring of the Dove (Tawq al-Hamama), like Plato's Symposium deals with love. In his portrayal of the psychology of love, and the picturesque details. Ibn Hazm's book is superior to the dialogue of the great Athenian. He gives a philsophical definition of love. Love is an inspired passion for unity between parts of the soul which separated in the physical world. Based on personal observations, ibn Hazm has woven a pattern of courtly and chivalrous love tinged with mysticism, in gorgeous prose strewn with short poems of his own. His *Kitāb al akhlaq*, ranks him with the Roman Seneca and the English essayist Francis Bacon[9]. He was also a philosopher of aesthetics. Once he was asked to define beauty. He gave his reply in his *Kitab al-akhlaq*. He classified beauty into different elements — comeliness *(shabaha)*, sweetness *(halawa)* symmetry *(qawam)*, etc., but about beauty itself i.e. *husn*, he frankly admitted that it was something which could not be translated in words, but only felt by the person who sees it.[10] Perhaps, he was right. Can we define beauty in absolute terms?

The summer of Hispano-Muslim philosophy was heralded by Abū Bakr Muhammad of Saragossa known as ibn Bajja. He was born at an unknown date towards the end of 11th century, and died at Fez in May 1139. Not much is known about his early life, his education, and other biographical details. He had several political appointments, but the restless man did not stick to any. Misfortune dogged him all his life after he left Saragossa when in 1118, the city was captured by the Christians. He left for the southern cities (Seville, Jativa, Granada) to seek his fortune. He moved from city to city as a wandering bureaucrat. Ultimately, he settled at Fez where he was poisoned to death allegedly at the instigation of Abū l-'Ala ibn Zuhr. Ibn Bajja had many enemies on account of his philosophical ideas which he expressed freely. He alienated people by his witty remarks couched in biting sarcasm. The famous anthologist ibn Khaqan was offended by his remarks at a gathering *(majlis)* of literary men. Ibn Khaqan was boasting of the many gifts he had received from his patrons. Just then, ibn Bajja saw a green drop dripping from his nose. Ibn Bajja remarked, 'and this precious green pearl is also one of the gifts you have received'[11]. Ibn Khaqan took his revenge, and quoting from his books out of context, he condemned him as a heretic in his anthology. Whatever his faults, there is no doubt that ibn Bajja was a man of versatile talents. He was a musicologist, a master lute player, a physicist, a botanist and a philosopher. He was not a writer of many books. The credit for preserving some of his books goes to ibn al-Imam, his most devoted disciple. About half a dozen of his books have survived, some in the original Arabic, and others in Hebrew translations. His well-known books are — The Treatise on the Unity of the Intellect with Man *(Risala ittisal al-'aql'b il Insan)*, the Farewell Letter *(Risalat al Wada')*, The Rule of the Solitary *(Tadbir al-Mutawāhhid)*, and the Book of Soul *(Kitab al Nafs)*. All these books have been printed in recent times.

Ibn Bajja had a tormented soul. He saw political chaos round him, and his own life was always in danger. He found solace in philosophy and music. The crucial question before him was as to how a philosopher should conduct himself in a hostile environment? The ideal state *(al madina al faḍila)* of a Plato or a Farabi was no where to be seen. The existing states were neither in the hands of the philosopher-kings of Plato nor the patriarchal caliphs of the first century of Muslim history. The philosopher was helpless as he could neither mend nor end the existing order. What should he do? The philosopher's most precious thing is his soul which is an emanation from the Active Intellect (the impersonal cosmic mind) and must return to it. The soul must be kept pure from the contaminating influence of matter if it has to reach its goal. This could be achieved either by mystic ecstasy or through an intellectual journey on the wings of philosophy. Ibn Bajja chose the latter. The philosopher should, therefore, turn into a *mutawāhhid* — a lover of solitude. He should give adieu to the world of matter, and return to his own realm of spiritual forms *(suwār ruhāniyya)* and rise higher and higher till he achieves union with the Active Intellect — the final destiny of his existence. Unlike Plato and Farabi who think of the masses, ibn Bajja leaves them behind, and concentrates only on the spiritual destiny of the philosopher, through escapist meditation. The social and political organisations of man, the tussel of economic activity have little meaning for him. His philosophy is obviously the testament of despair of a metaphysician who was tired of life. One wonders why he did not commit suicide. But he had fine views on ethics. He pondered on the eternal question of good *(khair)* and evil *(shr)*. He found evil a part of Divine Scheme *(tarteeb illahi)*. Both good and evil come from God, Without evil, there can be no good, but man has been granted the freedom of choice. Actions which are motivated by pure righteousness, and love of truth are divine actions. The persons who perform such deeds are the Friends of God *(auliya allah)* — men like Uwais al-Qarni, and Ibrahim ibn Adham.[12]

The concept of the retired sage *(mutawahhid)* was taken up by ibn Tufail (1110-1185) of Gaudix (Wadi Ash) a beautiful town near Granada. Although a physician by profession, he was dwarfed by the philosopher in him. He entered into the service of the Almohad governor, and slowly rose to the status of a court physician of sultan Abū Yaqūb Yusuf. The sultan liked him for his learning. Ibn Tufail was in fact his intellectual preceptor, and both of them discussed philosophy. When the sultan died, his son kept him in his service. Ibn Tufail is famous for his philosophical novel — *Hayy ibn Yaqzan* which in English

may be translated— 'Alive, son of the Wakeful'. The title of
the book is rather unalluring, but it is a pleasure to read it. The
plot of the story narrated below will give the reader a better
peep into the author's mind than a lengthy exposition of his
philosophy which (stated briefly) was an amalgam of current
neo-Platonic thought, sufism and Islamic beliefs.

Ibn Tufail takes his reader to an island in the Indian ocean.
It was a lonely place, and no one lived here. All of a sudden
an infant appears on the island without parents. The author has
given two possible versions about the birth of the child.
According to one version, it was born to a princess as a result
of a secret alliance with a man against the wishes of her father.
To hide her shame, she put the infant in a sealed ark, and left
it on the sea. The ark floated and drifted into the island. He
gives another version in which he discusses the possibility of
spontaneous birth of the baby. A mass of clay with an exact
proportion of the substances which make the human body,
fermented by chance. It developed into a cone-shaped object in
which a human embrayo grew slowly with protective membrance
as in the uterus. When it was ripe, the clay broke up and the
baby was born. A gazelle saw the crying baby and fed it with
her milk. The child began to grow under her motherly care. It
played with the gazelle, the birds and friendly animals. He had
no feathers, no protective skin, no claws and no horns for self-
defence. When he grew up, Hayy (the name of the child given
by the author) covered bis body with leaves, held at his waist
by twisted twigs and grass. He shaped a pointed stick to fight
animals. Soon after he was seven, the gazelle died. The
inquisitive boy wanted to know the cause of her death. He
ripped her body, but got no answer. He did not know what to
do with her body. He saw a crow being buried by another.
Hayy learnt that burial was a way to dispose of a dead body.

Hayy was now growing fast. Not long after, this adolescent Prometheus discovered how to make fire. The new discovery brought many changes in his life. He retired to a cave, and installed a gate at its entrance. He made threads from animals' hair, and dress and shoes from their skins. He made a number of crude instruments for cutting and breaking objects. He made a saddle, and became an expert hunter. He began to dissect animals, and discovered that there was a vital force inside the body. He learnt that the eyes helped him to see, the ears to hear, the tongue to taste, the nose to smell, and the skin to feel. The internal organs also performed certains functions. The liver digested the food, the nerves carried messages from the brain to all parts of the body. He opened the heart of an animal, and found that it was the chief organ of the body because when it stopped, the body ceased to function. He was now already twenty-one. He gained all knowledge of the physical world by sense perception, and empirical observation. He was already a budding naturalist. From now onwards, he delved into the world of philosophical thought. He perceived an underlying unity in all living things. He found order and beauty in created things. Pondering over the matter further, he came to the conclusion that there was a Supreme Being who created the world. But how did the Supreme Being come into existence? Did it emerge out of nothing? Did it exist from eternity? Was the world created in time? On further thought he found that the Supreme Being could not be perceived by the senses, because these could comprehend only objects which existed in time and space. In the middle of his thirties, Hayy the natural scientist turned into a monotheist. He began to look within, and in the next fourteen years he discovered that he carried within his body an inner spirit. This ethereal element was his soul which was the most precious part of his life. The soul endowed him with powers of intuition. At the age of 42 Hayy emerged from the *cul de sac* of sense perception into the world of mystic intuition and ecstacy because only in this way he could be near the Supreme being. For hours he would sit with his head bent, and his eyes closed in a state of deep meditation. Enraptured by the bliss of his new experience, he saw "what the eyes had never seen, the ears never heard, and the heart never imagined."

Ibn Tufail has devoted nearly the whole book to the saga of Hayy's intellectual and spiritual development. At the end of the book he introduces two more characters and the novels reaches its climax. Not far away, there was another island inhabited by human beings, and ruled by a king named Salman. The people of this island were the followers of a religion introduced long ago by a certain prophet. The teachings of this religion took a comprehensive view of all the activities of man- his secular demands and spiritual needs. Salman had a friend named Absal who was an equally devout follower of the religion, but he interpreted its teachings philosophically. He was a leader of intellectual elite of the island. As for Salman, he was a traditionalist of firm convictions, and would not entertain any arguments on religious matters. Absal was in search of a place where he could recluse in solitude — like ibn Bajja's *mutawāhhid*. He heard about the neighbouring island, and hiring a boat, he reached there. He was enchanted by the sylvan surroundings, and found the island an ideal place for contemplation. In the course of his wanderings, he met Hayy. Hayy had never seen a human being before, and his first reaction was to run away from Absal. By degrees they came closer. Absal taught him his language, and the two became friends. Hayy enfolded the story of his life from his miraculous birth to mystic consciousness. Absal was surprised to find that Hayy had reached the highest truth without any guidance, and that

Hayy's ideas were in consonance with the philosophy underlying the traditional religion professed by the people of his native island. He placed before Hayy, the fundamentals of his religion — the divine origin of the world, the prescribed prayers, fasting, the rewards and punishments in the afterlife, and the many rules for regulating the life of the people. Hayy recognised the wisdom of the religion followed by the people of the other island. He was anxious to visit the island, and to share with them his own mystical philosophy. Absal warned him that his people disliked philosophical debates, but Hayy insisted, and the two left for the other island. Hayy was given a warm welcome, but soon after, he realised that he had incurred the displeasure of the people after he propounded his mystical experiences. Hayy saw his mistake, and decided to leave the island. Before he left, he advised the people to strictly follow their way of life as it was based on Divine Wisdom.

It would now be clear that ibn Tufail's aim in writing this philosophical allegory was to demonstrate that reason and revelation, theology and philosophy are aspects of the same truth. Hayy ibn Yaqzan received enthusiastic reception in Europe. It was translated in Hebrew by Moses Joshua of Narbonne in 1347. An Englishman — E. Pocock rendered it in Latin at Oxford in 1671 under the title 'Philosophus Autodidactus'. It has been translated in English, Dutch, German, French, Italian, Spanish, and Urdu. It has been a favourite book of the Quakers. European scholars have discussed the probable impact of Hayy ibn Yaqzan on Defoe's Robinson Crusoe, and Gracian's Criticon. A.R. Paster in his work — The Idea of Robinson Crusoe (Watford, 1930) discussed the subject, but this theory has not found acceptance. Ibn Tufail died at Marrakesh leaving his book Hayy ibn Yaqzan, and his friend ibn Rushd. Who was this friend?

One day the Italian poet Petrarch (1304-1349), the colourful lover of Laura who was celebrated by him in his many sonnets, was sitting in his study, when a young enthusiastic student of philosophy dropped in for a tête-a-tête. During the course of discussion his friend dropped some unpalatable remarks about St. Paul. When Petrarch protested, his friend chuckled and said, 'You remain a Christian. As for me, I have no faith in old wives' tales. Your Paul and Augustine are idle-talkers. How I wish you had read Averroes and seen for yourself how superior he is to both of them'. The two friends nearly came to blows.[13]

Now, Averroes is the Latinized name by which qaḍi ibn Rushd of Cordova was known in Europe in the Middle ages. Contemporary with ibn Tufail, Abū l-Walid Muhammad ibn Rushd, was born at Cordova in 1126 in a renowned family of scholars and jurists. His father and grandfather were eminent judges of their time. He started his studies in Quranic disciplines, hadith and law. He knew imam Malik's *Muwatta* by heart. His commentary on Aristotle's Poetics, despite its flaws, is a testimony to his wide readings in literature. He enriched his knowledge by reading books on physics, biology, medicine, and philosophy. All through his life he was a book-worm; he read late hours in the night. Only on two nights he, regretfully, missed his tryst with books — the nuptial night, and the night his mother died. His vast learning did not remain hidden. He was summoned to Morroco to advise 'Abd al-Mumin, the founder of the Almohad dynasty, on educational matters. During his stay at Marakesh, he came into contact with ibn Tufail who saw in the bright youngman of twentyseven, the promise of a great thinker. Later, ibn Tufail introduced him to sultan Abū Yaqūb who succeeded 'Abd al-Mumin. Inspite of his orthodoxy, sultan Yaqūb was interested in philosophical discussions. Ibn Rushd has narrated the account of his first meeting with sultan

Yaqūb in these words: "When I was presented to the Amir, Commander of the faithfuls, I found him alone with ibn Tufail. The Amir turned to me and asked questions about any father and ancestors. Then, he asked me what the philosophers said about the Universe. Is it esternal or created? I made excuses, as I felt so much embarrassed, that I even denied that I knew anything about philosophy.; The Amir understood my embarrassment, and he himself initiated the discussion and put me at ease. I opened up and talked to him freely.' We do not know how long he remained at Marrakesh. In 1163 we find him at Seville where he held the post of qaḍi for several years. Later, he was posted as the Chief Judge of Cordova. For a decade he held this post with distinction. This period saw the publication of some of his greatest works — *Fasl al-maqāl*, *Kashf al manahij*, and *Tahafut al-Tahafut*. He was about fiftysix when (in 1182) Abū yaqub summoned him at Marrakesh, and employed him as his physician. Two years later, Abū Yaqub died, arid in 1185 ibn Tufail also died. The new ruler Yusuf al-Mansur confirmed him in his post. The relations between the two were very cordial, and so intimate that the philosopher addressed the sovereign as 'my friend'. But in 1194-95, ibn Rushd came under a cloud. By this time he was an author of several philosophical writings. The conservative ulemas kept themselves in readiness to discredit him in the eyes of the ruler. They poisoned his ears by concocting wild stories about his alleged heresy. They told him that: (i) ibn Rushd considered the planet Venus was a god, (ii) he denied that the tribe ʿAd, mentioned in the Quran ever existed, (iii) that in a work on zoology he had stated to have seen a giraffe in a garden of the king of Berbers — an obvious insult to the sultan who was the ruler of Spain as well. The conspiracy succeeded. Al-Mansur could not displease the ulema as he needed their support and blessings to fight the aggressions of the northern Christian states. He was at Seville when it was decided to try ibn Rusad. He was summoned in the mosque of Cordova for a trial at the end of which the sixtynine years old philosopher was exiled to Lucena, a small town near Cordova. He was only under house arrest. His books were banned. However, the period of disgrace did not last long as the whole drama was politically motivated. Through the intercession of some notables (including ibn Zuhr) ibn Rushd was recalled to Marrakesh and restored to his former post. Two years after (Dec. 11, 1198) he died aged seventytwo after putting posterity in debt for several books on philosophy. He was temporarily interred at Marrakesh, but his body was brought to Cordova and buried in the family cemetery. The mystic ibn al-Arabi was present at the time of burial. Gentle, abstemious, simple in living, ibn Rushd was a devout student of philosophy and equally devout in his religious duties. When someone criticised him for being kind to his enemies, ibn Rushd replied, 'There is no virtue in being kind to a friend, but he is virtuous who is generous to a foe.' He never imposed capital punishment, and when it was necessary, he transferred the suit to another judge.

Ibn Rushd is known for his commentaries on philosophical works, and also for his defence of philosophy from the attacks of the ulemas. We do not know the number of his writings, but his output was voluminous and varied. The historian ibn Usabia has given a formidable list of his books. The French philosopher, E. Renan who earned his doctorate in 1852 from Paris University on his learned thesis 'Averroes et l'Averroism', counted 65 works — philosophy (29), theology (5), law (9), astronomy (3), grammar (2), and medicine (17).[14] Some of his books have been printed while others are available in Latin and Hebrew translations. He was a great commentator specially of Aristotle whose teachings he tried to separate from the abracadabra of neo-Platonism. He had an immense respect for him. Aristotle was to him the very acme of human intelligence. He commented on Aristotle's De Anima, Physica, De Substantia Orbis, metaphysica, De Caelo et Mundo, Analytica Posteriora, De Generatione et Corruptione, Sensu et Sensibilibus, Ethica and Poetica. The commentaries are of three categories — the large, the intermediate, and the short. The last called 'Takhlis' was an abridgement meant for beginners.

Ibn Rushd will always be remembered as a great champion of philosophy. To, the philosopher, nothing is sacred, and he must judge every belief on the touchstone of reason. Al-Nazam who flourished in the East about the middle of the 9th century, preached that doubt was the beginning of all rational knowledge. The philosophers were sometimes patronized, and sometimes persecuted. During the time of ibn Rushd they were regarded as a bunch of heretics (Ar. sig: zindiq) in Spain as well as in the East. Under the impact of Greek philosophy, a crop of materialistic thinkers (dahriyyun) jettisoned God and religion in the sea of their heresies. They believed in a self-supporting cosmic system which came into being itself, and worked according to its own laws of existence. Belief in the soul, resurrection, rewards and punishments in the after-life were myths created by man. Many thinkers followed the neo-Platonic philosophers who advocated that God had dealings with the world indirectly through a series of beings or emanations: called intelligences. The philosopher Zakariya al-Razi (865-925) went further and made a direct assault on religions. He denied the miracle (ijaz) of the Quran, and affirmed that a better book with a better style could be written, although he never wrote a line to prove his theory. In Athens of Pericles, they would have given him a cup of hemlock to drink, but the Muslims of those days honoured him because, in addition to being a thinker, he was a genius in clinical pathology. It was left to the Abū Hamid al-Ghazali (1058-1111) to lead a revolt against the philosophers. Ghazali, it may be stated, was no ordinary mortal. Born in a poor family, orphaned in early childhood, Ghazali was gifted with exceptional intellectual powers. He was a philosopher to the very tips of his fingers. For years he studied philosophy only land himself in the wilderness of doubt. The eternal questions of philosophy which centred round God, His knowledge, His attributes, time, space, soul, causality and infinity befogged his mind — just as they do even today. He lost his faith in religion, and became a wanderer. He visited Mecca, Madina, Jerusalam, and the tomb of Abraham at Hebron. Through prayer, meditation and divine grace he returned to the warm embrace of religion. Ghazali turned into a champion of mystic religion. The former friend of philosophy turned into its bittest enemy. Armed to the teeth with dialectics he sat down to tear philosophy to shreds. His indictment of philosophy is contained in several books particularly The Incoherence of the Philosophers *(Tahafut al falasifah)*, in which he accused the philosophers of breeding heretic ideas in the minds of people. Ibn Rushd was pained after reading this book. He must have cried with anguish -Et tu Ghazali'! Soon he came out with a rejoinder in his Incoherence of Incoherence *(Tahafut al Tahafut)* and an equally famous book the *Kitab Fasl al maqal*. He condemned Ghazali as a hypocrate, and gave point by point reply to his objections. Ibn Rushd went straight to the Quran, and quoted several verses to prove that God Himself had ordained upon man to reflect on the universe. From these verses he concluded that philosophy is a search for truth, and its study is permissible. Working on these lines, he carried the war in the camp of the theologians, and even questioned their right to interpret the Quran. He argues that the philosophers are 'firmly ground in knowledge *(raasikhuna fil ilm)*.[15] He asserted that by virtue of their training in logic, they were more competent than the theologians to give independent judgement *(ijma)* in matters relating to Islamic jurisprudence. The ulemas, he said, were slaves of traditional thinking. These doctrines of ibn Rushd brought on him the wrath of the ulemas. But ibn Rushd was not anti-religion He thought that religion and philosophy were twin sisters because both contained wisdom, but while the former is for the masses *(jamhur)*, philosophy is for the intellectual elite. 'In short (says ibn Rushd) religions are according to the philosophers obligatory since they lead towards wisdom in a way universal to all human beings, for philosophy only leads a certain number of intelligent people to the knowledge of happiness and they, therefore, have learnt wisdom, whereas religion seeks the instruction of the masses.'[16] He places the prophets above the philosophers because 'every prophet is a sage, but not every sage is a prophet'.[17]

Some scholars are of the view that ibn Rushd had no original philosophy of his own. He was only a faithful disciple of Aristotle who was content with elucidation of his master's philosophy in his monumental commentaries. In this endeavour he was not doubt successful. Neverthless, he expresses his personal views on philosophical matters during the course of his commentaries, Don Arnaldez, a modern Spanish authority on ibn Rushd says — 'If one considers the whole corpus of ibn Rushd's works and the unity of his wide thought, it becomes apparent that the 'commentator' was a true philosopher'.[18] The subject most debated by the philosophers in those days related to the origin of the world. Ibn Rushd believed in God, but not in creation *ex-nihilo*. He envisaged a continuous creation which in his opinion was more worthy than that which is accomplished once for all. He postulated a world constantly evolving and taking new shape. The world and time are eternal. He did not believe in miracles as every phenomenon is governed by fixed laws, and causes are followed by effects. With a mild sarcasm he speaks against the theologians who base the truthfulness of a religion on the capacity of its founder to perform miracles. Coming to Islam, he says that the Quran does not attribute miracles to the Prophet. When the pagan Arabs told the Prophet that they would follow him if he performed miracles in support of his claim, the Prophet replied through God's revelation (Sura XVII.93) that he was only a human being and a messenger. The only miracle of Islam, says ibn Rushd is the Holy Quran itself and its message which contains all the rules of conduct for the good of mankind.[19] In his ethical thinking, ibn Rushd was of the view that God is the Creator of both good and evil. He created evil as a means to an end — the triumph of good. Fire is good, and of great service to man, but harmful only by an accident[20].

Ibn Rushd's political philosophy can be gleaned from his commentary on Plato's Republic which has luckily survived only in Hebrew translations. For ibn Rushd, the state was a necessity without which it is not possible for man to attain happiness. Some of his political views are still relevant. He was against all forms of totalitarianism. He regretted that Amir Mu'awiya perverted the political direction given by the first caliphs of the Muslims whose governments were in accordance with Plato's ideal republic The worst tyranny in his eyes was a government run by the priests. The state should be in the hands of elderly leaders. All the citizens should be given a good education - but not in Arabic poetry which he thought was dangerous for morality. The rule of the army should be to maintain law and order, and it should be kept aloof from politics.

What will happen (he asks) if the dogs instead of guarding a sheepfold start devouring the sheep. He pitied the condition of women who vegetated like the plants, and had no occupation but to feed the babies, and to look after domestic chores. As there were more women than men in the Andalusian society, he was pained to see that half of the population was simply idle and of no use to the state. He found no differences between the sexes in regard to performance of any work. In the army, the educational field, and other occupations, women could be as efficient as men. In certain fields, such as music, men could hardly reach the virtuosity of females.[21] Perhaps, Ibn Rushd was Spain's first feminist.

Ibn Rushd's defence of philosophy was of no avail. Triumphant orthodoxy gave no peace to philosophers. The 13th century monist, ibn Sab'in of Murcia (1217-1269) suffered all through his life at the hands of the *fuqaha* (theologians). They chased him wherever he went. He was forced to leave Spain for Ceuta with a group of his disciples. At Ceuta he shot into prominence when king Federick II of Italy sent him a questionnaire asking him to reply to some questions on philosophy. He sent his replies through the king's ambassador. The text of ibn Sab'in's replies has survived, and it was published in 1880 by M.A.F. Mehren. He was expelled from Ceuta, and he wandered in search of safety. He arrived at Tunis, but a theologian from Seville who lived there was after his blood. He left for Cairo, and met the same fate. Finally, he reached Mecca, but a Spanish émigré gave him no peace. Persecuted all his life, he obtained his release by opening the veins of his wrist. He was great during his life, as well as after his death. His most faithful disciple the Spanish Sufi al-Sushtri praised him as the 'magnet of souls *(mqnatis al-nufus)*. In our time, the French theosophist — L. Massignon of France was one of his admirers. Ibn Sab'in was the last rose of Andalusian philosophy. For the sake of brevity, it would be necessary to pass over in silence some philosophers and logicians who preceded ibn Sab'in, and also those who followed him. But a century after his death, a man of Spanish ancestry appeared in northwest Africa who laid the foundation of a new school of philosophy beyond the intellectual reach of even the Greeks. This was 'Abd ar-Rahman ibn Khaldun.

Ibn Khaldun belongs to the mainstream of Hispano-Muslim thought, and it is but fitting that we conclude on him this short account of Andalusian philosophy. He was a direct descendant of the Banu Khaldun family of Seville, we left behind in an earlier chapter. They lived in the little Eden of Seville — the celebrated Asharaf on their estate. Before Seville fell, they left for north Africa, and settled at Tunis. Ibn Khaldun was born there on May 27, 1332. He received the usual classical education. After memorising the Quran, he learnt hadith, law, philology, literature and philosophy. Most of his teachers were of Spanish origin because northwest Africa, at this time, was teeming with them. During the period ending 1382, he lived mostly in north Africa. At this time, the whole of the region was fragmented into small states which arose from the ashes of the Almohad empire. Their rulers fought for expansion and supremacy. In this atmosphere of plots, factional intriques, and wars, ibn Khaldun found an opportunity for self-aggrandisement as well as introspection into the affairs of the state. He held several secretarial posts. By nature a man of ambition, he used every public assignment as a spring-board for his progress. He kept moving from one court to another — sometimes at Fez, today at Tilimsan, tomorrow at Bougie. He worshipped the rising sun, and threw away his loyalties whenever his patron was in distress. He participated in the court intriques whole-heartedly.

He was lucky not to have been removed by a poniard for his many disloyalties. But he could not escape imprisonment on account of his involvement in a plot against the Merinid sultan Abū Enan. Late in 1362 he had to flee to Spain to save his head. The reader will recall that the Nasarite ruler Muhammad V once took refuge at Fez along with his minister ibn Khatib. Ibn Khaldun had befriended ibn Khatib, and when the Spanish king regained his throne, he followed them. Muhammad V. took him in his service. He was so much impressed by him that he sent him to the court of Pedro the cruel of Castile (in 1364) as a special envoy to negotiate a treaty of friendship. Ibn Khaldun met Pedro at Seville. The Christian king took a liking for him, and invited him to settle at Seville, the home of his ancestors, but ibn Khaldun declined the offer for obvious reasons. The intellectual life at Granada was congenial to ibn Khaldun. He moved in the circle of leading scholars like Abu 1-Barakat al-Bellafiqi, held discussions on philology, listened Andalusian music and poetry, and attended banquets and weddings. He sent for his family, and would have settled in Granada, but his Spanish honey moon was cut short. As Ibn Khatib grew jealous of his growing influences, he realised that he had no future in Spain. He sailed from Almeria for Africa, and arrived at Bougie, in March 1365. So capable was he that every ruler sought his services, knowing full well his past history. The Hafsid ruler Abū Abdullah employed him as his hajib, but when he died, ibn Khaldun deserted his successor, and took service at the court of the amir of Constantine Abū 1-Abbas in May 1366. But there was no end to his wanderings. Sometime in 1375, he was so much tired of the vicissitudes of life, that he left for Spain. He was disappointed again. The Spanish government declared him a *persona non grata*, and he was forced out of the kingdom of Granada. Through the efforts of his friend

Muhammad ibn 'Arif, who was a scion of a powerful tribe, he returned to Qal'at ibn Salamah, a fortress to the south of Oran. He spent three yeas there, and delved into the mysteries of social phenomena. During this quiet retreat, far from the sordid intriques of court life, and the sound of clashing swords, the ideas which had been flitting across his mind crystallised into creative thought. Let us hear his own words on the subject. 'I was inspired by that retreat with words and ideas pouring into my head like a cream until the finished product was ready.'[22] This product was the famous introduction — the *Muqaddimah*, to his general history — '*kitab al-Ibar* (The Book of Examples), which laid down the foundation of a new and independent discipline called by him '*Al-Umran al-bashari*', and sociology by us today.

The rest of his life is not without interest, and may be summed up briefly. Like a bird in a cage, he longed for freedom, and he decided to leave Tunis in 1378. For four years he led an unhappy life. The ruler Abū l-Abbas kept a vigilant eye on his activities, while the leading jurists were displeased with him. Under the pretext of a pilgrimage to Mecca, he bid adieu to northwest Africa forever. He arrived at Alexandria on Dec. 8, 1383, and moved on to Cairo. A year later, his family coming to join him perished on the sea. This bereavement did not break the spirit of the man. He enjoyed his stay at Cairo. In its crowded plazas, splendid buildings, hospitals, educational institutions, and the life-giving Nile, he saw another Granada. He spent the rest of his days in that great city earning his living either as a teacher of law, or as a judge. In Cairo, a most unusual adventure came his way. In Dec. 1400, he had to accompany al-Nasir on his expedition to relieve Damascus which was being threatened by the mighty Timurlang. If that city fell, nothing would stop the great Tartar from marching with his hordes into Egypt. Putting his life in danger, this bold thinker who was already seventy, had himself lowered in a basket from the walls of the city to reach the Tartar camp. He stayed there for forty days, and had several interviews with the Tartar leader. Ibn Khaldun has given an account of his interviews with Timur in his autobiography. He saved Egypt from a disaster. He returned to Cairo, and spent his time in revising the *Muqaddimah*. Sometimes, he would post letters to his friends including ibn Zamrak, the poet of Granada. On March 17, 1406, he died and was buried in a cemetery near Cairo's Nasr Gate.

Ibn Khaldun was gifted with a photographic memory, an analytical mind, and a keen power of observation which helped him to develop his empirical-historical approach to the drama of human destiny. Many streams converged into the reservoir of his vast learning in almost every field — history, philosophy, ethics, geography, law, literature, and Quran exegesis. The subjects are discussed in the *Muqaddimah* are: histriography; human relations; influence of geography on food, colour and character of people; group-consciousness; rise and fall of dynasties; administration; the art of warfare; relationship between demand and supply of goods; labour problems; self-employment; agriculture; commerce; marketing of goods; inflation and its impact on economy; town-planning; speculative philosophy *(qalam)*; sufism; music; poetry; calligraphy; pedagogy and curriculam; the world of dreams and clairvoyance. All these topics are fitted into a logically organized framework. "A better form of presentation for ibn Khaldun's ideas and material could hardly be imagined[23]." The *Muqaddimah* is divided into six long chapters and each chapter into essays written in a lucid style. The text is found in many manuscripts - the Atif Effendi copy in Turkey is unique as it has an autograph of ibn Khaldun himself.

The *Muqaddimah* opens with a dissertation on the nature and scope of history. History is not just past politics, It is neither a saga of select individuals. History is an enquiry into the laws that underlie events and episodes. Beneath the outward surface of historical evolution, there are certain laws, and it is a historian's function is to study them. He says, 'On the surface history is no more than information about political events, dynasties, and occurrences of the remote past, elegantly presented and spiced with proverbs. It serves to entertain large crowded gatherings and brings to us an understanding of human affairs ... The inner meaning of history, on the other hand involves speculation and an attempt to get to the truth, subtle explanations of the causes and origins of existing things, and deep knowledge of how and why of events. It is firmly rooted in philosophy. It deserves to be accounted a branch of philosophy'.[24] In order words, history should be written by philosophers, because of their capacity for analysis and objective study. The raw-material of history is to be found in the original sources which the scientific historian must utilise with the utmost care. He should guard himself against unfounded assumptions and fictitious stories. The historian should sift through his sources to reach the truth, and throughout his research, his attitude should be free from partiality. He cites several examples of the mistakes committed by the historians who, with one breath, attributed the fail of the celebrated Bermaki family of Persia, to the romantic attachment between princess Abbasa and Ja'far Bermaki. After analysing the matter, ibn Khaldun concluded that the fall of the family was due to their overweening ambitions. Ja'far lost his life because he arrogated to himself the prerogatives of the caliph. Again, ibn Khaldun mocks at the account of caliph Ma'mun's marriage with Buran. Most of the historians wrote that M'amun was roaming about at night in the streets of Baghdad, when he was pulled up by a silk cord flung from a window of a stately mansion. He was led into a sumptuous hall where he was surrounded by a bevy of beauties. He was struck by the beauty of Buran, and he fell in love with her.[25] All this was absurd gossip and not history in the eyes of ibn Khaldun.

The subject of the *Muqaddimah* is man and his social organisation. Ibn Khaldun invites his readers to look at the wonderful drama of creation — the emergence of life on the planet, and its gradual growth from minerals to plants, and from plants to animals, culminating in man. 'One should look (says he) at the world of creation. It started out from the minerals and progressed in an ingenious, graded manner, to plants and animals. The last stage of plants such as palms and vines is connected with the first stage of animals such as snails and shellfish which have the power of touch. The word 'creation' with regard to these created things means that the last stage of each group is fully prepared to become the first stage of the next group. The animal world than widens, its species become numerous, and in a gradual process of creation, it finally leads to man, who is able to think and reflect. The higher stage of man is reached from the world of monkeys in which sagacity and perception are found, but had not reached the stage of actual reflection and thinking."[26]

Of all the animals, man alone has the power to shape his destiny. Like the animals, he likes to live in groups. Civilisation is the product of man's faculty to think, his gregarious instinct, and his economic needs. He defines civilisation *(umran)* as the state in which human beings leave their nomadic life, and live together in fortified cities for satisfaction of their needs — food for the body, clothes to wear, and shelter from hostile environment.[27] Urban life gives birth to economic activity. No man can live on the fruit of his own labour. He needs the help and cooperation of his fellow human beings for satisfaction of his needs — classified as necessaries, comforts and luxuries. This leads to diversification of economic activity, emergence of trades and occupations for earning livlihood *(ma'ash)*, division of labour and production of goods and markets. As economic activity becomes complex many problems arise — transportation of finished goods, competition among producers, the rise and fall of prices. Ibn Khaldun was an advocate of *laissez faire* economy. He was against state-trading, and condemned forced labour. He desired stability in prices, because continuous low prices are harmful to trade. All economic activity is part of God's plan because He desires mankind to live and prosper on the globe. For this reason, he supported the citizens' right to property.

The core of ibn Khaldun's thought is his concept of group consciousness. He calls this *'asabiya'*. He does not use this word in a narrow and parochial sense of racial prejudice, but in a larger sense — a sort of nationalism. To him the asabiya was a feeling of oneness in a tribe, or a much larger group united by common ties of fellowship, community of economic interests, and outlook both cultural and religious. It was a feeling of deep attachment generated by the will to live together. It is the motive force which holds a state and a society intact. Man being a social animal, his natural gregariousness coupled with economic needs, urge him to unite under a leader for the sake of internal discipline as well as protection from external dangers. Under the urge of this *élan vital*, the roaming nomads join into tribes, the tribes into large groups, and build settlements according to availability of basic needs. This leads to growth of cities. The people living in cities get together under the bond of solidarity *(assabiya)* and a state comes into existence replacing the tribal chiefs by the most powerful leader among them. He is their king, their sultan or caliph who not only keeps the state united, but also acts as a restraining influence over the people. The state lasts so long as the asabiya, the source of its strength remains alive. Ibn Khaldun gives numerous instances from the history of Muslim states in support of his theory. The Abassids lost their group feeling, and fell a victim to the Tartars. Exactly the same happened to the Umayyads of Spain. When their group feeling was destroyed, the petty rulers seized power, and the Umayyad kingdom ceased to exist.

Ibn Khaldun found that the history of the Muslim world was a drama of dynastic changes founded by despots. He was intriqued by the rise and fall of dynasties, and sat down to think over this phenomenon. He saw history moving with a definite pattern of growth, maturity, and decay. Just as a man grows from infancy into adolescence, passes into manhood, reaches old age, and dies, so also dynasties pass through stages of birth, growth, and downfall. He saw five stages in the life-span of a dynasty. In the first stage a dynasty captures the state by force of arms, and crushes all opponents to secure its position. The leader of the dynasty serves as a model of benevolance to the people. He defends their property, and makes necessary arrangements for collection of taxes, soon after the restoration of peace. In the second stage, he consolidates his grip on the state. He recruits a body of loyal persons (motivated like him by group consciousness), to prevent any plot to remove him from power. In the third stage, a ruler enjoys life because of peace and stability. He builds monuments, plans new settlements, and beautifies his kingdom. He spends large sums on the army, to keep it in a good trim. In the next stage, the ruler lives in blissful contentment by following the policies of his forefathers. In the fifth stage, the ruler wastes his wealth on pleasures and amusements. He is generous to the low class of people. The important posts are given to this class even if they have no merits. The new-comers create a feeling of resentment among the old clients and supporters of his predecessors. By this time, the group-feeling melts into the thin air. He needs money and taxes his subjects to replenish the treasury already siphoned off by his reckless spending. All the vices of urban/ sedentary culture prop up. Immorality, and social vices (gambling, cheating, fraud, theft, perjury, usury) sap the vitality of the state. The dynasty reaches the stage of its biological decay. Its days are numbered, and anytime it could be overthrown by a leader inspired by a fresh group-feeling, or by attack from a peripheral power. Ibn Khaldun puts the life of a dynasty at 120 years.[28]

Ibn Khaldun has assigned a whole chapter on the art of war. He was no warmonger. He wrote on warfare because the military gave security to the state from aggressions. However, sometimes war became inevitable. After discussing the causes of war, he gives his views on reconnaissance, movement of troops, digging of trenches, logistics, equipment, strategy, and even military music. He advises fighting in close formations which are like a long wall or a well-built fortress. He knew that if the army was scattered everywhere it would not be strong anywhere. The capability of the commander, the morale of the soldiers, the adequacy of arms are some of the factors necessary to achieve victory. These *principes de guerre* are absolute, but there are some factors of a fortuitous nature which can change the fortune of a battle. "There is no certainty (he says) in war even when equipment and numerical strength that cause victory (under normal circumstances) exist. Victory and superiority in war comes from luck and chance. This is explained by the fact that the causes of superiority are as a rule, a combination of several factors. There are external factors such as the number of soldiers, the quality of weapons, the number of brave men, skillful arrangement of line formation, the proper tactics, and similar things. Then there are hidden factors. These hidden factors may be result of humane ruse and trickery such as spreading alarming news and rumours to cause deflection (in the ranks of the enemy); occupying high points so that one is able to attack from above which surprises those below and cause them to abandon each other; hiding in a thicket or depression and concealing oneself from the enemy in rocky terrain so that the armies (of one's side) suddenly appear when the enemy is in a precarious situation, and he must flee to safety. These hidden factors may also be celestial matters which man has no power to produce for himself.'[29] The element of luck on the battlefield cannot be ruled out. A sudden storm, and heavy rains can decide the issue of a battle. Napoleon knew that a trivial chance could cheat him. That is why he once said, 'I base my calculations on the expectation that luck will be against me'.[30]

Ibn Khaldun had sensible (almost modern) views on educational psychology. Man being a thinking animal, acquisition of knowledge is natural to him. The power to think is lodged by God in the cavity of the human brain. Ibn Khaldun divides the thought process into three stages. The discerning intellect helps man to obtain knowledge from things around him; the experimental intellect determines his behaviour towards his fellow men; and the speculative intellect gives him the capacity to think about abstract matters, the problems of philosophy and higher truths.[31] Education should aim at development of the aptitude *(malaka)* of a student. The curriculum should be phased realistically to suit a student's power of comprehension, and his capacity to assimilate what he learns. It should start from simple facts, and gradually proceed with complex controversies. Beating and spanking should be scrupulously avoided, as severity to students turns them into liars. Geometry sharpens the intellect and it should be included in the syllabus. He lauded Plato for making the study of geometry compulsory for admission to his academy[32]. The students should also be taught the theory of music. It seems he regarded music as the arithmetic of sounds. Harmony gives pleasure to the ears as the harmony of the human form gives pleasure to the eyes.[33] Higher education should be imparted through discussions. There should be no lack of communication between the teacher and the taught. He was against memorizing and the use of notes and abbreviated handouts for the students.[34] After higher education, a scholar should travel abroad to broaden his outlook, and to meet specialist in other countries. Travel was apart of his plan of education. And finally, the teacher should set an example of what he teaches.

The *Muqaddimah* was the world's greatest book of philosophy of the 14th century. Although Ibn Khaldun's focus was on the Muslim world, what he wrote was of universal interest. The whole of this book is full of gems of wisdom. He tells the social anthropologist that man is the child of customs and not the child of his ancestors. He tells the economist about many facts relating to the mechanism of prices, and the behaviour of demand and supply — facts which were true in his time as they true today. He advises the rulers to keep the judiciary separate from politics. He emphasises the importance of agriculture — man's oldest occupation. He has a kind word for labour which he called a state's capital. Ibn Khaldun saw before him deserted cities, falling monuments, and ruling dynasties lingering in the agony of death. He warned that injustice is the main cause of the fall of a state. He discusses the plight of nations who lose their independence. The rule of an alien people is an unmitigated disaster for the ruled. The subject nation loses its confidence, and worst of all it imitates the culture of its masters because of the latter's political domination. Finally, he tells the philosopher, in all humility, that there are many questions, the philosopher cannot answer. Any attempt to do so, is as futile as weighing a mountain with the pair of scales meant for weighing gold. We may quote the late Prof. Toynbee's tribute to this thinker of Spanish descent. 'In his chosen field of intellectual activity (says Toynbee) he appears to have been inspired by no predecessor and to have found no kindred soul among his contemporaries, and to have kindled no answering spark of inspiration in any successor, and yet in the Prolegomena (Muqaddama) to his Universal History he has conceived and formulated a philosophy of history which is undoubtly the greatest work of its kind that has ever yet been created by any mind in any time or place"[35]. A thinker of such a great stature left no impact either during his life or after he was gone. The fact is that ibn Khaldun was born before his time. He was like a bird that 'sings with full-throated ease', and is heard by none. During his life he had no disciples. Socrates groomed Plato, and Plato, Aristotle, but ibn Khaldun had no pupils to carry forward the torch lighted by him. For a long time, the *Muqaddimah* remained neglected. The West discovered ibn Khaldun in the 19th century when a French orientalist rendered it into French. When the translation appeared it was too late to exercise any influence because the several disciplines which ibn Khaldun had conceived, had already been initiated and developed. But the western intellectual circles were surprised to find in him a precursor of several great thinkers — Vico, Machiavelli, Montesquieu, August Comte, Adam Smith, Spengler, and even Marx.

We shall now leave the mansion of Andalusian philosophy, and pass into the world of the sufis who try to grasp reality beyond all dialectics. Sufism or *Tasawwuf* is an offshoot of Islam. The sufis are inspired by the Quran, the hadith, and the life of the Prophet. A story goes (it has been recorded by ibn Al-Arabi who was himself a famous sufi) that the Almohad sultan Abū Yaqūb once visited the sufi Abdullah Muhammad bin Al-Mujahid of Seville. During the course of discussions, he asked the sufi why he kept himself aloof from the people, and whether he did not feel lonely. The scholarly sufi who was sitting with books piled before him, replied that he never felt lonely because whenever he wished to commune with God he read the Quran, and when he desired to converse with the Prophet he would open a volume of hadith, and if he wished for the company of the Prophet's companions he read their biographies[36]. The sultan was impressed by his piety. He left him with a box containing one thousand gold dinars. The box remained unopened for 12 years until he died.[37] The sufis never hanker after political power, but they prefer to live in poverty, humility and devotion to God and His prophet.

For the sufis, God alone is the Ultimate Reality — *La illaha il la Allah,* and all else is perishable. They are a God intoxicated people with no loyalties except love of God and his creatures. They do not bother who rules the state. They are above law, not because they are anarchists, but simply because they do not have the capacity, nor the need, nor the time to break the law of the land. They would live as a decent people even if there were no state and no government. A sufi passes his days and nights in silent prayer, and complete obedience (ubūdiayat) to God. For a sufi it is not enough to offer prayers five times a day and fast for thirty days in a year obligatory on the Muslims. His whole life is a saga of prayer and austerity. The sufi cultivates the love of God as the supreme aim of his life. He completely dedicates his life to the service of God by placing his trust *(tawakkal)* in His Bounty *(ikram)*. He spends all his life in remembrance *(dhikr)* of God, and aspires only his pleasure *(rida)*, by leading a life of continence *(zuhd)*, and voluntary poverty *(faqr)*. Through fasting, prayer, vigils and ascetic living, he kills the evil instigating part of his psyche *(nafs al-ammarah)*. After suppressing his appetites, lust, anger, greed and passions, he passes through several stages *(maqamāt)* of self-illumination. His spiritual odyssey ends when he attains complete purity of thought and action and becomes a true representative of his Beloved — that is God.

Muslim Spain blossomed with sufis all through the 8 centuries, but it is in the 12th century that we are exposed to a full panorama of their lives and practices mainly through the two books of ibn Al-Arabi, viz. *Rūh al-quds,* and *al-Durrat al-fākhirah*[38]. A sufi expresses his submission to God by prayer, meditation and endless invocations of God's beautiful names *(asma al-husna),* and recitations from the Quran, and blessings on the Prophet. For the sufi, the Prophet was the Ideal Man, being as he was, the bearer of the Divine Word. Ibn al-Arabi gives a peep into the daily routine of a typical sufi - Abu 'Abdullah Muhammad bin Qassum with whom he associated in his youth. After the morning obligatory prayer in a mosque, the sufi started his individual prayer which continued till the sun had risen high. The prayer over, he would lecture to his disciples on the importance of ritual cleanliness and the need for prayer and other subjects relating to the sufi way of life. He finished each session with the recitation of the final section of *Sūr Baqr* of the Quran. On returning home from the mosque in the afternoon, he would take a brief nap proceeded by a frugal meal. He would return to the mosque and read one fifth of the Quran with complete absorption. After the noon prayer, he returned home, and was busy in invocation until the time of the sunset. He came to the mosque again, and delivered the call to prayer *(azan)*, and returned home. Before going to bed he recalled all that he had done during the day. At midnight he left his bed, and after a bath and ritual ablution, he retired to a corner of the house for prayer, medidation and recitations from the Quran.[39] Many sufis preferred a place of solitude — a cemetery or a wilderness or any place far from the madding crowd. Kindly and gentle, a sufi would never retaliate even when wronged. Abū Ja'far al-Uraani, a sufi of Loule near Silves in Portugal was attacked by a man with a knife. The pious sufi did not resist, but offered his neck to the assailant, and even prevented his disciples from interfering on his behalf. When the man raised his knife, it twisted into his hand. The man fell down at the sufi's feet with remorse.

It is said that some sufis could perform miracles through their spiritual powers. A few acquired weightlessness. A female sufi Zainab al-Qal'iyyah of Seville would rise 30 cubits from the ground during her prayers.[40] She renounced wealth and adopted the sufi path *(tariqa)*. A sufi named Abū Hajjaj could walk on water. Another relieved pain merely by touching the aching part of a patient. Abū Muhammad bin Ashraf of Ronda could light fire from grass.[41] Abū Ja'far al-Uryani mentioned above could bring down rain from the clouds. Shams (whose real name was Yasminah) was known as the 'mother of the poor'. She could exercise telepathic powers to communicate with her disciples. One day ibn al-'Arabi and several other sufis were on a visit to her. Suddenly, she called out, 'Ali return and pick up your handkerchief' Ali was one of her disciples, but he was not present. When she was asked to explain, she replied that Ali was coming to see her; on the way, he took rest near a stream, but when he resumed the journey, he dropped his handkerchief. That was why she called out that he should return to the spot to pick up the handkerchief. After an hour or so Ali himself arrived and narrated what had happened. He confirmed that he heard the voice of Shams telling him to return and pick up the hankerchief.[42] Another female sufi was Nūna Fatima who could excercise her will-power to summon any person whom she liked. Ibn al-'Arabi served her for many years before he left for the East. Fatima was married to a righteous man who was later afflicted with leprosy. She nursed him for twenty years, and after his death, she devoted all her life to prayer, fasting, and spinning. She took her suffering as a gift from God and never grumbled. When ibn al-'Arabi met her she was already eighty. She was thin and frail with a radiant face. He made a hut of reeds for her outside Seville. She was in communion with invisible spirits, and exercised her spiritual powers for the good of the people. Ibn al-'Arabi has mentioned one such act. One day a woman came to her in tears, and told her that her husband had left home for Sidonia to take a second wife. She begged for her help. Fatima recited the first verse of the Quran and uttered, 'Go, *Fateha*, and fetch her husband'. After three days her husband returned. Ibn al-Arabi interviewed him. The man revealed that everything was ready for performance of his marriage, when all of a sudden he felt as if his heart was contracting within, and his eyesight began to fail. He was struck with remorse, and returned home.[43]

The sufis lived by making caps, spinning and raising vegetables. They earned just enough to keep themselves alive. Many of them sensed the time of their death. When Abdullah Muhammad al-Sharafi, knew that his hour was near, he sent away his disciples on the plea that he was proceeding on a long journey. He left for his village, and soon after he died.[44] The sufis had no particular attraction for marriage. Some of them preferred to remain unmarried hoping that in their after-life, they would marry heavenly brides — the houries of Paradise. A sufi of 9th century who lived in the East saw a woman in a dream. She was the fairest woman he had ever seen. He asked her 'Who are you'? She replied that she was a houri from heaven. The sufi asked for her hand. She replied, 'Take permission from my master who is Allah'. Finally, the sufi asked her about her dowry. The fair phantom replied, 'That you shall keep your soul clean of all worldly passions'. There is an equally interesting story of a sufi named Ahmad ibn Abul-Hawari. The sufi saw a vision of a woman of unusual beauty whose face shone with celestial brightness. He asked her what made her face so bright. She replied, 'I collected the tears you shed during your prayers, and with these tears, I have anointed my face which shines with the radiance you see'[45]. In his al-Durrat al-fakhirah, ibn al-Arabi introduces his readers to a young sufi Abū Ali Hassan of Seville for whom he offered to arrange a suitable match. Hassan repeatedly declined to marry. One day ibn al-Arabi insisted on hearing his reason for remaining a bachelor. The sufi replied with all seriousness that he was already engaged, and his marriage would be celebrated on the coming Thursday. He said this on Saturday, and the next Thursday he suddenly fell ill and died, or 'entered heaven as bridegroom', in the words of ibn al-Arabi[46]. Many sufis, however, did marry because Islam looks upon celibacy as unnatural to man. Even after marriage the sufi led a life of piety and prayer. They converted their wives into their spiritual sisters, and they shared with them the ideals of piety and spiritual exercises. Ibn al-Arabi, the great sufi of Spain was married early to Maryum, the daughter of a wealthy parents, but she observed the sufi way like him. In his *Futuhat al-Makkiyya*, he has celebrated her piety, and their identity of mystical experience.

A study of Spanish sufism would be incomplete without a short of account of the life and doctrines of ibn al-Arabi who was according to Asin Palacios 'the prince of Hispano-Muslim mystics.' Muhiyyudin, commonly known as ibn al-Arabi, and honoured to this as *'Shaikh al Akbar* (the great doctor)' was a native of Murcia where he was born in 1165 in a family of sufis. The family descended from Hatim al-Ta'i, a name famous in history and legends for his selfless generosity and hospitality. The family moved to Cordova when ibn al-Arabi was eight. His father was in civil service. He rose in social status, and counted ibn Rushd among his friends. Ibn al-'Arabi received formal education in grammar, literature and theology, and he broadened his horizon by reading Plato, Aristotle, and the neo-platonic thinkers. A vision in his early youth converted him to the sufi way of life. Meanwhile, strange things were happening to him. He showed signs of unusual psychic states. He spent long hours in cemeteries, and it is said that he acquired the power of communicating with the dead. Probably, his father was alarmed. He wanted to wean him away from the sufi path, and for this purpose he took him to ibn Rushd who at this time was the qadi of Seville. The philosopher had no faith in mysticism, and asked him sarcastically what he had found through mystic illumination. The philosopher was deeply impressed by the reply of young ibn al-Arabi.[47]

Ibn a-'Arabi lived in close association with the sufis, and observed their ways. During the course of his apprenticeship, he served as a disciple to many sufis whose names he has recorded in his writings. He was a devoted disciple. The opinion of Nuno-Fatima, the lady sufi of Seville, shows how sincere he was. She used to tell her disciples, "Most of you come to me with part of yourselves, leaving the other part elsewhere. Ibn al-'Arabi visits me with his whole self."[48] He visited several towns in Spain and northwest Africa. Sometime in 1198 he visited his native city of Murcia. While returning home he broke his journey at Almeria to pay his respects to the renowned sufi ibn al-'Arif.[49] In 1202 when he was forty, he left Spain for good on a long career of wanderings in Africa and the East. He performed the hajj, visited Baghdad, Mosul, Hebron, Aleppo and Jerusalem. He stayed at Mecca for a long time, and it was there that he began his towering masterpiece the *Futuhat al-Makkiyya* (Meccan Revelations), and also addressed his highly lyrical verses to Shms Nizam, the beautiful daughter of an Isfahani aristocrat resident at Mecca. The public took him to task for these poems, and he had to intervene to convince his critics that the poems were allegorical in nature. At Mecca he met some pilgrims from Asia Minor. He accompanied them to Konya. At Konya which at that time was a centre of sufi thought, he met Sadr-ud-din who became his most devoted disciple. Later Sadr-ud-din was to teach his master's *Fusus al-hikm* to the great sufi Jalal-ud-din. He wandered all over Asia Minor, and shuttled between Konya and Mecca. Leaving Asia Minor, the peripatetic sufi laid down his pilgrim's staff at Damascus. He died there on Nov. 16, 1240. His disciple Sadr ud-dun was with him when he died. He was buried in a tomb at Damascus which is visited by sufis and scholars of all races and climes.

This great sufi moving from one country to another was one of the most prolific writers of his time. We are still uncertain about the exact number of his books. Brockelman put their number at 239, but recent researchers estimate that he was author of about 400 books. Most of his books are in the libraries of Turkey. About a dozen or more have appeared in print at Cairo, Istanbul and Hyderabad. His most famous writings are

Rūh al-quds, al-Durrat al-Fākhirah, Kitab al-Isra ila maqām al-asra, Futuhat al-Makkiyya, Fusus al-hikm, and *Tarjuman al-ashwāq.* The Futuhat al-Makkiyya which runs into 560 chapters is the testament of his mystical doctrines and experiences. In this book he expounds his views on God, soul, prophethood, revelation, pre-destination and after-life. Written in abstract style, woven with fantasies, and illustrated with geometrical designs, the *Futuhat* is a challenge to the most patient reader. The *Fusus al-hikm* of which an autograph copy exists at Istanbul, has been translated into several languages. He has claimed that the book was inspired by the Prophet who appeared to him in a dream and dictated the book to him. This book is divided into 27 chapters each named after a prophet starting from Adam and ending on the Prophet of Islam. Each prophet is a logos *(kalimah)* of God, the highest logos being the Prophet Muhammad who crystalled in him all the aspects of Divine Wisdom revealed separately to the prophets who preceded him. The *Tajaman al-ashwāq* is a collection of love songs inspired by Shms Nizam- ibn al-'Arabi's Beatrice. Prof. R.A. Nicholson the British orientatlist and friend of Iqbal has rendered the book in English. The *Kitāb al-Isra* (printed at Hyderabad in 1848) is an unusual book. Written in rhyming prose, it describes his own spiritual journey from the world of being *(kawn)* to God's presence.

Throughout his long life ibn al-'Arabi saw visions of a spiritual nature. He has narrated these visions in his Futuhat, and Kitab al-Isra. He saw Khidar, the patron saint of all sufis at Tunis while he was sailing on a boat on a moonlit night. In the same city he received the 'Seal' of sainthood. At Murcia, during his last visit, he received a command from God to communicate his spiritual experiences to all. At Bugie in the month of Ramazan (597/1200), he was transported into space and inducted into a spiritual union with the stars and the planets. At Mecca when he was circumbulating the Holy Kaba, he met a heavenly spirit in the form of youth engrossed in meditation. He approached him with reverence, kissed his right hand, and begged him to reveal his identity. The youth replied, 'Look at my form and you will know the answer. I am the knowledge, the known, and the Knower'. During another vision, he had discussions with all the prophets. His descriptions of heaven and hell, and the bliss of the Beatific Vision enjoyed by the virtuous, embody the spiritual experiences of a man of extraordinary intuition and imagination moved by the overwhelming ecstasy peculiar only to the sufis.

His mystical philosophy is abstract, and his language so dazzling in its complexity that scholars think twice before approaching him. The central theme of his philosophy was the doctrine of Unity of Being known in Arabic as *'wahdat al-wajud'*. He saw an undercurrent of unity in the multiplicity of natural phenomena. "He often uses (says Prof. Affifi, the Egyptian authority on ibn al-Arabi) symbols and similies in expressing the relationship between the multiplicity of the phenomenal world and their essential unity. The one reveals Himself in the many as an object is revealed in different mirrors, each mirror reflecting an image determined by its nature and its capacity as a recipient. Or its is like a source of light from which an infinite number of lights are derived. Or like a substance which penetrates and permeates the forms of existing objects: thus giving them their meaning and being. Or like a mighty sea on the surface of which we observe countless waves for ever appearing and disappearing. The external drama of existence is nothing but the ever-renewed creation *(al khlaq al-jadid)* which is in reality a perpetual process of self-revelation. Or again, we might say, the one is the real Being and the

phenomenal world is its shadow having no reality of itself'.[50]
All knowledge obtained through reason, inference, perception
is limited. The best knowledge comes through mystic experience.
This, he called 'ma'rifa', and the person who tries to seek this
knowledge is a traveller — a *sālik* who undertakes the journey
to reach God. Through spiritual exercise — silence, withdrawal
from men, control of hunger, vigils, the heart is purified. God
grants the 'sālik' the manifestation of His light *(tajalli)*. The
traveller's love *(ishq)* of God is achieved in his final union
(wasl) with Him. As ibn al-'Arabi saw unity in diversity, he
had no quarrel with followers of other faiths. In his oft-quoted
verses he says that his heart is open to receive the teachings of
all faiths:

> It is a meadow for gazelles,
> A convent for Christian monks,
> A temple of idols,
> The Kaba of the pilgrims,
> The Tables of the Torah,
> The Book of the Quran.

Inspite of political upheavals, the rise and disappearance of
despots and dynasties, sufism continued to flourish in Muslim
Spain. Theophile Gautier says in a poem that the marble statue
outlives the state. It is equally true of Islamic sufism which is
also an art—the art of living at peace with God, with one's own
self, and also with one's neighbour. In the 13th century Muslim
power shrank so much that only a little strip was left in their
hand. Their greatest work of art at Cordova slipped out of their
hands, but sufism defied the rough-and-tumble of the political
upheavals. The sufi way of life did not lose its appeal. Spain
continued to produce sufis — there was a crop of them. Out of
these sufis we may mention Abu 1-Hasan al-Fasi. He was born

(1212) at Shushter, a small village near Guadix. He followed the doctrines of ibn Masarra and ibn Sa'bin. He performed several pilgrimages, and became a friend of the famous sufi Suhrawardi. He fell ill at a sea-shore village called "Al-tinha" meaning "clay." Like all sufis he knew that his end was near, and he remarked to his disciples — "My clay longs for clay." Soon after he died and was buried at Damietta on Oct. 16, 1269 far from his native land. His bier was carried by his poor disciples who hovered round him wherever he went. He was also a poet of distinction. He has let a diwan of poems in the muwashshah style on which an Egyptian scholar has earned a doctorate.

The kingdom of Granada saw the impact of eastern influences on Hispanic sufism. Sufism was taking a new shape. It was turning into a cult of monasticism. When ibn Buttutah was in Granada, he sought out local sufis. He spend some days at their hospic called al-'Uqab (The Eagle) situated on a hill about eight miles from the city. He found several darwishes — one each from Samarqand, Tabriz, Konya, Khurasan, and two from India[51]. The Persian influence is seen in their sufi practices. Music becomes a part of sufi rituals. During the time of ibn Khatib a group of sufis (most of them were masons and weavers) built a mosque at Albaycin, where they held their gatherings[52]. After the night prayer, their session commenced with sermons, zikr, and recitations from the Quran, and ended with chanting sufi verses of the Persian Hallaj. As the music went into their souls, some of sufis would rise abruptly and maddened with heavenly love they would dance in a trance. The dance rose to a crescendo as the musicians repeatedly chanted those very lines which moved the sufis to dance. At last they fainted and fell exhausted. The music stopped, and the session ended. There were several hermitages (Ar.sig.Zawiya) all over the kingdom of Granada where the sufis lived a communal life. A famous hermitage was in the hills of Malaga. Its building was donated by a wealthy merchant. The inmates were all men of piety and learning, and fully conversant with sufi doctrines and practices. A shaikh managed the convents with the help of servants. Each sufi lived in his own room, and met his companions only at meals and prayer. Every morning, the servants visited every sufi to enquire about his personal needs. Each sufi was supplied with weekly ration of oil for lamp, sugar, soap and two sets of clothes. They were also provided with a pocket allowance of 30 dirhams each for personal expenses including daily baths. The sufis ate food in separate dishes. Most of them were bachelors, but those married lived in separate rooms. In its last phase, sufism in Spain turned into a monastic order — as in the rest of the Muslim world.

Notes

1. M.M. Sharif: A History of Muslim Philosophy, Vol. I, p. 424.

2. On Ikhwan al-safa, see the scholarly article of Dr. omar Farrukh at pp. 289-310 in M.M. Sharif's History of Muslim Philosophy.

3. Asin Palacios: Abenmasarra y su escula, Madrid, 1914. An English translation of this book has been made by Prof. Dunlop. Don Arnaldez, the Spanish scholar of Hispano-Muslim philosophy, has condensed the book in his article on ibn Masarra in the Ency. of Islam (N.Ed.).

4. Ibn Hazm: Kitab al Milal, Vol. I, p. 591.

5. Ibid, p. 597 (verse: 5 of Sur. XXXIX).

6. M.M. Sharif: History of Muslim Philosophy, Vol, I, pp. 281-283.

7. Ency. of Islam (N.Ed.) article on Ibn Hazm.

8. Hitti" History of the Arabs, p. 558.

9. The Tawq al-Hamama itself is full of asphoristic pronouncements, for example: (1) Of love - may God exalt you, the first part is jesting, and the last part is right earnestness. (2) Repulsion of opposites, accord between similars, attraction of like for like — these are facts taking place

all round us. (3) The soul being beautiful, is affected by beautiful things. (4) Fidelity is only praiseworthy when a man is in a position of being unfaithful. (5) Women are like aromatic herbs, which if not well tended, soon lose their fragrance. (6) The joy of one hour does not compensate for the sorrow of several. (7) Adultery violates the sanctity of the harem, confuses the lawful offsprings of wedlock, and separates husband and wife.

10. Nykl: pp. 99-100.

11. Ibid., p. 252.

12. On ibn Bajja, the reader may like to read (1) M.M. Sharif: History of Muslim Philosophy, vol. I, pp. 506-525. (2) Dr. E.I.J. Rosenthal: The Place of Politics in the Philosophy of ibn Bajja, published in the Jublee No. of the Islamic Culture (Hyderabad). pp. 117-211. (3) Dr. Saghir Hasan: Avempace: The Philosopher of Andalus, published in the Islamic Culture of Jan, and April, 1962, and his translation of ibn Bajja's Kitāb al Nafs. (4) the article on ibn Bajja in the Ency. of Islam (N. Ed). (5) Majid Fakhry: History of Muslim Philosophy, New York, 1970. pp. 290-294.

13. Renan; pp. 264-265.

14. Renan: pp. 48-59.

15. The Quran: Verse 3.7.

16. Ibn Rushd: Tahafut, pp. 360-361.

17. Ibid.

18. Ency. of Islam (N. Ed.) article on ibn Rushd.

19. M.M. Sharif, Vol. I, p. 564.

20. Ibid, p. 550.

21. Renan: pp. 126-127.

22. Ibn Khaldun: The Muqaddimah, Vol. I, (P:L iii) as quoted by Rosenthal from ibn Khaldun's autobiography - the At-ta'rif.

23. Ibn Khaldun: Vol. I, p. IXX, of the Preface by Prof. Rosenthal.

24. Ibn Khaldun: The Muqaddimah, Vol.I, p. 6.

25. Ibid, pp. 27-30 and p. 39.

26. Ibn Khaldun: The Muqaddimah, Vol. I, p. 195.

27. Ibid, p. 84 and 80-91.

28. In Khaldun: The Muqaddimah, Vol. I, pp. 346-356.

29. Ibn Khaldun: The Muqaddimah, Vol. II, 85-86.

30. Lt. Col. A.H. Burne: The Art of War on Land (Indian Ed.), Delhi, p. 6.
31. Ibn Khaldun: The Muqaddimah, Vol. II, pp. 412-413.
32. Ibid, Vol. III, p. 131.
33. Ibn Khaldun; The Muqqadimah, Vol. II, pp, 397-398.
34. Ibid, Vol. III, p. 290.
35. Arnold Toynbee : A study of History, London, 1953, Vol. III, p. 322.
36. Austin: The Sufis of Andalusia, pp. 146-147.
37. Ibid.
38. These books have been translated by R.W.J. Austin under the title: The Sufis of Andalusia, London, 1971.
39. Austin: pp. 84-86.
40. Ibid, p. 155.
41. Ibid, p. 119.
42. Ibid., p. 141-143.
43. Austin: pp. 144-146.
44. Ibid, p. 77.
45. The stories of these two sufis will be found in Asin Palacios: p. 132.
46. Austin: pp. 98-99.
47. Ibn al-Arabi is said to have replied to ibn Rushd, 'Yes, and no. Between the 'yes' and 'no', the souls take their flight from their matter, and the necks become separated from their bodies'. S.H. Nasr: Three Muslim Sages p. 63, and Austin: p. 24.
48. Austin: p. 143.
49. Ibn al-'Arif has left a small book on sufi doctrines — Mahāsin al majālis. This has been translated by Elliot and Adnan Abdullah and published by Aveberry & Co., London in 1980.
50. M.M. Sharif: A History of Muslim Philosophy, Vol. I, p. 413.
51. Ibn Buttutah: pp. 315-316
52. Ibn Khatib: Ihata, Vol. I, p. 289.
53. Al-Maqqari/Gayangos, Vol. II, pp. 405-406.

Chapter 25

Society and Social Life

Who were the Spanish Muslims? What was their population? The second question is difficult to reply as we do not have any demographic information, and it is not possible to prepare a conjectural estimate. But there is no doubt that the region south of Toledo (which now includes the modern province of Andalusia), the valley of the Ebro in the north, as well as the South of modern Portugal, there were hundreds of thousands of the Muslims, and they constituted a majority at many places. Not only the urban centres, even hundreds of villages were full of them. Regarding the other question, it may be stated plainly that the Spanish Muslims were not a homogeneous people. They were composed of three ethnic groups — the Semitic Arabs, the Hamitic Berbers, and the Muslims of Roman and Gothic ancestry whose forefathers converted to Islam after the conquest. The Berbers were the first to arrive under the flag of Tariq; they were only twelve thousand. They were followed by eighteen thousand Arabs under Musa. Some six thousand Syrian Arabs landed with Balj, and were settled in various parts of the peninsula. There is no evidence to show that the Arabs arrived in substantial numbers afterwards. On the other hand, the Berbers continued to reach Spain whenever they were recruited by the

Umayyads, and later by the north African dynasties who ruled Spain. Attracted by the climate, and the prospects of better life, the newcomers never returned to the countries of their origin. Broadly speaking, the Arabs, both the Yemenites and the Qaisites, settled in the smiling valleys of the Guadalquivir, the Xenil, and the fertile basin of the Ebro. Nearly all the famous tribes whose names appear in the early history of Arabia (before and after the advent of Islam) were represented by their descendants who migrated to Spain for permanent settlement. The eastern region south to the walls of Tarragona in the north was dotted with Arab settlements. Even in their colonies, the members of the same tribe lived together. Toledo was full of Banu Fihr and Kinana; Seville and Valencia were thickly populated by Banu Temim and Badajos had a large number of colonisers from Hadramawt. The Berber tribes (Sanhaja, Zanata, Masmuda, and Bani Birzal) hailed from the Rif and the Grand Atlas. They outnumbered the Arabs, and occupied a larger territory though much of it was cold and inhospitable. They were concentrated in the coastal Meseta, along the Tagus, and the semi-fertile plains of La Mancha (of Don Quixote fame), the Estremadura, and the bleak hills bordering Galicia. The urban centres particularly Cordova, Medina Sidonia, Beja and Merida had large Berber families. They had minuscule pockets in the heart of predominantly Arab settlements in Ronda and Malaga. Even long after the conquest it was possible to recognise the Arabs and the Berbers by their headdress. The Berbers used the turban (imama) while the Arabs put on the qalansuwa as in other Arab countries. The separate colonies (formed on ethnic basis) were fraught with dangers to the stability of the state. When the Umayyad kingdom went to pieces, Muslim Spain was broken up into Arab and Berber kingdoms.[1]

The immigrants, both the Arabs and the Berbers who entered

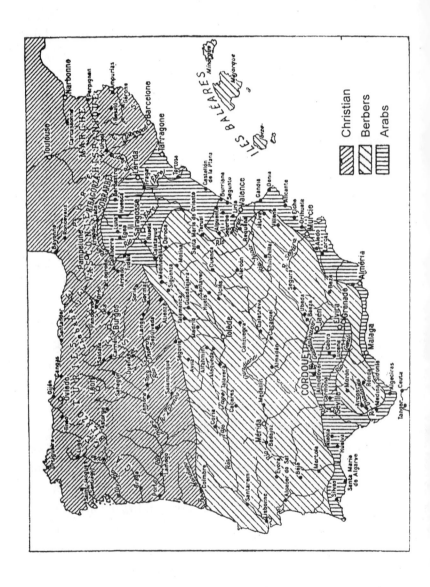

THE POPULATION OF ARABS AND BERBERS IN MUSLIM SPAIN.

into Spain with Tariq, Musa and Balj, did not exceed even fifty thousand. Although Muslim Spain came into existence as a result of conquest, at the specific invitation by a powerful section of the Christians, it differed from the colonial rule of the European warriors and marketers in Africa and Asia in recent history. The Muslims were not birds of passage. They did not exploit the country to enrich the far-flung countries of their origin. They did not live in arrogant isolation from the local population. They mingled with the people as Spain was a home to them. When they arrived in Spain, most of them were without wives. They married the local woman *(banat al ajam)*. These marriages between the Arabs and the Berbers with Roman/ Gothic women were instrumental in spreading Islam as their Spanish spouses adopted the religion of their husbands. Their conversion to Islam was necessary as otherwise these marriages, and the offspring would have been illegitimate in the eyes of the people. Even if a Christian or Jewish wife retained her faith, the Muslim husband claimed the children who were brought up in the Muslim faith. Thus, a new ethnic group came into existence. This was the group of Hispano-Muslims or *musalima/muwalladun*. After a century or more, the descendants of the Arabs and the Berbers were left with little trace of their ancestors in their haemoglobin. The Moriscos deported from Spain hardly knew whether their ancestors were Arab, or Berher or of Gothic origin; they called themselves Andalusian. At the same time it cannot be denied that the effects of colonisation of the Arabs and the Berbers, are easily perceptible even today among the Portuguese and the Spaniards. The present day Spaniard is proud of his *sangre pura* (pure blood) but facts belie this claim. On account of the concentration of the Berbers, the Portuguese of Algarve bear marked similarity to the Berbers of the Atlas mountains of north Africa. The Spaniards of rural areas in Andalusia and Valencia resemble the Arabs in their physical traits — men with straight nose and olive complexion, and women with black lustrious hair, and coal-black eyes burning with a slow fire. (It is confirmed by numerous travelogues written by western authors). This cannot be said about the Spaniards of the northern uplands, There were not many permanent settlements of the Muslims in these regions, and the people living there proudly claim that their blood is free from what they hatefully call the 'Moorish taint'.[2] A comparison of the features of a Galician or a Basque with those of a farmer in Valencia or a fisherman in south of Portugal will confirm the point.

The Berbers exceeded the Arabs, but the converted Muslims far out-numbered both of them put together. How and why the Spanish Christians adopted Islam, has been stated earlier. There is no doubt that hundreds of Roman and Gothic families took to Islam as the fish take to water.[3] Except a handful of them who embraced Islam with the tongue in their cheek, the vast bulk of them were sincere Muslims. Many of them were more orthodox than the descendants of old Muslims. The converted Muslims were seen all over Spain and in every walk of life. They adopted the Muslim way of life although some retained their Roman/Gothic surnames such as the Banu Angelino and Banu Sabarico of Seville. Even amongst prominent Muslims of Spanish ancestry there were many who were completely arabised such as ibn Qutia (son of the Gothic women), ibn Bushkuwal (son of *Pascal*), ibn Masarra, and ibn Hazm of Cordova, and the Banu Qubturnuth of Badajoz. After two or three centuries they too merged in the melting pot of Spain, and many even forgot the very names of their ancestors. The Muslim rulers utilised the services of the neo-Muslims in the civil and military set-up to compensate for the lack of enough immigrants from the

East. "The coexistence within Islam of elements of population of such diverse origin, led to their gradual fusion, a process which was aided by the adoption of an identical way and rhythm of life, and by the bilingualism which at least in everyday life, placed Spanish, Arabic and the Romance tongue *(al-'ajamiyya)* on the same footing'.[4]

Another element in the mosaic of the Spanish Muslim society worth mentioning, even though it was microscopic, was that of the slaves. All the slaves, whether black or white were foreigners. The black slaves (Ar. *'abid*) were brought from Sudan and Mali. They were employed as guards at the royal palace, and were distinguished under the Umayyads by their outfit — glittering swords, helmets, and white tunics. The negro women were employed as servants as they were known for their domestic virtues. The negro slaves continued to be employed in affluent homes up to the last days of Muslim rule. The white European slaves, the 'Saqaliba' as they were called, were imported by the Jewish slave dealers. The colour of their epidermis ensured their future. Their number increased steadily, and under the later Umayyads it was as high as thirteen thousand. These white slaves from France, eastern Europe, and northern Spain were managers of the royal harem. They came as unlettered brutes, but they picked up Arabic, and imbibed Muslim customs and courtly manners. Many grew rich, and lived in luxury, and even employed slaves in their homes to flaunt their wealth. One of them, Habib Saqalabi who lived during the reign of Hisham II, composed a book in which he celebrated the good qualities of his fraternity. Unfortunately, this high-sounding work — *kitāb al-istizhār wa-l-mugalaba'ala man ankara fada'il as-Saqaliba*, has perished. But we have another document which shows how conscious the European slaves were of their superiority over the Arabs. This is the epistle of ibn Garcia. Born in a Basque family in the extreme north, ibn Garcia was taken prisoner when he was a small boy. He grew up into a devout Muslim with a flair for Arabic literature. He was taken in service by the Slav ruler, Mujahid of Denia and the Balearic islands. In his epistle *(risala)*, preserved by ibn Bassam, ibn Garcia downgraded the Arabs in the most virulent language. In a very uncharitable remark, he called the Arabs slaves having descended from Hagar, the slave of the prophet Abraham.[5] These white slaves did not return to their native places. They were a greedy lot, and contributed in no small measure (along with the Berbers) to the dismemberment of the Umayyad kingdom. The Umayyads engaged them to counterbalance the influence of the Arabs and the Berbers, but they paid a heavy price for this mistake. Slavery was a necessary evil of the time. There were slaves in Plato's Greece, and imperial Rome, but the lot of the slaves under the Muslims was decidedly better. The slave, both male and female, could buy his or her freedom. Many lived as members of the family while pious Muslims manumitted their slaves as an act of mercy. Some slaves even inherited the property of their masters. (In India a whole dynasty which included a queen, ruled in the Middle ages.) In Muslim Spain, the white slaves set up small kingdoms which lasted till the coming of the Almoravids. There was also an abundance of female slaves in the nineth and the tenth centuries. Their number ran into thousands. They were mostly prisoners of war who remained in the Muslim territory if not ransomed by their guardians. A blonde Christian slave who imbibed Muslim culture, and who could also sing and dance after training, was simply irresistible. They entered the royal household and aristocratic homes. They were given beautiful names — *Sihr* (Magic), *Jawhara* (Pearl), *Subh* (Dawn), *Uns al-Qulub* (Joy of hearts). What is most surprising is that almost all the Muslim rulers were children of these white Christian slaves. This is why many rulers after Hakam I had blue eyes, golden hair and red beards — the hall-marks of European physiognomy. From this point of view, the Spaniards themselves continued to rule the country except for the period of Almoravid and Almohad intervention. They were not an alien race, but sons of the soil, the only differences being that they were not Roman Catholics. Seen in this perspective, there was no serious break in the continuity of Spanish history.

In addition to the above ethnic groups, there were also the Jews and the Christians. Collectively, they were called the *"ahl al-zimma"* a word used to signify that the Muslim rulers were responsible for their protection and well-being. The Jews were much less than the Christians. The former belonged to the Semitic race, while the latter were a mixed race of the previous conquerors — the Romans, the Phoenicians, the Goths, and the Vandals who settled in Spain long before the Muslims. The Jews lived side by side with the Muslims, spoke the same language, and gave Arabic names to their children. But though culturally integrated, they were not so emotionally. The Jews were persecuted under the Romans and the Goths, but they found in Muslim Spain a haven of security — the first ever they had after the Diaspora. Under the Muslim rulers they served as ambassadors, physicians, and ministers. They amassed wealth by trade with European countries and the Muslim East. The excise collectorate under the Umayyads was practically in their hands. They also shone in the world of letters. Some of the greatest Jews of all time — Hasdai ibn Shahprut the ambassador and physician, Ismail ibn Naghzalah the chief minister of the Zirid state, ibn Gibrol (1021-1070), the philosopher, ibn Maymun (1135-1204) the great physicians and thinker, Bahya ibn Pakuda the mystic, and the writer Yehuda Halevi (d. 1143) and several others were born in Muslim Spain.[6] But the Jews were loyal by compulsion of self-interest. The Spanish Jews had an infinite capacity to cut their sails to every changing gust of the wind. They stabbed the Gothic Christian state when the Muslims appeared in the peninsula, and when the Muslims fell on evil days, they turned their back on them. How ironic it is that after they were squeezed out of Spain in thousands by Ferdinand and Isabella in 1492, they migrated to Muslim lands for safety. As for the Christians living in the Muslim territory, they (mostly the priests and their fervent follows and the northern ruling families) never accepted the legitimacy of the state. Even though the bulk of them were arabised, in their heart of hearts, they looked to their northern brothers for salvation from the Muslim rule. For them the Muslims were, politically intruders, and theologically pagan. They longed for freedom forgetting they too were offsprings of Roman and Gothic pagans. When the Muslims grew weak through mutual fighting, they had no scruples in allying themselves with the northern Christian rulers. The arabised Christians — the *mozārabes*, played an insidious part in the liquidation of Toledo and other parts of the Muslim territory. In the later centuries, they were all saboteurs, and by their activities they facilitated the mission of the conquistadores.

The Muslims were proud of their beloved al-Andalus. It is not difficult to discern a deep feeling of love for their country — its prosperity, the beauty of its cities, the greenery of her valleys, and the glory of her cultural life. This feeling of intense nationalism peeps through their historical and literary works. They were proud of being Spanish Muslims — *Andalusi*. Many writers, theologians and thinkers added the word 'al-Andalusi' after their names. Some even specified the names of the very city of their birth, viz. *al-qurtabi* (born at Cordova), *al-ishbili* (hailing from Seville), *al-majriti* (born at Madrid) etc. The

sentiment of nationalism almost bordering on chauvinism is
seen in the epistles of ibn Hazm and Ash-Shaqundi which were
composed to prove that the Andalusians were in no way inferior
to the Muslims of eastern lands. Both of them thought that the
Spanish Muslims excelled the eastern Muslims in many fields.
In his epistle ibn Hazm says — 'I have read in the Gospels that
Jesus said: "no one is a prophet in his own country.' By this
biblical reference, he implied that the Spanish Muslims should
stop their fascination for the East, and think of the glories of
their own country. Another writer, the qaḍi Sa'id of Toledo in
his monograph 'History of Science/*Tabaqat al-umam*'
condemned the European races living beyond the Pyrenees for
their backwardness. He thought of them as a race of thickheaded
barbarians.[7] When ibn Khatib was an exile in Africa, he pined
for Spain. His famous muwashshaha addressed to sultan
Muhamamd V began with the following lyrical lines:

> Jada-k al-ghayth idh al-ghaythu hama
> Ya zaman 'l-wasli bi- 'l-Andalusi.
> May abundant rains refresh you.
> Oh! the time of meeting in Al-Andalus.[8]

This noble feeling of patriotism, this vibrant sentiment of
love for Spain was not exploited for noble ends. The selfish
rulers, and political adventures mad for power, fermented armed
conflicts resulting in their eventual downfall and extinction.

What was the position of women in Spanish society? Muslim
society, it may be admitted, was male dominated — just like
any other society of civilized homosapiens. The father, being
the head of the family, both male and female children, grew
under his authority and protection. No girl could marry without
the consent of her father. When Mu'tamid's daughter was
arrested and sold, her wealthy purchaser wanted her to marry

his son, but the brave girl refused. She wrote to her father who was then a prisoner at Aghmat. She informed him of her plight, and obtained his permission. 'Abd ar-Rahman V loved his cousin Habiba. He wrote to her in a poem that he was eligible for her hand became he had good looks *(jamal)* and also possessed good manners *(adab)*, but her mother (she had already lost her father) rejected the suit. A bride brought dowry *(jahiz)* with her according to the status of her father. The rich parents gave substantial dowry to their daughters, some even borrowed money for the purpose. The reader will recall that al-Mansur advanced money from the public treasury to his friend for his daughter's marriage. During the caliphate period Cordova was flooded with female captives. These girls were readily available and no dowry was demanded for them. The Muslim parents had, therefore, to spend lavishly on dowry to capture suitable grooms for their daughters.[9] The dowry was a voluntary gift; it included jewellery, a wardrobe of silks and brocades. Some virtuous ladies would find grooms for orphan girls and willingly parted with their clothes and jewellery for them.[10] Among the Moriscos, the dowry was the simplest — a bed and ten ducts because they lived under fear and uncertainty. An ideal marriage was a life-long relationship. In the society of the Spanish Muslims, marriage was easy, romance risky, and divorce difficult. Most of the marriages, though arranged by parents were successful. On the other hand, some of the famous romances — of Wallada and the poet ibn Zaidun, of Hafsa and Abū Ja'far Sa'id, never bloomed into marriage. A marriage was conducted by a qadi, and also liquidated by him. If a divorce suit came before him, the qadi did his best to avert the disaster unless it was found inevitable. A woman felt utterly helpless if she herself wanted a divorce from a cruel husband. We have seen how a humanitarian qadi paid indemnity to the husband of a woman who was prepared to commit suicide rather than live with her husband. Rarely, a divorced woman who abhorred her husband would refuse to take the custody of her child. When ibn Sa'd the 12th century chief of Valencia divorced his wife, she left her son with him on the plea that the child might grow into a rascal like his father.[11]

By and large, the women lived in seclusion, but there was no ban on their visiting markets and public baths. They could even visit a cemetery a freedom denied to Muslim women in many countries. The German traveller, Munzer who was in Granada in 1494, saw a burial ceremony near the Gate of Elvira. He found the imam chanting the prayers, while women dressed in white scattered branches of myrtle on the grave. The woman moved in the public places with their heads covered, and faces partially exposed. In the villages they worked without a veil. Educated women like the princess Wallada, Nazhun, Hafsa moved freely without a veil. The Andalusian women of the leisured class with slaves to look after housework, had ample time for cultured pursuits. Economically, women were dependent upon the males, but they were free to earn their living. The Andalusian women were excellent caligraphics. At one time in the 10th century, there were 170 female caligraphists in the city of Cordova[12]. Teaching was also a profession open to women. In the fields, they tended the silkworms. Spinning and weaving and even perhaps carpet-making at home, were popular female occupations. But the number of economically emanciplated women was marginal. The vast majority of them them lived at home, and looked after domestic chores — to the profound regret of the philosopher ibn Rushd. After the marriage, the husband had (theoretically) definite mastery over his wife, but in actual practice it was not so. The Muslim males (leaving aside men who were instinctively domineering, or were misogynists like the 14th century scholar Abu l-Barakat al-Ballafiqi of Granada) were henpecked husbands. In fact, the teachings of Islam and the Prophet's own life inculcated a spirit of chivalry towards women. Several rulers were the most obedient servants of their wives. The iron-willed Hakam I, the debonair 'Abd ar-Rahman II, danced attendance on their wives/mistresses. Once an angry Tarub shut herself in her boudoir and would not talk to 'Abd ar-Rahman. Royal messages failed to thaw the haughty beauty. At last, 'Abd-ar-Rahman ordered that a pile of gold be placed at the closed door. The magic worked, and the door opened. The pious 'Abdullah dotted on his 'Pearl' — the former Christian Iniga Graces. The caliph 'Abd ar-Rahman was ordered about by Zahra for whom he built the garden city of Madinat al-Zahra. His son Hakam II was in the hands of the Christian beauty Aurora (Subh). Al-Mu'tamid was led by the nose by Rumaikiya/Itimad. He went out of the way to meet every whimsical demand of the coquette. One day, she saw from the window some village girls walking on muddy puddles, and she recalled her days when she was a girl and walked bare-footed on the muddy bank of the river. Al-Mu'tamid ordered that a patio of the palace be covered with musk and ambergris, and rose-water, and the queen walked playfully with her maids on the fragrant paste. Long after, she reproached her husband for being unattentive to her, and the faithful prince retorted — 'wa la nahar at-tin — not even on the day of the mud." She recalled the incidence, and withdrew her remarks. The qaḍi Muhammad ibn Ali of Granada had a soft corner for women. He used to tell the people that women were like delicate crystals and should be handled with care.[13] The ladies of the royal harem steered clear of the garbage of politics — except Tarub, the wife of 'Abd ar-Rahman II, and Ayesha, the mother of Abū Abdallah, the last king of Granada.

The generality of Andalusian women were pious and devoted to their faith. The saintly and learned fisherman of Lisbon, Al-Marwāni (a contemporary of ibn Bajja) who lost his life in a battle with the Christians, left his wife and a daughter. The mother and the daughter (both were educated) earned their livelihood by spinning, and refused to take any gift of money from an admirer of the deceased head of the family.

But women in the royal harem and affluent families had to put up with bigamy of their husbands. Perhaps, there was always a surplus of women in Muslim Spain. In the 12th century, the philosopher ibn Rushd found that female population was double of men. Naturally, marriage was the only career open to them. Frequent wars decimated the male population; captive women arrived as trophies of a military victory, and these had to be absorbed in the social mainstream through a legal marriage or through concubinage. The latter relationship was short-lived because as soon as a concubine delivered a child she rose to the status of a wife with full rights for her, and her child. The ordinary Muslim like ibn Jubayr was happy with only one wife. But even when a wealthy husband had only one wife, the latter was always haunted by the fear that her husband might implant her rival in the house at any time. A most characteristic example is that of the handsome Abū Bakr of Cordova and his wife narrated by ibn Hazm. Abū Bakr was married to the beautiful Atiqa, a daughter of the Commander of the Upper Marches, under the government of al-Mansur. She was a nagging wife, and the two often quarrelled on petty matters, although Abū Bakr was loyal to her, and never set his eyes on another woman. Abū Bakr died of plague in June 1011 in the prime of his youth. After his death, the world lost its sunshine for Atiqa. She wasted away slowly, and joined her husband on the very day he had expired. When she was alive, she used to tell her mother that after the death of Abū Bakr, she had lost the will to live, but she had at least one comfort in her life that while he was alive, he never shared bed with another woman. The reader is free to draw his conclusions.

We do not know exactly how the Spanish Muslim women looked like A mixed race of the Arabs, the Goths, and the Romans, the Spanish Muslims were a handsome race. The women, by and large, were good-looking. But there was no Malborough, and no Rubens to transfer their beauty to the canvas. In the absence of painting and sculpture, we may turn to the versatile art i.e. poetry, to catch glimpses of Andalusian women. The beauty of a women was linked to all that is lovely in nature — the gardens, the flowers, the sun, the moon, the stars, the slowly gliding streams, the precious stones, and the dark-eyed gazelles. 'Abd ar-Rahman V praised the white bosoms of Habiba; the poetess Hafsa speaks of "the springs of sweetness" i.e. her lips, and invites her lover to the cool shade of her long and flowing tresses. A tall figure like the willow *(ban)* rising from prosperous hips was an essential element of female beauty. The lily-white neck of his beloved made ibn Khafaja almost mad. Nature fashioned Wallada (says her lover ibn Zaidun, in his qasida *'nunya'*) from musk, silver and pearls; so soft and delicate was her skin that even her bangles made the skin red like blood. Ibn Baqi compares the cool and serene beauty of his beloved to statues made of ivory and marble. Big and dark eyes like that of a gazelle, and langrous glances were the subject of many love songs. Ibn Hazm liked blue eyes in his early youth. The Granadine ibn Hayyan got intoxicated by the sight of dark eyes, a moon-like face, enveloped in the clouds of dark tresses, and a mouth with pearl-like teeth enclosed by scarlet lips. The Spanish Muslims were proud of their females. Here is ibn Khatib's eloquent tribute to the ladies of Granada.

"The women of Granada (says the historian) are distinguished
for their beauty, their gracefulness, their long and wavy hair,
the pearl-like whiteness of their teeth, the perfume of their
breath, the lightness of their gait, their mellifluous conversation,
and their good morals."[14] Their love for finery (he adds),
colourful and gorgeous raiments, passion for jewellery, have
reached the stage of competition among them. The long list of
costumes given by Pérès shows that the Andalusian women
were rather overdressed[15]. Their dress was no doubt elaborate
and picturesque. The Christian royalty and aristocracy of the
northern regions, derived much of the splendour of the female
trousseau from the Muslims. The inner garment, the *qamis* (from
which the French got the word chemise) was put on by all
women. On the qamis they wore a jacket *(mitraf)*. The lower
part of the body was covered with petticoats called *'sarawil.'*
The headdress covered the face leaving the eyes open. A long
robe or cloak *(qaba)* reached down the knees like the mantilla
of the Spanish ladies. The qaba was held by an ornamental belt
— the *washi*. The belt of wealthy ladies was made of brocade,
of many colours and adorned with jewels. In the kingdom of
Granada stockings became a fashion with ladies.[16] Their footwear
was like the colourful slippers of modern Algerian women. The
ladies of the privileged class who led a leisurely life took full
care of their appearance and coiffure. They perfumed their
bodies, scented their hair, applied maskara *(kohl)* to the eyes
(added poison to their glances as the poet ibn Hani said), and
dyed their fingertips with henna. The hair was tied in a chignon
at the nape. Some women, like their eastern sisters, allowed
their hair to dangle with studied negligence, while others would
'set' their hair like the letter 'lam' of the Arabic alphabet on
their temples. Gold and silver ornaments bedecked the female
anatomy. The most popular ornaments were the ear-rings,

bracelets, necklesses, bangles and pendants. We get much of this information from the poetry of the Spanish Muslims.

Illiteracy in a woman was regarded as a blot on her sex. Qamar, a slave-girl of Ibrahim ibn Hajjaj, the 9th century rebel chief of Seville, has left a poem in which she said that if a woman should be illiterate to enter the Paradise, she would prefer to go to hell.[17] In a chapter of his Nafh at-tib, the indefatigable al-Maqqari, while dilating upon the literary history of the Andalusians, says, 'we shall be guilty of negligence if before closing this chapter we do not say a few words about the wives and daughters of the Muslims who made themselves conspicuous by their talent and who showed their wit and eloquence in elaborate and ingenious poems.'[18] And then, he opens a small picture gallery of Andalusian women who were known for their learning and literary talents. There is enough evidence to show that the Spanish Muslim women did enjoy some freedom and initiative, but there is no evidence of separate schools for girls. Probably they could join the mosque schools and read in the company of boys during their early teens. The grown-up girls were taught at home by their parents, and those who could afford, by private tutors. For this reason higher education was limited to a small number of women. The majority of them could read the Quran and religious books, and were able to write at least elementary Arabic. Many could compose poetry, and several anthologies are full of their poems. Except poetry, not a single literary or historical work of an Andalusian woman, has come down to us. They had no Gulbadan Banu Begum, no Jahan Ara, no Zebunnisa, as in Mughal India, but there was more literacy among Andalusian woman than any Muslim state in the Middle Ages. In female literacy, Muslim Spain excelled ancient Greece, Rome, and even Byzantine empire.

The earliest poetess was Hassana al-Tamimiya who lived in the reigns of Hakam I, and 'Abd ar-Rahman II. The latter, we already know, was the father of Hispano-Muslim culture. Qalam who lived in his harem was widely read in polite literature, and wrote with a beautiful hand. Lubna, a talented poetess graced the court of Hakam II. She was equally good in arithmetic. She drafted the private letters of Hakam. Almost contemporary with her was Fatima who copied manuscripts for the library of Hakam. In the 2nd half of the 10th century Ayesha bint Ahmad was (according to ibn Hayyan) unrivalled for her learning *(ilm)*, and proficiency in literature *(adab)*. She was an expert caligraphist, and made copies of the Quran. She was skillful in composing extempore poetry. When al-Muzaffar received her in his palace, she improvised verses wishing his son (who was presented to her) would come up to his expectations. Dana al-'amiriya, a daughter of al-Muzaffar was a composer of melodies. She set ibn Hazm's poems to music.[19] The Andalusian girls were taught instrumental music so that after they were married they could provide solace to their husbands.[20]

In the twilight of the Umayyad kingdom, the princess Wallada daughter of the caliph 'Abd ar-Rahman al-Mustakfi, shone like the moon on the literary firmament. Ibn Bassam has given a pen portrait of this *femme fatale* of Cordova, who ran a salon at her mansion, which was a rendezvous of contemporary writers of prose and poetry. Warm-hearted, quick in making repartees, a master of classical literature, this blonde daughter of a Christian concubine was free from the inhibitions of her sex. She moved freely among her many admirers. She was dressed in the height of current fashion. Her flowing robe carried two inscriptions which read: By Allah, I am destined to eminence, and I keep my head high. My lovers may touch my cheeks, and if they desire they can even kiss me.'[21] Some European authors compare her to the Greek poetess Sappho, others see in her life and character, the French novelist Georges Sand. The unlucky ibn Zaidun was mad about her. For sometime, she reciprocated his feelings. Once she invited him to a secret meeting after sending the following missive.

> Meet me at night when it is dark,
> The night keeps all secrets.
> I love you so much that if the moon loved like me
> It would not shine,
> And the stars would not move.

The lovers continued to meet in a garden among flower-beds, but their romance came to an end when she became cold and formal. A materialist to the core, she preferred her intellectual inferior — the rich Cordovan ibn 'Abbdus who also visited her salon along with others. In all probability, she joined his harem, and said goodbye to the Muse. Ibn Zaidun addressed many poems to her. The qasida already referred to, (one of the gems of Hispano-Arabic poetry), was inspired by her. In a satire in prose he even ridiculed ibn 'Abbdus and cast aspersions on his dark skin, but nothing would melt the heart of this Andalusian *la belle dame sans merci*. She died in 1091.[22] Some authors say that she never married.

Spanish history from the 11th century onwards is crowded with blue-stockings, both Muslim and Jew. Maryam bint Abu Yaqub Ansari who was born at Silves, left for Seville in the early decade of the century where she set up a school for girls and taught literature. She was an ornament to her sex who combined in her both character and learning. She was also a poetess. Several poems of Maryam are extant, but the most touching is the one in which she gives a picture of her old age:

What do you expect from a woman of seventy-seven?
Frail as a spider's web,
Hobbling like a baby, supporting a stick
A prisoner loaded in chains!

Ummtul Aziz Sherifiya, a descendant of the caliph Ali, and a
grand-daughter of ibn Diyha author of 'Mutrib', was an eminent
poetess of her time. She was also a scholar of grammar, prosody,
and gave lectures on literature. Men were not ashamed at
learning prosody from her. The two beautiful princesses —
Umm ul-Karim of Almeria, and Umm ul-Ala of Guadalajara
were highly educated women of independent character. When
a man with grey hair proposed to the latter, she advised him
in a poem to keep his distance. In a well-known couplet she
told him that grey hair cannot seduce youth, and that he should
not behave in his old age as foolishly as he did when he was
young.[23] Al-Mu'tamid's daughter Buthaina inherited her father's
talent in versification. Her letter in the form of a poem addressed
to her father in which she sought his permission to marry, is a
literary masterpiece and it is enough to ensure her immortality
in opinion of Henri Pérès. During the Almoravid period Nazhun
of Granada earned fame in the literary circles as a poetess of
beautiful similes which conveyed the tenderness of her soul
and her mild disposition.[24] There were many others who
distinguished themselves in literature, — Hind and Asma of
Seville, Ummul Hanna, Hamda, and her sister Zainab of Alhama,
Nudar (d. 1338) the scholarly daughter of ibn Havyan, the
famous grammarian of Granada. Before we take leave of
Andalusian women, we may also meet Hafsa bint Hajjaj
ar-Rukuni of Granada, the most outstanding poetess of her time.
Ibn Khatib did not omit to include her in his biographies of
eminent persons of his beloved Granada. She was (says ibn
Khatib) the unique (farid) woman of her time in beauty, culture

and literary accomplishments. Although a liberated woman, she was not a gold-digger like Wallada. She was a poetess of great sensitivity and feminine grace. Much of her poetry was inspired by her love for the ill-starred aristocrat Abū Ja'far ibn Sa'id. Their romance ended in a tragedy. Many a time they would steal away to a kiosk *(qubba)* in the shady grove of Hauz Mu'ammal on the outskirts of Granada where they sat locked in each others arms. She had a premonition that their love would end in a disaster for both. In a sad proem she expressed her fears thus :

> By my life, the garden was not happy at our tryst.
> It was full of enmity and jealousy.
> The stream felt no joy at our union.
> The dove *(qumri)* sang only plaintive songs.
> Do not think your thoughts will help you in all conditions.
> I suspect that the stars in the sky are spying over us.[25]

She proved to be right. The Almohad governor wanted her hand, and finding no response from her, he got Abū Ja'far beheaded on a false charge of conspiracy. Poor Hafsa put on a mourning dress at the tragic end of her lover. She received threatening letters and settled at Marrakesh as a teacher to ladies of the royal harem. She never married and died in 1190.

For many Andalusians life was a long holiday of pleasure and fun. Like the Romans, they spent their lives in indoor and outdoor amusements — chess playing, picnics on gondolas, *fêtes champêtres*, feasts, banquets and drinking parties. Horse-racing and hunting were the most favourite outdoor games. The valleys of Andalusia abounded in pigeons, partridges, pheasants and cranes. The hunters had trained hawks to catch the birds. At home, chess swallowed the time of many indolent men.

This intellectual game, creation of the ancient Hindus, reached Spain from the Orient, and attracted the prince and the peasant alike. There were plenty of grand masters. Al-Muzaffar patronised master chess players, and several of them were on his payroll. Under the mulūk at-tawāif, chess playing, like poetry, became an obsession. Ibn Abbas, the pleasure loving bibliophile and minister of Zuhair of Almeria, was a great chess player of his time. He was so confident of his success that while playing he chanted his favourite lines: Bad luck is asleep, and defeating me is forbidden by fate. Once a game of chess saved Seville from massive destruction when Alfonso invaded the kingdom of al-Mu'tamid to recover the customary tribute from him. He found himself in a hopeless situation, but the resourceful ibn ʿAmmar who was a brilliant chess player, came to his rescue. He visited the Christian camp armed with a fabulous chess board worth a kings's ransom. When, the chess board made of gold, and sandlewood pieces, was displayed before Alfonso, he marvelled at its beauty and worksmanship. Ibn Ammar invited him to play a round on the condition that if Alfonso won he would have the chessboard, and he (ibn Ammar) won, he would demand whatever he liked. The greedy monarch agreed as he had set his heart on the chessboard. Ibn Ammar, who was the invincible king of the chess won the game. As the winner, he demanded Alfonso to withdraw from the Muslim territory. Alfonso went back on his word, but later agreed if he was given the tribute.[26] Abū Abdullah, the last king of Granada was also a reputed chess player. He played a game with Pedro Fajerdo, the governor of Lorca — the stakes being Almeria and Lorca. Abū Abdulla won the game, but Pedro refused to honour his pledge to hand over Lorca. Playing chess was a favourite pastime of the Muslim ladies. A miniature in the Book of Chess (compiled and illustrated under the orders of Alfonso the Learned shows a high born Muslim lady clad in a long robe and bedecked in jewellery, playing chess with a Christian lady. Chess was introduced in Europe by the Spanish Muslims. They called the game 'al-shatranj' after the original Sanskrit. The Spanish word for chess — ajedrez, and also the Portuguese 'xadres' are derived from the word al-shatranj. Alfonso's book on chess is based on Arabic sources, and describes the game and moves as known to the Muslims.[27]

Another popular entertainment was the magic show performed by an illusionist *(khayali)* behind a screen on which he casted shodows accompanied by a dialogue. Yet another most popular show was the 'kurraj'. It was performed by armed dancers mounted on a wooden horse — very much like the hobby-horse of today. Attack and withdrawal were special features of this show. The hobby-horse was called 'zāmil al-zain. This game is still performed in Spain, and among the Basques of north Spain, the hobby-horse is called zamalzain.[28] But of all the funs, nothing pleased the hedonists of Muslim Spain more than the dance of a ballerina. A class of professional dancers *(rawaqis)* existed in Spain during the days of the mulūk at-tawāif. The rulers of these small princedoms kept a battalion of musicians and female dancers. Ibn Abbas mentioned above had the greatest munher of dancers, but the figure of 4000 given by historians is grossly exaggerated. His was rather an extreme case because he owned fabulous wealth. (The man owned a library of half a million books) During the time of the historian Shaqandi (11th century) the ballerinas of Ubeda were famous for their beauty, vivacity, and fine play of the sabre dance. As all dance, whether performed before a deity or men, is basically lascivious, so also was the Andalusian dance. The repertoire of choreography was limited to amorous signals from the eyes and the hands. Some motions expressed the coquetry of the beloved, and the humility of the lover.[29] The wedding feast *(walima)* in the kingdom of Granada was incomplete if there was no dance performance. So endemic was this kind of festivity, that the sultan Yusuf had to restrict it in the public interest. The dances of the Muslims of Granada, and also the Moriscos were, the *zamras* and the *lailas*. These dancers were officially banned by the Inquisitions.

Although, all the vegetables grew in plenty in Spain, the Spaniards of those days — the Christians, the Jews, and the Muslims were a non-vegetarian people. Probably, the meat was boiled before being baked as in the East. The ordinary folk consumed mutton and fish (mostly sea fish), but those who were wealthy, preferred poultry, vension and meat of birds. Grilled fish, balls of minced meat, asparagus and artichoke were the favourite dishes of passionate stomachs. Wheat was the staple food of all the Andalusians. Very delicious breads were made at homes and public backeries, from flour, syrup of dates, and oil of almonds.[30] The Andalusian food was moderately spicy as all the major spices, — pepper, cloves, ginger, cardamon and cinnamon were cultivated in Spain. Vinegar was used for making a variety of pickles. Honey was an essential item of food thanks to the extensive rearing of bees in orchards and gardens. Desert truffles were made from figs, pistachios, almonds, eggs and nuts. A popular dish was the *halwa* of carrot which was prepared in honey and syrup of grapes. Another sweet, sold at all confectioneries, was '*mujabbanat*' made from cheese. The town of Jerez was famous for these sweets. On certain festivals, specially the noroz, they made big cakes of fine flour *(darmak)* perfumed with suffron *(muza' fara)*[31]. At all banquets and grand parties, the food was served a la Ziryab viz. by a succession of courses and not by placing all the food before the guests. The aristocratic families were fond of inviting friends at parties for the fun of a get-together. A Prime Minister of Granada (Muhammad bin Abd ar-Rahman al-Lakhmi) who kept an open house, was known to give banquets outstanding the feasts given by the Bermeki family of Baghdad.[32] Ibn Khaldun was all praise for the Muslims of Granada for their wonderful parties. The frank and eloquent confession of Abū Ja'far reveal the pleasures of life enjoyed by the aristocracy. He was a scion of the famous Banu Sa'id family of Alcala la Real distinguished for their wealth and intellectual pursuits. He was beheaded in April 1164, his fault being that he loved the poetess Hafsa. Ja'far's cousin visited him a day before his execution. A calm Ja'far consoled the weeping visitor thus — 'Why do you weep for me. I have enjoyed my life to the full. I have eaten the hearts and livers of chickens, used crystal cups, rode fleet steeds, dressed myself in silk, burnt the costliest candles, enjoyed the company of wives and concubines, and reposed on soft brocades. I am now in the hands of a cruel Hajjaj, and waiting the fate of Hallaj"[33]. The guests did not eat in silence. Witty jokes were exchanged as invitees did justice to the food before them. At a grand party given by al-Ma'mun, the ruler of Toledo, a certain pastry called 'the qadi's ears' was served along with a fruit popularly known as 'the cow's eyes'. When the guests were eating the pastry, al-Ma'mun turned to the qadi al-Waqqashi and remarked jokingly, 'Look qadi, they are eating your ears'. The quick-witted qadi picked up the fruit, and retorted, "and I am eating their eyes."[34]

Wine drinking was failry common among men of substance, the poets and freethinkers. As prosperity increased, drinking assumed alarming proportions in the 10th century. The teetotaller Hakam II once seriously thought of destroying all the vineyards in his kingdom, but the theologians advised that prohibition could not be enforced in that way as the addicts would find substitutes for wine[35]. Some of the zealous teetotallers (and they were always in a majority) would break into houses and destroy wine cups to record their protest against drinking. But all this was of no avail. Men like ibn Quzman who was a connoisseur of expensive wines, ruled out all repentance. In a zajal he tells an angry theologian *(faqi)* — "You want me to repent. How foolish of you! How can I repent when the garden is ablaze with flowers, the breeze is fragrant, and the flute is pouring out soulful music."[36] Ibn Madghalis who lived in the 12th century would not listen to his moralising critics. In a zajal, he advised them to go on a pilgrimage to Hijaz and leave him to his pleasures[37]. The place most preferred for drinking was not so much a carpeted hall, but a garden (bustan) on moon-lit and starry skies. The Andalusians raised drinking to an art. The names of cups and vessels connected with drinking would make a glossary. A sweet called 'naql' was served as snacks along with wine. The wine was served by effeminate boys, or by lissom girls with dreamy eyes. Ibn Az-Zaqqaq (d-1134) has celebrated an Ephebe in a poem.[38] The drinking sessions lasted a whole night and the revellers regretted when they heard the muezzin calling the faithfuls for the pre-dawn prayer. A shameless Umayyad prince sang with joy, — 'I spend my nights in drinking in the company of beautiful faces *(wuju milāh)* and I do not bother to listen the meuzzin chanting *"hayya alal falah".*[39] In the kingdom of Granada, drinking was not uncommon. Once a Secretary named Muhammad 'Abd al-'Abid came drunk and vomitted in the very presence of the sultan, and he lost his job.[40] Malaga wine was famous all over the country, and a dying prince desired Malaga wine even after death. Some addicts would visit a church where the priests were equally notorious for drinking, and would entertain their guests with hospitality. Cordova in the 12th century was famous for a variety of wine known as 'wine of the Convent' *(Khamr al-dair)*[41].

The pious Muslims had their own gatherings *sans wine*, and sans music. We have a warm description of one such assembly held at Toledo during the peaceful reign of Hakam II. The gathering was held at the house of Ahmad bin Sa'id Ansari a rich and religious minded person known for his learning and moral rectitude. Some fifty invitees attended the periodic meetings. The guests came from distant places and nearby towns. The invitees sat in a spacious hall tastefully decorated with silk hangings, and with carpets on the floor. If it was winter, a mettallic tube of burning charcoal was placed in the centre to warm the guests as they reclined on cushions. The session began with a recitation from the Quran. This was followed by a long discussion. The meeting ended with a princely banquet. Dish after dish of meat prepared in olive oil was followed by curd, desserts and fruits.[42] We hear about symposia of literati, poets and critics, held under the patronage of wealthy men of culture. At such meetings poetry was recited in a spirit of healthy competition. Some poets, with a sharpe memory, would recite verses ending with the same letter or rhyme. Others would give on the spot demonstration of their skill in versification by composing lines on any subject suggested to them. There would be discussions on classical masters, as well as critical evaluation of writings of emerging authors. Some would read from memory pages after pages from the Kitāb al Aghani of Isphani, or the maqamat of Hariri. Such warm gatherings as well as religious symposia — the *"maulood"* were a common ocurrence throughout the kingdom of Granada.

The birth of a child, the circumcision of the male child, the religious festivals (the two Eids), the Persian nauroz, and

wedding ceremonies were celebrated with gusto by the rich and
the poor alike. We have described the grand reception given by
al-Ma'mun of Toledo on the circumcision ceremony of his
grandson. The ceremony held at the Zahira palace was equally
memorable. On this occasion a mass circumcision ceremony of
five hundred boys from different families was held by al-Mansur
at his own expense. All marriages in Spain were solemnised by
a qadi with recitations from the Quran and the hadith. The
religious ceremony culminated in festivities, illuminations and
music. One of the grandest celebrations marked the marriage of
al-Mansur's son al-Muzaffar with Habiba. On the day of their
marriage, the bride dressed in silk and brocades and jewellery
left her home in the company of her relations and friends
followed by the qadi and the witnesses for the Zahira palace.
The garden, the lakes and the fountains were profusely
illuminated. The bride was received at the gate by maids each
holding an ivory wand inlaid with gold. She was led to the
pavilion where she was to wait for her husband. Music filled
the air as the guests feasted on the choisest cousin. At night the
groom arrived with his relations under a canopy of swords
made of gold, and he demanded entrance into the pavilion.
After a feigned resistence by the bride's maids he was allowed
to enter. The festivities lasted the whole night while the
musicians sang, and the poets chanted blessings for the new
couple.[43] The celebrations at the marriage of al-Mu'tadid of
Seville with a daughter of Mujahid of Denia and the Balearic
Islands, lasted a week. The wedding of al-Musta'in Billah (early
12th century) with a daughter of the minister of Valencia was
the grandest social gathering ever held in the northern kingdom
of Saragossa. The Jewish minister Abū Fadl ibn Hasdai was in
charge of all the arrangements. Guests arrived from all parts of
the country — brave knights, distinguished secretaries, ministers

and neighbouring princes. The splendour of the celebrations surpassed the wedding ceremony of al-Ma'mun, the Abassid ruler of Baghdad with the princess Buran. Feasting and merry-making continued for days and nights and nothing was left out to cater the comfort and pleasure of the guests[44]. There are reports of lavish wedding feasts (walima) in the kingdom of Granada. The marriage among the Moriscos was the simplest affair. A bed and 10 ducats were all the dowry they gave to their daughters.[45] The Morisco bride and the groom went to the church in borrowed Christian costume for the marriage ceremony. After they returned home, the marriage was performed according to the Muslim rites behind closed doors. After the nuptials, the bride's mother visited the groom's house, and scattered handfuls of sweets, perhaps, as a good omen for the newly-wed.

The venue of outdoor recreation was often a pleasure garden specially on full-moon nights. The garden was also a place for philosophical discussions, scintillating talks, and recital of poetry. Often the perfume of the flowers would mingle with the voluptuous music of a lute played in accompaniment to a tambourine, while a ballerina danced on the light fantastic toe. The Spanish Muslims built hundreds of gardens. In fact there were never so many gardens in the whole history of Spain before. The joy of owning a garden was shared by all. The sufi Muhammad ibn Tahir (d. 989) on his return after a long sojourn in the East, settled at Murcia, and built a garden in which he planted fruits and vegetables.[46] This sufi's garden was nothing compared to the vast botanical gardens. Prof. G.S. Colin tells us that Europe's first botanical gardens were created by the Spanish Muslims. In the rest of Europe (he adds), they appeared in the middle of the 16th century.[47] ʿAbd ar-Rahman was the first ruler to build a garden which was planted with seeds and fruit saplings imported from Syria. It is he who introduced the palm and the pomegranate in Spain. From his time to the 15th century, the Andalusian plains, hills and valleys smiled with gardens in whatever territory was held by the Muslims.

The Muslims' love for gardens is ascribed by some European authors to descriptions of Paradise reserved for the virtuous as a reward in their life beyond the grave. There are several verses in the Quran in which the bliss of after-life is metaphorically compared to the joy of living in a garden of perennial summer and running water. The terrestrial garden was, therefore, conceived as a reflection of the celestial garden (*firdos*) or Paradise. Many Muslims desired to be buried amidst flowery plants and ever-green shrubs. The burial gardens (Ar. sig. *rauza*) were dotted all over the Muslim world, of which, that dream in marble-the Taj at Agra, is the best example. There were several tombs in Muslim Spain, but not of that grand scale. The garden tombs of the Muslims have disappeared through vandalism, but a few epitaphs celebrate their beauty. A typical epitaph of the garden tomb of the Granadine sultan Yusuf III is preserved in the Alhamra museum. The epitaph reads — May rain clouds water the grave, and the moist garden carry to him, its fresh perfume'[48].

Writing about the cultural life of the Arabs, Dr. Draper says, "No nation has excelled the Spanish Arabs in the beauty and costliness of their pleasure gardens[49]." It is possible to reconstruct an authentic Andalusian garden. Ibn Hazm has described a garden-cum-orchard, the property of his friend where he spent many happy hours enjoying the broad panorama of fruit-laden trees, the running water and flowers of many colours.[50] Earlier ibn Zaidun described a garden in which he invited Wallada to meet him. A more realistic description is given by ibn Khaqqan in his *"Qala'id al-iqyan."* He describes the famous park — the *Khair al-zijjali* at Cordova built by the Berber aristocrat Abū Marwan al-zijjali for the benefit of the public. He was buried here by the side of his friend, the poet ibn Shuhaid who was a frequent visitor to the garden. Ibn Khaqqan writes about this garden in these words: "It is situated near the *Bab al-Yahud* (The Gate of the Jews). The Khair is one of the most marvellous, the loveliest places of joy. The portico *(sahn)* is made of pure white marble *(marmar)*, a brook *(jadwal)* runs swiftly through it like a serpent, and a reservoir receives all the limpid waters. The roof of the pavilion is ornamented with lapiz-lazuli. The trees are harmoniously planted in lines, and the flowers smile in their parterres.'[51] These descriptions sum up the elements of an Andalusian garden — water, greenery, flower-beds, and roofed pavilions. At least three specialists combined to lay out a garden — the botanist, the horticulturist, and the architect-cum-engineer. The first two selected and planted the shrubs and flowers, vines and fruit trees; the third designed and constructed water-courses, kiosks, pavilions, cascades, and traversal walks. At both the ends of a garden there was a richly ornamented pavilion for rest and repose. It is probable that there was also a third pavilion in the centre. It was open on all the sides to give a panoramic view of the long vistas on all the sides of the garden. Ibn Luyun, a famous botanist of Granada has left a blue-print for laying out a garden. The author's plan provides all the above features in addition to, shaded vines forming a pergola, for solitary walks. Far away, stood the fruit trees to protect the garden from strong winds. The flower-beds were laid in cruciform design pre-dating the gardens laid out by Baber at Agra, and Shah Abbas at Isphan. The flower-beds were at a lower level compared to the paths. This disparity was intentional, and part of the design because while walking on the path, a person enjoyed the illusion of treading on a carpet of flowers. Out of the hundreds of pleasure gardens of the Muslim period only one has survived. This is the Generalife *(jannat al 'Arif)* situated on a hill across the Alhamra. It dates from the 14th century. The enclosed garden is flanked by pavilions on both the sides with upper stories of great beauty for the ladies to repose and enjoy the beauty of the garden from a height. The Generalife evokes the sensuous solitude mingled with perfume of flowers and the soft sound of trickling fountains, enjoyed by the sultans of Granada. There are modest remains of a garden in the Alcazaba of Malaga, and another at Velez Benaudalla near Montil not far from Granada. The latter has all the features of a garden referred to above.

The Andalusian gardens were planted with ornamental trees like the cypress *(sarw)*, the palm *(nakhl)* and trees with colourful and sweet smelling blossoms like the pomegranate *(al-rummān)*, lemon-tree *(laimun)*, the orange tree *(narranj)*, the mulberry tree *(tut)*, the apple tree *(tuffāh)*, and the vine *(karma)*. The pools were planted with nailofar *(water-lily)* as in the garden of the Zahira palace. We know the favourite flowers of the Andalusian garden lovers. A list would include — myrtle *(raihān)*, Jasmine *(Yasmin)*, narcissus *(bahar)*, rose *(ward)*, basil *(habaq)*, lavender *(khuzāma)*, carnation *(qaranful)*, marjoram *(mardaqūsh)*, oleander *(diflā)*, red anemone *(shaqiq al-Nu'man)*, and blue iris *(khurram)*. The orientalist M. Pérès has given a much longer[52] list. For lovers of flowers, and the poets, some flowers and shrubs had symbolic values — the narcissus, of sadness, the myrtle, of tranquillity, the rose, of joy. During the course of an imaginary debate between the narcissus and the rose, the latter carried off the palm. The rose chided the narcissus for wearing the sad looks of an aged women. The rose claimed its superiority for being the symbol of radiant youth — a maiden clad in a red robe. The narcissus (said the rose) withered away, but the rose, even when it was dry, was sought after for extracting rose water.[53]

The Andalusians, like the ancient Romans enjoyed the luxury of a public bath. Even those who had their own bathrooms, they would prefer to visit a public bath which gave certain services (such as massage) not available at a home. The public bath was also an ideal place for gossip, as it was patronised by men from all walks of life. Poets got inspiration after a refreshing bath at a public bath. There were public bath in all the cities and villages. During the time of ibn Hayyan, Cordova had the greatest number of baths — 300 under the caliph 'Abd ar-Rahman, and double that number during the time of al-Mansur. There were also separate baths for females which were managed by women. On certain days, the general public baths were reserved for them, and on such days the entire management was placed in the hand of females. The working of all baths was supervised by state officials. A public bath was supplied with running water through metallic tubes hidden inside the walls. Many baths were decorated with pictures, and were paved with marble and mosaic. Some baths had pictures of embracing couples[54]. In the XI century there were even marble statues as in the Roman baths. These statues were escavated from Roman buildings and installed in the baths to attract customers. Such baths must have functioned in secrecy (perhaps as haunts of vice) in unfrequented localities so as not to incur the wrath of the people. A bath was a many-roomed complex. A client first entered into a lounge. When his turn came, he was led into a dressing-room where he removed his clothes, wrapped himself in long towel, and put on wooden slippers. He was given a massage with olive oil by servants wearing gloves. Thereafter, he entered into other chambers one after the other — the frigidarium *(al bayat al barid)*, the tepideria *(bayat al-wasti)*, and the calidarium *(bayat al sakhan)*. The water both cold and tepid was discharged by taps, and the warm steam rose through holes in the floor. The patrons were provided with leather producing soap. For the Spanish Muslims a bath was not simply a cleansing experience. Personal cleanliness was incomplete if the body and the clothes were not perfumed. After the bath, the perfumers *(tayabun)* anointed the clients with perfumes of their choice. The art of perfume making was brought to Spain from the orient. From ancient times, Arabia was famous for frankincense and aromatic herbs. When Shakespear's Lady Macbeth wanted to sweeten her little hands, she thought of the perfumes of Arabia. The use of perfumes was common to all classes of the Andalusian society. In several cities, there were separate bazars for the sale of perfumes. The perfumes extracted from musk *(misk)*, ambergris *('abir)* and aloes *('ud)*, and suffron *(za'faran)* were highly expensive and only the rich could afford them. The general public used perfumes extracted from flowers, particularly the rose and the jasmine. 'The Andalusian Muslims were very particular about their cleanliness in their person, dress, and beds and the interior of their homes,' says ibn Sa'id.[55] The poorest man would spend his last dirham on buying soap for washing his clothes, rather than appear in the street with dirty clothes. Ibn Ghalib is full of praise for the Spanish Muslims, and compares them to the citizens of Baghdad in their cleanliness, beauty of form and elegance of manners. In fact one of the serious allegations against the Muslims by their Christian rulers and also the inquisitors was that they washed and bathed daily even in cold weather. Personal cleanliness was heretical in the eyes of the priests. Even queen Isabella regretfully, confessed before her personal priest (Hernando de Talavera) that she washed her feet once in a month. The Spanish

government enforced strict laws to discourage cleanliness among
the Muslims, and their baths were destroyed.[56]

And now we come to Shakespear's 'food of love'. i.e. music.
The Spanish Muslims were divided into two groups — those in
favour of music, and those who were opposed to it. The latter
group condemned music as a forbidden pleasure (or *mālahi*)
and the musicians as an effeminate people *(mukhannathun)* who
sang dirty love songs, drank, and thus corrupted the youth.
They were mostly, the puritanical ulemas and their orthodox
followers. But inspite of their opposition (even fulminations
from the pulpit) music flourished during all periods of Muslim
history. 'Indeed the cultivation of music by the Arabs in all its
branches reduces to insignificance the recognition of the art in
the history of any other country', says Dr. H.G. Farmer, a great
authority on music both eastern and western.[57] Music flourished
throughout the Muslim period of Spain, and musicians and
their art were held in respect by men and women of liberal
education and culture. When Ziryab, the great musician of
Baghdad arrived in Spain, the reigning sultan 'Abd ar-Rahman
II rode out to receive him at the gate of Cordova. The views of
'Abd Rabbihi, Spain's earliest author, illuminatingly articulate
what music meant to the Spanish Muslims. Accordingly to him
music is 'the pasturage of the soul, the spring-grass of the
heart, the arena of love, the comfort of the dejected, the
companion of the lonely, the provision of the traveller ... often
times, man only appreciates the blessings of this world and the
next through beautiful music *(alhan)*, for it induces to generosity
of character in the performance of kindness, and of observing
the ties of kinship, and the defending of one's honour, and the
overcoming of faults. Often times man will weep over his sins
through (the influence of) music, and the heart will be softened
from its stubbornness, and man may picture the kingdom of

Heaven and perceive its joys through the medium of beautiful music'.[58]

The history of Hispano-Muslim music began with 'Abd ar-Rahman I who, like all the Umayyads, was found of music. A female musician named Afza enlived his leisure hours with her flute. The next ruler, Hisham I, was an orthodox man, and being a disciple of imam Malik, he had scant liking for music. His son, Hakam I, loved the good things of life. He had several virtuosi at his court, the most conspicuous being al-Abbas Nasai, Ulun, Zarqun, and the jew Mansur. The reign of 'Abd ar-Rahman II is marked by the arrival of a large number of musicians, and singing girls from Madina and Baghdad. The emirate of Spain had been firmly established, and several artists migrated to Spain urged by the prospects of better patronage. Among the female musicians who came to Spain were the famous Fadl and Qalam. Fadl was once in the service of Harun al-Rashid of Baghdad. She left for Madina, where she was purchased for 'Abd ar-Rahman II. Qalam was originally a slave from Navarre. She was carried to the East where she received training in polite literature and music. But the greatest musician to reach Spain from Baghdad, was Ziryab. He was an authority on music, both theoretical and practical. He had a golden voice, and was also a brilliant composer. He composed ten thousand songs and set them to music. His songs were collected by Aslam bin Abd al Aziz, but this unique book is now lost.

Ziryab knew from his experience at Baghdad that the demand for professional musicians was bound to increase in Spain. He opened a school in Cordova. His school is of paramount importance in the history of Andalusian music. He introduced the music of the Muslim East in Spain. This music had its basis in the *'huda'* i.e. the caranvan song of the pagan Arabs. Under the Abbasids this purely Arabic music was enriched by Persian and Byzantine melodies. In Spain, this music aborbed some local influences, but it is difficult to isolate the purely local music from the music imported from the East for lack of literature on the subject. The theory of ethos *(tathir)* was a part of this music imported from Abbasid Baghdad. The notes of the solfeggio were said to be related to the planetary influences, the signs of the zodiac, and the atmospheric elements like the wind and the seasons, the humours in the human body, and even colours and perfumes. On the practical side, the verse and the refrain were sung in different melodies. The melodies were ornamented by gloss *(zaida)* which Dr. Farmer defines as the 'science of decorating or festooning the melodic outline by graceful figurations such as we know of in Western music as the appoggiatura, shake, trill, and other graces, and including perhaps another note struck simultaneously, as with the Greeks. Harmony, in our sense of the word was unknown. Its place was taken by rhythm *(iqa)* which one writer on Arabian music has termed 'rhythmic harmony'[59]. Thanks to al-Maqqari, we possess interesting details about the method of instructions at the school of music set up by Ziryab. Before admission, the trainee's voice was tested. He was made to sit on a cushion; his waist was tied, and he was asked to raise his voice to the highest pitch. If he could not open his mouth or if he stammered, he was given a small of piece of wood to keep in his mouth for several days until his jaws expanded. His training began when his voice was found suitable for vocal music. To begin with, he was made to cry out, at the top of his voice, — *'ya hajjam.'* If he spoke with a clear and sonorous voice, he was admitted to the school, and Ziryab spared no pains to make a good musician out of him. We do not know the period of training, but we do know that the curriculum was divided into three portions. In the preliminary stage, the student was taught rhythm *(iqa')*; in the intermediate stage, he was introduced to melody, and in the final stage he was taught the art of gloss *(zaida)*. The students who passed out of the school of Ziryab were respected all over Spain. After his death, his work was continued by his son (Ja'far), and his two accomplished daughters, Hamduna and Ulayya.

From the 10th century the sound of music was heard in many homes from Silves to Saragossa. It was the chief entertainment of rich dilettanti as well as the common man. No wedding ceremonies were complete if there was no music. Like poetry, music too was an obsession with many Andalusians. Abū l-Asbagh, a son of 'Abd ar-Rahman III (all Muslims rulers of Spain and their children were men of culture like the Mughal Princes of India) had an inordinate love for wine and music. After constant persuasion of his brother Hakam, he abandoned drinking, but not his devotion to music. 'By Allah, I will not give it up until the birds stop singing,' was his eloquent reply to his critics. However, at big gatherings the musicians were separated from the audience by a curtain, as a concession to the orthodox. By this arrangement, the lovers of music would say that they only listened music, but did not see it performed before them. The public observed no such restrictions. Surprisingly, even some pious men came under the influence of music. We have a typical story of a qaḍi of Cordova (Abū Abdullah ibn Isa) who died it Toledo in 948. The story goes that the qaḍi on his way to attend a funeral stopped for a while at the house of his friend. He offered the qaḍi refreshments, and also summoned his slave girl *(jariya)* to entertain the guest with her songs. The qaḍi liked one of the song so much that he wrote it on his palm. The writing was visible when he raised his hands in prayer at the funeral![60]

This anedote reveals a special feature of Andalusian society—
the employment of female musicians in wealthy families. Imam
Malik who forbade music had advised that a slave-girl who
knew music should not be employed. This advice of the imam
was honoured more in breach than fulfilment by Spanish
Muslims. A slave-girl trained in music, both vocal and
instrumental, was conspicuous in distinguished families, like a
record-player in a modern home. For every demand, there is a
source of supply. Many slave-girls accomplished in music were
imported from the East in the early days. The Spanish patrons
paid exorbitant price for a really good musician. Ibn Hajjaj of
Seville purchased Qamar for a sum of three thousand dinars.
Tarab, who excelled in music (*ghina*) was sold to al-Mundhir,
son of 'Abd ar-Rahman II, by a merchant, for a thousand pieces
of gold. The songs of Uns al-Qulub filled the palace of al-
Zahira of al-Mansur. But there was also an indigenous source
of supply of female musicians. Many of them were Christian
captives (from Leon, Navarre etc.) who were trained in music,
and sold to prospective patrons. A beautiful slave-girl trained
in the art of seductive tête-a-tête, and music, would fetch a
handsome price for the owner. There were schools for training
these girls. We have a report about at least one such school
which was run at Cordova by ibn Kinani, a clever physician of
the 11th century. We should like to hear from him about his
business in this field. 'I can infuse intelligence in stones (says
the physician). I would like to tell you that I have at present in
my house four Christian girls (*rumiyyat*) who only yesterday
were illiterate, but today are versed in logic, philosophy,
geography, music and caligraphy.'[61] Proceeding further, he says
that scholars have tested their knowledge. In addition to good
looks, figure and gracefulness in walking, they can also sing
well. It was no wonder that he sold one of his treasures to the

ruler of Sahla, a small state near Saragossa, for a sum of three thousand dinars. Many of these female musicians lived like wealthy movie stars of today. They passed from one wealthy patron to another. Often a master would set her free, and marry her, rather than be deprived of her entertaining art. The taste for music spread all over the Muslim society almost like a virus. When Rome burned, Nero played on his fiddle. Even when the Umayyad dynasty was in the throes of death, the princes did not give up their passion for music. The palace of al-Mahdi, the Umayyad prince who fermented a civil war at Cordova, resounded with the sounds of a hundred lutes and reed-pipes (mazamir). When the muluk at-tawa'if ruled broken-up Spain, lilting music of voluptuous melodies and orchestra (sitara) was heard in every palace and pleasure-garden. The songs of the Sicilian poet ibn Hamdis were a rage among the people. A visitor in Malaga in the early 11th century who stayed in the city for sometime, heard the sound of the lute (ud), pandore (tunbur) and reed-pipes (mazamir) from all sides. The Cid was not wrong when he censured the Muslim princes for their excessive love of music. The Almorvids and the Almohads discouraged music, but it made no difference in the long run, as the cause of music was taken up by the intellectual class.

One noticeable feature of the 12th and the 13th centuries is the presence of a large number of musical theorists and writers. As in other fields, so also in musical literature, the inspiration came from the East. Some of the greatest writers on the subject were Farabi, ibn Sina, and al-Khawarizimi. Their writings reached in the 9th century with ibn Firnas, but from the 11th century, more and more intellectuals appeared in this field. Maslama of Madrid (d. 1007), al-Kirmani (d. 1016), spread the theories of the Ikhwan al-safa whose writings characterised music as a spiritual art beloved of all wisemen.[62] Abul-Salat

(1068-1134) of Denia wrote his Epistle on Music *(Risala fi l-musiqi)* which has survived only in a Hebrew translation. Yahya al-Khuduji of Murcia who probably flourished in the 12th century composed a Book of Songs on the lines of Kitāb al-aghani of Isphani. The philosopher ibn Bajja's treatise on music enjoyed the same reputation in Spain as that of Farabi in the East. Ibn Rushd also wrote on music. The 13th century philosopher, ibn Sab'in has left a work on Musical Modes. A Murcian savant, Abū Bakr al-Raquti of the 13th century taught philosophy, mathematics, and the theory of music. When the Christians annexed Murcia, Alfonso retained him to teach the Christians.[63] Several music theorists from Spain settled in the East.[64]

The Musical instruments used by the Muslims in the Middle ages are legions. Many of these instruments from the East were imported in Spain. Shaqandi has given a long list of the instruments in vogue during his time.[65] Broadly speaking they were of two kinds — the stringed ones and the others belonging to the wood-wind genre. The stringed instruments, most popular were, the qanun, rabab, 'ud, qitara and munis. Among the reed-blow type were the zulāmi, buq, shabbaba and mizmār. The timbrel genre were represented by the duff, ghirbal, and the tabl. The last was a cylindrical used only by the army on the march. But the 'ud was the most popular of all the instruments because it produced music of great aesthetic appeal. Ziryab was an innovative player of 'ud. He realised its importance and introduced several improvements. He discarded the plectra of wood, and replaced it by one made of the eagles' talons. The 'ud carried four strings of silk each representing, by their length and thickness, the four humours of the human body. Ziryab added a fifth string to represent the soul. The second, third, and fourth strings were made from the entrails of a young lion. The new lute *('ud kamil)* was complete and perfect, as it was supposed to touch every poignant feeling. It was fretted according to the musical scale. The manufacture of musical instruments was an art. Seville was a centre for manufacture of the best musical instruments. Even today, the best Spanish guitars are made in Seville. There was no dearth of manuals on the manufacture of musical instruments.

Notes

1. On Arab and Berber settlements, see L. Provençal: L'Espagne Musulmane au Xeme Siècle, pp. 18-28, Anayatullah: Andalus ka Tarikhi jughrafiya, pp. 58-72. Both obtained their information from Al-Maqqari.

2. During the reign of Philip II, the cardinal Francisco Mendoza Y Bobadella wrote a book entitled, 'Tizon de la Nobleza', in which he tried to prove that not a single noble family of Spain was free from Moorish and Jewish blood in their veins. This book was published last time in 1880 at Barcelona. (Pérès: p. 283).

3. L. Provençal: L'Espagne Musulmane au Xème Siècle, p. 32. The author says that the influence of Islam was attractive and not coercive. His actual words are — 'L'influence de l'Islam fut alors attractive, et non coercitive; les conquérants s' appliquèrent d'aillaeurs à respecter les clauses des traités de capitulation, qui n'engageaient en rien les convictions religieuses des tributaires'.

   The reader will recall Count Julian who helped Tariq at the time of Conquest of Spain. His grandson converted to Islam and took the name of 'Abdullah. In the 10th century his desendants were renowned theologian and jurists of Cordova. L. Povençal: Histoire, vol. I, p. 13.

4. Ency. of Islam (N.Ed.) article - Al-Andalus.

5. H. Pérès, p. 286.

6. Palencia: Historia Literatura: pp. 297-302, about the Jews who wrote in Arabic.

7. Ibn Sa'id: Tabaqat al-umam, p. 6.

8. Ibn Khaldun; The Muqaddimah, Vol. III, p. 450.

9. Al-Marrakeshi, p. 26.

10. Ibn Hazm: Tawq, p. 100.

11. Ibn Khatib: Ihata, Vol. II, p. 163.

12. Al-Marrakeshi, p. 366.

13. Ibn Khatib: Ihata, vol. II, p. 209. Ibn Hazm had similar views. See page 214 of his Tawq of Hamamah.

14. Ibn Khatib: Ihata, vol. I, p. 38.

15. Pérès, p. 318.

16. Palencia: p. 189. (La Espana Musulmana)

17. Ellen and Whishaw, p. 73; Dozy, p. 379.

18. Al-Maqqari/Gayangos: Vol. I, p. 161, and also ibn Bushkuwal, Vol. I, pp. 691-696.

19. Ibn Hazm; Tawq, p. 217.

20. H. Farmer: Article on 'Moorish Music' in Grove's Dictionary of Music.

21. Ibn Bassam, Dhakhira, Vol. I, p. 376.

22. A.R. Nykl; pp. 107-118.

23. Ibid, p. 211. (Both these women flourished during the XI century)

24. Al-Maqqari/Gayangos, Vol. I, p. 66.

25. Ibn Khatib, Ihata, vol. I, pp. 316-317.

26. Al-Marrakeshi; pp. 111-113. Dozy: pp. 677-678.

27. Arnold & Guillaume: The Legacy of Islam, pp 32-34. give interesting details about the terms and moves of chess derived from the Arabic sources.

28. Ibn Khaldun: The Muqaddinah, Vol. II, pp. 404-405, The Legacy of Islam, p. 373.

29. Nykl: p. 169.

30. Ibn al-Awwam: Vol. II, p. 294 & p, 157. We possess sufficient informative about Andalusian cuisine, its composition and quality in several books. One such book was published in 1934 at Mossoul, but this relates to the 13th century. (L Provençal: Le Civilisation arabe on Espagne. p. 161).

31. Pérès: p. 316.

32. Ibn Khatib: Ihata, Vol. II, p. 279.

33. Ibid, Vol. I, p. 97.

34. Nykl, p. 308. The qaḍi al-Waqqashi (Abu l-Walid ibn Ahmad) was born at Huecas (Ar. Waqqash) near Toledo. He was a walking encyclopaedia of knowledge, a philosopher and mathematician. He had a knack for solving puzzles. He believe that Truth is beyond comprehension. He said this in a famous distich:

I am sorry to say that all human knowledge
is of two kinds — and this is, all.
one, the acquisition (tahsil) of which is beyond attaining,
The other falsehood, not worth gaining.
He died in Dec. 1096.

35. Al-Maqqari/Gayangos, Vol. II, p. 172.

36. Nykl: p. 298.

37. Ibid, p. 310.

38. Nykl: p. 232. The poet asked the garden, 'Where are your daisies'? The
     garden replied that it had placed them in the mouth of the cup-bearer
     (saqi). The saqi denied it, but the truth was out, when he smiled.

39. Pérès: p. 360.

40. Ibn Khatib: Ihata, Vol. II, p. 207.

41. Pérès: 368.

42. Condé: Vol. I, p. 486.

43. Condé : Vol. II, pp. 12-13. (The night proceeding the nairuz was
     considered auspicious by the Muslims for consummation of marriage.
     (Pérès: p. 303.)

44. Pérès; p. 295.

45. H.C. Lea: p. 7.

46. L. Provençal: Revista de Instituto Egipcio de Estudios Islamicos (Ano
     Primero), Madrid, p. 168.

47. Ency. of Islam (N. Edn.) article 'Filaha,' by Prof. Colin. The botonical
     gardens appeared in the 11th century at Seville and Toledo.

48. James Dickie : The Hispano-Arab Garden, Its Philosophy and Function
     (published in the Journal of Oriental and African Studies, 1968), pp. 237-
     248.

49. Draper: Vol. II, p. 33.

50. Ibn Hazm: Tawq. p. 191.

51. Pérès: pp. 128-129.

52   Pérès: pp. 167-184. These are some of the most beautifully written pages
     of the masterly work on the society of the Spanish Muslims as reflected
     in the poetry of the XIth century. Much of what is contained in the book
     equally applies to the entire period of Muslim rule in Spain.

53. Ibid.

54. Pérès: p. 333. Probably they belonged to Roman times and were installed in some Andalusian baths.

55. Al-Maqqari/Gayangos: Vol. I, pp. 116-117.

56. Apart from the royal baths in the Alhamra, there are remnants of public baths in many places in Spain, some even in the Balearic islands also. On public baths, the reader may like to read — (a) The article, 'Hamam' in the Ency. of Islam (N. Ed.), (b) H. Pérès, pp. 338-343, (c) Torres Balbas: Los Edificos Hispano-Musulmanes (pp. 92-121), published in the Revista del Instituto Egipcio de Estudios Islamicos, (Ano Primero), Madrid. On enacments against bathing see H.C. Lea: Moriscos, p. 129, 131,162,216 and 229.

57. Arnold and Guillaume: The Legacy of Islam, p. 358.

58. H.C. Farmer: History of Arabian Music, p. 156.

59. H. Farmer: History of Arabian Music, pp. 109-110 and pp. 72-73.

60. Pérès: p. 61.

61. H. Pérès: p. 384.

62. M.M. Sharif: History of Philosophy, Vol. I, p. 300.

63. Al-Riquti returned to Granada when he was pressurised to embrace Christianity. He told a friend that he could not embrace Christianity. His reason, in his own words: 'I have worshipped only one God all my life, and I do not think I have pleased Him. How can I earn the pleasure of three gods. (Al-Maqqari (Urdu Trans: p. 495)

64. H. Farmer: History of Arabian Muslim : pp. 223-224.

65. Al-Maqqari/Gayangos: Vol. I, pp. 58-59.

Chapter 26

The Legacy of the Spanish Muslims

————•—•————

Europe in the early Middle Ages presented a spectacle of degrading illiteracy and deplorable backwardness. On the other hand, Spain under the Crescent was the only country on the continent with an advanced civilisation. For countries north of the Mediterranean, Muslim Spain was "a centre of refined civilization, a conservatory of polished society, and good taste".[1] The Papal records of the 8th and the 9th centuries show that the tapestries and the vestments for ecclesiastical use were imported from Spain. Long before the merchants of Venice, Genoa and Pisa appeared on the scene, the argosies of the Muslims plied from one end of the Mediterranean to the other. The traders and travellers — the usual carriers of cultural seeds spread the stories of the brilliant civilization of Spain. Europe looked upon Muslim Spain first with excitement and envy, followed by recognition, and ending with imitation. The reader will recall the praises of Cordova sung by the German Hrotswitha mentioned in an earlier chapter. The Ripoli MS. from Spain and the Alcandrius MS. from the south of France, give evidence of the literary and intellectual contacts with Muslim Spain.[2] There is a story that Pope Sylvester II (d. 1003) during his youth visited the Spanish March from where he came to Cordova to learn arithmetic and the art of making astrolabes. On his return, rumours went round that during his sojourn among the infidels, he learnt magic and necromancy. As the centre of western culture, Muslim Spain irresistibly attracted the semi-barbarous peoples of Christian Europe. J.B. Trend an authority on the history and civilization of Spain tells us that "whenever the rulers of Leon, Navarre or Barcelona needed such things as a surgeon, an architect, a dressmaker or a singing-master, it was to Cordova that they applied." They were such a backward people that they asked for help from the Muslims for measurement of their land. From all parts come travellers, bent on study as well as trade, and eager to behold the wonder of this new classic civilization of the orient.[3] By slow degrees, Muslim culture and learning filtered into Europe. But a tidal wave of cultural impact rose towards the end of the 11th century when the Cross was implanted at Toledo in 1085 A.D. The fall of Toledo is as important an event as the fall of Constantinople to the Turks which was to come in the 15th century. Both these events initiated the most fascinating epochs of cultural drifts in the history of intellectual enlightenment. We have already stated that Toledo was a centre of Hispano-Muslim culture. The Christians, the Jews and the Muslims were completely Arabised. In the dress of the people, their customs, language and music, Toledo was like other cities of Muslim Spain. The libraries of Toledo were full of the accumulated learning of the savants and scientists of Spain as well of those of the eastern lands under the Crescent. 'Conquered Islam took her savage conquerors captive and introduced the arts and civilization into the rustic life of Christendom' says Arnold Toynbee.[4]

The process of cultural transmission was set in motion by the famous school of translators which was established by Archbishop Raymund during the term of his office (1126-52).

He commissioned his archdeancon Dominic Gundisalvus, and the converted Jew ibn Daud (Latinized into Avendeath) to translate books from Arabic into Latin. As the fame of this school spread over Europe, scholars flocked to Toledo from England, France, Italy and Germany. Dr. Charles Singer has drawn a lively sketch of the activities of these visiting scholars and their efforts in getting access to Arabic books. 'We are (says Dr. Singer) at the beginning of the 12th century. An eccentric and restless European student dissatisfied with the teaching of Paris, of Bologna, or of Oxford, is attracted by floating stories of the wonders of Arabian learning and wisdom and power. He determines to try his fortune in Spain. After many adventures he arrives at Toledo, which passed to Christendom in 1085. The country is in disorder, and fighting between Muslims and Christians is still going on in outlying districts. He has crossed the frontier from the Spanish March, having evaded, or bribed the sentries. He brings with him a letter,'from a patron in his own land, to an official of the native Church. Such officials are in a state of apprehension, for Muslim rule is a recent memory. Our student seeks to establish his credentials. His host can converse with him in Latin, but only with difficulty for their pronunciations differ greatly. Even when our student is accepted for what he is, his troubles have but begun. The very last thing he is likely to get from his clerical friend is any help with the accursed science of the Infidel. For one thing the poor man knows nothing of it. It stands to him for all that is abominable; it is 'black magic', accursed, unclean. Moreover, the language of these Mozarabes, or native Christians, is a non-literary patois, of mixed Arabic and Latin origin, and quite useless for the investigation of Arabian philosophy. It is the patois, not the literary tongue, which our student picks up while looking round him for more efficient aid. At last, he sees

where help may be found. The Spanish Jews of that age had
entered with far greater spirit than the Spanish Christians into
the philosophical and scientific heritage of Islam. While ignorant
of Latin, with which they have not the same spiritual link as
their Christian fellows, many speak and write good literary
Arabic. Our student, now with some command of vernacular,
makes the acquaintance of a Jew of this type, and arranges a
series of secret meetings in some back attic of Jewish quarter'.[5]
The Jews, were no doubt an important link in the translation
of Arabic books. For atleast three centuries, hundreds of Arabic
books were translated into Latin. The translators belonged to
different European nationalities. The most important translators
of the 12th century were the Englishman Adelard of Bath (c.
1130), the Spanish Jews Avendeath (1090-1165), the Italian
Gerard of Cremona (1133-1187), Plato of Trivoli (c. 1150), and
Petrus Alfonsi (b. 1062). Gerard of Cremona was the prince of
the translators who alone translated no less than 80 books.
These translations included Jabbir ibn Hayyan's 'Book of
Seventy', on chemistry, Ibn Sina's *al-qanūn fi tib* on medicine,
Abūl Qasim's work on surgery, mathematical writings of the
three Banu Mosa brothers on the measurement of plane and
spherical surfaces, al-Khawarizimi's Algebra, and several works
of Galen and Hippocrates. Avendeath and Gundisalvus jointly
translated several books of ibn Sina, al-Ghazzali, and Avicebron
or ibn Gabirol The last was a great Jew of Muslim Spain who
lived at Malaga (1021-1058), and lectured on neo-Platonic
philosophy. He was the author of a celebrated work in Arabic
— the Source of Life *(Yanbu al-hayah)*. They also translated
books of Farābi, Thabit bin Qurra, which added greatly to the
mathematical and astronomical libraries of Medieval Europe.[6]

In the 13th century, the process of translation continued with
more tempo. A great Spanish king of catholic tastes appeared

on the scene as a patron of Islamic learning. Alfonso al Sabio (1252-1284) rose above religious hatred, and ordered translation of Arabic books on diverse subjects. He had several scholars at his court, particularly the two Jews — Judas ben Moses and Issac Bensid. The famous Alfonsine Tables on planetary movements which for centuries constituted the basis of scientific astronomy in Europe, were only the astronomical Tables *(zij)* of the Spanish Muslim astronomer Zarqali. The Jews mentioned above constructed an armillary sphere for the king, after the Hispano-Muslim models. Much of the material for the 'Crónica General' complied at his orders can be traced back to Arabic sources. His Book of Games (Libro de los Juegos) gives a first hand account of chess as played by the Muslims. The contents of a book on the properties of precious stones (Lapidario) are derived from Arabic literature on the subject. Along with Spain, Sicily also played the role of a fallopian tube through which the seeds of Arabic learning entered and spread over Europe. The Muslims were rulers of the island from 902 to 1060, and it is indeed a marvel that during this short period of one century and a half, Sicily was thoroughly Arabised. The island was a cultural appendage of the Muslim world, and a miniature Spain in all respects. Learning, science, poetry flourished on the island kingdom along with crafts including silk and paper manufacture. Some of the most important Sicilians were Idrisi, ibn Hamdis and ibn Zaffar. We have already met Idrisi. Ibn Hamdis, the poet, has left his collection of poetry. Ibn Zafar's 'Salwan' is composed of short stories like the maqamàt of Hariri. The Muslim rule came to an end in the 2nd half of the 11th century when the island passed into the hands of the Norman.[7] Under the Norman king Frederick Sicily became a centre of translations from Arabic. The Marseilles born Jacob Anatoli (1194-1256) was the first scholar to translate the works of ibn Rushd into

Hebrew. The adventurous English scholar Michael Scott who earlier had visited Spain to learn Arabic, moved into Italy, and reported at the court of Frederick, Scott Latinized ibn Rushd's commentary on Aristotle's De Anima. Farraj ben Salim of Girgenti known as Farachius or Farragut translated the medical works of Razi. In 1265 another Jew named Bonacosa turned into Latin the *'Kulliyat'* of ibn Rushd under the title 'Colliget'. Yet another Jew was Kalonymus who translated ibn Rushd's *Tahāfat al Tahāfut* at the orders of Robert the Good of Anjou who ruled from 1309-1343. The process of translation lost its momentum in the 15th century, but even during the Renaissance period, the Italian princes and wealthy noblemen rivalled one another in collecting Arabic manuscripts.[8] Among the earliest books in Arabic published by the famous Medici Press in Rome in 1592 was an abridged form of Idrisi's Book of Roger.

The impact of translations of Arabic books was tremendous. "It was like a fertilizing rain", says Max Meyerhof[9]. The Arabic learning awakened the slumbering curiosity of the European mind, and quickened the rational impulse. A translator himself has acknowledged this. Adelard of Bath who advocated rational enquiry in his 'Natural Questions' says, 'I have learned from my Arabian masters under the leading of reason; you, however, captivated by appearance of authority follow your halter. For what else should authority be called than a halter; just as brute beasts are led where one wills by a halter, so the authority of past writers leads not a few of you into dangers, held and bound as you are by bestial credulity'.[10] This is an unmistakable evidence of gradual revival of learning long before the Greek refugees arrived in Europe with their manuscripts after the fall of Constantinople in 1453 to usher in the glorious Renaissance. The Latin translations of Arabic books on science, algebra, philosophy, and medicine broke the dawn of humanism in

Europe. The Arabic learning prepared the soil for the seeds of the Renaissance to germinate. The Spanish Muslim civilisation was, therefore, a boon for Europe. 'It is for the Arab civilization (says John Owen) that we must look after those influences of free culture that directly affected the Renaissance.[11]

In the field of medicine, Europe came to possess some of the monumental works written in Arabic — Razi's medical encyclopaedia, the *al-Hawi*, his masterly treatise on small pox, ibn Sina's *al-Qanun*, ibn Rushd's *Kulliyat*, ibn Zuhr's *Taysir*, the surgical work of Abul Qasim Zahravi, and several books on gynaecology and opthalmology. These books in Latin dress, virtually created the science of medicine in Europe. The state of monkish medicine in the Middle Ages has been described by Dr. Singer in these words: 'Anatomy and physiology perished. Prognosis was reduced to an absurd rule of thumb. Botany became a drug list. Superstitious practices crept in, and medicine deteriorated into collection of formulae, punctured by incantations. The scientific stream, which is its life-blood, dried up at its source'[12]. All this changed as the medical works of the physicians of Spain and the East reached into the hands of European teachers of medicine, and Europe got rid of quacks, and witchcraft, as a body of scientifically trained physicians came into the field. Abul Qasim's surgical work contributed to laying the foundation of modern surgery[13]. Ibn sina''s Qanon was so much in demand in the medical schools of Europe that in the last thirty years of the 15th century it was printed sixteen times, and twenty times in the 16th century. In the subsequent centuries the Qanon held its field as text book in medical colleges in Europe, and in Latin America until the end of the 19th century. In pharmacy, the Spanish ibn Wafid's *kitab fi-l-adwiya* in Latin form was published fifty times in Europe, while ibn Baytar's Latin version entitled 'Simplicia' was in use upto the middle of the 19th century. The writings of Arnald of Villanova, and Raymund Lull are full of quotations from Jabbir. Many medical practitioners may not be aware that several words they use daily are derived from Arabic viz. alkali, alocohol, elixir, soda, antimony and sharbet are only modified forms of Arabic al-qali, al-kuhl, al-aksir, suda, ithmid and sharbat. In the Middle Ages, the two parts of the distillation apparatus were nicknamed 'Moors' Heads' and 'Moors' Noses'.[14] Today these are called alembic and aludel — words of Arabic parentage, the first from al-inbiq, and the other from aluthal. The mathematical sciences were equally revolutionized. The contributions of the Arabs/ Muslims in mathematics are now recognized by all historians of science like Libri, Cajori, and the great historian of science George Sarton of Harvard University. Libri, the historian of mathematics said: 'Efface the Arabs from history and the Renaissance of letters would have been retarded for several centuries'.[15] Through Spain the Arabic numerals and the zero reached the rest of Europe. (The concept of zero is of Hindu discovery.) This new language of mathematics replaced the cumbersome Roman numerals, while the use of zero gave new dimensions to calculations. The translation of al-Khawarizimi's *Hisab al-jabr w'al muqabalah*, opened the world of algebra for the European mind. This included not only equations but also the method of solving geometrical problems with the help of linear and quadratic equations. Europe is also indebted to him for trigonometrical ratios. It is now admitted that the concept of sine and cosine is a legacy of Muslim mathematicians of the East/Spain. Roger Bacon's Optics is based on the writings of the great physicist ibn Haytham.[16] Copernicus acknowledged the greatness of the Spanish al-Zarqali, and quotes him in his *De Revolutionibus orbium coelestium*.[17] During the Renaissance period Regiomontanus (15th century) worked out problems on the bases of the astrolabe — 'the noble instrument — the *safiha*' of the Spanish al-Zarqali.

Out of the philosophers whose books reached the Latin world, ibn Rushd of Cordova was, by far, the most important. Dr. Singer says about of him that he is "one of the most influential thinkers of all time".[18] Ibn Rushd was lauded as a commentator, but condemned as a thinker. He had a host of admirers at Oxford, Paris, Montpellier, Naples, Padua, Bologna and Venice. Roger Bacon (1214-1294) had a profound reverence for him.[19] Dante honoured him as 'the great commentator', but consigned him to hell in his Divine Comedy.[20] In a letter dated Oct. 1498, Christopher Columbus acknowledges ibn Rushd as one of the authors whose writings inspired him to discover the New World.[21] The great Italian Pico della Mirandola (1463-94) was among his numerous admirers. Books published about ibn Rushd began with words of praise for him. During the 14th and 15th centuries, he was considered an equal of Aristotle in wisdom. But he had many critics also. His belief in the eternity of the universe, his denial of miracles, and his theory of 'double truth', were unpalatable to the Church. His enthusiastic disciples gave the wildest interpretations to his doctrines with the result that in orthodox circles he was seen as an opponent of religion. In Paris in 1240, and again in 1269, he was censured by the Church. Robert Kilwardby, the Archbishop of Canterbury also joined the crusade against ibn Rushd. Thus, Christianity came in conflict with philosophy. Just as the study of Greek philosophy raised certain metaphysical and ethical controversies relating to revelation, creation, nature of God, free-will, the origin of multiplicity, the soul and the intellect, and which gave rise to speculative philosophy *(ilm al kalam)*, in the same way ibn Rushd's philosophy gave birth to Christian Scholasticism. A group of learned theologians came forward as champions of faith. Among these scholars, the most famous were Albert Magnus (1193-1280), and St.. Thomas Aquinas (d. 1274). Dressed as an Arab, Albert lectured at Paris on Aristotle in the light of the works of Avicenna, al-Farabi and Al-Ghazzali. They took ibn Rushd to task and asserted the authority of the Church. The *Summa Theologica* of St. Thomas is one of the masterpieces of Christian Scholasticism still read and reverred by the Roman Catholic clergy. He upheld that the soul of every individual is a separate entity, and attacked the theory that primeval matter existed before creation. The Saint drew most of his arguments from Ghazzali. The freethinkers of Europe loved ibn Rushd, but the Church looked to Ghazzali (even though an infidel Muslim) as their defensive bulwark.[22]

The virulent outbursts of Petrarch (1304-1374) against Arabian/Islamic learning in general, and ibn Rushd in particular prove the extent to which Arabian thought and culture permeated all Europe. His aversion is seen on every page of his writings says Renan. Petrarch was averse to the use of Arabic terminologies by the Italian physicians. In a letter to this friend Dondi he writes — 'I request you not to take any notice of the Arabs as if they never existed. I hate the entire race. I know the Greeks produced many thinkers, poets and men of eloquence, mathematicians, and orators, but the Arabian physicians! You know what they are. I have read their poetry which is all depressing and obscene. And still I fail to understand why highly educated men heap praises on them that they hardly deserve. I was surprised when I heard a physician saying (and he was supported by his colleagues) that he would not permit even a modern Hippocrates to produce any work if the Arabs had not already written on the same subject. On hearing this I felt stung, and my heart went to pieces as if pierced by a sharp weapon, and I thought of burning my books... O! the folly of it. O!

Italy's wisdom. Is it sleeping or is it extinct?'[23] In a letter to Luigi Marsigli, a monk of the Order of St. Augustine, Petrarch writes against ibn Rushd. 'I appeal to you to write, at your convenience, a book against the mad dog ibn Rushd who is incessantly barking on Christ and the Catholic faith'.[24] Even the painters of Italy did not spare the Cordovan sage. He appears in several frescoes as a representative of heresy. He can still be seen in a hell scene surrounded by snakes, painted in the Campo Santa of Pisa. This was painted in 1335 by Andre Orcagna. One of the most remarkable is the frescoe painting in the church of St. Catherine at Pisa. This was painted by Francesco Traini in the 14th century. Here, St. Thomas is seen sitting on a stool below an enthroned Christ. The Saint has a copy of his Summa in his lap. Below him is ibn Rush reclining in abject misery while a a ray emanating from the Summa falls on his commentary flung near him.[25]

The impact of Arabic thought on Christian Spain is equally significant. The influence is clearly seen in the writings of some thinkers who were actually trained to serve as missionaries of the Church. 'The failure to destroy Islam by the sword (says Miguel Asin Palacios, (who was once a Jesuit priest and Prof. of Arabic at the University of Madrid) begot in its turn the ideas of the pacific conquest of souls, and led in the thirteenth century to the establishment of the Missions to Islam'.[26] The Franciscan and Dominican Friars were the leaders of this movement. In this context three brilliant missionaries are of much importance. They are Raymund Martin (1230-1286), Raymud Lull (1235-1315) and Fr. Anselmo de Turmeda (D. 1420). Raymund Martin was a Dominican from Catalonia and was specially trained for spreading Roman Catholicism among the Jews and the Muslims. He studied the philosophical writings of Ghazzali, Farabi, ibn Sina and ibn Rushd. One of his books

entitled 'Pugio fidei adversus mauros et judaeos' was written
with the object of converting the Muslims (mauros) and the
Jews. In the process of his studies, he had also to prepare
himself to defend Christianity from the heretical tendencies of
philosophy of ibn Rushd's European disciples. Martin found a
readymade defensive arsenal in Ghazzali's Tahafut al-falasifa.
He extracted all his arguments from Ghazzali because he
believed that in combating heresy it was best to bring the
philosophers themselves into the arena.[27] The other Spaniard
(Raymund) was a Majorcan by birth, and belonged to the
Fanciscan Order. He came from an aristocratic family, but at
the age of 30 he renounced everything, even his wife and
children for a life of devotion. He began as a dedicated opponent
of Ibn Rushd as well as Islam. As Averroism and Islam were
heresies in his eyes, he set out to fight both. One dream of his
life was to destroy Islam — says Renan.[28] At the Council of
Vienna held in 1311, he appealed to the Pope Clement V to
promote a military order to destroy Islam.[29] He wrote many
Pamphlets against ibn Rushd. Renan has given a whole list of
these pamphlets. One pamphlet illustrates the thinking of this
Franciscan. The 'Lamentations' appeared in Paris in 1310. He
resorts to an allegorical form to explain that Christian theology
is superior to the doctrines of Averroes i.e. ibn Rushd. He
presents Dame Philosophy expressing her deep anguish at the
pernicious doctrines of philosophy, pleads her innocence and
asserts that she is a humble maid of theology, and invites all
scholars to come to her aid.[30] The fire that burned in him carried
him to Africa to preach the Gospel to the Muslims. He died
there in a scuffle. But before his death, a great change came
over him after a study of Spanish sufis — ibn al-'Arabi, ibn
Sab'in and al-Shushtri. The Spanish Arabist Julian Ribera called
him, 'a Christian sufi'. Lull was a master of classical Arabic,

and his writings betray close affinity with the sufi thought and practices. Imitating the 99 names of God *(isma al hasna)* he wrote his 'Hundred Names of God *(Els cent noms de Déu)*. In another book *(Blanquerna)*, he advocated sufi practices. He desired that the Bible should be recited in the manner the Muslims recite the Quran. He liked the honourific epithets used by the Muslims for the Prophet, and suggested that the Christians should also use similar phrases for Jesus Christ. And finally, he recommended that women should sit separately from men in a church as in a mosque.[31] The life of the third missionary is equally interesting. Anselmo de Turmeda was born at the island of Mallorca, and after his theological studies at Lerida and Bologna, be became a missionary. He was fascinated by the natural philosophy of the Ikhwan al Sufa, and wrote several books. In his 'Dialogue with an Ass *(Disputa del Ase)* he tried to establish that the animals are not inferior to the human beings. Surprisingly, this missionary left Spain, reached Tunis, converted to Islam, and took the name of Abdullah. He died at Tunis in 1420 (the date is given by Don Palencia), and was buried in a tomb which is held in great respect to this day. Before his death, he wrote a work against Christian doctrines using much of the material from ibn Hazm's *Kitab al-Milal.*[32]

For centuries Arabic was the language of culture and learning, and it is no wonder if it has left an indeliable imprint on Spanish. So deep is this influence that modern journalism has not been able to obliterate it. Today, Spanish owns thousands of Arabic words (many are nouns) representing all kinds of objects — flowers, fruits, colours, precious stones, culinary art, tools, measurements, musical instruments, games, costumes, and articles of daily use. Much of vocabulary of agriculture, irrigation, constructions, and carpentry is of Arabic derivation. A mason in Arabic is called 'al-banā; and albanil in Spanish;

a brick in Spanish is called 'adobe' after the Arabic at-tub; from the Arabic al-khayyat (a tailor), the Portugues got their word alfalate. The Spanish words borrowed from Arabic include many commonest articles of daily use — alcoba (bedroom), alfombra (carpet), almohada (pillow) gabān (overcoat), and bata (dressing-gown). The Spanish words — aduana (custom-house), alcalde (mayor), and fonda (hotel), tahona (a bakery) are only modified forms of Arabic equivalents. The Dutch Orientalist Dozy compiled a glossary of Spanish words of Arabic origin, in the last century. This book needs to be reprinted, and brought up to date. Spain's first Arabist, D.J. Condé recommended the study of Arabic to his countrymen because this language, according to him gave to Spanish some of the richest and most eloquent forms of speech! The educated people in the south of Spain (and even in Portugal) are fond of flowery expressions of courtesy unlike other Europeans. A host would tell his guest as a mark of hospitality to consider his home as belonging to him. The Spaniard begins a work with a prayer for God's help and utters the word 'ojala', which is a modified from of 'inshalla'.[33]

Even a casual glance at the map of Spain and Portugal will show the extent to which geographical and topographical names are derived from Arabic. The word 'algarve' for the south of Portugal comes from the Arabic 'al-gharb' meaning the west. A Muslim village called 'Fatima' (north of Santarem) in Portugal is now a world famous shrine for the Roman Catholics who gather here for prayer and penance because it was here that three children saw a vision of the Virgin Mary.[34] The Arabic words for river, mountain, hill, sandy-bank, lake, island, cave, tower, have endowed the whole peninsula with geographical names. The Arabic word for a river (wadi) is found in the names of several rivers and streams — the Guadalquivir (*Wadi al-kabir:* the great river), the Guadalajara (*Wadi al-hajara:* the river of stones), the Guadalcazar *(Wadi al-qasr)*, Guadalcoton *(Wadi al. qutn,* the river of cotton), Guadalmedina *(Wadi al-madina)*. The word 'wadi' appears in other places — Guadiana, Guadix, Guadalupe. In Portugal the word 'wadi' has been changed into odi or ode, as in such names as Odiana, Odivellas, Odelouca and Odeleite. Lagoons and lakes, both in Spain and Portugal carry their Arabic names based on the Arabic 'al-buhaira', as for example: Albuera, Albufera, Albuhera. From the Arabic word *'jabal'* (mountain), are derived names of numerous places — Gibraltar (Jabal l Tariq), Jabalcon, Jabalquinto, Gibralfaro, Gibraléon. The word *'al-qala'* (a fort) appears in Alacala de Henares, Calatayud (*qal'at* Ayyub), Calatanazor, and Calatrava. Several places have derived their names from the Arabic word *'madina* (city) These are: Medina Sidonia, Medina del Campo, Medina de Pomar, Medinaceli, Medina de Rioseco. The word *'al-qantara* (bridge) occurs in a dozen places. The famous place 'Trafalgar' comes from (taraf al-ghar, cape of the cave), just as Algeciras got its name from 'al-jazira' i.e. an island. The Arabic words for a village *(al-qarya)*, a mine *(al-ma'dan)*, a meadow *(al-marj)*, a suburb *(al-rabad)*, a fortress *(al-qasaba)* peep through many well-known places both in Spain and Portugal. Among the Alpujarras (Ar. *al-busharat)*, the scene of the bloody crusade between the Christians and the Moriscos, whole villages have retained their Arabic names to this day. The highest peak of Spain — the Mulhacen, is designated after Muley Hassan. There are many places/villages which begin with the Arabic' *bani'* after the Muslim families who lived there. Such names are very common in Valencia, Murcia and the Balearic islands. There are for instance — Benicasim, Benjarefe, Benaudalla, Biniadris, Binicalaf, Baniganim, and Binisalem. They are obviously Hispanised forms of Bani Qasim, Bani Ashraf, Bani Abdullah,

Bani Idris, Bani Khalaf, Bani Ghanim and Bani Salam— all famous Arabian tribes/families. The instances could be multiplied. In fact, a study of the impact of Arabic on the topography of the Iberian peninsula would be a subject of great interest, but it will need a lot of research and also a long stay in Spain and Portugal .[35]

The Spanish literature which appeared after the fall of Toledo was influenced by Arabic literature. Stories like the *maqamāt* of Hariri, the Indian Fables (the *Panchtantra*) and many legends and sea-voyages which are part and parcel of the Arabian Nights were popular among the Spanish Muslims as well as the Christians and the Jews. When the gates of Arabic learning opened both to Spain and the rest of western Europe, the earliest literary work to be rendered from Arabic into Latin was the Kalila was Dimna. This translation was made by Petrus Alfonsi in 1120 under the title Disciplina Clericalis'. Petrus was a converted Jew who later settled in England and introduced Arabic learning in the island kingdom. The first Spanish version of these tales appeared in 1251. This event is a milestone in the history of Spanish literature as it laid the foundation of short-story writing. More and more stories followed. Their objectives were entertainment as well as moral counselling exactly as in Arabic literature. A most significant work which appeared in Spain was entitled: Bocados de oro'. This was a translation of the 11th century Egyptian Mubashashir ibn Fatik's work relating to the sayings of ancient philosophers. It was rendered into English by Earl Rivers under the title — The Dictes and Saying of the Philosophers and was printed in 1477 by Caxton — the first book to be printed in England.[36] In 1253 appeared the romance of the Seven Sages in Spanish translation. This was specifically done for the Infante don Fadrique under the title. 'Libro de los engannos et los asayamientos de las mujeres (The

Book of the Tricks and Wiles of Women)[37]. The second half of the 13th century also saw the translation of the Buddhist legend of Barlaam and Josaphat. In fact there was no end to translations of stories from Arabic. In 14th century the Spanish writers began to stand of their own legs, but the Arabic influence did not die out. In the 14th century Don Juan Manuel (1282-1349), a nephew of Alfonso the Learned, wrote his Conde Lucanor which is one of the classics of medieval Spanish Literature. In this book, Patronio, the trusted aid of the Count answers questions on practical life in the form of a story to illustrate his replies. Most of the stories are taken from Arabic sources and there are even several Arabic phrases in it. Once the Count asked Patronio what to do if a person is pestered by the capricious demands of another person. In his reply Patronio narrated the romantic episodes from the life of Al-Mu'tamid. One of these episodes has been narrated in an earlier chapter of this book. Juan Ruiz the author of Libro de buen amor (The Book of True Love), tells the stories of his own love-affairs with oriental flavour in a language full of Arabic words and phrases. Spain's earliest book on chivalry/knight-arrandry is the Historia del Caballero Cifar written in the 14th century. It is an annoymous work, but its author says that it is based on material borrowed from a book in Chaldean i.e. Arabic. It is probable that the concept of chivalry at least in Spain was taken over from Arabic stories. Significantly, the word 'cifar' is the Arabic 'safar' meaning a journey, while the knight's wife is Grimma or Karima, an obviously Muslim name.[38] Stories like the Historia del Caballero Cifar, culminated in Cervante's Don Quixote. Not once, but several times, Cervantes (who once lived in captivity among the Muslims in north Africa) tells his readers that the original of Don Quixote was the work of a Moor named 'Cid Hamet ben Engeli'. Modern scholars hold the view that Cervantes said this humourously to give a semblance of truth and authority to his fantastic novel.[39] We are surprised that the man who justified the expulsion of the Muslim should attributes his great literary work to an infidel Muslim.

Arabic also influenced the syntax of medieval Spanish. This was a direct result of translation of Arabic texts during the formative period before it emerged as a vehicle of literary expression. The literary works produced during the time of Alfonso the Learned, and even after, were written according to Arabic syntax, and nothing but the sound of words distinguish them from Arabic writings.[40]

There is no doubt that Spanish poetry was also influenced by Arabic strophic poetry i.e. the zajals. The earliest impact is observed in the folk songs composed in mozárabic Spanish i.e. Spanish with Arabic words. Some scholars have recently discovered love songs of short lines in Romance language at the end of Arabic muwashshahs. They are said to be the oldest poetic texts in any vernacular language in Europe, says Don García Goméz. There is mystery about these tail pieces because their authors are exactly, not known, but they afford valuable proof of fraternity between Romance and Arabic poetry. Here is an example of a small poem with two significant Arabic words[41]:

> Vayse meu corachon de mib,
> ya rab, si see me tornarad?
> Ten mal meu doler li l-habibi
> Enfermo yed, cuand sanarad?

My heart is going away from me. Oh God when will he return? So great is the grief for my beloved. For he is ill. When will he be well?

A far deeper impact is observed by scholars in the prestigious Cantigas de Santa Maria, a collection of about 400 songs composed at the orders of Alfonso the Learned in the 13th century presumably between 1250 and 1280. The Cantigas are held in reverence by the Spanish Christians, like the Divine Comedy by the Italians. The songs narrate in ballad-style the miracles performed by the Virgin. The surprising fact about the songs is that they are modelled on the Arabic zajal poetry in their strophic structure. It may not be out of place to say that there were Muslims musicians at the court of Alfonso. There are Muslim musicians in the minatures in the Cantigas, and the performers are shown with instruments of Andalusian origin. The Spanish orientalist Ribera even maintained that the melodic strain of Moorish music is traceable in the Cantigas. But his theory, so far the musical part is concerned, has not found wide acceptance, The Bohemian Juan Ruiz also used the zajal from in his poetical compositions, as in the light-hearted song in aa, bbb, a form :[42]

> Mis ojos noveran Luz,
> Pues perdido he a Cruz.
> Cruz cruzada panadera
> Tomé por entendedera;
> Tomé senda por carrera
> Como (faz al) andaluz

My eyes will see no light since Cruz was lost to me. Crooked Cruz whom I took as my love Thus I took a wrong path for a straightroad, just as an Andalusian would do.

The continuous wars and skirmishes, and tournaments between the Christians and the Muslims inspired some of the greatest master-pieces of European literature — the Song of Roland in France, the national epic of Spain, — the Poem of my Cid, and the Moorish Ballads. The disastrous tragedy of Roncevalles in which Charlemagne lost the flower of his chivalry, is the subject of the *Chanson de Roland* (Song of Roland). There are several Saracens i.e. Muslim characters in this famous epic — Marsile, the Saracen king, Bramimonde his wife, and warriors like Malprime and Baligant. These are obviously European names, and it is not easy to exactly identify them in the light of contemporary history of Spain. Whatever its value in the eyes of the French, the fact remain that it is full of very uncharitable remarks against the Muslims and their faith. The Romanceros Moriscos or the Moorish ballads whose authors are still unknown occupy a unique place in Spanish literature. Most of these ballads were composed in the 15th century, some much earlier, and some after the fall of Granada as shown by internal evidence. The subject of those composed in the 15th century or thereafter, is love and chivalry. The Muslims of Granada were famous for their code of Chivalry — kindness to the weak, courtesy to the fair sex, and respect for a brave enemy. We are not surprised if their Christian foes addressed them as "Knights of Granada, gentlemen, although Moors". The whole setting of the ballads is Hispano-Arabic. The characters, mostly if not all, are Muslim. Zarifa/Sharifa, Fatima, Aisha, Maryam, Zaida, Zara/Zahra, represent the love-stricken maidens in love with gallant knights — Almanzor, Abenumeya, Mustapha, and Hamet Ali. The localities mentioned in the ballads were famous in the glorious city of Granada, and its green vega, the Vivramala *(bab al-Ramla)*, the Alcazaba, and the Albaicin. Some scenes are placed right inside the Alhamra. The Muslim knight, in his cloak, kaftan, plumes and his lance and scimitar, is a picture of manly grace. The Love of Boabdil for Vindaraja, the Song of Captive Zara, the Bull-fight of Zulema, the Warden of Molina, the Lovers of Antequera,

Zaide's Love, Abenamaar's Jealousy, and Zara's Earrings, are some of the most charming of the Moorish Ballads, narrated with artless felicity. A translation of Zara's Earrings will be found at the end of this book. This beautiful ballad (translated by Lockhard) must have been a part of the repertoire of Muslim folk songs sung by wandering ministrels.[43] The figures of speech, the tears, and sobs, the passionate confessions of love in these ballads remind us of the courtly love depicted in Arabic poetry. Even the God of the ballads is — Allah.

The Spanish Jews who lived in the Muslim territory were fascinated by Arabic literature, particularly poetry. They wrote in Arabic and Hebrew with incomparable elegance. The debt of Arabic in shaping Hebrew grammar as it stands today is recognised by scholars.[44] The Spanish poets of Spain composed muwashshahs in Hebrew imitating the Arabic poems both in form and contents. The earliest poems of this genre were composed by Samuel bin Nagrilla (d. 1056), the minister of the Zirid sultan of Granada, and Solomon bin Gibrol (d. 1060). 'The apogee of the Hebrew poetry in Spain is during the 11th-12th centuries, which coincided with the highest efflorescence of the Arabic muwashshaha'.[45] Two Spanish Jews — Yehuda Halevi, and Isacc, the son of Abraham bin Ezra, visited Egypt about 1140, and introduced the muwashshahs among their brethern in the Nile country. The poems were sung at gay parties, and there was such a craze for them that the Cordovan philosopher ibn Maymun (who at that time lived in Egypt) issued a fatwa/decree against the singing of these poems by his co-religionists.[46] A peculiar feature of these Hebrew muwashshahs was the use of Kharjas (last lines) in Arabic but transcribed in Hebrew characters. The American Arabist — Prof. James T. Monroe, of the University of California has collected a corpus of 93 Arabic Kharjas. Most of them run into two lines, but many poems have 4 to 8 lines. The Hebrew poems exhibit all the conventional features of Arabic ghazal poetry. The beloved is dark-eyed, and has a willowy waist The lover is paie and emaciated. The beloved is cold, and she avoids meeting the lover from fear of watchers and censors. The lovers employ messengers to exchange news of each other, or arrange clandestine meetings. In short, no stock-in-trade topic of Arabic love poetry has been left out. The Kharjas have an erotic appeal. The following kharja is a naughty reply to be conveyed to a lover by a woman's messenger:[47]

bi-l-lah rasūl	By Allah, messenger
qul li-khalil	Tell the friend
kayfa s. sabil	What route to take
wa-yabit 'indi	to pass the night with me.
khalfa l-hijal	Behind the curtain
na'ṭih dalal	I will give him curls,
'ala n-nikal	to torment him
wa-nazid nahdi	I will offer my breasts.

We shall now leave Spain and turn to the south of France where a great lyrical poetry unexpectedly bloomed towards the end of the 11th century. Its form and content were entirely new. The exponents of this poetry are known as the troubadours. These Provençal poets had a lightness of heart born of their pleasure in life. They expressed their feelings with fluent simplicity. They composed their lyrics in the romance dialect. There were many troubadours, but the chief of them were Guillaume, the Duke of Acquitain (1071-1127), Cercamon, Marcabru, Jaufre Rudel and Peire d'Alvernhe. The sudden appearance of this lyrical poetry of the Provençal troubadours without any precedent models, has intriqued European scholars. Many explanations have been offered. Some scholars have advanced the hypothesis that the early troubadours mentioned above composed their songs under the influence of Arabic poetry of Spain — the popular poetry in the zajal form. The alleged impact of Hispano-Arabic zajal poetry on the troubadours is one of the oldest debates in the field of comparative literature. The debate was initiated by the exiled Jesuit scholar Juan Andres of Spain who was librarian to the king of Naples. In his 'Dell' origine, de'progressi e dello stato attuale d'ogni letteratura, which appeared at Parma (1782-99), Andrés advanced the theory that we should look to Hispano Arabic poetry as a formative factor in the origin of the poetry of the French troubadors. Since then the debate has been going on. Many scholars have favoured the theory, while others have rejected it. In the last century Renan in France, and Dozy in Holland dealt a blow to the theory. Later on, it was realised that these two scholars were not well-equipped to give a considered view on the subject, perhaps because the first was a philosopher, and the second a historian. During the present century several scholars have studied the problem in greater depth. Julian Ribera, Don Menendez Pidal and Prof. García Gomez in Spain, Lévi Provençal in France, the German Hoenerbach, the Czech A.R. Nykl and S.M. Stern have tackled the problem more authoritatively because some of them are double specialists i.e. scholars who mastered the poetry of the troubadours as well as the lyrical poetry in Arabic, in addition to other peripheral subjects relevant to the issue.

The theme of the troubadours' poetry is love, and its psychology is, on the whole, similar to Hispano-Muslim concept of refined love (hubb al-muruwa). The love-game is exactly the same. The bewitching glances of the beloved, her tyranny and cruelty make the lover weep. He suffers from sleeplessness, and his body becomes pale and thin. In his submissiveness (obedienz), absolute humility, limitless patience, and insistence on secrecy of his passion, he is very much like the lovers depicted in the Tawq al-hamama. This is not all. Earlier, it has been mentioned that the raqib, and the hasid were enemies of lovers as they put hurdles in all romantic attachments. Exactly the same position prevails in the love poetry of the troubadours. The lover has to guard himself against the *gardador* (watcher or raqib), the *lauzanglers* (caluminators or nammam) and the *gilos* (the jealous or hasid). Further, there is a marked correspondence in the rhyming schemes between the zajal type of Arabic poetry and the songs of the troubadours. A zajal, we have seen before, has three sets of rhyming lines — the markaz, the aghsan, and the simt. A poem of the troubadours is also modelled on this very pattern. The estribillo is the markaz, the mudanza is the aghsan, and the vuelta is the simt.[48] In addition to thematic and strophic resemblances, there are other features also which are common to both the Provençal and Arabic poetry, such as the employment of messengers by the lovers, the use of masculine form of address for the beloved and fictitious names (senhal) like the kinaya of the Arabic poets. There have been debates about the origin of the word 'troubadour'. Some maintain that the word is derived from the Arabic word *'tarab'* meaning 'joy', and this answers the spirit of troubadour poetry. However, the view has not been accepted by all the scholars, although there is still no satisfactory explanation of the etymology of the word. Taking into consideration all these parallelisms, Prof. Nykl, one of the consistent supporters of the Arabic theory says, — 'The evidence points to the fact that the first troubadours were hospitable to the new way of combining rhythms and melodies, and were fitting their songs to new combinations or rhymes, according to their strongly differing personalities. If we compare Guillaume's, Marcabru's and

Rudel's forms of poetry with the forms current in contemporary Muslim Spain, as well as in the East, we cannot fail to find considerable analogies which can only be explained by imitation or adaptation, not by independent invention'.[49] Prof. G.E. Grunebaum is equally categorical. 'There can be little doubt (says he) as to the influence of Arabic poetry on the songs of the troubadours'[50].

The Arabic theory is not acceptable to many scholars. As none of the troubadours knew Arabic, "where is the question of their copying Arabic poetry", they argue. They recognise the parallelisms between Provençal poetry and the Arabic poetry, but want a positive proof of the actual transmission. The supporters of the Arabic theory argue that the south of France and the north of Spain were culturally very close. The Jews, and the Christians, the Muslims of Toledo, and the neighbouring districts were bilingual. The last were called moros latinados. There were Muslim minstrels at the court of many Christian rulers. They sang songs in the Zijal form. The Arabized Jews loved Arabic popular poetry and copied it, with consummate skill. The Jewish poet Yehuda Halevi of Tudela flourished about the same time as Willian of Acquitaine, the first troubadour. There was a constant flow of traffic between the Spanish March and the south of France. The influence could have reached by *viva voce* means. The Arabic theory is still alive and its supporters have not ben subdued. If this issue is finally settled in favour of the Spanish Arabic poetry, this will be the greatest single contribution of the Spanish Muslims, because the French troubadours are the founders of modern secular poetry of Europe, and their influence was felt in Italy and perhaps in Germany also.

Equally sensational is the discovery that the great Italian

poet Dante (1265-1321) was indebted to Islamic models for his epic — the Divine Comedy. As it is known to all students of literature, the famous epic is an imaginary journey through Hell, Purgatory, and Paradise, narrated with great eloquence. The admirers of Dante attribute the poem to his creative genius. The late Asin Palacios in his epoch-making book — *La Escatologia musulmana en la Divina Comedia* (Madrid, 1919), has claimed that Dante was deeply influenced by Islamic models in Arabic literature on the Prophet's ascension *(miraj)*. The nationalist Italians and the whole Catholic world were aghast at the thought that Europe's greatest Christian epic could be based on non-Christian sources. The hadith literature in Arabic depicts the Prophet's *'miraj'*, and what he saw in Hell and Heaven. The Spanish sufi ibn al-'Arabi had also similar visions which he described in his several books. Asin Palacios discovered similarities between the Divine Comedy and the Islamic literature on the Prophet's spiritual journey, and ibn al-Arabi's mystic visions. The parallelisms are not just superficial, but go deeper into the minutest details. As it will not be possible to condense the whole thesis of Asin Palacios, only some instances of the similarities between the Islamic visions and the Divine comedy are given. Both the visions, the Prophet's nocturnal journey *(isra)* and ascension *(miraj)*, and Dante's journey begin at night on being awakened from sleep. Their approach to Hell in both the visions is announced by a violent outburst of flames and deafening noise. The Prophet is accompanied throughout the journey by the angel Gabriel, and Dante was conducted by Virgil. A wolf stopped the Prophet at the entrance of hell, while Dante by a Panther and a he-wolf. The architecture of hell in Dante's epic and the Islamic literature is identical. Both the visions viewed hell as a colossal amphitheatre with a series of strata having separate tiers for each group of sinners. The torments in both the Hells are similar. The reptiles sting the tyrants; those who disobeyed God's commandments against drinking are afflicted by maddening thirst; the usurers walk with swollen bellies; the slanderers scratch their skin with their own nails; the disobedient children writh in burning lava; the murders are knifed and killed, and restored to life and hacked again and again; the adulterors are hurled up and down by a hurricane of flames: many sinners are stonned. The traitors are made to freeze in ice like sinners in 'Zamharir' of Islamic literature on afterlife. So much for the inferno. The features of the Dantean Paradise, are, likewise, found in the Islamic literature. In both the visions, colour, light and chanting of hymns suggest the supernatural character of the Beatific Life. At the gates of Paradise, the Prophet is received by a beautiful maiden, and so was Dante. As they pass through nine heavens (the Prophet in the company of Gabriel, and Dante of his beloved Beatrice), they meet in each sphere all the Biblical prophets surrounded by pious souls. Both were dazzled by the light in the celestial spheres, but they were blessed with special visual powers. In the sphere of Jupiter, the Prophet saw an angle in the shape of a cock singing hymns, while Dante saw an eagle singing biblical songs. The Prophet saw a ladder rising to the sphere of Saturn. Climbing on it he rose to the highest Heaven in time less than the twinking of an eye. Dante too rose up by a ladder in less time than it is taken to withdraw a hand from fire. At the last leg of the journey towards the Beatific Vision, the Prophet was wafted up by a luminous wreath, while Dante was carried on a cresset or circular diadem. The effect of the Beatific Vision on the Prophet and Dante is the same. Dazzled by effulgence, they fall into ecstasy which words can hardly describe. After a close study of the epic of the great Florentine, and the writings of the sufi ibn al-Arabi of Murcia, particularly his 'Meccan revelations *(Futuhat al-Makkiya)* and his book of Nocturnal Journey *(Kitāb al-Isra)*, Asin Palacios observed, — "Among all the Islamic thinkers, the Murcian ibn al-Arabi stands out as the most likely to have furnished Dante with this model for the hereafter. The infernal regions, the astronomical heavens, the circle of the mystic rose, the choirs of angels around the focus of Divine Light, the three circles symbolising the Trinity-all are described by Dante exactly as ibn al-Arabi described them. The similarity betrays a relation such exists between a copy and model. That it should be a mere coincidence is impossible'.[51] The very philosophy underlying the Divine Comedy and the writings of ibn al-Arabi is the same. Dante was enraptured by the metaphysical doctrine of light already found in the illuministic *(ishraqi)* school founded by ibn Masarra of Cordova. God was conceived as Pure Light, and the universe as an emanation of Divine Light. Ibn al-Arabi was a follower of the *ishraqi* school, and Dante uses the same symbols to express the metaphysics of light.[52]

Asin Palacios gives the likely channels through which the *'miraj'* literature could percolate to Italy. In a well-documented chapter he discusses the prestige enjoyed by Muslim Spain among the 'semi-barbarous peoples of Christian Europe'. The Latin translations of *'miraj'* literature were available in Spain, and it is very probable that these translations fell into the hands of Dante as during his time Spain and Italy were very close to each other. Dante associated with the Italian rabbis who were all versed in Islamic lore and learning. The learned Jewish rabbi Emmanuel of the Zifrani family was a friend of Dante. He was also close to Brunetto Latini, a scholar of encyclopaedic knowledge. Latini was an admirer of Arab learning, and he acted as a literary adviser to Dante. In 1260, Latini was sent as an ambassador of Florence to the court of Alfonso the Learned when the translation of Arabic books was in full swing. Among the works translated was a version of the *'miraj'* in Latin, and it is very likely that this was brought to Florence and came into the hands of Dante.

From literature, we pass on to architecture. The mingling of Gothic and Islamic architecture gave birth to a new form of architecture. The first carriers of this synthesis were the mozárabes — the Arabised Christians and monks who settled in the Christian north in the reign of Alfonso III (866-909). They introduced the horse-shoe arch and the Cordovan system of building the roofs. The ribbed vaulting, a characteristic feature of Gothic architecture is only an echo of similar vaulting seen in the ceiling of the domes of the grand mosque of Cordova. The Santa Maria de Lebena, San Miguel de Celanova, Santiago de Penalba, San Cebrián de Mazote, and several other religious places raised in the first decades of the 10th century are the earliest specimen of the impact of Cordovan tradition on Gothic architecture.[53] In the later centuries particularly after the Christians' massive conquests, the influence of Islamic architecture became more pronounced. The mudéjares (the Moslems who did not leave their homes and lived as vassals) enriched the Gothic architecture with delicacy and refinements. This came to be known as mudéjare architecture. In fact, the term 'mudéjare' applies to all the arts and crafts produced by the Muslim subjects for their Christian masters — buildings, pottery, illuminated leather bindings, and many articles of daily use. As these mudéjares were known for their skill in architecture, interior decoration and industrial arts and crafts, the Christian rulers, inspite of *odium theologicum*, relied on their services. The mudéjare engineers, builders, and craftmen introduced Islamic structural themes in the works executed by them for their patrons. This is how polylobbed arches, square minarets, slender arched windows, blind arcading — the elements of Hispano-Muslim architecture were stamped on the Christian architecture. The mudéjare architecture was so much liked that it infiltrated all over the Spanish peninsula.[54] A list of mudárjare buildings would be too long. Some of the famous structures are the Gate of Visagra at Toledo, the palace of Alfonso XI at Tordesillas, the monastery of Las Huelgas, the tower of San Martin at Teruel, and the tower of San Gil at Saragossa, In the opinion of Rafiq Ali Jairazbhoy, (a modern Indian authority on Islamic architecture who has travelled distant lands to see Muslim buildings of the past), Saragossa has the finest example of mudéjare brickwork with 'raised and recessed brick bonds forming chevrons, diapers, or basins of interlocking stars'[55]. The author has cited numerous examples of mudéjare influence in belfry towers, cloister vaults, the capitals of churches and monasteries of many northern cities. But the greatest single mudéjare work is the Alcazar of Seville built for king Pedro the Cruel (d. 1396) of Castile. The Alcazar is a miniature Alhamra, and it is believed that the services of workers from the kingdom of Granada were obtained for building and decorating the Alcazar. The palace was planned and decorated in the manner of the Alhamra. The open patios, the slender columns, the horse-shoe arches, the polychrome tiles, and endless arabesques give it the rank of a younger brother of the Alhamra. There are even Arabic inscriptions on the walls. One inscription reads — 'glory to our master the sultan Pedro'.[56] The palace built for king Jean (1385-1433) of Portugal at Cintra is also after the mudéjare style.[57]

We know the names of several mudéjare/Muslim master builders and artisans, and also their works[58]. In 1303 Muhammad built the Tower of Carpio in the province of Cordova; in 1306 Yahia worked at the Cathedral of Seville. A mudéjare architect of Saragossa named Muhammad de Bellico designed in 1354 the Trinity Chapel at Sigena monastry in the province of Huesca. 'Abd ur Rahman of Segovia erected in 1433-1440, the church of Cartuja del Paular in Lozaya valley at the orders of Juan II. About the middle of the 15th century, Ali Rami worked at the Cathedral of Saragossa. In the last quarter of the 15th century (1475) Yusuf built the library of the University of Salamanca, in collaboration with Master Ibrahim and master Ali. A Muslim named Mahoma de Borja and his two sons constructed the pews for the Cathedral of Huesca. A certain Ali of Ronda erected the lectern of the Cathedral of Saragossa. Several features of Muslim architecture of Spain spread all over Europe. Sir Christopher Wren realised this influence when he described the architecture of Medieval Europe as 'Saracenic refined by the Christians'.[59] The art of carving in plaster is still alive in several cities of modern Spain. As a result of long association with the Muslims, the Christians were accustomed to privacy within their homes, which is why in many of homes in Spain and south Portugal there is an inner courtyard surrounded with loggias, and living rooms with alcoves. The pattern was adopted as a standard feature of domestic architecture, and it is stated to be the origin of the Italian palazzo of the Renaissance period.[60] Hispano-Muslim ornamental forms were also introduced in France. The architecture of Muslim Spain is a living reality even today. The modern mosque at Paris, and the recently built mosque at Casablanca (one the most beautiful in the world) are some of the examples of Hispano-Muslim architectural traditions. We may also add the magnificent royal palace on the Red Sea in Hay al-Andalus locality of modern Jeddah.

The Christians came under the spell of Hispano-Muslim music. There is no doubt that they appreciated the music of their Muslim neighbours. One of the earliest examples is

furnished by the physician al-Kinani. Once he attended a
reception given in his honour by a daughter of Sancho Garcia,
the Count of Castile (995-1017) The musicians at the reception
were Muslim females from Cordova who were presented to the
Count by the reigning caliph Sulaiman.[61] There are numerous
instances of the Christian rulers employing Muslim musicians.
Pedro III of Aragon had 'moros trombadoes' at his court. The
court of his successor Sancho IV was full of Moorish musicians
— out of twenty-seven, thirteen were Muslim. Pedro IV (1336-
87) employed Ali Ezique who played rebec (rabab) for him. A
Muslim named Mahomet played fanfare at the court of Jaime
II of Aragon. A company of musicians from Valencia visited
the Court of Juan I (1387-95) to entertain guests at a wedding.
Muslim musicians are seen in the miniatures of the Cantigas
Santa Maria. In fact there were 13 Muslim musicians including
two women as his court of Alfonso the Learned. A most
illuminating example is seen in an Aragonese reliquary in the
Real Academia de la Historia, Madrid. There are figures of
angels on this relic with instruments of Hispano-Muslim origin
their hands. They stand on a floor of mosaic ornamented with
arabesques, and they are dressed as Muslim musicians with
stylised Arabic inscriptions on the hem and collars of their long
robes. It seems that Andalusian musicians were engaged at
religious functions because the Valladolid Council of 1332
disallowed hiring of Moorish musicians. Probably, they were
the best instrument makers. Even in the early 16th century, we
are told, that a Morisco named Mahoma Mofferriz was famous
for making key-board instruments for his wealthy Christian
patrons.

In the light of these historical facts, it was quite natural if
Hispano-Muslim music influenced Spanish music, and to some
extent even European. But the whole matter is fraught with

controversies. Some writers vehemently reject the very idea of any influence. The very first problem relates to the alphabate of music. There is a marked phonetic similarity as shown below between the Arab and European solfeggio :

Arabian: Mim, Fā, Sād, Lam, Sin, Dal, Râ.
European: Mi, Fa, Sol, La, Si, Do, Re.

Are the syllables of European solfeggio based on Arabian system? This is stated to be an old claim on behalf of Arabian music. It was repeated by Pigeon de Saint-Paterne, an orientalist at the court of Louis XVI of France, after a study of an Arabic manuscript in the Royal library. But it has not been possible to locate the manuscript. As there is no documentary evidence, all that is admitted is the phonetic likeness. Even Ribera's thesis that the melodic strain of Moorish music is to be found in that of the trouadours, and the great collection of poems — Cantigas de Santa Maria, has not been accepted by all the musicologists. But there is no doubt that in the Middle ages, when the musicologists debated the therapeutic value of music, they largely drew upon the writings of ibn Sina, and Farabi. Ibn Sina's *"Shifa'* and Farabi's *Kitāb al Musiqi* reached Europe through the partals of Tolado. Farabic was quoted extensively by Roger Bacon (1214-1280) in the musical portion of his Opus Tertium. The 13th century musicologists Walter Odington, Jerome of Moravia, and Engelbert also quoted the opinion of al-Farabi and the Sina - the former in his *De Speculatione musices* and the latter in his *De Musices*. The possibility of Arabic tunes in the old Spanish music cannot be ruled out. The 14th century poet, Juan Ruiz (author of Libro de buen amor i.e., the Book of Love) even quotes Arabic tune entitled "Cable el Orabin" or "Cabel el garbi."[63]

Europe owes a large number of musical instruments to the

Spanish Muslims. A brief list of the musical instruments used by them has been given in a previous chapter. Their actual number is much larger. 'Whilst the names of those used in Europe might be counted on the fingers, those of the Arabs can be enumerated by the dozen', say Dr. Farmer. That Spain and Europe borrowed these instruments in addition to instrumental tablature and mensural music, is now acknowledged by historians of music. These musical instruments were adopted in Portugal, and the rest of the Latin world in the Middle Ages. Many are still in use. Their names tell the story of their parentage. This is supported by iconographical evidence. The lute is the Arabic al'ud; the guitar comes from 'qitār'; the rebec from 'rabab'; the canon from 'qanun'; and the tabel/taber/tabor, from 'tabl'. The square al-duff, and the round bandair of the Arabs were baptized as adufe and pandere. The two reed instruments — zamr, and al-surna, were the parents of the shawm and the dulcyna. In Italy, these instruments became popular under the names — Liuto, rebecca, tumbura, and canone. In the paintings of Fra Angelico, Bellini, and Mantagna, the instruments shown are in their original Andalusian shape. The Spanish Muslims were the first Europeans to use musical instruments like the lute with places of notes fixed on the finger-board. The frets were determined by measurement. These instruments were easier to play than the Cithara and the harp among stringed instruments which had to be tuned only by complete dependence on the ears to produce the desired notes. That instrumental tablature was known to the Spanish Muslims is proved by the unqualified acknowledgement of a monkish writer in the 15th century in a Latin manuscript dated 1496-97, but of much earlier authorship. The manuscript says, "It is a marvel that the gift of the Holy Spirit should be poured down on infidels. I say this for the reason that a certain Fulan by

name, Moor of the kingdom of Granada, worthy of praise in
Spain among Spanish guitarists, by the impulse of the spirit of
learning, has discovered the art to be given to those who have
an inclination for playing the lumbutum, guitar, viol, and
instruments similar to these." He gives in detail the phonetic
system of notation which was in use (says Dr. Farmer) until
the eighteenth century under the name of "tablature" [64]. The
tablature given in the Latin manuscript is identical with that of
the Frenchman Adrien Le Roy of the 16th century — an obvious
fact that Hispano-Muslim tablature influenced both Spain and
France. The impact of the music of the Spanish Muslims is
palpably seen even today in the manner of performance — the
short, crisp strokes of the plectrum and the prolonged 'Ay' to
adjust the voice before singing. It is observed in the staccato
rhythm of the Cante hondo, and the firey flamenco punctured
by clapping of hands, and passionate cries of 'Ole, Ole', exactly
as the Muslim audience cried, 'Allah Allah' in chorus when
moved by music. The spirit of the Portuguese 'fado', and songs
of Andalusia of today which empahsise fatalism, and anguish
of unrequitted love, may also, perhaps, be traced to the music
of Spanish Muslims.[65]

We are now at the end of our story. Seen superficially,
history seems to be a graveyard of civilizations telling us like
Shelley's 'Ozymandias' that death and decay are the final end
of man's achievements. But this is not so. History destroys a
lot, but also saves some vestiges of the past to enable man to
measure his march ahead. The Spanish Muslims vanished from
Spain after writing one of the most glorious chapters in the
civilization of Europe. Their descendants do not exist any more
on the Spanish soil, where for centuries, they lived and toiled,
loved and fought, created beauty, and promoted learning. Like
the Greeks, and the Romans, they too have left their footprints

on the sands of time. In Spain, there presence can be felt even today. We hear their footsteps on the terraced streets, under the graceful arches, below the latticed windows in many towns of Andalusia. Their memories linger on the walls decorated with azulejos tiles, the white-washed houses with a weathercock at the top, the elegant patios heavy with the perfume of jasmine and orange blossoms, the murmuring fountains, the folk songs, the seductive beauty of their monuments, and above all the Spanish language itself replete with thousands of Arabic words. The subtle perfume of their culture pervades the whole of the south and east of Spain so says Lévi Provençal.[66] Day by day, their cultural legacy is being unfolded by scholars of Spain, France, the U.S.A., England, Morocco, Tunis, and Egypt. We should be grateful to them. May these scholars live long! May those who are no more rest in peace!

Notes

1. L. Provençal: Islam D'Occident, p. 303. The author says — "il est admis aujourd'hui que L'Espagne musulmane a représenté pour l'Europe méditerranéenne un foyer de civilisation raffinée, de vie luxueuse et policée, une sorte de conservatoire des belles manières et du bon ton."

2. H.G. Farmer: Historical Facts for the Arabian Musical Influence, London. (p 9, 24 and 33) The first two chapters of this book (pp. 1-47 are of general interest as they relate to cultural contacts between Muslim Spain and Europe, based on books which are not available n India.

3. Asin Palaces: p. 243, and Legacy of Islam, p. 9.

4. Arnold J. Toynbee: Civilization on Trial, Oxford, 1948, p. 185.

5. Charles Singer & E.R. Bevan: The Legacy of Israel, pp. 204-205.

6. On the Toledan School of Translators, the reader may like to consult : (i) Palencia: Literatura Arábigo-Espanola, pp. 313-315. (ii) The Legacy of Israel. pp. 202-245. (iii) Renan, pp. 158-173, (iv) The Legacy of Islam, pp. 33, 246,257,268,347. (v) O'Leary: Arabic Thought, pp. 261-274.

7. S. Riyast Ali: Tarikh Saqlia (2nd Volumes), Azamgarh, 1935. It is good work on Muslim Sicily. The second volumes gives a subject-wise account of cultural life.

8. Jacob Burkhardat : The Civilisation of the Renaissance in Italy, London, 1928, p. 209.

9. Arnold and Guillaume: Legacy of Islam, 1931, p. 351.

10. H.T. Kimble: Geography in the Middle Ages, London, 1938, p. 78. The book contains much information on Muslims' contributions to geography.

11. Dr. G. Schmidst, a well-known scholar says, 'As Humanism is founded on the writings of antiquity, which the Muslims had discovered, so the Renaissance is based on the fresh blood which Islam brought to Europe'. (See his article entitled 'The Influence of the Islamic World on European Civilization' published in the Golden Jubilee Commemmoration Volume of 1927-1976, of the Islamic Culture (Hyderabad) (p, 241). Also see John Owen: p. 66.

    It will be interesting to note that the translators latinized the very names of the Muslim savants. Thus, ibn Rushd was changed into Averroes, ibn Bajja into Avempace, al-Ghazzali into Algazel, ibn Sina into Avicenna, al-zarqali into Arzachel, Razi into Rhazes, Abul qasim Zahravi into Abulcasis, ibn Zuhr into Avenzoar, ibn Haytham into Alhazen, ibn Wafid into Abenouefit etc.

12. Arnold and Guillaume: Legacy of Islam, p. 345.

13. Ibid, p. 331.

14. Sidgwick and Tyler, p. 187.

15. G.H. Farmer: Historical Facts for the Arabian Musical influence, p. 3.

16. Arnold and Guillaume; Legacy of Islam, p. 395. In his article referred to above, Dr. Scmidst says that Copernicus would not be conceivable without the works of the Arab mathematicians.

17. Ibid.

18. E.R. Bevan & Charles Singer: The Legacy of Israel, p. 191

19. E. Renan: p. 210.

20. Dante: The Divine Comedy (Inferno Canto V. p. 23) of Eng. trans. by H.F. Cary, London.

21. E. Renan: p. 251.

22. D.L.O'Leary: Arabic Thought and its place in History, p. 286.

23. E. Renan: pp. 261-262. This is a long passage, but it has been shortened.

24. Ibid, pp. 267-268.

25. Renan: p. 242. The whole chapter No. XVI of chapter No. II of the second part of his book (Averroes et l'Averroisme) (pp. 238-248) is interesting in this context.

26. Asin Palacios: Islam and the Divine Comedy, p. 240.

27. Renan: p. 196.

28. Renan: pp. 203-204. (La destruction de Islamisme fut, on le sait, le rêve de taute sa vie.")

29. Ibid.

30. Renan : pp. 204-205.

31. Palencia: Historia Literatura Arábigo-Espanola, pp. 317-319.

32. Ibid, pp. 339-340.

33. Palencia: Historia de la Espagna Musulmana, pp. 197-200. Jan Read: The Moors is Spain and Portugal, p. 237. Arnold and Guillaume: The Legacy of Islam, pp. 19-23. Dozy's glossary entitled — Glossaire des mots espagnols el portugais derives de l'arabe, was published at Layden in 1869.

   Condé : History of the Dominion of the Arabs in Spain Vol.I, p. 4. E.G. Browne in his great work — Literary History of Persia (Vol. I. p. 9) writes that a debased form of Arabic is still used by the peasants in some valleys of the Alpujarras in their love-letters. Browne wrote in 1929. I have not been able to verify his statement.

34. Natural Goegraphic, Dec. 1980. Article : Fatima, Beacon of Faith. The author of the article says that the village was named after a Moorish princess during the time of Muslim rule.

35. The impact of Arabic on the language of Malta which was in possession of the Muslims from 810-1090 would be a rewarding work. The present language of Malata is in fact a dialect of Arabic, and there are numerous places of Arabic origin.

36. Arnold and Guillaume: p. 195, and Palencia: Literatura Arábigo-Espanola, p. 333.

37. Palencia: Literatura Arábigo Espanola, p. 337.

38. Palencia; Literatura Arábigo Espanola, p.345.

39. Cervantes: Don Quixote. Eng. Trans: Charles Jarvis, London. Even at the end of the book Cervantes says — 'The sagacious Cid Hamete, now addressing himself to his pen, said, 'Here O my slender quill! Whether well or ill cut her by this brass wire suspended.. p. 765.

40. Condé: Vol. I, p. 22. Also see the article of H.R. Huffman — Two Examples of influence of Arabic syntax in Spanish (Journal of the American Oriental Society, 1977, pp. 27-33).

41. S.M. Stern : Hispano-Arabic Strophic Poetry, p. 140. Also John A Crow: The Root and the Flower, New York, 1963, p. 63.

42. Palencia: Literatura Arábigo-Espanola, p. 361.

43. J.G. Lockhard: Ancient Spanish Ballads. London (John Murry & Co.), 1859. This book is available in Harding Library, Delhi. I should like to thank the staff of the library for allowing me to consult the book.

44. Palencia: Literatura Arábigo Espanola, pp. 297-302 give an excellent, but brief account of the writing of the Spanish Jews.

45. S.M. Stern: p. 78.

46. Ibid, pp. 79-80.

47. James T. Monroe: Ninety-Three Kharjas in Hebrew Muwashshahs: Their Hispano-romance Prosody and Thematic features. The Journal of American Oriental Society (97.2 of 1977) pp. 141-162. For the above Kharja see p. 157 of this article.

48. Palencia: Literature Arabigo-Espanola, pp. 116-117.

49. A.R. Nykl: p. 379. For examples of similarity between the zajals and poems of troubadors, see pages: 246, 272 and 393.

50. G.E. Von Grunebaum: Medieval Islam, Chicago, 1961, pp. 340-341.

51 Asin Palacios: The Spanish work of Asin Palacios was translated in English by Harold Sunderland under the title 'Islam and the Divine Comedy, and published in London in 1926. (see page 172 and pp. 237-272, of the Eng. trans.)

52. Ibid.

53. Palencia: Historia, p. 195-196.

54. Ibid, p. 210.

55. Jairazbhoy, p. 107.

56 G. Marcais, Vol. II, pp. 656-657.

57. Ibid.

58. L. A. Meyer, pp. 73,89,92,131 & 134.

59. Jairazbhoy: p. 142, and also pp. 106-109 on mudejare workers, and artisans, and their works.

60. Hugh Braun: p. 131.

61. Pérès, p. 386.

62. Grover's Dictionary of Music and Musicians : p. 784, and also pp. 726-728.

63. Farmer: Historical facts, p. 14.

64. G.H. Farmer. Historical facts for the Arabian Muslical Influence: pp 96-100, and p. 9 of Dr. Farmer's article — The Arabian Influence on Musical Theory.

65. The paras on music are mostly based on the writings of Dr. H. Farmer. These are : (a) Historical Facts for Arabian Musical Influence, London, 1930. (b) His splendid article: 'Moorish Music' in Grove's Dictionary of Music and Musicians (3) Arabian Influence on Musical Theory, published in the Journal of Asiatic Society 1925. (d) History of Arabian Music.

66. L. Provençal: Islam d'Occident, p. 314.

Appendix 1

———·•·———

A chronological Tables of the mulūk at-tawāif of the 11th century. A complete list will be found in Dozy's Spanish Islam (pp. 734-743, and Palencia's Historia, pp. 63-67). These kingdoms were liquidated by the Almoravids of north-west Africa.

1. Cordova
   Abū l-Hazm Jahwar   1031-1043
   Abū l-Walid Muhammad ibn Jahwar   1043-1064
   Abd al-Malik ibn Muhammad   1064-1070
   Thereafter Cordova was annexed to the kingdom of Seville.

2. Badajos/Banu Alaftas
   Sabur   upto 1022
   Abū Muhammad   1022-1045
   Abū Bakr Muhammad al-Muzaffar   1045-1063
   Yahya   1063-1067
   Omar al-Mutawakkil   1067-1094

3. Denia
   Mūjahid   1009-1044
   'Ali bin Mūjahid   1044-1076
   Denia was annexed by Muqtadir of Saragossa.

4. Granada

Zawai ibn Ziri	upto 1019
Habbus	1019-1038
Badis	1038-1073
'Abdullah	1073-1090

In 1057 Granada annexed Malaga also.

5. Murcia

Khairan (of Almeria)	1016-1028
Zuhair (of Almeria)	1028-1038
'Abd al-Aziz al-Mansur of Valencia	1038-1061
'Abd al-Malik al-Muzaffar of Valencia	1061-1065
Thereafter Murcia was held by Mu'tamid, ibn Ammar, and ibn Rashiq	..1090

6. Saragossa

Mundhir ibn Yahya Tujibi	upto 1039
Al-Musta'in	1039-1046
Ahmad Muqtadir	1046-1081
Yusuf Mutamin	1081-1085
Ahmad al-Musta'in	1085-1110
ʿAbd al-Malik Imad ad-dawla	1110
Saraossa was conquered by the Christians in Dec. 1118.	1118

7. Seville

Abū l-Qasim ibn Isma'il (the qaḍi)	1023-1042
Al-Mu'tadid	1042-1069
Al-Mu'tamid	1069-1091

Seville annexed the small kingdoms of Cordova, Algeciras, Ronda, Moron, Huelva, Silves, and Mertola.

8. Toledo

Ya'ish ibn Muhammad	upto 1036
Isma'il al-Zafir	1036-1043
Al-Ma'mun	1043-1075
Yahya	1075-1085

In 1085, Alfonso conquered the kingdom of Toledo.

9. Valencia

The two Slavs Mubarak and Muzaffar	1021-1061
'Abd al-Aziz al-Mansur	1061-1065
'Abd Rakr, the Qadi 'Usman etc.	1075-1092.
Ibn Jahhaf as the republican head	1092-1094.
Cid	1094-1102

In May 1102, the Almohad general Mazdali took control of Valencia.

Appendix 2

———•·•———

Moorish Ballad of 1568, Prior to the Rebellion of Granada[1]

Let the God of love and mercy's name begin and end our theme; Sovereign He o'er all the nations, of all things the Judge Supreme. He who gave the book of wisdom, He who made His image, man, He chastiseth, He forgiveth, He who framed creation's path.

> He the One sole God of Heaven, He the One sole God of
>   earth,
> He who guards us and supports us, He from whom all
>   things had birth;
> He who never had beginning, Lord of heaven's loftiest
>   throne.
> He whose providence guides all things, subject to His
>   will alone.
>
> He who gave us Holy Scripture, who made Adam, and
>   who planned
> Man's salvation, He who gives their strength to nations
>   from His hand;
> He who raised the Saints and Prophets, ending with
>   Mahoun the greatest—

Praise the One sole God of Heaven, with all His Saints,
    from first to latest!

Listen, while I tell the story of sad Andalusia's late—
Peerless once and world-renowned in all that makes a
    nation great;
Prostrate now and compassed round by heretics with
    cruel force—
We, her sons, like driven sheep, or horseman on
    unbridled horse.

Torture is our daily portion, subtle craft our sole
    resource,
Till we welcome death to free us from a fate that's ever
    worse.
They have set the Jews to watch us, Jews that know nor
    truth nor faith,
Every day some new device they frame to work us
    further scaith.

We are forced to worship them in their Christian rites
    unclean,
To adore their painted idols, mockery of the Great
    Unseen.
No one dares to make remonstrance, no one dares to
    speak a word;
Who can tell the anguish wrought on us, the faithful of
    the Lord?

When the bell tolls, we must gather to adore the image
    foul;
In the church the preacher rises, harsh-voiced as a
    screaming owl.

He the wine and pork invoketh, and the Mass is wrought
with wine,
Falsely humble, he proclaimeth that this is the Law
divine.
Yet the holiest of their shavelings nothing knows of right
or wrong,
And they bow before their idols, shameless in the
shameless throng,
Then the priest ascends the altar, holding up a cake of
bread,
And the people strike their bosoms as the worthless Mass
is said.

All our names are set in writing, young and old are
summoned all;
Every four months the official makes on all suspect his
call.
Each of us must show his permit, or must pay his silver
o'er,
As with inkhorn, pen, and paper, on he goes from door to
door.
Dead or living, each must pay it; young or old, or rich or
poor;
God help him who cannot do it, pains untold he must
endure!

They have framed a false religion: idols sitting they
adore;
Seven weeks fast they, like the oxen who at noon-tide eat
the more.
In the priest and the confession they their baseless law
fulfil,

We, too, must feign conversion, lest they work as cruel
   ill.

Albotado and Horozoo[2] shear us like a flock of sheep
Cruel judges and unsparing, who their tireless vigils
   keep,
And whoever praises God into destruction's net they
   sweep.
Vain were hiding, vain were flight, when once the spies
   are on his track.
Should he gain a thousand leagues, they follow him and
   bring him back.

In their hideous gaols they throw him, every hour fresh
   terrors weave,
From his ancient faith to tear him, as they cry to him
   "Believe!"
And the poor wretch, weeping, wanders on from hopeless
   thought to thought,
Like a swimmer in mid ocean, by the blinding tempest
   caught.

Long they keep him wasting, rotting, in the dungeon foul
   and black,
Then they torture him until his limbs are broken on the
   rack,
Then within the Plaza Hatabin[3] the crowds assemble fast,
Like unto the Day of Judgment they erect a scaffold vast.
If one is to be released, they clothe him in a yellow vest,
While with hideous painted devils to the flames they give
   the rest.

Thus are we encompassed round as with a fiercely
      burning fire,
Wrongs past bearing are heaped on us, higher yet and
      ever higher,
Vainly bend we to their mandates; Sundays, feast-days
      though we keep,
Fasting Saturdays and Fridays, never safety can we reap.

Each one of their petty despots thinks that he can make
      the law,
Each invents some new oppression. Now a sharper sword
      they draw!
New Year's day in Bib el Bonut[1] they proclaimed some
      edicts new,
Startling sleepers from their slumbers, as each door they
      open threw.

Baths and garments, all our old ancestral customs are
      forbidden,
To the Jews we are delivered, who had spoil us still
      unchidden.
Little reck the priest and friar so they trample on us yet;
Like a dove in vulture talons, we are more and more
      beset.

Hopeless, then, of man's assistance, we have searched
      the prophets o'er,
Seeking promise in the judgements which our fathers
      writ of yore;
And our wise men counsel us to look to God with prayer
      and fast,

For through woes that make youth ages, He will pity us
     at last!

I have done; but life were short our sorrows fully to
     recall.

Kind Senores, do not blame me, if I am too weak for all.

Whoso chants these rugged verses, let his prayers to God
     arise,

That His mercy may vouchsafe me the repose of
     Paradise!

Notes

1.   By Mohammad ben Mohammad aben Daud, the chief agitator in the movements which led to the rising. — Cartulario de Alonzo del Castillo (Memorial Hitorico espanol, 1852, Tom. III. p. 41).

2.   Albotado was a converso and a priest of the new Christians to whom Francisco Abenedem, a bricklayer at work on the Alhambra, revealed in confession the conspiracy on foot in the Albaycin. Antonio de Horozco was a canon of Sacromonte. The houses of both were attacked on the night when Abenfarax entered Granada — Marmol, Lib. iv. c. 2, 4.

3.   The Soq el-hattabin or the wood market.

4.   The Gate of the Banner — the principal plaza in the Albaycin.

Zara's Ear-rings

———•—

"My ear-rings! my ear-rings! they've dropped into the
    well,
And what to say to Muca, I cannot, cannot tell."

'Twas thus, Granada's fountain by, spoke Albuharez'
    daughter,
"The well is deep, far down they lie, beneath the cold
    blue water—
To me did Muca give them, when he spake his sad
    farewell,
And what to say when he comes back, alas! I cannot tell.

"My ear-rings! my ear-rings! they were pearls in silver
    set,
That when my Moor was far away, I ne'er should him
    forget,
That I ne'er to other tongue should list, nor smile on
    other's tale,
But remember he my lips had kissed, pure as those ear-
    rings pale—

When he comes back, and hears that I have dropped them
      in the well,
Oh, what will Muca think of me, I cannot, cannot tell.

"My ear-rings! my ear-rings! he'll say they should have
      been,
Not of pearl and of silver, but of gold and glittering
      sheen,
Of jasper and of onyx, and of diamond shining clear,
Changing to the changing light, with radiance
      insincere—
That changeful mind unchanging gems are not befitting
      well—
Thus will he think — and what to say, alas! I cannot tell.

"He'll think when I to market went. I loitered by the way;
He'll think a willing ear I lent to all the lads might say;
He'll think some other lover's hand among my tresses
      noosed,
From the ears where he had placed them, my rings of
      pearl unloosed;

He'll think, when I was sporting so beside this marble
      well,
My pearls fell in, — what to say, alas! I cannot tell.

"He'll say, I am a woman, and we are all the same;
He'll say I loved when he was here to whisper of his
      flame—
But when he went to Tunis my virgin troth had broken,
And thought no more a Muça, and cared not for his
      token.

My ear-rings! my ear-rings! O luckless, luckless well,
For what to say to Muça, alas! I cannot tell.

'I'll tell the truth to Muca, and I hope he will believe —
That I thought of him at morning, and thought of him at
      eve;
That, musing on my lover, when down the sun was gone,
His ear-rings in my hand I held, by the fountain all alone;
And that my mind was o'cr the sea, when from my hand
      they fell,
And that deep his love lies in my heart, as they lie in the
      well."

In the ballad Zara stands for Zahra, Muca for Musa, and
Abbuharez for Abdul Harith. The ballad will be found in
Lockhard: Ancient Spanish Ballads. This splendid work is
profusely illustrated. In one of the engravings Zara is seen in
a flowing robe and girdle sitting near a well in the garden of
a Moorish villa.

Appendix 4

Bibliography

———•·•———

Adam Mez: The Renaissance of Islam, English translation by
S. Khuda Bux Patna, 1937.

A.A. Afife: The Mystical Philosophy of Muhyuddin ibn al-
Arabi. Cambridge, 1939.

A-Daffa Ali Abdullah: Muslim contributions to mathematics.
London, 1977.

Al-Himyari: Kitab Ar-Rawd Al Mitar. Arabic text and French
translation by Levi Provençal, Leiden (1938).'

Anonymous: Kitab Akhbar Majmu'a. Urdu tanslation by Maulvi
Muhammed Zakarya. Delhi, 1942.

Al-Khushani: Quzat Qurtaba. Cairo, 1966.

Al-Marrakushi: Kitab al-Mu'jib. Amsterdam, 1968, and also
urdu translation by Naimur Rahman, Madras, 1921.

Al-Maqqari: (1) Nafh at-tib. English translation by Pascual de
Gayangos 2 volumes, London, 1843, under the title
'History of the Mohammadan Dynasties in spain. (2) Urdu
trans. by Maulvi Khalil ur Rahman, Aligarh, 1921.

Altamira, Rafael : A. History of Spain, translation by Muna Lee, new York, 1949.

Amir Ali: History of the Saracans, London, 1949.

Arberry (A.J.) : Aspects of Islamic civilisation London, 1964.

Arnold (T.W.) : The Preaching of Islam, London, 1932.

Arnold and Guillaume: The Legacy of Islam, Oxford, 1931.

Bertrand, Louis: The History of Spain, London, 1956.

Brockalmann: History of Islamic Peoples, London, 1949.

Brown, E.G.: (a) Arabian Medicine, Cambridge, 1921 (b) Literary history of Persia 4 vols. Cambridge, 1929.

Burkhardat, Titus : Moorish culture in Spain, London, 1972.

Bernard Lewis : The Arabs in history, London, 1966.

Bernhard and Ellen Wishaw : Arabic Spain. London, 1912.

Calvert, Albert : Moorish Remains in Spain, London, 1905.

Charles Singer and Bevan : The Legacy of Israel. Oxford, 1927.

Clement Huart : Arabic Literature, London, 1903.

Condé, A.J. : Historia de la Dominacion de los Arabs en Espana. 3 Vols. English translation: Mrs. J. Foster, London, 1854-55.

Creswell, K.A.C. : 1) A short account of early Muslim Architecture, London, 1958.

Davies, R.T.: Golden century of Spain, London, 1965.

Dozy, Reinhard : Histoire des Musulmans d'Espagne. English translation: F.G. Stokes, London, 1913.

Draper William: (1) History of the Intellectual development, of Europic 2 vols. 1909 (2) History of the conflict between religion and science. London, 1904.

Dulcie Smith : The poems of Mu'tamid of Seville. London, 1915.

Enan Abdullah : (1) Decisive moments in the history of Islam. Lahore, 1943. (2) Ibn Khaldun — His life and work. Lahore 1945.

Ernst Kühnel : Islamic Art and Architecture, New York, 1967.

E.N. Adler : The Jewish Travellers, London, 1930.

Emilio García Gómez : "Moorish Spain" pp. 225-236, published in "The World of Islam", Edited by B. Lewis, London, 1976.

Farmer (G.H.) : (1) History of Arabian Music, London, 1929. (2) Historical facts for the Arabian Musical influence. London, 1930. (3) The Arabian Influence on Musical Theory. London, 1925. (Journal of the Royal Asiatic Society).

Gibb, H.A.R. : Arabic Literature. Oxford, 1963.

Grube, E.J.: Islamic Pottery, London, 1976.

Grunebaun (G.E. Von): Medieval Islam, Chicago, 1901.

Henry Charles Lea : Moriscos of Spain, their conversion and expulsion. Philadelphia, 1901.

Hitti Philip : (a) History of the Arabs, London, 1953 (b) Makers of Arab History, London, 1968. (c) Capitals of Arab Islam, 1973, U.S.A..

Henri Pérès : La Poesie Andalouse en Arabe Classique, Paris, 1953.

Hugh Braun : Historical Architecture, London, 1953.

Hussani, H.A.Q. : Arab Administration, Madras, 1949.

Imamuddin : Economic History of Spain (711-1031), Dacca, 1963.

Ibn al'Arabi : (a) Ruh al-quds (b) Al-Durrat al-fakhirah Eng. Trans. by R.W.J. Austin under the title, "Sufis of Andalusia", London, 1971 (c) Tarjaman al-Ashwaq Eng. trans. R.A. Nicholson. London 1911.

Ibn al-'Awwam : Kitab āl-Filaha (2 vols) Urdu-Trans. Maulavi S.M. Hashim. Azamgrah, 1927, under the title kitab al-Filahat.

Ibn Bassam : Zakhira fi mahasin ahl-al-jazira 3 vols. Cairo, 1932.

Ibn Battuta : Travels: Eng. Trans. H.A.R. Gibb London, 1953.

Ibn Bushkuwal : Kitab al Sila, Cairo, 1966.

Ibn Hazm : (a) Kitab al-millal w'al Nihal 3 Vols. Urdu Trans. by Maulana Abdullah Imadi. Hyderabad 1945 (b) Tawq al-Hamama Eng. Trans. by A.J. Arberry. London, 1953.

Ibn Khaldun : (a) The Muqaddima, 3 Vols. Eng. Trans. by F. Rosenthal, London, 1958. (b) Tarikh ibn Khaldun (Urdu Trans.) by Hakim Ahmed Hussain. Allahabad, 1937. [Chaplers relating Muslim Spain]

Ibn Khallikan : Wafayat al-a'yan (4 vols.) Eng. Trans, by De Slane, London, 1843-71.

Ibn Idhari : Al-Bayan al Mughrib, Cairo, Vol. I, 1938 and Vol. II, 1951.

Ibn Jubayr : Rihla — Eng. Trans. R.J.D. Broadhurst, London, 1952.

Ibn Khatib: Ihata fil-Akhbar Ghurnatah, (2 vols.) Cairo, 1319 A.H.

Ibn Rushd: Tahafat al-tahafut, Eng. Trans. by Van den Bergh, London, 1954.

Ibn Sa'id: Tabaqat al Umam (Urdu Trans. by Qadi Akhtar Mian, Azamqarh, 1928.

Ibn Tufail : Hayy ibn Yaqzan. Eng. Trans. by L.S. Goodman, New York,1972.

Jairazbhai (Rafiq Ali) : An Outline of Islamic Architecture, Bombay, 1972.

John Heywood: Arabic Lexicography, Leidon, 1962

Jan Read : The Moors in Spain and Portugal, London, 1974.

John Owen : Skeptics of the Italian Renaissance, London, 1893. (This rare book is available in the library of Zakir Hussan College, Delhi. I am grateful to the Librarian for allowing me to consult this book.)

John Brookes : Gardens of Paradise, London, 1987.

Kimble, H.T. : Geography in the Middle Ages, London, 1938.

Lane-Poole : The Moors in Spain, London, 1912.

LeBon, Gustav: La Civilisation des Arabes, Paris, 1884.

Lévi Provençal : Histoire de l'Espagne Musulmane 2 Vols. Paris, 1950.

L'Espagne Musulmans au Xème Siècle: Institution at vie sociale, Paris, 1932.

Islam d'Occident. Paris, 1949. Le Civilisation Arabe en Espagne, Paris, 1948

Martin Hume : The Spanish People, London, 1901.

Majid Fakhry : A History of Islamic Philosophy, New York, 1970.

McCabe Joseph : The Splendour of Moorish Spain, London, 1935.

Mayer, L.A.: Islamic Architects and Their works, Geneva, 1956.

Marcais, Georges : Manuel d'Art Musulmane — L'Architecture, 2 Vol., Paris, 1926.

Michell, George : Architecture of the Islamic World, London, 1978.

Migeon, Gaston : Manuel d'Art Musulmane — Arts Plastiques et Industrials, 2 Vols, Paris, 1927.

Miles, George : The Coinage of the Umayyads of Spain, 2 Vols, New York, 1950.

Nicholson, R.A. : Literary History of the Arabs; Cambridge, 1914.

Nykl, R.A. : Hispano-Arabic Poetry and its Relations with the old Provençal Troubadours, Baltimore, 1946.

O'Leary : How Greek Science passed to the Arabs, London, 1951.

Arabic Thought and its Place in History, London, 1939.

Owen Jones : The Grammar of Ornament, New York, 1986.

Palencia, Gonzalez : (i) Historia de la Espana Musulmana, Madrid. 1945. (ii) Historia de la Literature Arábigo Espanola, Madrid, 1945.

Placios, Asin. : Le Escatologia musulmana en la Divina Comedia, Madrid. Eng. trans : Harold Sunderland, London, 1926.

Prescott, William : (1) History of the Reign of Fredinand and Isabella, 3 Vols, London, 1841.
(ii) History of the Reign of Philip II, London, 1857-58.

Renan Ernest : Averroes et L' Averroisme, Paris 1852.

Reinaud, M. : Invasions des Sarrazins en France. Eng. Trans: Prof. H.K. Sherwani, Lahore, 1964.

Rivoira G.T. : Moslem Architecture: Its origin and Development, Oxford 1918.

Roth Cecil : History of the Jews New York, 1965.

Rom Landau : Islam and the Arabs, London, 1958.

Sarton George : Introduction to the History or Science, Vol. 2nd, Washington, 1927.

Seyyed Hossein Nasr : (1) Islamic Science, London, 1976. (2) Three Muslim Sages, Harvard, 1964.

Sigewick and Taylor : A History of Science, New York, 1918.

Sharif M.M.: A History of Muslim Philosophy, 2 vols, Wiebaden, 1963-66.

Stern Samuel Miklos: Hispano-Arabic Strophic Poetry, Oxford, 1974.

Talbot Rice: Islamic Art, London, 1965.

Trend J.B. : Spain from the South, London, 1928.

T.B. Irving : The Falcon of Spain, Lahore, 1958.

Washington Irving : The Conquest of Granada (Everyman series)

Watt W.M. : The Majestry that was Islam, London 1974.

Watt H.E. : Spain from the Moorish Conquest to the Fall of Granada (711-1492), London 1920.

Warren E. Cox : The Book of Pottery and Porcelain. Vol. I, New York, 1946. '

Wiener P.P, and Aaron Noland : Roots of Scientific Thought, New York, 1957.

Reference Books / Periodicals

1.   The Encyclopaedia of Islam (New Edition)

2.   Grove's Dictionary of Music and Musicians.

3.   Islamic Culture, Hyderabad.

4.   Islamic Quarterly, London.

5.   The Journal of American Oriental Society.

6.   Andalus ka tarikhi jughrafia, (M. Inayatullah), Hyderabad.

Appendix 5

———•———

Calender of Events

710   Reconnaissance of Tarif in Spain.

711   Expedition of Tariq ibn Ziyad.

712   Arrival of Musa ibn Nusair in Spain.

718   Revolt of Pelayo in the Asturias.

719   Death of the Tabi Hanash as-Sana'ni.

931   Birth of Abd ar-Rahman I.

732   Battle of Poiters.

741   Revolt of the Berbers in Spain.

755   'Abd ar-Rahman lands in Spain.

778   Siege of Saragossa by Charlemagne.

788   Death of 'Abd ar-Rahman I of Spain.

796   Death of Hisham I & accession of Hakam I.

817   The revolt at Cordova.

822   Death of Hakam I, and accession of 'Abd ar-Rahman II.

825   Foundation of Murcia by 'Abd ar-Rahman II.

829   Foundation of the grand mosque at Seville by 'Abd ar-Rahman II.

852   Death of 'Abd ar-Rahman II and accession of Muhammad.

857   Death of Ziryab at Cordova.

886   Death of Muhammad, and accession of al-Mundhir, and construction of a bait al-mal at the grand mosque of Cordova.

888   Death of al-Mundhir, and accession of Abdullah.

889   Death of the jurist Baqi ibn Mukhlad.

905   Death of 'Abdullah ibn Qasim who introduced the 'Zahiri' school of thought in Spain.

912   Death of 'Abdullah and the accession of 'Abd ar-Rahman III

915   Birth of Hakam II.

918   Death of the agitator ibn Hafsun.

920   Taking over by the Umayyads of the cities of Osma, san Estaban de Gormaz, Clunia.

928   Fall of Bobastro in the hands of 'Abd ar-Rahman III.

929   'Abd ar-Rahman III declares himself a Caliph of Spain.

931   Death of ibn Masârra at Cordova.

932   'Abd ar-Rahman III takes over Toledo.

939   Defeat of the Umayyad armies at Simancas.

940   Death of the poet and man of letter ibn 'Abd Rabbihi.

944   Foundation of dock yard by 'Abd ar-Rahman III at Tortosa.

951   Construction of a new minaret at the mosque of Cordova

953   Arrival of the German ambassador Jean de Gorz at the court of 'Abd ar-Rahman III

955   Death of the historian Ahmad ar-Razi. Foundation of the city of Almeria by 'Abd ar-Rahman III

956   Construction of the grand mosque at Tortosa

961   Death of 'Abd ar-Rahman III, and accession of Hakam II

970   Death of Hasdai ibn Shaprut

973.   Death of ibn Hani

976   Death of Hakam II and accession of Hisham II

977   Death of ibn Qutia

987-988 Enlargement of the mosque of Cordova by al-Mansur and the birth of the historian ibn Haiyan

994 Birth of ibn Hazm

997 Expedition of al-Mansur against Santiago

1002 Death of al-Mansur at Madinaceli

1008 Death of al-Muzaffar

1010 Sack of Madina az-Zahra

1031 Fall of the Kingdom of Cordova

1068 Death of al-Mu'tadid of Seville and accession of al-Mu'tamid of Seville

1085 Fall of Toledo

1086 The Battle of Zallaqa

1091 Exile of al-Mu'tamid

1095 Birth of ibn Quzman

1106 Death of Zahravi

1118 Fall of Saragossa

1125 Death of ibn Zuhr

1138 Death of ibn Bajja

1147 Death of ibn Bassam

1148 Fall of Lerida, Fraga and Tortosa

1163 Birth of Ibn al-Arabi at Murcia

1171 Construction of the grand mosque at Seville by Abū Yaqub

1183 Death of ibn Bushkuwal

1185 Death of ibn Tufail at Marrakesh

1195 The Battle of Alarcos (al-Arak)

1212 Battle of Las Navas de Tolosa (al-Iqāb)

1230 Fall of Majorca

1231 Fall of Merida and Badajos

1236 Fall of Cordova

1238   Fall of Valencia.

1243   Fall of Murcia.

1246   Fall of Jaen and Jativa.

1248   Fall of Seville

1269   Death of Sufi ibn Sab'in at Mecca.

1273   Death of the Nasarite ruler Muhammad I.

1292   Fall of Tarifa.

1313   Birth of ibn Khatib at Loja.

1349   Construction of College (dar al-ilm) at Granada.

1351   Ibn Battuta visits Granada.

1365   Construction of a hospital at Granada by Muhammad V.

1369   Death of ibn Khatima.

1374   Death of ibn Khatib at Fès.

1410   Fall of Antequera.

1426   Death of the jurist ibn'Asim.

1469   Marriage of Ferdinand of Aragon with Isabella of Castile.

1479   Union of Aragon and Castile.

1485   Fall of Ronda.

1486   Fall of Loja

1487   Fall of Malaga and Almeria

1489   Fall of Baza

1492   Fall of Granada

1568   Revolt of the Moriscos in the Alpujarras

1609   Expulsion of the Moriscos by Philip III.

Index